D1025331

TO WIN OR
TO DIE

For Dan +
Candy —
in recognition
of your
first
decade in
the
Mideast;
and appreciate
for
friendship,
softball,
and much much
else —

Ned

TO WIN OR TO DIE

A PERSONAL PORTRAIT OF
MENACHEM BEGIN

NED TEMKO

William Morrow and Company, Inc.
New York

Copyright © 1987 by Ned Temko

PHOTOGRAPHIC EDITOR: LISA PLESKOW

Grateful acknowledgment is made for the following permissions:

Poem, "Slain cavalrymen never die . . ." by Amos Oz, reprinted with permission of Amos Oz.

Essay, "The art of speech . . ." by Menachem Begin, reprinted with permission of Harry Hurwitz.

Poem, "Even in poverty, every Jew is a prince . . ." by Vladimir Jabotinsky, reprinted with permission of Ze'ev Jabotinsky.

All rights reserved. No part of this book may be reproduced or utilized in any form or by any means, electronic or mechanical, including photocopying, recording or by any information storage and retrieval system, without permission in writing from the Publisher. Inquiries should be addressed to Permissions Department, William Morrow and Company, Inc., 105 Madison Ave., New York, N.Y. 10016.

Library of Congress Cataloging-in-Publication Data

Temko, Ned.
  To win or to die.
  Bibliography: p.
  Includes index.
  1. Begin, Menachem, 1913–   . 2. Prime ministers—
Israel—Biography. 3. Revisionist Zionists—Poland—
Biography. 4. Irgun tseva'i le'umi. 5. Israel—
Politics and government. I. Title.
DS126.6.B33T45 1987   956.94'054   87-1598
ISBN 0-688-04338-0

Printed in the United States of America

First Edition

1 2 3 4 5 6 7 8 9 10

BOOK DESIGN BY KARIN BATTEN

To my parents
And, above all, to Asti

Contents

8 CONTENTS

Acknowledgments

Dozens of people helped me write this book, yet some deserve special thanks. Menachem Begin himself was invaluable. After hinting he might receive me (as a reporter, I had met with him in 1980), he decided not to risk appearing to endorse a book over which he would have no control. Yet when comrades or subordinates asked him whether they could see me, he invariably said yes. To have said no, might have condemned this book to stillbirth, so great remains the loyalty Begin commands.

His older sister, Rachel Begin Halperin, was extraordinarily helpful. She gave me many hours of her time, razor-sharp memory, intelligence, and unflagging good humor. Members of Begin's political family were also generous: his personal aide, Yehiel Kadishai; former cabinet secretaries Arye Naor and Dan Meridor; Eliahu Ben Elissar, director of Prime Minister Begin's office and later his ambassador to Cairo; and Yaakov Meridor, Begin's deputy in the anti-British underground and during many of his years as a politician. I am also grateful to Shmuel Tamir and Ezer Weizman, the only men briefly able to challenge Begin within his own party. Two other men who served and left—Begin's U.S.-born press spokesman, Ze'ev Chafets, and military adviser General Ephraim Poran—also offered me their time, energy, and insight. Chafets also gave me much more: a friendship that long predated this project, and transcends it.

I thank the outsiders who spoke with me, among them, former President Jimmy Carter; Secretaries of State Cyrus Vance and Alexander Haig; former U.S. Mideast negotiators Sol Linowitz, Harold Saunders, and Morris Draper. Also, the veteran U.S. ambassador to Israel, Samuel Lewis—articulate, reflective, insightful, and soon-to-be author of what promises to be the single most valuable political memoir for students of Begin's complex political relationship with the United States. I am also grateful to the staff of Warsaw University's archives and to others—librarians and pedestrians, in Warsaw and outside—who helped me reconstruct Menachem Begin's childhood Poland.

Others, in different ways and on different continents, have given me support without which I could never have written this book. My editor, Bruce Lee, quite literally helped teach me how. Valued friends Avi Weinstein, Jon Randall, Jeff Price, Trudy Rubin, Alfons

Hamer, Bob Slater, Mary Curtius, Terry Wrong, Brooke Kroeger, Don and Sandra McNeil, Debby Seward, Lisa Pleskow (friend and photographic editor), Deborah Harris, Charlie Weiss, Alex, Kiki, and Christopher Beam, Roberta Fahn, Tamar Solnik, Dan and Candy Fisher, Rivka Zipper, and Yehoshua Arnowitz helped me in ways even they may not have realized. My friends at the *Christian Science Monitor*—above all, David Anable and Kay Fanning, who are also my bosses—not only gave me encouragement. They provided me the time to write this volume. And one friend mattered above all: my wife, Astra. Without her love, understanding, boundless patience, and backing, I could never have completed this book.

I thank, finally, a dozen men and women almost no one has heard of. Now Israelis, as boys and girls they lived alongside Begin in a town that history books call Brest-Litovsk—where Trotsky signed the treaty that took the Soviet Union out of World War I. Jews have always called it by its Yiddish name, Brisk-de-Lita: a town that is dead, a town they mourn. It is a town Begin rarely mentioned but which helped make him all he became.

N.T.

April 1987

We want to fight—either to win, or to die!

—MENACHEM BEGIN
Warsaw, 1938

Prologue

The Mystery and Tragedy

So jolting was his encounter with Menachem Begin, then just out of high school, that the youngster recalls every detail a half century later. Yehuda Rosenman lives twenty-five floors above Manhattan now. Yet, as a boy in the Polish town of Brisk-de-Lita, he would often scurry from his father's jewelry shop, up cobbled streets, to the apartment where the Begins lived. Usually Menachem's mother would be waiting with a batch of the sugar cookies Rosenman adored, and a steaming glass of tea. The Begins' living room—*literally* a living room, since Menachem and his older brother, Herzl, slept there—would be in chaos. Visitors streamed in and out, mostly to see Menachem's father, who was secretary of the town's Jewish community council. But on this day, Begin's parents were out. Menachem was alone—sprawled on the couch, reading—when Rosenman arrived.

Begin ignored him. For several minutes, the visitor—who knew Begin well, and looked up to him—waited for acknowledgment. Finally, he barked, "Menachem! Why the hell do you ignore me and lie there even though I am sitting here?" Begin put down his book and replied: "I am going to tell you something you must always remember. It is terribly important for an educated man, if he wants to *know* things, to read a minimum of a hundred and fifty pages a day." Says Rosenman, smiling, "I still remember the number! A hundred and fifty pages a day! Menachem said the more you could read the better, but that you had to set a *goal*—a minimum. And it had to be *important* reading, not just entertainment. You had to concentrate your mind." Begin said he didn't mean to insult the younger boy. "But there are *always* people coming in here," he said. "I can't hide myself, because we have a tiny apartment. So I just have to make time, and just lie like this and read."

"That," says Rosenman, "was the nature of the *discipline* this guy had."

It was discipline with a vengeance. It came early to Begin—partly because he grew up as a Jew in Poland between the world wars, partly because he grew up small, sickly, homely. He was a loner, who learned to shut out others before they could shut him out. Then he learned to lead them.

The story of Menachem Begin is a mystery—clouded by friends, foes, and Begin himself. The official version is that he grew up happy, except for schoolyard tussles with Polish anti-Semites. At sixteen, he devoted his life to Zionism. When the Nazis invaded Poland a decade later, he was forced to flee east, and was imprisoned in a Soviet labor camp. Released, he made his way to Palestine. There, he led an underground revolt that forced the British to leave, and helped create the State of Israel. For the next thirty years—the official story goes—Begin put nation above politics, principle above personal gain. He led his party through the wilderness of parliamentary opposition, then into brief stints in "national unity" cabinets. Finally, in 1977 the people rewarded him: They made him prime minister. He secured peace with Egypt, was reelected against heavy odds in 1981. Then he made war with the "terrorists" of the Palestine Liberation Organization in Lebanon. By the end of 1983, the war had gone sour, but through no fault of Begin's. His wife died. His health deteriorated. Neither blaming others nor explaining himself, he retired—to think, perchance to write—in peace.

To his rivals—the Labor Zionists of David Ben Gurion who dominated Jewish politics from 1900 until 1977—Begin is a fanatic, a "fascist," a racist. They accept the early chapters of the official story. But his "revolt" against the British was, they say, mere terror prettied up with slogans. After all, when Begin's underground soldiers blew up the King David Hotel in 1946, they killed civilians—and fellow Jews—alongside British officials. Two years later, Begin's men slaughtered dozens of Arabs in the village of Deir Yassin, near Jerusalem. As an opposition politician in Israel's first three decades—say Begin's foes—he was less democrat than demagogue. As prime minister, he was a supporting actor in peace with Egypt: President Anwar Sadat was the key. Finally, Begin's true identity—warmonger, not peacemaker—reemerged with the invasion of Lebanon.

The truth lies in between. The childhood was less happy than either side suggests. The stay in the Gulag was shorter: It lasted roughly a month. Begin neither understood nor decided the operational details of the King David bombing. (He assumed there would be few casualties, although he mourned only the Jews among the civilians who died.) The Deir Yassin attack, Begin did not even know about beforehand. (He always implied that he did.) Begin, as Israeli opposition leader, did generally observe the rules of democracy and decorum. Yet in the 1950s, he threatened to fight an Israeli–West German agreement on reparations money for Jewish survivors of the Holocaust. He warned of a new underground. At least two of his trusted deputies—unbeknownst to most of Begin's political rivals to this day—started planning terror, including the dispatch of a booby-trapped dictionary to the chancellor of West Germany. Two postal workers opened it: "It was," remarks one of the organizers, "the last dictionary they ever read."

Begin came to power in 1977 as much because of changes in Israel—and the incompetence and corruption of the Labor Establishment—as through his own actions. But he did want peace with Egypt, and played far more than a supporting role in achieving it. The same can be said of the war with Lebanon. The war—and the retirement and seclusion that followed it—were an outgrowth of all that was good and bad in Menachem Begin. They were the logical end point of the life, and era, of Menachem Begin.

Begin loved words—from the moment he made his first "speech," at age nine from atop a picnic table in Poland. During a political career that spanned more than half a century, he used words to encourage allies, shred rivals, or simply because he liked their sound. He came to attach an almost mystical significance to what was written, announced, spoken: What was *done,* by himself or others, was secondary. In negotiation, Begin used words with the precision of a courtroom lawyer. But in his speeches, writings, and interviews, he used them with the bombast of an orator. The word "great," from Begin, meant little. "Very great" was a mild compliment. "Very greatest" was the only meaningful accolade. His two volumes of autobiography often read like speeches. In them, as in his later writings, he reveals himself rarely, indirectly, inadvertently.

The biography of Begin is more than the story of a man. Begin built an underground army, a political party, a government, and finally an Israel in his own image. He left behind a changed nation: less Western and less trusted by America; more responsive to its own poor, but also more violent, and mired in economic crisis. He changed the map of the Middle East. He left Israel more powerful, less threatened by Arab neighbors—and inextricably tied to the West Bank of the Jordan River, biblical land captured in the 1967 Middle East war and long seen by the Arabs, the United States, and many Israelis as a bargaining chip for peace.

Begin's life is a lesson in power. Ridiculed at first, his revolt helped oust Britain's nearly hundred thousand troops from Palestine. Rebuffed by the Israeli electorate eight straight times, his party was then chosen to govern. David Garth, the New York consultant who has made a career of representing men of power, handled Begin's 1981 reelection campaign. No one Garth has ever met—with the possible exception, he says, of Lyndon Johnson—wielded power as deftly as Menachem Begin. No one felt that power more sharply than Jimmy Carter, then president of the United States and nominally the most powerful man on earth. More than once, Carter tried to face down Begin. Begin did not blink. Carter had to.

Begin's life is also a study in contradiction. He was the picture of a gentleman—honest, kind to the most lowly of associates, and often to foes. Yet, says a former aide, "he could end someone's political career in a matter of minutes." The victim, moreover, was often a man Begin had once called "friend." Begin devoted his life to securing Jewish control over the ancient Land of Israel. Yet he was barely more familiar with its hills and valleys—even in Judaea and Samaria, where he planted dozens of Jewish settlements—than the greenest immigrant. He had a saint's sensitivity to the suffering and needs of his own, Jewish people. But he was often blind to those of other peoples.

He adored his wife, whom he married in her teens. Never did he look at, much less sleep with, another woman. But Aliza Begin had one rival—Menachem's political life. The toll of the rivalry on his family was sometimes cruel. Begin either would not, or could not, temper it.

Begin could be petty. He would pull apart draft agreements comma by comma; refuse to budge on the tiniest of points. Yet when it mattered—the avoidance of civil war in Israel in the 1940s, or the signing of peace with Egypt—he proved he was more than a politician. He was a statesman.

The story of Begin is not just a mystery. It is a tragedy. Though he achieved great victories, he craved one thing above all: acceptance. He was a shy man, of whom Arthur Koestler noted after an interview in the 1940s: "He has the self-assured awkwardness of people who have learned to find a *modus vivendi* with their own shyness." From comrades, he came to value personal loyalty above all other qualities. The fact that his defense minister during the Lebanon War, Ariel Sharon, operated within these limits partly explains Begin's mishandling of the war, and his silence on it after retirement. From outsiders, Begin expected rejection—and adopted a preemptive combativeness that sometimes encouraged it. Yet he ached to be liked—especially by those Establishment Jews who had branded him a fascist. He wanted History to call him a peacemaker. Instead, he ended up a recluse—remembered more for war with Lebanon than peace with Egypt. Most saw him in the end as an object of pity and puzzlement. A few rivals could not resist remarking that they had told you so: Begin was a warmonger all along.

To understand Begin as an Israeli is impossible. He described himself as "a simple Jew, in Israel." This was in part affectation, a way of saying he wasn't going to pretend to be a *sabra* earth child the way Ben Gurion sometimes did. But it was also true. Begin remained a Polish Jew, molded by a world that was murdered by Adolf Hitler. More Jews lived in Poland between the world wars than to this day inhabit Israel. Their life, in the words of one of Begin's childhood neighbors, was in ways "more distinctly Jewish" than anything Jews have constructed before or since. Yet on the first day of September 1939, the Germans invaded, and Poland's Jews did one of two things in the war that followed. They died at the hands of the Nazis—like most of Begin's family. Or they fled—like Menachem Begin.

All Begin did afterward flowed from that flight. Never did he address the issue directly. But one of the dozens of political proclamations he wrote during his days as underground commander does: "Against the eyes of every son of the nation appear and reappear the carriages of death. The images come as if on their own volition— even during daytime diversions; and most of all, maybe, in the nights: The Black Nights when the sound of an infernal screeching of wheels and the sighs of the condemned press in from afar and interrupt one's slumber; to remind one of what happened to mother, father, brothers, to a son, a daughter, a People. *In these inescapable moments every Jew in the country feels unwell because he is well.* He asks himself: Is there not something treasonous in his own existence. He asks: Can he sit by and allow the terrible contradiction between the march to death *there* and the flow of life here. . . . And there is no way to run from these questions . . ."

Begin found a succession of answers: the revolt against Britain, peace with Egypt, war against the PLO. The last was an exorcism of the pain of a Polish survivor; the redemption of a pledge that Jews would never again have to march peaceably to death, or rely on anyone but themselves for survival. But the enemy was not Germany this time. Yasser Arafat was not Hitler. The threat was not a holocaust. Begin, elected by young and mostly Mideast-born Israelis, was speaking for a generation of Polish Jews whose time was passing. Even had the war gone better; even had there been no massacre of Palestinians in the Beirut camps of Sabra and Shatila; even had Begin's wife not died; and even had Begin not lost control of his government and touch with his constituency; still, the war in Lebanon would have been the penultimate chapter of his story. Only the end might have been different.

Yet it is the beginning, says Menachem Begin's sister, that is least understood and most important. "My God!" she sighs. "How that boy has suffered in his lifetime!" And to understand him, she says, "you must go back to the roots. To write the biography of my brother, you must also write the biography of a boy, in Brisk-de-Lita."

Chapter One

Arms and the Boy

Menachem Begin was born August 16, 1913—the final child in a family about to be torn apart by war.

He had two years of peace, in a Jewish market town ruled by czarist Russia, and would toddle along the porch of his grandfather's home while his brother and sister romped through the yard. Grandfather Begin was the last in a line of timber barons, and his house nestled near the Mukhavets River on the edge of town. Menachem's parents' home, in town, was not much smaller. They had a Russian peasant for a maid. "Before the war," recalls Menachem's sister, Rachel, "we had a wonderful life. We used to dream of going all the way to Saint Petersburg to study. But Menachem was born into *Gone With the Wind*! The war tore everything apart. My grandfather and grandmother died. My grandfather's house was burned. By the age of two, it was all over for Menachem. He did not have a childhood like me or my other brother, Herzl. He did not even remember his grandparents. He knew nothing."

World War I began far from Brisk. But the Germans, preceded by food shortages, neared in 1915, shortly before Menachem turned two. That spring his father was exiled, for telling anyone who would listen that a Russian defeat would be good for the Jews. Menachem's mother, a woman who spoke little and complained less, awoke a few months later to find the walls of Brisk plastered with a

Russian decree: Civilians must leave within three days. She bundled her infant son, and the other children, onto a train. They headed east, away from the front.

Menachem at first found flight an adventure, says his sister. But it soon turned to horror; then, to hardship. The family halted at an uncle's home in Drogitchin, a White Russian village bloated with refugees fleeing both the advancing Germans and the retreating Cossack-Russian cavalry. One day a cavalryman approached the room in which the Begins lived. "The window was small, so we saw only the horse," recalls Rachel. "The Cossack demanded whether there were *Zhidie* or *Russkie*—'Yids' or 'Russians'—within." Her uncle, who spoke Russian, persuaded the soldier to leave. But a few evenings later, the Cossacks returned. As the Begin children watched with other refugees in a nearby field, the town went up in flames.

The Begins moved back west. Brisk was by now a German army post, so they settled a few dozen miles east, in an abandoned country house near Kobrin. Menachem and the other children enjoyed this time; they spent hours exploring the nearby woods. But when his father returned—having wandered into Russia, then back west—he decided the children must grow up in a town. They must read and write, not race through forests. He rented a room in Kobrin, a place that offered him no work, and his family only the bare essentials of life. "There was a cake shop near our place there," says Menachem's sister. "We couldn't afford it. We didn't even dare *look* at it. One day, the son of the woman who rented us the room bought himself a cake. Menachem came up to him and said: 'Please, can I just *sniff* it?' " Mrs. Begin overheard and, for the first time since the start of the war, she cried. Menachem, as the youngest, did get special attention. He had a German baby-sitter, a blond boy named Joseph. "Menachem adored him!" says Rachel. But before long, he was summoned to battle. "We all," says the sister, "cried then."

The father left again in 1918, bored with Kobrin and anxious, as the war wound down, to return to Brisk. He persuaded the Germans to let him start repairs on the main synagogue, coming back to Kobrin each Sabbath to rejoin his family. In 1919 he brought the others home to Brisk. The two older children went by train. Menachem followed—with his mother, an aunt, and the baggage—in a horse-drawn cart.

He was six, and he returned to a town in ruins, torched by the departing Russians. It had been Polish for hundreds of years, Russian for a century before the war, and was now German. Its name had changed: Bzescz, Brest-Litovsk, Brest. But its Jews called it Brisk. They had first come in the 1300s, from Bohemia and southern Europe, when Poland offered a refuge from Inquisition and Crusade. Brisk sat between the Mukhavets and Bug rivers, a few miles west, and timber men like Menachem's grandfather used the water as a highway. The town was a rail junction, too, with a switching yard for the coal-driven trains that chugged from Moscow toward Warsaw, Brussels, and Paris in the West. The Russians had built a red-brick fort nearby. But this made the town no easier to defend: You could peer in any direction without seeing a hill, only black-green forests interrupted by peasants' half-acre plots.

When Menachem came home, the Germans were leaving and the Polish authorities returned—only to be ousted anew by the fledgling Soviet Army. The Begins crouched in a basement as the Russians galloped in. Not a shot was fired, however. A few weeks later, under threat of counterattack, the Soviets withdrew for good. Brisk was Polish again. It stayed that way until Adolf Hitler attacked, just after Begin's twenty-sixth birthday, nearly twenty years later.

Menachem's first memory, he says, was of Polish soldiers flogging a Jew in the town park. Though he wasn't there—two Jews, not one, were flogged—he might as well have been. One of the victims died, leaving behind a daughter whom Rachel knew. The doctor who had tried to save him was the Begins' downstairs neighbor, and himself died of a heart attack a few days later. "My father," says Rachel, "was beside himself!"

Such was the boy's reintroduction to Brisk. He was a small child—"frail," say classmates—and he craved affection. He did get more than his share from a mother who, in his phrase, sacrificed the "instinct of self-preservation . . . for the identification of her soul with that of her beloved son." But he had mixed feelings about her favor. In his memoirs he describes a World War II cellmate with empathy approaching confession: "A son was crying for his mother. A grown man who will always be her 'little son' . . ." Yet Begin rejects as "weakness" this "hankering for boyhood . . . for a mother's touch."

It was the father—Ze'ev Dov Begin—for whose affection Menachem and the rest of the family vied. He had a teacher's sternness and kept a teacher's distance. He set a "puritanical" tone, recalls

Menachem's sister. "We were deeply attached as a family, but one didn't *show* affection. One didn't embrace." Besides, he had little time for Menachem those first years back in Brisk. Grandfather Begin, the riverside home, the money and status were gone. The first task was to get twelve-year-old Rachel and Herzl, then nine, back to school. They had to learn Polish: Rachel's schooling had been in Russian, and Herzl had studied German and Yiddish in Kobrin. Menachem—an afterthought, since he had been too young to study during the war—learned to assert himself. One day he decided he needed schooling as much as Rachel or Herzl did. He wandered through town and found the kindergarten. "He was very small!" recalls Rachel. "He couldn't even pronounce the sound 'k' or 'g.' He walked in and stood in the hallway until someone asked him what he was doing. 'I am the son of Mr. Begin,' he replied. 'And I want to enter kindergarten.' "

At home, Menachem tried to draw near to his father. Ze'ev Dov loved chess. Of the children, only Herzl had a special aptitude for the game. But Menachem set out to learn: From the age of seven, he would hover near his father's brass-wheeled chess table. "I played a lot," he said years later. "My father taught me how to play, and he was my first 'partner.' " Still, Ze'ev Dov was a driven man, and it was not chess that drove him. He called himself a "proud Jew"—an identity taken late in life and passed on to those around him with the fire of a religious convert. He had spent forty years "finding himself" in a town and a time that scorned this as a luxury. The first of Grandfather Begin's nine children, he was sent to a Jewish yeshiva as a boy. He was expected to learn Hebrew and study the holy books, enter the timber business, marry, and have children. He did well at yeshiva. Yet he longed to be a doctor. After secretly poring through medical texts, he ran away to Berlin in hopes of entering university. Grandfather Begin ordered him back, and married him off to the daughter of a friend, but Ze'ev Dov divorced the bride. He worked grudgingly at the timber business, between trips to the cafés and bookshops of Warsaw, and remarried only a quarter century later. Then forty-three, he wed a twenty-year-old named Chassia. She had little education, but loved Yiddish books. Ze'ev Dov told her she could go back to school, and he might have kept the promise—but for the war, the birth of three children, and poverty.

Between weddings he found his life's cause, his "proud Judaism." He came to it with thousands of other European Jews under the pressures of anti-Semitism, late in the 1800s. Yet in Brisk, a fortress of rabbinical tradition, the credo was heresy. Most Jews there sought solace in the books of God. Only a few, poorer families drifted to the rebel rabbis known as Chassidim, who preached that faith and not book learning would bring redemption. Fewer still, taking their lead from Warsaw or Berlin, looked to the West, embraced secular writers, drifted away from religion. And at first, barely a handful made Ze'ev Dov's choice—Zionism, a creed that said Jews had only one weapon against the Pogrom: to leave for the Mideastern land of Palestine, and redeem a two-thousand-year-old claim to a nation.

Ze'ev Dov bellowed his Zionism, though he never left Brisk to go build a Jewish state. On the death in 1904 of Theodor Herzl—founder of the Zionist movement—he defied the town rabbis and called a memorial service. Family lore says he and two friends—one of them, the grandfather of future Israeli Defense Minister Ariel Sharon—took an ax to the padlocked door of the synagogue, held a service, and left. A neighbor has another version. "Many thousands gathered near the synagogue," recalls the man, grandson of the rabbi who he says had ordered the synagogue locked. "They called over the old attendant." He had no keys. "So some of the crowd visited the rabbi's house, broke windows, doors, furniture, and dishes. Neighbors called the police and arrested two men, who had headed the operation. One of them was Menachem Begin's father." The rabbi dropped charges, the man says, and the Herzl memorial was held a week later.

The next year, Ze'ev Dov and Sharon's grandfather helped organize Jewish "self-defense" groups. When the Russians found arms in Grandfather Sharon's yard, both men were told to behave themselves, and did. But in 1907 only the sex of Ze'ev Dov's first child kept him from turning the naming ceremony into a Zionist event. He had wanted to call the baby "Herzl." In 1910, when his first son was born, Ze'ev Dov did use the name.

Even in wartime exile, Ze'ev Dov's Zionism flourished. In Kobrin he organized a celebration of Lag b'Omer, the holiday marking the ancient Jews' revolt against Roman rule in Palestine. After returning to Brisk to help repair the main synagogue, he raised money for a Jewish hospital. He conducted a census of the Jews. Then, he was offered the post of secretary of the Jewish community, or *kehila*. His job was to record births and deaths, and liaise with the Polish authorities. He made it a platform for preaching Zionism.

Yet mainly, he preached at home, and Menachem became his disciple. Rachel had craved the role. When her father was exiled by the Russians before the war, the seven-year-old girl had no trouble figuring out why. The Germans, he had told her on one of her cherished daily strolls with him outside town, were not coarse like the Russians. "Just wait! They are a different culture." Rachel, however, had a drawback as heir to Ze'ev Dov's creed: She was a girl. Once, she publicly disagreed with her father on a point of Zionism. "He was very, very proud, on the one hand," she remembers. "But then I heard him complaining to my mother: 'She dared to go against me!' " When Herzl was born, three years after her, Ze'ev Dov exulted. "He was so happy when he had his son!" Rachel says, and others from Brisk agree. "My boy, Herzl," the father would proclaim, "is great. He has the name of the great Herzl!" Yet the son loved mathematics more than Zionism, which he learned competently but without passion.

Menachem was not named for a great Zionist, but by dictate of the calendar. He was born in the Jewish month of Av, the time for mourning the Romans' destruction of the Temple in Jerusalem. It was tradition to name sons born in Av, "Menachem"—Hebrew for "the consoling one." From the time the boy could toddle, Ze'ev Dov would hold him aloft and, pointing to object after object, ask in Hebrew: "What's that?" Yet this was Zionism by autopilot: He had done the same with the other children. At first, it was only Menachem's mother who gave him special attention. She would perform skits of ancient Jewish heroism for him and his playmates. Around the time the two Jews were flogged in Brisk, the Poles shot three dozen others in Pinsk. When a Yiddish paper published a protest poem, Chassia Begin taught it to Menachem. "He couldn't read then," Rachel recalls. But he had another gift: a nearly photographic memory. He learned the poem by heart, and would clamber atop a table in the Begin apartment and recite it to visitors.

Menachem's initiation as a Zionist came shortly before his tenth birthday—on Lag b'Omer, Ze'ev Dov's favorite holiday since he had organized the wartime celebration in Kobrin. In Brisk, he continued the practice. Pumping his walking stick up and down like a drum major, he would lead Jews on a march into the woods, then back to the town park for food, speeches, and song. In 1923 he reserved a role for Menachem. A few days before the event, he drew the boy aside and unfolded a hand-scrawled essay on the heroism of Bar Kochba, the leader of the revolt against Rome. Ze'ev Dov suggested Menachem deliver it. Delighted, the boy memorized, then practiced it. "He learned it by heart," says Rachel. "But he also *understood* what he was saying." When his moment came, he mounted a picnic table in the park and, hands clasped behind his back, held forth to the crowd. Years later he gave himself mixed reviews. "There were no loudspeakers then!" he boasted to one interviewer. In a volume of memoirs, however, he calls the debut "a fiasco." Rachel's recollection is that he was a success, and reveled in the attention. How magical was the experience, Menachem suggested only once, years later in an essay ostensibly about a Jewish leader whose oratory he admired. The phrasing was too vital not to suggest autobiography:

> The art of speech cannot be acquired by learning. All the schools of rhetoric, from the dawn of history until this very day, have not produced a single orator worthy of the name.
> And who is an orator?
> An orator is he who knows how to combine logic and sentiment, heart and intelligence. It is the speaker from whose heart and brain is spun a thread reaching to the hearts and brains of his audience. And at certain moments, his listeners become one entity, and that orator becomes a part of it. . . . All of a sudden the audience feels carried aloft, elevated toward another world . . .

Chapter Two

The Coming-
of-Age

Menachem Begin turned ten three months later. He attended a school run by the Mizrachi movement, which preached a mix of Zionism and Orthodox Judaism. Evenings, he spent in a Zionist scout troop his father had helped found. Around him, the town of Brisk settled into its postwar identity. It was a place where a Jewish boy could spend mornings studying Hebrew, or praying at one of dozens of synagogues or religious schools. He could pass his afternoons playing soccer at the Jewish Sports Club near the river, evenings singing Zionist songs. Then, he could get denounced, or beaten, as a "dirty Yid" on the walk home.

Two nationalisms collided in town, as two peoples, almost equally, accounted for its forty thousand citizens. One was Jewish, the other Polish, and you could chart the division on a map. Brisk was a grid of dirt alleys and cobblestones—"cats' heads," Jewish children dubbed them. It lay between the railroad in the north and the Mukhavets River in the south, with the Begins and most other Jews living nearer the river. Poles lived closer to the station, or in leafy suburbs across the tracks. Light came from kerosene or gas lamps. Water came from the river, in barrels mounted on horsecarts. Some families got indoor toilets after the war, but not many Jews. Not the Begins.

Both Poles and Jews were entering a golden age. For years both had cherished the dream of a separate nation. Now, the war had left a new world order, and the winners dealt the Poles and Jews into it. The Poles got Poland back. The Jews got a British pledge of a "national home" in British-ruled Palestine, and a guarantee of "minority rights" in Poland until that happened.

The three and a half million Jews of Poland were the largest Jewish community in the world, with roots going back six hundred years in towns like Brisk. Yet to most Poles, the Jews' "minority rights" seemed an insult. The war had left the country's economy in shambles. The Poles were mostly peasants, scratching a living outside town or competing for jobs and business inside. The Jews, barred from farming in the old days, were the merchants and moneylenders, artisans and accountants. They were better educated. They were also, after the war, savagely taxed. "If a Jew screams," scoffed one official in a remark Menachem's neighbors in Brisk repeat to this day, "that means he has money!" Feeling resented, rejected, reviled, even Brisk's older Jews started increasingly to embrace Zionism. Yet they rarely thought of leaving: Brisk was home. "I'm a Zionist *because* I live in Poland," Ze'ev Dov remarked to one of Menachem's schoolmates. Jews Menachem's age, however, were not only resented in postwar Brisk. They were harassed or beaten. They did not merely embrace Zionism as a creed. They began planning to leave.

Menachem, in primary school, was more a loner than a Zionist. His Lag b'Omer speech had made him a celebrity: He delivered the welcoming remarks when Rabbi Maimon, the Mizrachi movement's founder, came to visit. Yet Begin spent most of his time studying. He seemed painfully shy. (Fifty-five years later, when he had grandchildren of his own, his favorite was the littlest. "So bright!" he would say. "So bright, but physically so frail!") Menachem, recalls one classmate from Brisk, "was a *little* kid. When he was twelve, he looked six or seven." His eyes stared from behind thick, round glasses. He read constantly, and his strongest subject combined the magic of words with the rigors of memory: Latin. When his teacher asked what he wanted to be when he grew up, the boy answered, "A lawyer." He wanted to "protect the poor and the deprived." Yet this he planned to do in Poland, not Palestine. "He had his head in his books," says the classmate. While some children were, even then, "wondering how to get to Palestine, Menachem was studying."

He did enjoy the Zionist scout group, which met a few blocks from home in a cul-de-sac near the courthouse. Though the scouts went hiking on weekends, Menachem preferred the indoor meetings. He would sing Zionist songs, dance the hora—and speak Hebrew, in which he excelled. Although he was too young to take a leadership role, Rachel did, and he basked in her glow. (Once during a meeting of her scout troop, he scurried so nearly underfoot that Rachel's friends had to boot him out.) He might have excelled on his own before long; yet barely two years after Ze'ev Dov had helped found the scout troop, he pulled his children out. The chapter was linked nationally with a group called Hashomer Hatzair, "The Young Guard," and it had swerved suddenly toward the Communist left. Ze'ev Dov drew his children aside and announced: "First you must fight for *your* liberty. Only then, as equals among equals, can you fight for the liberty of the world." Other scout groups put down stakes in town. But until 1929, after Menachem turned sixteen, all failed his father's test.

In town they said Menachem was like Ze'ev Dov Begin. But this was only partly true, and became less so as Menachem grew. The physical resemblance was hard to miss. The father sported a cavalryman's moustache and side whiskers, yet had in common with his son features that, except for the prominent nose, were delicate almost to the point of femininity. Father and son also came to share a defiant Zionism, and the shield of bluster that often grows from shyness. Too, Menachem got from Ze'ev Dov a respect for Jewish tradition, deepened in synagogue each Friday. Like Ze'ev Dov, however, he never became a strictly Orthodox Jew.

Menachem's reminiscences of his father, if read literally, convey only admiration. He tells of Ze'ev Dov's progress from confrontation to confrontation with Polish authority, each showdown yielding vindication or victory. When Menachem was seven, he says, Polish troops came for his father after the Soviet Army's retreat. They said he had abetted the Bolsheviks. But Ze'ev Dov "was able to ward off arrest and eventually save his life when he put the question: 'Have you a warrant?' " Next, he faced down Marshal Józef Pilsudski—the Polish war hero and postwar president. Pilsudski, visiting Brisk, received a delegation including two rabbis and Ze'ev Dov. They wanted food for returning Jews, many of whom huddled in the rubble of war-torn buildings. Pilsudski asked for a list of speculators among the Jewish merchants, and said the authorities would ensure equitable food distribution. "Mr. Marshal," Ze'ev Dov huffed, "the Jewish community is not a group of spies!" Pilsudski, Menachem says, was livid, but later evinced "respect" for this "honest and proud Jew."

Not long afterward, the father saw a Polish officer take a knife to the beard of a local rabbi. Ze'ev Dov raised his walking stick and clubbed the Pole on the hand, only to be hauled away with the rabbi to the fortress near the Bug. "They were beaten until they bled," says Menachem. "But his spirits were high. He was sure he had done the right thing." He also wasted little time in again confronting Polish authority, and was again detained. "A rumor started that he would never return, for he had been shot and killed," Menachem recalls. "Indeed, one of the hooligans had aimed his rifle at my father, even squeezed the trigger and even fired—but missed." Years later Menachem would say of his father: "In all my days, I have not seen a more courageous man than him. I will never forget my father's fighting for the honor of the Jew."

Yet the ancedotes read like parables. Rachel suggests, for instance, that Pilsudski's apologetic "respect" for Ze'ev Dov after their confrontation was Menachem's invention. That a Polish guard could fire on the captive Begin and *miss* seems similarly implausible. The stories' tone suggests distance as well as admiration—almost as if the son is paying tribute to someone else's father. And they stop abruptly with the early 1920s: with Menachem's own coming-of-age.

As he neared high school age, Menachem came to despair of ever achieving intimacy—as opposed to Zionist partnership—with his father. In some ways Ze'ev Dov was father to an entire town. As he preached Zionism to Menachem, so he lectured other children. He talked politics with them, asked how school was going, quizzed them on the Bible. When they flubbed a question, he would remark with a wink: "I'll bet you even the school principal doesn't know the answer!" As he played chess with Menachem, he played chess with the rest of Brisk. During school holidays he would sit in the park, a chess board on the bench beside him. Humming as he played, he invited youngster after youngster to take him on. Many who grew up with Menachem don't remember much about him, but add: "I knew the *father*. I used to play chess with him." The Begin home was an open house—where a revolving debate on Zionism and other issues of the day would be held with the visitors of the moment. "It was a verbal place, very loud," recalls Menachem's childhood protégé, Yehuda Rosenman. "They'd *kibitz* with each other. They'd argue with each other." It was not, however, a place for closeness.

Menachem soon began to hear new things about his father. The town respected Ze'ev Dov's courage, his honesty. He was indeed, as Menachem wrote years later, "an example" to other Jews in town. But they made fun of him, too. *Meshuggener*, they called him good-naturedly, "the loony one." They said he put on airs. Everyone knew the Begins no longer had money, that the timber business was gone. Ze'ev Dov's job gave him a steady salary, and with unemployment raging, that was nothing to sneeze at. But the pay was meager: Menachem, Herzl, and Rachel tutored classmates to help make ends meet. Still, the father strutted around town like an aristocrat. He dressed like one, too—though one neighbor recalls, "You could see his suit was worn bare at the elbows." He carried a silver-headed walking stick. "My father was a great dandy," Rachel says, "even in times of great financial difficulty." And though Ze'ev Dov loved public speaking, he invited ridicule at the podium. He wore false teeth, and lacked the money to fix them. He had a "permanently hoarse voice," recalls one of Menachem's companions. "It was hard to make out what he was saying." None of this dampened his enthusiasm. But when he spoke, says another associate, "he'd get so worked up that, at some point, he'd be apt to put his hand over his chest and yell in Yiddish, 'Ohhh! My heart!' I never found out whether there was anything wrong with his heart . . ."

Menachem heard more serious jibes at Ze'ev Dov. The father's showdowns with authority, some said, made more noise than impact. His rebel's vocabulary belied a tendency to chum up with the authorities. The Russians had expelled him before the war. But Ze'ev Dov had loved to play chess with Russian officials—a pastime even Rachel feels saved him from far worse than exile. After the war, it was his fluent German, and admiration for Germany, that helped him return early to Brisk. When the Soviets briefly retook the town in 1920, he had little choice but to billet some of them in his apartment. But he also helped Red Army officers get food from Jewish merchants—and throw a party before their departure, while ordinary Russian troops, not to mention thousands of returning Jews, went hungry nearby. Menachem never mentioned this incident. Years later, he said only that his *mother* had chatted with a simple Russian soldier who "warmed his bare feet" in the kitchen. He did not say why feet needed warming in August of 1920.

There was one darker side of his father's personality Menachem could not ignore: its effect on his mother. Chassia Begin was not one to criticize her husband. Besides, says Yehuda Rosenman, the rest of the family talked so much that she "didn't have much of a chance to open her mouth." But Menachem saw how she struggled to feed a family on Ze'ev Dov's Zionism. As an adult, he would say he learned patience from his mother. He told the story of how, one Monday, she took Ze'ev Dov aside and said: "We have no money to prepare next Sabbath's dinner!" It was a week away, so Ze'ev Dov replied: "What's the worry?" Each morning that week, Chassia approached her husband only to receive the same reply. On Thursday Ze'ev Dov finally assured her he would provide: "Tonight, there is a drawing of the lottery!" When Chassia asked, reasonably enough, whether he had bought a ticket, Ze'ev Dov Begin chuckled: "Hah! Is it anything to win a lottery when you buy a ticket? *I* believe I'll win *without* buying a ticket!"

There were two Jewish high schools in Brisk. Ze'ev Dov helped to found the better one, a few blocks from home. It was Zionist, and it taught in Hebrew, except for required courses in Polish language and history. It was also one of three Jewish schools in Poland that had "official rights"—meaning its diplomas were recognized by Polish universities. But Ze'ev Dov did not send his sons there, nor to the other Jewish high school in town. Menachem and Herzl were enrolled at the Romuald Traugutt Memorial Gymnasium. It was farther from home, near the train station, and was named for a hero of one of Poland's doomed uprisings against Russia in the 1800s. Run by the Polish government, it was "an anti-Semitic *gymnasium*," says one of Menachem's companions. "Ze'ev Dov Begin, who educated all of his children to be Zionists, sent his own sons to a Polish government school!"

One reason for the choice was money. The Hebrew schools charged tuition. It was not steep, but Ze'ev Dov was a poor man. The government school—if you could get accepted—was free. It also offered a better career route for a Jew than any Hebrew school. Ze'ev Dov wanted his children to get ahead, to go to the city to study, make the escape his own father had denied him. Even Rachel ended up at Warsaw University, rare for a small-town Jewish girl in those days. When Menachem had told his primary-school teacher he wanted to be a lawyer, the words were his own. The dream was Ze'ev Dov's. Yet in every way but academic, Traugutt was hard on Menachem Begin. He was one of a handful of Jews to be admitted. He had earned that distinction, by excelling in primary school. For a Jew, however, brains alone were not enough: Ze'ev Dov had connections with the Poles via his work at the *kehila*. The father operated between two worlds, Jewish and Polish, and Traugutt now forced the son onto similar ground.

Begin remembers the school as "a large and awesome red-brick building," a place that "taught a foreign language, a foreign literature—and hatred of the Jews." In fact, the Jewish high schools also had to teach Polish language, literature, and history. They even offered Polish premilitary training, if not so elaborate as Traugutt's. The difference between the schools was in spirit. Traugutt celebrated Poland's postwar revival; encouraged in a largely poor, Polish student body a crusade to ensure that no one would ever humble Poland again. The children needed little encouragement—or, in a town brimming with Jews richer than they, much imagination—to pick their enemies. Barely a day passed without Polish teenagers beating up Jews on the streets, sidewalks, or soccer fields. Menachem, at Traugutt, was on the cutting edge of the conflict.

Looking back, Begin would turn philosophical: "We acquired knowledge at the cost of beatings. Every day had its 'quota'—a quota of insults and shoves and 'sieges.' . . . We learned to defend ourselves, to beat those who beat us, and to insult our insulters." Still, he fought with more desperation than effect. A neighbor recalls seeing him "messed up badly, with all *sorts* of bruises. Menachem wasn't the sort of guy to *pick* a fight. He was weak, physically. He had no choice in the matter. The Poles attacked *him*. It was standard operating procedure." Begin says the lesson he learned was not to run away: "We returned home bleeding and beaten, but with the knowledge we had not been humiliated."

He developed mixed feelings about the Poles. He had friends at Traugutt, "youths [who] began—one can say—to respect us more, as we explained our past." He reciprocated, abhorring Jewish passivity almost as much as Polish truculence. "A cruel person," said Begin later, "is a frightened person. He behaves with cruelty when he assumes he will not be hurt." Menachem did not shrink, moreover, from the Polishness Traugutt taught. His favorite teacher was an assimilated Jew who taught Polish literature, and introduced Begin to the work of Poland's greatest modern poet, Adam Mickiewicz.

Begin read, memorized Mickiewicz. Years later, he would refer to
him as a Pole who sympathized with Jews. This was an incomplete
picture. Mickiewicz did try to organize a Jewish legion in the 1850s
to fight in Turkish-ruled Palestine. But he did so largely out of a
fondness for glorious uphill causes—a trait more appropriate to a
Polish cavalryman, or a postwar Polish teenager, than a small-town
Jew. Before the attempt at a Jewish legion, he had organized a Polish one to fight with Garibaldi in Italy.

"He who has never tasted bitterness," Mickiewicz wrote, "will
never taste sweetness in heaven." The essence of his message was
best captured by an Israeli writer, Amos Oz, a century later. Assuming the persona of "Poland's national poet," Oz intones:

> Slain cavalrymen never die
> They fly high through the air like the wind,
> Their horses' hoofs no longer touching the ground ...
> Cavalrymen never die,
> They become transparent and powerful as tears.

Mickiewicz's masterpiece celebrates a soldier named Konrad
Wallenrod—a fifteenth-century Pole, kidnapped by foreigners and
raised by them. Caught between two worlds, he becomes one with
his abductors and finally leads them into war against Poland. But in
battle he becomes Polish again, and leads his troops into a trap.

Menachem led two lives and was a loner in both. He studied at
Traugutt, with Poles. After school he read: Polish poetry, French
and Latin classics. In Yiddish, he devoured Jewish literature and his
father's Warsaw newspapers, brimming with Zionism. Other Jewish
boys played soccer, swam in the Mukhavets, or skated on it when
winter got cold enough. They strolled with girls along the river, stole
kisses, proclaimed first loves. Menachem, however, did none of this.
The others saw him as odd—an impression, says Rosenman, not
helped by the fact that he remained "skinny, in an era when skinni-
ness was not a sign of health." Around town, there were rumors he
had TB. He didn't, but he did chronically sniffle and cough. He was
"an unusual boy," says a sometime companion named Shlomo
Kandlik. "He didn't really have close friends."

The girls thought him homely. "In those days," Begin said in a
uniquely intimate interview years later, "a boy would court a girl.
Both were high school students. For example, they held books under

their arms, and the flirtation between them would begin when the boy asked the girl: 'Ma'am, what is the book you are reading?' And she would tell him the contents of the book. And he would describe his book. Against such a literary background did nearly all love affairs begin. I think [sadness, says the interviewer, crept into Begin's voice] it is a lovely way of courtship." Yet if it happened to Begin, no one who grew up with him can recall it. One girl remembers a New Year's Eve party. She and her friends made up the guest list. They asked all the nice boys. They asked Herzl Begin, and considered asking Menachem. But they decided not to: He wouldn't have fit in.

Menachem seemed to resent Herzl. Rachel, who doted on her younger brother, was away at Warsaw University. Herzl was not only at the same school as Menachem, but in the same class. Like many his age, he had lost ground in the postwar changeover to Polish education. He didn't like the subjects Menachem did: Latin, literature, history. Herzl liked math, and had an ability for it approaching genius. But unlike Menachem, the older Begin was popular with the other boys: Sometimes he would stand outside the window of the Jewish high school and help friends cheat on math exams. He went to dances with the girls. Herzl also achieved a special intimacy with his father. When he wrote his first love letters in high school, he even showed them to Ze'ev Dov. Many years later, Begin would all but omit Herzl from reminiscences of home. In one rare exception, he told a reporter Herzl had been a "very capable" mathematician. Yet this was faint praise, given Begin's bent for superlatives. In the same interview, he says of Rachel: "My elder sister was also my teacher. She was one of the more brilliant students in town."

Still, Menachem shone in one area: oratory. He became an attraction at Zionist meetings his father helped organize at the main synagogue. Herzl was dismissive: "It was as if he felt sorry for Menachem, thought he was wasting his time," says a boy who knew them both. Yet hundreds came to listen. Menachem seemed entranced when he spoke. He spun Mickiewiczian hymns of glory to the struggles of the Jews—a message all the more powerful for its timing. By early 1929, depression hit the precarious Polish economy, igniting boycotts and even violence against Jewish shops. In Brisk, teenagers sported green ribbons—emblems of a "league" to "defend" the town against Jews. Says a neighbor of Begin's: "You must realize that all of us had grown up in Brisk. So had our fathers and grandfathers. We had a truly *Jewish* life there, which we loved. But now, we saw there was no future: We weren't wanted." Nor were they wanted in Palestine. There, resistance from local Arabs had boiled over that year with the slaughter of dozens of Jews in Hebron, the burial place of the Hebrew patriarchs in the hills west of the Jordan River. The British were backtracking from their pledge of a Jewish homeland. Menachem Begin's oratory was like a battle cry—a promise that, win or lose, to fight would bring glory.

One afternoon in the fall of 1929, a few weeks after he turned sixteen, Begin walked to the Jewish high school to hear a teacher who was setting up a new Zionist youth group. His name was Moshe Steiner. He had a Ph.D. in Islamic studies and oriental languages, and espoused a truculent Zionism known as Revisionism. Its founder-hero was a Russian Jew, Vladimir Jabotinsky, who was second only to Chaim Weizmann in the Zionist world. Jabotinsky felt that no matter what the British wanted, Jews should leave Europe by the hundreds of thousands. They must reclaim Palestine from its resident Arab majority—by numbers if possible, by force if necessary.

As the students filed in, Steiner recognized most of them. However, barely had he started talking when a boy he did not know sprang to his feet and asked, in Yiddish, for the floor. "Sure," Steiner complied, and the youth fired a salvo of barbed questions. "He heckled me," recalls Steiner: "How did we think we could *do* all this? How could we get anything from the British, when the British were saying there was no room in Palestine for so many Jews? How do you expect to become a majority?" Steiner parried the assault, suggesting the youngster drop by later to talk. It turned out, recalls Steiner, that "this small, physically unattractive kid was Menachem Begin, and he had a local reputation as an orator." The boy had read some of Jabotinsky's articles in Warsaw newspapers, knew they met Ze'ev Dov Begin's criterion for Jewish liberation. But he wanted to know more about the Revisionists' youth wing—called Betar. Steiner tried to explain, citing a poem by Jabotinsky that Betar had adopted as its battle cry:

Even in poverty, a Jew is a prince;
Whether slave or tramp
You have been created a prince.
Crowned with the diadem of David
In light or in darkness
Remember the crown . . .

By midnight, Begin was a convert. The anthem seemed to speak directly to him. "He really *believed* it, personally!" says Yehuda Rosenman, who soon joined him in Betar. Begin recalls being "fascinated by the total Zionism of Betar. . . . It brought together all those elements I'd found in reading and listening." He started spending every afternoon with Steiner's fledgling Betar cell. An older boy named Zigman, from the Jewish high school, had been chosen to head the group. Begin made no move to unseat him. There was no vote, or change of title: None was needed. Where Zigman had questions, Begin had answers. He exhorted the others to spread a Jabotinsky gospel he knew far better than they, charted a drive to recruit and organize classmates. "He had a special power," says Steiner. "He seemed to draw support without exactly recruiting it. Within two or three weeks, he was in charge."

Begin placed a distance between himself and his followers. He would offer to help them with schoolwork, and inside Betar never asked them to do what he wouldn't, or didn't, do himself. Before school he would knock on doors, soliciting Betar funds. But, says one protégé, Begin retained the initiative. "If you *asked* him for a favor, forget it. Never! It lowered your image in his eyes." He would sprinkle conversation with badges of erudition: proverbs in Latin, quotes from Jabotinsky. Though ready to hear others' political gossip, he offered none of his own. "Everyone else, in a town like ours, talked, visited, saw each other on the street, gossiped. We had an oral culture!" recalls Rosenman. "But Begin was more disciplined. You never knew what he was planning, who he was going to see, what he was going to do. He never shared that sort of thing with anyone. He told what he wanted to tell you." Another of Begin's Betar troops, Shlomo Kandlik, says Begin "placed himself above us," adding, "We looked upon him like a kind of god, someone better than the rest of us."

Begin loved the muscle in Jabotinsky's Zionism. He wore his Betar uniform—with its Sam Browne belt—everywhere but Traugutt. He acquired a Betar companion and bodyguard named Avraham Stavsky, a mountain of a boy everyone called by his nickname "Abrasha." The two looked like unmatched bookends: Begin was still slight and beardless. "He slouched," says Moshe Steiner, "even in his Betar uniform."

But on stage, he seemed transfigured. He now spoke at least once a week, celebrating Jabotinsky and Betar, and the ranks of the youth group swelled with each speech. Most of the recruits were poor, the children of Jews who were either unemployed or about to be. Wealthier youngsters tended to adopt a more gentle, "Labor Zionism." Typical was a youth group called Gordonia which preached that sweat and toil, not Jabotinsky's sword, would win Palestine. "Begin's followers," recalls an acquaintance who joined Gordonia, "were, in a way, from the wrong side of the tracks." Yet Begin shouted from the podium that this didn't matter, that they were all royalty. Every Jew was a prince.

"He would cast a spell!" recalls Rosenman. "He would start his speech on a high pitch, and then he would modulate it. Often, he would start with a quote from a German poet—Goethe or the like." Then he would switch to Yiddish—the singsong mix of Polish, German, Russian, and Hebrew that was the sidewalk tongue of East European Jews. "He spoke as one of them!" recalls a Lithuanian Jew who came to know him well. "They had no hope. Nothing. His great talent was to speak from the very soul of the *shtetl,** to make things simple—black and white—and to offer real salvation. Full salvation!" His power impressed even rivals. Israel Lev, a neighbor who had remained in Hashomer Hatzair despite its leftward swerve, was walking home one day when he spotted a crowd outside Brisk's main Jewish auditorium—the Sarver Theater, a few blocks from the river. Lev peered inside and saw Begin on stage. "I thought to myself: Why should *I* listen to *him*? He was a kid, my age! What could he possibly say?" Then Begin spoke. "He started suddenly, and with such incredible energy! I was nailed in place, and I stayed until the very end."

As Begin neared graduation in 1931—among the top in his class at Traugutt—Vladimir Jabotinsky came to town. Begin joined a crowd of thousands to greet him at the train station. The next morning Jabotinsky spoke at the Sarver Theater. Spouting a "juicy Yiddish" even Begin had not equaled, he whipped the crowd into a frenzy. So tightly packed was the hall, that Menachem had to squeeze into the orchestra pit. "I was," he says, "*more* than won over." He walked home determined to devote the rest of his life to Jabotinsky, and Betar. "Jabotinsky," says Kandlik of the Begin conversion, "became God for him." A story began making the rounds that he was practicing the Revisionist leader's speaking style

---

* The Yiddish term—literally, "village"—used for the Jewish towns and villages of Eastern Europe.

in front of a mirror. Rosenman doubts this, but adds, "Menachem did take Jabotinsky as his teacher, his model."

That fall, Begin left Brisk for the first time in his adult life—to study at Warsaw University. Registering for law school, he planned for Zion. On his university application, he was asked for his native language. He wrote: "Hebrew." And the first thing he did on reaching Warsaw, in October, was to seek out the followers of Vladimir Jabotinsky.

Chapter Three

The Jabotinsky Years

Begin arrived in Warsaw with one suit of clothes, a pair of shoes, and a plan: He phoned an office on the edge of the Jewish quarter, and asked for an appointment with a man named Propes.

Aharon Propes was in no rush to oblige. Nine years older than Begin, he had helped Jabotinsky found Betar, and now oversaw its 150 chapters throughout Poland. He told the teenager from Brisk he would meet him a few days later, on a street corner. Yet if Begin resented the snub, he did not show it. He arrived proclaiming that he longed to serve Betar and awaited only Propes's orders. Disarmed, the Betar chief recalls deciding "the moment I met Begin, to co-opt him." He offered the boy a job, as chairman of the group's Organizational Department. The post dealt with small-town branches, *shtetl* Jews like Begin, and paid only ninety-one Polish zlotys—about ten dollars—a month. But it carried with it a seat on the High Command through which Propes ran Betar. Begin thanked him, and sped off to see his sister, Rachel, to gush the good news.

He lived for the work, spending just enough time on his textbooks to notch Cs at law school. He spoke less often in class than in the second-floor meeting hall of the Jewish students' dormitory, across the Vistula River from campus. There, most evenings, rival Zionist orators squared off. "Begin was only a youngster," recalls a student who debated him for the Labor Zionist left. "But he was a very impressive orator at those student meetings. He became undisputed leader of the Revisionist group." A few years earlier, Begin's *shtetl* anger might have grated on city ears. Warsaw was theaters and fashion and café chatter, a city the Poles called the Paris of the East. Its one hundred thousand Jews prided themselves on sophistication—that is to say, assimilation. Yet by the early 1930s the depression that had savaged the *shtetl*s, hit Warsaw. Hitler came to power in Germany, and in Poland the anti-Semitic National Democrats gained strength. Revisionist Zionism, once seen as a lunatic fringe, gained credence. When the Zionists held their world congress in 1931, the year Begin left Brisk-de-Lita, Jabotinsky threw a scare into the Labor Zionists of Chaim Weizmann: In the election of congress delegates, the Revisionists fell just short of Labor—by 29 percent to 21 percent.

With the approach of the next congress, in 1933, Begin was suddenly thrust into the front line of a battle between Jabotinsky and Weizmann's heir-apparent, David Ben Gurion. The contenders hit the campaign trail in June, from *shtetl* to Polish *shtetl*. Ben Gurion called Jabotinsky a fascist: "Vladimir Hitler." Jabotinsky exhorted Jews to flee Europe, and retake Zion. The race seemed a tossup—until the seventeenth of the month, when news flashed from Palestine that a Ben Gurion protégé, Chaim Arlosoroff, had been gunned down on the beach in Tel Aviv the night before. Two men had ambushed him as he strolled with his wife. At first, it seemed the attackers were Arab. Two Arabs confessed in custody. Then Mrs. Arlosoroff pointed her finger elsewhere. Two Jews were charged—one of them a recently arrived Betar settler from Poland: Begin's bodyguard, Abrasha Stavsky.

Begin was home on vacation when the news came. Stavsky, he fumed, was the victim of a frame-up. On hearing that one of the town's Jews had given information on the suspect to the police, Begin sought out the man's son, exclaiming: "We will destroy your house!" Jabotinsky also felt Stavsky had been framed, all the more so because the charges were so convenient politically for Ben Gurion. But the Revisionist leader, now in Warsaw, called on his followers to stay "cool and steadfast." When a newspaper said Jabotinsky had canceled his campaign appearances for fear of Labor Zionist reprisals, he denied this and went back on the road. The next weekend, he boarded a train for Stavsky's—and Begin's—hometown.

Begin was waiting at the station, where he had posted uniformed Betar youths to hold back protesters. He stayed by Jabotinsky's side throughout the visit—so close that one neighbor assumed Begin was now "Jabotinsky's aide"—even as hecklers inside the theater hurled eggs and tomatoes. Ben Gurion, meanwhile, confided in his diary that he was less interested in whether Stavsky was really a murderer than in the political implications of the Arlosoroff killing. These became clear in the election for the Zionist congress delegates: Ben Gurion's allies loped to victory with 44 percent of the votes. The Revisionists got only 16 percent.

Begin returned to Warsaw—and Jabotinsky—later that summer with Abrasha Stavsky's mother. She had asked him and Moshe Steiner to arrange an audience with the Revisionist founder. Steiner seems to have set up the encounter; but Begin was by Mrs. Stavsky's side when it took place and said years later: "I brought Stavsky's mother to Jabotinsky. I still remember how he greeted her, comforted her." A few weeks later, Begin met Jabotinsky for a third time in as many months—in Brisk, at a dinner marking Steiner's departure to become editor of a Yiddish newspaper in Warsaw. The celebrants posed for a photograph: Jabotinsky and Steiner stand, side by side, in the center. Well apart from them are two of Begin's relatives—Ze'ev Dov and Herzl, looking bored. Menachem is two rows behind Jabotinsky and Steiner, in Betar uniform. He has just turned twenty, but looks, at most, sixteen. Craning toward the camera, he gives the impression of a very young man, not yet part of Jabotinsky's circle, but edging closer, drifting away from his own family and from Brisk-de-Lita.

Back in Warsaw, Rachel soon sensed the change. A Revisionist herself, she attended the debates at the Jewish dormitory. One evening, seeing that Menachem was battling a cold, she offered to stay the night, to "take care of him." But her brother said no. "He would not hear of it!" With each speech, Menachem's reputation was growing. "I was never a member of Betar," says one Warsaw Jew who heard him speak. "But I would sometimes go to the dormitory to hear speeches. That was where I heard Begin. He was debating Israel Schipper"—a prominent Jewish historian. "Begin was devastating! He debated Schipper in the other man's style, and defeated him! From that point on, I made sure to hear Begin speak whenever he appeared. He was head and shoulders above anyone else!"

He spoke, increasingly, on the road. As head of Betar's Organizational Department, he visited *shtetl*s throughout Poland. He would meet local Betar leaders on arrival, then deliver a speech. "He built up a tremendous reputation," recalls a Jabotinsky aide. "You must remember that Betar in Poland had become a mass movement, with close to a hundred thousand members. Usually, they were of the lower social classes. The youngsters who were heads of local chapters were in their early twenties, or late teens." They saw Begin as one of their own. "They always wanted him to speak at their rallies." A Betar activist named David Yutan, who sometimes accompanied Begin, says he "*looked* so frail that, if he was speaking somewhere for the first time, the organizers would hurriedly schedule a second speaker, just in case he couldn't hold up." It took moments to dispel the notion. He would speak for an hour, sometimes more, whereupon the second speaker was discreetly canceled. With each visit, Begin attracted new disciples, young militants like Yutan. "I first met Begin at a Betar conference," he recalls. "He had something very special. He had a way of making you *believe!*"

In January 1935, at a Revisionist conference, Begin—demonstrating a confidence well beyond his twenty-one years—moved once and for all from the world of his childhood, to Vladimir Jabotinsky's. Jabotinsky had called supporters to Krakow, a university town in southern Poland, to seek their endorsement of a truce with Ben Gurion. He liked Ben Gurion, who had served in the Jewish Legion Jabotinsky had helped establish during the world war, and felt Zionism needed unity to succeed. Yet Begin rose to protest the rapprochement. Turning to Jabotinsky, he declared: "*You* may have forgotten that Ben Gurion once called you 'Vladimir Hitler.' But we have a better memory." Jabotinsky replied, "I shall never forget that men like Ben Gurion once wore the uniform of the Legion, fought alongside me. I am confident that should the Zionist cause demand it, they would not hesitate to don this uniform again."

Jabotinsky carried the day, and Begin fell into line. The harmony, however, was misleading. Begin was a Jabotinskyite; yet he was not like Jabotinsky. He agreed that Jews must leave Poland, and fight for Palestine. He imitated Jabotinsky's podium style—and also began emulating his old-Russian practice of kissing the hands of lady visitors. Still, the differences ran deeper. Jabotinsky was a nineteenth-century liberal who had traveled Western Europe, translated Dante, written poetry. An assimilationist in his youth, he had chosen Judaism and Zionism more with his mind than his heart. By instinct, he remained a negotiator, a compromiser. He believed in the goodness of men, even Christian and Polish men. Begin was none of this. He fancied himself an intellectual. And he was, by the *shtetl* standards of his youth. However, Begin's was a dour, single-minded intellect. He read avidly—but only history, politics, biography. By instinct combative, he did not believe in the goodness of (non-Jewish) men—whether Poles in Poland, or Arabs in Palestine.

Time favored Begin's pessimism, and Jabotinsky seemed to sense this. The worse things got for the Jews of Europe, the more powerful became Begin's appeal among the *shtetl* poor where Jabotinsky's power lay. The poor idolized Jabotinsky. But in Begin, they saw a piece of themselves. This seemed both to entice and unsettle Jabotinsky. He felt a paternal fondness for the firebrand from Brisk. Indeed, one Begin admirer claims to have been told privately by Jabotinsky at the Krakow meeting that Begin would someday make a fitting leader of all Betar. Yet, a few weeks after the Krakow meeting, Jabotinsky turned to an aide and asked, "What do you think of Begin as a speaker?" The assistant said he had no idea, having never heard him speak. Jabotinsky offered, in good-natured imitation, a few phrases of gobbledygook. "Then he asked if I'd understood him," recalls the aide. "I said that *I* hadn't understood a single word, but that Begin's followers sure seemed to understand, and loved it!" Jabotinsky, beaming, agreed.

In 1936 he sent Begin to Czechoslovakia, whose Betar commander was complaining he lacked the funds even for postage stamps. Membership was low, morale lower, when Begin arrived in late February. He left the commander nominally in place. Assuming the title of deputy commander and head of the Organizational Department, he mapped out a countrywide recruitment drive. He scheduled martial parades for a dozen branches, and ordered posters drawn up, for the first time, in Hebrew. Then he went on a speaking tour, skipping meals to save money, which he in turn spent on posters and mailings. "We shall suffer a bit, starve a bit," he told one local. "Betar must have access to all funds, whenever needed." From mid-March through late April, he gave thirty-five speeches, nearly one a day. In *shtetl* Yiddish, he set the tone of his first appearance, in Bratislava. Slovak nationalists had been harassing Jews there. Begin said the Jews must defend themselves. But more than this, they must go on the offensive—do harassing of their own! By the time he arrived in the town of Volovo, Jews from miles around had braved torrential rains to fill the local synagogue for his appearance. He returned to Prague for the summer, worked from dawn to dusk, and spent evenings reading Zionist texts. Then, as word of his exploits filtered to Warsaw, Begin was recalled to Warsaw.

Propes waited with trepidation. As early as the Krakow conference, he had heard delegates whisper, after Begin's brush with Jabotinsky, "He's the successor!" The words haunted him—especially now, amid criticism from Jewish militants in Palestine of his own position as Betar leader. While Begin was away in Prague, Arabs had loosed their worse violence against Jews since the Hebron massacre of 1929. Some of Palestine's Jabotinsky Zionists had responded by reviving a national military organization—in Hebrew, *Irgun Zvai Leumi* (IZL). The IZL rejected the view of Zionism's senior spokesmen—Ben Gurion, Jabotinsky, Propes—that Jews must fight only in self-defense. The group, mostly Betar boys, began launching preemptive attacks on Arabs. Jabotinsky scolded the IZL leaders, saying they must at least issue warnings in order to spare civilian casualties. He insisted that the Irgun must also defer to his *political* strategy—to negotiate a new British commitment to a Jewish state; and seek Polish help, in the meantime, in Betar's campaign to smuggle European Jews into Palestine. When the IZL countered by saying *it* should take charge of Propes's emigration campaign, as a natural source of IZL recruits, Jabotinsky said no. So, of course, did Propes.

Begin, however, was not so sure. He shared Jabotinsky's distaste for violence against civilians: It wasn't fair, manly. Yet the Irgun was doing in Palestine what Begin had advocated in Bratislava: going on the offensive. When the IZL dispatched an envoy to Poland for talks with Betar, but used him to undercut Propes instead, Begin befriended the interloper, a sardonic philosophy student from Jerusalem named Hillel Kook. Kook got the Poles to help set up boot camps for IZL prospects among departing Jews. "Within a year," he recalls, "ninety-five percent of the Betar people over eighteen were *Irgun* people, trained in Poland. Mr. Propes—a very nice man, by the way—was left with all the school kids!"

Begin stopped short of an open break with Propes, although making an unsuccessful attempt to nudge Jabotinsky toward IZL militancy. But he courted Kook, who recalls him "as a pleasant guy who used to *shmooz* with me in cafés in Warsaw." Begin's protégé David Yutan agrees: "He staked out a militant position" on the IZL. Then, near the end of 1937, Begin suddenly asked Jabotinsky for a "leave of absence." With a World Betar Conference planned for the following fall, he said he wanted to apprentice in law in Galicia, the formerly Austrian southeast corner of Poland. Jabotinsky, hands full with the IZL-Betar dispute, agreed.

• • •

Begin had no intention of retiring. He was biding his time until the Betar congress. He settled near the Galician town of Drohobych, but he spent little time on his law. He toured the area giving speeches, kept in constant touch with Betar allies, began taking English lessons. Barely had he arrived, moreover, than an unfamiliar distraction buried thoughts of torts and dockets altogether: For only the second time in his twenty-five years, Menachem Begin fell in love.

Menachem, recalls his sister, had always been "very correct in such matters." One reason he had refused her permission to tend to his cold at the Warsaw dormitory was the fear of "even a remote possibility it might not be clear, the next morning, whose room I came out of." The sister of Yehuda Rosenman, Tsipora, remembers sharing a train coach with Begin on the four-hour journey from Warsaw to Brisk not long after he'd started law school. She was the prettiest girl in Brisk—"prettier than Sara Braverman, the blonde the boys fawned over!" gushes one friendly rival. Begin spotted her through the window of the compartment, and asked permission to join her. "He knew me from Brisk. I was not in Betar. But he knew me, because my *brother* was. He sat down next to me. Then, he asked me whether I'd read a certain article by Jabotinsky! Why he came over, I'm still not sure. But he had four hours with a pretty girl like me, and all he talked about was Jabotinsky!"

The first girl Begin courted, just after the mission to Czechoslovakia, was named Ela Neuberg. He was turning twenty-three, and she was nineteen—a Betar supporter in Warsaw who wanted to become a doctor. "They spent hours together!" recalls David Yutan, who later married the girl's sister. "I can't say whether it was love. But he had very close feelings for her. I got the impression there was a possibility of marriage." She left Poland, however—to study medicine in Italy. By the time she returned, Begin had found his second love: Aliza Arnold, of Drohobych.

He met her after a Betar speech: Her father, a lawyer and a leading Revisionist in town, invited Begin home for dinner. The seventeen-year-old Aliza, and her twin sister, were there. An asthmatic from childhood, she looked weak, and said little. She was a member of Betar, but always listened more than talked at meetings. She was not beautiful—wags were quick to say Begin liked her because she looked like Jabotinsky. But she had regular features, long dark hair, a sudden smile, and eyes that could bore into you like diamonds. That first evening, Begin's strongest impression was that she had nice table manners. Yet he fell for her with an abruptness and depth rivaled only by his romance with Jabotinsky Zionism. The next day, as he headed out of town to deliver another speech, he wrote: "I saw you, my lady, for the first time. But I feel as if I have known you all my life."

He spent every hour he could with her, and courted her by letter when he was away. He even managed to spirit her to Brisk, for a meeting with his parents. "They loved her," he would recall years later (although Begin's mother did remark to Rachel that the girl had an annoying, Galician manner of "embracing me all the time"). Menachem, for his part, had little doubt that he had found his life's partner. Only first, he had a political challenge to meet: the Betar conference.

As it approached, almost everyone expected Propes to come under pressure from pro-IZL militants, and Begin was their unofficial standard-bearer. They knew, recalls David Yutan, that "the real reason he had left [Warsaw] was because he disagreed with Betar policy." Propes, too, could not help but sense the brewing storm. Still, he knew something else as well: Begin and his allies could not confront Aharon Propes, without also confronting Jabotinsky.

It was a determined and self-confident Begin who returned to Warsaw in September 1938. The World Betar Conference was a homecoming, held, under Jabotinsky's gaze, in the Jewish dormitory near the bank of the Vistula. It opened amid new threats to the Jews of Europe. Hitler had convinced Britain's Neville Chamberlain that appeasing the Nazis could bring "peace in our time." In Palestine, Arab-Jewish violence had cowed the authorities into further curbing Jewish immigration. An Irgun youngster was hanged for trying to ambush a busload of Arabs in reprisal for the murder of a Jew. The condemned man walked to the gallows proclaiming: "Long live Jabotinsky!"

Begin spoke the first day of the conference. He said that for years young Jews had believed "moral pressure" would secure their homeland. No longer: "Everything has changed—both in Israel and in the world. We must draw conclusions. Most of all, the conscience of the world has ceased to respond. We regret this. But it is a fact. It cannot be denied." The British, he charged, "send the best of our young men to the gallows. We must face the truth: They must first and foremost consider the Arabs." And this, he said, was because

Arabs fought and killed, while the Jews just talked. "We have had enough of surrender!" shouted Begin. "We want to fight—either to win, or to die!" Playing to Jabotinsky's admiration for Garibaldi's liberation of Italy the century before, he proclaimed: "Italy would not have been liberated without Garibaldi!"

Jabotinsky broke in. "Sir," he said drily, "you may want to recollect the ratio of Italians to non-Italians in the country at the time." When Begin shifted ground, arguing that the "example of the Irish War of Independence" showed that a people could "fight for one's homeland on occupied soil," Jabotinsky persisted. "Tell me, sir, how you propose to get Betar soldiers into the country without foreign assistance?" Begin replied that once the Jews had an army, foreign backing would come. "What I want is for us to start creating an independent military force." If that decision were taken, military experts could do the groundwork. Yet Jabotinsky, like an attorney in cross-examination, remarked: "Have you taken note, sir, of the proportion between Hebrew forces and Arabs in Israel?"

"We will win with *moral* force!" Begin declared. "Even if we are to fall in battle, we will fight. The time has come for war. Without war, Zionism is being destroyed. Betar has no choice but to follow this road, in order to save Zionism." Then he threw down the gauntlet. Forcing a floor vote, he proposed to change the oath recited by Betar initiates since the founding of the youth group. It was an amendment the IZL might have written. The old version pledged recruits to prepare "for defense of my Homeland," adding: "I will raise my arm only in defense." Begin dropped that pledge, and proposed instead: "I will prepare my arm for the defense and the conquest of my Homeland."

"There are millions of Jews who have nothing to lose," he explained. "Our role is to exploit the power shackled within them."

Jabotinsky had had enough. "Allow me," he said, "to address some sharp words to the assembly. As your teacher, I have the duty to do so. Forgive me if I speak harshly. But there are various kinds of noise. Some are useful—the creak of machines or wagons, for instance—and we abide them. But the creaking of a door, by contrast, is futile, unnecessary. There is no room in Betar for such noise. Some noise is beautiful, but we must avoid the temptation to make noise for its own sake. Remarks such as those of Mr. Begin are like the creaking of doors, and in Betar must be ruthlessly repressed. Hebrew violence," said Jabotinsky, had its place, but only as a catalyst for "the world conscience." Now was a time for realism. Were

Jews strategically placed to emulate Garibaldi? No. "This is balder-dash and nonsense." The goal must be to transport Jews to Pales-tine, and this must "take precedence over shows of heroism." Arguing that past immigration had been won by appealing to the conscience of the world, he railed against Begin's pessimism: "If there are those who feel there is no way out but Mr. Begin's, you have weapons—commit suicide! If there is indeed no conscience in the world, you have the option of Communism, or"—arching his arm toward the river two blocks away—"there are the waters of the Vistula.

"If I am wrong," said Jabotinsky, "I suggest we disband Betar. . . . To say there is no conscience is to despair. We must sweep such no-tions aside. Of course we must all express our own opinions. But there is a limit to such freedom. Conscience rules the world. I re-spect this truth. To mock it, ridicule it, must be forbidden. I under-stand your pain. But to let pain produce despair is dangerous. It is the loud creaking of a door—futile and unnecessary."

Despite Jabotinsky's plea, the delegates accepted Begin's amend-ment. They chose the twenty-five-year-old *shtetl* orator over Betar's founder, now nearing sixty. Begin pushed no further. The confer-ence reelected Propes as Betar leader. It reiterated its devotion to Jabotinsky as honorary chairman, at which point Begin turned to him and added: "Sir, world Betar in all its branches and ranks awaits your command!" But word of the confrontation with Jabo-tinsky spread. "It made Begin famous," recalls Hillel Kook, who was in Warsaw but did not attend the Betar congress. Yisrael Scheib—a Revisionist professor who spoke on Begin's side at the conference—goes further. "Begin's speech made him what he be-came. Jabotinsky was a legend! A towering figure. Opposing Jabo-tinsky was not like opposing someone like Shimon Peres! Yet here was Begin, proving himself strong enough to get up and speak against Jabotinsky."

Propes emerged with his position intact but his power depleted. At the start of 1939, the IZL sent a second envoy, Mordechai Stre-litz, to Warsaw to beef up IZL membership and choose youngsters for the Polish training camps. Strelitz didn't even bother phoning Propes on arrival. Jabotinsky tried to rescue his Betar leader, firing off a note to the Irgun commander in Palestine, David Raziel, and ordering him to stop undermining Propes's authority. When this had no effect, Jabotinsky summoned Raziel to Paris in February and greeted him with a question: "Are you a militant of Betar?"

"By birth," replied Raziel, who genuinely admired Jabotinsky. "Are you prepared to accept any decision we come to?"

"Unhesitatingly," Raziel replied.

Jabotinsky was delighted. "I've been waiting for the last fifteen years," he said, "for such a man." But the grass roots of the IZL, and Betar, were in a more militant mood. "The Irgun delegation, with the exception of Raziel, was anything but cooperative," recalls a Jabotinsky aide who attended. "Jabotinsky somewhat dejectedly observed that Raziel in fact did not seem to have full control of his own colleagues." In the end, the Revisionist leader had little choice but to draft an agreement acknowledging the ascendancy of the Irgun Zvai Leumi. Nominally, Betar would still outrank the Irgun in Europe. But top priority in Betar would go to IZL activity—via a new "military command," nominally part of Betar but run by Strelitz. Propes was sent on a diplomatic mission to America, ending his tenure as commander. As successor, recalls Kook, "Jabotinsky chose a man who, though not a *member* of the Irgun, was known as an Irgun sympathizer, a man who Jabotinsky thought would make a good go-between." He chose Menachem Begin.

Begin, however, meant to be much more than a go-between.

Chapter Four

War

Begin moved into Propes's office, but spent much of his time in Mordechai Strelitz's cramped quarters down the hall. He sealed a partnership that gave Strelitz rein over the technical aspects of the Irgun training camps, but reserved political control for himself. Begin dazzled Strelitz. "He was only a young man, but he had already graduated from university," recalls the IZL veteran, who had not. "I was impressed." Begin peppered—flattered—him with questions about Irgun operations in Palestine, and implied that he hoped to enlist in its ranks one day. The curiosity was genuine, and Begin delighted in the military trappings of the IZL. When a senior Irgun officer visited Poland shortly after he took over, Begin brushed aside his aides' misgivings and ordered a welcome complete with honor guard. Strelitz, for his part, invited Begin along on visits to the Polish training camps. When Begin named a new Betar High Command—allies from the confrontation with Propes—he designated David Yutan as head of the emigration campaign the Irgun had wanted to control. Yutan was told to liaise with the IZL, but not defer to it. "There was coordination," he recalls. "There was none of the conflict that existed under Propes."

Begin enlisted three other members of his command to tighten political and ideological control over both Betar and the IZL in Poland. He told Yisrael Scheib to draw up a detailed plan to "strengthen the intellectual and spiritual education" of Betar recruits. To monitor progress, he included a school chum of Yutan's (and a onetime student of Professor Scheib's) named Yisrael Epstein. He assigned a friend of Epstein's, Moshe Stein,* to add political lectures to the arms training offered in the IZL camps. But it was Begin who ran the show. "He *ruled*," says Scheib. "The only other people who mattered at all were Yutan and Epstein: He would tell them everything *before* our formal meetings." However, both were younger than Begin, and they deferred to him. "They were nice boys," recalls Scheib. "But they were not people who could *discuss* with Begin as equals." Yutan agrees: "We were close—Menachem, Epstein, and I. We went through thick and thin. But even though we were friends, you always felt a distance." Like most young men, Yutan and Epstein told a dirty joke now and then. "But," says Yutan, "we didn't *dare* tell one around Begin. With Menachem— even though we were so close in those days—one felt the need for respect. It was not a matter of rank; there was just something inside Begin—a power—that you *felt*."

The second weekend of April 1939—Easter—Begin made one of his increasingly rare visits home to Brisk. Poland's Jews were shuddering in fear of Hitler, who had rounded up thousands of their brethren in Germany and dumped them over the border. Then, in a night of broken glass, German mobs had gutted synagogues and shops, as Nazi police gazed on. Hitler reacted by arresting twenty thousand more Jews, and sending them to camps. On March 15 he had taken Czechoslovakia without a shot. That same day, the British handed Zionist envoys the draft text of a new Palestine policy. A surrender to Arab demands known as the White Paper, it envisaged Jewish statehood after ten years—but meanwhile would curb Jewish land purchases in Palestine, and all but end Jewish immigration. A total of seventy-five thousand Jews could come in the next five years; any arrivals after that would need Arab approval. The trap around Polish Jews was tightening. To the west lay Germany. To the south, Nazified Czechoslovakia. To the east, Russia. There was one exit: the southeast border with Romania, in the foothills of the Carpathian Mountains. The British White Paper threatened to make even that irrelevant.

Barely was Begin home than he felt he should be back in Warsaw.

---

* Not to be confused with Moshe Steiner, the schoolteacher who introduced Begin to Betar in Brisk-de-Lita.

His parents wanted the family together through Passover, the next Saturday, and Rachel and Herzl were in no hurry to leave. Menachem, however, boarded the train back to the Polish capital, promising his father to return for the holiday. He told the town's Betar branch the same thing, whereupon it printed posters announcing he would deliver a speech. But when Ze'ev Dov walked to the station Saturday to meet his son, he did not appear. Once back in Warsaw, Menachem led a demonstration against the White Paper. The crowd marched on the British embassy. Begin hurled stones through the windows, was carted away by police, booked, and jailed. His head was shaved. "It was not an ordinary prison, not the worst kind," says Rachel. "Still, he was locked up along with some common criminals."

A Jabotinsky aide, working through the American embassy, soon got him out—with a warning from the head of Poland's security police to keep out of trouble. Menachem emerged from jail, found Rachel waiting for him, and returned to her apartment to rest—but only after she agreed to buy dozens of cigarettes for his Polish cellmates. Years later, Begin's memory would stretch the jail term to "nearly two months" and rehearse "rather harsh" trials at the hands of other prisoners. In fact, he seems to have got on well with them. He lectured thieves on politics. They in turn helped him adjust, did chores on his behalf. "He formed ties with the other prisoners," says Rachel. "This is why he immediately wanted me to get the cigarettes."

Begin led no more marches. He contented himself with Jabotinsky's conversion to IZL militancy when, in mid-May, London published the White Paper. "The Irgun is your salvation!" the Revisionist founder told a Warsaw rally. "The White Paper will be ripped to pieces. It denies you the right to save your lives!" Begin set about defying the White Paper on the ground, drawing up plans for Jews to leave through Romania and then travel by Black Sea ship to Palestine. He worked without rest. Scheib, unable to focus on drafting his Betar "education" plan, glanced up one morning to find Begin at his office door. "Menachem," he said, "I can't work in such circumstances! The world is in chaos. Everyone knows there's going to be a war!" Begin replied: "Everybody *must* do his job," and walked out.

He paused only once, to go to Galicia at the end of May to marry Aliza. "I told her life would be hard," Begin recalls. "I told her we would never have any money." He offered the prospect of "prison, too, for we would have to fight for the Land of Israel." Aliza said she was not afraid. They were wed wearing Betar uniforms, and attended by Jabotinsky, who wished Begin the happiness "I would wish for my own son." Begin stayed overnight, then returned to Warsaw. Aliza stayed behind for several weeks. She arrived in the capital "full of energy," recalls Yisrael Scheib's wife, Batya, who drew close to her. "She was a dynamic young girl, not yet experienced in life." She never complained, however, recalls Menachem: She understood the need "to work, to organize the big migration to Palestine."

Begin left for the Romanian port of Constanța to see off a first boatload of emigrants, and spent the rest of the summer trying to arrange a second exodus. By twos and threes, a thousand Jews from all over Eastern Europe gathered near Poland's southeast border. Begin sent an aide into Romania with a suitcase of cash to ensure safe transit. He had Moshe Stein run political lectures and weapons training for the refugees, camped near the border town of Sniatyn. He, too, felt war was coming—even after receiving a letter from Jabotinsky predicting that Europe would yet come to its senses. To Rachel, Begin showed the note and remarked: "Maybe he is just too humane, too kind, to contemplate so terrible a war." For the refugees on the border, Begin felt, emigration could mean the difference between life and death.

Yet suddenly, the British intervened, persuading Poland and Romania to halt the emigration attempt and order the Jews back home. The Jews, with nothing to lose, stayed put. Begin summoned Stein back to Warsaw, then thought better of this and sent him back to boost morale among the refugees, and to minimize free-lance attempts to escape across the border. Begin toyed with seeking an airplane to fly them to the Black Sea, but found the scheme unworkable. Then he boarded a train for Sniatyn. He arrived to find hundreds living in dirt and sweat by day, and, increasingly, risking capture by trying to escape at night. The Romanians had discreetly offered twenty-five transit visas—ensuring an uproar in camp over who should get them. Betar officials on the spot had planned to allocate the visas on the basis of a random list drawn up weeks earlier, when it was assumed everyone would get across. Begin, however, called the camp together. Shouting above the grumble of the refugees, he said it was a time for discipline. There was a number of particularly urgent cases among the camp population—Jews from Lithuania who, if not allowed to cross, would be arrested on returning home. Next in importance was the fate of draft-age youths: For them, an exit visa would mean the difference between fighting in Polish uniform in Europe, or battling as Jews in Palestine. "I appeal to you," Begin declared. "I ask the first twenty-five names on the original list to give up your own places, to sacrifice them, for the good of all!" David Yutan, who was there, feared a riot. "He was asking them to risk their lives!" It was, says Yutan, the single most powerful speech of Begin's career. "He found the twenty-five! He talked them into it!"

The next night—August 31, 1939—he took the train back to Warsaw. Yet before he arrived, Hitler's tanks and bombers invaded Poland. As bombs rained on Warsaw, Begin made his way through the chaos of the train station to Betar headquarters. Assembling the High Command, he spoke less like a Jew than a Pole—less like Bar Kochba than Mickiewicz. "We are citizens of Poland," he said. "Our responsibility as citizens is to help the government." He issued an order for Betar ranks to help the Poles dig trenches, and then set off to find the commander of the Polish Army. The commander was busy. "But we met with a general," recalls Yutan. "Begin proposed we organize special Betar battalions—Jewish battalions—in the Polish Army, for special missions." The general said he would pass on the offer.

In the several days that followed, Hitler sliced through the Polish Army—literally, like tanks through cavalry. Begin got no response from the army brass. He was issuing further instructions on trench digging when the door of Betar headquarters flew open and in strode Uri Zvi Greenburg, the closest thing to a Revisionist poet laureate. "What are you people still doing here in Warsaw?" he snapped at Begin. "You're crazy!" Gesturing toward a map on the wall, he said, "You see this? This is Poland. The Russians are going to take half of it, and the Germans the other half. It is already happening! Can't you see?" Yet Begin replied: "As long as we are here we are Polish citizens, we will not desert. We are not deserters."

It took two days for his resolve to crumble—under Nazi bombs and the certainty Hitler would take Warsaw. Begin decided to retreat southeastward, to Lublin, and return when the fighting subsided. He told Stein to bring the organization's funds and essential archives. With Aliza, Stein, and those Betar comrades who remained, he boarded a train at the end of the first week in September. Recalls one High Command member: "We figured England and France would rescue Poland, and destroy the German Army in six or eight weeks." In fact, Begin boarded one of the last trains to leave a free Warsaw. "We were bombed repeatedly," recalls Scheib. "We would get off when the bombers swarmed in, jump back on when they left." At Lublin—under air attack—Begin decided they must flee farther: to Kovel, then across the Romanian border, and on to Palestine. Minutes later, a bomb detonated a carload of Polish Army ammunition at the head of the train. Dozens died. Begin, in the rear of the train, was unscathed and unruffled. He drafted a note in Polish asking for food and other supplies from the nearest town. Stein delivered it, and got the supplies. But by the time he returned, the train had been repaired and was ferrying Begin and the others to Kovel.

Well to the north—in Brisk-de-Lita—Begin's parents and brother watched the Germans arrive. So did David Yutan, who had fled Warsaw by a later train and made his way, wounded, to Begin's birthplace. "Where is Menachem?" his mother asked. "Is he well? Where will he take refuge? He must write!" But Menachem's father was calmer: "Menachem," he said, "will find his way, no matter what the difficulties.

"You can rely on Menachem."

Chapter Five

Flight

Menachem moved by rail, cart, and foot toward Kovel—slowed by German bombs, then by a worsening of Aliza's asthma. He took her to her family in Drohobych, and suggested she rest there while he arranged the crossing into Romania. She refused. As they resumed their trek, Hitler was mopping up most of Poland, and ceding Stalin the rest. Within hours after the Begins reached Lvov with their re-assembled Betar comrades, Soviet police called in Menachem for questioning. He was released but, taking no chances, headed south—to the border post at Sniatyn. His comrades secured a pair of exit visas for the Begins. But Menachem said rank-and-file Betar members must cross first. "There is time," Aliza agreed. There wasn't; the Soviets closed the border.

The best of bad options came to Begin by radio a week later: the news that Stalin had taken Lithuania but had declared its capital, Vilna, a free city. The town had other advantages. It was home to Yutan and Epstein, and so vibrantly Jewish it was known as the Jerusalem of Europe. So the Begins headed for Vilna—"Three exhausting and perilous days in boxcars and train carriages," recalls Yutan, who had rejoined them—and halted there.

They moved in with Yutan's family for a few days, then rented an apartment, whereupon Menachem set about re-creating Betar's Warsaw organization without Warsaw. Hundreds of fleeing Jews had made their separate ways to Lithuania. The bagful of Polish zlotys Stein had hauled east was all but worthless, yet Begin secured a trickle of hard currency from Irgun backers abroad. He kept his men on salary, set up a dormitory for Betar and IZL refugees, and began giving political lectures. He directed Yutan and Scheib to resume "emigration" work, and founded a weekly newspaper. He had one of Strelitz's IZL officers lead a weapons course. Begin was a student in that class, but leader in everything else. "It was a little crazy," recalls Yutan. "All these activities despite the war. But I think it was mainly a question of morale."

Begin needed the boost most of all. For the first time since escaping Warsaw, he had a chance to reflect. He sensed that his family, who had not fled, would surely die. Yutan told him that while he had been in Brisk, the Nazis rounded up Herzl and others and lined them up along a wall. An execution squad assembled. The commander shouted, "Fire!" No one did: It was the Nazis' idea of a joke. In Warsaw, meanwhile, thousands of other Jews remained— including the leaders of other Zionist groups. Begin felt guilt, and it burst to the surface with the arrival of a letter from a veteran Betar-IZL organizer in Palestine, Shimshon Yunitchman, questioning his failure to stay put. "When the ship is sinking, the captain leaves *last*, not first!" the note said. Begin was "jolted," recalls Scheib, and promptly proposed that they all return to Warsaw. Scheib is unsure how badly Begin wanted to go back: He and the others knew this would amount to suicide. "Maybe he was not too sorry we voted against him. Maybe if he'd been determined, he could have convinced us, as he had on other issues. Or he could have vowed to return alone." Still, Scheib sensed an "underlying seriousness" in the suggestion—a measure of Begin's agony at having left.

He was torn, both aching to leave for Palestine and determined never again to abandon ship. When news came that David Raziel and Jabotinsky had agreed to an IZL truce for the duration of Britain's war with Hitler, Begin shouted: "This is a betrayal of our cause! A betrayal!" Yet when exit permits were bought, bribed or forged, Begin insisted he would not use one until everyone else had safely left. He pushed Betar activities to the limit of official tolerance, even as the Soviets were pressing the Lithuanians to keep order or risk losing Vilna. In late July of 1940, Begin organized a rally to mark Theodor Herzl's birth. Midway through it, he was handed a note: Soviet troops were entering the city. Others on the dais were shaken, but Begin called for order, and declared: "We shall conclude this meeting—maybe our last in this country—by singing 'Hatikva.' " Scheib says he "will never forget that 'Hatikva'—sung with tears in our eyes. It was typically Begin!"

He closed the dormitory, then the newspaper. He stopped paying

Betar salaries, as the Soviets choked off funds from outside. What money did get through went to secure passage for at least a few Jews on Soviet carriers. Refugees needed European "consular letters" to qualify, and Begin saw to the forgeries. To buy food, he and the others started looking for work.

Then Jabotinsky died—in American exile. "I felt," says Begin, "that the bearer of hope was gone, never to return; and with him— perhaps never to return—hope, itself." He summoned the High Command, and insisted on a commemoration. When a revered Talmudic scholar died days later, Begin and his comrades peeled off from the funeral procession and held a ceremony for Jabotinsky. In a graveyard speech, Begin said that since they could no longer fight for Zion, it was their duty to suffer for it. "His words," says Yutan, "were full of pain. All of us were thinking: Jabotinsky is dead. The world is at war. The Germans are winning. Everything is falling apart. So what are *we* doing *here*?"

The Soviets heard about Begin's speech and came looking for him, at Yutan's house. At the others' urging, Menachem and Aliza left for a village in the hills outside town. The Begins and the Scheibs shared a house there; Yutan and his wife got an apartment. Begin spent much of his time reading politics and philosophy, or playing chess with Scheib. Afternoons, the two men ventured into the surrounding woods to chop fuel for the fireplace. Even the fire did not always dent the autumn damp, which would leave the asthmatic Aliza wheezing for breath. Yet, when she was feeling well, Menachem would sometimes produce French- and English-language textbooks; and the Begins would sit and quiz each other on vocabulary. "He and Aliza never quarreled," recalls Scheib. Yet having fled again—if only a few miles—Begin's guilt gnawed deeper. A *shtetl* ally from the early Betar days, Yerachmiel Wirnik, had stayed behind in Vilna. He sent word that Begin's departure had hurt Betar's emigration efforts, and urged him to return. The plea hit a raw nerve. Begin scrawled in reply: "I am now living in the woods, with a wood-burning fire. Do you wish me to throw into the same fire the friendship between a young boy from Brest and a young boy from Kovel!"

The Soviets soon discovered Begin's refuge. In September he got a letter calling him to Vilna City Hall in connection with an inquiry he had not made. Plainclothesmen loitered in the village. "We knew it was a matter of only a few days," says Yutan, "before the police made their move." They pressed Begin to flee, but he refused, saying: "If they want to arrest me, I will face it. I am the commander of Betar. My arrest will satisfy them, so that others will not be arrested." Around lunchtime on September 20, 1940, the police came. Begin and Scheib were playing chess. "Three men arrived, in civilian clothes," Begin's companion recalls. "They asked why he hadn't come to City Hall." Begin said if they wanted to arrest him, he must insist they show a warrant. But the ploy, which had worked for Ze'ev Dov Begin twenty years earlier, did not work now. Scheib's wife started to sob. Aliza did not. "She was very strong," says Scheib. "She came in and asked the police whether they'd like to have lunch. They'd never seen such a performance!"

Begin retired to the bedroom to dress for jail. He donned tie and jacket. He packed a Bible, and a biography of Disraeli. He polished his shoes. He embraced Scheib, kissed Aliza, and, gesturing to the policemen like a country squire on the way to a foxhunt, declared: "After you, gentlemen." As he was leaving, Yutan arrived. "Tell Yisrael I concede the chess game," Begin chirped. He was, he said years later, "ready to get arrested. After the death of Jabotinsky, the whole world blackened for me."

Besides, arrest was an end to flight—a relief, and a challenge. Begin was not only ready to face his inquisitors. "He *wanted*," says Yutan, "to face them."

Chapter Six

Prison

Begin was taken to Soviet police headquarters and told that all he had to do was tell the truth, and he would be released. When he replied that he had done nothing wrong, the police officer accused him of lying and of organizing "anti-Soviet" activity. Begin scolded him: "I have read that representatives of the Soviet authorities behave courteously to citizens. Besides," he said, "I am not telling lies." They booked him, led him through the iron gates of Vilna Prison, and locked him in a third-floor cell with two other prisoners, both Polish. One was an aristocrat, whom Begin disliked. The other was a tailor by trade, and a corporal in the Polish Army. Begin started tutoring him: "in a number of subjects, principally the history of his own people and of other nations."

At night, the guards took Begin to a "small, warm, well-lighted room" for further questioning. His interrogator was a Soviet Jew, whom Begin baited, cajoled, and lectured on good manners. "You don't have to hurt my feelings," he protested when the officer cast aspersions on Jabotinsky, "even if I am a prisoner." When the NKVD* man said the prisoner's feelings didn't interest him, and lashed out at the "farce" and "fraud" that were Zionism, Begin retorted: "What right have you to say Zionism is a farce?" The debate lasted until dawn. Returning to his cell, Begin says he had been so

---

* The People's Commissariat of Internal Affairs, the controlling body of the Soviet secret police from 1934 to 1946.

caught up in the test of wills that he felt he was heading back to a hotel room from summit talks on the "future of my people." The sense was so real that he turned to the duty officer and asked whether there had been any mail in his absence.

The debate went on, intermittently, for several nights. At one point, when Begin quoted the Soviet constitution in his defense, the officer exploded: "What? You quote me the Stalin constitution, you damned lawyer!" Still, says Begin, there were no beatings, no torture—only threats of "other means," neither explained nor implemented. In the end he was handed a "confession" to sign, "admitting" he had headed Betar in Poland. Begin objected to the wording; he said he would "acknowledge" his Betar work but not "*admit*" it. Admission implied guilt. The investigator argued for a while, but gave in.

Menachem missed home. He missed his mother—the "comfort" of her embraces. He missed Aliza. He asked his cellmates whether he should send her permission to seek a divorce. When they said yes, however, Begin hesitated. He asked the advice of another prisoner, who persuaded him to drop the idea. Soon afterward a Betar girl, posing as Aliza, was permitted to visit. She told him that his wife had safely escaped to Palestine, with David Yutan.

Jail turned ugly as winter set in. Begin was overheard telling a joke that his warder thought disrespectful, and was sentenced to a week's solitary confinement. As he was led to his windowless cubicle, he took stock of himself—one of the prison "intellectuals, with thin puny bodies"—and wondered whether he would emerge alive. Yet he saw solitary as a test. He was given only bread and water. The cell was empty except for a slop pail that the guards never emptied. "For a pillow, I had to use my arm. . . . By day it was too hot, and at night freezing cold. In addition, I was entertained by a thriving colony of rats." Still, says Begin: "I survived."

On April 1, 1941, he was led to a jailhouse "trial" with dozens of others. Each was asked his name. Papers were shuffled, verdicts pronounced. Menachem Begin was declared "an element dangerous to society" and sentenced to a "Correctional Labor Camp for a period of eight years."

He was taken back to his cell to wait for the sentence to be implemented. When the Betar girl visited again, Begin told her to tell Aliza "I am proud of her. Write that I am proud of them all. Write that I am strong and healthy, and that I will come back." It was not until June, however, that he left Vilna. He was roused early one morning and taken with hundreds of prisoners to the train station. With seventy others, he was packed into a freight car with bars on the windows and two tiers of wooden slabs for bunks. The rumor started that they were headed for a labor camp one thousand miles north, near the railhead of Kotlas. The train chugged for days through unfamiliar countryside, stopped for days without explanation, then resumed the journey into Russia. The monotony and stench were interrupted only twice a day, by head counts and meals of cold fish preserved in salt. "The worst thing," Begin says, "was the thirst." At one station a guard responded to howls of "Water, water!" by scooping bowlsful from a puddle of green slime. The prisoners shouted in protest. But, says Begin, "the reply of the NKVD men was quiet and leisurely, even reasonable: 'The next station is far away. You wanted water, and this is the only water we can give you.' " Begin drank.

In the last week of June, good news came. It traveled by word of mouth, from soldier to soldier, siding to train siding. Hitler had broken his pact with Stalin. Having raced through Western Europe, the Nazis were ready to turn east, and make war on Russia. Begin recalls that the news "burst in with the force of a storm." The prisoners sensed it was true, from the surge of Soviet military traffic in the opposite direction. Polish prisoners, like Begin, were especially heartened: They had been jailed at least partly because the Soviets were at war with Poland. Now chances were that Moscow and the exiled Polish government would join hands against Hitler.

Still, the alliance would take time. The train chugged on to Kotlas, and beyond. In mid-July it came to the end of the line—at Koshva, a few hundred miles from the Arctic Circle, in east-central Russia. As Begin and the others were marched through mud for several hours to Pechorlag, a camp near the Pechora River, he struck up conversation with the guards. "They told us back in Vilna that if we worked well, we would get out sooner," he prompted. The guard replied, "People don't get out of here."

Begin spent the first ten days in the infirmary, having met two other Polish Zionists who talked him into trading a button-down shirt for a sick pass. Then he entered camp in earnest. Only a week later, the Poles and the Soviets signed their anti-Hitler pact: All Polish prisoners would go free when formal okay arrived from Moscow. Still, day after day passed without its arriving. Begin marched each morning to the banks of the Pechora to help unload iron crossbars for use on a new rail spur to Vorkuta, on the rim of the Arctic Circle. "We carried the iron supports on our shoulders from the ship along a narrow plank to the shore," he recalls. Then he would haul them to a truck three hundred yards away. His shoulders burned with pain. Tundra flies stung "face, hands, ears, nostrils. . . . Millions of them, billions!" Yet the common criminals—*urki*, in camp slang— made fun of his agony, of the bruises on his "delicate, white hands." Back at camp, he says, they delighted in "humiliating" him.

At first, he resented their jeers. He used his stock of dress shirts to bribe the thugs to leave him alone. When they stole most of his remaining clothes, he made a point of reporting the theft to camp authorities—flouting the law of the Gulag. Yet he quickly came to admire the *urki*'s expertise, and sought an accommodation with them. "They really *did* know what to do. They put pads made of rags on their shoulders to protect the skin" on work detail. "They put on masks made of netting, or rags punched with holes" to ward off the flies. After his initial show of independence, Begin good-naturedly accepted a nickname bestowed by the *urki*—"Four Eyes," for his glasses. He took to sharing a hand-rolled smoke with the camp elders on work breaks. The criminals—like an earlier breed in a prison cell in Warsaw—took him under their wing, and helped him haul the iron rails when the sun got too hot, or the flies too vicious.

After barely a week's labor Begin fell ill for real. Though not admitted to sick bay, he was exempted from work. As he sweated under a temperature of almost 103, lice attacked from his mattress. It was the first time since his arrest, he says, that he feared death. "It was the first time—I felt to my annoyance—that I was beginning to be sorry for myself." The fever lasted three days. The fourth day, feeling a bit better, he reported to the infirmary for convalescent advice. The medic ordered him back to work. "I'm still very weak," Begin protested, but had no choice but to comply.

Back at work, he helped those even frailer. There was a Russian youth in camp who had been so badly tortured by Stalin's police that he could no longer control his bladder. "Lavatory," the *urki* called him. "The poor fellow was shunned," Begin recalls. "Everyone despised him. It was really difficult to stand next to him." Yet Begin spent hours with him, listening to his stories, giving the man his own tobacco ration. The indulgence touched even the *urki*— whose leader, a convicted killer known as Redbeard, took Begin aside to tell him so.

In late August, after several weeks in Pechorlag, Begin and hundreds of others were ordered north to a second camp. A group of Polish inmates implored him to intervene with the authorities and find out what had happened to the release order from Moscow. At first, Begin refused, saying proud men did not ask Stalin's police for favors. But the others argued that pride was a luxury they could not afford, and he relented. Seeking out a Soviet official, he was assured that all Poles would go free as soon as he got the order from Moscow—even if this meant plucking them from the riverboat taking them to the new camp.

The boat left with nearly a thousand prisoners, from Begin's camp and an adjacent one, crammed below deck. The vessel wafted toward the Arctic for nearly three weeks. It crawled with lice, was ruled by common criminals. Redbeard's men left Begin alone, but the *urki* from the second camp collected lice by the handfuls, fed them through the bunkboards onto the political prisoners, and chortled at their panic. "Did you receive the presents?" they would shout from above. Begin weathered the assaults, at least once with the intervention of Redbeard. But a Russian Jew named Garin, a former *Pravda* editor purged by Stalin, broke under the pressure. He moaned that the *urki* were out to kill him. Begin said he would ask Redbeard to intervene. But before he could, Garin went into a final hallucination and died. In the man's dying minutes, Begin sang "Hatikva" to him, as the *urki* guffawed.

And then, suddenly, the voyage was over. The orders from Moscow arrived, in the form of a sentry's shout from above deck. "Begin!" the alphabetical rollcall of Polish prisoners started. As he hurried above deck, the *urki* protested: "He's a Yid, not a Polack!" But he was a citizen of Poland. "I felt very light," says Begin. "I could hear the whirring of the wings of freedom."

Decades later, he would say he had spent two years "in [Vilna] prison and a Soviet concentration camp." In fact, the confinement had lasted a year—September 1940 to about September 1941. More than two thirds of this was spent in Vilna Prison. Another six weeks, Begin was on the train to Pechorlag; three more weeks, on the river transport. Begin spent only about a month in the Gulag—a *summer* month, adds one Begin disciple in a rare note of criticism. Half the camp stint was spent in a sickbed. Moreover, Begin (and the other Poles freed with him) left Pechorlag just before it entered its most murderous winter ever. Forty thousand of its prisoners—four of every five men—would die of ice and toil in the six months following his release. Begin's confinement, however brief, was agony. The bruised limbs, the tundra flies, the taunts of the *urki* were no invention. Yet looking back, Begin seems to have felt the need to make the hell seem hotter; his stay longer.

He moved south. He hopped freight cars, slept on park benches and in train stations, and tried to make his way to Palestine. The countryside was a-crawl with freed Poles. By word of mouth, Begin located Rachel and her husband in a town near the Afghan frontier. But fearing reimprisonment, he resumed his flight. When he heard that a veteran Revisionist lawyer, Yohanan Bader, was in a Turko-man town some five hundred miles away, Begin sent word for advice. Bader came in person, and advised him to link up with the Polish army-in-exile, which Stalin was helping equip to fight pro-Nazi regimes in the Middle East. Yet when Begin tried to enlist, he flunked the physical because of a weak heart, and weaker eyes. He scrawled a note to the Poles' chief of staff imploring him to reconsider. He was granted an audience, and explained his fear the Soviets might rearrest him. The officer relented but added, as Begin proclaimed his gratitude, "I'll be keeping an eye on you. Don't get it in your head to run off to Palestine once we head south!"

He didn't have to. The army moved to Persia, then westward, and in May 1942 crossed the Arab-ruled Transjordan into Palestine. When the unit paused on the East Bank of the Jordan River, Begin wandered into the grass to "breathe the odor of the fields of my Homeland." Once across, it took him only hours to get word to Aliza and Yutan that he was well—and establish that Epstein and Yisrael Scheib and Moshe Stein of the old Betar command were safely in Palestine. He also learned something else: Irgun commander David Raziel was dead. After calling the truce with the British, Raziel had volunteered for a sabotage mission into pro-Nazi Iraq, only to perish in an air raid. Begin had lived to see the Land of Israel. But the IZL, his hope for a Jewish state there, lay in tatters.

Chapter Seven

Home

Begin reunited with Aliza: Their first child, Benjamin, would be born ten months later. But he had little time for family. He worked as a translator at Polish headquarters in Jerusalem. What free time he had, he spent with Palestine's Jabotinsky Zionists. He attended their meetings, and spoke at them—often fiddling with his wedding ring as he did, a gesture inherited from Jabotinsky. He was now, however, a celebrity in his own right: the leader of Betar for Poland, the man who had dared defy his master to raise the banner of the Irgun. Nearing thirty, he looked older than before—in Polish uniform, cap tilted rakishly over his right ear, a cigarette often dangling between second and third fingers. He reveled in the change, in being a soldier. "I met him a little while after his arrival in the country," says a comrade from Polish Betar days. "We were both in uniform. Begin wore that of a simple private in the Polish Army. I was a corporal in the British Army. And we found ourselves standing opposite one another. And Begin *saluted* me! I thought he was kidding. But no, he saluted my *rank*—quite seriously."

Begin briefly ran Betar in Palestine, supplanting Jabotinsky's son, Eri, who was in the United States with Hillel Kook, seeking American help to evacuate Jews from Europe. For Betar newspaper articles, Begin chose the pseudonym "Ben Ze'ev"—derived from Jabotinsky's Hebrew name and meaning "Son of Jabotinsky." But when the British put pressure on the Polish Army to rein Begin in, he left Betar. Following the lead of many Warsaw comrades, he sought an active, if discreet, role in the Irgun. Visiting Arye Altman, leader of the Revisionist party in Palestine since the late 1930s, Begin sought an introduction to allies of the late Raziel. Altman arranged a meeting with Raziel's sister, Esther. Almost exactly Begin's age, she sat on the IZL command cobbled together after her brother's death. "I met him in Dr. Altman's office in Jerusalem," she recalls. "Begin was in Polish uniform. He made mostly small talk, about Russia, conditions in Palestine." Yet he stressed, above all, an admiration for David Raziel. "He wanted to meet his friends, and his family and his followers." And, says Mrs. Raziel-Naor, they were equally anxious to meet him.

The Irgun had been at loose ends since Raziel's truce with Britain—when a group of top officers, led by a philosophy student named Avraham Stern, seceded. They formed the Fighters for Freedom in Israel—or LEHI—and mounted attacks on British officers and officials. On Raziel's death the Irgun leadership had passed to a Raziel protégé, Yaakov Meridor. He was brave but indecisive, more liked than respected. Dr. Altman was now setting overall Irgun policy, and his policy was to be on good behavior until the war was over. The IZL rank and file, however, ached to return to the offensive, all the more so since the British had killed Stern several months before.

Begin was their natural leader. One IZL novice recalls meeting with frustrated comrades in Tel Aviv when Begin strode in—"wearing khaki shorts, military boots, and wire-rimmed glasses, and a cap with the eagle of the Polish Army. I had never met him. I didn't know anything about him. But we'd been rambling until Begin spoke. He synthesized all that had been said in his absence. He defined the situation in which we lived, and the future—the struggle. He assessed the roles of the British, of Jews in the Diaspora. . . . He had an answer to all our questions." Veterans were equally impressed. "We were *frustrated* because of Raziel's death, the split with Stern, all these crises," says Eliahu Lankin, who had left active service since Meridor's accession. "I, of course, had heard of Begin—as Betar leader, as a speaker, as an opponent to Jabotinsky! I went to hear him at a meeting, and I was impressed." Along with other veterans, he sought a second meeting. "We talked with Begin. He was new to Palestine, which we were not, so he listened more than he talked. He asked us questions. And we told him— above all—that we felt the Irgun must no longer stay quiet." Menachem Begin agreed.

Days later, Lankin's group returned to Begin and asked him to assume command of the Irgun. "He was hesitant. He said he had to think it over; that he needed experience." Yet Lankin assured him that knowledge of military matters was not required: He and his friends wanted a "political leader—with *authority*. A commander." Besides, he explained, Begin had the advantage of being an outsider to the "intrigue, splits, and arguments" of the past two years.

As Begin mulled over the offer, debate over Lankin's move raged among grass-roots IZL members. Whatever the newcomer's strengths, many of the troops complained, he was an interloper. He could barely load a gun, much less fire one. "Word had passed from mouth to mouth that Begin had arrived and that some people wanted him as commander," says Moshe Stein, who began touring IZL units to push that view. "There was some strong opposition in all areas: Jerusalem, Netanya, Haifa. They wanted someone from the underground, a man with no shade of public reputation." Stein and other former Betar men "argued they were making a mistake: that Begin was a figure that people could *believe* in."

In the early summer of 1942, the Lankin group took its case to Meridor. They argued that only by installing Begin at the top could morale be rescued, and the fight for a Jewish state revived. Meridor seemed less surprised than relieved by the suggestion. Born in Galicia, he had revisited Poland for an IZL training course when Begin was in charge of Betar. Meridor had not met him, but recalls, "When I visited my father at the time and asked about Zionist developments, he said: 'You have a very able young leader, a fiery speaker, in this Begin; and I like him.' " Now he summoned Moshe Stein and asked him to bring Begin to IZL headquarters, a few blocks back from the seafront in Tel Aviv. Begin reported in Polish uniform, snapped to attention, and declared: "Commander, I am at your disposal."

Meridor was "amazed, embarrassed," recalls Stein. *No one* snapped to attention before Meridor in those days. Recovering, he suggested with equal formality that Begin "assume the burden of command." Begin proposed a compromise. He refused an immediate transfer of power, saying that as a public figure, still in Polish uniform, he couldn't possibly lead an uprising against British rule. Besides, said Begin, "I insist on going through proper channels." At least for the time being, he would "serve the Irgun as a simple soldier." Yet in fact, he quickly became much more. He offered behind-the-scenes political advice, and Meridor leaped at the idea.

Twice a week, the IZL chief traveled to Jerusalem to confer with the Polish Army translator. "I would put him in the full picture of what was going on in the Irgun. I consulted him on almost all matters."

It took only one meeting of the High Command, with Begin present on Meridor's invitation, for the others to see the new man could not remain a simple soldier. Rising to speak, Begin outlined a plan of action. Touching on history and politics, Europe and Palestine, he said he shared the others' urge to fight. But this time, the target must not be the Arabs; or the aim, revenge. The Irgun must fight the British, who were reneging on their Balfour pledge and sealing tight the gates to Palestine. "We must do more than fight," he said. "The world must be brought to understand *why* we are fighting." This, Begin implied, could be his job. "It was clear," says Esther Raziel-Naor, "that even though he asked to join as a private, his personality, breadth of knowledge, and understanding of political issues set him apart." He radiated a certainty and confidence beyond his years. Meridor would say, decades later, that one reason he felt Begin should assume command was "that I was too young for the job." He may have felt that way. In fact, he and Begin were both thirty.

As desperation deepened, the rank and file's opposition to Begin lessened. Rommel had only just been rebuffed at El Alamein, a few hundred miles south. From Europe came the first reports of the Holocaust. Thousands in Palestine received obituaries by word of mouth. The Begin name was among them. Ze'ev Dov was dead, and Chassia, and Herzl. The Germans had shot them. Menachem was told his father had gone to his grave in the Bug River, shouting a curse from the Torah: "A day of revenge will come unto you!"

Yet most of the IZL's veterans were, by 1942, seven thousand miles from Palestine. They were in America, where Hillel Kook was marshaling efforts to get Jews out of Nazi Europe. Serving under Kook were Jabotinsky's son, Eri, and the Revisionist founder's former aide, Shmuel Merlin. A pardoned Abrasha Stavsky was also there, with veteran IZL officers like Arye Ben Eliezer, a debonair Tel Aviv taxi driver who had been active in Irgun "immigration" work before Raziel's death. They all wanted Meridor out, and the Irgun's truce canceled. Unaware that his comrades in Palestine were well on the way to accomplishing both aims, Kook sent Ben Eliezer to Tel Aviv in the autumn of 1943—with a political platform advocating a "provisional Hebrew government"; and orders to encourage a leadership change in the IZL. Yet was Begin the man to lead? The name didn't even occur to the U.S. contingent. "As far as we knew, Begin wasn't even a member of the Irgun!" explains Kook.

Shortly after arriving in Palestine, Ben Eliezer wrote back suggesting that *he* take over from Meridor as military leader, with Kook as absentee political chief. Kook was cool to both ideas. Then, as Ben Eliezer canvassed fellow IZL veterans, Begin's name came up. Ben Eliezer, who had met him during the 1938 Betar conference in Warsaw, now invited him to discuss the future of the Irgun. Begin not only welcomed Kook's political platform. He said he'd been thinking along the same lines. The two men met several times: on Tel Aviv streets after nightfall, at the seaside Savoy Hotel, at Ben Eliezer's sister's house nearby. One night, Begin unfolded a typewritten "Proclamation of Revolt" against the British in Palestine. He said he had drafted it weeks before Ben Eliezer's arrival. Yet it resembled, in parts almost verbatim, Kook's platform. Ben Eliezer felt he had found his man.

Begin, however, was still a Polish soldier, and he refused to assume the IZL command as a "deserter." He had sworn an oath to the army. Ben Eliezer, and a veteran Warsaw Revisionist named Marek Kahan, now intervened. Contacting army headquarters, they proposed a deal. The Poles were desperate for U.S. support, and knew Kook's group had built up a congressional lobby unprecedented in U.S. history. If the army released Begin, he would go to America, join Kook, and lobby for Poland. The Poles agreed and discharged Begin in December. Yet he sped not to New York, but to Tel Aviv—where Meridor immediately handed over the IZL command.

Opposition to the handover remained, notably from Altman's Revisionists, who preferred the pliant and peaceable Meridor. When Begin went to see Altman's deputy in Jerusalem and served notice that the IZL's truce with Britain was about to end, the aide appealed for restraint. He said "Jewish unity" must claim top priority, and that other Jewish leaders would oppose Begin's move. Besides, how could a ragtag group of Irgun youngsters hope to humble Britain's nearly one hundred thousand troops in Palestine? Begin, replying that the time for timidity was over, turned and left.

Back in Tel Aviv, he resolved to cut ties with the Revisionists, lest they try to undermine his revolt. Calling a conference of Irgun field commanders, he asked for a vote of confidence. "I want to hear openly from each of you," he said, "whether you are ready to work with me." From a list handed to him by Meridor, he read out their names one by one. Says Raziel's sister, "Everyone had to stand up and say whether or not he was ready to accept." Several refused. One quit on the spot. The rest went along—although one officer, a nineteen-year-old *sabra* named Shlomo Lev-Ami, did so with an audible growl. (Meridor says, "Dr. Altman had wanted Lev-Ami to take over.") Begin co-opted him, making him "chief of staff" in a realigned High Command. He included Meridor as well, although easing him into several months' "vacation" during the transition. Rounding out the new team were Arye Ben Eliezer and Lankin. As an IZL alias, Begin took the name "Ben David," "Son of David." The reference, he said, was to Raziel.

Yet ending Raziel's truce was not as easy as Begin had hoped. If few among the Irgun's roughly one hundred active members doubted the peace must be broken, many feared breaking it too soon. "We had almost no guns," explains Eli Tavin, IZL intelligence chief at the time. Few shared Begin's confidence that a political strategy, forcefully argued to the Jews of Israel and the world, could make up for missing hardware. Though Begin pressed for an immediate declaration of war, it was well over a month before he felt strong enough to send a draft for typesetting. "Words. Just words!" scoffed the printer to Begin's "director of publications," David Yutan. When Yutan brought a sample to the High Command for approval, however, Begin tacked it on the door, read it in silence, and exclaimed: "Perfect!" Before dawn on February 1, 1944, dozens of IZL teenagers started pasting his "Proclamation of Revolt of the Irgun Zvai Leumi" on the walls of Palestine.

Chapter Eight

Revolt

Begin recalls waking up elated, thinking, "We are going to war." His poster, replete with boldface headings and exclamation points, demanded that the British cede power to a "provisional Hebrew government," which would proclaim a Jewish state. Those European Jews still alive must have a haven. Those who had escaped to Palestine owed it to their "slaughtered brethren" to stop paying taxes, call a general strike, march "day and night." Children must leave school, denounce the British for having "delivered our brethren to Hitler." Anyone who could not join—whether Jew or Arab— was told to stand aside. "The traitor shall be cursed, and the coward held in contempt," pledged Begin. There would be a fight "to the finish: for freedom—or death."

Yet his words fell flat. Eli Tavin, in Jerusalem, watched pedestrians cluster around the poster, chuckle and exclaim, "Dreamers! Revisionists!" There were no marches, no general strike, no school boycott.

Begin, bracing for a long struggle, left Aliza with their infant son in Jerusalem and moved into a Tel Aviv hotel under an alias. After nightfall, February 12, time bombs exploded at immigration offices in Palestine's three main cities: Tel Aviv, Haifa, and Jerusalem. There were no casualties, little damage, no arrests—only, the next morning, a new wall poster, in which Begin claimed responsibility for the bombings. He said the idea had been not to kill, but to make a political statement. Days later, the IZL hit Palestine's tax offices.

Still, Begin knew that it would take more than broken glass to convince the British—or fellow Jews—he meant business. The answer
to that problem came from Arye Ben Eliezer, emerging as the key
figure in Begin's High Command.

Ben Eliezer had Begin's grasp of strategy, plus the understanding
of military detail Begin lacked. He took aside the IZL "operations
chief," a brooding *sabra* teenager named Eitan Livni, and suggested,
"How about hitting police stations?" Livni, enticed by the challenge,
agreed. So did Begin, who then decided the *political* question of the
attacks' timing. On March 23, Ben Gurion's Labor Zionists called a
hunger strike to protest the murder of Jews in Europe. After sundown, IZL units attacked British police headquarters in Haifa, Tel
Aviv, and Jerusalem. Two bombs exploded. An attempt to plant a
third ended in a shoot-out with the British. In all, eight men died—
two IZL rebels and six Britons.

When Begin heard the news he turned to Ben Eliezer and said:
"Now it does not matter if we die." Addressing Palestine by wall
poster, he lamented the casualties on both sides, but he added:
"These victims fell in battle, in planned military attack. Soldiers of
the Irgun Zvai Leumi do not shoot from ambushes at accidental opponents. There is morality to their arms, and an aim to their war."
Begin said he, like David Ben Gurion, had fasted. "Yet we broke
our fast, not with a feast—but a battle."

Next morning, he traveled to Jerusalem for his son's first birthday. The British were combing Palestine for suspects, so he took an
Arab bus. His IZL escort, who spoke Arabic, relayed the passengers'
"mixture of amazement, fear, and admiration" at the bomb attacks.
Begin was heartened. Having never conversed with individual
Arabs, he saw them as a group—backward, but not necessarily dangerous. ("Woe to the cause that can be slaughtered by the knife of a
son of the desert," he would remark years later.) The bus gossip
confirmed in him a sense that the Jews could dazzle the Arabs into
neutrality. He drew up a message, had it translated into Arabic. It
said the IZL was not fighting the Arabs, only the British. If the
Arabs defied Begin, they would be punished. Far better, he said,
that they sit back and watch Jewish ingenuity and guts humble an
empire.

The British missed catching Begin by a hair, showing up at the
Jerusalem home just after he had returned to Tel Aviv. A few weeks
later, however, they caught a large number of IZL men—including
Arye Ben Eliezer and David Yutan. Begin's instinct was to move

deeper underground, and part from Aliza for the duration of his revolt. "It seemed healthier that she should live openly, not knowing
my whereabouts," he recalls. But when the British began harassing
her, Begin moved with Aliza and their son to an IZL safe house
near Tel Aviv. It had broken shutters. There was no heating or electricity. It did, however, have a large kitchen table, which Begin used
alternately for eating, reading, or receiving members of his IZL
command.

He reshuffled his inner circle—with the effect, if not intent, of
strengthening his own hold. He drafted Yisrael Epstein, who was
teaching school in Tel Aviv, as personal aide and confidant. Replacing Ben Eliezer as number two on the High Command was the
returning Meridor. Begin added two others to his cabinet: Operations Chief Livni, and a field commander from Haifa named Chaim
Landau. All had courage and military experience. On political matters, all except the loyal Epstein were neophytes.

The revolt sputtered after Ben Eliezer's arrest. It was two months
before the Irgun struck again. Guns blazing, Begin's troops captured
a British radio station near the Arab town of Ramallah. Yet when
they demanded to broadcast a Begin communiqué, they discovered
that they had attacked the wrong building: The radio's transmitting
station was in Jerusalem. For months afterward, the Irgun was silent. Morale sagged, amid taunts from Ben Gurion and Dr. Altman
in the political center and from Stern's LEHI heirs on the right. The
Establishment pressed Begin to abandon his sputtering revolt in
favor of Jewish unity. The Sternists—now including Yisrael Scheib
and another Begin colleague from Warsaw days, Nathan Yellin-
Mor—pressed him to join a campaign of assassination against individual British officials.

In July Begin chaired a secret "promotion ceremony" on the anniversary of Jabotinsky's death. In a pep talk to his troops, he maintained that public sympathy for the revolt was growing. He revealed
that the military wing of Ben Gurion's establishment, the Haganah,
had asked to meet with him. He had refused. "We have nothing to
say to them at present," he huffed. "They are emotionally unprepared for war." Begin was even more dismissive of the Revisionists.
"The movement belongs to us and not to Dr. Altman. It will support
us, because it is Jabotinsky's movement." And the Stern group?
Begin admired its militancy, but abhorred its lack of discipline. He
said he had been meeting with the Sternists, and saw advantages to
cooperating with them. But the Irgun must be in charge, he said,

adding icily that he had already "managed to convince them that their political slogans are inadequate."

Still, Begin knew his revolt was faltering. He told his troops they must find a way to escalate—go beyond symbolic strikes at the "prestige" of the British and "damage the administration's capacity to function as well." He then announced a symbolic strike, but of unprecedented daring. He called it the "Western Wall Campaign." The reference was to the Wailing Wall, the remnant of the Jewish Temple leveled by Rome almost two thousand years before. Since the Arab-Jewish violence of 1929, British troops had barred Jews from sounding the traditional ram's horn—or *shofar*—there on the Day of Atonement. "We have decided that on Yom Kippur this year," said Begin, "the shame with which this government of oppression has stained the last vestige of our past independence—the Western Wall, symbol of our country's sacredness—will be removed. This year, no foreigner will be allowed onto the plaza in front of the Wall. The traditional prayer will take place there without any interference from the oppressor's representatives. Also, the blowing of the *shofar* will be visible to all." He said the operation must go ahead, "at all costs." Aware that Yom Kippur was more than two months away, he added: "If the High Command is arrested before then, it is the duty of everyone who remains outside prison walls at the time to go ahead with the Campaign."

Not everyone, however, shared Begin's sense of priorities. With the arrest of Ben Eliezer, many felt it was time for a cease-fire. Energy should be directed to raising money, arms, and recruits for a more effective revolt. This seemed doubly logical when Livni's boys chalked up a fresh failure in the field that summer. They had planned an arms raid on four British installations, but the Stern group hit one of them first, forcing postponement of the attack. When the troops finally struck in late August, they captured only fourteen rifles.

Eliahu Lankin was among those who favored a truce. "What if none of our men can get close to the Western Wall?" he pressed at a High Command meeting in Begin's safe house. "All of our propaganda will go for naught. The impression of failure will be created." For months, said Lankin, the revolt had limped on without new recruits, guns, or money. Few veterans like himself, who had drifted off during Meridor's reign, were returning to the fold. Begin, however, stood his ground. With any luck, he said, "We won't even have to make good on our threat." The British might negotiate. Even if

they didn't, a truce at this stage would simply play into their hands:
Arrests would continue. The gates of Palestine would stay pad-
locked. And with the European war winding down, the last thing on
London's mind would be to redeem the tarnished promise of the
Balfour Declaration. Begin did hedge his bets, by telling Meridor to
plan Yom Kippur attacks on four British security fortresses around
Palestine. Yet with the others' grudging approval, he issued a staccato of escalating warnings for British troops to keep clear of the
Wall. "Any policeman who on the Day of Atonement dares to burst
into the area of the Wailing Wall and disturb the traditional service," vowed his final poster, "will be regarded as a criminal and
punished accordingly."

The fall-back attacks scored mixed results. Three units were
forced to retreat. The fourth killed four Britons, seized arms and
ammunition. But on the Temple Mount in Jerusalem, the British
blinked before Begin did. There, says a historian of the Palestine
conflict, the authorities were "intimidated into a humiliating withdrawal." The few policemen present were plainclothesmen, and
kept their distance. As the second star of the evening flickered into
life, a ram's horn wailed.

It was a victory not only for the Irgun, but for Begin. "I had always claimed we couldn't promise victory," recalls Lankin, "that all
we could do was to fight. How long the struggle would take, we
could not know. The Irish had fought for generations! But Begin
was so full of belief, so full of faith!" Begin himself declared by
poster: "A change has occurred. Our warning—and our willingness
to follow through on it—have borne fruit." He said he would not
pretend that the British were in retreat. "But the will of the rule of
oppression was broken; broken in a sensitive area, a potential starting point for Hebrew independence. We have shown we are free
men, proud, ready to face our oppressors—not slaves ready to surrender in the interests of 'peace.' "

At least for a while, Begin's position among his officers became
inviolable. He was no field general: They gently rebuffed his periodic requests to join "the boys" on attacks. He drew excitement,
instead, from the need for security precautions, safe houses, dis-
guises—including one, typical of the IZL's amateurishness in such
matters, that came with a doctored ID referring to Begin as a
"housewife." But Begin became the others' political oracle—"an
educator," recalls one officer, "whom we tried to release from details
and allow to sit and think." Rarely venturing outdoors, he spent

hours reading newspapers and listening to the radio—often, London's BBC. His poster communiqués evolved into a regular "wall newspaper" called *Herut*—"Freedom." He wrote scripts for an underground radio that broadcast brief bursts of analysis or exhortation introduced by the whistled tune of the Betar hymn—one step ahead of British detection units.

At meetings of the High Command, Begin adopted a professorial tone. He would enter the room after the others, shake hands with each, call the session to order. Aliza would bring tea, then retire. Abhorring votes, Begin sought "consensus." He would open with a lecture on events in Palestine and beyond, explaining how they helped or hindered the revolt. He avoided detailed involvement in organizational issues unless they touched on problems of politics or ethics. When Livni's elevation to the High Command sparked protests from local commanders, who feared for their autonomy, Begin said only that both sides' views should be considered. He said the same when confronted with questions on how forcefully IZL youths might solicit "donations" from well-to-do Jews.

But when Tavin turned up a British informer in the ranks and clamored for revenge, Begin intervened. Even when shown a list of IZL members the informer had handed to the authorities, he said *justice* demanded the man be told he was under suspicion and given a chance to rebut the charges. The spy, no fool, fled. In the summer of 1944, Begin was asked for permission to avenge the murder of a Jewish truck driver by an Arab near Haifa. After all, it was pointed out, the Irgun had acted similarly in the 1930s. But Begin refused, saying, "We are in a different period now, and a different war. We are waging a war of liberation against foreign authorities." He said the courts could mete out punishment to the Arab murderer. "The British," he argued, "are *hoping* we will respond, so that they can channel our struggle into civil strife." His final remark sounded almost rabbinical: "I take upon myself the moral responsibility for this issue, and release you."

He offered the others a certainty, a sense of purpose they found irresistible. "He had erudition, eloquence," explains Tavin. "He was head and shoulders above the rest of us in political vision." The triumph on the Temple Mount had vindicated that vision. "We began to become a power," says Tavin. "We became an organization that youngsters looked up to. Even if some of our military operations failed, they made an impression—a furor. And it was Begin who did this, through his writings and his broadcasts."

The British retaliated. They arrested dozens and, for the first time, deported them—to East Africa. Yet the main pressure came not from Britain. It came from other Jews, most of whose leaders opposed the Irgun revolt more than ever. The exception was the Sternists, whose support Begin saw as a mixed blessing. Their fondness for assassination and Russian-anarchist tracts offended him. "We were revolutionaries!" recalls Scheib. "Begin preferred a strong, military organization—like Pilsudski." In a series of letters before Yom Kippur, Begin and the Sternists toyed with a formal alliance. This failed when Begin insisted they accept his authority, although he did sign on to the Sternists' suggestion of a looser agreement that each group would keep the other informed of military plans and other "day-to-day issues." He needed all the friends he could get.

Still, the Revisionists, with whom Begin had cut ties, fumed at becoming targets in a crackdown by British police unaware of the breach with Begin. And the fury of David Ben Gurion ran deeper. With the world war limping to an end, he sensed Britain would finally quit Palestine. Yet he also feared that the Irgun attacks, while too piddling to humble the British, might so anger them as to deny the Jews a state.

He was determined, by force if necessary, to bring Menachem Begin to heel.

Chapter Nine

The Finest Hour

Begin thought Ben Gurion a dangerous dreamer, scared of a fight and wrong to believe he would get a state without one. The same was true of Dr. Altman; only he wasn't strong enough to be dangerous. When the Revisionists refused an Irgun request for funds in late 1944, and criticized the revolt in print, Begin wrote off Altman once and for all. "He is no longer an authority in our eyes since he has written those disgusting things about us," he told the High Command. He vetoed a suggestion he stage a *putsch* against Altman, but only because he wasn't sure it would work: He told his men to check with militants in the party and see if "they can control matters." Meanwhile, he sent a message to Altman: "Either you head a movement that becomes a factor in our war, or you must leave political activity—and the country."

With Ben Gurion, Begin neither could, nor would, be so dismissive. Begin both resented and respected, abhorred and envied him. Ben Gurion had vilified Jabotinsky and Abrasha Stavsky, dismissed the IZL as "dissidents" and "terrorists." Yet he was also the man with whom Jabotinsky had reconciled, a man who had made his mark on Zionism when Begin was in high school, and who was now the most powerful Jew in the world. He had displaced Chaim Weizmann as leader of Zionism's political council, the Jewish Agency. He controlled its army, the Haganah. There must be no illusion, Begin told his own commanders, that a Jewish state could function without David Ben Gurion, or that the IZL could be anything more than a "component" in a Jewish government.

At first, he tried to avoid Ben Gurion. He refused requests to meet with Haganah leaders—knowing they would simply try to get him to call a truce. But by late 1944, Ben Gurion's troops could no longer be ignored. They were staking out the British installations Begin sought to attack. For a while it seemed the Haganah might even try to prevent the sounding of the ram's horn on Yom Kippur. Begin told the High Command that this could not be tolerated, that the Irgun must confront the interlopers. When Lev-Ami, Lankin, and Livni all objected that this would risk a showdown the IZL couldn't win, Begin retreated. But he told them to start "mentally" preparing the troops for such a clash. "Sooner or later," said Begin, "it will be unavoidable." Meanwhile, he ordered an escalation of IZL operations. He directed Livni to draw up plans to attack British oil installations in Palestine—an idea abandoned earlier because of fears that the Haganah might intervene. Begin himself then scrawled a list of targets for the months ahead, including a stone building that dominated the skyline of Jerusalem and doubled as headquarters for the British rulers of Palestine. In Irgun code it was dubbed the "main kitchen." It was, in fact, a hotel—the King David.

Begin also, however, agreed to negotiate. He took his rivals' latest feelers as a tribute to the revolt, a hint they might even be ready to join. Dismissing warnings from Tavin of a possible trap, he accepted an invitation to meet Haganah leader Moshe Sneh, whom he had often debated at the Jewish students' hall back in Warsaw. Begin assumed Ben Gurion himself would be there; and he told the High Command he would propose an alliance, a united revolt against Britain—under Ben Gurion's overall command.

But Ben Gurion did not show: "I don't know why," Begin mused a bit sadly to the Haganah chief, whom he would blame years later for having prevented such an encounter. When Begin raised his proposal anyway, Sneh argued the time was not yet ripe for rebellion. Calling the IZL a group of "putschists sabotaging a revolution," he asked Begin to cease fire, at least for a few weeks. Begin refused this, refused even Sneh's fall-back request for an "unannounced" pause: A truce would set a precedent of retreat at the very time that Ben Gurion should be raising the banner of battle. For several hours, the two men talked past each other. Finally, Sneh issued something close to an ultimatum: If Begin would not agree to a cease-fire, the Haganah had "the authority to demand this of the IZL, to command it." The Irgun was risking a civil war, cautioned Sneh: "Not because any decent Jew *wants* this, but because the logic of your action will cause it."

Begin left the meeting shaken, disappointed in his bid for an alliance and no longer eager for a showdown. He summoned the High Command and said they must "not be drawn into conflict." The IZL must do "everything possible to avoid civil strife." He said if the Haganah left them with no choice, they would fight to survive. But he lay low: Although not announcing the truce Sneh had wanted, Begin made no effort to mount any military operations during the weeks that followed.

Still, he sensed a showdown was near. It made no difference, Begin told his commanders, that "we have no plans, now or in the future" to challenge Ben Gurion for leadership. The fact was that the IZL was generating more grass-roots respect than even Begin had expected. Though the British weren't yet leaving, the revolt had at least cowed the Arabs in a way the Haganah had never managed. "A great fear has overtaken them," crowed Begin. Even without electioneering, he said, the Irgun posed a long-term threat to Labor Zionist dominance, a dominance so smugly exercised that "many people, and not only on the right" were starting to resent it.

Three weeks later he met with the Haganah a second time. Again Ben Gurion opted out, sending his military aide, Eliahu Golomb. The meeting lasted five hours, and Golomb did most of the talking. He patted Begin on the back for giving Jews a new sense of pride and self-confidence. But the Irgun's "terrorist activities"—and wall-poster invective in which Begin had come within a hair of likening the British to the Nazis—were threatening the entire Zionist enterprise. "We don't want a civil war," he told Begin. "We do not want Jews to suffer, or to kill Jews. But we are prepared for this if faced with the threat that Zionism will be damaged or destroyed. We are through sitting still. We have no choice but to take our own measures to prevent your actions."

Begin replied with ice and fire: "You categorically demand that we stop our war. You are threatening us with destruction. Sirs: We did not have to meet in order to hear this demand, and these threats. We are not afraid of 'destruction.' We have made our private reckoning at the start of the road. We do not believe you will succeed, in all frankness, in destroying us. We say openly: 'We will not halt our war!'" For three weeks, he pointed out, his men had observed a de facto truce, only to be rewarded with a demand for a longer one. Why not stop leaning on the Irgun, asked Begin, and start trying to "use us to add force to your own political demands" with the British? Why not accept that even Ben Gurion and the "pacifist" Haganah would eventually have to take up arms? Begin repeated his

willingness to defer to Ben Gurion if and when he joined the fray:
"We feel that Ben Gurion—not Altman or one of the Revisionists—is the man who can today best lead youth into war." Until that
time, however, the IZL would not take orders from Golomb, Ben
Gurion, or anyone else. "We consider ourselves capable of independent judgment. . . . We cannot give up our fight—and if you are not
ready to join, we ask only that you do not interfere. If you do not, no
civil war will occur. It all hinges on you. Our weapons are not
directed at Jews, and will not be. If you refrain from civil strife,
nothing will happen."

That nothing would happen, however, seemed unlikely. After the
meeting, Begin took his case to the people. In a pamphlet called
"We Believe," he publicized Golomb's threat, defended the revolt.
The Irgun had shown the world that Jews were ready to die for Israel, would resist the rule of "a minority of camel herders and their
British patrons." It was only a matter of a year or two, Begin predicted, before Ben Gurion would have to abandon a policy of
"never-ending compromise," and fight. The Irgun would accept Ben
Gurion as leader; the ideal choice, Jabotinsky, was gone. Meanwhile, the IZL would survive. Begin predicted the Haganah would
try to make good on its threat, but figured only "a few degenerate
types" would agree to fire on fellow Jews. The IZL would *not* fight
back. "Others will rise in our place—from all sides—even the side
that today curses us. Our blood," wrote Begin, "will not have been
spilled in vain."

He told the High Command they must "act carefully and wisely,
and not be drawn into a civil war." Though still rejecting the idea of
formally declaring a truce, he made no move to press the point with
an early breach of a de facto cease-fire that had now lasted more
than a month. He ordered Livni to tell his men to ignore any Haganah provocations. Then, sensing that this order might not stick in
the field, he instructed commanders to brief their units on the political reasoning behind it.

As it happened, however, there was no time for briefings, re-
straint, even for a resumed revolt. Days later—November 6—two
Stern group youths in Cairo ambushed and killed Lord Moyne,
Britain's minister of state for the Middle East and a confidant of
Prime Minister Churchill. Summoning his commanders into emer-
gency session, Begin fumed at this "treacherous" violation of the
Sternists' own suggestion that the two groups coordinate efforts.
Still, this was beside the point: The murder of Moyne removed any
doubts about a Haganah crackdown on Jewish "terrorists." Begin

knew the Irgun was sure to suffer every bit as much as the Sternists. "We must not take fright, or go on the defensive," he said. But he ordered his commanders to "exercise personal caution" in a bid to escape capture. In its last recorded act, the High Command empowered Begin to draw up an "order of rank ... to allow for the event of his own arrest."

Ben Gurion acted on November 20. He called on Jews to deny all succor to the "terrorists"—and help hand them over to the British. The Stern group retired from the field, which virtually exempted it from reprisals. This left the Irgun. Dozens of IZL suspects were hounded from their jobs, tailed through city streets, detained for Haganah questioning, or denounced to the police.

Begin ordered his men to turn the other cheek. "We *ached* to react," recalls Eli Tavin. "People in the field complained, and I agreed with them. I was getting the intelligence reports—about mistreatment of people merely *suspected* of being in the Irgun." A half dozen of Tavin's subordinates were detained. "I thought Begin's orders were crazy," agrees Yaakov Amrami, who took over as intelligence chief when Tavin himself was kidnapped by the Haganah. "Begin said we must not fight back because one day the Haganah would fight alongside us. It was absurd! They were following us openly, denouncing us, and we couldn't even slap their faces. And they *knew* this! Begin was saying *openly* we wouldn't fight back. At first, I think they couldn't believe their ears!" One by one Begin's comrades disappeared. Meridor, Lankin, Lev-Ami were hauled in by the British and deported. As the crackdown proceeded, Begin's troops grumbled over his insistence on restraint. "We had come to accept Begin's judgment without question," recalls Yehuda Lapidot, an IZL officer near Tel Aviv. "This time, however, we disagreed."

Still, to a man, the Irgun held its fire. "I find it hard to explain, to this day," says Tavin. "We were people with our very lives at risk! Yet even those of us who did not agree with the order, obeyed." He says one explanation is that many IZL members had been weaned on the discipline and honor code of Jabotinsky's Betar. But he feels the main reason people followed Begin was that he made them into a power in the land. Lapidot agrees. Though he and most other IZL troops had never actually met Begin, they "well remembered the difficult days before he became commander. We knew that if we disobeyed him, we risked having the whole Irgun fall apart."

Begin recalls the period as the Irgun's toughest. "There was a cri-

sis of trust between myself and Irgun soldiers. Many could not understand how we allowed their own commanders to be captured."
He agonized over each new denunciation or arrest. Yet, publicizing
his pledge of restraint by wall poster, he was reduced to warning the
Haganah that if the IZL were indeed wiped out, "Your children will
spit on your graves!"

The IZL revolt went on hold, except for the heist of two sacks of
uncut diamonds in Tel Aviv at the start of February 1945. Begin
never left home. He wrote, read, listened to the radio, and played
chess with Operations Chief Livni. There were no High Command
meetings: Except for Livni and Chaim Landau, there was no High
Command. "We never knew what would happen the next day," says
Livni, who would emerge at night to keep tabs on his dwindling
forces. The diamond theft brought a glimmer of cheer. "Who would
have thought," Begin said chuckling, when Livni returned with the
stones, "that the father of little Benny Begin would ever hold so
much wealth in his hands!" More often, Begin would ramble on
about Ze'ev Dov, Poland, Vilna. "He told me about his last chess
game with Yisrael Scheib," Livni says. In February Begin's frustration finally boiled over—in a wall-poster howl against Ben Gurion
and his Haganah brass:

> You rampage, Cain, in the streets of Jerusalem, in Tel Aviv,
> in the towns and villages. You have used your might, Cain. But
> you did not use it when millions of our brothers perished as
> they turned their eyes to Zion.
>
> You chose an ally, Cain. To them, you turned over your
> brothers—into hands stained with the blood of millions thrown
> back from the gates of the homeland into the ovens of Mai-
> danek . . .
>
> Cars chase cars. Telephones ring. Signals are given and de-
> tectives appear. Tommyguns are raised. 'Halt!'—the foreign
> rulers command. 'Out of the cars,' the enslavers order. 'Which
> one?' the detectives—your allies—ask. And you, Cain, walk
> over, raise your hand, and point: 'That's him. Take him!'
>
> Your mouth brims with socialist rhetoric, Cain, but you are
> an exploiter. You incite, inform, betray, abduct, and hand men
> over, Cain.
>
> And we, the soldiers of Zion, are commanded not to repay
> you. Though our blood boils, it is blood that is totally dedicated
> to the nation and the homeland. Our eyes are directed, even

today—especially today!—toward love of our brothers, toward the redemption of our nation.

But, said Begin, a day of reckoning would come. "And it is not far off. The nation will rise up, its anger will burst forth. And for your treachery and crimes, for your informing and libel; in the name of the maligned nation, in the name of the enslaved homeland, in the name of its martyrs, in the name of our imprisoned brothers, in the name of our bereaved mothers and deserted children, in the name of our sacred war and in the name of our spilled blood—we shall repay you, Cain!"

Then, in the spring, the assault began to slacken. Fewer Haganah men were willing to participate. Fewer IZL men remained to denounce. New men—unknowns—were taking the place of those arrested. In Europe Ben Gurion found that his hope for postwar concessions to Zionism was misplaced. He could not get Britain to scrap the White Paper, let alone sanction a Jewish state—even when Churchill was ousted by the avowedly "Zionist" Labour party. In late spring, Begin tried to regain the initiative by petitioning some 250 of Palestine's most prominent Jews with a draft declaration of a "Hebrew government." There were no takers. But by autumn an exasperated Ben Gurion ordered the Haganah to stop chasing Begin's men, attempt to patch up their quarrel, and prepare to take on the British.

It was a vindicated Begin who accepted a Haganah invitation to talk. Operationally, his army was in tatters. Even with the easing of Haganah pressure in mid-1945, the IZL could muster only a few abortive mortar attacks. Yet, in political terms, Begin had won. Ben Gurion, attempting to destroy the Irgun, had legitimized it instead. Begin's discipline and restraint, writes historian J. Bowyer Bell, had won "the sympathy and understanding of many who abhorred his politics, suspected his motives and even doubted his sanity." The IZL's "politics and revolt might still [have been] unpalatable, but its character was for many now above question, and its primary loyalty to Zionism undeniable. The Haganah had maimed without killing, created sympathy where none had existed before."

Begin won much the same respect inside the IZL, whose command he now reshuffled to replace the missing. Says Amrami, a member of the new High Command, "Begin had been proven prophetic. He had told us the Haganah would one day fight the British alongside us. I never believed it—never. Almost none of us did. But now, it was happening!" The most powerful endorsement, however, came in a Tel Aviv safe house late in 1945—from Eli Tavin. The Haganah had kept the IZL intelligence chief themselves, rather than risk sharing his secrets with the British. He had been blindfolded, subjected to a mock execution, beaten, chained to a steel cot in a darkened storeroom for weeks on end. Begin insisted he go free as part of any rapprochement with the Haganah. A day after his release, the two men met. Tavin says he did not bother raising the issue of retaliation against Ben Gurion's men: "I didn't feel I needed to," he explains. "We were about to start a united struggle.

"Besides, I came to realize Begin had been right to insist on restraint. I agreed with his decision."

Chapter Ten

To Unity and Back

Begin joined the Haganah and the Sternists in a Joint Resistance Movement. He refused to disband the IZL, saying there was no guarantee Ben Gurion would not back out of the fight with the British. But he did give the Haganah veto power over IZL operations—with the exception of "confiscation" raids against British arms stores. The alliance took the field on the last night in October. The Haganah, IZL, and Sternists staged bomb attacks throughout Palestine, interrupting rail lines, damaging train carriages, and sinking a pair of police boats in Haifa Harbor. There things rested until December 27—when Begin moved to test the limits of the new alliance. In what he disingenuously defined as a simple "confiscation" raid, IZL and Stern forces coordinated attacks on British police headquarters in Jerusalem and Jaffa. The assault forces damaged the buildings, killed ten people, seized no guns, and triggered the largest British security crackdown in over a year. Jerusalem came under curfew. Dozens of Jews were searched, questioned, or arrested. Ben Gurion was called on the carpet: The British wanted an explanation, and a disavowal. Yet he refused to provide either, delivering what Begin called "a fine and refined reply."

In the first three months of 1946 the Irgun found its war feet. Along with the normal quota of miscues, Begin's men gutted two dozen British planes on the ground, stole a truckload of arms, blew up railway bridges, and ruptured tracks. The rail assault, April 2, had a sour ending: the arrest of Eitan Livni. But Begin was determined not to let this break the IZL's stride, all the more so given a growing Haganah's tendency to veto many of his proposed attacks. Barely pausing for breath, he named as new operations chief, Amichai Paglin.

Paglin went by the code name "Gideon"—or to most, simply "Giddy"—and Begin had started wooing him almost immediately after assuming the IZL command. He had approached Meridor the year before: a teenager with family links to the Haganah who had set up a three-boy underground and wanted to borrow dynamite to kill the British high commissioner. Meridor gave Paglin the explosives, then got cold feet and ordered him to cancel the attack. Paglin did, but bombed a British construction firm instead, and put up wall posters in Tel Aviv the next day proclaiming: "This is the beginning! We give Britain two months to leave Palestine."

In late 1943, Begin sent word to Paglin inviting him to join the IZL. Paglin agreed. (One of his two student comrades went on to join the Stern group, and shot Lord Moyne.) He became IZL commander for Tel Aviv and a member of the Irgun's military-planning council, earning a reputation for nearly reckless courage in the field, and for inventive genius in his arms workshop. Over six feet tall, with thick hair and a menacing toothbrush moustache, Paglin spoke softly, except when the mercifully slow fuse ran out on his temper. Now Begin summoned him to a late-night encounter in an orange grove near the safe house, and named him to replace the captured Livni. In a burst of energy during the next two months, IZL troops raided arms from a British police station; robbed a bank; hijacked, evacuated, and dynamited five train carriages.

Then, on June 13, the British Mandate raised the stakes: It announced that it was sending two Irgun captives to the gallows.

Begin ordered Paglin to find British men to hang, and Giddy kidnapped six. Begin would fight gallows with gallows. For a host of reasons, he could not let his boys hang. He considered the Irgun an army. Its fighters were *soldiers,* and when captured, they were prisoners of war. The Mandate could not be permitted to execute them like common criminals—or "terrorists." Yet, more than this, the army was a family. It had been set up that way—on Betar principles—long before Begin's arrival. Inductees swore an oath pledging "preference at all times to the Irgun above my parents, my brothers, my sisters, and my entire family." Begin had added a patriarchal style of his own. He demanded filial devotion from those around and below him; assuming in the bargain responsibility for their actions, their moral dilemmas, their lives. The approach hardened with the arrest of officers who might have shared this sort of responsibility—Arye Ben Eliezer or Eliahu Lankin—and their replacement in 1945 by an inner circle that rarely dabbled in political issues, like Chaim Landau or former Jabotinsky aide Marek Kahan. "In my presence," Begin recalled several years afterward, "my [IZL] friends called me 'the commander.' But among themselves, they called me 'the old man.' I admit I liked it."

There was a final reason Begin could not abandon his boys: the gnawing sense that he had already abandoned another family, in Brisk-de-Lita. He had confessed his anguish only indirectly, in a wrenching, rambling preface to his proclamation of restraint when Ben Gurion ordered his crackdown on the IZL: "Against the eyes of every son of the nation appear and reappear the carriages of death. The images," Begin said, "come as if of their own volition—even during daytime diversions; and most of all, maybe, in the nights: The Black Nights when the sound of an infernal screeching of wheels and the sighs of the condemned press in from afar and interrupt one's slumber; to remind one of what happened to mother, father, brothers, to a son, a daughter, a People. *In these inescapable moments every Jew in the country feels unwell because he is well.* He asks himself: Is there not something treasonous in his own existence? He asks: Can he sit by and allow the terrible contradiction between the march to death *there* and the flow of life here? . . . And there is no way to run from these questions; no refuge from the answers."

With the British captives in hand, Begin called a brief halt to wall-poster or radio statements on the death-row captives. There was no need to publicize the abductions; the British did that for him. He figured the more noise he made, the harder the British would find it to retreat. But retreat, he felt sure, they would. Symptomatic of his confidence was one poster he did publish during the crisis: warning the British to stop trying to locate and silence the IZL's underground radio. He threatened "blood, much blood," if they succeeded. When Marek Kahan asked him what would happen if the Irgun had to make good on the threat, Begin replied, "We won't have to. The British won't risk it. Look at the odds. They'll catch three, maybe four men, and a small suitcase with radio equipment. We would get another transmitter. And they would risk paying human lives for such a raid? The stir in Parliament would be unbelievable!"

That bluff worked. But the issue of the gallows was much less open to finesse. Pressure on Begin mounted daily. British troops threw a dragnet over Palestine. Ben Gurion voiced "distress and horror" at the IZL kidnappings. The first break in the crisis came soon: One of the Britons escaped. Begin, fearing further mishap, ordered Paglin to free two others and concentrate on preventing the escape of the remaining three. Yet he also worried that the British might raise the stakes by passing a death sentence on Eitan Livni and two dozen other IZL prisoners still awaiting trial. Breaking his silence with a statement read out on IZL radio, he said if the others were sentenced to death, "We shall set up whole *avenues* for the hanging of Britons." He said he did not want this: "We are soldiers of a great and cultured nation. We slay in battle and we die in battle. Harming defenseless prisoners is alien to what we believe in." But, he said, "We also know that beyond the normal rules of warfare there is in every conflict the law of reaction; of reflex. And we shall implement this law ruthlessly."

The British ordered hefty jail sentences, not the noose, for the latest IZL convicts. Leaning on Ben Gurion to lean on Begin, however, they swooped down on Labor Zionist settlements and arrested nearly a thousand Jews, including some of Ben Gurion's aides. Four people were killed, and eighty injured resisting arrest. At the end of June, Begin got a note from the Haganah's Moshe Sneh saying he had received informal assurances that no Jews would hang if Begin freed the hostages. Yet Begin wrote back that an "anonymous promise" was not enough. On July 3 London finally surrendered; the high commissioner in Palestine commuted the death sentences. Begin resisted the urge to crow. Instead, he drafted an "internal memo" to his field units. He said there was a moral to the story—"a phenomenon which perhaps we alone can understand. It is the quality which has pervaded our hearts, mingled with our blood. It is a simple quality, but there is none nobler: It is the quality of *loyalty*."

He had won another, windfall victory—the revival of Ben Gurion's commitment to the Joint Resistance. The Haganah resented Begin's brinkmanship. However, fuming at the arrest of dozens of its members and supporters, it now gave Begin the green light for an operation he had first dreamed of two years earlier. He would attack the "main kitchen"—British headquarters in Jerusalem's King David Hotel.

The King David was the political and social hub of Jerusalem—six stories of fieldstone across the street from the YMCA, between the residential areas of Rehavia and the German Colony. Private Begin of the Polish Army had visited it shortly after arriving in Palestine, only to be told that since he wasn't an officer, he would have to use an outside staircase. Now he told Paglin to figure out how to blow up the place. Never one to meddle in military details, Begin was staying out of them altogether with Paglin as operations chief. Giddy had won Begin's heart with his inaugural burst of activity—the heist of British guns and ammunition, the bank robbery, the gutting of nearly a dozen railway coaches. Whereas Livni had come to High Command meetings to report on prospective operations for Begin's comment, Paglin sensed Begin's urge to escalate the revolt, encouraged it, played to it. He would brief Begin on the latest inventions from his arms workshop and delight him with suggestions on how they might be put to use. "Gideon—our Giddy," recalls Begin, "was a combination of traditional Jewish brains and reborn Jewish heroism . . . both a planner and executor." When Begin shared either of these roles, it was only to ask whether precautions would be taken to avoid needless casualties and ensure an escape route for the attackers. Paglin would answer, as Livni had, "There can be no guarantees. But we've taken every possible precaution."

At the King David, Paglin intended to smuggle "Arab" delivery boys into the basement with booby-trapped milk cans crammed with explosives. In keeping with Begin's code of battle, he suggested affixing a warning in English, Hebrew, and Arabic on each can, and making a telephoned bomb threat as an extra precaution. Begin okayed the plan. So did the Haganah, but it pressed Paglin to cut the alloted evacuation time from forty-five minutes to thirty. "They want to be sure we blow up any documents linking them to us!" Begin snickered to Giddy, but he said the change was fine with him.

As the attack neared, the Haganah had second thoughts. On July 19, Sneh wrote Begin asking him to postpone it for several days. Begin agreed. But he said a few days was all he would wait, and told Paglin to strike on July 22. Paglin ordered the necessary eight hundred pounds of explosives brought into Jerusalem from around the country. When on July 20 Sneh wrote again—asking for just a few days' further delay, and promising that Ben Gurion would meanwhile publicly declare a "policy of noncooperation" with the British—Begin ignored the request. On the morning of the twenty-second, Sneh repeated his plea. Again, Begin did not reply: No second thoughts could change the fact the Haganah had approved the attack three weeks before. Besides, Begin reasoned, a delay would risk allowing the British to uncover the explosives.

As the assault got under way, Begin sat with Chaim Landau in the Tel Aviv safe house waiting, ears turned to the radio, for word that mighty Britain had been forced to evacuate her headquarters and watch it collapse. The bulletin came that afternoon: A bomb had indeed gutted the south wing of the King David Hotel. But under the rubble lay dozens of dead. Fresh bulletins followed, like obituaries. Some of the victims were British officials. Most were not. In all, twenty-eight Britons lay dead or dying; also two Armenians, one Russian, one Greek, forty-two Arabs. And seventeen Jews. Begin stared at the radio in dumb horror, until Landau clicked it off, declaring: "This must stop! You must not listen to these reports." Early that evening, Paglin arrived. He told Begin that as far as he knew, all had gone according to plan—except that the British, for some reason, hadn't evacuated the hotel. Begin cut him short, saying: "I understand the casualties were out of your control. You should not blame yourself. We all share responsibility." A note arrived from the Haganah command, demanding that Begin take the blame for the tragedy. Ben Gurion denounced the attack and expressed condolences to the families of the victims.

Begin issued a communiqué that, for one paragraph, was stock IZL prose: "At 12:05 P.M., soldiers of the Irgun Zvai Leumi attacked the central British administration, the secretariat of the occupation regime, and headquarters of the occupation army. The attack was executed in battle with military and police guards." Then, he turned defensive. The "tragedy which occurred" was not the IZL's fault, he insisted. Blame lay with the British: They had ignored warnings to evacuate while their "military experts" tried to defuse the explosives. If this was intended as an account of what went wrong, it bristled with inaccuracies. No British "experts" had approached the booby-trapped milk cans. Though the communiqué said an Irgun warning had been phoned in some twenty minutes ahead of the blast, it in fact arrived only eight minutes before. While the statement cited additional warnings to foreign news agencies, the only such call had gone to *The Palestine Post*. Begin spoke of a pitched battle between Paglin's "delivery boys" and British guards. In fact, only one Briton had gone into the basement, to check reports of a heist by Arabs; he was shot. The ensuing chaos, the delayed telephone warnings, and the misfiring of a small diversionary bomb

Paglin had planted outside, all contributed to the tragedy. Whether Begin knew any of this at the time, is unclear. What is certain, is that he ordered no investigation, then or later, of precisely what had gone wrong. Nor did he seem to feel that the details mattered much. The key was that some warning—no matter when, no matter how— had been conveyed, that the *intention* had been to avoid casualties. "The rules of Land Warfare," he said, "had been observed."

There was one detail, however, that he could not wish away: Well over a dozen Jews had died. "We mourn the Jewish victims," said Begin's communiqué, in a note of selective regret. "They are tragic victims of the Hebrew War of Liberation. There is no greater tragedy—and no more exalted cause." Meeting with the High Command the next day, he confessed special pain for "sympathizers of the Irgun" among the dead. But in an Irgun radio statement, he said he would not pretend to mourn the Britons who had died. "We mourn the *Jewish* victims. . . . The British did not mourn the six million Jews who lost their lives, nor the Jewish fighters the British have murdered with their own hands. We leave the mourning for the British victims to the British." The largest group of dead— Arabs—Begin did not mention at all. He sent a condolence note to only one of the wounded—an American news reporter who had written sympathetically of the Irgun.

Begin pressed his case against the British as outrage at the attack grew—all the more so when he got wind of a Haganah intelligence report that the British high commissioner, Sir John Shaw, had received the bomb warning, but tossed it aside with the taunt "We don't take orders from Jews!" The British denied the allegation—it turned out, years later, to be false. Yet Begin repeated, and embellished, it. He charged at one point that the commissioner had actually posted guards to keep people from evacuating the hotel, then had left and saved himself.

Still, the King David attack made Begin a pariah, and buried the Joint Resistance. Ben Gurion pronounced the Irgun "the enemy of the Jewish people." Begin tried to shrug this off, retorting that even before the King David, the Labor-Zionist leader had turned over IZL boys to the British. But the words stung. Years later, Begin would recall the brief period of united revolt as the "happiest days of my life." For a while he had been spared the label of "a dissident commander, whose every victory is denounced as failure, every failure as catastrophe." For a while, "the whole people were behind us."

Now, the whole world was against him.

Chapter Eleven

Two
Fronts

The British were determined to make Begin pay. They papered Palestine with Wanted posters: "Polish . . . 5 feet, 9 inches; medium build; long hooked nose; bad teeth . . . horn-rimmed spectacles." Happily for Begin, the description bore scant resemblance to his latest underground persona: a bearded, squinting Rabbi Israel Sassover of north Tel Aviv. Still, the British closed in. Twenty thousand men threw a cordon around Tel Aviv, and closed in block by block. They set up interrogation tables and detained hundreds of Jews—including another ersatz rabbi, the Stern group chief of operations, Yitzhak Shamir. For four days a British unit camped within yards of Begin's house, where he lay squeezed into a secret wall compartment. Young Benjamin Begin was told his father was away on business. The Begins' second child toddled underfoot—a daughter, Chassia, born weeks earlier. When the troops took Aliza away for questioning, a British officer glanced at her pallid features and huffed: "Send her home." But then they searched the house. They threw open cupboards, at one stage even rapped on Begin's hideaway. He recalls a thirst so "terrifying" he could hardly worry about being discovered. When Aliza finally sounded an all-clear, he tumbled to the floor, lurched to the kitchen sink, and doused his head in water. "We should have caught him," remarked the British commander years later. "The men did not search his house properly."

David Ben Gurion called a truce with the British until the end of the year, when the World Zionist Congress was to meet for the first time since before the war. He was leaning toward compromise with the Arabs, a "partition" of Palestine to create adjacent Arab and Jewish states. In London, after the King David tragedy, Britons seemed to start wondering whether Palestine was worth their trouble—whether *empire* was worth it, at a time when colonies everywhere sought freedom, and England reeled under the food rationing, power cuts, and its worst weather in memory. Yet if the nearly universal horror over the King David seemed to be hastening a British retreat, it seemed just as likely to have dealt Begin and the IZL out of the political spoils.

Begin churned out wall posters and radio commentaries—against the Haganah cease-fire; against partition of a Jewish state that he said belonged "on *both* sides of the Jordan." After a lull of more than a month, Paglin resumed operations—with a spate of attacks on the railway system, including a bombing that reduced a Haifa train station to rubble. Yet, as an increasingly self-confident Ben Gurion prepared for the World Zionist Congress, Begin was left to warn him against any fresh attempt to wipe out the Irgun by force. This time, he vowed, "We will react to every attempt to crush our revolt." Physically, the strain showed too: For several weeks Begin suddenly lost his appetite, and could retain no solid food. The ailment passed, however, as suddenly as it had come.

Under mounting pressure in Palestine, he turned his gaze to Europe, where he had sent Eli Tavin to open a "second front" for IZL Zionism. Tens of thousands of Holocaust survivors festered in "displaced persons' camps," still barred from Palestine by the White Paper. Though Ben Gurion toured the camps like a messiah—on the need to bring the refugees to Palestine, all Jewish leaders were united—Begin sensed in this desperate horde without a country a natural constituency for the Irgun. He formulated a legal argument for counting the refugees as citizens *in absentia* of the undeclared State of Israel. He proposed proclaiming statehood in the name of its Jewish "majority—composed of citizens of the country living here and citizens [potentially] returning to it." He felt Europe, too, might offer other commodities his hard-pressed revolt desperately needed: money and arms.

In October he sent Yisrael Epstein, his most trusted underground comrade, to help bring the second front alive. It sprang to life several days later with a force not even Begin had anticipated: Tavin's fledgling IZL cell in Rome blew up the British embassy. With no casualties on either side, Begin exulted in the prospect that the post–

King David crisis might finally be ending. Yet there, the Irgun's European recovery jolted to a halt. The Italians arrested Tavin—and Epstein, who had tarried in Rome to help draft a communiqué on the embassy blast. And as the European Irgun sought to reassemble—under the direction of Eliahu Lankin, who had escaped from a British jail in Africa and made his way to Paris—Begin found himself embroiled in tension with some of the very IZL veterans who had helped make him commander four years earlier. With the defeat of Hitler, Hillel Kook and his comrades were making their way back from America to Paris, with a vision of policy, priorities and a postwar Palestine strikingly different from Begin's.

Looking back years later, both sides reject the idea that power was at stake. Yet, a division of political roles was. Kook's group had long ceased to see itself as a part of the Irgun. They had resigned in order to found a Hebrew Committee for National Liberation (HCNL) and a series of other lobbies and political organizations that operated with an effectiveness then unprecedented in American history. Enlisting the backing of several hundred thousand Americans, including dozens of congressmen and other public figures, Kook had pressed variously for creation of a Jewish army; an end to the Roosevelt administration's willful neglect of the European Jews being marched to death in Hitler's camps, and the proclamation of a "Hebrew government" in Palestine.

It was this last aim that first brought the tension between Begin and Kook to the surface. The idea of a "Hebrew government" had appeared in the political platform Kook sent to Palestine with Arye Ben Eliezer in 1943—and in Begin's "Proclamation of Revolt" the following February. During Kook's wartime activities in the United States, contact between him and Begin had been limited to the occasional, generally polite, exchange of letters. Yet by 1946 it had become clear that the two men held different views of what such a "Hebrew government" would mean. Begin envisaged an exclusively Jewish state. Kook defined "Hebrew" with a secular and pluralistic flavor picked up during the years in America. He felt the new state must embrace Jews—but also those Muslims and Christians who accepted its authority. Judaism was just a religion. A "Hebrew"—or Israeli—state must have a wider identity. There could be "Hebrew Jews"—and Hebrew Muslims—in the same sense there were "American Jews" in New York.

At first, the friction was largely semantic, and only Begin and Kook seemed to take it seriously. Their separate representatives in

Europe—Tavin and Shmuel Merlin—even managed to negotiate a division of functions between the two groups shortly before Tavin's arrest. Kook's men would act as the "political representatives" of the IZL, and organize aid for those Holocaust survivors who "viewed Israel as their home and desired to go there." Yet both Begin and Kook rejected the accord. Begin balked at the idea of endorsing help for *those Jews who viewed Israel as their home.* He fired off a letter to Europe, Tavin recalls, "explaining in very forceful terms [his differences with Kook on] the Jewish-Hebrew issue." Kook, who was still in New York at the time, rejected the agreement for other reasons. "I did not for one moment," he recalls, "consider giving up the [independent] existence of the Hebrew Committee."

Begin was insistent that he must do so. With Epstein, he sent a proposal that Kook's men in Europe join a single Irgun political "representation" for the Continent. The new body would include Betar and Revisionist veterans from the camps—diluting the Kook group's importance. That plan never got beyond a jail cell in Italy, however. Lankin, on assuming the European command, was blissfully unaware of Begin's concern. He knew and respected Kook from earlier IZL days—and owed his escape from Africa in large part to the Kook group's funding, organization, and political contacts.

Inexorably, the tension with Kook moved from the semantic to the political. In New York, Kook sought to counter Ben Gurion's drift toward acceptance of a partitioned Palestine by advocating the early proclamation of a Hebrew government. Begin resented the pressure. He was suspicious that the HCNL envisaged *itself* as the Irgun's voice in such a coalition—while he, and the IZL in Palestine, would be relegated to a purely military role. Begin had a different vision: The Palestinian Irgun must remain the leading force, militarily *and* politically, in the battle to oust the British and found a Jewish state. Kook must bend to those priorities. Most of all, felt Begin, the HCNL should redirect the hundreds of thousands of dollars it had raised in America to arming the IZL's units in Palestine. By letter, Begin rejected the idea of proclaiming a government that Ben Gurion was sure to boycott. Kook countered that *with* Ben Gurion, the government would prance happily into partition. As things stood now, he argued, Begin's men were providing the military leverage with which Ben Gurion was pressing his own political platform on the British. They had become "a shooting agency for the Jewish Agency!" Begin retorted that there *would* come a time to proclaim a Hebrew government, especially if the upcoming Zionist congress endorsed partition. But there must be no hasty action. The proclamation would come "only if we are sure of the participation of others—or if there is no other choice left."

Holding out hope the congress might yet produce a reunified struggle for all of Palestine, Begin ordered Paglin to cease fire for its duration. He had Shmuel Katz, a South African Jew who was the most articulate member of the current IZL High Command, go to Europe and distribute a bulky IZL pamphlet to the delegates. It called for the revival of the Joint Resistance and the proclamation of a similarly wide "Hebrew government." The congress, however, endorsed neither. It did stop short of explicitly endorsing partition, and chose Ben Gurion's relatively more militant approach over that of Anglophile Chaim Weizmann, whom it reduced to a figurehead. But the emphasis was on diplomacy: Barely had the congress ended than Ben Gurion left for negotiations in London.

Begin denounced the congress, canceled the cease-fire. But he still hesitated to declare a "Hebrew government" Ben Gurion would surely reject. Only an unexpected tragedy, then a new crisis with the British, deferred renewed tension with Kook. In Italy, Tavin's men tried to spring Epstein from jail. The attempt was bungled, and Epstein was shot dead. Begin heard the news on the BBC. "He was my comforter," Begin would recall years later. But fearing arrest, he could not even go to synagogue to recite the prayer for the dead. And hours after Epstein's death, came the sudden announcement that the British had sentenced an Irgun teenager to eighteen years' imprisonment—and eighteen lashes. Begin summoned his aides— "one had to go on," he says—and read them a draft wall poster he had written in stilted, yet perfectly understandable, English:

> We warn the occupation Government not to carry out this punishment, which is contrary to the laws of soldiers' honour. If it is put into effect—every officer of the British occupation army in Eretz Israel will be liable to be punished in the same way: *to get 18 whips.*

He told the British that Palestine was not colonial Africa: "Israelites are not the Zulu. You will not beat the Israelites in their homeland. And if you beat them—His Highness's officers will be beaten publicly." This time, the British moved to call Begin's bluff. They flogged the Irgun prisoner, and sentenced a second one to a whipping. Paglin promptly kidnapped two British officers—and gave each of them eighteen lashes before setting them free. When Begin threatened that if there were any more floggings, Britons would be shot and not just flogged, the British retreated. They amnestied the second prisoner.

It was, for Begin, a political triumph. But he had little time to savor it. In the U.S., Hillel Kook—taking Begin's pre-congress letter as a go-ahead—told a news conference that he was traveling to Europe to organize the creation of a Hebrew government. It would be operated partly "in exile," partly by Begin's Palestinian IZL. Begin made no move to repudiate the announcement. Receiving one of Kook's colleagues a few days later, however, he reiterated that now was not the time for such a step. He accused Kook of grandstanding instead of raising money for the IZL's revolt. In January 1947 he sent Katz to Paris on the mission initially assigned to Epstein: to establish a new IZL office responsible ultimately to him.

Kook had no intention of complying. He did drop any immediate plans to organize a provisional government. Katz made it clear that Begin was flatly opposed, at least until Ben Gurion formally accepted partition, and Kook knew that "without at least the Irgun's participation, the idea was ludicrous." But he was equally intent on retaining the HCNL as a separate entity. He concentrated on plans to transport Jews back to Palestine, purchasing two ships with hundreds of thousands of dollars raised by his Hebrew Repatriation Fund in the United States. Begin fumed. "I am enraged," he wrote Kook in mid-1947, "to think that the Irgun representatives are not coming across with all possible assistance. Our boys get out of jail and are forced to wander around hungry. We have lost repeated opportunities to purchase weapons. Operations have been canceled because of lack of funds—and only because of that. . . . Five hundred and fifty thousand dollars, you spend for two ships! With that kind of money we could organize a small revolution. If we could have both the ships and the money—well and good. But we have received not a farthing for battle while thousands go to an activity that is essentially demonstrative." He concluded with a "recommendation" that priorities be reordered: "Everything, but everything, must go for the front line!"

Kook held firm. To sell the immigration ships, even had he wanted to, would have vindicated the allegations of critics in the

United States—America-firsters, and more than a few Jews who were fearful that his lobbying would encourage anti-Semitism—that the HCNL was merely a slick front organization for "IZL terror" in Palestine. Begin—through Katz—then pressed harder. Sensing alarm among some of Kook's comrades that the tension with Begin might cause the IZL to self-destruct before the Mandate did, Katz moved to co-opt them one by one. Shmuel Merlin seemed particularly torn. In January 1948, with Kook briefly out of town, Begin preemptively named Merlin head of the HCNL. At first this made little difference. Kook and the HCNL were inseparable entities; Merlin lacked the standing to assume Kook's mantle, much less to turn over the group's coffers to Begin. Still, the tension did gradually subside. After the first of the HCNL immigration ships had been intercepted by the British and rerouted to Cyprus, Kook joined with Begin's men in efforts to equip the second ship to ferry more than a thousand Irgun and Betar activists to Palestine.

There, amid the dispute with Kook, Begin's battle with the British had been hurtling to a climax.

Chapter Twelve

Dissident Commander

By communiqué and radio message, Begin celebrated Irgun violence, lashed out at Ben Gurion's caution, and taunted the British. Paglin organized assaults on banks, trains, railways, police vehicles. He devised roadside bombs, suitcase bombs, barrel bombs—even a homemade flamethrower which, Begin boasted by wall poster, "was made by our specialists." Whereas at one time the Irgun had struck about once a month, it now quadrupled that pace. More and more Britons died—not on the scale of the King David, but relentlessly, in twos and threes. "We in Palestine had no doubts about Begin's leadership," recalls Intelligence Chief Amrami. "On the contrary, it began to dawn on us that he had been right all along, that maybe we would see a Jewish state in our own lifetimes! We saw that our revolt was starting to affect the public in England, and that *world* opinion was more and more opposed to British rule here.... We felt our struggle was appreciated, recognized more."

The British hit back in early 1947. They sentenced another IZL prisoner to hang—a teenager named Dov Gruner, captured on his maiden mission. They confined troops to quarters in fear of kidnappings. But Begin ordered Paglin to find hostages, and he did: a retired major and a civilian judge. From prison, Gruner wrote Begin a farewell note: "Of course I want to live. Who does not?" But the message also said, "I swear that if I had the choice of starting again I would choose the same road, regardless of the possible consequences to me." It was signed: "Your faithful soldier." Begin celebrated the boy's courage, took his case to the world. The British delayed the execution, pending an appeal to the Privy Council in London. Yet when Begin ordered a reluctant Paglin to set his hostages free, the British passed death sentences on three more Irgun youths—not saying when the execution would take place. They withdrew military and civilian staff into barbed-wire "security compounds," and hinted that if trouble continued, all Palestine would be clamped under martial law.

Telling his High Command that the British were on the run, Begin called their bluff. He issued a vow that the IZL revolt would continue, moved to a new safe house, and turned full control of his army over to Paglin and his field commanders. IZL units would no longer have to issue warnings before attacks, and were told to hit "targets of opportunity" countrywide. On March 1, 1947, they mounted sixteen separate attacks, including a bomb blast that gutted a British officers' club and left twelve corpses under the rubble. GOVERN OR GET OUT! screamed a headline in London's *Sunday Express.* Choosing the first option, the British imposed martial law. They slapped a curfew on Jewish residential areas. Bus services, trains, taxis, and mail delivery screeched to a halt. Food was distributed by the army. Military courts were set up to try curfew violators. Paglin's field commanders struck anyway—three attacks the first day, three more, then three more. They bombed a tax office in Haifa, penetrated British "security zones" in Tel Aviv. By mid-month more than a dozen Britons had been killed; and on March 17 martial law was lifted. Moments later, Paglin arrived at Begin's safe house. When the operations chief snapped to attention, Begin dispensed with Irgun discipline, threw his arms around him, and exclaimed, "You've won, Giddy, you've won. Our boys have won!"

But he had crowed too soon. The British moved Dov Gruner and the other three death-row prisoners to the most formidable prison in Palestine, the Crusader fortress at Acre. On April 16, Begin was listening to Haganah radio. A sobbing announcer suddenly declared: "This morning, Dov Gruner, Dov Rosenbaum, Mordechai Alkoshi, and Eliezer Kashani were executed by hanging."

Begin ordered Giddy to take hostages, and announced: "We shall no longer be bound by the normal rules of warfare." He directed Irgun units to set up "courts-martial of the Jewish Underground Movement" and try any Briton they could catch. The charges: "illegal entry into Palestine; illegal possession of arms and their use against civilians; murder; oppression and exploitation." There would be no appeal; conviction would carry a sentence of death. But the British sentenced two more Jews to hang, and foiled Irgun attempts to snare hostages. Begin was left to okay the smuggling of a grenade into the prisoners' cell, where, the night before their execution, they pressed it between them and pulled the pin.

Begin publicized their heroism, taunted the British for cowering in barbed-wire "ghettos" for fear of Irgun attack, but ached to reply to the hangings with more than words. Sensing this, Paglin summoned Intelligence Chief Amrami and chastised him for failing to find Britons to kidnap. He bundled Amrami into a car and set out on a fresh search for hostages. Finally, in a hotel bar they found one. About forty, puffing on a pipe, he looked perfectly English. They seized him and drove to the outskirts of Tel Aviv. Yet when they produced a noose, the man stammered: "I'm ... a Jew!" Amrami challenged him to prove it: Could he speak Yiddish? Paglin ordered Amrami to get on with the execution, feeling there was neither time, nor need, to check with Begin. But at the last instant the hostage began muttering the Kaddish, the Hebrew prayer for the dead. The Irgun men drove him back to the hotel.

Still without hostages, Begin briefly recaptured the momentum from Britain several days later, when an IZL team breached the Acre fortress and set free 251 Irgun, Sternist, and Arab captives. It was, proclaimed Begin, "the greatest prison break in history—an act of liberation, planned to the last detail." The British, however, caught two of the attackers, and, in June, sentenced them to die. Though Paglin managed to kidnap two British policemen, they escaped.

As efforts to find Britons to hang continued, Begin was sought out by the United Nations committee detailed to investigate the Palestine conflict and make recommendations for its resolution. Publicly, he dismissed Britain's decision to refer the question to the UN as a maneuver—taken under IZL military pressure—to win a few months' breathing space without abdicating control. Still, he grabbed at the chance to receive the three senior committeemen, if only for the political recognition the encounter would imply. The envoys—the Swedish committee chairman, a Chinese, and American diplomat Ralph Bunche—were brought to his safe house. When he asked them to try to visit the two IZL members on death row, they said there seemed little hope the British would agree. He then delivered a nearly three-hour review of the Irgun's history, Dov Gruner's courage, and the futility of British rule. Asked what might happen if Britain left, Begin replied: "I do not believe the Arabs would actually go to war . . . unless a third party encourages and aids them. But if they do, we will smite them hip and thigh. In modern war, it is not numbers that decide the issue, but brains and morale." As for brains, he said, "I need not elaborate. As for fighting spirit, you have heard of the attackers of Acre Fortress. You have read of the men who went to the gallows . . ."

When the men left, he wrote a memorandum for his troops. "We do not overstate the impression our words have made on a few goyim*," he said. But he added that the "atmosphere really was comfortable. The fact that the IZL was the only element in the country to which the commission turned of its own accord, demonstrated the importance of the IZL—of its war—in the eyes of international parties."

On July 8 the British announced they would hang the two Irgun men eleven days later. Begin pressed Paglin for hostages, and this time two unarmed sergeants were abducted to a basement hideaway near the coastal settlement of Netanya, the hometown of the death-row prisoners. The British clamped the area under martial law, enlisting a terrified local population to help find the hostages. By Irgun radio, Begin denounced the town's Jewish mayor as a "collaborator, no better than the European Jews who had cooperated with the Nazis." But, declared Begin, "You—Netanya—are not Warsaw or Lodz, in spite of the fact that the head of your Council has taken upon himself the respectable job of Head of a Ghetto. You, Netanya, are a working town, a town of national pride. You do not surrender. You *will* not surrender. We know full well that even your Haganah members rejected with a decisive majority any offer for treacherous collaboration with the enemy forces that are plotting against us. . . . You are besieged, Netanya. But the siege will not last long. We will not abandon you, Netanya, to the unruly persecution of the oppressor."

Pressure on Begin mounted. First the Haganah, then Palestine's chief rabbi, appealed to him to free the British soldiers. Though he

---

* Literally meaning "nations," the Hebrew word has come to connote the non-Jewish nations: the Gentiles.

could not risk a formal meeting of his High Command, he summoned its members one by one. He asked how they felt about hanging the officers and, extraordinarily, did not preface the question with any hint of his own view. All the others favored retaliation. A few days later he received two more UN envoys, South Americans with leftist leanings and sympathy for the Irgun's uprising. When both appealed for release of the British, Begin said, "We never execute a man without judging him first." Yet one of the envoys persisted, arguing that the hostages had had no part in sentencing IZL men to death. Begin replied: "They are soldiers of an army invading our soil. Britain must suffer the consequences if she refuses to respect the laws of war and executes our soldiers."

Before dawn July 19 the British hanged the prisoners. Paglin hurried to Begin's safe house. Several other officers were already there, and Begin said that in principle he felt there was no choice but to hang the British hostages. But he seemed nagged by doubts that this was feasible, at a time when Netanya was literally crawling with British troops. Paglin, asking to see Begin alone, assured him he would find a way to hang the sergeants. There was a small chance of failure, but, argued Paglin, it must be risked. IZL credibility was at stake! Begin gave his okay. Paglin rushed back to Netanya and hanged the hostages, one by one, on a rafter in the basement hideaway. Then he drove the corpses to a eucalyptus grove and dangled them from a limb, hands and feet bound, heads hooded. He planted a mine on the road out. It blew one of the corpses to bits as a British soldier dragged it away for burial a few hours later—but not before photographers had recorded the two dead British soldiers hanging, intact, for front pages worldwide.

The Jewish Agency accused Begin of murder. A Ben Gurion aide proclaimed: "It is mortifying to think that some Jews should have become so depraved by the horrible iniquities in Europe as to be capable of such vileness." In Tel Aviv British troops junked cafés, smashed windows, beat up passers-by. Five Jews were killed. Typical of the response to the hangings was a diary entry by the British mayor of Jerusalem: "The murder looks like the work of the Stern Gang, who are just a little more murderous than the Irgun. . . . It is safe to say that ninety-five Jews out of a hundred condemn it."

Begin announced the Irgun's responsibility—by military communiqué:

Two British spies, Martin and Paice, under arrest in the underground since July 12, 1947, have been court-martialed following an investigation of their criminal, anti-Hebrew activities.

He said they had been convicted of illegal entry, membership in a "British criminal terrorist organization known as the British occupation force," illegal possession of arms, espionage, and "premeditated attacks on the Hebrew underground." A "request for pardon," said Begin, "was rejected."

The statement added insult to injury, and Begin seemed to regret it almost immediately. Publicly, he stood his ground. But in a memo for field units, he acknowledged that his "legalistic" tone might have been unwise. The principle involved, however, was important, and he tried to explain it to his troops. The hangings were not mere revenge, but "perhaps the most revolutionary act in the history of revolutionary wars." It was "the first time in the history of the British Empire that the sons of the 'Master Race' have been hanged in this country." This was the message he had meant to convey in the communiqué, "establishing the execution in the context of a *sentencing,* not of reaction to the murder of our prisoners. . . . It was important to communicate our heartfelt sense that it is the *oppressors* who are illegal here; that they are terrorists, they are murderers, they illegally possess arms; and that they will be tried in court. . . . The *trial,* not the execution, is our response."

Begin told his men to brace for "hard times," but not to lose heart, or be distracted by the invective of fellow Jews. "It is bred of fear," he assured them, "fear that has blinded their eyes—as it blinded the eyes of their predecessors in the ghettos of Poland, prevented them from seeing the danger of liquidation that faced them all." The IZL had offered "the imperative sacrifice of the few for the many—to ensure the establishment, and independence of the Jewish State."

He tried to reassure himself as he reassured the others. He took some heart from the second UN visit. After the two South Americans had left, Begin recounted how one of them had gasped on arrival: "So you are the man!" "I realized then," said Begin, "to what extent the underground fired the imagination." Yet the envoy, Guatemala's Jorge Garcia-Granados, remembers no such gasp—although he does acknowledge admiring Begin's success in eluding capture by the British. He says Begin delivered a tiresome lecture, "like a schoolmaster," which Garcia-Granados politely cut short with an unsuccessful bid to get Begin to cede the Arabs a state too.

He recalls the IZL chief as being "in appearance, disarmingly mild."
Now nearing his mid-thirties, Begin was rapidly balding, pale from
his indoor revolt. But, says the envoy, "he had a manner of looking
at one with eyes that seemed almost to have a mystic gleam, and a
smile which flashed suddenly and which for some reason—perhaps
of the contrast of sharp white teeth in an otherwise placid face—
gave an impression of ruthlessness."

The Irgun's "ruthlessness"—at the King David and in the eucalyptus grove near Netanya—was helping hasten London's retreat. A
British officer would later complain that his men had been "kidnapped, killed, even flogged" in Palestine. Says historian J. Bowyer
Bell: The hanging of the sergeants proved the "straw that broke the
Mandate's back." Still, the victory was bittersweet. When the UN
committee announced its findings in August, it envisaged the partition of Palestine into adjacent Arab and Jewish states, and Ben
Gurion went along. When the General Assembly endorsed the plan
in November—and set May 1948 for Britain's departure—Palestine's Arabs howled in protest at even a truncated Israel, and took
up arms. The great majority of Jews danced in the streets—and appeared to look to David Ben Gurion for defense and leadership of a
state whose mere existence mattered more to them than its size.

Menachem Begin seemed destined at most for a walk-on role in
whatever came next.

Chapter Thirteen

Friendly
Fire

Begin steered a collision course with Ben Gurion, who saw no place for rival Jewish armies in his fight for Israel. Ben Gurion called on the IZL and the Sternists to disband, disarm, and join the Haganah. Begin still agreed in principle that Ben Gurion was best placed to lead the Jews, and pledged to fight alongside "our persecutors of yesterday." Yet he would not abandon his own campaign against partition: the struggle to redeem Jabotinsky's vision of an Israel filling not only all of Mandatory Palestine, but the Arab kingdom of Transjordan, east of the Jordan River. Nor did he believe Ben Gurion was finally trading diplomat's garb for battle dress. The Haganah, he charged, were essentially bargainers. "We," by contrast, "fight." When Haganah units tried briefly again to subdue the Irgun by force, Begin vowed to retaliate: "In this struggle, which Ben Gurion, in his madness, wants to force upon our people, only one kind of liquidation will be possible: Mutual liquidation!"

After a clash near Tel Aviv that seemed to sober both sides, the fighting subsided. Still, Begin railed against partition by wall poster and radio, and questioned Ben Gurion's mandate for accepting it. "Have you held a referendum? Has the IZL taken part in free, general democratic elections under its own banner?" he asked. He charged that Jews were being led to betray their "sacred" homeland in swap for a mere "ghetto state." He vowed to oppose partition even if "the Jewish Agency opens a Jewish concentration camp and we face imprisonment"—even, indeed, if Ben Gurion *could* demonstrate majority support for it. "No majority of this generation of the Jewish people," Begin insisted, "has the right to give up the historic right of the Jewish people to their entire country, which belongs as well to all Jewish generations to come."

Though he kept this largely to himself, he figured his defiant words would make little practical difference. Partition was an accomplished fact, if only because the international community was likely to ensure it stayed that way. The most he could do—and he was determined to do so—was use IZL gunfire to press out Israel's "partition borders" wherever possible. Begin shifted battle fronts: from the retreating Mandate to the Arabs, who had begun staging hit-and-run raids on Labor Zionist farm settlements, and sniper attacks on the main road from Tel Aviv to Jerusalem. The Haganah fought off the attackers, but was reluctant to embroil itself in all-out war. Begin, however, responded by again ceding operational control to his field commanders, who launched attacks on Arab villages. In Jerusalem Paglin's boys revived the scattershot brand of violence that had brought the Irgun afoul of Jabotinsky, and Propes, in the 1930s: They exploded a bomb on a crowded thoroughfare outside the walls of the Old City. In the last three weeks of December alone, 216 people died in the undeclared war for Palestine: 126 Jews and 90 Arabs.

Begin went through the motions of advocating peace. He issued an Arabic-language call for restraint, vowing to "sever the hand" of those who ignored it. He still held to his view that Arabs were backward folk who, if they thought things through, would find little reason to fight the stronger, brighter, and more determined Jews. Yet if they fought, Begin thought to himself, so much the better! A peaceful Arab acceptance of the partition plan would be disaster. This was Begin's "greatest worry," he would acknowledge decades later. War, by contrast, offered a chance to scrap the partition accord by force of arms. "This silly agreement will not be binding on the whole people," he proclaimed by wall poster at the end of 1947. "The war that will break out will establish the existence of the state." It was a war that Begin meant to wage without quarter. Retrieving a pledge he had first spoken in a conference hall near the Vistula nearly a decade earlier, he proclaimed: "We will prepare ourselves for the defense of the people and the liberation of the homeland." At year's end he called for a Jewish "offensive" against "the [Arab] murderers' bases"—the prelude to "the Hebrew [war] of liberation."

With the British in retreat, Begin started to peep out from underground: He and Aliza spent Saturday mornings visiting Shmuel Katz and his wife in a Tel Aviv suburb. The rest of the week, however, Begin would leave at dawn for the nearby apartment of Marek Kahan. There, in a pattern established early in the revolt, he would spend the day listening to the radio, reading newspapers, receiving comrades, and writing policy proclamations—as Aliza knitted, read, waited, at home. Mrs. Kahan served him breakfast, though, she recalls, he was "usually so engrossed in his work that he wouldn't notice what he was eating!" Late at night Begin would walk home to Aliza, and sleep. In late February 1948, he broke that pattern too. Hearing that Haganah youths had tossed grenades into an IZL fund-raising meeting in Tel Aviv's Mograbi Square, Begin went to look. "That night," he says, "I came into direct, though one-sided, contact with thousands of Hebrew citizens. I stood among dozens of debating groups. Here and there I caught the surprised, questioning glance of a comrade who had recognized me. But the eyes would turn away as though they had not seen. . . . Not all the debaters in the street were friends of the Irgun, but almost every one of them denounced the cowardly act of intimidation."

Hurrying home, he scrawled a warning: "With grenades, the students of Ben Gurion have tried to silence us. But the emissaries of Ben Gurionist Fascism will not shut our mouths. Nor will they frighten the public. He who dares, out of dictatorial stupidity, to raise his hand against us, against our messengers, against our audience, against our donors—that hand will be cut off." Nor, said Begin, would Ben Gurion be allowed to run a state this way. "We are warning: such a regime, a regime of bloody tyranny, a regime of torture and Gestapo tactics will not be allowed to be found in Israel." Begin said he would not set up a rival government. But "if a government of the style we have seen in Mograbi Square is founded—we shall bring it down. And we have proven with our life and death that no price is too dear for us in our war for Hebrew liberty and honor."

Yet Begin's Irgun was changing, and his role changed with it. War was coming, and hundreds of volunteers flocked to the IZL banner. They were mostly the young, urban poor whom the Haganah settlement infrastructure had overlooked. Begin needed them, if only as a counterweight to Ben Gurion's "majority." They had guts, fire. But they lacked the ideological grounding of the early IZL. War also meant converting the Irgun to a battlefield army, whose intricacies the Irgun commander was ill equipped to handle. He turned over the job to Paglin, head of a "planning and retraining" council, and kept in only intermittent contact with the officers in the field. Begin would rule on strategy. Early in 1948, he called a joint session of the High Command and Paglin's planning group, and gave his army four "strategic objectives"—all of them outside the partition boundaries announced by the UN. He wanted the Arab port of Jaffa, abutting Tel Aviv, the nearby coastal plain, and the Arab Galilee in the north. Above all, he said, the IZL must take the provisionally "international" city of Jerusalem.

An escalation of Haganah attacks on the Arabs in early 1948 stirred mixed feelings in Begin. He was glad to see Ben Gurion's men take the field: By March he joined Jewish Agency leaders in an "agreement in principle" to coordinate activity under overall Haganah command. The IZL would join the Haganah-led army—as separate units, with separate officers. But Ben Gurion made no move to ratify, much less implement, the accord. And Begin, meanwhile, resented the credit the Haganah was getting, at home and abroad, for a fight the IZL had been waging since 1944. When Irgun units in Jerusalem rebuffed a local Haganah bid to disband them—instead demanding, and getting, a widened combat role—Begin was delighted. When told, in intermittent radio contacts, that his troops were planning to take the offensive against Arabs on the outskirts of the holy city, he cheered them on.

Not until it was too late did he know precisely where they were headed: into the Irgun's single most controversial act of violence since the King David bombing. "We didn't like to talk about *details* of operations on the radiophone," recalls Yehuda Lapidot, by now the Irgun's deputy commander in Jerusalem. On April 9—a week after the Haganah's much celebrated capture of the Arab stronghold of Castel, above the main road from Tel Aviv—the IZL and Stern group launched an assault on an Arab hill village on the other side of the road. It was called Deir Yassin and, unlike Castel, it had stayed out of the fighting, refused to station snipers there, even chased off a group that tried to defy the ban. The only hint of trouble had come in reports of sniper fire from the area on April 2. Then things fell quiet again. Yet IZL Jerusalem commander Mordechai Raanan argued that control of the village was crucial to any eventual fight for Jerusalem. The Haganah commander agreed: "I have no objection," he wrote Raanan, "to your executing this action on the condition you have forces to hold the village." His one caveat was not to blow up any houses, since the villagers would flee and "foreign forces"—Syrians and Iraqis trickling into Palestine since December—might take over.

The attackers struck at dawn: a few IZL and Sternist veterans backed by dozens of recently enlisted volunteers. Raanan, in keeping with Begin's underground code, had a sound truck broadcast an order for the villagers to evacuate. It never got close enough to make much difference before the hillside exploded in gunfire. With word of the Jews' advance, the villagers of Deir Yassin—each householder with his rusted flintlock—set about fighting off the assault. For hours they did so. Raanan, on a nearby hill, called for Haganah reinforcements, and ordered a change in tactics—"the method we used against British buildings. . . . One man would take a small explosive and blow a door or a window, and a second man would toss in a bag of ten or twenty kilograms of TNT." Shouting a warning before each bombing, the IZL troops dynamited eleven homes. The twelfth surrendered, with the rest of the village. Amid the rubble lay not only young men—Raanan says he still shudders at the memory—but old people and women and children. When the Haganah's strike arm—the Palmach—finally arrived, it angrily ordered Raanan's men out—and buried the dead, including at least some who had been cut down in a hail of IZL and LEHI gunfire after most resistance had fallen away.

Begin, assembling a garbled picture from radiophone reports, issued an exultant communiqué: "You have heard, Saturday night, the official announcement of the Haganah command: You heard about the Castel. But you have been told nothing about the conquest of the village of Deir Yassin! You were told nothing about how a great battle developed there in which, for the first time, soldiers of the IZL and of LEHI and of the Palmach together took part." The blackout was intentional, he complained: "There is no end to the envy of the mean-minded people in charge of writing official communiqués." He added details—citing, in chronological order, radiophone reports from its men on the scene on the day of the attack. First came "a reinforcement [of the village] by Iraqi and Syrian soldiers." The Arabs were firing from "fortified positions." Then: "During the attack an announcement was made by loudspeaker that women and children should evacuate immediately." After the evacuation "the fortress positions were bombarded. Dozens of enemy men were buried under the ruins." Then came more reinforcements on all sides—including Palmach men. Finally, came victory. The moral was clear: "On the Jerusalem front, all He-brew forces stood together; without the agreement of the [Ben Gurion] separatist leadership; and in spite of it. A covenant of blood, a covenant of conquest, of victory, was made among the IZL, the LEHI and the Palmach. . . . This is the thread to victory." Losses, concluded the communiqué, totaled "four dead, four seriously wounded, 28 lightly wounded. Until present, we have counted 240 Arab dead. . . ."

To Raanan, Begin sent a separate message: "Congratulations on this splendid act of conquest. Convey my gratitude to all the com-manders and soldiers. We shake your hands. We are all proud of the excellent leadership and the fighting spirit in this great attack. We stand at attention in memory of the slain. We lovingly shake the hands of the wounded. Tell the soldiers: You have made history in Israel with your attack and your conquest. Continue thus, until vic-tory. As in Deir Yassin, so everywhere shall we attack and smite the enemy . . ."

Then Begin found that most of the "enemy dead" were not sol-diers at all. The British thought him a murderer. Ben Gurion evinced "horror and disgust," and sent condolences to King Abdul-lah in Transjordan. When Arabs ambushed a convoy of Jews on the way to a Jerusalem hospital a few days later, Begin's critics charged it would never have happened if not for the "barbarities at Deir Yassin." Most Arabs voted with their feet: Thousands fled to Trans-jordan, Syria, or Lebanon with the words "Deir Yassin" on their lips. Begin, in a phrase that remains in the Arab political lexicon to this day, was dubbed "the butcher of Deir Yassin."

He replied by wall poster, in a mix of defensiveness, truculence, and inaccuracy reminiscent of the King David aftermath. The Ha-ganah itself had often caused civilian casualties, Begin said. Every-one knew Deir Yassin had to be taken for the Jews of Jerusalem to be secure. There had been fierce fighting. "The large number of wounded on our side, the large number of weapons we took and the numbers of Iraqi and Syrian soldiers killed—part of the regular [Arab] army stationed in the area—bear witness to this." There had been a warning by loudspeaker—"forfeiting the element of sur-prise." Most civilians had fled. "Some did not obey our warning and were hurt during the house-to-house fighting." Yet in fact, says Lapidot, there were only a few Syrians or Iraqis. Raanan adds that no civilians fled, until it was too late. As in the King David crisis, it is unclear whether Begin knew this at the time. He did add a note of condolence, albeit hedged: "We express our great sorrow that among the wounded were women and children." But this, he said, was "not the fault of our fighters. They fulfilled their human duty, and much more."

When Raanan showed Begin the Haganah's okay of the attack, he took the offensive. He broadcast it, charged the Labor Zionists with hypocrisy. Besides, had Deir Yassin's results been all tragic? "From an Arab source," said Begin, "we have heard since the conquest of Deir Yassin that demonstrations have taken place in the Old City demanding, for the first time since the fighting began four months ago, a peace with the Jews."

The one thing he did not say was that he had known almost nothing about Deir Yassin until the last body was buried. This would not only have implied a lapse in his own command, and a surrender to Haganah invective, it would have sapped Irgun morale. And it would have violated the code of loyalty and responsibility by which he had led the Irgun—and Betar—from the start.

A few days later Begin left the underground for good, joining Paglin in the IZL's most audacious bid yet for a major role in the war: an attack on Jaffa. Paglin had been planning it for weeks, raiding a British armory and a supply train in preparation. Begin addressed the troops before battle. "It was years," he recalls, "since I had given a public speech. Perhaps for the first time in my life I suffered from acute 'stage fright.' Most of the men did not know me, except as a name and a symbol." With Paglin alongside, he shouted: "Men of the Irgun! We are going out to conquer Jaffa. We are going into one of the decisive battles for the independence of Israel. Know who is before you, and remember whom you are leaving behind you. Before you is a cruel enemy who has risen to destroy us. Behind you are parents, brothers, children. Smite the enemy hard. Aim true. Save your ammunition. In battle, show no more mercy to the enemy than he shows mercy to our people. But spare women and children. Whoever raises his hands in surrender has saved his life. You will not harm him. You will be led in the attack by Lieutenant Gideon. You have only one direction—forward."

He set up headquarters in an abandoned Tel Aviv schoolhouse. As the battle raged, Paglin showed up intermittently to brief him.

The morning after the attack, Begin awoke, read the newspapers as usual, and was indignant at their dismissive references to his army's "abortive" bid to take Jaffa. Yet only hours later, he was summoned to Haganah headquarters, where Commander Israel Galili* and Operations Chief Yigael Yadin said they were in fact impressed with the IZL attack—so much so that they were ready to implement Begin's long-fallow proposal that the IZL enter the army as separate units. The Haganah men added, however, that it was imperative that Paglin try to break the stalemate at Jaffa, and take the town.

Begin returned to the front, summoned Paglin and his officers, reported the Haganah's encouragement, and asked whether a breakthrough was possible. Begin had his doubts: "I do not think we should go on battering our heads against these fortified positions, which are in any case covered by British tanks. We have done our best for two days. In these circumstances it is no disgrace—not even for the Irgun—to suspend the direct assault. We shall defend the line we have taken with a strong holding unit. The rest of our troops we shall withdraw." Paglin agreed. But at nightfall, says Begin, "deputations" arrived from the front to ask him for one more chance at capturing the Arab port town. Paglin arrived, saying he had found "new weak points in the enemy's positions," so the assault was resumed. For another two days the fighting raged. British tanks and gunners intervened in an effort to beat off the attack. Yet in the end, an IZL banner fluttered atop Jaffa's Hassan Beq Mosque by the edge of the Mediterranean. Begin called his first news conference since going underground. "Gentlemen," he delcared, savoring the sarcasm, "we have invited you to see the results of the futile, showy, abortive attack of the Irgun Zvai Leumi. . . ."

To Ben Gurion, the IZL's victory was a mixed blessing. With the British departure only a month away, he still wanted Begin's men to disband—not just defer, as envisaged in their March agreement with the Jewish Agency. They must meld into a single army, commanded by the Haganah. Yet Begin, all the more so after Jaffa, felt the Irgun had a special vocation to fulfill. He had long since stopped toying with the idea of opposing Ben Gurion frontally, or keeping the Irgun in business once Israeli statehood was declared. This would mean civil war; and worse, a war the Irgun could not possibly win.

---

* Galili had replaced Moshe Sneh in that capacity.

But he was determined, meanwhile, to use the IZL to force Ben
Gurion to proclaim at least "partitioned" statehood without delay.
It was starting to look as if he might hesitate to do even that, amid
pressure from a jittery outside world, and from many Jewish Agency
colleagues more moderate than he. Begin issued a series of appeals,
demands, warnings, with a common theme: If an Israeli government
were not declared, "rebellion" against a "capitulationist ... Vichy
leadership" would be justified. On May 9, Begin implied by wall
poster that if Ben Gurion didn't announce a Hebrew government,
the IZL would do it for him. Yet just before Sabbath, on the evening
of May 14, David Ben Gurion proclaimed the modern State of Israel. He became its interim prime minister, and his inner circle, its
government.

Begin replied by IZL radio the next night—speaking, not writing,
to the country for the first time. When he arrived at Paglin's Tel
Aviv apartment, where the transmitter had been set up, his own
inner circle was waiting. Landau was there, and Shmuel Katz. So
was Yaakov Meridor, who had escaped from Africa and made his
way home earlier in the day. Also on hand was Hillel Kook, who
had returned on the same plane. Begin embraced them all, then took
a seat behind the microphone and began his address. At first, in the
sticky heat, he seemed nervous. Yet as soon as he started speaking,
recalls Katz's wife, he became "the very picture of poise." He announced that he was disbanding the Irgun within the borders of the
new state. "There is no longer a need for a Hebrew underground,"
Begin said. "In the State of Israel, we shall be soldiers and builders.
We shall obey its laws—for they are our laws. We shall respect its
government—for it is our government." But *outside* the UN partition lines, he declared, the IZL would fight on as a separate army.
And inside, he would establish a political movement—an opposition
party, in effect. He called it *Herut*—"Freedom"—the name borne by
the wall newspaper so indispensable to his leadership of the Irgun.

When Begin finished talking, an IZL officer recognized Hillel
Kook and suggested he be included in the Irgun leadership's next
meeting with Ben Gurion. "What meeting with Ben Gurion?" Begin
retorted. "You want me to meet with Ben Gurion? With this informer? With this British collaborator?!" Kook turned to Begin:
"Menachem, I just heard you recognizing Ben Gurion as prime
minister of Israel! Don't you think you should meet with him?"
Begin did not reply, so Kook sought out Paglin, who had just arrived from IZL positions at Ramle, on the road inland to Jerusalem.
"What's going on?" he asked. "Are there two armies now? Three?"

Begin answered for him: "No, we have a liaison man in touch with some shmuck from the Haganah named Cohen."

But Begin could not admit the truth: It was Ben Gurion who refused to see *him,* and the slap hurt. In two rounds of talks—in 1944 and, now, in 1948—the Labor Zionist leader had sent deputies instead. Begin craved "this collaborator's" approval, still felt the mix of resentment and jealousy that had marked the two men's rivalry from the start. The next day, Kook again met Begin, who drew a carefully folded piece of paper from his breast pocket. It was signed by David Ben Gurion. "You see?" Begin crowed. "He says he was impressed with the way we ran things in Jaffa!"

After the radio speech, Begin met senior Haganah men and told them he was in a position to contribute a commodity Ben Gurion needed desperately: arms. The second of Kook's "immigration" boats was docked in France, and could bring back weapons as well as men. Begin proposed selling the ship to the Haganah—for $250,000. He would use the cash to buy arms for the separate IZL units in the army and those of the Irgun that survived outside the partition borders. The Haganah could send back arms on the ship too—Begin would split the cargo space. But Ben Gurion replied by note two days later: Now that there was a state, there was no room for the Irgun, in any form, anywhere.

Begin sent Katz and Marek Kahan to Paris to keep tabs on the arms boat—a U.S. Navy tank transport reconditioned and renamed *Altalena,* Jabotinsky's nom de plume as a journalist. In Israel he kept negotiating with the Haganah. At the start of June he gave some ground, pledging to dissolve the IZL military staff, make no further arms purchases, and demand no separate allotments for IZL men inside the army. He insisted only that the Irgun survive in Jerusalem. When news reached him from Paris on June 5 that the French were ready to provide twenty-seven truckloads of arms and ammunition, Begin's instinct was to inform the Haganah. But when some aides suggested holding off, Begin did so. He decided to wait until the deal had been finalized, and the *Altalena*'s sailing date set. Ben Gurion's agreement to a June 11 cease-fire with the Arabs—a mistake, Begin felt—did nothing to change his mind. Yet several hours before the truce took effect, Begin got an update on the *Altalena,* via the BBC news: The ship had just left for Israel.

Begin fired off a cable to Katz saying the vessel could not possibly land now, adding: "Why did she leave?" He dictated a second message—to Eliahu Lankin, who was in command on board—telling him to keep clear of the Israeli coast until further notice. He met Haganah commander Galili the next day and told him what the whole world now knew: The ship was at sea. He detailed what arms were on board: crate upon crate of grease-packed rifles and ammunition. He told him the boat was also carrying IZL and Betar survivors from Europe. He now proposed giving most of the arms to the Haganah, reserving 20 percent for the IZL in Jerusalem plus a "fair" share for the Irgun units most recently integrated into the army. But when briefed on Begin's offer, Ben Gurion exploded. One army meant one army, he said. No more deals. No more percentages.

Begin returned to his headquarters. Its location, since the British had left, was an open secret: the Freund Hospital, a few blocks back from the Tel Aviv coast. He radioed "keep clear" messages to Lankin. Three nights later, he received Galili in his office, and asked what Ben Gurion wanted him to do with the ship. Galili softened the edges of Ben Gurion's ultimatum. But there was coldness in the Haganah man's tone and Begin, laments one IZL officer who was there, seemed not to notice it. When Galili proposed buying all the arms aboard and turning them over to the army, Begin replied that money was not the issue: "The arms belong to the Nation." Galili left, saying he would talk it over with Ben Gurion and report back. Later that day he phoned Begin with a terse directive: Tell the ship to head full throttle for Israel.

Begin figured he had won. The next day, Galili suggested the boat avoid UN detection by landing north of Tel Aviv—at Kfar Vitkin. Begin agreed, even though this was a Labor Zionist stronghold. He asked the Haganah for help in unloading the arms, to which Galili agreed. Begin also suggested that the IZL store its share of the ammunition in IZL depots, to which Galili mumbled that this sort of thing could be worked out later. The next morning—June 18—the *Altalena* plowed south of Crete, one day's sail from Israel, and Begin confidently phoned Galili with a newly toughened proposal. He wanted assurances that 20 percent of the arms would go to the IZL in Jerusalem. All the rest must go to Irgun units in the army. Galili hedged: He said 20 percent could go to Jerusalem—though pointedly omitting mention of *who* in Jersualem would get them. The army must decide where the rest would go. Begin "argued and pleaded" the point, says an IZL man, but to no avail.

The next day he phoned Galili to press harder. Meridor and Landau were in the office and, as Begin spoke, Hillel Kook arrived. Sensing trouble, Meridor motioned Kook to restrain himself. But no sooner had Begin hung up than Kook roared at him: "You're crazy! You don't know what you're doing. . . . This is not our *first* arms ship. It's our last! And if you're going to discriminate against the Haganah people with these arms, what do you think will happen in the long run? I mean, they may have six ships on the way. *They* are in charge here. We are joining *their* army. And you want to create a precedent for discrimination? In later battles, our people will be left without arms. They'll be slaughtered."

Begin said nothing. He looked at Landau, then at Meridor. Finally, he asked Meridor: "Yaakov, what do you think?" To which Meridor replied: "I agree with Hillel." Kook apologized for the outburst, whereupon Begin phoned Galili again. "I had a talk with my colleagues," he said, "and we have a new proposal." He would settle for the 20 percent consignment for the IZL in Jerusalem. The rest of the weapons belonged to the army. He asked only for a face-saving concession: that "an Irgun representative" be allowed to make a speech when the main part of the arms were delivered to the army, "explaining where they had come from." The two men signed off, with Galili noncommittal.

Before dawn June 20, Begin and his comrades gathered on the beach at Kfar Vitkin as Monroe Fein—the U.S. Navy veteran skippering the *Altalena*—brought the boat toward shore. Begin, not wanting to risk blame for a UN truce violation, shouted: "Go back out and come back after nightfall." Fein did so, and Begin returned to headquarters. But Ben Gurion summoned his cabinet. Not mentioning the Galili talks, the prime minister charged that Begin had hidden the existence of the *Altalena* until it was already at sea. He told them if the IZL chief weren't humbled once and for all, he would saddle Israel with two armies. To the cabinet, Ben Gurion proposed two choices: "Hand over the government to Begin, or tell him that if he does not stop these actions—we will shoot!" Put that way, it was no choice at all.

Begin returned to Kfar Vitkin before nightfall. When some recently laid camouflage netting prompted an aide to suggest that the *Altalena* might be sailing into a trap, Begin dismissed the idea, saying, "Since Jaffa, the Haganah boys adore Giddy!" Paglin, Meridor, and other officers were waiting with IZL volunteers on the beach to unload the arms. After dark the ship pulled offshore. Begin went on by launch, and climbed aboard to a burst of applause. Dozens pressed forward to touch the commander who had humbled an empire. Some cried. Begin shook hands stiffly, nodded acknowledgment, and boarded the launch back to shore. But when the unloading started, an Israeli Army envoy showed up with a message: "Surrender" and turn over the cargo to the army—within ten minutes.

Begin rejected the "stupid ultimatum," and told the envoy he wanted to meet with the officer who had sent him. The officer replied within minutes: no. Begin told his men to keep unloading, and sent word to Tel Aviv to call a news conference for foreign journalists at Kfar Vitkin. Then he noticed that not only had the unloading stopped, but the arms already on the beach were being ferried back to the *Altalena*. Begin located Paglin, who said, "Yes, I ordered it." When Begin asked why, Paglin said there was still time to escape, with the arms. "We can wait out the cease-fire. . . . We can land in Gaza, or El Arish. We have enough strength to take over an Arab area." Begin reassured him: "The army has no ill intentions." But Paglin said that was absurd: It was time to fight, he said, implying that killing Ben Gurion and the rest of the cabinet might be part of the counterplan. Begin pleaded, persuaded, cajoled, then finally declared: "I hereby remove you from operational command in this area." Paglin replied that if he wasn't in charge he was leaving, and left. Begin told Meridor to take over the operational details: He, Begin, would assume overall command.

Pacing the beach like a field officer, he addressed the others in Yiddish and Hebrew slang. "These Haganah guys are a bunch of *kakers*!" Begin snorted. When a group of Jewish mayors arrived in hopes of mediating, Begin snapped: "What? Do you think we're going to negotiate with these *bozes*," appropriating the Labor Zionists' own epithet for reactionaries. When two UN officials showed up to ask what the *Altalena* was carrying, Begin had them turned back, then exclaimed with delight: "They thought I was a sergeant!" At one point, an alarmed Irgun youngster approached him and asked, "Sir, what are we planning to do?" Begin replied, "Don't worry. Everything will be all right." When asked what would happen if things went wrong, Begin said, "Then, we'll go to Tel Aviv. We will discharge our cargo there." The youngster protested that the Haganah would open fire if they did, but Begin replied: "Jews do not shoot at Jews!"

By next morning, the beach was surrounded by Haganah-army units. The Jewish mayors returned to press Begin for a compromise:

Twenty percent of the arms could go to the IZL in Jerusalem. The rest would be handled as the army decided—although stored under joint army-IZL guard. Begin agreed. But Ben Gurion wanted surrender. Begin decided to send the ship to Tel Aviv, where he figured a more sympathetic public and the foreign press might bring the prime minister to his senses. Merlin suggested sending it back to Europe instead, but Begin would not hear of this. "You want us to run away?" he exclaimed. He suggested that Meridor take command of the ship: Begin would stay at Kfar Vitkin with a rump force to face the Haganah. Yet when Meridor suggested swapping roles, saying the *ship* should be the main concern, Begin agreed, and summoned the men for a situation report. Motioning for quiet, he declared, "The Irgun has once again been proven right . . ." He got no further. Rifle fire erupted from all sides. Begin, Lankin, Stavsky, and a wounded Merlin clambered onto the launch, sped to the *Altalena* and set course for Tel Aviv.

On the beach, Meridor raised the white flag. On board, confusion reigned. Two cruisers from Israel's infant navy shadowed the *Altalena,* briefly firing as she neared Tel Aviv. From shore, the Haganah's David Cohen announced through a loudspeaker that a government official would board the boat to arrange for unloading. Begin sent a message of acceptance—on condition that members of his High Command were first brought on board for consultations. The loudspeaker blared no. There things rested for several hours. When someone on deck suggested that Begin put on a hat to avoid recognition from shore, he refused, huffing, "Nothing is going to happen!" As a crowd of startled IZL veterans and civilians gathered along the coast, he raised the ship's loudspeaker and appealed to army troops positioned on the rooftops: "Do not open fire! We have brought weapons for ourselves and for you. We have come to fight together! We shall not fire; we shall not fight our brothers. We have brought you arms! Come and take them!" Then, he sent the launch ashore with a first batch of rifles. The army opened fire, and began strafing the *Altalena*. Ashore, IZL boys and the Haganah army units exchanged shots. On the terrace of the nearby Kaete Dan Hotel, foreign reporters, diplomats, and UN officials stared, aghast.

The *Altalena*'s American captain—knowing Begin only as "this short, wiry character with a small black moustache"—took over. He ordered a group of fellow navy veterans to man the guns, and respond to any incoming fire. Begin shouted at them to halt, but no one listened. Then, Fein got on the radio and requested a cease-fire, in order to evacuate Merlin and others wounded in more recent Haganah fire. The reply came in midafternoon: An army field gun blasted several shells just beyond the ship. Fein radioed shore again to protest, and, when the firing stopped, hoisted a white flag. Begin had the IZL men take it down, and went below to commiserate with Merlin. "Do you know what has happened? Fein ran this white rag up the mast without asking me!" Begin favored martyrdom: "We must all perish here. If we do, this will be a sign and a symbol of Labor's true colors. The people will rebel. A new generation will come to avenge us." Merlin, who had no intention of perishing, told Begin to hoist the white flag again. He did so, telling Fein he would make a new stab at negotiation.

Moments later, however, the army opened fire for the last time. A shell hit the cargo hold. Rifle shells exploded everywhere, and Fein gave the order to abandon ship. At first, Begin vowed to go down with the *Altalena*. But in the end, he took the last launch ashore. Soaking but uninjured, he rushed to the IZL radio transmitter. Paglin, and about four hundred others, had been rounded up and jailed. Yet Ben Gurion had decided not to risk arresting Begin, who now went on the air to address the nation. Dozens of IZL men lay wounded. Sixteen were dead—including Abrasha Stavsky, cut down as he trudged ashore, yards from the scene of the Arlosoroff murder fifteen years earlier. Begin spoke for well over an hour. Alternately shouting in rage and pleading for his people's understanding, at times weeping into the microphone, he called the attack on the arms ship "the most dreadful event in the history of our people, perhaps in the history of the world." He denounced Ben Gurion as a "foolish idiot"—a man, he said, who had so desperately wanted to kill the leader of the Irgun Zvai Leumi that he was ready to risk civil war to do so. "Vain fools!" Begin shouted. "Do you know what would have happened if they had succeeded in their plot? They would have sunk us to the depths of Hell!" Begin demanded freedom for the IZL men who had been jailed. If Ben Gurion and his men—some of them, "real Nazis"—dared to harm the captives, he vowed, "Their fate is sealed!" Yet he also cried out an order to his own men: Hold your fire; sheath your weapons. "There must not be a civil war with the enemy at our gates!" God would protect the brave men of the Irgun. The people of Israel would see through Ben Gurion's designs. "For the people of Israel are not Ben Gurion!"

Begin returned to Kfar Vitkin the next morning. Several hundred IZL youths milled amid a few arms crates. He called the troops together. "I still remember his words!" says one: " 'Not one bullet against the Jews! Our enemy is the Arabs!' "

Begin moved into the Katzes' apartment for a few days, leaving Aliza with the children. For the first time in years, his inner circle wondered whether he was capable of leading them out of crisis. The radio speech had moved but also disturbed them. Recalls one officer: "His charismatic image as the vigorous resistance leader was badly tarnished." Katz, back from Europe, agreed. He thought Begin's broadcast "disastrous. . . . He had a shattering story to tell, but he did not realize he was in no state to tell it. . . . His voice broke and he wept. He sounded incoherent, out of control." It was, felt Katz, a speech that had played into the hands of Ben Gurion, who promptly harrumphed: "Blessed be the cannon that shelled that ship. It should be placed in Israel's war museum!"

Begin just wanted to be alone, says Mrs. Katz. He read a bit, talked less. "He was a completely broken man. In all the time I had known him in the days of the underground, I had seen him worried and distracted, but never hopeless." But now, she says, "he touched the very depths of depression."

Chapter Fourteen

Terms of Peace

He toyed with moving to Jerusalem, to command the IZL there. But Meridor, Katz, and the others insisted he stay in Tel Aviv—to restore his image, confront Ben Gurion, launch Herut. This would be no easy task. Though two ministers resigned over the *Altalena* incident, the rest of the government, and the country, accepted Ben Gurion's version: Begin was a traitor. He had been planning a coup. He had to be stopped.

Begin told his side to the few who would listen. To Arthur Koestler, who visited a few days later, he spoke in a near whisper that conveyed more sadness than rancor. By the time he received an American reporter later in the summer, however, some of the old fire had returned. "We were led into a trap, and we fell for it!" Begin said of the *Altalena*. For vindication, he seemed to look to the future—to Israel's first election, which Ben Gurion had set for January of 1949. Begin predicted Herut would win "30 to 40 percent," and that Labor would get about the same.

Still, he was torn between his urge to lead Herut to the polls, or the Irgun in vengeance. "If a free state is created here, with free competition, there is no possibility of internal armed conflict," he told the American interviewer. "We shall never use arms against our fellow Jews. We want ballots, not bullets." But he said that if "this government should create a form of life under what Ben Gurion has called 'the blessed cannon,' with mass arrests without trial and masked investigators . . . then this is a rule of tyranny and the possibility exists of a new underground." Begin said he would not actively encourage it; he would not have to: "Our new, proud and regenerated youth" would not stand for another *Altalena*. Yet what, he was asked, if Herut were *voted* into oblivion? What if Begin got 5 percent—not 40—of Israel's vote? "We would," he retorted, "voluntarily disappear from public life." Then, he seemed not so sure. Asked the next day to approve a typescript of the interview, he scribbled in a softer phrase: "If Herut gets five percent, we might perhaps voluntarily disappear . . ."

He sent Katz to run the IZL in Jerusalem. He offered advice, but Katz—and Raanan—ran their own show. In Tel Aviv Begin the party leader gradually crowded out Begin the commander-in-revolt. The old rage did reappear, briefly, when Ben Gurion accepted a UN truce with the Arabs, who were in retreat. It was, Begin charged, "one of the most deadly conceivable blunders." The government had forfeited, "by the stroke of a pen, the advantages gained through blood and the sacrifice of our finest sons." Yet when Katz's boys wanted to attack the Arab, eastern half of Jerusalem in spite of the cease-fire, Begin said no. He said the IZL would have to be disbanded, if only because Herut needed what little money there was. He and Katz agreed privately that once peace was signed, a Jerusalem branch of Herut would be set up instead.

Begin meanwhile paid a visit to Jerusalem—so triumphant the *Altalena* disaster might never have happened. He toured IZL clinics. He waded into his two natural constituencies: the Orthodox Jews of Mea Shearim, and the originally "Arab," or Sephardic, Jews of the market quarter, Mahane Yehuda. He even paid a call on a Haganah training school. Everywhere he was cheered—as the man who had led a revolt, who wanted *all* Jerusalem to be Israeli. When he strode onto a second-floor balcony in Zion Square to deliver his first public address since Poland, hundreds jammed nearby streets. When he had finished, and pushed through the throng to a nearby restaurant, they craned for a look, reached out to touch him. After dinner, Begin personally oversaw the printing of his speech for Jerusalem's main Revisionist newspaper. The next day he reviewed his troops, who stood at attention on a soccer field on the western edge of the city. Leaving, he was escorted by an "honor guard," complete with motorcycle outriders, and was applauded by crowds on the road's edge.

But his political home was Tel Aviv. It was the closest thing Israel had to a European city: a place for the poor, the young, the brash, and the angry. Begin addressed them for the first time that summer, at an open-air theater called the Gan Rina, two blocks back from the sea where the iron corpse of the *Altalena* slept. The crowd started arriving before noon. By the time Begin appeared hours later, there were thousands, and they exploded in applause. When a cantor had intoned a blessing, Begin stepped to the podium. Suddenly there was silence. "It was," recalls one who had watched as a child from his father's shoulders, "quiet, like a temple." The boy would become one of Israel's top journalists; he would, however, "never forget that moment. . . . Everyone just wanted to *see* him. Here he was: The British had put a price on his head. I'm convinced most people didn't even come to hear him—just to set *eyes* on him!" Begin savored the silence. Then, slowly, he howled a greeting to the throng—five words borrowed from Jabotinsky, who had meant them as a metaphoric tribute to Tel Aviv, the first city built by Jews in Palestine in two thousand years. Now the words applied doubly—as a symbol, drawn in the colors of the Zionist flag, and as an ode to this whitewashed city by the Mediterranean: "Tel Aviv, *kakhol ve lavan!*" he shouted. "Tel Aviv, blue and white!"

The waterfront erupted in shouts and song. Begin, between ovations, lashed out at Ben Gurion, proclaimed the ideal of a Jewish state in all Palestine, stirred what Koestler recalls as "blind enthusiasm and rage." But for Begin it did what the Jerusalem reception had only started to accomplish: It recharged his batteries. It made him hunger for battle, not a military one this time, but political.

Ben Gurion was the enemy. Begin portrayed him as the "weak" man he had always been, and said Israel, more than ever, needed a voice of defiance, a guardian of the true faith. In his party platform the Herut leader vowed to keep the peace; yet also to prepare Jews for some future "war of liberation" that would undo the partition Ben Gurion had accepted. Internationally he would seek good relations with the major powers: Moscow, Washington, Paris—in that order. Begin envied the Americans their democracy. But what help had it given the European Jews, whose cries for rescue had gone unheard? The Soviets—if for their own "anti-imperialist" reasons— had *applauded* the revolt against the Mandate. At home Begin promised the Palestinian Arabs civic and cultural autonomy in an unabashedly Jewish state: They were, after all, a minority; against the *potential majority of* world Jewry whose country was Israel. His economic program was vague, utopian. He wanted state control of key industries, but promised to protect "little people" from big business. Beyond this, Begin vowed to look out for his own: ensure pensions, medical help, for IZL boys who had "risked their lives and shed their blood for the liberation of their homeland."

He concluded: "The Hebrew Herut Movement, founded by the Irgun Zvai Leumi, has come into being to continue to battle for freedom and in order to install in the life of our State the principles which form the basis of the war for complete independence. The Hebrew Herut Movement will resist any attempt to enforce on our State and country any regime of oppression. The Hebrew Herut Movement will resist any attempt at one-party rule."

To Ben Gurion, it all sounded like an *Altalena* through the ballot box. He set out to create once and for all the "one state, one army" that still eluded him. After moving against his own left wing by disbanding the Haganah's elite Palmach, he turned again to the question of the Irgun. Begin, in negotiations that Ben Gurion as usual sat out, assured the government he would demobilize his men in Jerusalem. Yet he wanted—and got by late summer—the release of the IZL supporters jailed in the battle for the *Altalena.* He then pressed for integration of the Jerusalem fighters into the army as a symbolically separate unit. This, too, the government negotiators agreed to in mid-September. Yet when Stern group holdouts murdered a Swedish UN negotiator who was proposing international control in Jerusalem—and Begin assigned part of the blame for the "tragedy" to the government's "appeasement" and "tyrannical rule"—Ben Gurion gave a final battle order. He ordered all Sternists arrested or, if they resisted, shot. He ordered the Irgun to disband and hand over its weapons. He did not blame Menachem Begin for the murder. But the Irgun must *choose*—between "unqualified loyalty to the state, and elimination." Begin saw little choice but to comply: He disbanded the IZL. The real battle with Ben Gurion, he felt, would be waged at the polls.

After January, the government would *have* to listen.

Chapter Fifteen

The People Speak

But first, Begin faced a new challenge, from an unlikely source. Eli Tavin was keeping an Irgun underground alive in Paris. Begin, hoping to live down charges of terror and treachery before polling day, wanted him to disband the operation and return home. Tavin refused. He saw the European operation as a last chance to pressure Ben Gurion to retreat from "partition," free from the constraints of parliamentary democracy. "We were planning attacks on diplomatic missions, British and Arab ships," he recalls. The idea enticed many of the Irgun veterans who were in Europe on the way back from exile in Africa, including Arye Ben Eliezer. Worst of all for Begin, Amichai Paglin had slipped out of his Israeli jail cell and joined Tavin in Paris.

Begin at first spoke to the holdouts as their rabbi. "Gather together, brothers, as a council of sages," he had written to Paris months earlier, in a first bid to win Tavin over. "Give us good counsel, that we may trust in it, since it will surely be worthy and wise." He promised not to impose his own thoughts on the matter. He figured he wouldn't have to. When Tavin and others, however, insisted on staying in business, Begin dropped all pretense of rabbinical consultation. He told his Paris comrades that he shared their desire to keep pressing for an end to partition. But he argued it would be impractical—and "politically dangerous"—to do so from underground. He added drily that unless the surviving European Irgun could dispatch guns, bullets, bombs, and thousands of troops, there was little point in keeping the organization there alive.

With most of Tavin's circle, the argument gradually succeeded. Ben Eliezer returned to Israel, and to Begin's side. Yet Paglin stayed on. Begin asked Tavin to send him home. When Tavin refused— noting that Paglin was a big boy, and was free to return if he wanted—Begin increased the pressure. "I got cables, letters, messages," Tavin recalls. He knew full well he could not operate for long "without at least the tacit okay of Menachem." Yet he resisted surrender. In late 1948 he and Begin worked out a compromise: They would thrash out the question face to face. Tavin sent Paglin home for the time being, on the understanding he could return to Europe if the IZL survived.

Begin needed money for his infant political party, and wanted to go to the United States to raise some. As an IZL "terrorist," he was briefly unable to get a visa. But he persuaded the U.S. ambassador to have the label removed, flew to New York, where Shmuel Merlin feted him among the Kook group's old supporters, and stopped in Paris on the way back. Tavin had gathered his officers from around Europe, and opened the conference by presenting the case for Irgun survival. Then, he gave Begin the floor. "Menachem launched into a report on the situation—with his point of view of the *Altalena* and the aftermath, the creation of Herut," Tavin recalls. He said the Irgun in Europe had performed heroically, but that its time had passed: The battle for an unpartitioned Israel must be won at the polls. Tavin says he could almost *see* his comrades surrender, one by one. "Menachem was convincing my friends. He was still their commander. By the revolt, by his conduct, he had built up an incredible personal influence." In the end there was a vote: unanimous, for dissolution. "I went along with it," Tavin says. "What could I do? I had to face the facts, in Israel as well as in Europe."

Begin returned home to campaign from border to border—as the architect of the revolt, as Raziel's heir, and as Jabotinsky's. The nominal Revisionist leader, Altman, begged for a few slots on the Herut ticket. The new state had decided to create a 120-seat constituent assembly by having each party submit a list of 120 names to the voters. If a party received 40 percent of the vote, the first forty-eight names on its list would join the assembly. Begin refused even to talk to Altman, who got so desperate he asked Hillel Kook to arrange an audience. Kook tried and failed. "Begin," he recalls, "was intent on forcing the Revisionists to run separately." Begin did put Kook high on the Herut list. Tension between the two had eased since the *Altalena:* Kook had been one of the dozens jailed. Besides, he came as part of a package. His closest comrade from the U.S. group was Ja-

botinsky's son, Eri. Rounding out the top of the slate were Arye Ben
Eliezer and Shmuel Merlin—both graduates of Kook's operation,
but by now more closely tied to Begin. Also on the list were Raziel's
sister, Yaakov Meridor, Eliahu Lankin, Shmuel Katz, the Revisionist lawyer Yohanan Bader, and the poet Uri Zvi Greenburg. Begin
included Chaim Landau too, despite misgivings among at least
some of the others, who viewed him as little more than an underground factotum. All in all, Begin figured, it was a formidable team.

He led parades, torchlight rallies. What violence there was, was
verbal. Before tens of thousands, Begin denounced Ben Gurion's
"surrender," said Jews had not survived the Holocaust to whimper
and beg for a partitioned homeland. He no longer ventured exact
predictions of Herut's share in the assembly, beyond telling friends
if he got fewer than five seats, he would retire. When IZL veterans
set up a betting pool, however, the spread ran from thirteen to thirty
seats. "Most guesses were closer to thirty," recalls Kook. To the U.S.
ambassador, Begin said he expected to finish second, but not far behind Ben Gurion. No one would get an outright majority; Herut
would hold the balance of power.

Voting day was a holiday. The country cast its ballots, then pic-
nicked. The results came the next morning. Begin finished fourth—
with fourteen seats, roughly 11 percent of the vote. Dr. Altman,
running on a separate Revisionist ticket, won no seats. But Ben
Gurion galloped to victory with forty-six. He formed a government
with the Orthodox religious bloc and two splinter factions, one representing small-business men and the other, the Sephardic Jews
with roots in southern Europe and the Islamic world.

Begin accepted the defeat well. He knew it could have been
worse, and took comfort in the pundits' consensus that only his
leadership had enabled at least a partial recovery from the political
damage of the *Altalena*. He made no attempt to insert Herut in the
governing coalition. (Neither, of course, did Ben Gurion.) Begin
and his comrades would guard the true faith in the new assembly:
Fourteen seats was an ample platform for that.

In a sense, he stayed underground. With Aliza and the children,
he set up house in the last of his IZL hideouts, the one-bedroom
apartment on Rosenbaum Street in the heart of Tel Aviv. It was on
the ground floor and had a small garden in back. Begin spent hours
at his writing table, consulted or commanded by telephone. Saturday afternoons, he received IZL comrades in the garden. Afterward,

he and Aliza would sometimes go to the movies—American westerns. This was his only diversion, and even in the theater, occasionally he seemed to be rehearsing a speech, a debate, a riposte to David Ben Gurion. With IZL driver Yoske Giladi at the wheel, he traveled three times a week to Jerusalem for the constituent assembly sessions. Seated beside Yoske in the front seat, he read throughout the trip. Unlike Ben Gurion, he did not tour farm settlements, crouch by roadsides and let the soil of the Bible run through his fingers. When he traveled to rallies or meetings, he would read on the way, deliver a speech to a throng of supporters, then ride home. He dismissed Ben Gurion's popular touch as disingenuous: the theater of an avowed Israeli earth child who had shown his true colors—those of the East European autocrat—by shelling the *Altalena.* Said Begin: "I am just a simple Jew in the Land of Israel."

He ran Herut as he had run the Irgun: a Fighting Family without guns. Party meetings, suggests Esther Raziel-Naor, were like IZL meetings. "When Begin had a plan to do something, he would make a presentation. He never liked to vote. We would talk it over. Then he would summarize. Generally he had a very strong power of persuasion, and we would agree." Begin still addressed some of the delegates—like Landau—by their underground names. He ruled through an unofficial high command: Meridor and Ben Eliezer. "I don't understand it!" moaned Uri Zvi Greenburg to a friend early in the assembly session. "We come to a committee meeting. I talk and I talk, but none of it matters. Begin has already finished all the business *before* the meeting, with Ben Eliezer and Meridor. The meeting is run very formally, very nicely. It all looks good. But everything has already been *decided.* And during the meetings, these two—Ben Eliezer and Meridor—are constantly sending Begin little bits of paper."

A few others resented this arrangement, but Begin ignored, froze out, or co-opted them. In the rare instances when issues came to a vote, Begin won easily. His comrades knew that if they wanted a political role in Israel, only Begin could provide it. Ben Gurion and Labor wanted no part of them, and there was no other practical alternative. Dr. Altman's demise at the polls had proven that. Besides, Begin offered something positive to his party, to this mix of IZL veterans and urban poor excluded from the new state's Labor Zionist aristocracy: He assured them that they—their revolt—had mattered; that he would end their spell as political backbenchers just as his revolt had ended an empire's mandate.

His most vocal opponents were Hillel Kook and Eri Jabotinsky.

Begin parted ways with them in the first days of the assembly—over the constitution it was supposed to write. Kook saw a constitution as a vehicle for recording his distinction between Jews and "Hebrews," between religion and nationality. Begin rejected the concept. He (and Ben Gurion) were also sufficiently shrewd to sense that such issues were best left for later, given the Orthodox bloc's swing vote in the present assembly. Begin did have a draft constitution drawn up and considered by a party committee, but he omitted Kook and Jabotinsky from both exercises. When Ben Gurion moved to shelve the constitution altogether and convert the assembly into a parliament, Begin went along. So did the rest of Herut, with only Kook and Jabotinsky dissenting.

Shmuel Katz, who had been on the constitution committee, was also uneasy at Begin's approach, but kept his feelings largely to himself. When he protested privately, Begin would invariably say he had a point, then ignore it. "He had this way of disarming you by pretending to agree with you, and then going his own way," wrote Katz years later. A few weeks after the constitution vote, Herut had to tackle the question of attempting to join the Histadrut national trade-union federation, a Labor-dominated group that dispensed jobs and housing, promotions and transfers, and discriminated against Herut sympathizers whenever it could. Begin agreed to hold exploratory talks with the union, then changed his mind. When Katz protested, Begin heard him out, said he had a point—and abandoned the negotiations.

Begin co-opted the eldest and potentially most important of the dissidents, Yohanan Bader. He gave Bader control of all economic-policy issues, an area where he himself lacked expertise or interest. He tolerated occasional criticism from the veteran lawyer in other areas as well, but with the understanding that on issues that Begin felt were important, his word would be final. The extent and limits of Bader's autonomy came into focus on Israel's first anniversary, in May 1949, when Ben Gurion hosted a reception. Begin called a Herut counterreception that morning and, while vodka glasses were clinking, declared, "Of course, we will all boycott Ben Gurion's event." Kook retorted that he, for one, was *not* boycotting it—even though he so resented Ben Gurion's behavior over the *Altalena* that he had not spoken to him since. "Ben Gurion is the prime minister of the State of Israel!" Kook argued. "If we boycott the Independence Day celebration because of him, we might as well boycott the Knesset!" Eri Jabotinsky agreed. Begin ignored them, but then

Bader spoke up. He said Kook had a point, and suggested a vote on the question: Begin won it, since only Kook, Jabotinsky, and Bader voted for attending the official gathering. Bader declared: "I will, of course, abide by the majority," at which Begin smiled approval. (Then, Bader attended anyway.)

In the Knesset, however, it was Ben Gurion who still shunned Begin. The prime minister proclaimed Herut and the pro-Soviet Communist party the only two groups he would never invite into his government. He made a show of his distaste by often refusing even to refer to Begin by name. He would call him "the member of Knesset sitting next to Dr. Bader." Begin spoke often during the parliament's first two-year session—always, in one way or another, to advocate a self-reliant, defiant Israel. Jews must choose their friends on the basis of who had helped, or would help, the Jews— and must rely on no one absolutely. The formula left Begin sounding softer about Moscow than the socialist Ben Gurion; and prompted Begin to reject suggestions of a formal alliance with Washington. But above all, Begin decried the government's efforts to secure peace with Arab neighbor-states. Ben Gurion had always lacked backbone, Begin charged. Now the prime minister was going to formalize his surrender, set partition in stone. Begin said the government must instead "tell us how we can achieve victory over our enemies, and how it plans to bring us *real* peace." When one of Ben Gurion's supporters asked Begin whether he had forgotten that there were two peoples—Jewish and Arab—in the area, Begin dismissed this as irrelevant. What mattered was the Jews' claim to the Land of Israel—all of it. Ben Gurion did not bother with such interjections. He would listen to Begin for a while, then shout, "Who killed Arlosoroff?" or a similar taunt, and send the debate tailspinning into a slanging match.

Begin was quickest to anger when Ben Gurion mocked his leadership of the Irgun, implying that all he had done to oust the British was write wall posters and murder civilians. "When did you actually fight?" he would challenge Begin. After one such occasion, recalls a Herut activist, Begin turned on the rest of his Knesset delegation and complained, "You left me alone! You left me alone against Ben Gurion." Katz, increasingly bitter over the abandonment of the constitution and labor-union talks, felt Begin was allowing the prime minister's invective to distract Herut from serious policy debate. He went to Begin and urged him "not to let Ben Gurion provoke him into these outbursts." The plea had no effect: Begin still craved the old man's approval. One day Begin arrived at the Knesset chamber, a building so cramped he had to walk by Ben Gurion to get to his seat. When the session recessed, Begin motioned to the Herut delegate nearest at hand—who happened to be Kook—and whispered: "Ben Gurion smiled at me!"

Ultimately, however, Begin craved the endorsement of his people. He set out to win it with the approach of Israel's second election in the summer of 1951. He orated throughout Israel, achieving a trancelike communion with the crowds who came to listen. A reporter for the party newspaper, failing to keep pace with Begin when taking notes at one speech in Haifa, approached him afterward to get the text. There was none. But the Herut leader—pacing back and forth, eyes half shut—obligingly ran through the performance again, verbatim. During the run-up to the country's second election, Begin also published his first volume of memoirs. Called *The Revolt,* the book's main purpose was to rebut the Labor Zionists' version of his uprising against Britain and of the IZL's role in the rebirth of Israel.

Having consolidated Herut, Begin felt strong enough to take Dr. Altman back into the fold as a Herut candidate. Kook and Eri Jabotinsky huffed their way into retirement. Of the old U.S. group, Merlin stayed on; and he was later rewarded with the post of party secretary. Begin sensed the *Altalena* was fading from the national psyche. A new issue had taken its place: the arrival of tens of thousands of Jews from Arab countries. Ben Gurion had brought them; but his country's economy could provide most with only squalid tent camps. His Labor Zionism pressed on them the option of becoming "real" Jews—meaning socialist settlers and farmers, a role that offered little temptation to immigrants who considered themselves real Jews already. The newcomers were hungry, angry—natural Herut constituents, eager ears for Begin's campaign broadsides on economic chaos and Ben Gurion's "illusion" of peace with the Arab world.

Israel's second election day dawned hot, and Begin awoke early. He walked with Aliza to the polling station, returned to the apartment to receive admirers and wait for the verdict. But far from rewarding Begin, the people rejected him. They shaved his fourteen seats to eight, reduced Herut to a splinter faction representing 6.6 percent of the electorate. The slap left Begin, almost thirty-eight years old and ending his second decade in politics, a broken man.

Chapter Sixteen

Underground Revisited

Begin summoned Herut the following night and said he could not go on. He would retire, practice law. His disciples rose one by one and implored him to stay. The meeting ran until dawn—when Arye Ben Eliezer, in an act of catharsis for them all, departed in tears. But Begin was adamant. When the Knesset reopened August 20, he did not even show up to take the oath of office.

He shut himself in his apartment, receiving party and IZL comrades, who pressed him to return. "Ben Eliezer and the others had devoted their whole life to this cause, and now Begin was simply walking away!" recalls one Herut activist. "They were shattered." In response, Begin conveyed variously a sense of guilt, resentment, fatigue. He felt he had failed his party. "He said it was his *duty* to retire," says Esther Raziel-Naor, "since he had not brought success in the election." But he also felt that some in the party—Kook, Jabotinsky, and their sympathizers—had failed *him*. "In the Irgun," explains one IZL veteran who visited him, "Begin had no rivals. There were no intrigues. No one was vying for office. Herut was different." Meridor, who spent hours with Begin, adds: "The internal strife in the party—with Kook and so on—had worn him down. He was not in a mood to carry on." Worse, he felt rejected by the people of Israel: They had forgotten his revolt, chosen Ben Gurion and partition.

In the weeks ahead, Begin saw few visitors. The most frequent were Ben Eliezer, who took over as interim party leader, and Meridor, who soon retired into private business. Begin made no move to return to parliament, or to study law. He sat with Aliza, whom he saw more than at any time since their wedding. She told him the voters had been duped: There would have been no Israel without Menachem Begin! Even she, however, could not lift his spirits. In the fall they left for Europe. They rested in the Swiss countryside. They visited Paris, where Begin reunited with Eli Tavin, who was still living there. To Tavin, he still seemed shattered by the electoral rebuff—but also homesick for Israel, politics, and Herut. In December, when Ben Eliezer phoned to fill him in on government moves for a war-reparations deal with West Germany, Begin for the first time hinted he might return.

Ben Gurion had raised the reparations issue the previous spring. Begin had not been against reparations in themselves. It would have been fine had Israel automatically been placed on the list of postwar beneficiaries alongside the Allies. But he held that for Jews to meet with Germans, *negotiate* blood money for the Holocaust, was something else. Ben Gurion had let the matter lie. But now—with Begin absent, and amid signs that German payments might run to nearly a billion dollars—the prime minister was determined to pursue the issue. After hearing from Ben Eliezer, Begin and Tavin walked along the Seine. Begin, though still "very down," yearned to "*do* something. He didn't say exactly what; but he felt the need to be involved." Any doubts evaporated days later, when Ben Eliezer collapsed with a heart attack outside the Knesset. Begin rushed back to public life on a cold, cloudy Monday—a few hours before the reparations debate of January 7, 1952.

The Knesset met on the ground floor of a gray stone building with curved edges that made it look like a tugboat plopped into downtown Jerusalem. A crowd of several thousand cheered when Begin emerged to speak three blocks away, from the same Zion Square balcony that had provided his first aboveground platform in 1948. Police, expecting trouble, were out in force. Begin drew a piece of paper from his pocket, held it up, and announced: "This note has just been handed to me. It says the police have grenades which contain gas made in Germany—the same gas used to kill your fathers and mothers!" The charge proved false, but it hardly mattered. Begin railed against Ben Gurion, "that maniac who is now prime minister," and said Jews must wage "a war of life or death" against a reparations deal. Then he marched up Ben Yehuda Street—the city's café thoroughfare—toward parliament. His supporters followed, many carrying stones, and broke through a barbed-wire barrier outside. The police fired tear gas and warning shots, but the demonstrators were not cowed. Rioting raged for hours, leaving 200 protesters and 150 police injured.

Inside the Knesset, Begin charged: "This government is about to negotiate with murderers!" For Jews, he said, there could "be no German who is not a Nazi, none who is not a murderer." He asked the chamber: "In what tribe of men, however primitive, does the son of a murdered man go directly to the murderer and ask reparations?" The Holocaust had left Jews with one thing only: their dignity. Now the government wanted "to destroy what honor we achieved in our suffering, all for a few dirty million dollars." Staring at Ben Gurion, he cried: "I appeal to you not as a political rival, but as a fellow Jew, a fellow orphan! I ask you: Do not go ahead with this deed. Go to the people. Call a referendum. What have you got to lose?" As the sting of tear gas seeped through shattered windows, Begin then read out a list of rabbis, poets, professors—all of whom, he said, opposed reparations talks. Ben Gurion retorted: "The people whose names you mention are not of an ilk with your mob of hooligans!"

"*You* are the hooligan!" Begin yelled back. When the speaker of parliament demanded an apology, he refused. Ordered to his seat, he shouted, "If I am not permitted to speak, no one will!" The session was adjourned and resumed only when Begin agreed to apologize.

"I have apologized," he said, "not out of fear of losing my Knesset seat. That issue is trivial compared with the issue we confront today. I have apologized because there are things I must say, a role I must fulfill—perhaps my last, but I must do it." Again peering at Ben Gurion, Begin shouted: "When you aimed your guns at us and I was standing on the deck of the *Altalena* as it burned, I gave the order: 'No. Do not answer fire with fire.' Today, I give the order: 'Yes!' For there are things dearer to a man than life; just as there are things more terrible than death. These 'reparations' are an issue for which we shall give our souls, for which we are willing to die. We will leave our families, say farewell to our children. But there will be no negotiations with Germany! People have died for lesser issues. We who saw our fathers dragged to the gas chambers; we who heard the rattling of the death trains; we who saw our fathers thrown into the river with 500 other Jews from glorious Brest-Litovsk, and saw the river go red with blood. We who saw an old mother murdered in hospital; we who saw events unequalled in history— shall we hesitate to sacrifice our souls to prevent negotiations with the murderers of our fathers?"

Begin concluded with a cry of anguish, and resolve: "You have power," he said, glaring at the prime minister. "You have prisons and concentration camps, an army, police, detectives, guns, machine guns. No matter! On this issue all your power will crumble like glass against rock. We shall battle this issue of right until the end. Physical power, in such battles, has no value. Power is vanity. . . . I know you will drag us off to concentration camps. You have arrested hundreds today. You could arrest thousands. It doesn't matter. They will go and serve their sentences. We shall go with them. And if necessary we shall die with them. But there will be no 'reparations' with Germany." Then, like a reservist girding for battle, he announced he was forfeiting his own parliamentary immunity.

Ben Gurion went on radio, and accused Begin of having taken "the first steps toward the destruction of democracy" in Israel. "A wild mob composed of Irgunists and Communists stormed the Knesset," he said. "I consider it my duty to tell the nation of the gravity of the criminal and treacherous plot, and to assure the nation that we have taken all appropriate measures to safeguard the security and peace." He said he did not "underestimate the declaration of Menachem Begin that he is preparing for a war of life or death. I know it is not difficult to carry out acts of murder against members of the government. Nor am I ignorant as to who is the principal target of Mr. Begin's plans." But, he said, "Israel will not be turned into a Spain or a Syria." The next day, the Knesset voted on reparations. Begin was back. So was Arye Ben Eliezer, carried in on a stretcher. The vote was close, 61–50, with nine abstentions. But Ben Gurion won.

Begin was under suspension from parliament—on charges of threatening the chamber with violence—when the reparations talks got under way. He called the punishment "cowardly," but otherwise ignored it. At a rally in Tel Aviv, he exhorted supporters to stop paying taxes to Ben Gurion's government. In a series of marches and demonstrations, he implored Ben Gurion—"despite the great differences between us"—to bring the negotiators home. If he didn't, and if the talks produced agreement, the "life and death struggle" would begin. "Imprisonment will not cow us! We shall not pay taxes to the government. Its decrees will be tossed in the trash basket. . . . This government exists by force of bayonets. Yet we have experience in breaking the force of bayonets."

To charges that he was advocating rebellion, Begin replied that he meant only to "vent the public feeling which has not been allowed expression in Knesset." But to Begin's deputies, his words sounded like a battle cry, a call back to the underground. Tavin, in Paris, was contacted by "a former member of the Irgun high command," who was now high up in Herut. The man, whom Tavin declines to name, asked him to mount a "military" operation against the Germans. Tavin arranged to have a leather-bound dictionary fitted with explosives, smuggled into Germany, and mailed to Chancellor Konrad Adenauer. Two post office employees opened it, and were killed. Back in Israel, a second senior Herut official, Chaim Landau, contacted a young party activist in Haifa and, saying he was acting in Begin's name, asked him to smuggle a package of explosives onto a ship bound for Marseilles, in southern France. Landau, the man says, told him the consignment would be used to establish an antireparations "underground" in Europe. (The package came back, unclaimed, and when the man asked Landau why, he was told: "We changed the plan.")

In September 1952 the reparations accord was signed. In October a twenty-nine-year-old Dachau survivor—and Begin admirer—named Dov Shilanski was stopped by police outside the Israeli Foreign Ministry. They seized his briefcase and defused a bomb set to go off minutes later. Shilanski had arrived aboard the *Altalena*. He had been in the crowd that surged alongside Begin to the Knesset for the reparations debate, was arrested, then released. Now jailed again, he chose as his attorney a protégé of Begin's named Shmuel Tamir. Tamir hastened to deny any Herut involvement in acts of violence. He said he had been phoned only because "Shilanski is my regular client in civil matters." This was untrue; but his denial of Herut involvement in the affair seems not to have been. Israeli newspapers at the time concluded Shilanski was part of a "dissident" rump of the Irgun that felt Begin had erred in disbanding the underground.

Begin himself shunned contact with Shilanski, who was sentenced to twenty-one months in jail, and left party comment on the matter to Bader and a few others. Though it was Begin's rhetoric that keynoted the revived underground, he seems to have avoided involvement in, or knowledge of, specific acts of violence. Whether he knew or at least suspected what Landau and others were doing, is impossible to say. Tavin, who returned to Israel and met with Begin shortly before the dictionary attack, says they discussed the reparations issue. Tavin told Begin in so many words that he favored violence; but Begin ignored the remark. Shortly after the move to smuggle explosives into France, too, Begin visited Haifa for a party rally. The youngster who had organized the shipment approached him and said, "Our group—meaning our underground—wanted to meet him." Again Begin ignored the remark. "He gave no sign he knew what I was talking about," the man recalls. "Whether he really did know, I can't say."

Shmuel Merlin, as secretary of the party, confronted Begin after Shilanski's arrest and accused the Herut leader of "organizing an underground." He told Begin it was impossible to run a political party and an underground at the same time: A choice must be made. Begin replied, "Shmuel, don't worry. Things will work out." Merlin quit, and the two men never spoke again.

The reparations issue cooled with time, and Begin shifted his assault on the government to two other issues. One was the lot of the Sephardim—Jews whom Ben Gurion had brought from Arab countries to Israel, but had failed to include in the promise of their promised land. The reparations, in effect if not design, were the latest affront to them. The millions of dollars paid to European Holocaust survivors further widened the gap with Israel's Sephardic underclass. "Many of the excited hooligans who swarmed through the barbed-wire barriers, attacked the police and threw stones at the Knesset windows," lamented a pro-Ben Gurion newspaper after the January 1952 riot, "were immigrants from eastern [Arab] countries." Begin also hammered away at Israel's relations with the Arab world: Despite the post–1948 armistice with Egypt and Jordan, both states were sanctioning cross-border raids into Israel. Begin admired the army's counterstrikes—under Chief of Staff Moshe Dayan and a brash field commander named Ariel Sharon. But he said the violence could only get worse unless Israel disavowed Ben Gurion's "illusory" approach to peace, the acceptance of a "ghetto state."

Begin instinctively rebuilt Herut around a new coalition. Its main components were the Sephardim and Orthodox Jewry, whom he hoped to woo away from their marriage of convenience with Ben Gurion. Some IZL veterans, who had transferred loyalty to Herut, began to drift away. Typical was Yaakov Amrami. He resigned after one of his regular Saturday afternoon visits to the Begin apartment. The two men were playing chess in the garden, when the talk turned to politics. At issue was the donation of sculpture to the Israeli Museum by Billy Rose, whom the Kook group had befriended in America. Herut had moved against accepting the artwork after Orthodox spokesmen objected to the inclusion of nudes. Amrami tried to argue Begin into accepting the donation, pointing out that Begin himself was not Orthodox and asking, "Why don't you tell the Herut members to stop this sort of thing?" Begin replied: "Are you aware that twenty-five percent of Herut voters are Orthodox?" Yes, said Amrami, "but why should the other seventy-five percent suffer?" It was a rhetorical question: He and Begin both knew the importance of Orthodox backing in the Knesset. But to Amrami, party politics seemed "a moral compromise of a sort Begin did not have to make in the Irgun."

Begin, meanwhile, got a sudden boost to his hopes of recouping Herut's electoral decline. At the end of 1953, with the next election two years away, an exhausted Ben Gurion retired to the Negev Desert kibbutz of Sde Boker. Replacing him was the dovish foreign minister, Moshe Sharett, and Begin instantly went on the offensive. At rallies in Jerusalem and in the Negev town of Beersheba, he assailed the government's "fatal complacency"—and advocated a preemptive war against the Arabs. In the Knesset he said any delay would simply benefit the Arab armies. "Tomorrow, they will be stronger than we are, or at least they will *think* they are, and they will attack us." He denied the need to wait until Arab raids escalated, saying Israel was already justified in going to war. "There is already a constant, bloody war—called *guerrilla* in Latin. Any military man, Israeli or foreign, will tell you that in our century—despite two world wars—there is no war more dangerous or difficult to win than a guerrilla war." In these circumstances, a conventional Israeli attack "would be just. Not a war seeking bloodshed but a war to end bloodshed; not a war to conquer foreign land but to liberate our own mortgaged homeland; not a war for war, but a war for peace!" Maybe there would still be cross-border raids. Maybe "our reaction will not stop Arab murder. But lack of reaction," said Begin, "will guarantee only more of it!"

Israel's third election was due in mid-1955, and he was determined to win it. Summoning Meridor back from private business, Begin directed him to shore up party cohesion for the campaign.

"The message to the rest of the Herut," recalls Meridor, "was that if you don't agree with our line, go somewhere else. . . . It reinforced those who recognized only Begin as leader." Even when Ben Gurion returned from his Negev "retirement" as abruptly as he had left, Begin remained confident. He toured Sephardic resettlement camps. He lashed out at Ben Gurion and his Labor Zionist elitism, amid shouts of support from the crowd. Yet Ben Gurion lashed back: Begin was an outlaw who had led a mob on the Knesset barely two years before!

The election trimmed Ben Gurion's party from forty-five Knesset seats to forty. Begin got only fifteen seats, but he did recoup his losses of four years earlier. Outpacing both the moderate General Zionists and the Orthodox bloc, he made Herut the country's second largest party. "The people are dancing in the streets!" he shouted by long-distance phone to one supporter. He also took heart from Ben Gurion's travail in assembling a new coalition, which took three months. "Correct me if I'm wrong," he joked when the government presented its program to the Knesset, "but I doubt there have been more difficult birth pangs since Adam and Eve!" He saw an omen in Ben Gurion's "relative defeat" at the polls: "You have ruled. But one day, you will be in opposition!"

First, however, Begin set out to prod his country to war.

Chapter Seventeen

Family Quarrels

By late 1955, Begin was not alone in the urge to take up arms. An undeclared conflict of raid and reprisal was building along Israel's frontier with Egypt when, in September, Egyptian President Gamal Abdel Nasser suddenly announced a deal to buy East Bloc weaponry from Czechoslovakia. The question in Israel became not so much whether the army should fight the Egyptians as whether it *could*. Was war justified? Would it work? Most of all, would the Americans stand for it—now that Eisenhower and Dulles had followed Harry Truman, and had taken to referring to parts of Israel outside the UN partition lines as "occupied" Arab land? Begin told the Knesset it must ignore American innuendo: "There are no territories 'occupied' by Israel." Accusing Ben Gurion of chumming up to Washington, he ridiculed the idea of "security guarantees" from the White House. "If the Mexicans invade America, we'll rush over to save the day and drive them back across the border!" But if the Arabs attack, "from America, we'll get a mere promise." He said security could come only from within. "To ask for a guarantee is a mistake," he said. "To beg for it is a humiliation. To receive it: a catastrophe!" Israel must go to war: "a war of self-defense, a war to put an end to an undeclared war that gets worse with each day." And if the Americans didn't like it, Begin suggested, that was the Americans' problem. At the start of 1956 he strode to the Knesset podium and delivered what would prove a seminal statement of his views on Israel and the superpowers. At issue, he said, was "the decisive question of our day: Whether a small state can resist the pressure of great powers." He declared:

> In the thirties the impression was that it could not. In the fifties it has been proved possible, provided the small powers found they had something hard in their grip. There are the examples of Yugoslavia, and Formosa. . . . The small state must not be ready to make concessions, for once it offers concessions at a time of pressure it only invites more pressure upon itself.

As the border violence flared anew in the spring of 1956, Begin dramatized his alarm at Israeli caution by calling on the Knesset to vote the government out of office. Yet it was a vote he knew he could not win, and it promptly degenerated into a shouting match with Ben Gurion. Sooner or later, Begin proclaimed, Israel would *have* to fight. The only question was when Ben Gurion would wake up. "You," Ben Gurion shot back, "did not fight in the last war and will not fight in the next!" Begin leaped to his feet and barked, "*You* were a traitor to Israel! Traitor!"

But David Ben Gurion did, in fact, feel war was inevitable. In mid-1956 he forced Sharett out of the government. Telling no one—least of all, Begin—he responded to increasingly truculent Egyptian demands, and tacit U.S. acquiescence in them, by sealing an arms deal with the French. In late October, Nasser announced an alliance with Jordan and Syria. On the twenty-eighth, a bronchitic Ben Gurion summoned Menachem Begin to his bedside in Tel Aviv, and informed him Israel would invade Sinai the next day. Begin was less surprised by the war than by being told beforehand. Moving close to Ben Gurion's bed, he drew himself to attention and declared: "I applaud your courageous decision. Rest assured of our support." Then he grasped Ben Gurion's hand—says Bader, who was there—and held it "as if they were lovers."

Begin rhapsodized as the army seized the Gaza Strip and all Sinai, and Israeli-allied French and British forces secured the Suez Canal. "I know that if our teacher and master, Vladimir Jabotinsky, were alive today," he told the Knesset, "he would declare—no matter what our differences, past or future, with the government—that we congratulate the Prime Minister and his associates for having made the wise and right decision the Sunday before last. More power to them!" But then Israel came under pressure to pull back.

The Americans and the Soviets, in unlikely alliance, led the out-cry. Moscow warned Israel it was "playing with the fate of its own people." Barely less chilly was the message from Washington, especially when Ben Gurion told the Knesset that Israel intended to keep the land it had captured. The Americans joined in a United Nations call—passed by 65–1—for Israel to withdraw. Eisenhower warned Ben Gurion that he risked endangering "the friendly collaboration between our two countries." A State Department official hinted that the United States might cut off aid, the UN might expel Israel, and that the Soviets might attack her. The Americans vowed to counter any Soviet move against Britain or France, but pointedly omitted mention of defending the Israelis. Ben Gurion saw no alternative to retreat—the only dissenting voice among his advisers was General Dayan's. Thirty minutes after midnight, November 8, the prime minister announced that he was ordering the army to leave Sinai.

He had in mind a gradual pullback, wanting at least to keep Gaza. Yet if even this was anathema to Begin—who tried and failed to block it in the Knesset—it was not enough for Washington. The Americans started cutting back aid. When the Israelis left El Arish, the Sinai's provincial capital, Begin again failed in an attempt to defeat the government. Why, he asked the Knesset, was the army retreating? "Is it because of the pressure of the superpowers, especially the economic and financial pressure of the United States?" To cede, he said, was a dangerous precedent: "Can the government promise us that after one such retreat under pressure, there will not be further pressure?"

Begin flew to the United States in February 1957 to lobby against such pressure. But Ben Gurion could hold out no longer: On March 1 he had Foreign Minister Golda Meir, at the UN, announce Israel's decision to leave the rest of Sinai and Gaza, in exchange for an American guarantee that Egypt would not interfere with Israeli shipping. Begin, sitting in the UN visitors' gallery, canceled the rest of his visit, rushed back to Israel, and embarked on a public campaign to force Ben Gurion out of office. "This government bowed not to Nasser, but to the United States!" he cried at a Tel Aviv rally. In the Knesset he pronounced an end to his pre-Sinai tryst with Ben Gurion: "We were opponents and are opponents, and will remain opponents until the day when we both obey the command of the Almighty," he said. He added a promise to the nation: "We will yet liberate Gaza again!"

But the next election was two years away, and few in Israel

seemed to feel Begin could lead the country better than Ben Gurion. The prime minister had bowed to the inevitable. Besides, he had secured one gain he did not have to hand back: peace on Israel's borders. Begin, restless, left with Aliza on a series of trips overseas. He resumed his United States visit, then went to Canada. He and Aliza toured South Africa, then France. Begin did not criticize Ben Gurion abroad: That was a family affair—for Jews to tell Jews in Israel. But he assailed the Americans and Soviets, and refined the theory that small states could and should resist pressure from superpowers. The key, he had said before the war, was that the small nations must possess "something hard" for leverage. Now, Begin said, Israel had proved it possessed an army capable of humbling Nasser. If the Americans had any sense, they would beg for Israel's friendship.

He stopped wandering with the approach of the 1959 election—one he sensed he might finally win. Sephardic resentment had never been higher: A coterie of sometimes corrupt Labor Zionists with hefty paychecks seemed to have a stranglehold on the Israeli economy. Tens of thousands of new Sephardim had arrived in the mid-1950s. Most were Moroccans—proud of their traditions, strong in their sense of community, and stung by the welcome they received. Setting its tone was a 1949 report in *Ha'aretz,* the Israeli equivalent of *The New York Times,* when the first North African Jews were arriving. The Moroccans, it said, were "a race we haven't known before in Israel. We are dealing with a people of record primitiveness. Their level of education borders on total ignorance.... Generally speaking they are only slightly better than the Arabs, Blacks and Berbers among whom they used to live." And, said the newspaper, "more than anything else there is one basic fact—their total inability to adapt to life in Israel and, above all, their chronic laziness and hatred of work."

Begin wooed them. "The primitive element," Ben Gurion lamented in his diary before the 1959 election, "is subjected easily to [Begin's] political and social demagogy." The Herut leader told the newcomers they had a right to demand a better deal. He charged that Ben Gurion and his cronies had hoarded the national wealth—and turned Israel into a divided country of "*Ashkenazim* and non-*Ashkenazim.*" And he vowed to roars and ovations from audience after largely Sephardic audience: "We shall sweep away the discriminatory and corrupt regime of Labor!"

Begin also sought the support of others who resented the Labor Zionist oligarchy. The party of small business, the General Zionists, had bolted Ben Gurion's coalition in the 1955 election—only to see its Knesset strength trimmed from twenty seats to thirteen. Begin had suggested a new alliance in 1956—under his leadership—and been rebuffed. Still, the parties had in common an urge to break the Labor Establishment's stranglehold on power, and would clearly need each other to do so. Begin counted on the businessmen to bond with Herut if it did well in 1959. He also hoped for help from the Orthodox, whose alliance with the government was under strain. In mid-1958, Ben Gurion tried briefly to liberalize the criterion for considering a person Jewish: A Jew would be able to declare himself a Jew, without rabbinical validation. Two Orthodox cabinet ministers quit, and Begin rushed to their side. "Israel," he declared, "was born with a divine promise." Addressing parliament as he had addressed Hillel Kook a decade earlier, Begin demanded: "Does this government truly believe that, with regard to Jews, one can differentiate between religion and national identity? If it does so believe, then I must ask: Can a member of the Jewish nation be a Catholic? Can a member of the Jewish nation be a Calvinist, Anglican, Baptist, Anabaptist?" The government shelved the proposal.

Yet Begin had an image problem. To many, he remained the man who had attempted a "coup" from the *Altalena,* led a mob on the Knesset: He was trigger-happy. With the approach of the 1959 election, he inadvertently strengthened the impression. When Israel Radio broadcast a message calling up several reserve army units— why, was unclear—Begin heard the news in the Knesset and promptly asked for the floor. "The General Staff of our army has declared a general mobilization," he said. "If our army, mobilized as a result of what has happened, is called into action, we shall all stand behind it!" The call-up—not a general mobilization, in any case—soon turned out to be a mistake. As if this were not damaging enough to Herut's bid to convince Israelis it was sober enough to govern, Begin misstepped again on the campaign's final day. Pressed to meet a packed schedule of speaking obligations, he resolved it in a way that played into the hands of those Labor rivals who had so often branded him "fascist." He borrowed a supporter's sleek Cadillac to speed him from rally to rally, escorted by leather-jacketed IZL youths on motorcycles.

On November 3, Israel voted. Begin picked up two seats—getting seventeen—and Herut remained the second largest party. But Ben Gurion did his best ever, winning forty-seven seats and easily assembling a new government.

Menachem Begin as young Betar
movement leader in Warsaw,
1938. Israel Government Press Office

Ze'ev Jabotinsky meeting with
Betar leaders in Warsaw, 1939.
Bottom row: From left, Menachem
Begin, Aharon Propes,
Jabotinsky. Jabotinsky Institute

Menachem Begin and Aliza after their wedding in Truskaviech, May 30, 1939. Israel Government Press Office

Menachem Begin, in Polish Army uniform of General Anders's forces in Palestine, with Aliza and David Yotan (at right), 1942. Top row: Moshe Stein, Israel Epstein. Israel Government Press Office

Menachem Begin, in Polish Army
uniform, with Aliza in Tel Aviv,
1942. Israel Government Press Office

Wanted poster. Top row: From
left, Menachem Begin, Arye Ben
Eliezer.
Description of Begin:
Age: 36 years
Height: 173 cm.
Build: thin
Complexion: sallow
Hair: dark
Eyes: brown
Nose: long, hooked
Peculiarities: wears spectacles,
   flat-footed, bad teeth
Nationality: Polish
Occupation: Clerk
Jabotinsky Institute

False passport used by Begin in the name of Dr. Jonas Konigshofer. Jabotinsky Institute

Menachem Begin with Aliza and son Benjamin; Ze'ev Dov during his
"Rabbi Sassover" period in Tel Aviv, 1946. Israel Government Press Office

March of solidarity on Allenby Street in 1948 after members of
underground came out of hiding. From left: Eitan Livni, Amichai
Paglin, Yaakov Meridor, Begin, Moshe Rosenberg (first leader of
Etzel), Benyamin Zironi. Israel Government Press Office

Begin's historic first speech at Zion
Square in Jerusalem after coming
out of hiding, 1948. Fred Csasznik

Menachem Begin and Yaakov
Meridor watching the burning ship
Altalena, June 1948. Jabotinsky
Institute

Herut party convention in Tel
Aviv, August 14, 1948. Israel
Government Press Office

Begin honors Irgun flag in
Jerusalem. Chief of Irgun Zvai
Leumi Menachem Begin, moving
freely again after being
underground with a price on his
head during the British occupation
of Palestine, kisses the flag of Irgun
during a parade in Jerusalem,
August 4, when he presented the
banner to the Jerusalem
commander. Jabotinsky Institute

M.K. Ḥaim Landau and opposition leader M.K. Menachem Begin in Knesset. Behind them is M.K. Faris Hamdan, June 1959. Israel Government Press Office

Former Prime Minister David Ben Gurion, General Ezer Weizman, and Minister Without Portfolio Menachem Begin, December 11, 1967. Israel Government Press Office

Prime Minister Begin and former
Director of Government Press
Office Ze'ev Chafets. Israel
Government Press Office

Prime Minister Menachem Begin
and Foreign Minister Moshe
Dayan during flight to Ismalia,
December 25, 1977. Israel
Government Press Office

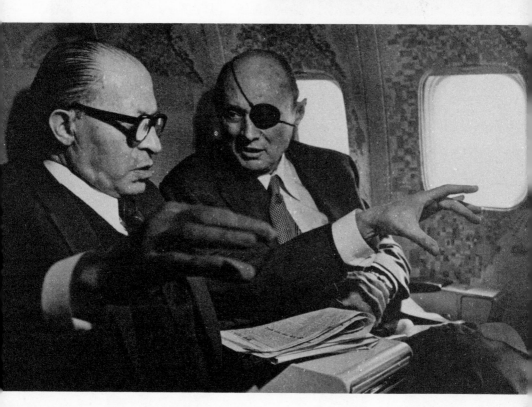

Prime Minister Menachem Begin welcoming President Anwar Sadat to the dinner given by him at the King David Hotel, Jerusalem, November 20, 1979. Israel Government Press Office

Prime Minister Begin and Nazi-hunter Beate Klarsfeld in New York, July 17, 1977. Israel Government Press Office

Prime Minister and Mrs. Begin
studying articles in American
publications at his Waldorf-Astoria
suite in New York, July 16,
1977. Israel Government Press Office

President Jimmy Carter and Prime
Minister Menachem Begin at
Sabbath eve supper, March 2,
1979. Israel Government Press Office

"The Triple Handshake" after signing the peace treaty, March 26, 1979. Israel Government Press Office

Major Haddad, commander of the Christian militias in South Lebanon, greets Prime Minister Begin in Kiryat Shmona, June 25, 1979. Israel Government Press Office

Prime Minister Begin speaks at a
dinner held in his honor by
President Sadat, April 1979. Israel
Government Press Office

Begin-Sadat summit, May 27,
1979. Israel Government Press Office

Prime Minister Begin speaking to a Jewish rally at Lincoln Center in Manhattan, March 28, 1979. Israel Government Press Office

Prime Minister Begin, accompanied by Minister of Agriculture Ariel Sharon (center) and Minister of Interior Yosef Burg (at Begin's left), hearing explanation about the settlement at Elon Moreh, February 27, 1981. Israel Government Press Office

Menachem Begin speaking at a meeting in Hechal Hatarbut in Tel Aviv celebrating Ze'ev Jabotinsky's centennial anniversary, June 6, 1980. Israel Government Press Office

Prime Minister Begin praying at the Wailing Wall on the eve of Jerusalem Day, May 31, 1981. Israel Government Press Office

Menachem Begin with walker,
1981. Gustavo Feinblatt

Prime Minister Begin, confined to
a wheelchair, conducts the Knesset
debate on the annexation of the
Golan Heights, December 14,
1981. From left: Yitzhak Shamir,
Simcha Erlich, Begin, Yosef
Burg. Gustavo Feinblatt

. . .

Begin's fourth straight election defeat sparked what would become the most serious Herut dissent since he had founded the party.
The first public sign came from a Begin protégé, the lawyer Shmuel
Tamir, within days of the vote. Tamir said the spectacle of Begin's
motorcycle outriders had not been an aberration, but a symptom of
inept leadership. Begin, he charged, was too busy reveling in his
own podium power to deal with the issues of substance facing
Herut. He had lost touch with Israel, and unless he overhauled his
party's "bankrupt" political message and moved toward the center,
he would never come to power. Shmuel Katz—who had left party
politics before the 1951 election—criticized Begin's leadership, less
brashly, by letter. Dozens of younger Herut activists, unexcited by
the prospect of a lifetime on the Knesset back benches, seemed to
harbor similar doubts. So did at least one Herut Knesset member, a
Revisionist who had long been at odds with Begin and finally sensed
the chance to do something about it. This was Eliezer Shostak, veteran leader of the Revisionists' National Labor Federation (NLF).
In 1948 he had favored merging with Ben Gurion's Establishment,
rather than battling it in quixotic opposition. After several years of
intermittent feuding, Begin had hit back hard. Calling the NLF a
"fiefdom . . . a power eating at the marrow of my bones," he emas-
culated it, by removing its ability to dispense jobs or pensions. Now,
Shostak saw in Shmuel Tamir a natural ally for a challenge to
Begin's leadership.

For a while, Begin deferred the reckoning—with an assist from
Ben Gurion, whose own party was entering a slow-burning succession crisis. First, a group of young Ben Gurion protégés forced
out another cabinet member on trumped-up charges—in turn forcing Ben Gurion to call a snap 1961 election in which his margin of
victory eroded by five seats. Herut held steady. Next, Ben Gurion
faced a challenge from his chief of intelligence, who leaked an exaggerated warning that Nasser had imported German scientists to
develop space-age rocketry. Begin used the first crisis to dramatize
his charges that Israel was being run by a corrupt establishment; the
second, to accuse Ben Gurion of letting the heirs of the Nazis "send
microbes to our enemies."

Within Herut, he continued to play patriarch to a Nonfighting
Family. Even if a secretary couldn't type, he refused to fire her, remarking, "She has children to support!" He insulated himself with

the abiding adoration of the old guard: Ben Eliezer, Mrs. Raziel-Naor, Chaim Landau, Lankin. You could find them any Saturday afternoon in the back garden at Rosenbaum Street. "It was a tradition," recalls one party member who often attended. "Begin would sit on his chair, his favorite, mustard-yellow armchair. And his good friends—at least they *thought* they were his good friends—they sat around, and everyone spoke to the god: 'Mr. Begin, your article yesterday in the *Herut* newspaper was a *marvelous* article. You really showed them!' And 'them' was Ben Gurion. *Herut* must have been one of the lowest-circulation newspapers in the world. But to watch this scene on Saturdays you would have thought Begin's article had been the major political event of the week! It was, literally, the faithful coming to see their god."

Begin did sense trouble, however. After the 1961 election he revived talk of an alliance with the small-business men. They had reconsolidated and renamed themselves as the Liberal party, and pulled even with Herut at seventeen seats. Yet Begin argued they needed his own image as a national leader if they were ever to become more than "a party of small merchants and landlords." Then—when Ben Gurion suddenly retired for good in 1963, with a parting charge that Herut was led by a "Hitlerlike" figure with a fondness for "racism and murder"—Begin moved to co-opt Shmuel Tamir, his critic of 1959, into a drive to win the election of 1965.

Begin liked Tamir, who was two years his junior, a *sabra* with smarts, ambition, and family ties to the Labor Establishment—a bit like Gideon Paglin of old. Begin had first met him at an IZL training exercise, where Tamir was called on to demonstrate a new sabotage technique. "This," Begin gushed, "is our advantage over our enemies: the Jewish brain!" Tamir went on to become IZL commander in Jerusalem for a spell, and after 1948 was Herut's press spokesman. But he left the party to practice law—with an eye for political cases like Dov Shilanski's and, on the eve of the 1955 election, Joseph Kaestner's. Kaestner was a Labor Zionist, suing for libel over a pamphlet that accused him of having favored cronies when arranging the escape of Jews from Nazi Europe. Tamir defended the pamphleteer, and used the case to highlight Labor Zionism's "conspiracy of silence" during the Holocaust. When Tamir won, Begin was delighted. Herut's final campaign poster in 1955 had pictured Kaestner above the slogan HE VOTES LABOR. YOU VOTE HERUT.

Now Begin included Tamir in accelerated talks with the Liberals.

In April 1965, barely six months before election day, the alliance was announced—even as Labor's image was tarnishing further. Labor's new leader, former Finance Minister Levi Eshkol, rehabilitated Pinhas Lavon, the cabinet minister who had been unfairly ousted by Ben Gurion's protégés. The Ben Gurion supporters—including Shimon Peres, Moshe Dayan, and Yitzhak Navon—seceded to form a rival labor party called Rafi, with Ben Gurion's endorsement. "It is a sad thing," Begin told a visitor, "to see those who were such staunch comrades for so many years engage in a bitter slanging match. It is just as sad to see what was once a united party break up." Still, he sensed, it would not be at all bad for Herut. At the signing of his alliance with the Liberals, he declared: "Gentlemen, we shall not be serving in the opposition much longer." He placed Tamir high on his candidates list—grooming him for high office in a Herut government and, to the alarm of some of the old guard, as an eventual party leader. "I have complete confidence in him," Begin told one of the veterans who objected to Tamir's meteoric promotion.

But in the November election, Begin's new alliance got only twenty-six seats—fewer than its component parts had mustered separately. Rafi won only ten. Labor, under Eshkol, dropped five, but still emerged with forty-five and formed a new government.

Eliezer Shostak, who had been left out of the coalition talks with the Liberals, said the results proved once and for all Begin could not bring Herut to power. "Begin has always said: 'Give me the chance and I will prove to you the movement will succeed my way. . . .' Many things the members did not understand, not even *agree* to, they accepted on hope and faith." But, Shostak told a party conference after the election, those days were over. Begin responded by trying to force the issue. Saying he knew there had long been "whisperings" of opposition in the party, he asked for a vote of confidence by the party executive. He got one—of sorts: He won by twenty-eight to five. Although the dissenting minority was small, it proved Shostak's point: The days when Begin could rule Herut unchallenged and unquestioned were over. When the party staged its regular convention six months later, Shostak showed up with allies. The most important was none other than Shmuel Tamir, pressed into increasingly open opposition by disgruntled members of Herut's youth wing.

Tamir proclaimed loyalty to Begin, but said the old guard around Begin must go. When Tamir and Shostak supporters presented an alternative list for the conference's honorary presidium, they humiliated the loyalist slate by a margin of two to one. The party's student leader from Hebrew University called on Begin and his allies to resign, provoking hoots of protest from old guarders in the crowd. Then Tamir spoke. He named no names, but said the party cried out for new voices, especially *sabra* ones. The message, recalls Yaakov Meridor, was clear: "The target was me, Arye [Ben Eliezer], Chaim Landau, Bader—the core." Begin tried once more to force the issue: He told the shocked convention he was resigning as leader—agreeing, after pleas from the old guard, to remain a member of the party executive. But Tamir said this begged the issue; he produced a guest speaker—a comrade from the IZL who had been his neighbor since the mid-1950s. The man, tall, with black hair and a toothbrush moustache, needed no introduction. Gideon Paglin strode to the podium and told the crowd Tamir was right: "You have surrounded Begin with a wall of iron!"

Begin was stunned. "You could *see*," says Meridor, "how it hurt him." He rose and, in the suddenly hushed hall, began to speak. For three hours Menachem Begin bared a soul that sought only acceptance from the Jewish people he had served—from Ben Gurion, perhaps most of all—and a bit of peace. He said he was tired, and had long been thinking of retiring anyway: Maybe without him, Herut and Ben Gurion's Rafi could constitute an alternative government. "But there is a limit to what a public figure can bear!" Begin cried. There is a limit to public cruelty towards a man. They called on me to retire from public life. I did not retire, neither because I was hated nor because I was beloved. But what *wrong* did I do to this people all my life? What wrong did I do to Mr. Ben Gurion that he hated me so? Was it because I and my friends fought for the State, of which Ben Gurion became the first premier with our consent?" Begin accused Shostak and Tamir of treachery. "They worked behind my back. They set up a coalition. They did not inform me. They left me like a blind man groping in the dark. Did they think I was the Premier of Monaco to have a Cabinet thrust upon me without my knowledge!" As many in the crowd wept, he announced he was leaving the party—never to return. Meridor could run Herut; Bader, its delegation in parliament. He would stay at home.

He did. Meridor, with Begin's okay, tried briefly to negotiate a compromise with Tamir. But when the rest of the old guard found out, they persuaded Begin to rescind his approval. He withdrew even more. Refusing to participate in any party meetings, he stayed in his apartment, reading, brooding, taking phone calls from Herut admirers. He lost his appetite, dropping more than twenty pounds in the weeks after the convention. "He seemed so hurt!" recalls Mrs. Raziel-Naor. "He felt he had opened himself to Tamir." Aliza tried, but failed, to persuade him that the needs of party and country demanded he snap out of his isolation. Even Paglin tried. He asked him to forgive Shmuel Tamir. "He is a wounded soldier on the battlefield. You, as commander, cannot leave him there!" But Begin refused. Finally, Meridor convened the Herut equivalent of a court-martial, which drummed Tamir out of the party. "I *had* to do it," he recalls. "There are a lot of things I did for Begin because I knew he wouldn't do them on his own, but that had to be done. I never asked him. I did them. Later, he might shout at me, say I shouldn't have. But I knew it was for his benefit."

With Tamir gone—and the old guard still in place—Begin finally returned to the party. He put on weight, soon acted in both Herut and the Knesset as if he had never been away.

And barely had he returned than he was suddenly invited to join the government of Israel.

Chapter Eighteen

A Taste of Power

With Eshkol's cabinet still traumatized by the Rafi electoral split, Nasser moved the Egyptian Army into the Sinai in May 1967 and ordered the UN peacekeepers there to leave. He blocked Israel's outlet through the Red Sea, at Sharm el-Sheikh. When Eshkol reacted with caution, Rafi's Dayan and Peres clamored for action. Begin wanted an ultimatum: If Nasser took one step more, war! The press called for the formation of a national unity government. And Eshkol, who was receptive to the idea, summoned Begin for consultations.

Yet Begin, finally within reach of his first share of government power, hesitated. Maybe he was used to being leader of the opposition, a role which, he had repeatedly argued to his Herut comrades, was every bit as crucial in a democracy as the premiership. Maybe, too, his thirst to settle scores with Labor had slackened with the departure of David Ben Gurion. Begin liked Levi Eshkol. The new prime minister treated him with none of Ben Gurion's disdain, and had even acquiesced in Herut's long-standing request to allow the reburial of Jabotinsky's remains in Israel. But Begin arrived for the national unity consultations with an offer Eshkol could only refuse: Herut would join a widened coalition—*if* Ben Gurion returned as prime minister. Though Begin had sworn publicly after Israel's retreat from Sinai in 1957 to oppose Ben Gurion until Judgment Day, he now insisted that a "truly critical situation" demanded his rival's leadership. And if he, Begin, could see his way to accepting Ben

Gurion's political revival, why shouldn't Eshkol do the same? Eshkol said no: He and Ben Gurion were by now "two horses that cannot pull the same wagon."

Begin, undeterred, went to call on Ben Gurion at his Tel Aviv apartment. He saw the mission as an exercise in patriotism, putting nation above party. But he was also, some colleagues felt, enticed by the chance to act as an agent for Ben Gurion's return, now that Ben Gurion oversaw a Knesset faction junior even to his own. So powerful was the urge that Begin ignored a fact widely known among Israeli politicians: Ben Gurion, now in his eighty-first year, had tired, mellowed. He did not want a war. When Begin suggested that the ex-prime minister lead the country into Sinai, Ben Gurion suggested that the army simply "take Sharm el-Sheikh" and wind the crisis down. "It emerged that he did not have much grasp of the situation on the ground," says a Herut aide. Begin had no choice but to abandon his campaign to bring back Ben Gurion.

There the matter rested until May 28, when Eshkol went on radio in an attempt to rally Israel behind him. The attempt turned into a disaster. Reading from a hastily edited text, he stumbled. He created not unity, but alarm, and raised to fever pitch the clamor for a widened cabinet coalition. Still, even as Nasser escalated—sealing a joint Arab military command—Begin continued to balk at Eshkol's overtures. Now he insisted that Rafi's Moshe Dayan be defense minister in any unity cabinet. The move puzzled even Begin's inner circle. His political secretary, a young IZL veteran named Yehiel Kadishai, had been called up for reserve army duty, but rushed to a pay phone to complain. He recalls tracking down Begin at Arye Ben Eliezer's home. "Arye answered the phone, and I asked: 'Why does Menachem oppose joining the cabinet without Rafi?' Arye—who agreed with me—said I should speak to Begin myself, and handed Begin the phone." Begin replied: "It will be okay, Yehiel." But Kadishai pressed: "Why should we fight Dayan's battles?" Begin simply repeated, "It will be okay."

Eshkol, as it happened, had nothing against Rafi's joining the cabinet, as long as Ben Gurion wasn't part of the bargain. Late June 1, he appointed Dayan defense minister, made Begin a minister without portfolio, and announced a national unity government. Begin summoned Meridor, Ben Eliezer, and Bader to accompany him to the doorway of the cabinet room for the inaugural session. When Eshkol had greeted everyone, Begin asked for the floor and delivered a biblical paean to the unity of the people of Israel, whereupon

Eshkol chuckled, "Amen! Amen!" Before the cabinet got down to work the next day, Begin led a group of supporters to Jabotinsky's grave, where he proclaimed: "Sir, we have come to inform you that one of your followers is now serving as a minister in the government of Israel."

The government's function was to make war, and Begin's initial role was to join, late June 4, in rubber-stamping the plan of attack. Before dawn the next day, Israel destroyed Egypt's air force on the ground. Begin agreed to a cabinet message sent to King Hussein of Jordan that if he stayed out of the war, Israel would not try to take East Jerusalem or other Jordanian-held land. But when Jordan attacked, the war widened: Israeli jets obliterated the Jordanian Air Force, and cut Syria's in half.

Begin now embarked on a war of his own: to reverse at least one result of Ben Gurion's partition, by taking the Arab, eastern half of Jerusalem. He enlisted the backing of Yigal Allon, the former Palmach commander who was now Eshkol's military aide. Shortly after noon on June 5, in Eshkol's Tel Aviv office, Allon made the pitch to the prime minister: "Begin and I want Jerusalem." Eshkol replied, "It's an idea," but did not commit himself. So Begin headed for Jerusalem, where the Knesset was convening in its recently inaugurated chamber of glass and marble on a hill near the western edge of town. He posted Kadishai outside, to intercept Eshkol on arrival, and persuaded the prime minister to convene the cabinet before parliament opened. Begin wanted a formal agreement on taking East Jerusalem. As Jordanian shells fell on the lawn outside, the ministers repaired to a bomb shelter, usually used for storing mops and detergent. But they gave Begin what he wanted.

He stayed overnight in Jerusalem. He checked in at the King David, which had displayed a delicious sense of irony since Israeli independence by extending him a discount. The hotel, like the city, was blacked out. Begin ate dinner in the basement restaurant that Paglin had mined with his milk cans, strolled outside for a while, then retired for the evening. But he slept fitfully, and returned to Tel Aviv the next morning brimming with excitement. A Dayan aide recalls running into him. "I was in uniform, and he came up and threw his arms around me—even though I didn't really know him personally—and said how wonderful it was that I was serving the army of Israel!"

At sunrise June 7, Begin was listening to the BBC and heard of UN efforts to secure a truce. Haunted by the possibility of a rerun of 1948, when a cease-fire had helped deny Israel East Jerusalem, he phoned Dayan and got him to persuade the prime minister to convene the cabinet. Needing no convincing, the ministers told Dayan to order the army into the Old City. The assault met scant resistance, and by sundown an Israeli flag flew on the Temple Mount. Begin entered the next day, winding through stone alleyways past shuttered Arab market stalls to gaze, with neck-jolting suddenness, on the overgrown mass of the Western Wall. "I cried," he recalls. "I suppose everybody had tears in his eyes. . . . Nobody was ashamed."

The war ended June 10. Israel, now more than quadrupled in size, had taken East Jerusalem and the entire West Bank of the Jordan River from Hussein. It had captured Gaza, Sinai, and the Suez Canal from Egypt; and Syria's Golan Heights. Eshkol had mixed feelings about the fruits of victory. He feared Israel would find it hard to administer the Arab territories, or even to get rid of them under acceptable terms of peace. Yet Begin had no such worries, and was determined that Israel not hand back captured territory as in 1956. An Israeli journalist recalls meeting Begin after the war. The man—Yehuda Litani—shares his last name with the river that meanders through Lebanon some fifteen miles north of the Israeli border. "Ah, Mr. Litani," Begin crowed, "we shall yet reach the Litani!" When the reporter noted the problem of the tens of thousands of Palestinian Arab refugees between Israel and the Lebanese river, Begin replied with a smile: "Mr. Litani, you must not mix geography with *demography!*"

The victory of June 1967 seemed suddenly to legitimize Begin and Herut. For years he had been branded as a lunatic, or worse, for keeping alive the dream of an "unpartitioned" Israel. Now the only part of the old Irgun emblem outside Israeli rule was the East Bank of King Hussein's Jordan, a prize so remote that even Begin had all but stopped mentioning it. In the summer of 1967 thousands of Israelis—left, right, and center on the political spectrum—voted with their picnic baskets, reveling in the chance to hop in their cars and drive to biblical places like Hebron, or to the overgrown sites of Jewish settlements lost in the 1948 war. Even Eshkol got caught up in the tide. He allowed Jews to resettle a portion of old Jerusalem— swallowing up dozens of Arab houses and shops in the process—and approved several settlements on the West Bank as well. The rest of the land, he figured, he could swap for peace with the Arab world.

Begin loved his cabinet work, which he saw as a platform for preventing any withdrawal from the territories won in the war. Eshkol treated the Herut leader as a full partner, giving him access to diplomatic cables and policy documents. Begin was faultlessly respectful of the prime minister, never publicly criticizing him or anyone else in the government. The picture of a Polish gentleman, Herut's minister without portfolio wore a tie and jacket to cabinet meetings and addressed fellow ministers as "Sir," both practices joltingly out of sync with the informality deeded by Ben Gurion. Before long, with no trace of irony, the others were addressing the Herut leader as "Mr. Begin." One cabinet colleague recalls how "Begin used to come into my office to see me, and would invariably kiss my secretary's hand. . . . Since she was a *sabra* girl, not used to that sort of thing, she would cringe whenever he appeared!"

Inside the cabinet room, recalls an Eshkol aide who became friendly with Begin, "he would speak at great length—much greater length than others—on the need to hold on to our battlefield gains." In the period after the war the issue was moot: There was no immediate prospect of a land-for-peace deal. But Begin wanted to ensure there was no hint to the contrary, a task he pursued most vigorously as a member of the three-man committee that drew up the cabinet's weekly communiqué. The other draftsmen were Foreign Minister Abba Eban and Israel Galili, Begin's rival from the days of the *Altalena*. "Begin *loved* drafting the cabinet statement!" says the Labor aide. Eban ignored the exercise, dismissing it as semantics. "But Begin and Galili—by now very friendly adversaries; Galili was the only one in the cabinet who called him 'Menachem'—would argue over every comma!"

For a while, Begin so enjoyed government that he rounded off the sharper edges of Herut ideology. He made no effort to short-circuit a series of secret contacts with King Hussein over peace terms. He did oppose the government's so-called Allon Plan for handing back most of the West Bank if King Hussein made peace. Still, he did not object to other ministers' pushing the option publicly—although, says Eban, "I remember how Begin chuckled when he heard the phrase 'total rejection' in Hussein's reply." When Eshkol succumbed to a heart attack in February 1969 and was replaced by Golda Meir—who had a record of strident opposition to both Herut and Rafi—Begin accepted her invitation to prolong the unity government at least until the next election, in the fall.

In the spring, however, Israel came under pressure for the first time since the war to ponder trading land for peace. Air and ground skirmishes erupted on the southern border. Egypt was getting new planes, arms—and thousands of military advisers—from Moscow. Gaza's Palestinian camps also ignited: Youths hurled rocks, even grenades, at Israeli patrols. In Washington, the new Nixon administration sought to reenter Mideast diplomacy. As the October election approached, Begin made no move to bolt the unity government: He seemed determined to press his opposition to negotiating concessions quietly, from within the cabinet. During the campaign, he observed his self-imposed stricture on criticizing other cabinet members, reducing the fire of his oratory to an occasional flicker. He emerged with a victory of sorts. His Herut-Liberal alliance held steady, at twenty-six seats, while Mrs. Meir and a nominally reunited Labor coalition dropped an aggregate seven seats. She asked Begin to stay on.

Yet Begin was not at all sure he wanted to. For weeks he spurned Mrs. Meir, even when she offered him four additional ministerial positions and a say in drafting the government program. She agreed to omit specific mention of handing back the West Bank in exchange for peace. Begin, however, countered by pressing on two domestic-policy issues. He wanted compulsory arbitration of a recent wave of strikes, and a national health-insurance scheme that would break the Histadrut's near monopoly in that area. To those who knew Begin, his demands rang hollow. To be sure, they were consistent with Revisionist party tenets he had written into the Herut platform in 1948. But never before had Begin taken much personal interest in them, or in any domestic issue. He had left these matters to Bader and, since the 1965 election alliance, to the Liberals. His sudden shift seemed to reflect deeper misgivings about staying in government—misgivings highlighted by the fact that most of Herut, and all the Liberals, desperately wanted to stay. They assured him he was needed in the cabinet, that only there could he keep Golda from dealing away the West Bank.

For Yaakov Meridor, remaining in government was a foregone conclusion. Why return to the opposition if you didn't have to? Two weeks before the election, he had recruited one of Israel's war heroes to join Herut, by promising him a seat in the new national unity cabinet. The newcomer had helped develop the Israeli Air Force, and now ranked second on the General Staff. He had also, however, done piecework for the Irgun before 1948, was hawkish on defense questions, and shared Begin's desire to keep the land taken in 1967.

He had ambition to match his guts, but knew he was too brash, and hawkish, to rise higher in the military hierarchy. He was Chaim Weizmann's nephew, Ezer, and he leaped at Meridor's offer of a Herut cabinet slot.

Still, Begin held out—all the more strongly as he sensed his own hold on his party was weakening. Arye Ben Eliezer was nearing death from cancer. Shmuel Tamir had set up a party of his own, which won two seats in the election. Meridor was in favor of bringing at least some younger blood into the leadership. And the Liberals were threatening to scrap the alliance with Begin if he insisted on dragging them back to the opposition benches. When Begin suddenly raised a new demand with Golda—that she give the Orthodox religious party a deputy minister's post, the Liberal leader, Yosef Sapir, exploded: "How *dare* you commit us without asking us!" By early December, Sapir was hinting at cutting a separate deal with Mrs. Meir.

Then on December 10, American Secretary of State William Rogers announced a joint bid with Moscow for Mideast peace. The implication was that the Soviets could pressure the Arabs, Washington would deliver Israel, and land would be traded for peace. "Perhaps this," Sapir remarked to a colleague, "will convince Begin!" That evening Golda summoned the old national unity government, which was continuing in caretaker capacity. To Begin's relief, even she favored rejecting the U.S. move. But minutes after the meeting, Begin phoned Sapir. "I have an idea," he said. "At times like these, the human brain doesn't stop inventing ideas. I suggest we propose that the clause on compulsory arbitration be dropped from the coalition agreement." He told Golda he would join the government. When Bader heard the news—on the radio the next morning—he phoned Begin and asked what had happened to the demand for national health insurance. "I slept on the issue," said Begin, "and finally decided I will fight for national health from inside."

The deal gave Begin six cabinet seats, the heftiest political patronage that had ever been his to dispense. Three seats belonged to the Liberals, one to Begin himself. With Ben Eliezer on his deathbed, Begin initially chose Landau and Yaakov Meridor for the remaining posts. But Meridor refused, saying he wanted to return to private business, and telling Begin he had already promised a cabinet post to Ezer Weizman. Begin, who knew he would face a rebellion by other old guarders if he whisked Weizman to the head of the line, pressed Meridor to stay on. Meridor was adamant.

And the more Begin thought of it, the less he could resist the allure of Weizman. In military panache, Weizman made Giddy Paglin look like a novice. His *sabra* credentials and Establishment blood made Tamir seem a parvenu. "The mere name 'Weizman' evoked in Begin some sense of vindication, I'm sure of it. You could tell!" remarks one Begin protégé. "For that matter, I'm sure if *Ben Gurion's* nephew had joined, *he* would have rocketed to a senior post, too." At first, Begin toyed with keeping Weizman out of the cabinet for a decent interval. "He should go through the motions," he told Meridor. "To instantly make him a minister just isn't done!" Besides, he remarked to another colleague, "the man is still in uniform!" But Meridor had anticipated both problems. He suggested naming his own son-in-law, Tel Aviv party leader Yosef Kramerman, to the cabinet post. Weizman would resign from the air force, Kramerman would resign from "his" cabinet slot and hand it to Weizman. Begin said he would play no role in such a device. "It's not kosher!" he remarked. But he also agreed that if Meridor could pull it off, and win Herut approval, he would play along.

The maneuver was the most open of secrets by the time Herut convened to vote. Bader, who felt that decades of dues-paying made the cabinet post rightfully his, told Begin he would fight for it. Begin refused to get involved, and when Bader entered his name on the party ballot against Kramerman, he lost. "Begin," Kadishai recalls, "sensed that the party was for Ezer—for Kramerman, the straw man. To fight for Bader would have meant strife, a quarrel." The next day Weizman—still not even a member of Herut—phoned Begin. "At seven in the morning," he recalls, "following a prearranged scenario, I [told] him I was prepared to resign from the army, so as to take my oath" as a member of the cabinet. "Yes, yes," said Begin, "you must resign." By ten in the morning, the deed was done, and the next day, Ezer Weizman became Herut's minister of transport.

"Begin enjoyed the cabinet debates," recalls a Labor colleague. "He came to feel he was playing a role of tremendous political importance—to keep Israel from committing the 'crime' of handing back land." He also came to respect Golda. To her fury, he would address her as "our senior sister." Sometimes, he would bestow on her his supreme compliment: "proud Jewess." The U.S. initiative had made concrete the issue of land for peace, and Begin's antennae were tuned for the slightest hint of retreat by fellow ministers. He would interrupt Labor rivals with the taunt, "You didn't say at all the same thing in the past," and send out for the minutes of past cabinet sessions to prove the point. "He was invariably right," says a Labor member of the government. "He had a photographic memory for such things!"

In early 1970 the war of attrition with Egypt escalated. Some 250 Israelis had died; 1,000 were injured. From Washington in June, Rogers proposed that Israel and Egypt enter peace talks under the UN aegis, and declare a three-month truce. The aim would be to implement the UN resolution adopted in 1967: land for peace.

When Nasser unexpectedly accepted the Rogers Plan, Begin agreed to the idea of a cease-fire. But he retreated from the UN resolution, which the first national unity government had accepted. Complaining there had been no cabinet debate, much less a vote, at the time, Begin now insisted Nasser must sign a treaty of peace with Israel before there could even be talk of withdrawal. Golda pressed Begin to moderate his opposition. She assured him she, too, had misgivings about the Rogers Plan. "But we won't have any cease-fire unless we also accept some of the less favorable conditions. . . . We won't get any arms from America." Retorted Begin, "What do you mean we won't get arms? We'll *demand* them." Begin, writes Golda, figured "all we had to do was to go on telling the United States that we wouldn't give in to any pressure whatsoever. And if we did this long enough and loud enough, one day that pressure would just vanish."

In early August the Knesset accepted the Rogers Plan. Begin's delegates voted against it. But Golda, who still wanted him in the government, let the matter drop. Begin did not. He announced he was leaving the government. Golda bent over backward to oblige him: She said he could stay inside the government even while opposing her on the Rogers Plan. Begin replied that the issue was too important. From the Liberals, he faced rebellion. In Herut there was also grumbling—not least from Meridor, and Weizman. The issue came to a head at a joint meeting of the Herut-Liberal alliance. Reminding the Liberals that it was he, and the IZL veterans in Herut, who had fought the British while they stood aside, he declared: "You cannot ask a man to deny his lifelong credo!" When the votes were counted, Herut backed Begin. Several Liberals did so as well, and he won by a whisker. At the start of August, he took his alliance back into opposition.

He thrived there. "I swear," he said, "that in all my life I have never been more at peace with myself and my conscience than I am now." Golda's foreign minister recalls thinking, on hearing Begin orate in parliament with his fire of old, that "he had exchanged the cabinet table for the Knesset rostrum with a measure of relief." The alliance with the Liberals, the taste of government, Ben Eliezer's death in late 1969, and Weizman's rapid elevation had all diluted Begin's control over a Herut universe he had created in his own image. One of Golda's colleagues recalls a cabinet vote not long before Begin's departure. At issue was Foreign Minister Eban's planned visit to West Germany. Begin railed against the idea, and Landau railed with him. But Weizman voted to let Eban go. "He was sort of an *enfant terrible*. I still remember Begin's look of utter astonishment when Ezer broke ranks!" One of the Liberals' cabinet ministers, Arye Dulzin, adds, "Begin was always used to being Number One, and suddenly he felt the ground shifting beneath him. . . . He preferred to go back into opposition, where he would be Number One again."

More than this, Begin feared that Herut's ideological identity was at stake. A few weeks later, one of Mrs. Meir's Labor party aides asked Begin why he had spurned her terms for staying. "It is not totally unrealistic," Begin replied, that if he had stayed in government, the day would come "when Golda presents a peace treaty to the nation, and a lot of those people who today shout, 'Begin! Begin!' would vote for you!"

Chapter Nineteen

The Battle
Within

The Rogers initiative collapsed soon after Begin left the government. Nasser used the truce to move new Soviet missiles to the edge of the Suez, and the Americans contented themselves with tapping him on the wrist. Golda said all deals were off until the Egyptian violations were corrected. Then, in September, Nasser died, and Vice-President Anwar Sadat took over for what everyone assumed would be a mere transition period. Adding to the sense of political flux, civil war erupted in Jordan between King Hussein and Yasser Arafat's fledgling Palestinian guerrilla movement.

Begin lashed out at the United States. He warned President Nixon that he risked going down in history "as a man who traded the blood of Jewish children for material deals with the Arabs." Nixon, he told the Knesset, was "playing chess with the fate of Israel." He resisted the Americans'—and some Israelis'—urge to rescue the beleaguered Hussein, or encourage the newly elevated Sadat, as political alternatives to increasingly assertive Palestinian guerrilla armies. Hussein, Sadat, indeed "all the Arab rulers," were on record as favoring the "liberation of Palestine," Begin reminded readers in a newspaper commentary in October 1970. The self-proclaimed "realists" who favored accommodation with misproclaimed Arab "moderates" were deluding themselves. When Secretary Rogers attended a Knesset committee session in early 1971, Begin lectured him for having said he was impressed by Nasser's successor. "We remember Hitler and Stalin speaking of peace," Begin exclaimed, adding icily,

"Besides, what do we have to discuss after you have, in your plan, given the Arabs everything?" When Rogers tried to cut him short, Begin snapped: "We are accustomed to parliamentary interruptions in our democratic House. But please, Mr. Secretary, I have the floor."

Inside Herut, however, Begin faced trouble. The party had gone along with his decision to leave the government—but with reluctance. Begin now moved to co-opt the doubters in the person of Ezer Weizman, their most dazzling, if junior, exponent. Begin was more charmed by the war hero—who preferred to be called simply "Ezer"—than by anyone since Shmuel Tamir. Egged on by Meridor, he promoted Weizman in 1971 to chairman of the party's executive committee. Although nominally the number two post in Herut, it was by tradition a distant second: Begin made policy decisions himself. "It was like being the chief executive officer of a company," says Meridor. The post was always filled after, rather than during, party conventions. "Begin felt only *one* chairman should be elected at the convention," explains a Herut veteran. "This was chairman of the *party*—Mr. Begin."

Yet Weizman had other ideas. He saw no point in heading "the executive arm of an opposition party, with very little to execute." While careful to avoid challenging Begin, he set out to refashion Herut into "a party that wins." Touring local branches, he touched base with natural allies in a quest to replace the Chaim Landaus and Esther Raziel-Naors with a new breed, and bring the party out of opposition once and for all. Though an affront to the old guard, the vision proved irresistible to many others: Begin as prime minister, backed by Ezer's flash and energy. Among the dozens attracted were Eliahu Ben Elissar. By the time Weizman came along, Ben Elissar recalls, Herut had lost seven straight elections. "There were almost no *young* people—people my age—ready to enter the party." Ben Elissar was the survivor of a family murdered by the Nazis. He had reached Israel at age ten, joined the Irgun, and helped paste Begin's proclamations on the walls of Palestine. In 1950 he joined the Mossad, Israel's CIA. He first met Begin, accidentally, on a train from Paris to Brussels in the 1950s. He could not resist blowing his cover when Begin asked, in French, to share a compartment. *"Ken, ha mefaked,"* replied Ben Elissar in Hebrew, snapping to attention: "Yes, commander." Back in Israel in the 1960s—with a Ph.D. in history, fluency in three languages, and a future in journalism—Ben Elissar accepted Begin's invitation to join Herut. Now Weizman phoned—and offered him the job of party spokesman, with Begin's okay. Yet Ezer was also promoting others, united in resentment of an old guard that had yet to win Herut an election. These owed their first loyalty not to Menachem Begin, but to Weizman.

At the end of 1972, Herut held its convention to plot strategy for the next election, due in the autumn of 1973. Weizman arrived determined to accomplish what Tamir had tried six years earlier: clear out dead wood. Hoping to unseat the old guard without offending Begin, he anticipated resistance. "No one in Begin's position, after not having won an election for twenty-five years, likes having someone come along and—even indirectly—say, 'Look, what you've done up to now didn't bring you into power,' " recalls Weizman. "Nobody likes to be told: 'You shmuck, look what you've done up to now! Let me do it my way, and you'll be a winner.' "

Still, at first Begin seemed to feel Weizman had a point. He also knew Weizman had backing—from younger, local party leaders who craved a share of power. Amid panic and protest from the old guard, Begin agreed to a compromise steering committee for the convention that included a contingent of newcomers. When Weizman proposed his own man for committee head—and said that this group should in turn choose the party's central committee—Begin agreed. Only then did Ezer push one step too far: He proposed transferring various powers from the party chairman—Begin—to the *executive* chairman, himself. From that moment, the convention was at war.

At past conventions Begin had developed the tradition—the fiction—of attending as a simple delegate. He would sit in the sixth or seventh row and when he wanted to intervene, he would whisper instructions to an aide, who would rush to relay them. Now Begin abandoned the practice. He went personally to the steering committee to ensure election of a Herut central committee he could trust. Recalls Ben Elissar, who remained loyal to Begin, "He had never so much as set foot in a steering committee meeting before." Begin told the group that Weizman was trying to form a faction within the party. "So I, too, have decided to form a faction." It was up to the committee to decide which faction they wanted. He added, for good measure, "I will find it more difficult to work with a central committee unacceptable to me."

The choice was not really a choice, and Weizman knew it. He went to Begin and tried to argue him back to the sixth row. Begin was a commander. "You belong to all of us below you, to the entire party!" *Commanders,* said Weizman, should not sully themselves by forming factions. "Why not?" asked Begin. "This is a democratic movement." He buttonholed Weizman's candidate for steering committee chairman and ordered him not to take the post. Then he sought out another key Weizman supporter—Meridor's son-in-law, Yosef Kramerman—and told him that if the "Weizman faction" did somehow triumph, it would have to figure out how to run for election without Menachem Begin. One by one, Weizman's allies caved in. Before the final session that evening, Begin and Weizman crossed paths in the hallway. Weizman upbraided the Herut leader for having left the national unity government, and predicted that at this rate he would *never* get another chance at power. Begin ignored the taunt, and spread the word he would deliver a major address.

Sensing victory, he drew Ben Elissar aside and remarked with mock irony, "Imagine, Eli! There I was shaving this morning. I had got up early, listened to the BBC, and I was *shaving,* and I got this idea. Why should I let Weizman go to the committee and sway them? *I* will go there." By the time Begin strode to the podium, the conference hall was jammed with Irgun veterans, their wives and children. Begin spoke for two hours—shifting from serious to sardonic and back again. Calling Weizman *"Mon général,"* he shouted: "We cleave to principles here, not to cabinet seats!" He savaged Weizman's suggestion that the party form a shadow cabinet to dramatize its bid for power. "For the first time in my life, I have been appointed prime minister! And by none other than the former renowned commander of our Air Force, Ezer Weizman!"

By the time the convention voted, Ezer was in no position to appoint anybody as anything. He grumbled that Herut wasn't a party, but a collection of IZL foot soldiers who still swore by their "commander." This was, in large measure, true. "We weren't used to the idea of anything less than deference to Menachem Begin," agrees Ben Elissar. "This is what Ezer didn't understand. Neither did Shmuel Tamir, but especially Ezer." Begin told the convention that Weizman had misunderstood the party rules: The steering committee would not select the party's central committee. The convention floor would. The vote was held, and Begin's supporters triumphed.

Before dawn, Weizman rose to address them. "I have learned in the past four days some very serious lessons about the democratic process," he said. "I believe that the party chairman and the chairman of the Party Executive should work in harmony.... I wish to make it clear I do not stand at the head of any faction. I joined this movement because of its ideological line, and I am not disappointed with it. But I am very disillusioned with other things that I have encountered here." He said he would remain a member of the central committee, but was resigning as executive chairman. "Having been told that there are two factions in the party, and that I head one of them, I find no other way."

Begin left the convention on a high. Interviewed on Israel Television, he said, "Ezer is a naughty boy—with considerable charm, but you can't create a policy out of naughtiness." To Ben Elissar, he chuckled, "Everything was going so *well* for Ezer. And then Houdini had to come on stage and ruin everything!" Yet having humbled Weizman, he tried to avoid losing him altogether. He leaked reports that Landau would be the new executive chairman, but then summoned Weizman for a tête-à-tête, and said he, Begin, would take over the position for an interim period. The seat would be warm if Weizman returned. He added that Ezer would still be welcome to manage the 1973 election campaign.

But it would be on Begin's terms. One by one, he purged Weizman's protégés from the leadership, and promoted his own men in their place. One was Yitzhak Shamir, the former Stern group operations chief and a Herut newcomer. A second was Isser Lubotsky, whose main distinction had been to preside over the party "court" that had ousted Shmuel Tamir. Ezer phoned Begin, protesting that he would find it hard to run the campaign after such a purge. But Begin replied that there had been no purge: He was just getting on with the day-to-day duties of the executive chairman. On January 14, Begin nominated a new executive committee heavily weighted with his own men. He invited Weizman and Yosef Kramerman to join. Kramerman accepted, but Weizman refused. Begin took the slate to the central committee for endorsement. Weizman demanded a secret ballot, but Begin insisted on a show of hands, and won, 155–23. "This," Weizman protested, "is a movement of passive people, fearful of change. It does not project—to put it mildly—an image of a vital political movement."

Begin retorted that he had "struggled to bring Weizman into the government. And believe me, he was given precedence over a long waiting list of party veterans." When Weizman replied that he had simply tried to rearrange the furniture in a hopelessly outmoded chamber, Begin cut him short, charging, "You wanted to *smash* the furniture!" When an Israeli reporter asked Begin whether Weizman hadn't been wise to try to revitalize Herut before the election, he replied: "We have never changed, because we have never *needed* to change." He seemed to drive home the point, after the convention, by calling for a fresh probe into the Arlosoroff murder.

Still, one Labor official could not resist chortling after the Begin-Weizman bloodbath: "Herut is incapable of setting up a *shadow* cabinet, let alone a real one." A pro-government newspaper added, "If Menachem Begin didn't exist, Labor would have to invent him." Begin, having demonstrated his sensitivity to criticism within the party, now reacted with yet keener resentment to the newspaper's taunt. He barred the offending reporter from future Herut meetings.

Fortunately for Begin, Labor was having problems of its own. With Eshkol gone, Mrs. Meir was under fire from Rafi pretenders to her throne. The country was strained by tensions between rich and poor, the Labor aristocracy and a frustrated middle class. As the 1973 campaign approached, a former Ben Gurion protégé named Yigal Hurwitz drew up a chair one afternoon at Begin's windowside table in the Knesset dining hall. Hurwitz had helped found Rafi, but had broken away, along with its more conservative members, to form a new "Rafi-State" list when the others rejoined Labor in the 1969 election. Now Hurwitz proposed enlarging Begin's Herut-Liberal alliance. "Only *you* can unify all of us," he told him. Begin, recalls an aide who was there, was noncommittal. Yet the idea enticed him; he'd tipped his hand during the *cri de coeur* against Tamir at the 1966 convention. And others soon raised similar ideas—notably another *sabra* war hero with Labor Establishment roots, General Ariel Sharon.

Sharon had even more medals—and scars—than Weizman. In the 1950s he had headed a commando unit that staged reprisal raids against the Arabs. In the 1956 war he led the storming of the Mitla Pass in the Sinai, gateway to the Suez Canal. In 1967 he fought again in the Sinai and after the war, bulldozed "security roads" through the shops, homes, and shanties of Gaza refugee camps in a crackdown on Palestinian unrest. Controversy dogged him: Yes, said critics, he got things done; but wasn't the *cost,* in life and property, combatants and civilians, too high? Begin had sided with Sharon: Arabs respected force, he said, and Sharon embodied it.

Sharon earlier had attempted to enter Begin's Herut-Liberal alliance—through its weaker link, the Liberals. Handling the Liberals much the way he had handled Gaza, he huffed that they were a colorless bunch of shopkeepers who could use a war hero on their slate. They told him they would do fine without him, so he beat a tactical retreat back to the army. Now, however, Sharon struck on several fronts at once: the Liberals, Shmuel Tamir, Weizman, Hurwitz's Rafi-State faction—and Begin's Herut.

"Sharon was not only a catalyst in these negotiations," recalls a Begin aide. "He was a physical force!" He had a separate pitch for each of the parties. He himself would join the Liberals. But for the alliance to gel, he insisted that Weizman and Tamir must come back too. He told them, in effect, that they had been right all along: Herut needed a change of style and image if it were ever to come to power. To the Rafi-State leaders, whom he met in a café near the Tel Aviv seashore, Sharon stressed the need for "a *big* alliance. The key is that I must know that *you* will join it." Sharon said he simply would not feel at ease in an alliance without them: "without people like myself, who began with Labor. . . . These are the people I grew up with."

At first, he trod gingerly with Begin. "I'm afraid of Begin!" he confided to Weizman. But Begin was enticed, and cowed, by Sharon. The war hero's roots ran back to Brisk, where Sharon's grandfather had enlisted Ze'ev Dov Begin to militant Zionism; and Sharon's grandmother had midwifed Menachem Begin's birth. However, Begin seemed to find more curiosity than allure in that connection. What mattered was that Sharon was the prototype of Begin's Fighting Jew, more so than Paglin, Tamir or even Weizman. Sharon seemed to sense this. "His approach to Begin during the talks depended on the day, the goal of the moment," recalls Eliahu Ben Elissar. Sharon moved from charm to bullying, and back again. In one meeting, when Begin objected to one of his suggestions, Sharon exploded: "You people are civilians. You never fought! You never shed blood!" He—then Ezer—stormed out of the room and slammed the door like a rifle shot.

Begin was not eager to bring Weizman and Tamir into a new alliance. When Weizman sulked back into retirement over Begin's attempt to relegate him to a junior place on the evolving candidate slate, Begin called the bluff and left him out. On Sharon's insistence, however, Tamir was allotted a safe spot. So were the Rafi-State leaders—but Begin needed no persuading there. His rivalry with Ben Gurion had long been more Ben Gurion's making than his own. Now more than ever, Begin craved his rival's acceptance, and the Establishment acceptance it implied. Ben Gurion, aging and ailing, finally seemed ready to concede it. During an accidental encounter at the King David Hotel after the 1967 war, the two men had exchanged good-natured banter over who had known what before Paglin blew up the place. Not long afterward, Ben Gurion wrote Begin: "I was very much opposed to some of your policies and actions, both before and after the establishment of the state. Nor do I regret my opposition, for I believe that I was right (anyone can err without realizing it). But on a personal level, I have never held a grudge against you." To Rafi protégés, Ben Gurion added with a chuckle: "Begin did, after all, offer me the prime ministership in 1967. Maybe there's room for a second opinion!" Now, Begin boasted, Sharon's alliance negotiations presented the opportunity to make more than a mere political deal: "We shall wed the followers of Ben Gurion, and the followers of Jabotinsky!"

In mid-September 1973, six weeks before election day, Sharon's shotgun marriage—Herut, the Liberals, plus the Rafi-State party— was announced. All that remained was to find a name for the alliance. Begin proposed *Ha Likud ha Leumi*—"The National Unity Bloc." Rafi members objected, saying this smacked of Begin's desire for an Israel on both banks of the Jordan. Begin conceded. They settled, simply, on *Likud:* "Unity."

Then, barely a week before the election—on Yom Kippur, the holiest day on the Jewish calendar—it all suddenly seemed trivial. Begin was at synagogue in Tel Aviv. His younger daughter, Leah, unable to enter the men's section, passed a note that he was urgently needed. When he came out, she told him to phone Golda's office. He did, and thus became among the first to experience the shock the rest of the nation would feel when the sirens wailed shortly afterward. The Egyptian Army had stormed back across the Suez. In the north the Syrians were advancing on the Golan. Israel, ripped from the complacent afterglow of 1967, was back at war. Reservists, like Sharon, rushed to the front. Begin sped to Golda's office, breaking Yom Kippur's stricture against motor travel, and she filled him in. He assured her of his political support.

It took roughly a week for Israel to halt the Arab attack and start to turn the tide—a week that cost the country more lives than any other in its history. Some in Herut pressed Begin to denounce Golda, and above all Defense Minister Dayan, for failing to prepare the country for war. But when Dayan sent a note asking him to forgo criticism until the fighting was over, Begin agreed, and ordered the party into line. As the war raged on, Moscow resupplied the Arabs. Golda begged arms from a Nixon administration so deep in Watergate that the president would resign less than a year later. Nixon, in a last gasp of international leadership, ordered an airlift. In the Sinai, Sharon waged war against the Egyptians: He took his tank division back across the Suez and surrounded Egypt's Third Army. In the north, taking new casualties with each new advance, Israel reclaimed the Golan, and then some. On October 22—with the Arabs and Soviets eager to halt the fighting—the UN declared a cease-fire. General Sharon ignored it. Yet two days later, after Washington and Moscow had gone on simultaneous nuclear alert for the first time ever, he acquiesced. Israel had won the 1973 war. But the victory had cost it three thousand dead, hundreds more crippled; forced it to turn to American transport planes for survival; and shattered the spirit of 1967 forever.

With the guns silent—and the election rescheduled for December 31—Begin went on the offensive. Staring down at Golda in the Knesset, he charged she had known "well in advance" that the Arabs were girding for war. "Yet you did not even admit this to your own government, and you overruled your own chief of staff when he wanted to stage a preemptive attack! What moral authority do you have after this failure?" He demanded to know why she had not called up reserves, moved reinforcements to the canal. "One may well say: 'Blessed is the nation which has such soldiers to fight for it!' But one cannot say: 'Blessed is the nation which has such a government to lead it!' " Sensing a real chance to unseat Golda, he vowed to recruit "the best brains in Israel" to form a new government. He stressed he was running alongside the "heirs of Ben Gurion," and when Ben Gurion died at age eighty-seven a few weeks before the vote, Begin went to Sde Boker for the funeral of the man he had once called a traitor.

Begin's Likud did well in the election—winning thirty-nine seats, seven more than the previous sum of its parts. Not only did he draw support from the young, the poor, the urban Sephardim, but also from the *moshavim,* semiprivate farm cooperatives long dominated by Labor. Golda dropped five seats; she won fifty-one, however, and assembled a new coalition. Begin summoned his Likud allies and told them not to lose heart. *This* time, he told them, they were on the road to power. "Even if Labor has won *these* elections, after something like the Yom Kippur War happens to a country, and to a government, they *must* lose power. They *will* lose power.

"It is only a matter of time."

Chapter Twenty

The Matter of Time

Nearly everywhere Golda Meir or Moshe Dayan went, in the months after the war, they met the venom of the crowd. Bereaved parents shouted, "Murderer!" Begin, in the Knesset, was barely more charitable. He charged the government was compounding the tragedy of the war, by acquiescing in U.S.-mediated "disengagement" talks with Egypt and Syria. He called it folly for Israel to pull back troops for anything less than formal peace treaties. He reprimanded U.S. Secretary of State Henry Kissinger, warning him from the Knesset: "You are not the first Jew to achieve high office in the country of your residence. Remember the past. There have been such Jews, who out of a complex that they might be accused of acting for the benefit of their people *because* they were Jews, did the contrary." When parliament endorsed the disengagement with Egypt in January 1974, Begin attacked it as a surrender. As an Israel-Syria accord drew near, he cut short a trip to the United States to address protest rallies back home. The campaign had little effect. But when an official inquiry commission questioned the government's handling of the war, Golda and Dayan saw little choice but to share the blame. They resigned.

Begin tried, and failed, to force new elections. Yet he sensed vulnerability in Golda's successor, Yitzhak Rabin. Although a *sabra* war hero like Weizman and Sharon, Rabin lacked their public presence. In interviews he spat out replies like a suspect on a police lineup. In his own party, he faced pressure from a rival, Defense

Minister Shimon Peres. Begin quickly challenged the new prime minister by leading hundreds of demonstrators onto a hill outside the West Bank's largest Arab town, Nablus, in support of Jewish squatters from a new pro-settlement group called *Gush Emunim*— "Bloc of the Faithful." The settlers called the site by its ancient name, Elon Moreh—where, the Bible says, God promised Abraham the promised land. Within days the free-lance settlement had attracted two thousand militants. Yet Rabin ordered them out, and Begin backed down, calling on the newcomers to leave, which they did. He vowed to fight the issue in parliament.

By the end of 1974, Rabin felt secure enough to boast that Likud would never come to power. "Begin," he said, "is an archaeological exhibit!" But the fossil hit back. "Mr. Rabin says I'm an asset to the [Labor party] Alignment," Begin scoffed to a radio interviewer. "It's a pity I can't say the same for him." A few weeks later, in January, he opened his own new alliance's first convention—in the West Bank settlement of Kiryat Arba, outside Hebron. Welcoming delegates to "the city of our Fathers, of Caleb ben Yefuneh," he demanded early elections and unveiled what amounted to a campaign program. He proposed peace with the Arabs—on his terms: "No further disengagements—no further withdrawals, which merely endanger the security of the nation." Instead, he called for a three-year truce on all fronts, with the aim of negotiating full treaties of peace. To the more than one million Palestinians of the West Bank and Gaza, he offered the deal he had tabled for Israel's Arabs in 1948— "autonomy." But he added a concession. The Palestinians would get Israeli citizenship if they wanted it—and the right to vote in Israeli elections.

It was peace through strength. If the Arabs reciprocated, so much the better. Yet he warned them of trouble if they did not. Gesturing toward Sharon and a surprise visitor, Dayan, in the audience, Begin declared: "Beware of the Fighting Jew—he who commands the few against the many." He is, said Begin, "a human being—the son of a Jewish mother, that most marvelous of all God's creatures, with all the softness of her love and the heavy burden of her concern. The Fighting Jew loves all children—Arab children, too. He loves books, loves liberty, and hates war: like Garibaldi. But he is prepared to *fight* for liberty. And," Begin warned, "if you ever raise a hand against this people, know this: The Fighting Jew is fearless, his heart is of steel, his hands are trained for war and his fingers for battle."

Begin would be a Fighting Prime Minister. If the Arabs attacked, he would ensure them "a crushing defeat!" He vowed to meet U.S. pressure with pressure: through pro-Israeli congressmen and American Jews. Where there was poverty, he would give succor: He would undo Labor's cronyism and corruption, restore old verities. "Ever since we joined Ze'ev Jabotinsky's banner," he told the convention, "we have represented the poor in possessions and the rich in faith. We are entitled to say: Let us return to the values of personal and public morality. . . . As leaders, let us give a personal example of modest living, of keeping promises, of sincerity and truthfulness in speech—of credibility in political and economic affairs." For the good of Israel, he said, let us above all oust the Labor coalition. "We are cursed with the weakest government in our history!"

Still, Begin could not force an election without defeating Rabin in the Knesset; and after the convention, Rabin gave him a lesson in the politics of power. He offered General Ariel Sharon a job, as his "security adviser." Sharon, who had now taken to telling anyone who would listen that Begin had to move to the *center* if he wanted to rule Israel, accepted the post.

If Begin was shaken, he did not show it. "I will yet teach Arik a lesson in battlefield tactics." He shrugged to a group of Likud members. Visiting New York shortly afterward, he told Avraham Stavsky's widow, "I think we are really going to succeed this time. You'll see: Abrasha did not die in vain." Back home, he consolidated Likud. At biweekly meetings of its joint executive, he deferred to his partners when he could, often prompting Chaim Landau to break in with a plea for Herut orthodoxy. Begin would respond with a soothing assurance, referring to Landau by his IZL code name— "Okay, Avraham, that's fine"—but ignore the substance of his protest. Yet, on issues that mattered to Begin, his word was still law. A Liberal aide recalls one meeting when Likud was deciding whether to propose holding municipal elections on the same day as national balloting. Begin invited discussion. One by one, the others backed holding simultaneous elections. But when a junior member suggested the opposite, Begin quickly "summarized" by agreeing with him. The rest dutifully switched sides, and Begin declared the point agreed on. Suddenly, a cry of protest came from another Likud newcomer: "What do you mean: 'agreed,' Mr. Begin? You've just heard everyone at the table say the elections should be held together, and now you simply decide the opposite! On what basis?"

Begin smiled. He told the youngster that since this was a democracy, there would be a vote. When hands went up—some with alacrity and some with caution, but all for Begin—the dissenter turned on the others. "What are you afraid of?" he shouted. "You've just voted against yourselves . . . against your own positions!" There was silence. He glared at Begin and asked: "How do you do it?" Begin answered softly, "Well, my friend, we seem to be in general agreement here. Your view is a minority opinion. But we are a democratic group, and we value the rights and dignity of the minority as we do those of the majority." He added, however, that he preferred unanimity. "Let me ask you, on behalf of our colleagues here, to reconsider your vote." The dissenter raised a finger in assent, to shouts of approval from the rest.

In Herut Begin prepared the old guard for pasture. Landau, Meridor, and Bader remained, but he relied on them little. He passed over both Landau and Eitan Livni to place Yitzhak Shamir as chairman of the party executive—and relied on him even less. He formed a new inner circle, with just two members. They were Eliahu Ben Elissar and Yehiel Kadishai. Both were bright, tireless—and consumed with dedication to Menachem Begin.

Kadishai was in his fifties. Begin had hired him a decade earlier, on the recommendation of his IZL driver, Yoske Giladi, to take dictation. (No one in the office could decipher Begin's writing.) He used Kadishai to answer the roughly fifty letters he received each week, and to record twice-a-month political commentaries that appeared, like speeches on paper, in the Tel Aviv daily, *Ma'ariv*. It took issues of enormous starkness—like the choice in 1967 of whether Herut should finally join an Israeli government—for Kadishai to deliver a political opinion of his own. "I am not," he notes, "the kind of person who *evaluates*." A Betar member as a boy, Kadishai had served in the British Army during the war, returned to Palestine on the *Altalena*, helped arrange pensions for IZL widows after 1948. Soon after, he left to manage a movie theater. Now Begin found solace in him. With the others, every word he uttered was a political statement. With Kadishai, he could say what he wanted: It would not be challenged, repeated, perhaps not even understood. Kadishai had the quality of an ideal butler: He sensed, anticipated Begin's moods. He laughed at Begin's occasional Yiddish jokes, applauded his repetitive anecdotes and parables from the underground days or earlier. He even collected *shtetl* humor of his own, for use when Begin seemed down. "Begin," recalls Kadishai, "almost always knew the punchlines before I got there!"

Begin soon shifted the dictation sessions to Rosenbaum Street. On Saturdays he and Aliza would ask the Kadishais along to the movies. He elevated Kadishai—whom he, and everyone else, called Yehiel—to the role of the compleat aide. "Yehiel was the one person with whom Begin had a completely relaxed relationship," says a Likud official who worked with them both. "He was the only one who could visit when Begin was in his pajamas." Almost constantly at his boss's side, Kadishai arranged his schedule, hired or promoted secretaries, intercepted and deflected visitors. "Most of the time Mr. Begin and I understood each other without speaking," he says. On political issues there was no need to speak. "He made his own decisions. He did not consult—with me, or with anyone. Others consulted *him*." Sometimes, when he sensed opposition, Begin would ask for advice. "But this," says Kadishai, "was a formality—it was a process of his sharing *his* views with the others, convincing people of the correctness of his opinion."

Begin found in Eliahu Ben Elissar, whom he made his press secretary, the intellect of a Ph.D. grad, the fighting Judaism of a Mossad veteran—and a devotion nearly as total as Kadishai's. This last quality, always important, became doubly so in the wake of Tamir's "betrayal," Weizman's, and now Sharon's. Even Begin's office secretary, who came from a Labor family, recalls, "He would remark when others were in the room, 'Yona is not one of us. But she is *loyal!*'" Ben Elissar was more than loyal. "He was like a kid around Begin!" says a friend. Ben Elissar explains: "Begin was a man who played a very great part in my formation—a heroic figure—and only afterward the man whom I worked for in Herut." As a Holocaust orphan pasting up IZL posters, he had looked on Begin "as an *otherworldly* figure—the Commander of the Irgun underground, a man whose name we never mentioned out loud, until the British left the country! I guess I did have a sort of son-father complex toward him." Begin responded as a kind, if distant, patriarch. Once, when Begin took the press aide on a working visit to New York, the two men were dining at the Waldorf. "I'm going to have the omelet," Begin said. "But you'll probably have the shrimp. I know you're fond of shrimp." Though shrimp aren't kosher, even some observant Israelis are more lax on such matters when traveling overseas. Yet Ben Elissar could not bring himself to commit such a lapse in front of Begin. "No," the aide said, "I'd prefer the omelet too."

Still, in one sense Ben Elissar could not rival Kadishai. "I had *ambitions* within the party," Ben Elissar explains. "Begin of course knew this. He knew Yehiel did not. Yehiel's lack of ambition was not only something verbal. It was authentic, absolutely beyond doubt! It was only in Kadishai that Begin had full trust. He once told me precisely how he felt about Yehiel. He said Yehiel was his alter ego."

By 1976, Begin had grown confident he could bring Likud to power. He no longer pressed for an early election—the next was due in late 1977. He contented himself with watching Rabin and Peres battle each other. He pointedly asked a reporter from a pro-Labor newspaper whether he had seen the latest Israeli opinion poll. Commissioned by Labor, it had found that 26 percent of Israel wanted Menachem Begin as prime minister, topping both of the bickering Labor frontrunners. When the government was suddenly confronted with the Entebbe hijack in July, Begin took the high road. He assured Rabin of support, even when the prime minister told him it seemed Israel might have to consider meeting the Arab terrorists' demands in order to save lives. "I understand the problem," Begin told him. "Whatever you do, you shall have our backing." Partly, Begin was responding to Rabin's goodwill. The prime minister, like Ben Gurion in 1956, was taking Begin into his confidence. In a similar crisis the year before, he had not done so—and Begin lashed out at him for being weak on terror. A few days after the hijack, Rabin summoned Begin again and told him he had decided on a rescue mission. Begin gave more than approval: He offered admiration and, as he turned to leave, Likud's prayers for his success. When success came, it was with the bittersweet news that among the casualties was an IZL veteran who had led one of the attack units. Begin met the returning hostages at the airport, where they hoisted him to their shoulders. But when the Knesset met, he heaped praise on Rabin. Recalls one Rabin aide: "Begin noted that had the raid failed, none of the others now scrambling for credit would have accepted responsibility!"

After Entebbe, Rabin's government sank back into crisis. Begin could not have scripted things better. With Peres poised to make his own bid for the premiership, Rabin reeled under a series of scandals. The manager of the state-controlled Israel Corporation was jailed for bribe taking and embezzlement. Next behind bars, on similar charges, was a Rabin protégé in the Histadrut. Then the minister of housing, accused of corruption, committed suicide. Finally came allegations that Abba Eban was secreting funds in a foreign bank account. After a post-Entebbe surge in the polls, Rabin's rating sagged back to 35 percent. (Peres, however, scored 50 percent.) In mid-December Labor's longtime Orthodox partners threatened to bolt the coalition—when Rabin violated the Sabbath by accepting delivery of a batch of U.S. fighter planes too close to sundown on Friday. Exhausted, Rabin announced he was resigning, in order to seek a fresh mandate to govern. Elections were brought forward to May 1977.

Begin put out feelers to Peres, suggesting they unite in a caretaker government. But Peres said no. And Begin—it soon became inescapably clear—faced a party-image crisis of his own. It had first broken the surface in the spring, and, especially after Rabin's shock announcement, the Israeli media began probing its roots. The issue was not so much corruption as mismanagement—of Herut's coffers. The party was neck-deep in debt. How, asked relieved Labor supporters, could Begin run a government if he couldn't even balance the party's checkbook? Begin hit the road in panic, making fundraising trips to France, Canada, the United States, Belgium, Latin America, Switzerland, then back to New York. He resisted the temptation to shift the blame, though he had never so much as glanced at the party accounts, and direct responsibility for financial matters now rested with Weizman's onetime ally, Yosef Kramerman. "I take and took responsibility for everything that is done in the Herut movement," Begin declared.

On the road, he was despondent. "He felt that finally Israelis were coming to the point where they would award a majority to the Likud, but that now there was this crisis," says Ben Elissar, who joined him on part of the trek. The aide tried to offer reassurance: "You are going to be Israel's next prime minister!" But Begin replied: "Eli, were it not for this financial crisis, you might have been right." One index of his alarm was a decision to invite Ezer Weizman back. Begin had extended a measure of forgiveness a few years earlier, by hosting a reception to mark publication of Weizman's autobiography. But he had rebuffed moves since then by Weizman—and Meridor—to rehabilitate him in Herut. Now he relented, and offered Weizman the post of campaign manager. When Weizman demanded absolute control of the campaign in the bargain, Begin agreed to that, too.

He returned to Israel in January to keynote Likud's campaign convention—inserting in the election platform a softened position on land for peace with Egypt that annoyed Chaim Landau—but then left to raise more money. With the government in disarray, a pro-Labor newspaper wondered whether Begin's absences might yet save it. Reporting on a Knesset debate, the paper delighted in Landau's "sonorous nasal tones," adding that "Begin would have had Rabin squirming in his seat." Still, little by little, Begin's road appearances enlisted help from old-time Revisionist, IZL, and Herut sympathizers, and rescued the party's finances.

At home, however, Weizman ran the show. "The trouble with most generals," he crowed, "is that they tend to prepare for the next war in terms of the last one. I'm preparing to wage the Likud's present electoral campaign on the basis of an analysis of the current situation." He said he would use Menachem Begin as his "greatest asset," but then set about rebuilding him to campaign specifications. Weizman drafted a full-page campaign manifesto that ran, over his own signature, in Israeli papers. There was no mention of a greater Israel, of the need to hold on to land won in 1967, or of the need to be tough with the Arabs. Lest the omissions be missed, Weizman told reporters: "Look for what *isn't* there." When Shamir phoned to ask how Herut could afford to splash full-page ads with Begin straining to ward off party bankruptcy, Weizman shot back that once he got Begin *elected*, the issue would be academic. He hired a friend, who ran Israel's top advertising firm, to help market the new Begin: FAMILY MAN AND DEMOCRAT. Posters went up with the soft-lit photograph of a balding and bespectacled gentleman who couldn't possibly have blown up the King David. Weizman organized a newspaper supplement profiling Begin as homebody, with Aliza as Everyman's wife.

Begin found it obscene—all the more so when Weizman excluded him from the daily strategy sessions which Begin, in previous campaigns, had run. But he needed Weizman too much to object. "This was the first time he had been *exhibited* in this manner," recalls Kadishai. "It was the first time any Israeli candidate had actually been pictured on campaign posters." But when Ben Elissar tried to get Begin to rein Weizman in, Begin replied, "What do you want me to do? *You* know what little I can do!" Says the aide, "He felt weakened by the financial mess." He busied himself with fund raising, cheering a Labor campaign that seemed to be run by lemmings, and planning what he would do as prime minister—despite the fact

Labor still led in the polls. When Rabin barely survived a leadership challenge from Peres, Begin told reporters: "We're relying on him to fire a couple of shots from the hip, with the sort of aim that will help the Likud. We wish him success in this endeavor."

He returned to the United States and Canada early in the spring. A Canadian-Jewish supporter, Leo Marcus, recalls dining with him at a Montreal hotel, when Begin suddenly declared: "I will soon become the first Israeli leader to sign a peace treaty with an Arab state!" He proceeded to outline his domestic policy: to upgrade housing, education, and recreational facilities in Israel's poorer, Sephardic neighborhoods.

Then, only days after returning to Israel in March, Begin was rushed to the hospital.

The diagnosis was exhaustion. While in the hospital, however, he suffered a heart attack. He was bedridden until the campaign homestretch in mid-May. When Herut chose its election slate—Begin at the top, Weizman in second spot—he was helpless to deliver on his earlier assurances to youngsters like Ben Elissar and Arye Naor, the son of Esther Raziel-Naor, that they would be on it. When Sharon tried to return to the Likud in April—only to be spurned by the Liberals—Begin received his prodigal general, and approved his return. But he could not get the Liberals to relent. "He was," recalls Ben Elissar, "physically too weak."

Labor, as Begin had hoped, continued to self-destruct. A newspaper report that Rabin's wife had an illegal U.S. bank account forced him to step down as a candidate for reelection, whereupon Labor chose Peres as its standard-bearer. But as the election drew near, Begin watched Herut's campaign on TV and wondered whether he would live long enough to become prime minister. Weizman refused to let Yitzhak Shamir, or Liberal leader Simcha Ehrlich, have even a moment of Likud's television time. ("I will not put someone on TV who has more hair between his eyebrows than I have on my balls!" he joked to aides after rebuffing Shamir.) The media campaign, recalls a Liberal party official, was "full of meaningless slogans and happy jingles; Begin hated it, but he was stuck in bed." Summoning Kadishai, he handed him a will. It asked that he—and Aliza when she died—be buried on the Mount of Olives, next to the two teenagers who had blown themselves up with a grenade rather than be executed by the British.

Yet by May, Begin was on the rebound. He managed the strength to scold Weizman for airing a series of anti-Labor ads that offended his sense of fair play. He began giving interviews. And several days before the election, he joined Peres in a television debate. He looked frail, but his mind wasn't. In repartee he was the Begin of old, quoting Peres's past statements back at him verbatim. It was, the papers said, a draw. In the circumstances, the draw was a victory for Begin.

He and the rest of Israel voted in the country's ninth national election on May 17. That evening he awaited the results in the yellow armchair on Rosenbaum Street. A few hours after sundown, Weizman's advertising friend phoned to tell Begin he could prepare an acceptance speech. Begin dismissed the suggestion as absurd. At eleven, a startled-looking television newscaster announced: "Based on the television's sampling, there is an indication of a decisive victory for the Likud. . . . According to this sample, Menachem Begin will head the next government." Now Kadishai phoned. He told Begin a mob awaited him at party headquarters a few blocks away. "It's too early, Yehiel," Begin replied. "This is just a guess by the boys at television." Yet Israeli security police, taking the guess seriously, showed up to offer protection. Congratulatory phone calls poured in, and IZL veteran Moshe Stein arrived to pronounce a biblical blessing. After midnight, Begin left for headquarters.

Weizman, who was in charge, had resisted the temptation to pop champagne corks. "We must wait for Begin," he said. When he arrived, hundreds of Irgun and Herut veterans, with tears streaming down their faces, reached out to touch him. Cornered by a reporter, the prime minister-elect refused comment. "I will not say a single word until I have spoken to my colleagues." But when the reporter persisted, asking Begin whether this was the biggest moment in his life, he shot back: "Oh, no! There were bigger ones—in the underground." He made his way to the podium, donned a skullcap, and intoned a blessing. He said he wanted to thank Aliza most of all, and his comrades from the underground. "We have come a long way together, and we have never ceased to believe that a day like this would come." He quoted Abraham Lincoln: This was not a time to settle scores. It was a time to bind up wounds—not a time for malice, but for charity.

Then, Menachem Begin set out to demonstrate that charity need not preclude muscle.

Chapter Twenty-one

The 180 Days

One of Begin's first decisions as prime minister-elect was to return to the Jewish squatter site of Elon Moreh—defying both U.S. alarm and the haziness of his mandate. The returns showed that Labor had lost the election more than Begin had won it. The Likud gained four seats, ending up with forty-three; Labor dropped twenty-two. Most of the swing—fifteen seats—went to a new, good-government party called the Democratic Movement for Change, known in Hebrew by its acronym, DASH. Dovish on Arab-Israeli issues, it was run by Haganah veteran Yigael Yadin, and included Shmuel Tamir.

Weizman advised Begin against the West Bank visit, but Begin ignored him. Trailing a gaggle of reporters, he climbed the Nablus hillside and declared: "In a few weeks or months, there will be many Elon Morehs!" Asked whether this meant Begin would "annex" the West Bank, Begin replied: "We don't use the word 'annexation.' You annex *foreign* land, not your own country." Besides, what was this term "West Bank"? From now on, the world must get used to the area's real—biblical—name, "Judaea and Samaria." Why, Begin asked, interviewing his interviewer, "is it so difficult for you to use these words?"

Begin was rushed back to the hospital several days later with "post-cardiacal complications," but the setback served only to reinforce his defiance. While Weizman and other Likud leaders began coalition talks—the Liberals' Simcha Ehrlich told reporters that Begin "can be prime minister if he doesn't drive himself too hard"—Begin drew up his own cabinet from bed. As the others concentrated on wooing DASH leader Yadin, Begin set out to assemble a leaner coalition without him—with the support of an Orthodox bloc delighted to be rid of its strange Labor bedfellows. He held four posts open for DASH as enticements to join the government later, on Begin's terms. While the others figured who in the Herut old guard would get the plum posts, Begin plotted a cabinet and staff of Herut novices, Labor holdovers—and outsiders. He set the tone in his choice for foreign minister: There were two eager contenders, the Liberals' Arye Dulzin, and Chaim Landau.

Begin wanted neither, but did not tip his hand. When the U.S. ambassador asked whom Washington should contact on foreign-policy matters, Begin suggested Dulzin. He told only three people— Aliza, Kadishai, and Ben Elissar—whom he really had in mind. All three said he was making a mistake. Still, he phoned Moshe Dayan, the tarnished *sabra* war hero, and offered him the job. Dayan had always given the Irgun credit for the revolt. He was hawkish, by Labor standards, on the future of the West Bank. He was also so blemished by the 1973 war that Begin's offer would amount to a rescue mission, ensuring loyalty. But most of all, Dayan was a celebrity. "Yes," Begin told Kadishai, "Dayan has lost standing as a leader here in Israel, since the Yom Kippur War. But in the world—both to our friends and our enemies—he remains a symbol. He is the man with the eyepatch! He stands for staunch Zionism. He stands for strength—he is the military man, commander, for years chief of staff, minister of defense." Dayan was "a man whom no foreign dignitary would dare meet without checking to make sure his pants are pressed!" When Dayan accepted, Begin rejoiced. "Who was Dulzin? Who was Landau?" recalls Ben Elissar. "Dayan, to the outside world, was like a De Gaulle!"

Begin reveled in proving he was in charge, that he was not about to rule like the gentle grandfather Weizman had marketed. Weizman, boasting to friends that he had "elected Begin," got no word of gratitude from the prime minister-elect. Begin did make him defense minister, but kept him squirming a few days before doing so. After offering Weizman the job, Begin chuckled to an aide: "Ezer wasn't *absolutely* sure I would offer it to him. He was so happy when I told him!" Though Begin gave Liberal leader Simcha Ehrlich the Finance Ministry, he passed over Herut's old guard. At least three were lobbying hard: Landau, Livni, Bader. Instead, he promoted a street-smart Moroccan, David Levy, as minister of immigration and absorption. He gave the party's most coveted Knesset post—chairman of the foreign affairs and defense committee—to Moshe Arens, a Betar veteran who had spent much of his life in America. (Telling almost no one, Begin had decided to give Arens the Foreign Ministry if Dayan said no.) He made up for his lapsed promises to put Ben Elissar and Arye Naor in the Knesset, by naming Ben Elissar director of the prime minister's office and Naor the cabinet secretary. But the quintessential new-breeder was a Michigan-born Jew named Ze'ev Chafets, twenty-nine years old, who had stumbled into a job as a Liberal party press aide a few years earlier. On election night, Chafets recalls embracing a grizzled Irgun veteran and exclaiming, "We won!" The old-timer retorted: "What do you mean 'we,' you little shit? You've been here for three months. I've been waiting all my life for this!" Begin made Chafets director of Israel's Government Press Office.

But he wanted one more *sabra* general aboard—the one he admired, and seemed sometimes to fear, most of all. Spurned by the Liberals, Ariel Sharon had rustled together a party of his own, and won two Knesset seats. Begin wanted Sharon so badly that at first he was ready to jettison a cardinal principle—opposition to unchecked police power in a free society. Sharon had suggested a new ministry to coordinate all aspects of law and order, and Begin decided to create one, under Sharon. But so strident was the outcry from Kadishai and Ben Elissar—and Dayan, too—that Begin relented. Sheepishly, Begin summoned Sharon and offered him the Ministry of Agriculture, stressing that the job would include control of West Bank settlement. When Sharon said yes, Begin confided to Kadishai with relief: "Can you believe it? I didn't think Arik would settle for the Agriculture Ministry . . ."

Recovered from his heart scare, Begin took office in late June with a three-seat Knesset majority. His first words to the cabinet set the tone: "There will be no smoking." The meetings were brief, discipline tight, and leaks—in contrast to Rabin days—nonexistent. "Begin ran the cabinet like a teacher in a kindergarten," recalls one of several Labor men he kept on as aides. He told reporters he would stay in office for at most six years: He would retire, at seventy, to write. But he had a crystal-clear vision of what he would accomplish before then. Item one was Middle East peace. He told the U.S. ambassador, Samuel Lewis, to pass the message to Washington. When the envoy handed him a summit invitation from President Carter—a newcomer himself who had wasted no time in charting the most pro-Arab course in White House history—Begin instantly accepted. He arranged to visit Romania, the only East Bloc state with an embassy in Israel, after the U.S. trip.

He spent every waking hour preparing his pitch for Carter. He pored through transcripts of the Rabin-Carter summit that had been held before the election. Anticipating pressure, he drafted a preemptive strategy—designed to surprise the Americans with concessions but stand tough on the issues that mattered most to him. Israel would give Carter a Geneva peace conference; consider handing back a large chunk of the Sinai as hinted in the Herut election platform—even, perhaps, part of the Golan. But the Palestinians would get only Begin's long-standing offer of "autonomy"—not the "homeland" Carter advocated. And Judaea and Samaria would be Israeli, forever. Begin, breaking with Labor tradition, would present the plan on a take-it-or-leave-it basis. To invite suggestions, he told aides, invited U.S. pressure.

He arrived in Washington July 19, and was welcomed by Carter on the White House lawn. Dressed in a gray suit, purchased days earlier when aides realized he owned only several threadbare outfits, Begin declared: "Mr. President, I have come from the Land of Zion and Jerusalem as the spokesman for an ancient people and a young nation. God's blessing on America, the hope of the human race. Peace to your great nation." He was nervous. "You had to know him well to see it," recalls Ben Elissar. "But it was there." Before the White House welcome, Connecticut Senator Abraham Ribicoff had called on Begin to chat, suggesting areas where Israel and the Arabs might compromise for peace. Begin was convinced Carter had sent the senator, a Jew, and that it was just the start of the pressure Washington would bring to bear.

The White House talks ran two days, and both Carter and Begin had prepared themselves for the worst. Carter, who says he had found Begin's postelection statements "frightening," recalls the talks as a "pleasant surprise. . . . He was much more moderate in words, and much more moderate in concept"—also, "a strong leader, quite different from Rabin." The new Israeli leader stressed his concessions: Geneva, Sinai, the Golan. When the president pressed for an end to West Bank settlement, Begin avoided an explicit rebuff. But he did not sign on. He responded with a paean to the biblical history of Palestine, and got Carter to endorse a final communiqué agreeing to disagree: "The president assured the prime minister that any differences that may occur from time to time should not be allowed to obscure America's, and his personal, dedication to this historic American commitment . . . to the security and well-being of Israel." Emerging from the talks, Begin told aides: *"Ein imut,"* "There was no confrontation."

He was in high spirits, and top form, at a news conference before heading home. Asked whether he would accept Palestine Liberation Organization participation at a Geneva conference, he drew good-natured laughter by saying that "a Jew usually answers a question by asking another question." Then he answered, as delicately as he had Carter's pressure for a settlement halt. He said the PLO could not participate, but that Israel wouldn't check credentials at the door. When another reporter asked if Carter had pressured Begin, he replied in a Yiddish-accented singsong: "We had a discussion. There were questions. There were answers. Sometimes the President asked a question. Sometimes I asked a question. The questions were good, and the replies were even better!" He delighted in transmitting a routine message of thanks to Carter from the plane home, and boasted to a crowd of Israeli reporters on arrival, "I was informed by the captain that it was transmitted direct to the White House!" Pronouncing the summit a success, he said Labor governments had created a "grave error" by attaching importance to securing full U.S. agreement on Israeli negotiating strategy. That ensured pressure—and friction. "I have read the contents of the conversation between the president and the former prime minister, Mr. Yitzhak Rabin. The talks he had with the President were extremely acerbic." Begin, by contrast, claimed "a very important promise on the part of the U.S. president—namely that we have differences of opinion . . . but the differences that exist, and which also may arise in the future, will never result in a breach between the United States and Israel."

Yet he took that assurance more literally than Carter. The next day Begin legalized Elon Moreh and two other free-lance settlements on the West Bank. Carter was upset—but fearful of condemning a Geneva conference to stillbirth. He said only that the move "obviously increases the difficulty in ultimate peace." Begin, for his part, declared: "As free men, as friends and, in my conviction, as allies, we shall discuss every question within the bounds of differences of opinion. We shall make every effort to reach agreement, or, if need be, to agree that we have not agreed—but the friendship will be preserved and intensified." He had gambled, and won. "He made the settlement move in full knowledge it would anger the Americans," says Ben Elissar. "But he took the step as a demonstration to the world of what and who he was; he wanted to serve notice that Prime Minister Menachem Begin remained true to the old Menachem Begin."

Yet he preferred being *Prime Minister* Begin, and no longer bothered with the disclaimer that nothing could compare with his years underground. He enjoyed remarking what a *surprise* he had sprung by getting elected. "He repeated the comment so many times it got embarrassing," says an aide. Adds Ben Elissar: "You could see how he loved the job! It was the fulfillment of all his dreams." With Labor in tatters, even the Establishment press gave him credit for restoring leadership to the country. Begin, who read every word, drew energy from the acclaim. He would rise at dawn, tune in to the BBC and Israel Radio news, read the morning newspapers, and head to the office by 8:00. Ben Elissar gave him a press briefing. But the exercise was academic: "He had already read every newspaper." The rest of the morning, Begin would receive visitors, sign letters, read policy reports or diplomatic-cable traffic. At 1:00, he would go home for lunch with Aliza, take an afternoon nap, and return around 3:30 for another three to four hours' work. Before leaving at night, he summoned Kadishai and General Ephraim Poran, the military aide he had inherited from Rabin. They would hand him two files: one on domestic issues and the second on foreign affairs and defense. Begin would spend the evening reading them, retire before midnight, to resume the routine at dawn.

At the office, even among those who owed him no Herut or Irgun obeisance, Begin inspired loyalty. Ilana Beaninstock, a Yemenite girl in her twenties who had been hired as a typist, recalls that at first she didn't like Begin. "I didn't like the people *around* him. Every time I would say, 'Let's do this or that,' they would say in hushed voices, 'No. Begin won't agree.' They held him in such respect!" Gradually, he converted her. "When I'd see him in the hallway, he would say, 'Good morning, Ilana.' I couldn't just say: 'Hi!' That's not the way to greet a prime minister. He gave you so much respect—gave *everybody* respect there—that you had to answer him in kind, with respect. I noticed that when I was in his presence I never felt that *he* was more important than I was. Even if there were important aides around—if I was there, he gave me a personal greeting. He'd say it to me especially, as if I were someone important. I began to love him. The human feeling for people, it sticks to you. You see that the prime minister cares—and what is this small woman? I felt, in my position, that I had to do a thousand times more than he did."

Aliza Begin, though she hid it from her husband, enjoyed the new life less than he. She missed the old days, before the Likud, when Begin and she and the Fighting Family had been alone against the world. The change had come slowly. By the mid–1970s, the Saturday night movie outings had become rare. Now they disappeared altogether. "What is this?" she remarked half-jokingly to Ben Elissar. "My husband is prime minister, but he still has to go to work at eight like a civil servant!" For a few weeks she did savor being Madam Prime Minister, enjoy a brief share of the limelight. Right after the election, with Begin hospitalized, she was interviewed on Israel Television. Fielding questions about her husband, she suddenly exclaimed, "Look, if you want to know about Begin go ask *him.*" On the way to visit Begin the next day, she turned to Ze'ev Chafets and remarked with a grin, "I really let that interviewer have it, eh?"

But she was an ill woman. Her childhood respiratory problems, stoked since by thousands of cigarettes, worsened. She had emphysema—though family and friends gingerly called it asthma in her presence. She felt that the shift from Tel Aviv to the hilltop air of Jerusalem had aggravated her condition, confiding to a friend that it had been a "mistake" to move. "She said the city was very difficult for her physically. But she accepted it; she knew one coudn't be prime minister and not live in Jerusalem." She disliked the constant presence of security guards. (Begin, who shared the dislike, eventually barred them from certain areas of the residence.) She was also uneasy with the sudden invasion of well-wishers, telling one old friend, "Now that Menachem is prime minister, *lots* of people want to be our friends. But we shall value above all those who wanted to be our friends *before.*"

She made another sacrifice as well. Much as she warmed to the glare of the television lights, she avoided them once her husband was up and around. "I have an aptitude for putting my foot in my mouth," she told a friend. "I'm afraid if I speak up I might just as easily hurt Menachem's cause as help it. . . . I've learned over the years to stay in the background." She found another role instead, throwing herself into an array of volunteer projects as her husband ruled.

Begin relied on Aliza as he did on no one else. Over lunch and dinner, he would share the events of the day with her. After a major speech in the Knesset or elsewhere, when Aliza could not be present, Begin would phone her to report. "That was Mr. Begin," she remarked to one visitor after such a call. "He was telling me how his speech went. It's been like that for forty years!" Rarely would Aliza deliver an opinion on a particular issue; almost never would she disagree. This, Begin neither sought nor needed from anyone. Her role was to listen, support. In times of crisis she gave Begin a haven for recovery, encouragement to carry on. "She was his *foundation,*" recalls a close friend. "She provided Begin someone unique: For him to talk with her was not like talking to a politician, or with anyone else. He was not a man who trusted other people. There was only Aliza."

He took *strength* from Aliza. "She was like a close aunt to him sometimes ... only tougher," recalls Ilana Beaninstock, who became Aliza's personal aide not long after the election. "She had this no-nonsense ability to see through people around her husband, judge whether they would do him good or harm, and she could say, 'Steer clear of this person.' " Her voice suited the role—so deep that more than one caller mistook it for that of the prime minister. Targets of her wrath—Tamir, Ezer, David Yutan, or Yisrael Scheib—remember it well. Scheib says he sensed from the day the Soviet police had come to get Begin in Vilna—with Aliza dry-eyed, defiant—that she was "the stronger of the two Begins." He and Menachem had drifted apart over the years, with Scheib sometimes writing sharply critical assessments of the Herut leader in the Israeli press. But when Begin fell ill, his old Betar colleague asked to visit. "Aliza," he recalls, "forbade it." Yutan, excluded from the Begins' home after siding with Shmuel Tamir in 1966, says, "He—Begin—cannot understand the idea of remaining friends while disagreeing, taking a different political approach. But I think this is true of Aliza even more than of him. She is a very tough woman."

Begin, says one of his staff, came before everything for Aliza—even before the children. They were grown now, and each seemed to show signs of the strain Aliza felt. Benny, after a brief attempt at politics in the early 1970s, was studying geology in far-off Colorado. The elder daughter, Chassia, had married—though she alarmed friends with a brief, sudden, steep loss of weight shortly afterward. The younger daughter, Leah, an El Al ground stewardess and unmarried into her thirties, still lived with her parents. (At Rosenbaum Street she had occupied the bedroom; Menachem and Aliza slept on a living-room couch.) But Begin himself could not have lived without Aliza. "At some time, a man like Menachem Begin needs one thing above all—peace, love," remarks Yisrael Scheib. "She gave him this."

. . .

Back from Washington, Israel's new prime minister assaulted the challenge of peace-through-strength with an obsession last shown—as opposition leader in 1955—when he sought to take the country to war. He ignored domestic issues, except for his campaign to upgrade Sephardic slums. He turned the economy over to Simcha Ehrlich. Having chosen Moshe Dayan for international celebrity, Begin now made use of his entree. The foreign minister held secret talks with the leaders of India and Iran—then, in London, with King Hussein. Begin even let Dayan offer the king a Labor-vintage proposal for territorial compromise on the West Bank, although he "gloated," recalls an aide, when the Jordanian monarch rejected it out of hand. Then, aching for a personal role, Begin made a secret visit of his own to Tehran. But he returned convinced the shah was in no shape to mediate. Seeking above all a conduit to the Egyptians, he felt only the Americans were likely to provide one.

Begin either did not, or would not, see the signs of pique in the Carter administration. He shrugged off U.S. criticism of his West Bank policy by reciting Carter's summit acceptance that friends could agree to disagree. He embarked on another round of preemptive diplomacy, sending a draft peace treaty to Washington for relay to the Arabs. Worded like a pact between Andorra and Liechtenstein, the document drove home Begin's insistence that any Mideast peace must ensure fully normal relations, not just the kind of peaceful belligerence Kissinger had mediated. Begin added a note for U.S. eyes only—detailing the parts of the Sinai and the Golan he would consider giving back. On the West Bank, however, he pressed to consolidate Israeli control. He ordered "equalization of services" there, hoping to hook West Bankers, Arab and Jew, to Israeli water and electricity as a first step toward hooking them to Israeli government. Typical of Begin's style of rule, the move had more symbolic than practical effect. An aide recalls approaching Begin a few months later with a complaint from Arab policemen, who were striking for more pay. "I told him that they really were underpaid, and that he had, after all, promised 'equalization' for the West Bank." Begin replied, "But you *know* we don't have the money for equalization!"

Symbolic, too, was Prime Minister Begin's second trip abroad—in early August. The visit was far shorter, in time and distance, than his first. Yet it generated practical effects that would come back to haunt Begin, Israel, and the world. He visited Marjayoun, the Christian militia's hilltop stronghold in south Lebanon. Begin arrived there with sympathy for the militiamen—under Rabin, Israel had secretly armed and trained them as a counterweight to Syrian and PLO influence. But he returned home feeling something more like a familial bond, and he soon converted Rabin's commitment to a crusade. The Christians, Begin said, were like the Jews of Nazi Europe: an island in a hostile "sea" of Syrian, Palestinian, and Lebanese Muslims. "They suffered ten massacres in one hundred years!" This was history according to Begin: a reinterpretation of a Lebanese conflict in which Muslims *and* Christians had maltreated and massacred each other with equal vigor. But, says an official who knew Begin well, "He *took aboard* this idea. Once he did so, he became incapable of seeing anything that didn't agree with it." Addressing an Israel Bonds delegation the day after his return, Begin did allow that the Nazi Holocaust may have been worse than the Lebanese Christians' predicament. "We, the Jewish people," he said, "suffered more." But in Lebanon, too, "an attempt is being made at genocide—to kill off a religious minority." The minority *would* win: Begin had met a "beautiful" Christian girl who "even spoke to me [in] Hebrew!" But the minority needed help. Shocking the Lebanese government, the Americans and his own aides, Prime Minister Begin proceeded to go public with Israel's involvement. "We help them militarily," he said. "It shouldn't be a secret. . . . Without our military help, the Christian minority would long ago have been wiped out. We cannot acquiesce in the attempts to destroy them."

The trip to Romania, which came in late August, ended up less as a peace mission than a window on the complex moods of Prime Minister Begin. Damp-eyed, he prayed with remains of Bucharest's Jewish community. Addressing them in Yiddish—"the language your mothers used to speak to you"—he lamented his failed attempt, in 1939, to get a final group of Betar refugees across the Romanian frontier. Many, no doubt, had perished at Hitler's hand. After his talks with Ceaucescu, Begin made a tour of the surrounding countryside. A carload of Israeli reporters pulled ahead at one point, stopped on the otherwise deserted roadway, and waved as he drove by. Back in Bucharest, Begin gushed absentmindedly: "What a reception! A group of Romanians even waved to me as I rode past!" On the plane home, Begin seemed pensive, a bit sad, until he suddenly turned on Jacob Ahimeir, the son of the militant Zionist who had been charged alongside Stavsky with the Arlosoroff murder. The son was a respected newsman at Israel Television, but had apparently angered Begin by proving anything but the dutiful Revisionist in that capacity. When some of his fellow newsmen now good-naturedly asked Begin whether he had ever bounced the infant Ahimeir on his knee, the prime minister replied: "No. And you know why? Because he was a big, fat baby. As a matter of fact," he added, to embarrassed silence among Ahimeir's colleagues, "he is *still* a big, fat baby!"

Politically, Begin felt the Romanian visit had been disappointing. The road to a Mideast peace treaty, he concluded, did not lead through Bucharest, as it had not led through the shah's Iran. Only when he sent Dayan on the road again—to Morocco—did Begin sense the first faint hope of progress. Morocco's King Hassan revealed that the Egyptians were willing to talk. Hassan suggested two options: Dayan could meet an Egyptian envoy, or Begin could meet Sadat. Begin leaped at the idea of a summit. But Sadat backed off, and sent an envoy to meet Dayan in Rabat. Dayan returned home with a message: Sadat *would* meet Begin; but the Americans must not be told, and Begin must first accept the principle of handing back all the land captured in 1967. Much as he wanted a summit, Begin rejected the latter condition. He also insisted on telling the Americans about Israel's contacts with Egypt—omitting the name of the Arab country involved, knowing that even a White House janitor could fill in the blank. Then he sat back to await Dayan's next scheduled meeting with the Egyptian envoy, near the end of the year.

The wait, however, turned stormy. The Carter administration's ire at Israel's West Bank policy boiled over in September. When Dayan was in New York for the UN General Assembly, the Americans read him the riot act. Then, they told him they planned to join Moscow in a Mideast "peace" declaration recognizing "the legitimate rights of the Palestinian people." Begin summoned Ambassador Lewis to lodge a protest; Carter ignored it. On the heels of this first, minor, setback to his preemptive approach to U.S. pressure, Begin faced the first challenges to his authority at home. One of them—a wildcat settlement attempt by Gush Emunim—was snuffed out quickly. Begin okayed a request from Weizman to have the army move the squatters out. Yet his two other *sabra* generals, Dayan and Sharon, meanwhile began defying his magisterial hold on the cabinet. Dayan, who had initially acquiesced in Begin's demand that he clear all foreign-policy moves with the premier beforehand, now insisted he be allowed to act as "a foreign minister, not a courier." The flap in New York over the American-Soviet declaration had forced the issue. Though frozen out of Begin's ultimately futile efforts to head off the U.S. move, Dayan had joined the Americans afterward in drafting a U.S.-Israel "working paper." He discussed it with Begin only when he got back. Begin chided him for the lapse; but accepted the draft, and the foreign minister's demand for greater running room. He promised to stop phoning the Israeli embassy in Washington for progress reports when Dayan was in the United States, and agreed to deal directly with his foreign minister instead.

Sharon's challenge was public. Taking Begin's assurances literally, he had assumed personal control of West Bank settlement. Then, without telling Begin, he announced plans to implant two million Jews in Judaea and Samaria. The remark not only alarmed Washington; it stirred questions in Israel over just who was making West Bank policy. Yet Sharon retreated a half step, saying he had been speaking in a personal capacity and did not mean to imply that the cabinet had already approved the plan. Begin avoided comment until pressed by an Israeli reporter who wanted to know if the prime minister was comfortable with the Sharon statement. "No," Begin said, but added, "That kind of thing can happen in any government. I want to say that the Minister of Agriculture is excellent in that capacity, he is truly interested in agriculture. But he is chairman of the Ministerial Committee on Settlement, and sometimes he makes statements. And he has corrected his statement. I have read the correction. It is better that he corrected it himself, than that I should have to issue a correction. But that, too, is part of life. Nothing tragic has happened. . . . There is no need to exaggerate."

Still, for the first time since taking office, Begin seemed unsure of himself—an impression reinforced when he was briefly rehospitalized with chest pains and fatigue. Pressured from all sides over the West Bank, he grabbed at Dayan's suggestion that he try sleight of hand. It was announced there would be no new settlements on the West Bank for the time being—only Jewish "military" encampments, with Gush "reservists." The move fooled no one. "It was not," recalls Ben Elissar, "worthy of the usual Begin." By October Begin felt the need to shore up the coalition—by adding DASH. He did so despite Yigael Yadin's opposition to West Bank settlement, and at the price of dropping objections to making Shmuel Tamir his minister of justice. Begin named Yadin deputy prime minister—the cabinet's fourth war hero.

The night of November 9, 1977, Begin went home at the usual time, dined with Aliza, and settled down for an evening's reading. No great decisions pressed. Peace was an issue, but the ball was in the Americans' court. Washington was trying without much success to nudge Arab leaders toward reconvening a Geneva conference. The Arab states disagreed on how and whether to attend such a conference, and Arafat was reluctant to accept a proposed compromise formula that would relegate the PLO to an indirect role. Israel had heard nothing from Egypt on plans for the further meeting in Morocco with President Sadat's envoy. Begin figured there was little to do but wait. Ben Elissar was also at home when an Israeli reporter phoned for his reaction to remarks Sadat had just made to the Egyptian parliament. In a rambling address, the president at one point had said he would go anywhere on earth for peace—even to the Knesset! Ben Elissar, smiling to himself, told the reporter that if Sadat wanted to come, he would of course be most welcome. So absurd did the notion seem, that he didn't bother phoning Begin.

Begin heard the news at dawn, on the radio. After reading the papers as usual, he left for the office. There, he issued a statement along the lines of Ben Elissar's: If Sadat wants to visit, let him come. Begin, too, figured the Egyptian leader had been carried away with his own rhetoric. But, he told an aide, "we must put him to the test." Within hours, events took on a momentum of their own. Sadat insisted the suggestion had been serious. The Americans—government and TV networks—played middlemen. Begin issued a statement, read out in Arabic on Israeli radio and television, formally inviting Sadat to Jerusalem.

Sadat replied, via Washington, that the broadcast invitation was insufficient. Begin was more certain than ever the whole affair was an exercise in public relations—until Ambassador Lewis called to relay an Egyptian request for a written letter of invitation. "It was then that we realized Sadat might really be coming," recalls Ben Elissar. Begin dictated a note. He had it typed on official letterhead, addressed to "His Excellency, the President of the Arab Republic of Egypt." The next day Lewis phoned with Sadat's RSVP: acceptance. Now, Begin sensed, history was in the making. And, he remarked to an Irgun friend moments afterward, it would *not* be made by the heirs of David Ben Gurion:

"After all the years of my being slandered and vilified as a warmonger and a terrorist, *I* am the one Sadat has decided to visit!"

Chapter Twenty-two

Waging Peace

Begin hid his elation as Sadat's arrival neared. He felt to do otherwise would be undignified—and bad negotiating tactics. The only hints of how he felt came in the Knesset, where Begin likened the approaching visit to Ben Gurion's founding of the state, and in a remark to reporters that he hoped "soon" to become the first Israeli leader to see Cairo. Although calling for a new era in Arab-Israeli history—"no more war, no more bloodshed, no more threats"—he avoided suggesting Israel would make negotiating concessions simply because Sadat was coming to Jerusalem. When those around Begin could not control their excitement, he did it for them. He refused Weizman's pressure to fire the chief of staff for suggesting Sadat's visit might be a trick, and gave the officer only a closed-door reprimand. When Ben Elissar, in charge of welcoming the Egyptian advance team, rushed back from the airport to share the details, Begin kept him waiting in the outer office. "It was the first time we'd seen an Egyptian plane, with Egyptian markings!" the aide recalls. Twice Ben Elissar tried to enter, finally bursting in, explaining that it was urgent he rejoin the Egyptians at their hotel. "So what?" replied Begin. "So it will wait a few minutes."

Sadat arrived after sundown Saturday. Begin greeted him at the airport—polite, not effusive. At lunch the next day he proposed establishing a "hot line" to Cairo, but turned aside the Egyptian's bid to tackle bedrock issues like the West Bank. A few hours later Sadat addressed a Knesset so mesmerized that even the usually rowdy

Communists behaved. Some delegates cried. "You want to live with us in this part of the world," said Sadat. "In all sincerity, I tell you, we welcome you among us, with full security and safety. This, in itself, is a tremendous turning point. We used to reject you. We had our reasons and our claims. Yes. We used to brand you as 'so-called' Israel. Yes. We were together in international conferences and organizations and our representatives did not—and still do not—exchange greetings. Yes. . . . Yet today I tell you—and declare it to the whole world—that we accept to live with you in permanent peace based on justice." Then the other shoe dropped: Such a peace, said Sadat, would require that Israel hand back all Arab land taken in 1967, and recognize "the Palestinian people and their rights to statehood."

Weizman scribbled to Begin, "We have to prepare for war." But Begin, rising in reply to Sadat, chose restraint. He was warm in tone, if firm in substance. He gave a speech that, like Weizman's campaign ads, was startling for what *wasn't* there. Working without a prepared text—he had received no advance copy of Sadat's—he said, "Until last night the distance between Cairo and Jerusalem was not only geographical. President Sadat showed courage in crossing this distance." Begin presented a vision of peace: when Egyptian and Israeli children would wave each other's national flags, borders would be open and busy with visitors in both directions. He omitted explicit claims to specific lands: the West Bank, even Jerusalem. He did not bat down Sadat's call for Palestinian rights. He contented himself with saying that the Egyptian's courage, in itself, would not weaken Israel's negotiating stance. "President Sadat knows, as he knew from us before he came to Jerusalem, that our position concerning permanent borders between us and our neighbors differs from his," said Begin. "However, I call upon the President of Egypt and upon all our neighbors: do not rule out negotiations on any subject whatsoever. I propose, in the name of the overwhelming majority of this Parliament, that everything will be negotiable. . . . No side shall say to the contrary. No side shall present prior conditions. We will conduct the negotiations with respect. If there are differences of opinion between us, that is not exceptional. . . . We shall conduct the negotiations as equals. There are no vanquished and there are no victors. All the peoples of the region are equal, and we will all relate to each other with respect. In this spirit of openness, of readiness of each to listen to the other—to facts, reasons, explanations; with every attempt at mutual persuasion—let us conduct the negotiations ... until we succeed, in good time, in signing a peace treaty between us."

Begin was protective of Sadat when they faced a phalanx of reporters at the end of the visit. Amid howls of denunciation from the Arab world, the Egyptian leader was badgered by Israeli reporters to invite Begin to Cairo. Begin ran interference. "I would like to see Cairo," he said. "But I do understand the reasons why, at this stage, such an invitation was not issued." When another reporter pressed Sadat further, Begin cut him short: "You heard from the President that I have a right [to visit] and that we have only postponed the exercise of that right." Besides, said Begin, "the time was so short" on the present visit "that I think, before I go to Cairo, I will have to invite President Sadat to Jerusalem for a second time." Still, the last word was Sadat's—and it was a plea from a leader at sea: "May God guide the steps of Premier Begin and the Knesset, because there is a great need for hard and drastic decisions. I already did my share in my decision to come here, and I shall be really looking forward to those decisions. ..."

Within days, Begin faced pressure to answer that plea. Sadat announced a follow-up peace conference—to be held in Cairo in December—and relayed through Washington a request that Begin help him by at least hinting at concessions on the West Bank or the Palestinians. Begin parried this appeal, and set out to preempt any further ones. He accepted the invitation to send a team to Cairo, and named Ben Elissar to head it. Instead of concessions on the West Bank, however, he dangled the offer of a near-total withdrawal from Sinai—sending it via Dayan, who met Sadat's envoy in Morocco. Then, Begin withdrew to his office and scrawled on a yellow legal pad his "Palestinian Autonomy Plan." It was the offer he had repeated and refined over three decades. He sweetened it with a proposal for an elected Palestinian council that would exercise autonomy. But he said the Israelis would retain "security" control of the Palestinian areas and the right to "acquire land and settle." Upstaging the Cairo talks, he convinced Carter to invite him to Washington with his "new proposition ... [to] break the deadlock."

He told the cabinet of the Sinai withdrawal offer, the Palestinian plan, and the U.S. visit, the day before flying to Washington—also, the day before the Cairo talks. Weizman was furious, feeling the defense minister should have been consulted on the security implications of leaving the Sinai. There was also thunder on Begin's right. Irgun veteran Shmuel Katz, whom he had hired as a press adviser, felt the Palestinian autonomy plan violated IZL orthodoxy, by omitting an explicit claim to sovereignty over the West Bank and Gaza. Begin ignored Weizman, and stroked Katz by taking him along to Washington. He sent Ben Elissar to the Cairo talks with the months-old draft of his peace treaty, and the knowledge that he, Begin, would be doing the real negotiating at the White House.

In Washington Begin surprised Carter by offering to give up virtually all the land Israel had captured from Egypt. And in presenting the autonomy plan, he agreed—over Katz's protests—to append a series of new sweeteners suggested by the Americans. Israeli troops might be "withdrawn" to security enclaves within the West Bank. He abandoned his long-standing opposition to the return of Palestinians who had fled in 1948 or 1967, saying they could come back "in reasonable numbers" to be negotiated with the eventual Palestinian council. He said the whole arrangement could be reviewed in five years. And when pressed at least to *discuss* the issue of West Bank sovereignty at some later stage, Begin amended his draft to read: "Israel stands by its right and claim of sovereignty to Judaea, Samaria and the Gaza District. [But] in the knowledge that other claims exist, it proposes, for the sake of the agreement and the peace, that the question of sovereignty in these areas be left open."

He felt the concessions well worth it—the price for recapturing the diplomatic initiative from an Egyptian president who had captured the world by flying to Jerusalem. Carter phoned Sadat and persuaded him to invite Begin to present the plan in Egypt, so delighting Begin that even when asked on American television how he felt about a Palestinian state, he refused to rise to the bait. "There can always be a review" of the autonomy proposal, he said. "But the first man to hear from me should be President Sadat." Of the White House talks, he declared, "If I came here a hopeful man, I am leaving as a happy one." Carter, who seemed no less happy, jotted in his diary: "I feel protective of Sadat, and in a strange way so does Begin."

But whatever "protectiveness" Begin felt had ended with Sadat's return to Cairo. Begin resented the Egyptian's pipe-puffing ease with the press, his status as international folk hero, his success in implying that Israel's response to the milestone Knesset visit had been tight-fisted. Begin's trip to Washington was intended as an end run around Sadat's charisma, a move to demythologize the peace process. When Ben Elissar phoned from Cairo and gushed about the beauty of the Pyramids and the hospitality of Egyptians, Begin retorted: "Skip the poetry, Eli." Now, covering his right flank by having Katz stay on in the United States to meet Jewish leaders, he joined Sadat Christmas Day in the Suez Canal town of Ismailiya.

From the outset, Begin took command of the talks. In a closed-door meeting he got Sadat's instant agreement to establish two "follow-up committees" to deal with specific political and security issues. He emerged beaming. When the full-dress summit opened—with Weizman, Dayan, Egyptian ministers and aides—Begin proceeded to read out his draft peace treaty, clause by clause. Sadat seemed uninterested, except to frown at mention of Israel's retaining its Sinai border settlements. When Begin finished reading the treaty, he started on the Palestinian autonomy plan. Weizman whispered that the recital seemed to be getting on Sadat's nerves, but Begin whispered back, "I, too, am nervous," and kept reading. Finally, Sadat interrupted, as Begin was running through a list of legal experts who had complimented him on the autonomy proposal. The Egyptian suggested that the summit concentrate instead on a set of negotiating *principles,* including eventual Israeli withdrawal from all occupied land, and a "solution to the Palestinian problem." Yet Begin replied that this would be rushing things. After Dayan failed to narrow the divide with compromise wording, the meeting ended—without so much as a joint communiqué.

When Sadat and Begin faced hundreds of reporters in a converted wave tank near the Suez Canal, the Egyptian leader announced the agreement on establishing follow-up committees. But he added, glumly, that there had been no agreement on the Palestinian question—"the crux of the problem here in this area." Begin shrugged off Sadat's complaint, and resurrected the phrase he had uttered on leaving Washington a week before: "I have come here a hopeful prime minister and I am leaving a happy man."

Back home, he pronounced Ismailiya a success. "Within the first five minutes, the decisive result was obtained": the follow-up committees. The heat was off Israel. There would be no time limit for the committees' work. "For the first time," he told the Knesset, "there is an *Israeli* peace plan. The whole world is arguing about the Israeli plan. . . . We used to be isolated in America and Europe. Now *we* isolate someone else. This is a most important development." He said Sadat had failed in his bid to enlist U.S. backing for his "anti-

quated" demands. "With the conclusion of the meeting at Ismailiya," Begin said, "we have given our share."

Yet not everyone agreed. Begin soon came under fire from old
guarders who thought he had given too much; and from Sadat, who
felt he had miles left to travel. The first challenge occurred in the
Knesset, where a handful of Herut veterans objected to the autonomy plan. Begin argued them down. He declared that it was painful
to confront people he loved, comrades "through thick and thin," but
that history demanded "responsibility . . . courage." Saying he felt
sure Israel was "on the right path," he forced a vote, and won. Labor
abstained en masse, disagreeing with the autonomy plan but unwilling to risk the role of spoiler. Among the Herut critics, only former
Sternist Geula Cohen and a fellow backbencher went so far as to
vote against Begin.

But Katz, who was not a Knesset member, persisted. Showing up
at Begin's residence, he resigned as press adviser, refused an offer to
return to America as UN ambassador, and vowed to challenge
Chaim Landau for the one chair still open in the cabinet. Begin exploded: "I'm the prime minister. You can't dictate ministerial ap-
pointments to me!" Katz said he wasn't dictating, simply planning
to seek the backing of Herut's central committee. "How," Begin
shouted, "can you be a member of a government when you oppose
its policies?" When Katz said that would be for the party to decide,
Begin ridiculed his pretension to "save Israel," and demanded he
desist from his challenge. Katz refused, left, and girded for a showdown.

Begin opened the central committee meeting January 8 by playing to the old guard. Not *only* had Israel given its last concession. It
might invoke a "great principle of international law": If Sadat rejected the Israeli plan, Begin would reserve "the right to declare that
the proposal is no longer valid." He played down his agreement to
leave open the question of West Bank sovereignty. "I proclaim from
this rostrum," he said, "our belief that the sole right to sovereignty is
vested in the State of Israel." He diluted the Sinai offer, too, by
promising that "all Israeli settlements will remain intact, and an Israeli defense force will be their sole defender."

As Katz rose to speak, he heard Begin whisper he would be lucky
to sway 10 percent—at most, 15 percent—of the seven hundred delegates. Yet a storm of applause greeted the challenger. Katz, taking

care to avoid personally criticizing Begin, turned the prime minister's own time-honored arguments against him. By leaving the issue of sovereignty open, Katz said, Israel would merely invite U.S. pressure to cede sovereignty. This, Jews must never do. Not only principle was at stake: "Our lives depend on it." Landau spoke next, about what he knew best: loyalty to Begin, a quality he contrasted with Katz's withdrawal from Herut politics after the first Knesset. Now Begin sensed trouble, and he rose to speak again. Unsheathing the weapon he had used years earlier against Tamir and Weizman, he said that if the party chose Shmuel Katz, the party could not retain Menachem Begin. Then he called the vote. Landau—that is, Begin—won it. Yet the tally was 306–206. "It was," recalls Eliahu Ben Elissar, "a very small majority for a candidate whom Begin had personally supported. Less than sixty percent! It was no great victory, either for Landau or for Begin."

The next week, when a despondent Sadat pulled out of the follow-up "political-affairs committee" agreed to at Ismailiya, Begin was more relieved than alarmed. He issued a statement blaming the crisis on Sadat's "illusion" that Israel would "surrender to demands that at no time were acceptable." This, he said in a jaunty address to a group of visiting French Jews the next evening, had been presumptuous. "I have *another* word for it: in the language of Corneille and Baudelaire and Descartes and Proust; in classical French, it is *chutzpah!*" Saying that he still hoped peace would come, Begin declared his readiness to resume talks as soon as Egypt relented. In the meantime—quoting Jabotinsky, without attribution, in more "classical French"—Begin said Israel must stand *kalt und fest*—"cool and steadfast."

But the insouciance forced a crisis with the Americans. Having hoped Begin would remain "protective" of Sadat, President Carter now felt the Israeli leader was making light of the risks Sadat had taken. Where Sadat craved peace, it seemed to Carter, Begin craved land. In February the Americans hit back. They publicly declared illegal the Sinai settlements Begin had vowed to keep. Then, Carter replied to an Israeli bid for new U.S. fighter jets by announcing a package deal that would also send planes to Egypt and Saudi Arabia. Begin was angered by the political slight, but more deeply hurt by the personal one. "He so *wanted* Carter to *like* him," recalls one top American official. "And he realized that it was Sadat whom Carter admired." After Carter's initial welcome of the autonomy plan, Begin boasted he had won the "goodwill and understanding" of a truly "great" American leader. Now he felt cheated: The only way to retain Carter's goodwill would be to make concessions Begin saw as a betrayal to himself, and Israel. He also felt he *deserved* to be admired more than Sadat, whom he considered an intellectual and political lightweight. "Sadat says he is not interested in details," Begin told a group of visitors. "But details, may I say, are quite important." To the Knesset, he complained that Carter and Sadat were ganging up on him. Only months earlier, Washington had praised him for the Palestinian autonomy plan. "Just because the other side did not accept a certain proposal, did those who praised the plan as a whole have to say: 'We, too, oppose this proposal'?"

In March the Americans called Begin to the White House, and only war, briefly, deferred that reckoning. Several days before the prime minister was due to leave, a PLO commando team breached the Israeli coast by rubber raft, and hijacked a bus north of Tel Aviv. Army roadblocks stopped the terrorists short of the city; however, in the ensuing shoot-out, thirty-five Israelis were killed, some seventy-five wounded. Begin announced he was delaying his U.S. visit for a week. Summoning his generals, he told them to hit back hard at PLO-controlled areas of southern Lebanon. Precisely how and where, he left to the army—as he had left military details to Paglin thirty years before. But, he told the Knesset, "gone forever are the days when Jewish blood could be shed with impunity. We shall sever the arm of iniquity!" Before dawn March 15, Israeli jets, tanks, and troops struck into Lebanon—driving hundreds of PLO guerrillas, and thousands of civilians, north toward Beirut. By the time Begin left for Washington on March 21, the Israeli force had halted near the Litani River.

Carter opened the talks with words of condolence on the bus massacre—but followed with a plea for concessions to Sadat. Begin refused. He complained the Americans had taken Sadat's side. "I was wounded in the heart," he told Carter, by the erosion of U.S. support for the autonomy scheme. Carter, however, would not be deflected. Surely, he said, Begin could at least provide a hint at later concessions if peace came closer. Begin said Israel had given all its concessions: It was now Sadat's turn.

Carter had had enough. When talks resumed the next day, he ticked off the list of Egyptian-Israeli problem issues and faulted Begin on all of them: West Bank and Sinai settlements, West Bank sovereignty, the principle of land for peace. The president added that he planned to summon congressional leaders and make the same presentation. Begin looked dumbstruck. In a near whisper, he protested that the charges were unfair, that Sadat's one "concession" had been a plane trip to Israel. Then, recalls Dayan, the "drawn and ashen" prime minister "leaned back in his chair and closed his eyes, weakened physically" by the onslaught. There, the summit ended.

Begin flew home to find his postelection honeymoon with the Israeli media definitively over—and his cabinet in disarray. Sharon drew up settlement plans with fanatical resolve. But Yadin's DASH—and, increasingly, Weizman—demanded the settlements stop, fearing they would make peace impossible. When Sharon's ministry announced a Jewish "archaeological" outpost near biblical Shiloh, a visit by reporters tore loose the settlement's fig leaf and, in the words of one Israeli pundit, caught the government "with its pants down, plainly lying to the Israeli public and the Americans at the same time." Once leakproof, the cabinet now made Rabin's look disciplined by comparison. Sharon and Weizman fought over settlement policy through client reporters, soon reducing Naor's formal cabinet communiqué to an academic exercise. "The leaks must stop. We cannot go on like this!" Begin told the ministers. "It must stop for the sake of our country and our government." Begin warned that they risked forfeiting the "confidence of the people, if we behave like this." Then, recalls Naor, "he heard the appeal leaked back on the radio an hour later." Only once—when leaks of a new settlement plan occurred as Dayan was off soothing the Americans' furor—did Begin intervene more directly. He phoned Sharon and demanded he issue a denial, which Sharon did.

But Begin's heart wasn't in it—nor his body, which was in the throes of another minor bout of postcardiac fatigue. He shared Sharon's thirst to settle Judaea and Samaria, confiding to a BBC reporter that no issue mattered to him more. He was dazzled by Sharon's battlefield determination to put settlements in place. When Sharon suggested a scheme to erect Potemkin settlements in the Sinai and abandon only *these* in the talks with Sadat, Begin briefly encouraged him, jettisoning the idea only when he sensed it would fool no one.

Besides, to surrender to Weizman's or Yadin's objections meant surrendering to Carter and Sadat. Begin returned from the summit defiant. In Lebanon he flouted a U.S.-backed effort to replace his troops with UN peacekeepers. He did pull out most of the Israeli incursion force, but handed over its positions to the Lebanese

Christian militia. He ignored American complaints that the Israelis had used U.S.-made "cluster bombs" in Lebanon, a violation of U.S. legislation that such arms be used only defensively. His one concession to American ire came when there was no choice: Satellite photos caught him out in a misstatement that Israel had not transferred U.S. armored-personnel carriers to the south-Lebanese militia. Carter, in an eyes-only reprimand, ordered the vehicles removed. If they weren't, he said, he would inform Congress. Begin backed down and, recalls a top U.S. official, even added an increasingly rare note of admiration for the president. "He seems to have respected Carter for having beaten him fair and square."

But when pressed by Secretary of State Cyrus Vance to promise a final decision on West Bank sovereignty five years after a treaty with Sadat, Begin offered only to "consider and agree upon future relations" between Israel and the Palestinians. It was, the Americans felt, a "Delphic sidestepping." At the end of June, he turned down a fresh Egyptian call for "total withdrawal" before it had even been formally presented. In July he rejected Sadat's request—relayed through Weizman—that Israel hand back Mount Sinai and the Sinai coastal town of El Arish as a good-faith move to revive the peace talks. "You will certainly agree, Mr. President," Begin wrote Sadat, "that no state takes unilateral steps." To U.S. Ambassador Lewis, he remarked: "Sam, no one gets anything for nothing!"

At the end of July, Vance did finally get Israeli agreement to negotiate "sovereignty" after a five-year peace transition—but wrested this from Dayan, not Begin. The secretary of state summoned the Israeli and Egyptian foreign ministers to a conference near London. Vance told Dayan that the agreement to "close" the sovereignty question after five years was the minimum Sadat needed to counter Arab charges that Begin would never cede anything more than Palestinian autonomy. Dayan scribbled an undertaking on a piece of note paper: "Israel will be prepared to discuss after five years the question of sovereignty (or permanent status). . . . Although these provisions do not call for a decision on the subject, it is the personal view of the Foreign Minister that an agreement on this question is possible."

When Dayan got home, Begin accused him of having exceeded his authority. Dayan rebutted, disingenuously, that he had merely conveyed Israeli intentions as he understood them. Begin convened the cabinet. To Dayan's astonishment, he proposed that both it *and* the Knesset endorse the foreign minister's concession. As the

rest of the cabinet berated Dayan, Begin ignored the storm, munch-
ing on a sandwich and sipping a glass of tea. "He let the others' fury
have full rein," recalls Arye Naor. Then, in a near whisper, he interrupted them: "Look, gentlemen. The Foreign Minister represents
the government of Israel, and through that government, he represents the State of Israel. As such, there is no such thing as a 'personal
opinion' for a foreign minister in an international forum. Therefore,
we have no choice but to approve what Mr. Dayan offered as his
'personal opinion.' " Turning to Dayan, Begin said, "Usually—and
I am confident that in the future this will be the case—the Foreign
Minister would consult his cabinet *before* delivering an opinion in
an international forum or to representatives of foreign governments.
But what was done, was done; and we must approve it." Then, he
went on: "I want to tell you one other thing. In May, when this issue
arose, I thought of proposing to the cabinet precisely the reply the
Foreign Minister has given. But at the time I was ill, and did not
have the energy to struggle with my friends who were not willing to
give such an answer. I think that this is the proper reply to the
Americans."

However, Begin now proceeded with renewed vigor to serve notice that Dayan's concession would be the last. In Lebanon, he let
the Christian militia use Israeli-supplied artillery to ward off an
American-backed attempt by the regular Lebanese Army to move
south. On the Mideast front, he lashed out at Sadat for attempting
an end run by meeting Shimon Peres, and he prevented Peres from
trying for a similar encounter with Hussein. "Peres can have my
prick!" Begin suggested, in Russian, within earshot of reporters. It
was Begin's favorite barracks curse because it allowed him to tell the
tale of its origin, which he now proceeded to share with Knesset critics. Czarina Catherine, it seems, discovered some old papers from
the reign of Peter the Great—including one in which a provincial
official had requested a favor. "He can have my prick!" Peter had
scrawled in the margin, to which Catherine is said to have appended
"With me, he can't even have that!" It was *Catherine's* remark, not
Peter's, that Begin had meant to borrow for Peres. He apologized for
the lapse. Days later, he replied to a Labor party suggestion that he
was "senile" by striding to the Knesset podium like a teenager and
quoting back to the Labor leaders a battery of names that they had
called each other over the years. When Peres objected, Begin chided
him: "Shimon, sit still."

When Carter proposed a triangular Mideast summit for September, Begin felt equal to the challenge. He had ceased hoping for the American president's favor: He expected to be ganged up on by Carter and Sadat. Yet he took their frostiness as proof that he was a better bargainer than they. He would go to America. He would talk peace. But if Carter and Sadat wanted a treaty, it would be on Menachem Begin's terms. If pressured, he would stand his ground. It would be an important meeting, Begin told the nation before leaving—but not a *"fateful"* one: "Our people lived thousands of years before Camp David, and will live thousands of years after Camp David.... If we are told that this is the last chance to arrive at peace, we shall not agree."

Chapter Twenty-three

Camp David

Begin's helicopter arrived last of the summitteers'—after Carter and Sadat had reunited and agreed that Camp David's setting, in wooded Maryland hill country, invited an informality which boded well for negotiation. Begin, sensing that informality meant pressure, set out to resist it within yards of the helipad. He asked Carter when the first meeting would be held, how or whether written records would be kept. When Carter said that Sadat seemed worried the talks might get bogged down in details, at the expense of major issues, Begin shot back: "I can handle both." Then, when Carter's wife, Rosalynn, suggested opening the summit with an interfaith prayer invoking Christian, Muslim, and Jewish blessings, Begin took out a pen and vetted the text line by line. While Carter suggested casual dress for the duration, Begin told the Israeli delegation: "When you see the president, you should always be properly dressed." In the event, Carter wore jeans. Sadat favored a jogging suit. Begin, with rare lapses, wore a jacket and tie. Carter and Sadat called each other by first names, but Begin insisted on addressing them by title. Carter was at first touched by the "formality." Then, he came to realize it carried at least one worrisome effect: "to limit the personal relationship" possible at the summit.

Begin breathed a sigh of relief when Sadat opened the negotiations—their first encounter since Ismailiya—by reading a proposal so full of old-style Arab demands that it shocked even Carter. It blamed all past wars on Israel, said that all captured land on all fronts must be returned, and proposed a full-fledged Palestinian state on the West Bank and in Gaza. Sadat also insisted the Israelis pay indemnities to Egypt for having dug oil wells in the Sinai. When Sadat finished reading his proposal, Carter joked to Begin that the Israelis could save everyone a lot of trouble by simply signing the document then and there. Begin, after a clipped chuckle, replied: "Would you advise me to do so?" Carter said no, and suggested the leaders recess to consult with their aides. Begin returned, defiant, to Dayan, Weizman, and the others. "What *chutzpah!*" he said of Sadat. He proposed drafting an immediate counterproposal, but bowed to the others' suggestion that it not be formally presented for the time being.

Carter called on the Israelis in the morning. He shrugged off Sadat's plan as mere negotiating tactics, and asked Begin to focus on core issues instead—especially, a West Bank settlement freeze. Begin refused to discuss a freeze. Carter said okay: If not that, what next best concession could Israel offer? Begin replied by lashing into the Sadat proposals, at which point Carter barked that Begin was dodging the real issues. "What do you actually want for Israel if peace is signed? How many refugees, and what kind, can come back? I need to know whether you need to monitor the border, what military outposts are necessary to guard your security. What else do you want? If I know the facts, then I can take them to Sadat and try to satisfy both you and him." However, Carter told Begin, "I must have your frank assessment. My greatest strength here is your confidence—but I don't feel I have your trust." Begin made no move to disabuse him of the assessment, whereupon Carter accused him of preferring land to peace—and of camouflaging the fact with a bogus proposal for Palestinian self-rule. Begin exploded. Weizman tried to cool tempers. But it was an acrimonious pair of peacemakers who broke to join Sadat for the summit's second three-way meeting. Begin picked up where he had left off, lambasting Sadat's proposal. Sadat shouted back. For three hours the two men yelled, glared, accused, fumed—oblivious to the presence of the president of the United States. At the end, Begin made a *pro forma* remark that he retained complete confidence in Anwar Sadat. Sadat said nothing, and left.

"We broke the ice," Begin reported back to the other Israelis. However, what had broken were the few surviving tatters of the personal tie established between Sadat and Begin in Jerusalem ten months earlier. So unsettled was Carter that he shelved the idea of

further meetings between Sadat and Begin. He would play go-between instead. Begin saw the change in tactics as a tribute to his own
toughness, a quality he was determined to project at all opportunities. When Carter aide Zbigniew Brzezinski dropped by and suggested a game of chess, Begin lied that it was the first time he had
played since Stalin's NKVD had hauled him away in Vilna. During
the game, he glared at Brzezinski as if the board were a battlefield.
On issues of substance, meanwhile, Begin told the Americans there
would be no settlement freeze, no evacuation of Jewish dwellings in
the Sinai, and no further sweetening of the autonomy plan he had
offered the Palestinians.

Begin's toughness left its mark. The Americans, realizing there
were only so many concessions they could pull like teeth from the
Israeli leader, used his autonomy plan as the core of their draft.
Their strategy was to prick enough loopholes in it, graft enough
phrases of their own, to create at least the theoretical possibility that
autonomy could develop into something more. Their hope was that
this—and unceasing pressure on Begin to surrender on the issue of
West Bank and Sinai settlements—might yet allow Sadat to sign an
accord without risking political suicide. "I would draft a proposal I
considered reasonable," Carter recalls, "take it to Sadat for quick
approval or slight modification, and then spend hours or days working on the same point" with Begin. "Sometimes, in the end, the
change of a word or phrase would satisfy Begin, and I would merely
inform Sadat." Still, on many issues, the Israeli leader stood firm. A
senior U.S. negotiator recalls Begin's "staking out a very hard position, which he didn't retreat from; then engaging in all kinds of exhausting legalistic tactics. You had to argue over every last comma;
get tied up in every last word." Another American official remembers hearing Carter at one point exclaim: "I don't know how to get
out of here. Every time I solve one problem, Begin has three more!"
He "wore down" the Americans, "conveyed a sense that he wasn't
going to give."

When the president relayed assurances that Sadat would retreat
from the opening proposal, Begin retorted: "I do not see how hon-
orable men can put forward one thing publicly and say a different
thing privately." When Carter suggested settlement concessions,
Begin replied that he would never deal away the birthright of the
children of the Holocaust. And when Carter tabled a U.S. draft—
the autonomy plan mined with new phrases like "self-government"
and suggesting a West Bank plebiscite as an element in deciding

eventual sovereignty—Begin accused the Americans of siding with Sadat. He rebutted the draft, clause by clause, his voice unflinching. Carter shifted tack, agreeing to shelve self-government in favor of the "national rights of the Palestinians." Begin replied: "Out of the question." He objected, too, to Carter's inclusion of language from UN Resolution 242 of 1967 proclaiming "the inadmissibility of the acquisition of territory by war." He said the Americans had plucked it out of context, as a trick to deprive Israel of Judaea and Samaria. Carter boiled over, saying if Begin was going to retreat from a UN decision the Israelis had accepted eleven years earlier, the summit was pointless. "You will have to accept it!" he shouted.

Begin replied, "Mr. President, no threats, please."

When the meeting broke up, Carter strolled back to his cabin with Dayan, muttering that Begin was "an obstacle to progress." To his wife, Carter was more blunt: "Begin is a psycho." He came to abhor meeting Begin. At times, recalls a U.S. negotiator, the president seemed ready to pack up and leave rather than weather another word-slinging session with the Israeli leader. "You've *got* to see Begin tonight," Vance remarked at one U.S. strategy session, to which Carter protested, "I don't *want* to see him!"

Yet gradually, Begin discovered there were costs to his toughness—and limits to his theory that small powers could dictate to huge ones. Carter increasingly ignored him. The Americans began working through Dayan, Weizman, and other aides—notably Israel's attorney general, Aharon Barak. This forced Begin to change the way he had always ruled: He would have to consult, if not heed, the others. In Carter's own encounters with Begin, meanwhile, he lost no opportunity to remind the Israeli that the power and prestige of the American presidency had been committed to the summit—and that failure would be "catastrophic" for U.S.-Israeli ties.

If the threat was slow to cow Begin, it had its effect on the others. Of these, Dayan and Barak were the most important; Weizman had long since lost the trust of his prime minister. Begin respected Dayan—in part because Dayan, unlike Weizman, showed respect for Begin. The prime minister felt even more at ease with Barak. He was younger, in his forties. A slightly baby-faced, pipe-puffing technocrat, Barak left political issues to others and talked to Begin in the language he liked best: legalisms, semantics, detail. Recalls a U.S. negotiator, "You had Begin. You had Dayan, who was no softy—

basically hard-line on security issues, but more *pragmatic* than
Begin, recognizing the need somehow to reach an understanding
with the Arabs, for *Israel*'s interest—and capable of putting himself
in the other fellow's shoes." And Barak? "Well, Moshe Dayan
would go to Begin and explain why it was *politically necessary* to do
certain things. . . . Barak could go in and show Begin how it was
'legal.' Barak would go and say, 'Now, Mr. Prime Minister, if we put
the word "also" in here, that will give you some flexibility. You're
not committing yourself irrevocably to one interpretation of this
sentence. . . . Or if we put a comma in here . . .' " And Begin, recalls
the American, "would latch onto those things like a dog onto the
biggest bone he ever got hold of!"

At first, says Dayan, Begin would get "angry and dismiss any
suggestion that did not appeal to him as likely to cause inestimable
harm to Israel." He entered the second week of the summit looking
for an escape route home. He requested a meeting with Carter for
"the most serious talk I've ever had"—barring one, he said, he had
held with Jabotinsky decades earlier. He told the president he could
not bring himself to sign the kind of accord the Americans wanted,
and suggested that all sides cut their losses and leave with a joint
statement acknowledging failure. Carter was tempted to agree but,
with periodic infusions of hope from Dayan and Barak, plowed on.
Through Barak, the Americans embarked on several days of word-
by-word re-drafting. The UN reference, for instance, was changed
to an endorsement of Resolution 242 "in all its parts." A "side-let-
ter" was drawn up—saying Israel could read any reference to the
West Bank to mean "Judaea and Samaria."

The Americans were able to insert phrases Begin had rejected out
of hand, by letting Barak embellish them with escape clauses. The
emerging draft proposed a "transfer of authority" on the West Bank
and in Gaza over a five-year "transition" period. After the transition, the Palestinians would get "full autonomy" via a "self-governing authority." This would be chosen in free elections, and would
"replace" Israeli rule. The areas' "final status" would "also recognize the legitimate rights of the Palestinian people." None of this
sounded like an assurance of the eternal Israeli control on which
Menachem Begin had insisted. But by "also" recognizing Palestinian rights, Barak persuaded Begin, the agreement implied that other
rights mattered too—notably Israel's claim to "security" in Judaea
and Samaria. Where the document referred to a "self-governing authority," Barak managed to add in parentheses the phrase "admin-

istrative council." Finally, Barak's rewording stipulated that "full autonomy" would apply to the "*inhabitants*" of the West Bank and Gaza. The idea—as Barak told Begin and Begin told himself—was that the *land* could remain Israel's forever.

"I dealt primarily with Barak," Carter recalls. "I don't know of any time in the last crucial days when Begin did modify his position, to moderation, that Barak was not the key one who spoke to Begin privately. And what I came to, was that my main strategy was to work with Barak on a particular statement of paragraph, and then let him go to Begin and try to sell it. And sometimes Barak would come back and say, 'Mr. President, if you change this or that word in the paragraph, I think the prime minister would accept it.' "

Yet at least one issue—settlements, in both Sinai and on the West Bank—resisted word games. Without resolving the settlement question, Carter and Sadat unswervingly insisted, there could be no agreement at all. On a stroll with Brzezinski around Camp David, Begin declaimed: "My right eye will fall out, my right hand will fall off, before I ever agree to the dismantling of a single Jewish settlement." When Carter sought out Barak, the Israeli told him only Begin could address settlements. When Carter braved Begin, the prime minister invoked the Bible, the Holocaust, and stood firm. And when Carter briefed Sadat, the Egyptian began packing his bags, and Carter started drafting a face-saving communiqué of failure.

The Israelis met in crisis session. Weizman hammered at Begin to retreat, but Begin barked, "I heard you!" Dayan argued more coolly: Israel could not avoid at least some concession on settlements, could not afford to cause the collapse of Carter's summit. It was an unexpected voice, however, that mattered most. General Ariel Sharon—back in Israel and no doubt aching for a piece of Camp David history—got a call for help from an old friend whom Begin had taken with him, Army Planning Director Avraham Tamir. Sharon in turn phoned Begin, who reconvened his aides and announced—"deeply moved," recalls Weizman—that "Sharon is in favor of evacuating the settlements if they are the last remaining obstacle to a peace agreement."

Begin was alone now, and the Americans knew it. Carter tightened the pressure, sending word that he would close the summit in two days—Sunday—no matter what. On Saturday Carter invited

Begin to his cabin—and was relieved when he showed up with Dayan and Barak in tow. Only Begin spoke, however. He opened with a quote from the Bible, extolling the importance of the Jews' return to the land God gave them. But he offered a concession: He and Sadat would spend the next three months negotiating a peace treaty. *If* they resolved all other issues, Begin would let the Knesset decide whether to give up the settlements in Sinai. Carter said that was not enough: Neither he nor Sadat could leave the settlement issue to chance. The battle lasted hours. Begin, recalls the president, "was shouting words like 'ultimatum,' 'excessive demands,' and 'political suicide.' " Yet in the end, Begin budged a step further: He said he would take the settlement question to parliament within fourteen days. Would Begin remain neutral, Carter pressed. Not necessarily. But he would let individual Likud deputies vote their conscience. This was *nearly* enough, felt Carter. Exhausted, he pushed for at least a fig-leaf concession on West Bank settlements. Would the Israelis freeze settlements for the duration of the peace talks? Begin said—or the Americans thought he said—yes.

Almost immediately Begin began agonizing over his retreat. He assured the other Israelis—and himself—that he had covered all his flanks. Yes, he had agreed to the phrase "legitimate rights" for the Palestinians, rejected in the past as a code word for Palestinian statehood. "But what is the ultimate importance of the term 'legitimate rights'?" he asked the others rhetorically. "The word 'legitimate' comes from the Latin word for 'law.' There is no such thing as an *illegitimate* right!" Still, the settlement concession ate at him. Summoning Barak, he set off for Sadat's cabin—the two leaders' first meeting since their opening confrontation—and attempted to reword the Sinai phrasing. Running into Carter on the way out, Begin said, beaming, that everything was now fine. Carter turned to Barak and asked what, exactly, Sadat had agreed to. When Barak tried to answer, Begin repeatedly interrupted. Says Carter, "I finally asked the Prime Minister point-blank to let Barak answer my question." When Barak did so, Carter realized Begin was greatly overstating what Sadat had in fact said, and was now planning to re-draft the settlement concession. Carter refused the change, and Begin saw no choice but to acquiesce.

The summit ended with two accords—one pledging Israel and Egypt to negotiate a treaty within three months, and Begin to present the settlement clause to parliament. The second agreement, with Barak's escape hatches, proposed to follow the treaty with negotiations to implement Palestinian self-rule on the West Bank and in Gaza.

Helicoptering to the White House with Carter and Sadat to sign the accords, Begin seemed elated. In the summit's homestretch, recalls a U.S. negotiator, he had seemed "stretched almost to the breaking point." Now, at least for the moment, the pressure was off. "We were all in a state of euphoria," says Carter. The Camp David talks, Begin declared at the signing ceremony, "should be renamed. It was the Jimmy Carter conference!" To applause from all sides, he added: "We still have a way to go until my friend President Sadat and I sign the peace treaties. We promised each other that we will do so within three months ... [But] I would like to say a few words about my friend President Sadat. We met for the first time in our lives in Jerusalem. He came to us as a guest, a former enemy. And during our first meeting we became friends." There had been tensions. But this, said Begin, "belongs to the past." Nor was his elation mere rhetoric. After the ceremony Begin met an old friend, who found him "on a high, an enormous high!" Said Begin, "I have just signed the greatest document in Jewish history!"

Then came the morning after.

Chapter Twenty-four

Full Stop

Begin refused to sign one of the Camp David "side-letters" delivered to the Israeli embassy on the heels of the White House ceremony—containing the U.S. understanding of what he had ceded on the West Bank settlements. The Americans expected a settlement freeze for the several years needed to negotiate peace with Egypt and autonomy with the Palestinians; but Begin insisted he had agreed only to a freeze for the three *months* of treaty talks with Egypt. The Americans accused him of reneging. Begin called the dispute a misunderstanding, an explanation endorsed by the U.S. diplomat who had drafted the settlement note, Harold Saunders. He remarks that by the end of Camp David, Begin's and Carter's proven ability "to talk past each other" had been further bloated by fatigue and mutual suspicion. Proven, too, was Begin's "tendency to hear selectively"—whether it was Sadat addressing him as "friend" in an otherwise testy meeting, or, at the first White House summit, Carter's commitment to Israeli security amid pleas for a settlement freeze.

Yet there could be no misunderstanding Begin's next moves—designed to serve notice that although he would unflinchingly implement the letter of Camp David, he would give not one jot more. The Americans and Sadat saw the accords as the start of a "process," building on a separate Israeli-Egyptian treaty and Palestinian autonomy, but leading, through the "transition" of autonomy, to full Palestinian self-government. The accords, after all, spoke of the Palestinians' "legitimate rights," promised a "self-governing authority" and a "transfer" of power. Barak's escape clauses, Carter figured, were semantics. Most, he recalls, entailed "an insignificant change, in my opinion." Besides, he reasoned, once Begin had concluded the Mideast's first peace treaty the muse of History would seduce him. He would soften. Other Arabs, like King Hussein and the Palestinians, would be tempted to join the process.

Before heading home Begin told an Israeli reporter, who told the world, that the Americans were wrong. "Legitimate rights" was a Latin tautology: "We conceded no principle." The Israeli Army would "remain in Judaea, Samaria, and Gaza. Full stop." When Carter warned him such remarks would make it impossible to woo other Arabs into peace talks, Begin responded, on a stopover in New York, by reiterating the remarks.

He returned home to cries of "traitor" from IZL veterans, and Gush militants. He ignored them, or shouted them down. Inviting Eli Tavin to his residence, Begin castigated him for opposing Camp David: "How *dare* you not trust the summit agreements! I—not Moshe Dayan—was the one who signed them!" When even Landau charged he had sold out, Begin struck back savagely. Landau was torn between the urge to be faithful and the ideology of a lifetime. He consulted a lawyer to establish just what Camp David meant, and when the cabinet convened, charged that Israel had given away too much. Begin turned on him—omitting, for the first time in decades, his disciple's IZL code name—and declared, "*Mister* Landau. You are just an engineer! You are not qualified to speak on this subject." Landau stared back, recalls one minister, like a wounded puppy. "It was literally sickening to watch." Yet after facing the cabinet for seven hours, Begin emerged with a near-unanimous endorsement of the peace accords. Then, refusing calls to seek a separate mandate from Herut, he took both the accords and the Sinai settlement question to the Knesset.

He said the accords must survive, the settlements must go—and, with tactical genius a General Sharon might have envied, insisted the two issues be linked in a single vote. He promised parliament to deliver a treaty with Egypt—maybe in two months, not the allotted three—but also to retain eternal Israeli control of "Judaea, Samaria, and the Gaza District." He brushed aside the likelihood of U.S. pressure once it came time to determine the "final status" of the territories: "We left no doubt," he said, "that after the five-year transition period, when the question of sovereignty comes up for decision, we shall assert our right to sovereignty over Judaea, Samaria, and Gaza. If an agreement is reached against the background of counterclaims, very well. If no agreement is arrived at, the result will be that the arrangements for autonomy and Israel's security will continue to remain in force."

Then Begin turned to the issue of the Sinai settlements. Intoning an amended version of the Jews' Passover litany, he said: "What makes this night different from all other nights? Tonight, we are discussing the signing of a peace treaty!" Without abandoning the settlements, he said, there could be no treaty. He had tried desperately to avoid bringing the settlers out. But Carter had refused. "As Prime Minister, I say to you—my dear and honored friends, and opponents: In my own heart, in my self, in my conscience, with all my soul, I knew that this way the Camp David summit would have broken down—that the State of Israel could not stand up in the face of this. Not in America; not in Europe. Not before American Jewry. Not before the Jews of other lands. We could not have faced this. All blame would have befallen us." Begin said he had spent his life resisting pressures. "But if the Camp David Conference had agreed on everything and broken up just because of the settlements, Israel would not have been able to stand up, all of Israel, in no way before the Western world. On such a day, or in the future, it would have had no choice but to announce surrender. This is my estimation. This is my belief. This is my view without hesitation. . . . There is no other way. This I believe, and will believe until my final day—that this is the right choice." Then, parliament voted. Eighty-four of its 120 members said yes to Begin's peace agreement.

One third of the Likud either voted no or abstained. Yet if assailed by the old guard, Begin also had earned a brief taste of the Establishment acceptance he had always craved. In the airport crowd that greeted him on return from Camp David was a member of "Peace Now," the citizens' lobby that had sprouted with Sadat's visit to Jerusalem and criticized Begin for being niggardly in his response to it. "Courage!" read the demonstrator's placard. "You're pointed in the right direction." Opinion polls gave Begin the approval of 78 percent of Israelis, an explosion of 16 percent from his presummit mark.

He seemed to exaggerate his pain at the defection of Herut veterans—in a bid to ward off American pressure for new negotiating concessions. The Americans—with diplomatic shuttles, telegrams, even videocassettes, challenging Begin's literal interpretation of the Camp David texts—set out to entice other Arab leaders to join the peace process. Carter sent Harold Saunders to Jordan with a letter detailing Washington's view on the end point of such negotiations: "Sovereignty" on the West Bank and Gaza must rest *not* with Israel, but with the Palestinians who lived there. There should be an "election by the inhabitants" to determine the areas' ultimate status. When Saunders crossed the Jordan River to Jerusalem, Begin was waiting with the text of an attack on Camp David by Geula Cohen, the former Sternist who was leading the old-guard assault inside Herut. He did not bother telling the American that Mrs. Cohen was an old guarder only in age. (In LEHI, she had helped broadcast underground radio commentaries. She had joined Herut well after Israeli independence and, once there, had sided with Ezer Weizman's abortive exercise in interior redecorating.) "You *see* what I have to deal with?" Begin exclaimed to the envoy; and then proceeded to answer each of the U.S. assurances to Hussein with one of Barak's escape clauses from Camp David. There would be no Palestinian "sovereignty," the prime minister said. There would be no U.S. "interpretations" beyond the deliberately hedged letter of the accords.

Begin sent Dayan to Washington for the first round of Israel-Egypt treaty talks, with orders to stick to details—exchange of ambassadors, border posts, cultural and political ties. As the Americans and Egyptians sought to "link" the treaty to a tighter Israeli commitment on Palestinian self-rule, Begin told Dayan to refuse. The meetings ended ten days later. The treaty details were in place, but a firestorm raged over the "linkage" issue. Begin announced preemptive "acceptance in principle" of the treaty draft, but said he wouldn't sign until the Americans removed a vague reference to linkage in its preamble. Then he retreated from even the three-month settlement freeze, unveiling plans to "expand" existing Jewish settlements. He also leaked his intention to transfer the prime minister's office to the eastern, Arab side of Jerusalem. When the Americans protested, he told them he had to give *something* to his old guard.

He pressed his assault on the Americans all the more energetically when it was announced that he—and Sadat—had won the Nobel Peace Prize. Though emphasizing that he would accept the accolade in the name of the People of Israel, Begin saw in the award a personal vindication. Interviewed by Israel Television, he was asked whether he had ever dreamed, during his IZL struggle and the decades of parliamentary opposition, of receiving such an honor. His reply was uncharacteristically devoid of rhetoric: "What can a member of the opposition do? He can try to influence but he cannot decide. Decisive action is only taken by members of the Government. And from the day I received this [prime minister's] task, I began to work on behalf of peace . . ."

Israel's Nobel laureate met America's secretary of state in New York, days later, en route to Canada. Begin insisted that "linkage" must go. He brushed aside the American's protest that even the present language had required pressure on Sadat. Shifting the subject, he told Vance Israel needed U.S. money to relocate the air bases it would be giving up in Sinai. After the meeting, Vance reverted to Camp David tactics, working with Dayan on a linkage clause and bringing the foreign minister along for a second encounter with Begin—at Kennedy Airport as the prime minister was heading home. Yet when Vance raised linkage, Begin answered with talk about Sinai airfields. Discouraged, Vance suggested that maybe Dayan might want to say a few words. When Dayan asked his boss, in Hebrew, if that would be okay, Begin shot back: "It was not *I* who asked you to speak. It was Vance, who seems to have taken over the running of the Israeli delegation." Dayan deferred to him. But Vance persisted, until Begin himself asked Dayan to speak. The foreign minister replied that he personally favored accepting the latest compromise language—a "target date" for completing preliminary Palestinian autonomy talks within a year of the Israel-Egypt treaty. Begin barked that he had heard enough of the foreign minister's personal opinion, and headed home.

He convened the cabinet on his return and phoned Carter, announcing preemptive acceptance of the existing treaty draft—with a woolly reference to linkage in the preamble but none in the main text. Begin pressed for an early signing. Carter refused, and Sadat wrote Begin pleading for some linkage in the treaty itself. Begin stood firm, however. With the ticking down, in late December, of the three-month period envisaged for treaty talks, Vance flew to the Mideast with compromise language on linkage. The new proposal, in the form of side-letters, specified a "good-faith target" of holding elections for the Palestinians' autonomy council within a year. Vance's first stop was Cairo, where Sadat asked him to press Begin for more explicit linkage—between the exchange of Egyptian and

Israeli ambassadors and the operational start of Palestinian autonomy, at least in formerly Egyptian Gaza. However, Sadat implied that even without that additional link, he would sign the treaty. With Carter publicly calling the Egyptian's attitude "very generous," Vance flew on to Israel.

Begin shouted him down, accusing the Americans of siding with Sadat. He said the side-letters were an unacceptable addition to a treaty draft Israel had already accepted. Where was "linkage" mentioned in the Camp David accords? "New proposals," Begin declared, "do not bring a peace treaty closer," and proceeded to reject the linkage proposal, phrase by phrase. Late that night Vance—despondent at the prospect of watching the treaty collapse; feeling "utterly incapable of getting past the minutiae," called on Begin at his residence. It was a rare face-to-face encounter: Begin, since Camp David, had tried to confine negotiations to larger, formal meetings. Vance, with an abruptness all the more jolting for its departure from his usual lawyerly calm, told Begin, "Look, you are likely to go down as an important figure in the history of your country, perhaps even in this history of the world—*if* you get this treaty, this peace. But if you allow this goal to be sacrificed for these relatively unimportant points, then you are going to be only a mere footnote!" Begin said nothing for several minutes. When he spoke, he made no reference to Vance's warning. But for the first time since Camp David, he did stress that he would work hard to help Washington work out a compromise. To a U.S. aide, he later mused sadly, "Carter *likes* Sadat more than me, doesn't he?"

Still, Begin would not give in on linkage. He had felt the pressure generated by one "target date"—the goal of signing the Israel-Egypt treaty in three months—and was more determined than ever to resist others. "We now have an example, on the basis of experience," he told the Knesset. "Lo and behold—and not through any fault of our own, since we were ready to sign the [draft] peace treaty on the 11th of November—the peace treaty was *not* signed within three months. Nonetheless, there are those who blame Israel for not honoring a target date." He said Israel must be prepared to weather pressure. He would "reject Egyptian proposals which endanger our nation's well being—even if they be supported by the Government of the United States, until the U.S. Administration sees its mistake, and sees that the State of Israel is indeed an important factor in the free world, and must not be weakened." To a group of Israeli newspaper editors, he added that the West Bank settlement restrictions were gone. "There is no freeze in the spirit of Camp David," Begin declared. "There has been, and there will be, settlement."

He sent Dayan back to the United States. But while Vance pressed for linkage—presenting his seventh draft on the issue by late February—Begin stood firm. He rescinded Dayan's earlier negotiating autonomy, empowering him only to discuss and explore American suggestions. Any Israeli proposals would require not only Begin's okay, but that of the rest of the cabinet, which increasingly resented Dayan's international stardom. Dayan protested, remarking at one point that it was "inconceivable that we should sit tongue-tied [with U.S. officials], and have to keep rushing to the telephone before we [can] tell them whether we accept or reject their proposals." But Begin, buoyed by the rest of the cabinet, said that was just too bad.

This, the Americans soon discovered, gave Begin the advantages of summitry with none of Camp David's pressure. Summoning Dayan, Carter issued something very close to an ultimatum: Begin must either give the foreign minister more leeway or join the talks himself. The treaty could—must—be wrapped up within ten days. When Dayan phoned Israel, Begin stalled. He said he had no objection to joining the talks but wanted to check with the cabinet first— a meeting that would have to await Dayan's return two days later. When the ministers had assembled, Begin told them he had not the slightest intention of going to the United States, where he would surely be subjected to a new dose of presidential pressure. To avoid an outright rebuff, he told the Americans that since *Sadat* was represented at the U.S. talks by a prime minister who lacked ultimate decision-making power, his own arrival would upset the conference's symmetry. Yet Carter would not be dissuaded. He phoned Begin and invited him to a one-on-one meeting, to be followed by a separate summit with Sadat. Begin grudgingly agreed to come—a week later. When Carter said he must come immediately, Begin said he would arrive within several days. But he added that he, too, would lack the authority to change the treaty draft without full cabinet approval. He also decided to leave Dayan and other colleagues home, ensuring that this cabinet approval would be seven thousand miles away.

Before Begin's departure, the other ministers gave him authority—on Dayan's acid insistence—to make any change he wanted. But Begin kept this from the Americans. He had Ben Elissar announce that the Washington visit was merely "personal." He took just Aliza, and two legal aides along—Barak was not one of them—and told reporters on leaving that despite "hints of pressure," he had no intention of caving in. "Israel has withstood many tests," he declared. "With God's help I will withstand pressures if they are applied." Asked about the then expired target date for signing a treaty with Sadat, he said, "Sometimes, negotiations carry on for years."

On arrival in the United States, he told the press he would not be railroaded into a "sham" agreement with Egypt. At the White House, Begin at first tried to avoid discussing the treaty altogether. He spoke of grander issues: an eventual alliance grouping the United States, Israel, Egypt, and maybe even the Saudis against foes like Libya's Qaddafi. He offered the Americans landing rights at the airbases to be relocated from the Sinai. Yet Carter pressed hard for linkage. Begin replied by questioning whether Sadat really wanted peace, and rattled off eight textual discrepancies between the latest U.S. draft and the Camp David agreement. When Carter tried to direct the discussion toward specific changes, Begin rejected them all—even one or two Israel had originally suggested.

But Begin was feeling the pressure. When the talks broke off for the night, he feared risking an irreparable breach with the Americans. After a fitful sleep, he returned to the White House reconciled to giving some ground—as little as possible, and on everything but linkage. He suggested verbal formulas that made Barak's seem straightforward by comparison. Addressing a Sadat request that the treaty not impinge on his Arab alliances, Begin proposed, in part: "It is agreed by the Parties that there is no assertion that this Treaty prevails over other Treaties or agreements or that other Treaties or agreements prevail over this Treaty." When the talks broke off for a second night, and the Carters had invited the Begins for dinner, the president left his wife with Aliza and took Begin aside. Verbal formulas were not enough for peace, he told Begin, and asked him to ponder Israel's future if peace were allowed to slip away. Ignoring the remark, Begin turned the discussion to specific treaty clauses, at which point Carter excused himself and retired for the evening. Yet the next morning, Begin finally proposed a verbal formula on linkage. Although there would be no target dates, Israel would accept the "goal" of completing the autonomy talks within a year. After that, West Bank and Gaza elections for the autonomy council would be held "as expeditiously as possible." Begin said he had to check with the cabinet for its approval, phoned Israel during the weekly cabinet meeting and read out the new draft. He had won, he said, a "complete turnabout" in the American position. Dayan failed to see any such turnaround, but he and the rest of the ministers said it all sounded fine. Begin reported the cabinet agreement to Carter—although adding, in a final show of toughness, a new counterdemand: the right to buy Sinai oil once the wells went to Egypt. Carter said if the Egyptians didn't want to sell, Washington would guarantee an alternative source. Begin said he wanted Sinai oil.

When Begin left to pack his bags, Carter phoned Sadat, then summoned the Israeli leader back to the White House. Carter said he had decided to travel to Cairo and Jerusalem himself to wrap up the treaty. Begin, who confessed he had been sleepless after their initial White House shouting match, said he welcomed Carter's shuttle effort. Then he flew home, determined to prevent the president from turning the journey into a Camp David summit without Camp David.

Begin had worn Jimmy Carter down. Before leaving, the president sent Zbigniew Brzezinski to Cairo to beg Sadat's support, in the hopes of winning a second term in the White House and pressing Israel for gradual concessions in the years ahead. Carter says he planned to let "Begin have his way with particular phrases and depend on Sadat to be flexible on language and to take the long view concerning the effect of the agreement." While in Cairo, Carter got Sadat to agree to most of the U.S. draft. But the Egyptian leader, with political problems of his own, still wanted tighter linkage. He now proposed a tie between the exchange of ambassadors and Israel's final pullback from the Sinai. Sadat also wanted Israel to agree to a liaison office in Gaza, as a symbolic commitment to eventual Arab control there. Additionally, he repeated his request for an early return of El Arish. Finally, in a show of anger at Begin's litigiousness, Sadat insisted on changing a few words in his verbal formula on Egypt's Arab alliances. Begin had said such commitments "shall not derogate" from the Israeli treaty. Sadat substituted "shall not be inconsistent with."

Carter arrived in Israel with foreboding, an unshakable preference for Sadat over Begin, and the determination to wring a treaty from the Israeli leader before returning home. He drove directly to the prime minister's residence for a private meeting. Carter said he thought peace was within reach. Begin said he hoped so. But he added that even if he and Carter *did* wrap up the treaty, he would of course have to submit it to Knesset debate before signing it. Carter exploded. He asked Begin what was the point of his staying in Israel if he had to go home empty-handed. Begin said he could not bypass parliament. For forty-five minutes the two leaders argued. On leaving, Carter said it seemed that if Begin really wanted a treaty, he was going about it in a strange way—"doing everything you can to obstruct it, with apparent relish." Drawing within inches of the president, Begin replied, "Look into my eyes. How can you say I am a man who does not truly want peace!" Carter—who says he felt "very dejected, and angry"—wheeled and left, convinced the only way to salvage the treaty was to "go over Begin's head—to cabinet members, to the Knesset, to the citizens of the country."

Begin showed up at the first round of talks flanked by his seven senior cabinet colleagues. Carter opened with an appeal for peace, adding that he had promised to phone Sadat that evening to report whether a treaty was within reach. Begin replied that Israel would not bow to such timetables: Treaties took time; the Knesset must debate. He proceeded to reject each of Sadat's final demands, digressing to denounce the "anti-Semitic" slant of Egypt's state-controlled press. Carter said that if Begin objected to the Egyptian changes, he must offer constructive counterproposals to address Sadat's concerns. Begin said he would be glad to, but needed time to formulate them. "It took us two days of talks at the White House," he said, prompting Carter to exclaim: "I don't have two days!" When Vance raised the linkage question, Begin again rejected Sadat's suggestions one by one, adding that the latest U.S. draft had failed to include the parenthetical stipulation that "autonomy" meant only an "administrative council." When the Americans asked Begin about Sadat's rephrasing of the formula on Arab alliances, he rejected even this. He offered an even more acrobatic compromise: "shall not . . . be construed as contravening."

When the Americans had left, Begin did, briefly, seem fearful of pushing Carter too far. He told his ministers that Israel would accept one Sadat demand: linking the exchange of ambassadors to the Sinai withdrawal. Still, there would be no linkage to Palestinian autonomy. The matter of the Gaza liaison office would be hedged. Sadat could raise it at the later talks on autonomy. He would not let Carter bully him: "The heavens will not fall," Begin told the cabinet, "if it takes longer than a few days to arrive at an agreement."

Inviting Carter to a full cabinet meeting the next day, he resumed arguing the U.S. draft, clause by clause. When Begin rehearsed his objections to the Gaza liaison office, however, Carter interjected: "You must agree." He said Egypt had to be able to influence its Gazan allies to accept the autonomy scheme. "It is," said Carter, "a matter of the national interest of the United States!" The room fell silent. Begin rolled his eyes skyward, then stared at Carter and declared: "Mr. President. Please consider the following: It is in *Israel*'s national interest *not* to agree to Egyptian officers. And we shall do what we have earlier decided to do." Carter, almost red with fury, ran his fingers through his hair, paused, then said, "All right. Let us proceed."

Carter left the cabinet meeting to address the Knesset, telling the chamber that while the *people* of the Mideast seemed ready for peace, "the leaders have not yet proven that we are also ready for peace." That afternoon talks resumed, but Carter sat them out, while Begin pressed his demand that Egypt agree to sell Sinai oil to Israel. In the evening, Carter packed to leave. Begin reconvened the cabinet and drafted a communiqué of failure: Peace would come eventually; work would continue. He handed it to Vance to hand to Carter, then headed home.

But the rest of the cabinet felt Israel could not send the president back to Washington empty-handed. With a nod from his colleagues, Dayan phoned Begin and read out a compromise proposal on Sinai oil. If the Egyptians didn't want to sell it, the Americans would meet Israeli needs at market prices. Could Dayan take this suggestion to Vance? Begin agreed but said he would have to report back to the cabinet before finalizing anything. That night, Dayan and Vance— keeping Carter briefed by phone—agreed on the oil question. Dayan also persuaded the Americans to consider deferring the issue of Gaza's liaison office for the autonomy talks, by assuring Vance that Israel would happily consider visa applications for liaison officers through normal channels.

Having scheduled a farewell breakfast with Carter at the King David, Begin awoke to a briefing from the foreign minister. Remarking that Dayan's progress the night before would help Carter push forward with treaty talks back in Washington, he left with Aliza for the hotel. Yet when they arrived, Carter gently suggested that Rosalynn and Mrs. Begin do some last-minute sightseeing, and

sat Begin down for a final attempt at a treaty. He said the Vance-
Dayan compromises brought a signing much closer. Begin agreed,
but countered that at a minimum, the *cabinet*'s approval would be
needed. Would Begin then at least hint at what *his* position would
be on the present draft? No, Begin replied. That would preempt his
fellow ministers.

Carter excused himself, phoned Vance, and summoned him and
Dayan to join the talks. When they arrived, he placed a copy of the
revised oil clause on the tablecloth and asked Begin to take it to the
cabinet for approval. Then, he nudged Dayan to repeat the compromise suggestion about Sadat's liaison officers—a victory for Israel—
to which Begin nodded assent. Finally, Carter asked a favor: Could
Begin help out the dangerously isolated Egyptians with a good-faith
agreement to ease political restrictions on local Palestinians? Begin
made no promises. But he told Carter to draw up something in writing: It would be considered sympathetically. Carter pressed no
more. He left for Cairo, promptly persuaded Sadat to abandon explicit mention of the liaison officers and settle for Begin's nonbind-
ing "goal" as linkage, and announced history's first Arab-Israeli
peace treaty.

Begin sailed the draft through the cabinet, then took it to parliament. He said he had weathered pressure after pressure, demand
after demand, from the Americans. He had even refused Carter's
summons to join the Dayan talks in the United States! The result, he
said, was a treaty without target dates, without a liaison office in
Gaza. "We do not exult," Begin concluded. "There is no reason for
exultation. We do not boast. There is no cause for boasting. All the
previous governments wanted what this Government is proposing to
you today." But, he said, "it has so happened that at this particular
time we have reached the point where we can sign a peace treaty.
Therefore, without exultation, without boasting, but with subdued
heart and with abundant love and with profound faith; on behalf of
the Government and with its concurrence, I ask the Knesset to approve the Treaty of Peace between Israel and Egypt." It did: 95–18,
with two abstentions and three delegates absent.

Begin ended the session on a personal note: "I want to tell my old
friends in this chamber—which is my second home, since I have
spent half my life in this house: What is my innermost feeling? True,
it is good that we have attained such a moment. There is concern for
the future, as there must be. There is also apprehension in the heart,
totally natural. But despite all this, we feel in our heart that we have

reached a certain turning point. May it be one which is entirely positive—for us, for the Egyptian people, for other peoples around us. For with all our hearts and all our soul—all of us together—want to attain the goal, compared to which none is simpler and none more human: Peace."

Begin suggested signing in Jerusalem. Sadat refused, so the ceremony was held on the White House lawn. Afterward, however, Sadat finally invited Begin to Cairo. On leaving Tel Aviv for Egypt, Begin declared: "Would *any* of you—citizens of Israel—have imagined two years ago that today, the 2nd of April 1979, a person holding the position of Prime Minister of Israel would be going to Cairo, there to be welcomed by a presentation of arms and the playing of *Hatikvah*?" He took with him a delegation that included veterans of the Irgun, Haganah, and Palmach. "For thirty-five years," he said, "I have been dreaming of the day of a meeting of the hearts among all these fighters. That day was long in coming—but come, it did." In Cairo Begin received the foreigner's traditional welcome: crowds, smiles, handclasps, cheers. Never before, even on assuming the prime ministership, had he been so exultant. He toured the Pyramids, prayed at Cairo's synagogue, dined in splendor with Sadat. At one point he bounded from his official limousine and waded into the sidewalk crowds. On the plane back, he plumped down next to a startled Israeli radio correspondent, borrowed his tape recorder, and conducted an "interview" in which Begin played reporter to the newsman's prime minister. "What could I do?" recalls radio correspondent Shalom Kital. After a few brief, unremarkable questions and answers, Begin said into the mike: "This is Menachem Begin. Now, back to the studio." Says Kital, "Begin seemed in a state of euphoria!"

On landing, he declared: "We came back on the wings of an eagle . . . after thirty hours which are not only memorable, but unforgettable in our lives." Praising Sadat for the welcome, he gushed that the Egyptians had mobbed him and shouted, "We like you," when he had escaped his limousine. "Their security boys were quite perturbed," Begin remarked. "I was not." Phoning Carter, he said he had had a "wonderful visit to Cairo!" Then, he addressed the Knesset: "Today, I can say by the opinion of the two nations, that the state of war which has lasted between Egypt and Israel for thirty years and more, has come to an end."

. . .

But Begin's work had not: With the treaty signed, he was determined to protect it from Jimmy Carter and Anwar Sadat; from Dayan and Weizman. From anyone who said the road to a "wider" peace, with wider concessions, had only just begun.

Chapter Twenty-five

Fortress Peace

Begin hastened to shut doors the Americans wanted open. He drafted a policy statement proclaiming Israel's right to sovereignty over the West Bank and Gaza. He added that Israel—even with Palestinian autonomy—would insist on control of water use, and all land not provably owned by Arabs. Settlement would escalate. "Security" would be ensured by the Israeli Army. To parliament and the press, Begin quoted back the hedges Barak had written into the summit agreements. "Anwar Sadat," he crowed to aides, "doesn't *understand* what he agreed to at Camp David!"

Never had Begin felt so sure of himself. Moshe Dayan, whom he had felt he needed in 1977, became dispensable, all the more so since Begin knew the Americans considered him *in*dispensable to Israeli concessions in Judaea and Samaria. Begin rejected pressure from the old guard to fire the foreign minister. He forbade Landau to raise the "Dayan issue" in the cabinet, told Herut leaders to show equal restraint in public, then told Dayan he had done so. But he froze Dayan out of the Palestinian autonomy talks. For delegation chief, he chose the interior minister, Orthodox-party leader Yosef Burg. When Dayan proposed that Israel unilaterally dismantle the military administration in the West Bank and Gaza as a boost for the autonomy scheme, Begin rejected that option: It went beyond the letter of the Camp David accords.

In early June, when he announced that Gush Emunim could take two hundred acres near Nablus and settle Elon Moreh in earnest,

the Americans protested. Begin replied that West Bank settlement
was not only right, "it is a vital security need, to prevent the murder
of our citizens and children." But a group of Palestinians, with title
to some of the land in the area, rejected both arguments, petitioned
the Israeli Supreme Court, and won. The Court ruled that the settlers were trespassing. Begin ordered Weizman, whom he knew opposed the settlers, to have Chief of Staff Rafael Eitan draft a
counter-argument that the settlement was crucial to Israel's security.
When the Court rejected this as well, saying Gush must leave, Begin
saw no choice but to comply. However, he would not send the army
to escort the determined settlers away, telling Weizman, "In the underground, I avoided bloodshed. We will not raise our hands against
Jews." Instead, he had the prefab settlement dwellings helicoptered
to an adjacent hill.

Begin eagerly implemented the provisions of his treaty with
Egypt: an inaugural voyage by an Israeli ship through the Suez
Canal; the opening of borders; the return of El Arish. But he rebuffed U.S. proposals to widen Palestinian autonomy: "legislative"
rights for the autonomous council; a vote for Jerusalem Arabs in an
eventual West Bank election. The initial U.S. autonomy negotiator,
Robert Strauss, called Begin "Menachem"—generally "tried to jolly
him up," recalls a fellow U.S. negotiator. Begin budged not an inch.
The Americans' second mediator in the talks was soft-spoken attorney Sol Linowitz. Begin respected him as the architect of the Pan-
ama Canal treaty, liked him as a Jew with a record of support for
Israel, but gave him no major concessions either. Recalls one Linowitz aide: "There were times when, in the hotel room before a
round of talks, we really had to pump Sol up to get him to go and
see Begin!"

Dayan, meanwhile, felt powerless to intervene. Even a further
heart scare—in July—did not stay the prime minister's course. Back
at work, Begin radiated what Dayan called "a sense of intellectual
superiority, as though he harbored not the slightest doubt that if he
himself directed every move in our foreign policy, he would do it
more successfully." On October 2 the foreign minister tendered his
resignation. Begin said he was sorry to see Dayan go: Politically, it
would "make things difficult." Yet he made no effort to get Dayan
to stay, and asked only that he let Begin make the resignation announcement. On October 21, Begin did so, adding that he would
become foreign minister himself until a suitable successor was chosen. In November he gave Mount Sinai back to Egypt two months

early. Then, however, he announced plans to move more Jews into Judaea and Samaria—and ordered a survey of land to which Arabs could not prove title, to head off future court challenges.

When a handful of ultra-Orthodox women from Gush Emunim decided unilaterally to "reclaim" a formerly Jewish hospital in the heart of Hebron, however, some aides feared Begin's unrestrained urge to settle the West Bank was becoming dangerously contagious. True, Hebron was the resting place of the Hebrew patriarchs, a town where Jews had lived for two millennia before the massacre of 1929. But it was also a bustling Arab town, the second largest on the West Bank. One of Begin's inner circle implored him to order the Jewish squatters out: Government authority was at stake. Yet Begin replied, "Hebron is *also* Israel. I will not have any place in Israel made *Judenrein!*" He did summon Gush representatives and ask them to cancel the sit-in. He assured them the cabinet would take up their case. But when the women stayed put, he did nothing. In early 1980, Begin told reporters: "The ladies should not have come on their own to that house. They should go home. Buildings are not seized in Israel—not in Hebron, not in Tel Aviv, not in Haifa. It is not nice." He said the unauthorized settlement amounted to "an expression of violence." He called it "impermissible," an affront "to the body politic." He added, however, that he would not force the women to leave. He had *asked* them to leave, and would keep asking them. They stayed, and three days later Begin issued a cabinet statement affirming the right of Jews to live in Hebron.

After awarding the foreign minister's post to Yitzhak Shamir, who had abstained in the Knesset vote on the treaty with Egypt, Begin flew to the United States for the first time since its signing. He arrived there secure in the knowledge that Carter, hamstrung by the seizure of American hostages in Tehran and a Soviet invasion of Afghanistan, was in no position to exert the kind of pressure he had at Camp David. Besides, at Camp David Carter had been in a position to offer Begin something he dearly wanted: Israel's first formal peace with an Arab state. Begin had that now. Carter did press him for autonomy concessions—the May 26 "goal" date Begin had accepted was approaching—but Begin offered none. When Carter suggested allowing Jerusalem Arabs to vote in the Palestinian autonomy elections, the prime minister said that would contradict Camp David, and quoted the relevant passages. At a White House dinner after the talks, he declared, "No pressure was exerted." He said he hoped there would be agreement by May 26. But if not, "the sky is not on our heads. We shall continue negotiating." He told an American interviewer that the latest Egyptian proposals in the autonomy talks amounted to "a Palestinian state all but in name. Israel will never accept it." And when Sadat responded by suspending the autonomy talks, Begin barely blinked. He called the rupture unfortunate, but said that since Sadat had caused it, only Sadat could repair it. To another reporter, he added that Egypt's tactics would not win Israeli concessions. "This is not," he said, "an Arab *souk.*"

When Weizman became the next cabinet dove to rebel, Begin cut him loose with delight. For months, Ezer had been leaking resignation threats, then retreating. To friends, he referred to Begin as "the late prime minister"—an aging *shtetl* Pole who would never have gained power without Weizman's campaign. During Begin's White House talks in April, Weizman had gone on Israel Television and called for early elections. Now he resigned for real. In a letter leaked to the press, he charged that Begin had frittered away "the expectations we nurtured in the election campaign." Israel seemed more divided than ever, he said. Though "the road leading to the strengthening and consolidation of peace is indeed wide and open, it is not being used. Instead of taking determined steps toward a stable and comprehensive peace, we are marching in place."

"Thank you," Begin retorted by letter, "for the important lesson you have given me in patriotism, in true Zionism." He played back remarks from a more pliant Weizman of earlier months—how lucky Israel was to have Begin as prime minister, how gently history would remember the man who signed a peace agreement with Egypt. Then, Begin attacked: "A shocking frivolity has guided you, through a desire to appear in certain foreign countries as the only 'pursuer of peace' in a government composed of peace saboteurs. I assure you, my esteemed Mr. Weizman, that we shall concern ourselves with remedying this injustice you have done to truth, to the people, to the government, and to each one of its members." He accused Weizman of "trying to depose me, both openly—on television while I was in the US on an important mission—as well as by intrigue, which could not have remained a secret." Finally, Begin settled a score that had rankled for two years: "You mention the election campaign for the Ninth Knesset, in which you participated together with the Dahaf advertising agency. Yet for some reason, you did not find it necessary to remind the public that you led the entire campaign with a call to the people to elect *me* as prime minister." With that, he accepted Weizman's resignation. He announced he would take over as interim defense minister.

Begin loved his new job. To some IZL veterans, it seemed that Defense Minister Begin was reliving the role of Irgun commander, writ large. To an inherited Labor aide, Begin's new job seemed to settle a score with history: Ben Gurion, too, had been both prime minister and defense minister. Begin delegated most of his new duties to his military adviser, General Poran, if only because the Defense Ministry was the only one still headquartered in Tel Aviv. "Begin never went into the purely military details," Poran says. But every Thursday—"like a Swiss watch"—he would trade his tie and jacket for an open-necked shirt, make the hour's journey downhill to Tel Aviv, and receive Israel's top brass in the defense minister's office. "Certainly I enjoy myself. What's wrong with that?" he told a reporter from army radio. In the evening he and Poran would ride back to Jerusalem. Begin's remarks were always the same: "What a tremendous breed of guys we have in the military!" When Begin was asked by an interviewer whether—as prime minister *and* defense minister—he might be pushing himself too hard, he replied: "Look at me! Tell me what you see. A broken man? Tired? Shattered? Unable to answer questions?"

With Dayan and Weizman gone, however, Begin's view of an eternally Jewish Judaea and Samaria came under fire from others. "Peace Now" demonstrators turned out in their thousands—forming a human chain from Jerusalem to Haifa, standing vigil outside the prime minister's residence. Begin accused them of "anarchy," and said even if one assumed that "10,000 . . . or even *50,000*" protesters howled abuse, "that would represent two-and-a-half Knesset seats in the next election." He said Peace Now could "demonstrate along the whole road from Jerusalem to Tel Aviv and Haifa and *back* again, and nothing will avail them."

Nor did West Bank violence—Arab and Jewish—deter Begin's drive to settle the territory. Seven settlers were gunned down in Hebron; Palestinian mayors were maimed in bomb attacks. Settlers' cars were stoned near Ramallah; Arab cars were attacked by Jews. Begin's sympathies lay with the settlers. He did condemn the bomb attacks on the Arab mayors as "crimes of the gravest sort," and vowed to punish the attackers. Yet he cautioned against assuming Jews were responsible. When settlers rampaged through Ramallah, vandalizing Arab cars in retaliation for stoning incidents, he was reluctant to arrest the vandals. At least one aide pressed him to do so—especially when it transpired that police had caught, but released, a Jew fleeing the scene with axes and hammers. "This was a genuine pogrom," the aide argued. "The particular Arabs whose cars were stoned might have had nothing to do with attacking Jews!" Begin said that wasn't the point: "Stones can *also* be very dangerous. You can even take out someone's *eye* with a stone. You can kill someone!" The aide countered that he had not meant to endorse violence against the settlers. He was saying only that the Arabs involved should be punished by law, not by the mob: "That is collective punishment! It's what the Germans used to do!" Still, Begin was unconvinced: Stonings, he repeated, could be fatal.

The aide made a final plea: to Begin the lawyer. "Think," he asked him, "of the Arabs whose cars were destroyed. Legally, they have no redress, no one to complain to—unless you want them to petition King Hussein. But he's not their king anymore, and you don't *want* them to complain to Arafat. If you want them to be part of Israel, then *you* are their prime minister. And *you* must help them and listen to them."

Begin promptly ordered the suspect arrested.

Still, his hesitation revealed a lapse in leadership, which burst to the surface in mid-1980 even as a more familiar woe—his own illness—returned. At the end of June, Begin collapsed on the Knesset floor from another heart seizure. It turned out to be a minor one. But it forced him back briefly into the hospital, and redoubled media concern over the accompanying political problem: Begin's genius for articulating the grand issues of peace and war—and the steel that allowed him to stare down the president of the United States and *dare* Washington to pressure the prime minister of Israel—were gifts less suited to the day-to-day business of running a country, tackling ostensibly littler issues. By the summer of 1980 at least one such issue—Israel's economy—howled for resolution.

Begin had never understood, nor much cared about, economic detail. In Herut he had left this to Bader. In the government he left it to the Liberals, except to proclaim his drive to uplift Sephardic neighborhoods; and, after the Liberals' Simcha Ehrlich had been dazzled by the theories of American economist Milton Friedman, to order a reduction in government economic controls. His first finance minister, Ehrlich, lifted foreign-currency regulations, scrapped a host of import duties, lowered taxes—and printed money. Inflation soared. Begin, who had lashed out at Labor a few months before the 1977 election for allowing inflation to float dangerously near the 30 percent mark, was soon faced with a price surge twice that high, and rising. Alarmed, he told Herut officials that the government could no longer get away with blaming the crisis on decades of Labor mismanagement. In 1979 he suddenly ordered a price freeze—ill prepared, ill implemented, widely criticized. Just as suddenly, he lifted it, and inflation leaped higher. He then announced a "courageous" initiative to slash government spending and hike interest rates, but did neither. At the end of the year, he accepted Ehrlich's resignation, and replaced him with Yigal Hurwitz.

The new man started well. He told the country hard times awaited. He pledged to cut government spending, raise interest rates, slow the money presses; and freeze both public-sector hiring and state construction projects. Begin praised the program. But by June 1980, when Hurwitz pressed for an across-the-board slash in government spending, interim Defense Minister Begin balked. He told Hurwitz he would try to help as best he could to bring other ministers along. But he declined to *order* any cuts, adding tellingly to one Israeli interviewer: "I'll reveal a secret: This is [also] how I operated in the underground. I try to bring about consensus." When Hurwitz threatened to resign, Begin implored him to remain—knowing he risked losing not only a second finance minister, but the rest of "Ben Gurion's heirs" with him. For a while, Hurwitz acquiesced. But at the turn of the year, the issue could be finessed no longer. Hurwitz wanted 10 percent shaved from ministry budgets. Begin at first agreed, hoping to keep him aboard. But when other ministers resisted, Begin again declined to force the issue, and Hurwitz, with his Rafi-State colleagues, bolted the coalition.

With yearly inflation topping 130 percent, Begin called early elections, for June. He feared losing them. His rating in the polls sagged. He and Peres ran neck-and-neck—though Likud as a party alliance trailed Labor by nearly 30 percent. Begin named a Herut stalwart, Yoram Aridor, to take over the Finance Ministry and promised to haul inflation down "from three digits to two." He also took some heart—briefly—from grander issues. Pressure for autonomy concessions was waning amid the diplomatic equivalent of battle fatigue in Cairo—and with the election of Ronald Reagan in America. But the economy was what mattered to Israelis, and Begin knew it. He lost weight, gave fewer interviews, seemed distracted at meetings. "He was in quite a deep depression," recalls a friend who saw him frequently. "He was doggedly going through the paces, assuming the party would lose and lacking the psychic energy to do something about it." An aide recalls Begin was "mopy, sulking, pitiful to watch, in those months."

It was Yaakov Meridor, back in private business, who mounted a rescue mission. He contacted a street-tough PR genius from New York, David Garth, and asked him to map out the election campaign. Garth, who had turned down a similar bid from Peres after finding him abrasive, flew to Israel and took an exploratory poll of his own. It showed Labor leading by 26 points. But Begin's individual "favorable rating" as a leader hovered around 50 percent; "unfavorable" at 25 percent. Peres's readings were the reverse. "Look," Garth told Begin, "these guys have nominated somebody—if you had to *pick* a guy to run against you, this is the guy you would pick!" Begin, for the first time in weeks, laughed out loud. Begin struck Garth as a man hurt by the country's rejection: "He could not understand why these people were *against* him." Garth took the job.

Begin rebounded in the spring. The shift started in April, barely two months before election day, with the Histadrut's own national election. Likud ran Begin's favorite Sephardi, cabinet minister David Levy. Labor won, but Likud held its ground. "We can really win the election," the prime minister told aides afterward. In strategy sessions with Garth, it was suddenly Begin who did the reassuring. "Relax, David," he told the American. "If we're short two or three or four seats, we'll still control the thing! We can assemble a coalition."

In the weeks that followed, he erupted in a burst of foreign-policy energy. When Reagan decided to go ahead with an inherited decision to sell radar planes to Saudi Arabia, Begin cried fowl. "If you sell these planes to the Saudis, Israel will be militarily transparent," he complained to Secretary of State Alexander Haig in Jerusalem. When Haig told Begin that Israel's concern was exaggerated, the prime minister decided on brinkmanship. Well north into Lebanon, in the Bekaa Valley hill town of Zahle, Lebanese-Christian militia leader Bashir Gemayel had decided to challenge the Syrian Army to a contest Syria could ill afford to lose. The town lay near the main road from Damascus to Beirut. The militia moved in, began carving out a security road from its own coastal headquarters to Zahle, then, when the Syrians started shelling, cried "genocide." Begin told Haig that if the Americans sold radar planes to the Saudis, data would no doubt be relayed in future to a Syrian Army that was even now threatening to slaughter innocent Christians. Israel could not stand for this, and might have to intervene in Zahle before it was too late. Haig counseled caution. As the administration pressed ahead with plans for the Saudi aircraft sale, Begin did play down *that* issue, saying it was no cause for a "split" with Washington. But at the end of April, he ordered the air force into action near Zahle—downing two Syrian transport helicopters. Damascus responded by moving three batteries of Soviet anti-aircraft missiles into eastern Lebanon. Begin demanded their removal, and hinted that Israel would bomb them otherwise. President Reagan summoned diplomat Philip Habib out of retirement and sent him on an emergency shuttle mission.

Begin exuded confidence. He said war was unlikely: The Syrians could achieve "nothing from war but defeat." Though announcing full support for the U.S. mediation mission, he added, "We do not rely on miracles. We will do what we have to do." The Syrians would not be allowed to treat Bashir Gemayel as the Nazis had treated the Jews, he told Knesset members, aides, and Ambassador Lewis in a succession of briefings. When West European leaders counseled restraint, Begin told them to mind their own business. One of them—Germany's Helmut Schmidt—he came very close to calling a Nazi. "I have never felt better," he told an Israeli interviewer as the crisis mounted. He said his health was good. And "from the mental point of view, from the point of view of morale, I feel much better today than I have in the past four years, because now I am in a fight. That has been my element, all my life."

He told a cheering Likud audience that if Habib couldn't remove the missiles from Lebanon, Israel's air force would do it for him. A day later, flouting Israeli security tradition, he told the Knesset that he had actually *ordered* a bombing strike, but that bad weather had grounded the planes. He declined to say whether, or when, he would call them back into action. As Habib shuttled, Begin hiked, then loosened, then hiked pressure on him. On May 19—six weeks before the election—Begin said he would not attack Syria unless Syria struck first. But he did not rule out attacking the Syrian *missiles* in Lebanon. Grumbled one pro-Labor newspaper, "The prime minister is keeping half a dozen balls of different colored rhetoric up in the air at the same time," with the result that he could hardly miss going to the polls as "either a war hero or a peace hero."

Begin felt the election would be close, and he had never wanted victory so badly. To aides, recalls Naor, Begin said a few seats "might make the difference. . . . We must do anything we can in order to ensure our victory. He said it was not only a question of who would be the next prime minister—but of whether this Land [Judaea, Samaria, and Gaza] will continue to be ours." He eagerly endorsed Finance Minister Aridor's contribution to the cause. Though inflation was now jerking toward the 200 percent mark, Aridor coined the theory that this was a problem of "consumer psychology." Buyers, anticipating higher prices, were rushing to buy. His solution was to slash import duties on a host of luxury goods and appliances: videotape recorders, color TVs, refrigerators. A new phrase entered the language of Israeli politics: "election economics." By mid-May—the statutory start of TV campaigning—Likud had narrowed the opinion-poll gap to ten percentage points. Where Weizman had filed down Begin's rough edges, Garth celebrated them. "We found," he recalls, "that Begin's *personality* was so strong that he seemed to convey a feeling of direction. Even people who *didn't* like Begin felt that there was something to react to." The campaign's motto was: "Vote Likud . . . Now Is the Time to Choose: Forward or Backward."

Begin and Garth made a perfect team. Begin reveled in the American's expertise. "He was fascinated by the technical stuff we were doing," says Garth. "He'd ask questions like: 'What are you basing that poll prediction on?' "—and would listen, rapt, to the reply. But Begin was the senior partner. When Garth is asked how he addressed the candidate, he pauses, then replies: "I called him 'Mr. Prime Minister.' I never had the inclination to call him anything else. And it's very funny: He may be the only client I had, *ever* had, who I addressed in private, in conversation, by his title." In larger strategy sessions, Begin would nod approval of decisions he supported. He would tune out of those he opposed—ensuring their natural death. Typically, he would launch into a string of anecdotes on life in Poland, or the Irgun. "At first, I thought his mind wandered," Garth recalls. "But I discovered it was his way of changing the agenda. Like a fox, his mind wanders! Other people would remark how Begin was always *lecturing*. But in lecturing, he was controlling the turf, the dialogue, the territory of the meeting." He adds: "I can't think of anybody in my twenty-five years in political life who executed power better by not having to use power—and by letting you kind of do your thing, but keeping you always in your place."

Begin, keeping the missile crisis a-simmer, embarked on a speaking campaign more vitriolic than any since the reparations debate of the 1950s—lashing out at Labor's clubby corruption, and setting the tone for Likud youths' heckling disruption of Labor rallies around the country. Labor lost its cool. "We screwed the Arabs and we'll screw you the same way," cried ex-Chief of Staff Mordechai Gur at one group of Sephardic hecklers. Peres accused another group of "Khomeini-ism." Late in May the prime minister ordered the heaviest air-and-artillery barrage in weeks against PLO positions in southern Lebanon. The Reagan administration, still fearing war in eastern Lebanon, protested. But Begin told a campaign rally that the Americans should worry about America. *He* would take care of Israel. By month's end, Garth's polls showed Likud within four percentage points of Labor. In early June, Likud pulled four points ahead.

On June 5, Begin summoned the cabinet to his home. He asked military aide Poran to phone each minister separately and tell none that the others were invited. A few, having never set foot in the prime minister's residence, sensed promotion. Puzzled on arrival, they were stunned when Begin came downstairs to announce: "Our planes are on their way to Baghdad." When one minister interjected, "You mean *Damascus,* Mr. Prime Minister," Begin said he had meant Baghdad. The air force was minutes away from bombing a nuclear reactor near the capital of Iraq.

The mission had taken root at a cabinet meeting months earlier—October 1980—when Begin had raised the possibility of attacking the reactor. Arguing down strong opposition, he had won standby approval to bomb the facility if and when necessary. The final decision would be taken by an "inner committee"—Begin, Shamir, and Chief of Staff Rafael Eitan. Several times since, Begin had been on the brink of ordering the attack, but had reconsidered. Late in 1980, he went so far as to summon Peres to brief him on plans to bomb the reactor. Peres warned him off, saying the international backlash would be crippling. Begin shelved the mission, but for a different reason: He feared it might help Jimmy Carter get reelected. But that the reactor must eventually be bombed, Begin never doubted. He dismissed Iraqi protestations that the facility was "peaceful," and felt Israeli inaction would risk a second holocaust. When his military experts voiced nearly unanimous objection—a reading which, in other circumstances he would unquestioningly accept—he pressed for specifics. Was the mission impossible, or merely dangerously difficult? They admitted it could be done—but said the strike must come sometime between arrival of the reactor machinery and introduction of its nuclear fuel; by late autumn of 1981, says one expert involved. Begin—without warning the cabinet, Peres, or Ronald Reagan—chose June to act. Military aide Poran feels he did so partly in awareness of the approaching election. "Begin was a politician. He knew that operationally, such an attack would have to be mounted within two or three months anyway. So from his point of view, why not do it *before* the election?" But Poran is equally sure that the prime minister did not act "specifically *because* of the election. He was not the sort of man who would have done such a thing—if he thought it was *wrong*—in order to gain power. He had no doubt that the attack was correct." As the planes sped toward their target, Begin's ministers sat in his living room and stared at each other in silence. A phone call broke the tension. It was from Eitan, at command headquarters. Begin listened, hung up, turned to the cabinet, and declared: "Our planes are returning in peace."

He rushed to headquarters to offer congratulations, telling Poran to phone Peres with the news. "Peres was shocked!" recalls the aide. So was President Reagan, all the more so when informed that U.S.-made bombs had been used in the attack. Reagan ordered the impounding of four F-16 jets that had already been paid for by Israel. Peres, meanwhile, charged that Begin had played election politics with the potentially most dangerous operation in Israel's history.

Begin ignored them both. "There will not be another holocaust in the history of the Jewish people," he told reporters. "Never again!" He said that people now denouncing the air strike would someday thank Israel for what it had done. Shouts of "Begin, Begin, King of Israel!" greeted the prime minister at his next campaign rally, in Tel Aviv's blue-collar suburb of Petakh Tikvah. "I am not a king," Begin shouted back, "but just a simple, ordinary man." Raising his arms skyward, he proclaimed: "Let us together, with one heart and one soul, lift our hands to heaven and give thanks to the Almighty for having blessed us with such fine sons as our pilots." Lashing out at America for impounding the F-16s, he charged, "This is the morality of Sodom and Gomorrah! It punishes the righteous for their act of self-defense; but rewards the murderous, dictatorial aggressors!" Then, he turned on Peres. Election politics? "Look around you!" Begin shouted. "Do I need such a ploy? Could I *ever,* if it were not absolutely necessary, send Jewish pilots to a possible death or a fate worse than death, which captivity and torture would be?" The crowd roared: "No!" Labor, said Begin, had ruled the country "by doing favors for their own, dispensing patronage, writing their little notes" to each other beyond the gaze of the people they ruled. When he scribbled a mock note on his palm, the crowd erupted in laughter, shouts, and applause. Then, he motioned for quiet. He said he had heard Peres was scheduled to appear in Petakh Tikvah, and said, "Don't disrupt his meeting. Just put the right slip in the ballot box!"

The homestretch was close, and violent. The Baghdad raid caused only a bleep in the polls; then Likud settled back to its four-point edge. When Peres spoke in Petakh Tikvah, Likud toughs rolled barrels of flaming refuse into the crowd, then vandalized Labor campaign headquarters. Determined to catch Begin at the wire, Peres and Rabin mended fences and pledged common cause in a new government. But at their final rally, a pro-Labor comedian made a fatal miscue—greeting the crowd by remarking how nice it was to see an audience of *real* Israelis, not Menachem Begin's *chakh chakhim*! The slang term—somewhere between "redneck" and "nigger" in tone—referred to the Sephardim. The prime minister heard of the slip the next morning when a reporter dropped by for comment. Begin had no idea what the slang expression meant. When the reporter explained, an aide who was there says, "You could almost *see* Begin working himself into a frenzy." He held his fire until nightfall, when he appeared in Tel Aviv for his own closing rally. "Did you *hear* what they called you?" Begin shouted. Drawing a crumpled scrap of paper from his pocket—squinting as if to get the odiously unfamiliar term just right—he repeated, in mispronounced Hebrew: "They called you *chekh chekhim*!" When he yelled, "Is *that* what you are?" the crowd roared back: "No!" Begin told them to go home now, phone their relatives, and tell them what Labor thought of them—then answer its taunt with their ballots!

He was in high spirits on election day. When Garth delivered his final prediction—a squeaky, fifteen-thousand-vote victory—Begin smiled. "David, you're a very nice boy. But you aren't going to tell me from a *poll* how the people of Israel are going to think?" He voted, and waited. Garth had been on target: Likud emerged with forty-eight seats, to Labor's forty-seven. It was enough, barely, for a new coalition.

Yet Begin proceeded to assemble a cabinet very different from his first, with aims just as different. He began his new term feeling he owed almost no one for the victory, needed almost nobody to help him greet History with a flourish.

With just one exception: General Ariel Sharon.

Chapter Twenty-six

Vision of
Victory

Begin approached Sharon after the election with the awe small boys reserve for big firecrackers. For months the hero of the Sinai had been lobbying to be made defense minister, questioning how an aging lawyer like Begin could presume to do the job himself with a war veteran like Sharon in the wings. Asked for comment, Begin had replied, "I never argue with friends in public. He said whatever he said. We are still friends." When Sharon lobbied harder, Begin quipped: "He'll ring the prime minister's office with tanks!" When Garth suggested during the election campaign that the Sharon appointment might mean extra votes, Begin replied, "I understand what you mean—that politically, it would be advantageous. But I can't do it at this time. It's wrong at this time."

Now was the time right? Begin reserved judgment for weeks after the election. He did feel a debt to Sharon, who, military maps in hand, had whipped campaign crowds into ecstasy with his defiant vow to keep Judaea and Samaria forever. Also, only Sharon, before success made such endorsement easy, had backed the bombing of the Iraqi reactor. "The experts are wrong!" he had told the other ministers. It was an operation that demanded daring, and guts—and Menachem Begin's vision. Begin sensed he might *need* Sharon, too, since arithmetic showed that any defections from Likud risked jeopardizing his coalition's Knesset majority. But above all, Begin entered his second term with a vision to which Sharon seemed an important complement. Having made peace, preserved the textual purity of "autonomy," Begin would now make war. With words if possible—guns if necessary—he would destroy once and for all the one force that might still threaten, or even rule, the West Bank and Gaza: Yasser Arafat's Palestine Liberation Organization. In keeping with the title of the memoir he said he would write after retirement, Begin now hoped to lead his "generation of Holocaust" to final Redemption.

The weekend after the election, Begin contemplated bombing Syria's Bekaa missiles. He retreated under pleas from Washington. But amid a surge in the PLO's intermittent shelling across the Lebanon-Israel border, he ordered air attacks there instead. For five days the jets bombed the area. When the Palestinians resumed shelling—killing three Israelis—Begin ordered the bombing of a PLO headquarters in western Beirut. Dozens of civilians died. The Americans fumed. Reagan extended the embargo on shipping the F-16s.

Begin shrugged this off. Meeting a *Wall Street Journal* reporter after the U.S. announcement, he seemed more indignant than sobered by the reprisal. When the reporter opened by saying he had read *The Revolt,* Begin quipped: "Ah, so you'd been having trouble sleeping at night!" Then, he turned serious: "We didn't attack *Beirut,*" he said. "We wouldn't, because there are civilians. . . . But we had to attack the headquarters of various organizations and points of the so-called PLO. And they placed themselves—probably intentionally—near or within the civilian population." Barely had the interview ended, however, than the "so-called PLO" unleashed its most sustained barrage of shellfire and ground-to-ground missiles in months—for the first time sending thousands, mostly Moroccan Jews, fleeing Israel's northern settlements. Begin beat a tactical retreat. When Philip Habib rushed to mediate, Israel gave him leeway to mediate in the Syrian-missile dispute—and secure a cease-fire with the PLO. So relieved was the prime minister at Habib's success on the second issue that he kept his promise on the first.

But he had deferred, not abandoned, his vision. Assembling his new coalition through late July, Begin was deluged with pleas to deny Sharon the ministry he craved. Ben Elissar, Naor, General Poran, all lobbied against Sharon. Yadin, who had retired with heart problems before the 1981 vote, called on the prime minister with a similar message. (Dayan, who won two seats for a new party advocating that Israel unilaterally implement West Bank autonomy, told colleagues much the same about Sharon—but lacked the clout to push the line with his old boss.) Still, when Begin presented his cabinet to parliament in early August, Sharon was defense minister. Shamir retained the Foreign Ministry. Rounding out the new cabinet were a returning Yaakov Meridor, six Liberals, and a number of lesser Herut lights. The government program stated: "At the end of the interim period determined in the Camp David agreements, Israel will raise its claim, *and act to realize its right,* to sovereignty over Judaea, Samaria and the Gaza District."

Begin flew to Washington in September for his first meeting with Ronald Reagan. The F-16 embargo had been lifted a few days earlier. Begin opened the talks by playing to the new president's unrefined anti-Communism, proposing "strategic cooperation" against Soviet influence, in the Mideast. Reagan agreed, and empowered Sharon and U.S. Secretary of Defense Caspar Weinberger to work out the details. Then Begin motioned to his chief of military intelligence, who unfurled maps of the Mideast, and tried to get Reagan to retreat on giving the Saudis radar planes. He lost the point, but did win from Reagan an assurance that Israel would always take regional priority in U.S. arms sales. He returned home satisfied that, finally, he had a firm ally in the White House—a man, he told Ambassador Lewis, "who looks on Israel as an ally, and doesn't mind saying so." To an Israeli reporter, Begin played down the Saudi aircraft question, stressing the accord on strategic cooperation. "President Reagan, in his first talk with me, already made a decision without giving a thought to the cries that arose in the Arab and radical states." Yet the one serious issue of discord—of which Begin said nothing—was Lebanon. In a last-minute meeting with Secretary of State Haig, Begin had been warned of "grave effects in the United States" if he went too far in his battle with the PLO gunners. Asked about the Haig meeting back home, Begin replied: "Permit me not to tell you what he requested. I was unable to comply with his request, and I told him so."

Begin—though this he kept to himself—sensed an even closer bond with Haig than with Reagan. Begin had met Alexander Haig nearly a decade earlier when the two men were paired at a dinner during President Nixon's visit to the Mideast. Haig, then Nixon's White House chief of staff, had delighted opposition leader Begin by volunteering outrage at American pressure, after the 1956 war, for Britain and France to retreat from their assault on Egypt. After the

Nixon visit, Begin autographed a copy of his *Revolt* and sent it to Haig in Washington.

Yet Begin's rapprochement with Washington lasted only weeks. On October 6, Anwar Sadat was assassinated at a military parade in Cairo. Begin attended the funeral, praised the slain Egyptian as a statesman and a "friend." Condoling Sadat's successor, Hosni Mubarak, he grasped the Egyptian's hand in his, and proclaimed "peace between us forever." Yet it would be, more than ever, a separate peace. When Haig, also in Cairo, pressed Begin for a settlement freeze, he replied, "No. I never promised Carter or anyone else that there would be no new settlements." He added that Israel was considering military action in Lebanon—although care would be taken not to bring the Syrians into the fray. When the Saudis reacted to the Sadat assassination by launching a new Mideast "peace plan"— earning backing from Western Europe, and from Reagan—Begin rejected it out of hand. He would not go beyond the letter of Camp David. "Israel is but a small country," he told the Knesset. "But it is, nevertheless, 50 percent of any agreement in the Middle East."

He proceeded discreetly to press friendly U.S. congressmen to vote down the Saudi aircraft sale. He was careful to avoid an overt challenge to the president, but that hardly mattered. By the time Reagan had squeaked the sale through Congress, says Haig, Begin had "lost the sympathy of powerful figures in the Administration and sorely tried the tolerance and understanding of the President." Said Reagan, publicly: "It is not the business of any other nation to make American foreign policy."

At home, Begin established a two-man government: He was its brains; Sharon would be its brawn; the PLO in Lebanon would be its target. Begin seemed both to admire and fear Sharon. In 1977 he had come close to being cowed into making him super-minister of police. When Agriculture Minister Sharon had allegedly leaked cabinet debates, openly denounced or threatened other ministers around the cabinet table, even flashed an obscene hand gesture at Labor foes in the Knesset, Begin had shied from bringing him to order. After the Knesset incident, he excused the general by remarking, "He is someone whose heroism will be remembered by future generations, while his critics will be forgotten!" On the rare occasion when Begin issued a reprimand, its tone was that of a father to an adored, if sometimes wayward, son. Sharon would offer a hedged apology, and the matter would be put to rest. Now the supremely confident defense minister was suddenly polite to his cabinet colleagues, indifferent to Labor foes, and deferential to the prime minister. A Begin aide calls the transformation "incredible. Sharon's approach to Begin was: 'You are the greatest! I adore you! I'll do anything you tell me.' " Besides, if Begin still feared Sharon, so, he figured, did others: more dovish cabinet ministers, Yasser Arafat, the Americans. To wage war in Lebanon would demand no less fearsome an ally. And, Begin told aides, he could always rein in Sharon if necessary. He, as prime minister, was the horseman—with a prize stallion, a Fighting Jew, in harness.

Sharon froze out competitors in the early months of the second-term government, and Begin saw no reason to intervene. When General Poran resigned as military aide, Begin appointed Sharon's preferred candidate in his place, a junior officer who lacked the clout and expertise to be the defense-policy actor Poran had been. Begin also obliged Sharon by easing out Deputy Defense Minister Mordechai Zippori, hawkish on Sharon but dovish on Lebanon. Inside the defense establishment, Sharon halted the intelligence division's practice of reporting directly to the prime minister. Begin made no move to protest. The effect, recalls Ambassador Lewis, "was to leave Begin intellectually dependent on Sharon, alone, for military information and advice." In the event, Sharon was giving Begin the advice he *wanted* to hear: Arafat's bases in southern Lebanon were vulnerable. Israel should hit not only them. The army could, must, go farther: to Beirut. There it could finish off the PLO leadership, and force the replacement of Lebanon's fragile post–civil war government with a man Israel could trust—Christian warlord Bashir Gemayel. "It seemed an outrageous idea, on the surface," remarks an official close to Begin. "But it was indeed the sort of thing which Begin, subliminally, was tempted to undertake." He told Sharon to keep refining the war plan, although deciding not to present it for full cabinet approval for the time being.

In late November Begin returned home from the office one evening, read the day's diplomatic dispatches, and went to wash up before dinner. In the bathroom, he slipped on the tile floor and broke his hip. He was rushed to the hospital. The press questioned how long Begin—after sixty-seven years and a series of heart scares—could go on. Begin, gritting his teeth in pain, dictated a riposte: a blow-by-blow account of the hip injury, the anesthesia, the pills, culminating in an assurance that he was feeling better, and a vow to carry on. Then he summoned the minister of justice and set out to prove the point. He told the minister to draft a law that in effect annexed Syria's Golan Heights. After returning home to convalesce in December, Begin convened the cabinet there and, having given most ministers no more warning than on the reactor bombing, declared: "Gentlemen: I am very pleased to propose to you the Law of the Golan Heights. Mr. Justice Minister, please read the text ..." Some ministers had misgivings—the move was certain to provoke an outcry at the White House—but they acquiesced.

When Begin announced the decision on December 14, Reagan froze "strategic cooperation," along with plans to sell Israel some $200 million in military hardware. Begin summoned Ambassador Lewis and, from his wheelchair, told him Israel was sick and tired of America's punitive "suspensions." Is Israel, he asked, "a vassal state? A banana republic? Are we 14-year-old boys who, if they don't behave, have their knuckles smacked?" Though careful not to attack Reagan by name, he accused the administration of bad faith, bullying—even anti-Semitism. Of course, Israel hadn't *warned* Washington about the Golan law! Begin said this would only have ensured an attempt to talk him out of the move, which he would have ignored. "I will tell you of whom this government is composed," he lectured Lewis. "It is composed of men who fought, risked their lives, and suffered. You cannot and *will not* frighten us with 'punishments' and 'threats.' Threats will fall on deaf ears. . . . You have no right to 'punish' Israel, and I protest the use of this term." As for the memorandum on strategic cooperation, "the people of Israel have lived for 3700 years without a memorandum of understanding with America, and will continue to live without it for another 3700 years!" Rescind the Golan announcement? Never, said Begin. "The word 'rescind' is a concept from the time of the Inquisition. Our forefathers went to the stake rather than rescind their faith!"

Begin summoned the cabinet again. He told the ministers what he had told Lewis, and directed Arye Naor to read the speech to the press. Then he motioned for Sharon to unfurl his maps and present his Lebanon war plan: a push by ground and air some forty-five miles north of the border, to the edge of the Lebanese capital, Beirut. The ministers were stunned; a few were horrified. Begin called first on Yosef Burg, who had a record of caution on Lebanon and suspicion of Arik Sharon. Burg asked whether it made sense to seek instant cabinet approval for a full-scale invasion of a neighboring state. "Yes," answered the prime minister. "It may be necessary to put the plan into action at any moment." Then the Liberals' minister without portfolio, Yitzhak Modai, asked for the floor. Never especially dovish in the past, this time he felt Sharon had gone too far. As Begin watched in disapproval, Modai's boss, Liberal leader Simcha Ehrlich, added: "Wait until you hear what *I* have to say!" Begin cut off discussion. "I see," he said, "how feelings are running. And I understand that it is pointless to continue." He dictated a postscript to Naor's declaration for the press: "As regards Lebanon, I have asked the Secretary of State be informed that we will not attack. But if we are attacked, we will counterattack."

He mentioned the war plan again in the cabinet in the weeks ahead, but the ministers were still skeptical. Also doubtful, in rare consensus, were the civilian and military intelligence services. But Begin and Sharon were determined. "There are people around this table who know from their own experience that hitting Beirut would solve the problem of Palestinian terrorism!" Begin told one cabinet session. In January Sharon secretly visited Christian-held East Beirut and met with Bashir Gemayel, the man he would make president. In February Begin sent word to Haig that if the PLO caused further trouble, Israel would push all the way to "the southern suburbs of Beirut." When Haig warned him off, he and Sharon started work on a fall-back contingency: a limited incursion into Lebanon along the lines of the 1978 war.

Yet another issue—related, in Begin's mind—briefly intervened: the future of the peace signed at Camp David. Israel's final pullout from Sinai was due in April. The border settlers were vowing to stay put. Begin was determined they must leave. But he was equally intent—with Sadat dead, the Saudis pushing a new peace plan, and the outside world welcoming it—that Israel get assurances that neither Mubarak nor Reagan was about to abandon Camp David. He wrote Reagan. Buried in an otherwise unexceptional appeal for Israeli-American friendship was an implicit warning: "The question that is being asked today in Israel is how Egypt will act after April 1982 if it is already—three months before completion of the withdrawal—demanding that the Palestinians be given the right of self-determination."

As April neared, the Sinai settlers' defiance grew. A few of them, American-born disciples of Rabbi Meir Kahane, threatened suicide.

Begin received their parents, said he shared their anguish, but made it clear the settlements would have to go. He barred Kahane from visiting them. But to Washington he sent a series of protests over Egyptian behavior: Mubarak was making demands that violated Camp David and had failed to stop small-arms smuggling from the Sinai. In the first week of April, Begin drafted a cabinet decision threatening to "consider postponing our final withdrawal from Sinai" if these alleged wrongs were not righted. He had Dan Meridor,* who had replaced Naor as cabinet secretary, translate the statement into English, and phoned Ambassador Lewis to read it to him. Reagan dispatched a team of State Department officials to Jerusalem, where they were received by Begin and Sharon. Sharon did most of the talking, rattling off some two dozen alleged Egyptian "violations" and saying Israel would be crazy to hand back the Sinai on schedule. Begin, playing good cop, stressed that Israel wanted to honor its commitment but needed assurances to do so. He then asked the president to send Haig. The Americans, pleading the Falklands crisis, dispatched two senior aides instead. But the Egyptians sent a delegation of their own, led by presidential adviser Osama el-Baz. "They all," relates Dan Meridor, "came running to Jerusalem."

Begin repeated his demand for assurances. On April 16, Mubarak sent a letter reaffirming his commitment to peace. Begin told the Americans this wasn't good enough. Four days later Mubarak sent a second note, pledging to stop the arms smuggling and otherwise observe the treaty. Reagan, whose patience with Begin had long since frayed, sent a letter of his own. In effect if not by intention, it beat Begin at his own verbal formulas. It did affirm Washington's commitment to Camp David, and to preserving Israel's "qualitative technological edge" in the Mideast arms race. But the letter offered no promises on *quantity:* a loophole through which arms sales to the Egyptians and Saudis could be threaded. It also failed to give Begin an explicit pledge not to talk to the PLO; or promise that America would not seek to extend Camp David by supporting other peace plans if they seemed workable. Begin stood down. He said the Reagan letter had tendered "important American commitments, in the political realm and in that of security." It was "one of the most im-

---

*No relation to Yaakov Meridor. Dan Meridor's father—Eliahu Meridor—was, however, a veteran Herut member who served in the Knesset from 1959 until the late 1960s.

portant letters, may I say, which was ever written by an American president to a prime minister of our country." He sent Sharon—armed with a multimillion-dollar golden handshake from the government—to flush out the last settlers.

But Begin felt little joy as his sixty-ninth birthday neared. He sensed he was racing against time—against Washington, and Israel's Labor Establishment—to secure his vision of Redemption. Pain gnawed at him from the old hip fracture. "Pain," recalls Ambassador Lewis, "was constantly etched on his face." Craving the drugs his doctors prescribed, Begin feared their dulling of the mind. More often than not, he chose pain over pills. Worse, Aliza was ill, and getting more so. Sometimes barely able to breathe, she was in and out of the hospital. To friends, she confided a dream: Menachem would make good on his old promise to retire at seventy—barely a year away. They would move back down to the cramped apartment at Rosenbaum Street near the sea. She began having the Tel Aviv home remodeled.

Begin *did* want to retire, to write his epic of "Holocaust and Redemption." But he had work to do first, battles to fight, scores to even. In May, he glared at Shimon Peres from the Knesset podium and complained that Labor *still* did not accept him, still would not "acknowledge that we brought Israel peace . . ." Saying he thanked God that Peres was not in power—"a vital danger to the State of Israel is being prevented"—Begin won parliamentary approval for a proclamation that Israel would never again evacuate settlements for peace. He knew, however, that resolutions could be changed. If his legacy were to last, it would have to be secured on the ground. One solution was to settle the heartland of the West Bank—Samaria. Labor had placed one settlement there; Begin had founded thirty-eight, and would add more. Yet there remained other ground to secure: the PLO's home away from home, Lebanon.

Throughout the spring he lay the diplomatic foundations for war. Although Habib's cease-fire was holding, Begin argued that the PLO was violating the truce by stockpiling new Soviet-manufactured artillery near the border. He also argued that attacks on Jews or their property in Europe constituted a PLO violation, punishable in Lebanon. When an Israeli soldier was killed inside Christian militia territory, he rejected the U.S. contention that Israeli troops did not belong outside Israel in the first place. "Can anyone imagine that we will permit the shedding of Jewish blood?" he countered. "That is simply unreasonable." On April 21 he ordered the army to shell "carefully selected terrorist bases" in south Lebanon. For nine months, he said, he had been guilty of "overrestraint." If the PLO responded to the gunfire, Israel would "hit them much harder." So loud became the rumors of war in Israel, and alarm in Washington, that Begin found himself assuring one interviewer that the cabinet "has not adopted any resolution for an invasion of Lebanon, or on starting a war." When asked whether Sharon might *push* Israel into war, Begin dismissed this as absurd. Both he and the defense minister were men of peace.

Few seemed to believe the denials. Begin's former aide, General Poran, heard whispers that Sharon was planning a push to Beirut, and went to the prime minister to plead for caution. "Don't worry," said Begin. "It won't happen." The escalation, however, continued. In May Israeli sappers defused two bombs, near a school and a commuter bus. Begin, charging a sin of intention, ordered air strikes into south Lebanon. This time, PLO gunners answered back. The shelling, whether by luck or design, claimed no casualties. Yet Begin summoned the cabinet, and gave Sharon the floor. Sharon unfurled his maps, this time seeking approval for a "police action," an air-and-ground incursion into southern Lebanon. Asked how long it would last, Sharon said the troops would be home in twenty-four hours. When former Defense Deputy Zippori asked why Israel needed to use the air force for a police action, Begin cut him off with the suggestion that if Zippori weren't so jealous of Sharon he wouldn't protest. When the deputy head of Israeli military intelligence cautioned against invading while the UN General Assembly was in session, Begin snapped: "*You* are telling *me* when the assembly is in session?" But the intelligence man's main objection was that even a "police action" might draw Syria's forty-thousand-strong army in Lebanon into the fray. "Never," Begin chided him, "predict anything in an absolute way." He brought the meeting to an inconclusive end. Then, six days later, he and Sharon called in the Labor leadership to brief them on the planned incursion.

The Americans summoned Begin to Washington, feeling an anguished urgency to dissuade Israel from war. Sharon had visited in late May, and presented both the Beirut plan and the fall-back "police action" to U.S. officials. He was told that either risked "devastating" political fallout. The prime minister agreed to come in June. But on the third of the month, Arab gunmen in London ambushed and critically wounded the Israeli ambassador. Begin ordered the chief of staff to draw up plans for an air strike against Beirut. The next morning he called the cabinet together and proclaimed: "We will not stand for their attacking an Israeli ambassador! An attack on an ambassador is tantamount to an attack on the State of Israel, and we will respond to it." He gave the floor to Eitan, who outlined the planned bombing raid but suggested delaying it for a day so that PLO leaders might be caught off guard. Begin refused: Israel must strike back now. Dismissing the ministers, he told them to gather at his residence the following evening. By then, he said, "we'll see what happens." The next afternoon, the PLO responded to the Beirut attack with a barrage of shell and rocket fire on northern Israel. By the time Begin reconvened the cabinet, after nightfall, he was determined to take Israel to war.

He had Sharon outline an incursion forty kilometers—twenty-five miles—north of the border. The defense minister assured the cabinet the whole thing would be over in barely a day. Begin hinted at longer—but made it clear that American pressures alone would ensure the troops would soon be home. In 1978 the Israelis had stayed in south Lebanon for three weeks. "This time," he said, "I'm not sure we'll have that long." Both men hoped the Lebanese Christian militiamen would promptly make Israel's war their own. "Who knows?" mused Sharon. "Maybe out of this operation— although not as a part of the goals of the war—the Lebanese will take part, and Lebanon may be changed, and we might even get the Syrians out and have a peace treaty with Lebanon!" Zippori objected that the Syrians, unlike in 1978, might join the battle. Begin interrupted him. "May I have your attention? I have said that we will *not* attack the Syrians!" When Zippori said that this didn't mean the Syrians wouldn't attack *him;* Begin replied that if they did, they would be asking for trouble. When Zippori cautioned the prime minister against believing that he could "wipe out the PLO" on the battlefield, Begin said he had "never suggested that." He called for a vote on the invasion plan. He won it, unanimously.

Having done so, he was poised to unleash the most powerful military machine Israel had ever known. As in his revolt against the Mandate, Begin would wage a political war, with statements to the Knesset and letters to Washington taking the place of IZL wall posters. As his operational partner he had harnessed not just an Eitan Livni, a Paglin, but General Ariel Sharon—the most fearsome Fighting Jew, Begin exulted to aides, since the Maccabees. Had only the Palestinians and Syrians been British; had Lebanon been Jaffa; and most important, had Arik Sharon been Eitan Livni, it might even have worked.

But the world had changed since 1940s, while Menachem Begin, it soon became clear, had changed much less.

Chapter Twenty-seven

Fighting
Jew

Begin awoke at dawn on the day of the war. Ambassador Lewis had driven up from Tel Aviv to tell him that Washington, through intermediaries, had won a pledge from Arafat to hold his fire. Sending Lewis off with the retort that America "must never equate *us* and the PLO," Begin huffed, "They had the *nerve* to tell me they had turned to the Saudis, and the Saudis to the Syrians, and the Syrians to the PLO, and the PLO had agreed to a cease-fire!" He wrote Reagan that Israel was going to war—in "self-defense," like Mrs. Thatcher in the Falklands—and would halt about twenty-five miles north of the border. Then he reconvened the cabinet and pushed through Sharon's final battle plan—failing to notice, since he remained the Irgun commander who left military detail to his Fighting Jews, that it would take the central invasion column well beyond twenty-five miles, to the main road between Beirut and Damascus. "A tactic worthy of Hannibal!" Begin exclaimed as Sharon rolled up his battle maps. He drafted a cabinet statement warning Syria's troops in Lebanon to stay silent: If they did, Israel would leave them alone.

When the troops, tanks, helicopters, and warplanes roared into Lebanon—and the Palestinians, as in 1978, fell back—Begin helicoptered north to invasion-command headquarters. He boasted to the men in uniform of how he had refused Ambassador Lewis's eleventh-hour plea for peace. Before returning to Jerusalem the next morning, he told Chief of Staff Eitan that the army would have thirty-six hours to advance and hold its ground. He would take care of any pressure to halt until then.

That afternoon, he headed north again—this time into Lebanon, with Sharon, to celebrate the ouster of PLO gunners from the twelfth-century crusader castle at Beaufort, perched high above the Litani River. Begin turned over the position to the Christian militia and heaped praise on the Israeli unit that had captured it, he assumed, without a single casualty. Six Israelis had in fact died, but Sharon didn't bother to ask before the ceremony; nor did Begin. After the handover, the prime minister flew back to Jerusalem, to stall mounting U.S. pressure. Reagan had sent Philip Habib back into action, but Begin kept him waiting into the evening. When he finally received Habib, Begin told him to carry a message to Syrian President Hafez al-Assad in Damascus: If he let Israel secure its twenty-five mile "security" line in Lebanon, no Syrian soldier would be harmed.

Sharon, however, was running the war. Begin, as in IZL days, limited his operational involvement to pressing the defense minister to avoid casualties. Begin did at one point veto Sharon's urge to push toward the east Lebanese town of Shtaura—Syria's stronghold on the Beirut-Damascus highway. He said this would risk unacceptably high Israeli losses. But by the time Begin arrived to address the Knesset June 8—to go public with his call for Syrian restraint and pledge to halt Israel's advance at the forty-kilometer line—Sharon's jets had bombed two Syrian radar posts inside Lebanon. Ground forces had advanced farther than forty kilometers, and opened fire on the Syrian-held hill town of Jezzin. To the northwest, beyond the declared twenty-five-mile line, a second Israeli unit engaged the Syrians near the town of Ein Zehalta. The next morning—day four of the invasion—Sharon urged field units on toward Beirut. He ordered preparations for a possible air strike on the Syrian missiles in the Bekaa Valley. Some seventy kilometers north of the border, on the coast road to Beirut, the army also was readying an attack on the PLO-held town of Damur.

Sharon helicoptered to Jerusalem—to join Begin and a cabinet that had not discussed, much less okayed, any of this. At least two ministers, Zippori and Orthodox leader Burg, were waiting with claws bared. They had only to read the battle communiqués to see that the army was pushing well beyond the forty-kilometer line, and had begun engaging the Syrians. Now Sharon wanted to challenge Syria head on, by hitting its missile batteries! Sharon ridiculed Zippori, countered Burg with the argument that his troops were under Syrian fire. They needed air cover; and air cover dictated an attack on the missiles. Then, Begin intervened. He asked—as he had asked Livni and Paglin so many times before—if there would be casualties in the attack on the Syrian missiles. Told that there could be no guarantees, but that casualties would almost surely be minimal, he directed Sharon to bomb them, which, after excusing himself to phone headquarters, Sharon did. The jets screamed north, knocked out the missiles, downed twenty-nine Syrian jets that had scrambled in reply, and suffered no casualties.

When Reagan responded with a call for a cease-fire, Begin summoned the cabinet and read out his proposed reply. He would agree to the truce, but append what amounted to terms of surrender for Arafat—and the Syrians. The PLO must stay at least forty kilometers north of the border. Syria would have to withdraw to prewar positions, and move no new troops or missiles into Lebanon. When Haig came on the phone in midsession, Begin read out Israel's terms, and suggested he hasten to Jerusalem to tie up the details. After hanging up, Begin told the cabinet, "It will probably take a day for him to get here."

But Reagan refused to send Haig. Instead, he sent Ambassador Lewis to tell Begin that Israel would first have to cease fire and withdraw its invasion force to the ostensible forty-kilometer security line. Reagan added that the United States would undertake no mediation unless the Syrians approved. Sharon—reporting intermittently to a cabinet that was now in virtually continuous session—announced that his troops would secure the Beirut-Damascus highway within eighteen hours. He said they wouldn't take Beirut, but might shell it. Begin got in touch with the Americans to say he would order a cease-fire at noon the next day. He told Chief of Staff Eitan he meant it—refusing even an "exemption" for a unit still in fierce combat with the Syrians.

But noon came and went, and an Israeli unit on the coast road pushed toward Beirut. When the Americans—Habib and his deputy, Morris Draper—protested, Begin told them he had never agreed to a "cease-fire in place. . . . There will be no turning of the other cheek. If someone fires on us from a hill in front of us, it is our right to take that position." Sharon helicoptered to the outskirts of Beirut, met Bashir Gemayel, and arranged for a linkup with his Phalangist militia near Baabda, the hilltop southeast of the city where the Lebanese presidential palace sits. Two days later a forward unit of the Israeli Army reached the site and drove on into Christian East Beirut.

Begin heard the news on Israel Radio, and denied it, having been told nothing. The next radio bulletin carried Begin's denial—and a live broadcast with Israeli soldiers in East Beirut. Begin did not hear it. He was meeting Habib, to whom he repeated his denial. Habib bellowed back: "Your tanks are already in Baabda! Our ambassador in Beirut has already reported the presence of Israeli tanks next to the presidential palace!" As if on cue, an aide told Begin that Defense Minister Sharon was on the phone. Excusing himself, Begin took the call and recapped the scene with Habib. Sharon replied: "So, we'll move the tanks."

Begin was more embarrassed than angered by Sharon's performance. He remained the IZL commander who had responded to a similar excess by Paglin's army—a raid on a British armory—with a slap on the wrist and the remark "In the old Austrian Empire there used to be a special decoration for acts of heroism performed by soldiers in breach of formal military discipline." He told Sharon the Israelis could stay where they were, but ordered him to go no farther. And he told the cabinet the war was almost over: It remained only for Gemayel's militia to move into the Muslim western half of Beirut and finish off the PLO. On June 15, two days after the Israeli move into East Beirut, Begin drafted a cabinet statement: "IDF forces will not enter West Beirut. . . . This job will be done by other forces." Then he dispatched a message—in Irgun wall-poster prose—to Bashir Gemayel: "Arise, and lead your warriors out to liberate your occupied capital!"

But Begin had misjudged Gemayel, and misunderstood Beirut. This "occupied capital" was home to hundreds of thousands of Lebanese civilians, not to mention foreign diplomats and reporters. Gemayel's "warriors," moreover, had spent much of Lebanon's civil war engaged in smuggling, protection rackets, looting, and indiscriminate murder. He misjudged his enemies too. The PLO and the Syrians—the Phalangists' equals in killing and corruption—were not inclined to let Gemayel arise and liberate anything. Sharon, who knew better, ordered air and artillery attacks on West Beirut.

Begin flew to Washington, for the summit that had been due before the war, unaware of Sharon's new offensive. Landing in New York, he was told that if the bombardment of West Beirut didn't stop, there would *be* no summit. He phoned Sharon and told him to cease fire until his return. Yet Sharon replied that this would risk Israeli casualties, and kept firing. By the time Begin reached Washington, the Americans were waiting with a fresh ultimatum. Begin phoned Israel again. This time he got Deputy Prime Minister Simcha Ehrlich, and told him to order Sharon to desist. But Sharon didn't, and closed in on the Beirut-Damascus highway, the Syrians' escape route from Beirut.

Begin arrived at the White House on June 21 and tried to portray the thrashing that Sharon had delivered to Syria's Soviet-supplied missiles as proof that "strategic cooperation" worked. "The combination of American planes and Israeli pilots is an excellent commercial symbol," he cracked. Far from amused, Reagan ignored the remark and, reading from file cards, ticked off a series of U.S. protests to Israel's broken promises in Lebanon. Begin was polite in rejecting Reagan's objections—but told Defense Secretary Weinberger to "be quiet" when he reasserted them in much stronger terms—and returned home determined to get on with the war. He still felt there was more that united than divided him and an American president who saw the world in terms of good and evil, and who equated evil with the Communist world.

On arrival in Israel, Begin declared that the summit had been "very important, very warm, friendly." The president, he added, "asked me to address him by his first name." The prime minister, recalls Ambassador Lewis, seemed convinced that it was only men like Weinberger who were souring the president on the war. "He didn't *want* President Reagan to believe bad things about him; because he admired Reagan, and believed they were basically on the same wavelength. He believed Israel was doing America's job in the Middle East."

Sharon continued to bombard Beirut after Begin's return, and Begin made no move to stop him. But on June 25—when Habib was jolted awake by the blast of Israeli shellfire in Beirut, and the Israelis were alerted that their one sympathetic U.S. negotiating partner, Haig, was about to be replaced—Begin finally ordered Sharon to halt. He informed Washington that Israel would cease fire, and delay any ground advance into Beirut for at least forty-eight hours—only to be told by Haig, in a parting message, to stop fighting once and for all or risk a breach with Reagan.

Begin's cabinet was in disarray. A narrow majority still backed the war. But the rest of the ministers were in rebellion. They objected to each new bombing, each advance on the ground, as a mockery of the war's initial aim and a dangerous step toward a bloodbath, a break with the Americans, or both. Begin either kept silent or defended Sharon—and repeatedly implied that Zippori, one of the strongest critics of the defense minister, was simply acting out his resentment at not being made defense minister in Sharon's stead. Publicly Begin had rebutted criticism of Sharon, calling him "my friend, the minister of defense." He said the war was going well, and charged that American reporters under bombardment in Beirut were slanting their dispatches to embarrass Israel.

Sharon did not cease fire. He tightened his noose on West Beirut—cutting off water and electricity. Begin acquiesced: He hoped this would prod the Americans to negotiate a PLO and Syrian surrender. He assured Habib of support in this endeavor—even if it meant allowing the PLO to save face, by leaving Beirut with their side arms. The prime minister told a sympathetic U.S. congressman on July 1 that this negotiated victory seemed within reach. The next evening, Begin felt it was closer: Lewis relayed news of a tentative agreement on the evacuation of Arafat and the PLO by ship; it remained only to find states to receive them. The PLO would retain a "political office" in Beirut and a token force of about six hundred men in the northern Lebanese city of Tripoli. After the PLO evacuation, the Israelis and Syrians would each begin a phased pullout from Lebanon. An international peacekeeping force—American and, possibly, French—would oversee the arrangement.

But Sharon wanted a more clear-cut victory. He was determined to force the PLO to surrender, not escape. And this he could do only by launching a full-scale ground assault on West Beirut—a strike so audacious that it could be risked only with Menachem Begin's prior approval. "He must back it," Sharon told his staff. As the Americans continued their bid to negotiate an end to the impasse, Sharon kept the city under siege and shellfire. Then, in mid-July he went to the cabinet with his plan of attack. The United States was fast running out of patience: The president sent a letter hinting that in order to contain the regional crisis Begin's war had provoked, Washington might even abandon its Kissinger-era promise not to negotiate with Arafat. In the cabinet just short of half the ministers now objected to Sharon's proposed ground strike, including two more Herut men, David Levy and Finance Minister Aridor. But Begin was not among them. He mustered a majority for turning over the final decision to a cabinet committee, as in the Iraqi-reactor bombing.

As opposition to Sharon's plan mounted, Begin stood his ground. Yosef Burg leaked news of the planned assault to the leader of Agudat Israel, a small religious faction that did not sit in the cabinet but whose support in the Knesset was important to Begin's majority. The Aguda leader phoned Begin to voice his opposition to Sharon's advance, but Begin did not retreat. When an army field officer, Colonel Eli Geva, resigned rather than participate in an invasion of West Beirut, Sharon sent him to see the prime minister. Begin asked the officer how many Israeli casualties were likely in an advance on the city. When Geva replied, "Dozens, for sure," Begin countered that Chief of Staff Eitan had predicted far fewer. Did the officer dispute his chief of staff? "I do," answered Colonel Geva, adding that many women and children would certainly die when Israel attacked. Begin cut him short. "Did you receive an order to kill children?" the prime minister demanded. When Geva replied that he had not, Begin remarked, "What, then, are you complaining about?"

On August 1—with the Americans still seeking states that would accept the PLO after evacuation from Beirut—Sharon ordered his heaviest bombardment since the start of the war. Israeli jets swooped down nearly 130 times in a space of ten hours, pounding a capital the Lebanese once called the Paris of the Middle East. In Washington the president—like millions of Americans—watched the carnage on TV. The next day, he received a message from Menachem Begin: "May I tell you, dear Mr. President, how I feel these days when I turn to the creator of my soul in deep gratitude? I feel as a Prime Minister empowered to instruct a valiant army facing 'Berlin' where, amongst innocent civilians, Hitler and his henchmen hide in a bunker deep beneath the surface. My generation, dear Ron, swore on the altar of God that whoever proclaims his intent to destroy the Jewish State or the Jewish People, or both, seals his fate, so that what happened from Berlin . . . will never happen again."

Reagan did not answer. When American newspapers splashed a photograph of a Lebanese infant injured by Israeli bombardment, the president had the picture placed on his desk. Begin's riposte was to place on *his* desk a photograph of a Jewish child being marched from the Warsaw ghetto to the Nazi death camps. In Israeli newspapers—as on the walls of Palestine decades earlier—Begin delivered an analysis of the two-month-old war. It was, he said, Israel's first "war of choice." And it was about to end—in victory. "There is no other country around us that is capable of attacking us. We have destroyed the best tanks and planes the Syrians had." No Arab had dared intervene, including the once-truculent Egyptians. "The treaty stood the test of the fighting in Lebanon." When the war was over, promised Begin, Israel would enter "an historic period of peace."

On August 4, Sharon resumed the bombing— and moved his troops forward. They stopped a few hundred yards short of the Palestinian refugee camps that marked the start of West Beirut. Reagan demanded that Sharon pull back and stop bombarding Beirut. Publicly Begin backed Sharon, declaring, "Jews do not kneel—except to God." Privately he told Sharon to advance no farther. The defense minister complied. But in readiness for the final assault, Sharon also ordered a call-up of reserve units. Begin might never have known had not Yosef Burg's son, Avraham—a vocal critic of the war— been among them. "I told my father, and my father told Begin," Burg recalls. Summoning the defense minister, Begin rebuked him, for the first time since the start of the war. Yet the prime minister seemed less upset by the call-up than by his embarrassment at having known nothing about it. When Sharon tried to shrug this off, saying the need for reserves had been "self-evident," Begin shot back: "What does 'self-evident' mean? You cannot take a step like that without approval. So many people know about the mobilization—and the Prime Minister knows nothing!" Sharon apologized, and by the time the cabinet convened, Begin made light of the lapse: "I know about all actions," he quipped. "Sometimes before they're carried out; sometimes after . . ." When the other ministers resumed their assault on Sharon, Begin again rose to his defense. He told them, in effect, that until they could muster a majority of the cabinet he would pay them no heed.

Yet a week later, Ariel Sharon pushed the cabinet—and most important, Begin—too far. As the Americans wrapped up the details of the evacuation of the PLO and introduction of Western peace-keepers, Sharon kept bombarding West Beirut. On August 11, Begin decided to accept "in principle" the American blueprint. The next day, however, Sharon—who had argued against accepting the U.S. terms—ordered the heaviest bombardment of Beirut since the first of August. The jet bombers screamed in seventy-two times. Artillery fire rained from the hills. When it was over, some three hundred people lay dead.

When the cabinet convened, minister after minister rebelled. At first, Begin stood aside, and Sharon was dismissive of the rebels. When Yosef Burg went on the attack, however, Sharon fired a barb at the dovish son: "Is your source by any chance a member of the family?" Begin turned to Sharon and remarked: "What kind of talk is that?" Turning to Burg, the prime minister added: "The Minister of Defense apologizes to you." Only when Sharon, addressing no one in particular, proclaimed, "We mustn't cave in," did Begin explode. "*I've* caved in? Do you know what pressure I've been subjected to, and I haven't even bent. *Three times* I've said 'nyet' to the Americans!" Sharon, scrambling to recover, assured the prime minister he had meant nothing personal. He was merely arguing that, with Arafat so close to defeat, "any decision not to advance is a bad one!"

But Begin now said Israel would not take Beirut.

When Sharon asked for the floor, Begin refused. When Sharon persisted, Begin snapped: "Do not raise your voice! I want it to be clear who is running this meeting." Before dismissing the cabinet, he formally divested the defense minister of authority to order any more air force missions. Then, exhausted, he retired for his afternoon nap.

He was awakened by a phone call from the White House. Reagan, unaware of Begin's cabinet rebuke to Sharon, demanded that Israel end the "unfathomable and senseless" bombardment of Beirut. If the bombing didn't stop, Reagan would bring Habib home and scrap the mediation mission. The Israelis, Reagan barked at the prime minister, were unleashing a "holocaust" against a defenseless city. Begin interrupted him. "Mr. President," he said, "you do not know the meaning of the word 'holocaust.' " Yet the issue was academic: Sharon ended the bombardment except for the occasional afterburst. Arafat packed his bags. Begin, convening the cabinet on August 15, said it was time for his ministers to make up, to accept that Israel had fought a difficult war but had won. On August 23— as the PLO evacuation drew near—Israel dotted the "i" in victory. Sealing access to Lebanon's parliament building from West Beirut as the Phalangists trucked in a quorum from the east, the Israelis watched the Lebanese elect a new president: Bashir Gemayel.

The victory soured quickly. A week later Begin flew north (ostensibly to vacation in the Mediterranean town of Nahariya) for a secret meeting with Lebanon's president-elect. Before it could start, Ambassador Lewis, citing urgent business, requested an audience.

Begin tried to put him off, but Lewis drove up from Tel Aviv anyway. He delivered a message from Reagan—the advance text of a Mideast-policy address set for three days later. In it, Reagan intended to declare what Begin had battled Jimmy Carter into abandoning: refusal to accept Israel's "annexation or permanent control" of the West Bank and Gaza, and U.S. support for Palestinian "sovereignty" there "in association with Jordan." The ambassador added that Reagan planned to include East Jerusalem Arabs in the equation. Begin was stunned. "This," he told the ambassador, "is the saddest day of my life since I became Prime Minister." When Lewis left, Begin turned to aides and declared: "The battle for Eretz Yisrael has begun."

To Begin's shock, the saddest day became sadder when Gemayel was ushered in. The prime minister, expecting a love feast, ignored his anguish over the Lewis message and the pain in his hip to stand at attention as the Lebanese warlord entered. "Welcome, Mr. President," he declared. But Gemayel, even before the perceived insult of having been kept waiting by Begin, was rueing his alliance with the Israelis. He was determined to end Lebanon's civil strife once the PLO and Syrians left, and feared that an open partnership with Israel would hinder that aim. When Begin asked him how and when Lebanon and Israel might sign a formal peace treaty, Gemayel hedged. He said he did want peace, but thought it would be best to delay a formal pact. Begin, ignoring the chill, continued. "We believe the first thing you must do as president is to visit Jerusalem, or at least Tel Aviv. Such a visit is of great importance in terms of assuring the people of Israel of your sincerity and desire for normal relations. Isn't that," he asked, "why we went to war and paid the price of hundreds of dead?" Bashir was noncommittal, but Begin persisted. He suggested a "target date"—December 31—for the treaty. Gemayel replied with a promise that he *would* be the second Arab leader to visit the Knesset—but did not say when.

The meeting ended with an agreement to get back in touch before inauguration day, September 22—and with a request from Gemayel that Begin keep the Nahariya summit a secret. Begin assured him he would. However, he helicoptered back to Jerusalem badly shaken, telling one aide that though Israelis had been dying for Bashir Gemayel, "When we come to him and say, 'All right. Now it is all in your hands. Let's make peace,' he starts to beat around the bush." It was, said Begin, a breach of faith. Within hours, his aides struck back, by leaking the "secret" summit to the press.

Begin phoned Lewis and pleaded for a few days' delay in Reagan's peace plan so that he could consult his cabinet. He seemed to feel, Lewis recalls, that "if he could only *talk* to the president, he could straighten things out." But Reagan refused to delay, and instead pushed his address forward by a day. That morning Begin summoned the cabinet. He complained that, like Gemayel, the Americans were desecrating the graves of Israeli soldiers. "We have just handed them the PLO, Syria, and Lebanon!" He drafted a communiqué of rejection: Israeli settlement would continue; there would be no "Arab sovereignty" in "Judaea, Samaria, and the Gaza District." Israel, said Begin, would hold to the letter of the Camp David accords. Then he wrote the president. He asked him to remember that Israel had sacrificed 350 lives—and more than 2,000 wounded—in the war. He said he had broken no promises. It had been a war of self-defense that had escalated only when Syria refused his appeal to stand aside. Besides, when the Syrians had fought, Israel had "destroyed 405 Soviet-Syrian tanks," downed "102 Soviet-Syrian MIG's," and obliterated the Syrians' missile posts. Instead of American gratitude, Begin complained, the presidential address conveyed the impression that Philip Habib and the U.S. marine peacekeepers were the heroes of the affair. "I protest," added Begin, "the failure to consult us prior to forwarding your proposals." He concluded:

Mr. President, You and I chose for the last two years to call our countries "friends and allies." Such being the case, *a friend does not weaken a friend,* an ally does not put his ally in jeopardy. This would be the inevitable consequence were the "positions" transmitted to me to become a reality.
I believe they won't.
For Zion's sake will I not hold my peace, and for Jerusalem's sake I will not rest. (Isaiah, chapter 62)
Yours respectfully and sincerely,
Menachem

The PLO left Beirut by the start of September, followed by the U.S. peacekeeping troops. But on the afternoon of September 14, Begin's aides rushed to him with news that a bomb had ripped through Phalangist headquarters in Beirut. Though it was not yet clear, they said, whether Bashir Gemayel had been killed, Begin insisted Israel must act to head off civil war. As aides shuffled in and out with contradictory reports from Beirut, he ordered Sharon to post troops between the city's Muslim and Christian neighborhoods. Shortly before midnight, Begin was told Gemayel was dead. Fearing a vengeful rampage, he gave Sharon expanded orders—to take strategic positions in West Beirut itself.

Yet Sharon, and Chief of Staff Eitan, expanded them further. That night, they decided the assassination offered an opportunity. This was to capture the teeming Palestinian refugee camps of Sabra and Shatila on the southwest edge of the city—denied to them first by Begin's refusal to allow Israel to take West Beirut, and then, only days before his assassination, by Gemayel's similar refusal. Sharon charged that "2,000 terrorists" remained inside (a figure he could not substantiate when the Americans had challenged him for evidence.) If the Israelis had been unable to take the camps, maybe the Phalangists could now be unleashed on them.

The next day Begin kept in phone contact with Sharon, who made no mention of the Palestinian camps even as he lay the groundwork for the slain president's disciples to capture them. About noon, Begin assured Lewis and U.S. envoy Morris Draper that the Phalangists were under wraps. There would be no "pogroms" in Beirut. Gemayel's deputy had survived the bomb blast. "He is a good man," Begin said. "We trust him not to cause any clashes." Yet at around dusk the next day, the Phalangists entered Sabra and Shatila. Facing no resistance to speak of, they began slaughtering anything that moved. By late that night, rumor reached the Israelis' forward command post that as many as three hundred people lay dead—at least some of them civilians.

That evening, Begin convened the cabinet and gave the floor to Sharon, who arrived by helicopter from Beirut along with Chief of Staff Eitan. Sharon revealed that the Christian militia was inside Sabra, though he made no mention of Shatila. He said the Phalangists would be left to operate "with their own methods," and that the *Israelis* would do no fighting in Beirut. When Eitan added that the Phalangists seemed intent on "terrible" vengeance for Gemayel's murder, however, David Levy expressed alarm. "When I hear the Phalangists are already entering a certain neighborhood—and I know what the meaning of revenge is for them, what kind of slaughter—then [it is clear that] no one will believe we went in to create order there, and we will bear the blame." But Begin did not hear: He was drafting the cabinet communiqué—a riposte to American criticism of the Israeli advance into areas of West Beirut since Gemayel's assassination. The move, he wrote, was a bid "to forestall

the danger of violence, bloodshed and chaos, as some 2,000 terrorists, equipped with modern and heavy weapons, have remained in
Beirut, in flagrant violation of the evacuation agreement."

By noon the next day—the Jewish new year—rumors of massacre
were rife. Israel's premier defense correspondent, Ze'ev Schiff of
Ha'aretz—contacted Zippori in anguish. Zippori phoned Shamir,
who took no action. Yet that night Eitan called Sharon: The militiamen had indeed "gone too far"; he had ordered them to leave Sabra
and Shatila by dawn. No one phoned Begin, however—either then
or the next day, Saturday. No aide recalls interrupting Begin's holiday Sabbath with the first gruesomely worded news-agency reports.
Saturday evening, Begin switched on the BBC news as usual. Its
lead item was that the heirs of Bashir Gemayel had slaughtered
dozens of Palestinians in the camps of Beirut as the Israeli Army
stood guard outside.

Begin phoned Eitan and Sharon, who told him the Phalangists
had been ordered out of the camps. Convening the cabinet at 9:00
P.M. in his living room, he opened with a defiant disclaimer: "*Goyim*
kill *goyim*," Begin protested, "and they blame the Jew!" Others,
however, were less sanguine. The Liberals' Yitzhak Modai asked
how Israel was supposed to reconcile the killings with its claim that
the advance into Beirut was to "protect life" after Bashir's assassination. Begin answered, "This was our pure and genuine intention.
That night I also spoke of this with the Chief of Staff. I told him we
must seize positions precisely in order to protect the Muslims from
the vengeance of the Phalangists." Then why, probed Education
Minister Zevulun Hammer, did Israel let the Phalangists into Sabra
and Shatila? "Days have passed," replied Begin. "What are you ob-
jecting to? That night, I said that we must prevent this." Now, he
drafted a communiqué. It expressed sorrow that a "Lebanese unit"
had entered the camps—"distant from an IDF position"—and
killed people. He said the Israelis had "forced the Lebanese unit to
leave." And he rejected suggestions that Israel must share responsibility for the killings: "No one," he declared, "will preach to us
moral values or respect for human life, on whose basis we were educated and will continue to educate generations of fighters in Israel."

The next morning—in a meeting set up well before the Beirut
massacres—Begin received an old Irgun comrade, former deputy
Jerusalem commander Yehuda Lapidot. The prime minister remarked that Burg was complaining that the cabinet had not been
informed that the Phalangists were being ordered into Sabra and

Shatila. "But that," Begin told Lapidot, "isn't the point!" Burg was shirking his responsibility: "As a member of a government one must take responsibility, whether one knows about it or not. They must act as I did, with Deir Yassin."

Begin rejected calls for an inquiry. Writing an American congressman, he said the uproar "seems to me—an old man who has seen so much in his lifetime—to be almost unbelievable, fantastic and, of course, despicable. Arabs murdered Arabs. Israeli soldiers stopped the carnage." But Begin failed to sense the trauma of his own people. In late September, four hundred thousand Israelis jammed central Tel Aviv to vent their anguish at the killings, and at Begin's reaction to them. On September 28, he did grudgingly acquiesce in the creation of a commission of inquiry. Ambassador Lewis, who continued to see Begin, noted new pain in his face. Even during the toughest hours of the war, it had seemed to him that "Begin loved his job." Only days before the Beirut killings, the prime minister had summoned a lifetime's fire to dress down Lewis for the Reagan peace plan. "He was tired," recalls Lewis. "But he was *up*—he was angry, strong!" After Sabra and Shatila, says the ambassador, "you could see he found no pleasure of any sort in the job. Everything seemed to come apart."

For a while he leaned on Aliza. But for nearly a year, she had been getting weaker, intermittently hooked to a respirator. One of the Begins' closest friends, Mrs. Batya Scheib, recalls visiting them shortly before Sabra and Shatila. "The two of them sat in a park. Aliza was in a wheelchair. I was *shocked* at how she looked. He, too, was still recovering from the hip injury. But she looked terrible!" To Ambassador Lewis's wife, after Sabra and Shatila, Aliza confided a fear: that Begin "wouldn't snap out" of his deepening sadness. But by early November Aliza was back in the hospital. Doctors inserted a tube in her throat. Unable to speak, she could only scribble notes. Begin briefly thought of resigning, telling Lewis: "I must devote myself to *her,* in whatever time she has left."

First, however, he had to answer a summons from the inquiry commission. The panel was chaired by a Supreme Court justice, Yitzhak Kahan. But also included was another recently appointed judge: the former attorney general, Aharon Barak. Arriving to testify, Begin looked weak, only slightly less shattered than his young aide, Dan Meridor. "My name is Begin, Menachem," the prime minister announced. He said he would prefer not to make a statement, but would take questions. Speaking in a clipped monotone, he said he had first heard of the massacres on the BBC, and "could not imagine" the Phalangists were capable of such murder. Politely, the panel pressed for specifics. They noted that Begin had told Morris Draper the day after the Gemayel assassination that the Israelis wanted to avert "bloodshed" in Beirut. What kind of bloodshed? Begin replied that he had meant "acts of revenge by Christians against Muslims, ordinary Christians. Not just Phalangists."

"But also Phalangists?" Barak pressed him. "Of course," replied Begin. "Their leader, the president-elect, had been murdered and we saw all the anguish that burst out as a result of the murder, and therefore I assumed that there could be acts of revenge from all sides." Then why, asked Barak, was there "not room to ask whether the Phalange should be allowed to enter the camps?" Begin answered: "Your Honor, I can only return to my previous statement that in those days none of us thought the Phalangists who were introduced into these two camps would not fight [only] terrorists."

Yet hadn't Begin himself warned Eitan to beware of the Phalangists? Yes, the prime minister said. But no one had told him there were actually plans for the militiamen to take the camps. When asked whether Sharon had erred in not keeping him informed, Begin answered no. He had told the defense minister to keep order in Beirut. The Phalangists had entered the camps to keep order—to root out "2,000 terrorists" there. Israel, said Begin, "already had enough casualties in this fighting."

Days later, Begin was due in the United States to meet President Reagan. His instinct was to cancel: He drove to the hospital and told Aliza he would stay by her side instead. But, asking for a notepad, Mrs. Begin scrawled her refusal: "You *must* go! It is a meeting with Reagan!" Begin sought out her doctors, who said it seemed safe for him to leave. So, with Aliza exultant over her victory—"He *went!*" she celebrated on notepaper to one visitor—Begin flew first to Los Angeles for a fund-raising dinner. He was resting in his hotel room when Benny Begin phoned from Israel and asked the switchboard to connect him to Kadishai: Aliza was dead. Kadishai summoned Begin's heart specialist and together they broke the news to the prime minister. Begin burst into tears. "Why! Why did I *leave* her?" he mumbled. "The doctors *said* it was all right for me to leave . . ." Kadishai canceled the dinner, and a few hours later Begin limped aboard his plane for the flight home. He said almost nothing, except to moan every now and then, as if suddenly reminded of the enormity of his loss. On landing, he motioned to Kadishai, telling him to make sure a grave site was ready on the Mount of Olives, next to the tomb of the two resistance fighters who had blown themselves up rather than submit to a British hangman.

Begin buried his wife the next day. In the week that followed he received the dozens who came to the residence to mourn Aliza and console the prime minister she had left behind. Among the first was Yisrael Scheib, who grasped Begin's hand and said, "I will pay a compliment to your late wife which no one else can match: She *hated* me! She hated me because she *loved* you, and could never forgive me the things I wrote about you." Begin replied softly: "She forgave you. Do not speak in her name." To Morris Draper, he offered his gratitude for his coming—and a historical explanation of how Jews mourned their dead. When Canadian-Jewish activist Leo Marcus arrived, Begin embraced him and said: "Next to me, she loved you best." Among a later batch of mourners was a teenage girl from a women's prison that Aliza had supported. The youngster had been a whore, jailed for killing her pimp. Begin greeted her politely, called her a "good girl," and asked what her father did for a living. "He's an airline pilot," she lied, prompting Begin to turn to the waiting line of mourners and exclaim, "You see? Here is someone from a good family. This kind of thing can happen to anyone." To Aliza's helpmate Ilana Beaninstock, who was standing in the line, the remark seemed a reminder of what Begin had lost with his wife's death. "Had *Mrs.* Begin been there when this girl came up and said her father was a pilot, she would have turned to me and said, 'She's lying, but it doesn't matter; one has to help her anyway.' You couldn't fool her. She was no-nonsense. And when she died, she left a huge empty space."

Begin slid into despair when the mourners left. "She always stood by me," he remarked to aides as he went through the motions of work. "But when it counted most, I wasn't there. I was thousands of miles from her!" The outcry over the war—and the camp massacres—grew by the day. Protesters kept vigil outside the prime minister's residence, another group outside his office. Begin tried to get them evicted, but relented when the attorney general told him it would be illegal. "What will I tell my grandchildren if they visit?" Begin mused to Dan Meridor. "How will I explain why I am here, inside, while they are out in the cold?"

Ordinarily, Aliza might have propped him up, forced him to rebound. Meridor, who tried in her place, says Begin would occasionally open up to him—or to Kadishai. "But it was *incomparable* to what he had with Aliza. She was the only person whom he really spoke to; the only person he could really speak his heart to, and lean on. Now he had to come back home—from four, five, six, seven, eight hours of work—to an empty big home, with *nobody* there. Aliza was the one who—when he had, might have had, crises in the past—would have taken him out of it, helped him out. And this time," says Meridor, "Aliza wasn't there."

The month after her death, the Kahan Commission warned Begin that its final report might accuse him of errors of "omission," and invited him to help avoid this by testifying again. Begin declined. He wrote a letter instead, repeating that no one in the government could reasonably have foreseen the massacre. In early February 1983, the commission released its report, maintaining that Israel must share responsibility for the tragedy. Sharon and Eitan were singled out. But the report added: "We find no reason to exempt the Prime Minister from responsibility for not having evinced . . . any interest in the Phalangists' actions in the camps." Maybe, the commission speculated, Begin could have prevented the massacres. "The Prime Minister's lack of involvement in the entire matter casts on him a certain degree of responsibility." The commissioners hinted broadly that Sharon should resign, and that if he didn't, Prime Minister Begin should "consider" firing him.

For a brief period, some of Begin's old energy returned. When Sharon resisted leaving, even though much of the cabinet wanted him out, Begin refused to sack him. As the ministers' calls for Sharon's resignation escalated, Begin finally went halfway: He removed him from the Defense Ministry. But he kept Sharon in government as a minister without portfolio, and also retained him on the cabinet's defense committee. "This man," he told the Knesset, "withstood all of Israel's wars, and in all of them led our army to victory with bravery and initiative." The Kahan report "left me a free choice"—to "*consider*" firing Sharon. Begin said he had fulfilled the letter of the commission's dictates: That had been hard enough. "Woe is us that we had to accept them! I will claim this for the rest of my life." When Labor responded by raising a no-confidence motion, Begin retorted: "Topple the government? Every Monday and Thursday you want to topple the government! If the people fire us, we will go home. But we will not volunteer to you our resignation. As long as we have a mandate from the people and as long as we have the confidence of the Knesset, we shall continue to serve."

But the people seemed more divided than ever, and Begin's flame more tenuous. In the marketplaces and Sephardic development towns, publication of the Kahan report ignited shouts of support for Menachem Begin—and Ariel Sharon. However, in Jerusalem Peace Now mounted a huge demonstration. Pro-Likud youngsters heckled, then scuffled with the protesters. Suddenly, a hand grenade was thrown and a Peace Now marcher died when it exploded.

Begin, recalls Dan Meridor, ruled with "precisely the same intellectual capacity" as before. But week by week, he lost weight. "The collars of his shirts stopped fitting!" says the aide. At the cabinet table, the prime minister spoke less and less. In public he spoke hardly at all. When a nationwide doctors' strike erupted in the spring, Begin all but ignored it for months. "He was less *involved*," acknowledges Meridor. "I tried to fill in, as far as *I* could, for many of the things. But I'm not the prime minister. I can't be. Nobody could be." By late spring, the Americans had mediated something very close to a formal peace treaty between Israel and Lebanon's new president, Bashir's brother, Amin Gemayel. Begin didn't seem to care. "He was much less able to deal seriously with issues," recalls one U.S. diplomat. In the Camp David days, "he would greet us by cross-examining us on our latest draft. He was assiduous about every bit of language. This time, he left things almost completely to others. . . . He would listen. But he would not have read any of the documents before the meetings."

Begin still, on occasion, summoned brief spurts of energy. "He tried hard to pull himself out" of the tailspin, says Ambassador Lewis. When Reagan publicly suggested that the United States might offer security guarantees to Israel, Begin hurled back a vintage protest that, after the Holocaust, Jews could not afford to rely on mere guarantees. In April, when delivering the traditional prime minister's message for Independence Day, Begin said the country could be proud of its achievements. "We must ensure the fruit of victory in the justified defensive war against the terrorist organizations," he said. In late June he finally intervened in the doctors' strike, now nearly four months old. But it was a sudden, erratic intervention: Eliezer Shostak, by now health minister, convinced Begin to give in to the doctors' pay demands—infuriating Finance

Minister Aridor, paddling against an ever-increasing flood of inflation.

Begin's physical decline fed an emotional one. When admirers called to beseech him to bounce back, he would say, simply, "I cannot." With the Israelis still in southern Lebanon, still taking casualties, Begin confided he could not summon the strength to "go to the people." He cared deeply, too, about his personal appearance, knew he looked skeletal, and found it difficult to summon the will to appear in public. In July the Americans suggested he resume the summit visit aborted eight months earlier. Meridor urged him to go. "But he said he could not. He *felt* he could not. Maybe it was his appearance. He was so thin! Maybe there were deeper things." On July 19 it was announced that Begin was delaying the U.S. trip for "personal reasons." As the summer wore on, he sometimes seemed to lose all ability to concentrate. One American-Jewish lobbyist who visited, recalls Begin remarking as they parted: "Keep writing those postcards!"—as if the Israel lobby were still living in the 1950s and scribbling notes to congressmen. One military officer recounts that Begin nodded off at a briefing, only to awake with a start and ask, to everyone's puzzlement, "Where is the ambassador?"

The polls showed that Begin remained most people's choice as prime minister, if by a slightly narrowed margin. Yet, inside the cabinet he ceased to rule. He said little, sometimes drifted off. By mid-August things got so bad that a junior coalition minister—from the newly created Sephardic party, Tami—publicly likened the government to "a ship without a captain ... scrambled eggs." On August 27, 1983, Leo Marcus visited Begin, chatted for a while, and returned home, remarking to his wife, "We will have a new prime minister within a month." Yet only two days later, Begin told his three closest colleagues—Kadishai, Yaakov and Dan Meridor—that he was quitting. He convened the cabinet, and when the ministers were seated, he declared: "I cannot carry on shouldering my responsibilities, with things as they are, the way I would like to, and the way I ought to." One by one, the others begged him to stay. A few followed him downstairs after the meeting to press their pleas. Sharon, among them, told Begin that the *people* of Israel needed him. Begin thanked them all.

But he said quietly, "I cannot go on."

Chapter Twenty-eight

Underground Farewell

From his second-floor bedroom, he could hear the crowd outside chanting, "Begin! Begin, King of Israel!" Ministers and party men visited, imploring him to return. By law, he was still prime minister. He had told the cabinet and press, not the Israeli president, that he was leaving. But he attended no cabinet sessions. He made no policy statements, much less any policy. He left behind an unfinished war, a divided nation—and no chosen successor. He had always refused to name one, saying that Herut was a democratic political party, not a monarchy. Now the party had no choice but to name one for him: Yitzhak Shamir, whose colorlessness and advancing age helped defer the question of who would lead the party in the long run. Begin offered neither congratulations nor advice to his successor. On September 15, he had Dan Meridor take a resignation letter to the president.

For weeks Begin stayed in the prime minister's residence. He could not face returning to Rosenbaum Street, or think of anywhere else to go. He did not venture outdoors, even in November to mark the first anniversary of Aliza's death. By December, Kadishai, the two Meridors, and some overseas supporters found and rented an apartment for him. It was a new, well-lighted place—down a winding, hillside road near the western gateway to Jerusalem. A guard booth was installed in the driveway. Early on December 10, a skeletal-looking Begin shuffled into a waiting car and was driven to his new home. From the back terrace there was a view of the Jerusalem

Forest—and, if you knew where to look, of a place that had once been an Arab village: Deir Yassin.

But the irony was academic; Begin kept the curtains drawn. He lay in bed, in his pajamas. Even when healthy, he had never learned how to press a shirt, fry an egg. Aliza had freed him from such concerns. Now, Kadishai and Begin's unmarried daughter, Leah, took up the slack. Except for them, other family members, and Dan Meridor, Begin received almost no visitors. Kadishai came practically every day; Dan Meridor, on Friday afternoons before the Sabbath. From time to time others stopped by: Yaakov Meridor, Harry Hurwitz, Jewish admirers from abroad. Begin's sister, Rachel, was largely kept away. She was still bristling with energy in her seventies, and might just have ordered her little brother to cut the nonsense, get out of his pajamas, and return to the business of living. It was a message that the others sensed Begin was not yet ready to hear.

Beyond Begin's self-imposed solitary confinement, a cottage industry arose: punditry on why he had retreated, when or whether he would rebound. Some said Aliza's death had broken him. Others cited Begin's own health. Most blamed the war, to which some added hints that Begin had come to realize it was *Sharon*'s fault the venture had turned sour. As for predictions, typical was one from an American academic. He said Begin might "head the ticket at an early election and then turn over the reins of government to his chosen successor."

The election was set for July 1984, after Shamir's cabinet fumbled its way to collapse in the spring. Begin's admirers told themselves he might even return as prime minister. He had "retired" before, lost weight, retreated—after the *Altalena* incident, the 1951 election, Shmuel Tamir's challenge in the 1960s. Kadishai, Dan Meridor, and others now tried to nudge Begin back aboveground.

Begin battled with himself. When *Ha'aretz*'s Ze'ev Schiff and Israel Television reporter Ehud Yaari started assembling an authoritative history of the war, Begin sent word he wanted to see them "off the record." Then, he canceled. When Shamir asked him to accept the symbolic 120th slot on the Likud election list, Begin refused. But he did push open the door of isolation a crack: He began conducting long phone conversations with old comrades, party men, admirers. To Israel Radio he offered occasional, terse comments on issues of the day. The voice was weak, but the mind was sharp. Kadishai brought him the newspapers most mornings. He devoured them, a bit more slowly than before but no less thoroughly. When it was suggested that he see a psychologist, Begin is said to have politely but firmly declined. Yet, when prodded by the wife of American-Jewish admirer Hart Hasten—a trained physiotherapist—Begin got out of bed for the first time in months, and practiced, one step more each day in the confines of the apartment, the forgotten art of walking. With each step, recalls Hasten, he seemed to regain confidence.

Begin *knew* the party needed him. Shamir's campaign appearances were greeted by chants of "Begin! Begin!" Only Sharon and David Levy, who had adopted a podium style imitative of Begin, drew any enthusiasm from the crowds. Shamir was reduced to telling reporters he had *talked* to Begin, and that Begin wished him well. Mrs. Raziel-Naor, now in her seventies, was stopped by a nodding acquaintance and told: "Please tell Begin we are waiting for him like the Messiah!" When she did tell him, Begin simply smiled, and said, "It is amazing." Kadishai, Meridor, and Hasten did not even bother suggesting he appear in public—despite wishful leaks from lesser party officials that he would be the surprise star at the closing campaign rally. But the inner circle did press him to record a television message, at least a radio interview. With Peres and Labor leading in the polls, they argued, the future of Eretz Yisrael was at stake. Begin said he knew he should intervene; but he could not yet bring himself to do so. *"Yesh zman,"* he assured the others. "There is time." Finally, sensing Begin was ready in late July, Hasten invited a friend to the apartment with an assortment of tape recorders. Begin balked, however, saying, "I cannot."

Two days before the election—the last day on which campaign statements could legally be broadcast—Hasten pushed harder. "Look," he told Begin, "you're in perfectly good shape. Your mind is sharp. You must have taken a *neder* [a religious vow] not to participate in the campaign! Otherwise, I can't understand why you're not helping the Likud, helping Shamir. It's beyond me."

Begin stared Hasten in the eye and said, "No. I did not take a vow."

"Why then?" asked Hasten.

Begin did not answer. But when a French journalist phoned him long-distance moments later, he accepted the call—and endorsed Shamir. Then, he agreed to tape a voice message for broadcast in Israel. Begin's nephew, who worked at Israel Television, was summoned to record it. He rushed back to put it on the air, but arrived just after the statutory ban on campaign messages took effect.

On election day Begin did not vote. His son, Benny, told reporters that "personal reasons" had kept the former prime minister at home. The race was close; but Labor won by a nose. By telephone Begin issued a spurt of comments to reporters. He told an American news agency that Shamir should remain prime minister. When the photo finish forced Peres and Shamir to open talks on a national unity cabinet, Begin told an Israeli reporter that he supported the move. He was feeling, he added, "very well." When Shimon Peres became head of the new government, under an agreement to "rotate" the post to Shamir halfway through his term, some in the old guard fumed, feeling that even a hint of participation by Begin might have propelled Likud to victory. Those closest to Begin, however, took heart from his last-minute attempt to join the campaign. They hoped to build on it.

Then, in late September, Begin was rushed to Shaarei Tzedek Hospital, a half-mile from home, for prostate surgery. The crisis had come quickly, though the ailment that prompted it had been building for months. At first, Begin had said nothing to anyone—not to his doctor nor to Kadishai. Yet even before leaving office, he had sometimes been seized by a sudden need to urinate. The condition had worsened in the weeks before the election, further sapping Begin's appetite, stripping more of his dwindling weight, and finally becoming so acute that the doctor ordered surgery. The operation went well. Heading home, Begin paused at the hospital exit and—without the cane and limp he had carried since his hip injury—strode to waiting reporters to issue a statement of thanks to the hospital staff. It seemed to Kadishai that Begin was finally on the road to recovery. "The crisis was a real godsend!" he remarked days later. "One of the doctors explained to me that for weeks—maybe *months*—it must have been so painful for Begin to urinate that, although he didn't say anything to me, he'd been drinking a lot less and eating a lot less." About two months later, Kadishai remarked that Begin seemed "much better. He is starting to see people again—one friend from Belgium, a friend from Canada. . . . Not just politicians. He hadn't wanted to be *seen*, because he felt he looked pale. But when he left the hospital the doctor told him he looked fine. Now he has also put on some weight."

On November 23 he emerged to attend the second-anniversary commemoration of Aliza's death, on the Mount of Olives. It was a sunny afternoon. Begin shook hands with well-wishers after the ceremony—Shamir, Arens, Ben Elissar, Arye Naor, Dan Meridor, and dozens of others. *"Toda,* Yitzhak," Begin said, "thank you," as Shamir filed past. He said exactly the same to each one. Back home, he continued to spend his days reading. He received political figures—including, on occasion, Arik Sharon, whom he wished well in his libel case against *Time* magazine in connection with the Lebanon War. Begin also would talk politics by phone—until the calls became so relentless that, in early 1985, he changed his number. He told me in February, "I think it should be possible" to meet in connection with the biography. He told the inner circle he might start on his memoir.

But there the recovery stopped. He lost weight again, started spending each day in his pajamas. He stopped talking about writing his book. He decided against my interview as well, relaying the message through Kadishai, who explained that Begin seemed to have settled back into seclusion. By the autumn of 1985, when Benny Begin's twenty-year-old daughter injured herself in a fall from an apartment window, Begin could not even summon the will to visit her. (When she later insisted on visiting *him,* her parents tried to dissuade her. "You're not well enough. . . . All those stairs!" said Benny's wife. "Besides, we're angry at grandpa for his not coming to see you.")

In March 1986 the party faithful again pressed Begin to emerge, for Herut's first convention since his retirement. He declined, and the conference collapsed in turmoil as Levy and Sharon mounted separate challenges to Shamir. The only Begin present was Benny. He agreed to run as Shamir's candidate for a convention committee. Yet General Ariel Sharon ran against him, and won easily—positioning himself, said some Israeli pundits, for eventual inheritance of the party Menachem Begin had created.

Begin's disciples still pressed him to bounce back. Failing that, he must set straight the record of history—above all, on Lebanon. Begin had fought great battles against great odds. He had risen to prominence in Betar, then in world Zionism. He had declared, and helped win, an impossible revolt in Palestine. He had given a voice to the voiceless: the *shtetl* poor in Europe, the Sephardim in Israel. Then—vilified by the Establishment for decades—he had won the prime minister's chair in 1977 and 1981. He had made peace with Egypt, without relinquishing the Jews' hold on Judaea and Samaria. But now—mourned the faithful—Menachem Begin's foes would have the last laugh. The world would forget the victories, remember only the hundreds of Israeli dead in Lebanon, the shame of Sabra and Shatila. Begin's disciples seemed to feel the war had gone wrong because others, above all Sharon, had wronged Begin. Yet they lacked the ability, authority, or endorsement to make that case in Begin's stead. "I will say nothing as long as Begin doesn't speak about it," remarked Dan Meridor. Mordechai Zippori wrote Begin suggesting he "lay the facts" of the war before the public for judgment. When he got no reply, he told an Israeli newspaper, "Begin knows who led whom astray. . . . He knows who was responsible for what happened in the wretched Lebanese war."

Begin stayed silent. For he could not set the record straight with a few words on Lebanon, a disavowal of Arik Sharon. Other issues would need addressing. In making peace with Egypt on his own terms, Begin had badly frayed Israel's ties with the United States. In driving the PLO from Lebanon, he had helped encourage a new Shiite Muslim terror in its place. (By the summer of 1986, Syrian troops were also back in Beirut.) In humbling Damascus, moreover, Begin had driven President Assad closer to the Kremlin. At home Begin had left an economy in shambles. (A few years earlier, he had batted down a reporter's impish suggestion that Begin's picture might one day adorn a ten-thousand-pound note. No such note was in circulation, and Begin said even if he lived another twenty years, there wouldn't be. But by the time he left office, ten thousand Israeli pounds were worth barely ten American dollars.) Finally, in championing the Sephardic underclass, Begin had left behind unprecedented divisions in Israeli society. They would have appeared anyway, some critics acknowledged, but perhaps not so deeply or so violently as the 1981 election campaign revealed.

Besides, Begin could not and *would* not cut Sharon loose, apologize for the war. He still saw it as a just war, and a victory. He admired Sharon for helping wage it. He blamed weaker Jews at home, and enemies abroad, for forgetting that the PLO had indeed been crippled, that Jewish control of Judaea and Samaria had become a fact—and for harping on the unavoidable tragedy of Sabra and Shatila instead. Even had he wanted to disavow his defense minister—and nothing he said to anyone around him suggested this—he could not have done so without disavowing himself. In his more than fifty years of public life, he had—for reasons personal and political—asked absolute loyalty from those around him, and given absolute loyalty in return. Says Dan Meridor: "Begin will never repudiate anyone unless *they* repudiate him. And Arik is much too smart to do that." It was little surprise that when one Begin admirer told a reporter that the former prime minister could no longer stand to hear Sharon's name mentioned, Begin dialed Israel Radio with a denial. He had always led by assuming responsibility for both victories and defeats—Camp David and Deir Yassin—and he was proud of this. To blame Sharon or anyone else for the war, would have cheapened all he had accomplished. *He,* not Sharon, had been prime minister of the State of Israel. "I will yet teach Arik a lesson in tactics!" he had boasted more than a decade earlier. How could he say it had turned out the other way around?

His belief in the war, and loyalty to Sharon, were matters not of intellect, but of soul. Begin was not consciously a political leader. He led by instinct. Had things been otherwise, he would not have so misjudged his own nation's torment over *"goyim* killing *goyim"* in the Palestinian camps. Begin was one of those rare persons who sum up an entire people, an entire generation. He was a hurt, insecure, angry *shtetl* Jew—an ugly child, a weakling, and a loner forced to find ways to prevail. The battle had not been easy. It was made harder by his sadness and guilt at having survived the Holocaust as his own flesh and blood went to their deaths; and by the constant scorn of the Labor Zionist Establishment, the British, and much of the world. The struggle did not make of Begin an especially likable man. But it did help make him a symbol and an inspiration for many thousands of Jews who learned—before or after the Holocaust—the lessons of pain and perseverance Begin had first weathered in a schoolyard in Brisk-de-Lita. Begin's words, his personal battles, his own stable of Fighting Jews had somehow comforted thousands of other hurt, and often bitter, people. It gave them hope.

By the end of the Lebanon War, the role was finished. The voiceless had been vindicated: Both Labor and Likud spent much of the 1984 election campaign courting the Sephardic vote. The weak had been proven strong: Militarily, not even the most skeptical could consider Israel vulnerable to challenge from beyond her borders, or to outside demands for a change in those frontiers. By the spring of 1986, none other than Yitzhak Rabin—defense minister in Shimon Peres's cabinet—would publicly rule out any return of the Golan Heights to Syria. The *problems* that accompanied Begin's victories, he was not qualified to address. His eloquence and anger offered no formula for ruling the 1.3 million Arabs who *lived* in biblical "Judaea, Samaria, and the Gaza District." His proud Judaism could not reduce inflation, heal rifts inside Israeli society—or, for that matter, salvage a Herut party created in his own image, once that image was gone.

Begin himself acted until the end like the *shtetl* rabbi he resembled. Even his supporters complained that an elected prime minister owed his electorate at least an explanation for his disappearance. He refused: Rabbis owe wisdom, not explanations, to *cheder* children. By the spring of 1987, the seventy-three-year-old Begin had not written his promised tome. But the title he planned to give the book was, in itself, a self-portrait. Begin epitomized a "Generation of Holocaust and Redemption." When its time had passed, he retreated to the haven where he had always functioned best: the underground.

After many months there, Begin was visited by Marek Kahan of the Irgun Zvai Leumi—the man who had rented the Rosenbaum Street apartment for him under a false name forty years earlier. Kahan was now in his eighties, but read, talked, argued, and preached like a man half his age. Seeing the skeleton that once was his hero, Kahan was shocked. Returning to Tel Aviv, he remarked to his wife, "He looks as bad as in the underground!" Then, he sat down and wrote Begin a note: "A man *needs* air. Sun. And light. You're not helping anyone by locking yourself inside; between four walls."

The call went unheeded, the walls unbreached.

Sources

Menachem Begin's life intersected—clashed sometimes—with others'. There were family, neighbors, protégés, allies, and foes. Some had died by the time I started work on this book. Begin's parents and older brother were murdered by the Nazis. Among his early political associates, Yisrael Epstein was shot in an Italian jail-yard in 1946. Underground comrade Amichai "Giddy" Paglin died in a car crash in 1978. Chaim Landau, Begin's protégé from the 1940s, died, after a long illness, in October 1981. Begin's wife, Aliza, succumbed to emphysema in 1982. However, others survive, and many agreed to talk with me. Their recollections, insights and observations—recorded in dozens of interviews during eighteen months of research—were of crucial help in assembling a picture of Israel's most controversial prime minister. Some, Menachem Begin's childhood companions, had never been interviewed before. His later associates, by contrast, had often recounted their political experiences with Begin. These men and women, too, obligingly entered new territory: searching their own lives for clues to what made Menachem Begin tick, cry, work, despair—what made him the leader he became.

Since many of the events in Begin's political life have stirred bitter dispute, it is little wonder the accounts of rival participants sometimes differ. Where relevant to the story, these differences have been noted. Where not, they have been omitted—in favor of those details on which all, or most, participants agreed. I have handled the more mundane problem of translating Hebrew names into English by opting for the most common form, except where the source or subject involved preferred another spelling. Where sources have gone by more than one name—as is the case for some of Begin's underground comrades—I have used the most common, or, in some cases, the least confusing for the reader.

In addition to the Israelis interviewed, foreign political leaders, diplomats, and Begin supporters spoke at great length of their experiences with him. Some of these figures are well known: former President Jimmy Carter, Secretaries of State Cyrus Vance and Alexander Haig, Ambassador Samuel Lewis. Others are less familiar: a ranking Egyptian official whom I have known for many years and who requested anonymity, or New York political consultant David Garth.

. . .

I have also used many written sources in preparing this book. Some—such as Begin's two volumes of autobiography—are widely available. Others are less so. Of particular help were long-forgotten, firsthand writings by journalists, academics, diplomats, or laymen on the birth and infancy of the State of Israel. These volumes, plucked from dusty shelves in the secondhand book stores of Tel Aviv and Jerusalem, often included references to Begin or events in which he was involved. Most of these works were published in English, or in English translation. Those in Hebrew, I read with the help of my bilingual research assistants, Naomi Miller and Felice Ziskin.

A further source, untapped by previous Begin biographers, was suggested to me by Eli Tavin, the chief of intelligence in the anti-British Irgun underground Begin headed in the 1940s. This was a series of Hebrew-language minutes from the underground's High Command. They run for much of Begin's first year as Irgun chief, and are on file in the archives of Jabotinsky House in Tel Aviv, headquarters of the Herut political party, which Begin founded in 1948. The records were discontinued in late 1944—judged a security risk once the mainstream Haganah began cooperating with the British against the Irgun.

Among other written sources are the memoirs of Begin's political contemporaries, and their biographies; histories of Poland, Palestine, and Israel; the official record of Israeli parliamentary debates. Particularly useful was a six-volume documentary record of Israeli foreign policy from 1947 to 1980, compiled by Meron Medzini under the auspices of the Israeli Foreign Ministry. I am also grateful to Rivka Zipper of the Israel Government Press Office for letting me rifle through file copies of Begin's statements and interviews, and Israeli press clippings, from his period as prime minister. Finally, my thanks—and respect—to earlier Begin biographers Eric Silver, Gertrude Hirschler, and Lester Eckman. Although I have written a very different sort of book, a certain amount of media source material is necessarily common to all biographies on a common subject. I would never have known where to start without two such thoroughly researched volumes. The Hirschler-Eckman book, additionally, pointed me toward Johannesburg's *Jewish Herald* as a source of detailed coverage of Begin and Herut—invaluable when I became the *Monitor*'s South Africa correspondent at the tail end of this project. Alas, the *Herald* was "amalgamated" into a second South African-Jewish newspaper shortly after my arrival. But its archives survived—and were kindly placed at my disposal by one of the paper's founding editors, Jedidiah Blumenthal.

In the next few pages I have included a list of people I interviewed for this book, and a brief note on each. Key sources—like Begin's sister, Rachel, and close political associates—were interviewed more than once. After the source list come individual chapter notes. These include a recap of written sources and interviews relevant to the particular chapter—followed by textually keyed notes on specific passages. The use of initials (e.g., EBE, for Mr. Eliahu Ben Elissar) in the textual notes means the information came from a personal interview. Use of the source's full name indicates the information came from a previously published statement or interview. The exception is Begin himself, who declined requests for a formal interview, but to whom I have referred throughout the notes by his initials. A full bibliography follows the chapter notes.

Interviews:

Yaakov Amrami: intelligence chief of the underground Irgun Zvai Leumi for much of MB's tenure as IZL commander.

Mike Arnon: cabinet secretary during much of MB's period as minister without portfolio in Israel's national unity government in the late 1960s.

Michael Aviasher: native of Brisk-de-Lita, where MB was born and grew up.

Ilana Beaninstock: secretary in MB's office at the start of his premiership. Later, personal secretary to MB's wife, Aliza Begin.

Moshe Ben David: native of Brisk-de-Lita, MB's hometown.

Eliahu Ben Elissar: member of IZL as a youth. Later, press aide to MB during his period as Israel's opposition leader. Director of the prime minister's office when MB became prime minister in 1977.

Chief Israeli delegate to Israel-Egypt peace talks in Cairo in late 1977. Then, Israel's first ambassador to Egypt.

Yitzhak Berman: member of IZL. Energy minister in MB's second government, after 1981 election. Resigned in the aftermath of the September 1982 massacre in Beirut's Sabra and Shatila refugee camps.

Avraham Burg: Son of veteran Israeli cabinet minister Yosef Burg. Prominent opponent of Lebanon War. From 1984, aide to Israeli Prime Minister Shimon Peres. (Interviewed by telephone.)

Jimmy Carter: president of the United States. (Interviewed by telephone.)

Ze'ev Chafets: director of the Israel Government Press Office during most of MB's term as prime minister.

Bill Claiborne: Jerusalem correspondent of *The Washington Post* during MB's premiership.

Morris Draper: deputy to Special Ambassador Philip Habib, President Reagan's envoy to the Mideast.

Batya (Scheib) Eldad: close friend of Aliza Begin. Wife of Yisrael Scheib, who worked with MB during his tenure as head of Betar in Poland. In Vilna the Scheibs shared a house with the Begins in the early part of the Second World War. (Interviewed by my research assistant, Felice Ziskin.)

Roberta Fahn: associate director of the Jerusalem office of the Anti-Defamation League of B'nai B'rith.

Eliezer Fein: MB colleague during his days as teenage Betar activist in Brisk-de-Lita.

Abe Foxman: deputy national director of the Anti-Defamation League of B'nai B'rith.

David Garth: political campaign specialist who masterminded MB's second-term campaign in 1981.

Eitan Haber: activist, then journalist in MB's Herut party as a youth. Later, one of Israel's leading military-affairs journalists for the Tel Aviv newspaper *Yediot Aharonot,* and author of a 1978 biography of MB.

Alexander Haig, Jr.: White House chief of staff under President Nixon. Secretary of State under President Reagan.

Rachel Begin Halperin: MB's older sister.

Hart Hasten: American businessman and philanthropist; political supporter and associate of MB. Presently, head of Herut in the United States.

Harry Hurwitz: longtime editor of Johannesburg's *Jewish Herald.* Later, adviser to MB during his tenure as prime minister.

Rafi Hurwitz: deputy director of the Israel Government Press Office when MB was prime minister.

David Ignatius: former Middle East correspondent of *The Wall Street Journal.* Presently editor of the *Outlook* section of *The Washington Post.*

Yitzhak and Tsipora Inbari: natives of Brisk-de-Lita, MB's hometown.

Yehiel Kadishai: MB's chief personal aide from the 1960s onward. By far MB's most frequent visitor after his retirement from the premiership.

Marek Kahan, his wife, and daughter, Brurya Kahan: Marek Kahan was one of MB's closest aides during the underground period. He, his wife, and daughter remained close friends of the Begins'. Mrs. Kahan and Brurya were interviewed by my research assistant, Felice Ziskin.

Shlomo Kandlik: native of Brisk-de-Lita. Member of Betar with MB there as a youth. Active in anti-Nazi underground in Poland during World War II.

Shmuel Katz: member of IZL High Command when MB was commander. Member of Knesset for MB's Herut party, 1949–1951. For a short time, aide to MB when he became prime minister in 1977. (Brief phone conversation.)

Shalom Kital: Israel Radio reporter during MB's premiership, frequently traveled with and interviewed Begin during this period.

Yona Klimovitzki: MB's receptionist-secretary before and during premiership.

Hillel Kook: under the alias "Peter Bergson," was senior IZL officer in the United States, then founder of the Hebrew Committee for National Liberation during the Second World War. Member of the Knesset for Herut, 1949–1951.

Akiva Kravitsky: organizer of Zionist youth group, Hashomer Hatzair, in Brisk-de-Lita with MB's father. MB and the other Begin children were briefly members of the group.

Doris Lankin: member of IZL when MB was commander. Wife of High Command member Shmuel Katz. Later, married Eliahu Lankin, another High Command member. (Brief phone conversation.)

Eliahu Lankin: member of IZL High Command. Commander of the ship *Altalena,* which figured in a bitter 1948 showdown between David Ben Gurion and MB. During MB's premiership, Israeli ambassador to South Africa.

Yehuda Lapidot: deputy IZL commander for Jerusalem during the controversial IZL–Stern group attack on the Arab village of Deir Yassin.

Israel Lev: native of Brisk-de-Lita, MB's hometown.

Shlomo Lev-Ami: member of IZL High Command when MB was commander.

M. Levine: native of Brisk-de-Lita. Later, member of IZL when MB was commander.

Samuel Lewis: U.S. ambassador to Israel during MB's tenure as prime minister.

Sol Linowitz: chief U.S. negotiator in the Palestinian autonomy talks pursuant to the 1978 Camp David accords.

Yehuda Litani: one of Israel's premier journalists, first for the newspaper *Ha'aretz* and presently on *The Jerusalem Post.*

Eitan Livni: IZL operations chief when MB was commander. Later, prominent member of MB's Herut party.

Asher Mabel: native of Brisk-de-Lita, MB's hometown.

Leo Marcus: longtime regional director of United Israel Appeal of Canada. Later, moved to Israel and became close friend of MB and Aliza Begin.

Meron Medzini: aide to former Prime Ministers Golda Meir and Levi Eshkol.

Dan Meridor: cabinet secretary during MB's second term as prime minister. Presently, Herut member of the Knesset. Among few aides and associates who continued to see MB regularly after his retirement.

Yaakov Meridor: IZL commander when MB arrived in Palestine in the early 1940s. Remained member of IZL High Command when

MB became commander. Later, senior member of Herut. Cabinet minister in MB's second-term government. Continued to see MB after his retirement.

Shmuel Merlin: associate of Hillel Kook in Hebrew Committee during World War II. Herut member of the Knesset after 1948, then the party's secretary (nominally MB's number two) in the early 1950s.

Arye Naor: cabinet secretary during MB's first term as prime minister. Nephew of David Raziel, former commander of the IZL.

Yehoshua Ophir: longtime journalist for Herut party newspaper. Author of several books, including the most detailed on the conflict between MB and colleagues Elizer Shostak and Shmuel Tamir inside Herut.

Moshe Pearlman: prominent Israeli writer, aide to Moshe Dayan during 1967 war.

Ephraim Poran: Israeli general, chief military aide to Yitzhak Rabin and, then, to Prime Minister Begin during his first term in office.

William Quandt: member of National Security Council staff under President Carter; participant in Mideast peace negotiations. (Informal conversation at the Washington home of WQ and his wife, Mideast affairs writer Helena Cobban.)

Mordechai Raanan: IZL commander for Jerusalem.

Alex Rafaeli: IZL veteran. Member of Hillel Kook's Hebrew Committee during World War II.

Esther Raziel-Naor: IZL underground radio operator. Later, longtime Herut member of Knesset. Sister of former IZL commander David Raziel.

Yehuda Rosenman: native of Brisk-de-Lita, MB's hometown. MB protégé in Betar there, and frequent visitor to the Begin home.

Harold Saunders: assistant secretary of state for Near East affairs under President Carter. Participant in peace negotiations, prominently involved in drafting Camp David accords.

Yisrael Scheib: member of High Command when MB was Betar commander for Poland in 1939. YS and his wife shared a house with the Begins in the early part of World War II after fleeing Warsaw for Vilna.

Moshe Sheinbaum: New York publisher. Lived in Warsaw when MB was a student and Zionist orator there in the 1930s.

Zelman Shoval: senior figure in the Rafi-State list, a spinoff from Labor party after Ben Gurion's resignation as prime minister. Involved in negotiations on founding MB's Likud coalition in the 1970s. Close associate of Moshe Dayan, foreign minister during MB's first years as prime minister.

Mordechai Sontag: native of Brisk-de-Lita, MB's hometown. Active in left-leaning Zionist youth group there when MB was prominent in rival Betar.

Bronka Stavsky: wife of the late Avraham Stavsky, who was an MB colleague in Betar in Brisk-de-Lita and figured in various aspects of MB's IZL career. Now remarried and living in New York.

Moshe Stein: Member of Betar High Command in Poland when MB was its leader. Helped lobby for MB's accession as IZL commander in Palestine.

Moshe Steiner: schoolteacher in Brisk-de-Lita. Helped found the local chapter of Betar, where MB began his life in Zionist politics.

Regina Steiner: MS's wife, who comes from Brisk-de-Lita and knew the Begin family there.

Michael Sterner: State Department Middle East expert, participant in peace negotiations from Kissinger era through Carter administration. (Interviewed in 1978 when author was covering Mideast for *The Christian Science Monitor.*)

Mordechai Strelitz: IZL envoy to Poland. Later, member of Betar High Command there when MB was commander.

Shmuel Tamir: IZL member when MB was commander. Aide to MB during his first visit to the United States in 1948. Later, member of Herut; expelled after clash with MB, but became cabinet minister for part of MB's tenure as prime minister.

Eli Tavin: chief of intelligence in IZL during early part of MB's tenure as commander. Later, head of IZL's European command.

Yitzhak Teneh: native of Brisk-de-Lita, MB's hometown.

Yaakov Timyanker: native of Brisk-de-Lita, attended primary school with MB there.

Cyrus Vance: U.S. secretary of state under President Carter.

Y. Vinikov: native of Brisk-de-Lita, member of Betar with MB there.

Ezer Weizman: Herut minister of transport during the party's participation in national unity government in late 1960s. Then, chief of

Herut party executive until clash with MB. Minister of defense during MB's first years as prime minister.

Yerachmiel Wirnik: MB associate in Betar during late 1930s in Poland.

Ehud Yaari: Israel Television expert on military and Arab political affairs. Author, with *Ha'aretz*'s Ze'ev Schiff, of a definitive history of the 1982 Lebanon War. (Yaari, a friend, made the remarks used in this book during an informal conversation in 1984.)

David Yutan: MB associate in Betar in Poland in 1930s. Member of High Command there when MB became commander in 1939. Neighbor of Begins' during early part of World War II. Briefly, MB aide in IZL; later longtime member of Herut.

Chaim Zadok: at Warsaw University when MB was student and Zionist orator there in 1930s. Prominent Labor party figure; later, Israeli minister of justice.

Mordechai Zippori: member of IZL when MB was commander. Deputy defense minister during first MB government; minister of communications in second-term cabinet.

Tuvya and Tanya Zussman: natives of Brisk-de-Lita, MB's hometown. Active in Labor Zionist youth group there when MB was prominent in rival Betar.

Notes

Acknowledgments

Interviews: Yehiel Kadishai, Yaakov Meridor.

Textual notes: **Dozens of people:** a full list of sources interviewed immediately precedes this notes section. **decided not to risk:** when I spoke to MB by phone in February 1985, he said, "I think it will be possible" to meet in connection with my book research. Some months later, he decided against this—relaying the message through YK, who said, "I think he always felt this would lend a certain authority to the book in question, which he did not want to do." **To have said no:** often MB associates whom I approached for interviews would request a few days "to think it over." YM, MB's closest surviving political associate, said quite frankly, "I would not think of giving an interview without asking him." MB said okay. Nathan Silver, a Canadian-Jewish activist and fund raiser who first agreed to see me, then reconsidered, saying: "I would have to ask him . . . and it is clear to me he wants his privacy." **His older sister:** Five and a half years older, she was living in Tel Aviv. At first she declined to see me, and her son, then working for Israel Television, told me it was pointless to press. She, however, warmed gradually to the idea—notably, after my visit to Warsaw and interviews with child-hood acquaintances from Brisk-de-Lita. During 1984 and 1985 she agreed to discuss her brother—herself and their family—on more than a half-dozen occasions. She was invaluable: a vital and witty woman whom I grew to consider a friend. When I got married in the summer of 1986, she gave me a gift of dark Israeli chocolates called "Splendid," and explained with a smile: "The name of the choco-lates is 'Splendid,' but notice that like all marriages, they're bitter-sweet." **staff of Warsaw University's:** I traveled to Poland at the start of 1985 in connection with my research for this book. **a dozen men and women:** four of MB's contemporaries initially responded to ad-vertisements I placed in Israeli newspapers, and, in turn, soon led me to others. I also attended a commemorative meeting in Tel Aviv in which Holocaust survivors from Brisk mourned friends and rela-tives murdered by Hitler's occupation force.

Prologue: The Mystery and Tragedy

Books: Begin, Menachem, *In the Underground,* Vol. I; Koestler, Arthur, *Promise and Fulfillment: Palestine 1917–1949.*
Interviews: Eliahu Ben Elissar, Ze'ev Chafets, Rachel Begin Hal-perin, Dan Meridor, Arye Naor, Yehuda Rosenman.
Textual notes: **above Manhattan . . .** in an apartment on West End Avenue, where I interviewed him in January 1985. **because he grew up as a Jew in Poland:** this and other general observations in the Prologue are expanded and explained in the main body of the book. **a "fascist," a racist:** when his rivals referred to him at all. Establish-ment historians relegated MB to a walk-on role in the foundation and development of Israel, until 1977, when he suddenly became the country's prime minister.

The childhood was less happy: this paragraph draws on material de-veloped at much greater length in the main body of the book. Source references appear in text notes for the relevant chapters. **The word "great":** ZC tells of the response from MB, then in retirement, to the publication of Chafets's *Double Vision,* criticizing U.S. media coverage of Israel. MB told Ben Elissar the work was an "important" book. "At first, I was flattered," recounts ZC. "But coming from Begin, the remark meant nothing. If he'd said it was 'a very important book,' that would have meant he liked it. 'An important book,' meant he had his reservations."

Never did he look at, much less sleep with: inevitably, as with any public figure, there were rumors. Two women, one of them a political ally and the other the former wife of an ally, were mentioned most often. I checked out both reports: the first with a close friend of the woman involved, and the second in an interview with the woman in question. I found no reason to believe either tale—all the more so given the unwavering belief of all who knew MB well that he was faithful to Aliza. **"the self-assured awkwardness":** Koestler, p. 266. **Sharon, operated within these limits:** see Chapters 26–28, interviews with AN, DM, EBE. Sharon declined to see me for this book, citing a reason strikingly similar to that which Kadishai attributes to MB: to grant an interview would imply some sort of endorsement. AS said, in a phone conversation in the summer of 1986, that he was concerned he would have no control over the finished product.

"a simple Jew, in Israel": MB said this on many occasions, for instance in a videotaped interview September 7, 1981, with Rabbi Alexander Schindler of New York. "I'm a simple man; I'm a simple Jew. I didn't say I'm a simple *Israeli*." **"Against the eyes of every son":** Begin, p. 169; proclamation issued December 2, 1944. **redemption of a pledge:** see MB letter to President Reagan during the Lebanon War; Chapter 27. **Yet it is the beginning:** RBH.

Chapter One: Arms and the Boy

Books: Begin, Menachem, *The Revolt* and *White Nights (WN);* Haber, Eitan, *Menachem Begin;* Heller, Celia, *On the Edge of Destruction: Jews of Poland Between the Two World Wars;* Hurwitz, Harry, *Menachem Begin;* Steinman, Eliezer, editor, *Brisk-de-Lita Volume: Encyclopedia of the Diaspora;* Soviet tourist brochure, "Brest"; Trotsky, Leon, *My Life;* Watt, Richard M., *Bitter Glory: Poland and Its Fate—1918 to 1939.*

Interviews: Rachel Begin Halperin (RBH), Yitzhak and Tsipora Inbari, Israel Lev, Asher Mabel, Yehuda Rosenman, Mordechai Sontag, Yitzhak Teneh, Yaakov Timyanker (YTi), Tuvya and Tanya Zussman.

Articles, broadcasts, pamphlets, etc.: MB interview for Israel Television series, *Pillar of Fire*, 1980, Hebrew transcript courtesy Israel TV; Halperin, Rachel Begin, interview on Israel Radio series, *The House of My Father*, 1978, Hebrew, transcribed and translated from tapes provided to the author by Mrs. Halperin; Israeli, Amichai, "When I Was Sixteen," profile based on interview with MB, in *Ma'ariv LaNoar*, February 4, 1969, Hebrew.

Textual notes: **He would toddle along:** RBH. **his father was exiled:** RBH. **Menachem's mother:** YR. **Russian decree:** a copy of the Russian-language proclamation appears in *Brisk-de-Lita Volume: Encyclopedia of the Diaspora*, p. 82. **She bundled:** RBH. **found flight an adventure:** RBH, who is the source for further details on the period of exile. **returned to a town in ruins:** Brisk-de-Lita survivors interviewed by author. Trotsky (p. 383) says when he was in Brisk for the Soviet-German treaty negotiations of 1918, "Barring a few buildings that stood apart from the old town, and were occupied by the German staff," Brisk-de-Lita "strictly speaking no longer existed." It had "been burned to the ground in impotent rage by the Tsar's troops during their retreat." However, Brisk survivors, and the Brisk encyclopedia, say some parts of the town survived the blaze—including, of course, the apartment the Begins moved into on return. RBH says it was owned by a family that stayed in Russia after the war, returning only in 1923, when the Begins moved again, to a plain, cramped apartment in a wooden house on Zigmontovska Street. **They had first come in the 1300s:** Brisk encyclopedia. For general background on Jews in Poland, see Heller and Watt. **Brisk sat:** with the help of interviews with Brisk survivors, and maps in Brisk encyclopedia and present-day Soviet tourist brochure, I was able to reconstruct a plan of the town as it existed between the world wars. Details in this paragraph come from interviews with Brisk survivors. **Russians galloped in:** RBH; Watt, Ch. 6.

Menachem's first memory: MB in *Pillar of Fire* interview. **he wasn't there:** RBH, who recalls even the name of the Jewish doctor downstairs: Shereshewski. The Begins lived on the second floor. MB himself acknowledges in various interviews over the years to Israeli reporters that his memory of the first years in Brisk, through primary school, is patchy and uncertain. For example, in *Ma'ariv LaNaor* in 1969, he recounts details of his primary-school years, then adds: "That is what my sister told me. She remembers much more than I do about my own life as a boy." However, he tells the flogging story on various occasions in a manner implying he was there; for instance, in the *Pillar of Fire* interview and in *The Revolt* (p. 232), where he says: "The other Jews were herded into the central park of the city and compelled to witness the spectacle. . . . I was seven years old at the time, but the horror of that degrading scene has never faded from my mind."

a small child—"frail": RBH and Brisk survivors, including YR, YT. **sacrificed the "instinct of self-preservation"**: *White Nights,* p. 104. **"A son was crying"**: *WN,* p. 111. **rejects as "weakness"**: *WN,* p. 30. **It was the father**: this paragraph draws on interviews with RBH about her family, and with YR, who contributes the perspective of a frequent visitor. **only Herzl**: RBH, SK, others from Brisk. **From the age of seven**: Haber, p. 22. **"My father taught me how"**: MB in *Ma'ariv LaNoar*. **not chess that drove him**: this entire section is drawn from RBH; also from a sketch on MB's father in the *Brisk-de-Lita Volume* of the *Encyclopedia of the Diaspora*. **told her she could go back to school**: RBH.

On the death in 1904: RBH, who says a third man, Mordechai Niemark, was also involved. **grandfather of . . . Sharon**: several Brisk survivors interviewed add that Sharon's mother, a midwife, delivered Menachem Begin when he was born nine years later. **another version**: essay in *Brisk-de-Lita Volume* of the *Encyclopedia of the Diaspora* by the grandson of Rabbi Yerucham Shatz (p. 185). This version is not at all out of character for MB's father as portrayed by other Brisk survivors interviewed. RBH stands by the tamer version. She says the rabbi involved in the incident was not Shatz, but Chaim Soloveitchik. **The next year**: Brisk encyclopedia, biographical sketches of MB's father and Sharon's grandfather. **But in 1907**: RBH, who provided the other details on MB's father in this section.

Rachel had craved: RBH. **"He was so happy"**: RBH. **others from Brisk agree**: several survivors interviewed mention father's evident fondness for firstborn. **"My boy, Herzl"**: YI. **loved mathematics**:

unanimous account by RBH, Brisk survivors, and in MB interviews with Israeli reporters. Says RBH, "Herzl was less engaged" in Zionism than either she or MB. "He was crazy about mathematics."

Menachem was not named: religious explanation provided by Rabbi Avi Weinstein. **it was only Menachem's mother:** RBH. Also, Mrs. Halperin's interview for Israel Radio's series, *The House of My Father.* **When a Yiddish paper:** RBH. **Menachem's initiation:** RBH. **Pumping his walking stick:** YR. **A few days before:** RBH. **"There were no loudspeakers":** MB in *Ma'ariv LaNoar.* Neglecting to mention that his father had actually written the essay, MB says, "I made my first speech. I spoke in Hebrew to a crowd of some five thousand people. And with no loudspeaker. There were no loudspeakers then!" **"The art of speech":** MB essay, published in 1965, entitled "Ze'ev Jabotinsky—What Did We Learn from Him?" reproduced in Hurwitz, p. 42.

Chapter Two: The Coming-of-Age

Books: Begin, Menachem, *The Revolt* and *White Nights (WN);* Haber, Eitan, *Menachem Begin;* Heller, Celia, *On the Edge of Destruction: Jews of Poland Between the Two World Wars;* Mendelsohn, Ezra, *The Jews of East Central Europe Between the World Wars;* Milosz, Czeslaw, *The History of Polish Literature;* Oz, Amos, *The Hill of Evil Counsel;* Steinman, Eliezer, editor, *Brisk-de-Lita Volume: Encyclopedia of the Diaspora;* Watt, Richard M., *Bitter Glory: Poland and Its Fate—1918 to 1939.*

Interviews: Michael Aviasher, Moshe Ben David, Eliezer Fein, Rachel Begin Halperin, Yitzhak and Tsipora Inbari, Yehiel Kadishai, Shlomo Kandlik, Yona Klimovitzki (YK1), Akiva Kravitsky, Israel Lev, Asher Mabel, Yehuda Rosenman, Yisrael Scheib, Mordechai Sontag (MS), Moshe Steiner (MSt) and wife, Regina Steiner, Yitzhak Teneh (YTn), Yaakov Timyanker (YT), Y. Vinikov, Tuvya and Tanya Zussman (TaZ).

Articles, broadcasts, pamphlets, etc.: Bashan, Raphael, "Begin on Begin," interview in *Yediot Aharonot,* September 12, 1977, Hebrew; Begin, Menachem, "Three Things," MB autobiographical essay in

Brisk-de-Lita Volume: Encyclopedia of the Diaspora, 1954, Hebrew; Dolav, Aharon, "White Nights and Tempestuous Days," based on interviews with MB and associates, *Ma'ariv LaNoar,* June 10, 1977, Hebrew; Halperin, Rachel Begin, *The House of My Father,* RBH interview for Israel Radio series, 1978, Hebrew, transcribed from tapes provided by RBH; Israeli, Amichai, "When I Was Sixteen," based on MB interview, in *Ma'ariv LaNoar,* 1969, Hebrew; Kaufman, Michael, "The Importance of General Jaruzelski," in *New York Times Magazine,* December 9, 1984; Schindler, Rabbi Alexander, "A Conversation with Menachem Begin," videotaped interview, September 7, 1981, transcribed from video; Soviet Government Tourist Office, "Brest," Byelorus Publishing House, 1977.

Textual notes: **He attended a school:** MB interview with Rabbi Schindler. **Zionist scout troop:** RBH, and other Brisk survivors, including MS, YT, and AK, who was one of the leaders of the scout chapter and says, "The [Begin] father helped us found it. . . . He was the patron." Brisk encyclopedia identifies MB's father as "chairman of committee of patrons" for the group. **It was a place:** details from Brisk survivors, whose recollections are strikingly similar. (In further source notes, phrase "Brisk survivors" indicates that all or most who were interviewed gave similar account.)

Two nationalisms: Brisk survivors, and Mendelsohn, who cites Jewish population of 21,440 for 1931 and says Jews made up about 45 percent of total Brisk population (p. 24). Brisk encyclopedia gives different figure for 1931: a total population of nearly sixty thousand, of whom about forty thousand were Jews. Of the rest, about half are Russian, half Poles—there was a large Polish contingent even under czarist rule. Brisk survivors who grew up alongside MB generally cite a population figure of forty thousand, about half Jewish. **Brisk was a grid:** details come from interviews with Brisk survivors, and Brisk encyclopedia. Physical layout reconstructed from those two sources, Soviet brochure on present-day Brest, and my 1985 visit to Polish border area just across the Bug River. Remarks from Brisk survivors or friends who have revisited the town—and correspondence from Polish Jews to Brisk native EF, now living in Tel Aviv—establish that virtually none of the landmarks of the old Jewish town survived the Second World War. The Great Synagogue, fulcrum for many survivors' memories, is now a movie theater. **"cats' heads":** MS. **indoor toilets:** YR. **Both Poles and Jews:** for excellent accounts of postwar periods, see Heller and Watt. **"If a Jew**

screams": several Brisk survivors mention this, notably AM, who attributes the comment to "the finance minister, Grabski." If the reference is to Wladyslaw Grabski, he was in fact prime minister—in 1920 and again in 1923. **"I'm a Zionist *because*":** Brisk survivor, in brief conversation before the annual commemorative meeting of Brisk Holocaust survivors in Tel Aviv (November 8, 1984). "If I were in Israel, I would no longer be a Zionist," the man says he recalls having been told by MB's father.

He delivered the welcoming: MB in *Ma'ariv LaNoar* interview. **Fifty-five years later:** YK1, MB's secretary. **"was a *little* kid":** YT, who also attended Mizrachi primary school and is the source for other details. **"A lawyer":** MB in *Ma'ariv LaNoar* interview. He says that he doesn't personally recall this, but that his sister, Rachel, does. **"He had his head":** YT. **cul-de-sac:** MS, other Brisk survivors; Brisk encyclopedia. **Menachem perferred:** Brisk survivors interviewed all describe MB as an indoor boy, stress his fondness and talent for Hebrew; Brisk encyclopedia. RBH and YTn, who was in Hashomer Hatzair with Rachel, are sources for further scout detail. **"First you must fight":** RBH.

In town ... point of femininity: Brisk survivors, plus photos of MB's father from the period. **defiant Zionism:** RBH. **Polish troops came for his father:** *White Nights,* p. 17. **Pilsudski, visiting Brisk:** "White Nights and Tempestuous Days," detailed separately by RBH to author. **knife to the beard:** "White Nights and Tempestuous Days," also MB in *Pillar of Fire* interview. **"Indeed, one of the hooligans":** MB essay in Brisk encyclopedia. **"I will never forget":** MB quoted in "White Nights and Tempestuous Days." **Rachel suggests:** RBH.

was father to an entire town: details on father from Brisk survivors, notably YR, MBD, YI, SK, IL, YR, TZ. **he would remark with a wink:** TI, YR. **he played chess:** MBD, TZ. **"I knew the *father*":** MBD; similar remarks from several other Brisk survivors interviewed. **"very verbal place":** YR. **The town respected:** almost without exception, even among those otherwise critical of MB or his father, Brisk survivors credit the father with furthering Zionism and serving the Jewish community of the town. **"an example":** MB quoted in "White Nights and Tempestuous Days." **they made fun of him, too:** YI, TZ. **pay was meager: Menachem:** RBH, YR; other Brisk survivors. MB, in *Ma'ariv LaNoar* interview, mentions tutoring in "Latin—literature and history" in order to help a household that was "poor, but full of love." **"suit was worn bare at the elbows":** YI. **walking stick:** YR. **"My father was a great dandy":** RBH in Israel Radio interview. **false teeth:** YI. **"permanently hoarse voice":** YR. **But when he spoke:** MSt. **tendency to chum up:** implied in remarks by SK, YT. **pastime . . . saved him from far worse:** RBH. **fluent German, and admiration:** RBH, who is also source for account of Soviet period. **Years later, he said only:** MB essay in Brisk encyclopedia. **he would say he learned patience:** YK, who is also source for the anecdote, which, he says, "I heard from him many times." **There were two Jewish high schools:** the account of education in Brisk is assembled from interviews with Brisk survivors and from MS, who taught at the better Jewish school, called the Tarbut School. **"Ze'ev Dov Begin, who educated":** SK. **reason for the choice was money:** Brisk survivors. **Ze'ev Dov wanted his children to get ahead:** RBH. MB, in *Ma'ariv LaNoar* interview where he recalls the lawyer episode, remarks: "All the children received higher education, and all this with the fundamental effort of the parents." See Heller's *Edge of Destruction* (pp. 240–241) on son-father tensions, and importance of mother's role, among Jews in Poland. One source for her narrative is autobiographical essays by Polish Jews. She cites "numerous references by young Jews to the weakness of their fathers; their lack of [economic] initiative, persistence, energy or practical sense. . . . In contrast, the mother is almost never presented in a negative light. . . ." Most essays "project a positive image of her, which comes close to the traditional idea of the *'yidishe mame,'* the incarnation of goodness and self-sacrifice."

Traugutt was hard: MB in *Pillar of Fire* interview and autobiographical essay in Brisk encyclopedia. In other interviews—notably the 1981 video conversation with Rabbi Schindler—MB omits reference to Traugutt. In that interview, recapping his education, MB says he attended *cheder,* "where I started to learn the first book of the Bible. Later on, I went to a Hebrew-speaking school." **He was one of a handful:** Brisk survivors. **brains . . . connections:** SK, YT, and YR. YR says, "Money was an important part" in the decision, but an additional factor might have been tension between MB's father and the Tarbut School principal, a Galician Jew regarded by many Brisk Zionists as overly assimilationist. **Begin remembers:** MB essay in Brisk encyclopedia. **Jewish high schools also:** Brisk survivors; also Heller book on Polish school system between the wars. **even . . .**

premilitary training: YR. **difference ... in spirit:** Brisk survivors.
Barely a day passed: Brisk survivors. Nearly all of those interviewed
recalled personal run-ins with Polish anti-Semites—on sidewalks or
streets. Several survivors, including YR and SK, mentioned soccer-
field brawls, especially on occasions when a Jewish team had defeated a Polish one. **would turn philosophical:** MB essay in Brisk encyclopedia. **A neighbor realls:** YR. **"We returned home":** MB
quoted in "White Nights and Tempestuous Days."

He had friends ... : MB in *Pillar of Fire* interview. "Others continued to hate us," MB says. "We sometimes had good friends among
the [Polish] students. But the foreignness between us remained." **"A
cruel person":** MB quoted in "White Nights and Tempestuous
Days." **an assimilated Jew who taught Polish:** MB, in *Ma'ariv La-
Noar*, calls the man ". . . a poet. Of Jewish origin, though he never
spoke of his Jewishness. He influenced me, and nourished by love
for classical literature." **Adam Mickiewicz:** MB, in *Ma'ariv LaNoar,*
says Mickiewicz "influenced [me] especially." **Years later, he would
refer:** MB, in *Ma'ariv LaNoar,* refers to having quoted Mickiewicz
from the podium of the Israeli Knesset. "I quoted some of his poetry
that I remembered by heart from my early days." **a Pole who sympathized:** MB in *Ma'ariv LaNoar:* "Mickiewicz himself loved Jews."
"He who has never tasted": Mickiewicz quoted by Milosz, p. 215.
"Slain cavalrymen": Oz, p. 42. **His masterpiece:** Published in 1828
and cited by Kaufman in *NYT Magazine* article. Milosz, pp.
220–221, notes that the fictional Wallenrod was in fact a Lithuanian,
captured in one of the periodic forays by the Teutonic Knights
against the then-united Polish-Lithuanian state. "The [allegorical]
political content," adds Milosz, "was evident to every Polish reader."

After school he read: MB in *Ma'ariv LaNoar;* RBH, YR (see Prologue), and YK, who says, "I think the last novels he read were the
classics. . . . Not those published in the last three decades. But *The
Brothers Karamazov* or *Crime and Punishment,* and Ibsen and
Shakespeare and all the French, Balzac and Anatole France. . . . All
the classics. This was his upbringing; his education." MB learned to
speak and read Hebrew, Yiddish, Polish, some Russian and German
while growing up. Yiddish was the main language in the home, although YR says MB's father also spoke excellent German as well as
good Russian and Polish. **Other Jewish boys ... Menachem, however, did none of this:** Brisk survivors, whose portrait of MB in this

regard is unanimous. Several interviewed say they recall Herzl doing such things, but not MB. **remained "skinny" ... cough:** YR. **"an unusual boy":** SK. **The girls thought:** RS, who was born and grew up in Brisk and met him when he came to teach in the Tarbut School; also YT and his wife. **uniquely intimate interview:** MB in *Yediot*'s "Begin on Begin." He adds: "In those days we read Tolstoy, Dostoyevsky, Proust, Shakespeare, Goethe and Schiller, and of course Bialik, Ahad Haam, and Brener." **One girl remembers:** RS.

Menachem seemed to resent: several Brisk survivors. YI, for instance, remarks of MB and Herzl: "Maybe they were like brothers at home, but outside we never saw them together." **in the same class:** MB in *Ma'ariv LaNoar*. **Herzl liked math:** Brisk survivors, also RBH. **unlike Menachem:** ZI, YT's wife, MSt and wife. **cheat on math exams:** YI, RBH, **special intimacy with his father ... showed them to Ze'ev Dov:** RBH. **Begin would all but omit:** typical is a passage in *WN* describing the plight of a prisoner: "He must know that a mother's loving hand will not comfort him any more. . . . There is no home, no mother, no sister, no friend." There is no mention of either his father or brother Herzl. **"very capable" mathematician:** MB in *Ma'ariv LaNoar*. **Herzl was dismissive:** Brisk survivors. Herzl seemed utterly disinterested in MB's Zionism and oratory. **"wasting his time":** SK. **hundreds came:** Brisk survivors. **"league" to "defend":** MS, RBH. **"You must realize":** IL. **Nor were they wanted:** historical background from Brisk survivors; Heller book.

One afternoon: background, as well as account of MB's first weeks in Betar, are from MSt. **as its battle cry:** YR. I have borrowed the English translation from Haber, p. 39. **no vote:** MSt. MB, in *Ma'ariv LaNoar,* says his formal title was Betar "instructor." **would knock on doors:** MSt's wife recalls awakening to his knock one morning. **"If you *asked* him":** YR, along with fellow Brisk Betar members SK and YV, is source for details in this section. **wore his Betar uniform ... everywhere:** MSt, echoed by other Brisk survivors.

on stage: Brisk survivors. **Most of the recruits were poor:** Heller book; MS, who is the Gordonia member quoted in this passage. **"cast a spell!":** YR. **"They had no hope":** YS. **even rivals:** IL. **Sarver Theater:** geography from IL, YR, TaZ. **among the top in his class:** YR. **"juicy Yiddish":** SK. **whipped the crowd into a frenzy:** IL, who, like MB, crowded into the orchestra pit. **"*more* than won over":** MB,

WN, p. 35. He says the speech left him "consecrated to the ideal, forever." He felt "in every fibre of [my] body" that he was being "borne aloft; up, up up . . ." In 1981 video interview with Rabbi Schindler, MB says he was "really conquered" by the Jabotinsky appearance, a word he also uses in *Ma'ariv LaNoar* to describe the scene. **story began making the rounds:** several Brisk survivors mention this, some as a story, some as if proven fact. **left Brisk for the first time:** RBH. **wrote: "Hebrew":** MB's university application and other university papers were sent back to Israel by Polish authorities after MB became prime minister. The papers are in possession of RBH, who showed them to me. Date of MB's arrival at Warsaw University—October 19, 1931—is in MB's file (No. 37882) still in the university archives and produced by a clerk when I visited January–February 1985. MB is recorded as having graduated from "R. Traugutt Government School" on June 12, 1931. Interestingly, his date of birth is listed as July 13, 1913, instead of August 16, the date given in official and family accounts of his life.

Chapter Three: The Jabotinsky Years

Books: Begin, Menachem, *The Revolt* and *White Nights (WN);* Ben Ami, Yitshaq, *Years of Wrath, Days of Glory;* Gervasi, Frank, *The Life and Times of Menachem Begin;* Haber, Eitan, *Menachem Begin;* Heller, Celia, *On the Edge of Destruction: Jews of Poland Between the Two World Wars;* Interpress (Polish Government Press Agency), *The Polish Jewry: History and Culture;* Katz, Shmuel, *Days of Fire;* Kurzman, Dan, *Ben-Gurion: Prophet of Fire;* Mendelsohn, Ezra, *The Jews of East Central Europe Between the World Wars;* Schechtman, Joseph B., *The Jabotinsky Story: Fighter and Prophet;* Schechtman, Joseph B., and Yehuda Benari, *History of the Revisionist Movement;* Tavin, Eli, and Yona Alexander, *Psychological Warfare and Propaganda: Irgun Documentation;* Watt, Richard M., *Bitter Glory: Poland and Its Fate—1918 to 1939.*

Interviews: Ze'ev Chafets, Rachel Begin Halperin, Yehiel Kadishai, Hillel Kook, Shmuel Merlin, Yehuda Rosenman, Yisrael Scheib, Moshe Sheinbaum, Mordechai Sontag, Bronka Stavsky, Moshe Steiner (MSt), Regina Steiner, Mordechai Strelitz (MStr), Y. Vinikov, David Yutan, Chaim Zadok.

Articles, broadcasts, pamphlets, etc.: Babetchuk, Y., "Sixth Meeting of the Third World Conference of Betar—Warsaw, 1938," Jabotinsky House archives, Tel Aviv, Hebrew; Bashan, Raphael, "Begin on Begin"; MB interview for Israel TV series, *Pillar of Fire;* Ben Yerucham, H., "History of Betar—Story and Source," Jabotinsky House archives, Tel Aviv, Hebrew; Dolav, Aharon, "White Nights and Tempestuous Days"; Fuks, Marian, "Jews in Warsaw," Interpass (Polish Government Press Agency) background article, Warsaw, 1984; Halevi, Yehoshua, "History of Betar in Czechoslovakia," Jabotinsky House archives, Tel Aviv, Hebrew; Kanaan, Haviv, "Menachem Begin: First Station," based on interviews with MB and associates, in *Ha'aretz* magazine, April 17, 1977, Hebrew.

Periodical: the *Jewish Herald* (Johannesburg) *(JH).*

Textual notes: **one suit:** RBH, YR. **Propes was in no rush:** account of MB's first encounter with Propes, salary, from RBH; dollar exchange rate in Watt. **helped Jabotinsky found:** background on Propes from Schechtman's *History,* Ch. 21. **deciding ". . . to co-opt":** Propes, cited in Kanaan interview, and Gervasi book. The remark seems to have been colored by time, and MB's later success—all the more so since it transfers the venue of Propes's first encounter with MB from a Warsaw street to Betar's offices. **He lived for the work:** RBH. MB's yearly law-school grades come from his listing in the "Diploma File" at Warsaw University law school—provided to me on a visit January–February 1985. MB's end-of-year mark for each of his four years was a 3. The Polish clerk explained that this was on a scale running from 2 to 5. A 2 was a failing mark; a 3, 4, and 5 were passing grades—in ascending order. MB received his law diploma on June 3, 1935. **meeting hall of . . . dormitory:** the building, called *Dom Akademidski in Polish, and an example of one of the less pernicious aspects of the Poles' interwar anti-Semitism, still stands: Number 7 on what is today J. Sierakowskiego Street. Stretching an entire block, it is a six-story building a few blocks from the Vistula,* across the river from Warsaw University. Facing away from the river, the dormitory building is of red brick, covered with yellowish-painted plaster and adorned with pleasant bas-reliefs. Above the doorway appear the initials AAJ, presumably a reference to the Jewish Students' Association. However, people in the neighborhood say it is now a government building. One Pole whom I met in the vicinity implied it belongs to the secret police. **"Begin was only a youngster":** CZ, who later became a member of the Knesset and minister of justice in Israel. **Warsaw was:** this section from RBH,

Heller, Watt, Interpress book, and article on Jews, and from Mendelsohn, who provided 1931 estimate of city's Jewish population. **Zionists held their world congress:** Kurzman, pp. 176–180. **approach of the next congress:** Kurzman. **news flashed from Palestine:** Kurzman, Ch. 6; Ben Ami, pp. 314–317; Schechtman's *Fighter and Prophet,* Ch. 10.

Begin was home: YV, who was the boy to whom MB barked, "We will destroy your house!" YV says the remark seemed "half serious," but that nothing came of it. He explains that his father, a leading Zionist in Brisk, had provided Stavsky with the immigration certificate—under the false name "A. Caspi"—that got him to Palestine. When investigators were trying to establish "Caspi"'s identity after the Arlosoroff murder, YV's father did provide Stavsky's real name. **Jabotinsky also felt:** Schechtman's *Fighter and Prophet,* Ch. 10. **"cool and steadfast":** Jabotinsky in the Yiddish newspaper *Moment,* June 22, quoted in Schechtman, pp. 187–188. **When a newspaper:** the anti-Jabotinsky Yiddish paper *Haint,* quoted in Schechtman. **Begin was waiting:** Schechtman; Brisk survivors (see Chapter Two notes for list). **one neighbor assumed:** SK. **Ben Gurion, meanwhile, confided:** Kurzman.

Begin returned . . . with Abrasha Stavsky's mother: MB in *Pillar of Fire* interview; Schechtman, Ch. 10; and MSt, whom MB and Schechtman write out of the encounter, but who says—with some credibility in view of his own relationship with Jabotinsky, seemingly closer than MB's at the time—that he helped set up the meeting. "Mrs. Stavsky asked me to go to Jabotinsky. Begin accompanied us. But when we got to the hotel, Jabotinsky came out and called me alone—not Begin," MSt says. **said years later:** MB in *Pillar of Fire* interview. **Begin met Jabotinsky for a third time:** MSt, who also allowed me to copy the photograph marking the occasion. **Rachel soon sensed the change:** RBH. **"I was never a member":** MSh, who is now a publisher in New York City. **"He built up a tremendous reputation":** SM. **"*looked* so frail":** DY. **January 1935, at a Revisionist conference:** Schechtman, p. 252. Also, general "History of Betar," assembled after Israeli statehood by MB's Herut party and kept in archival library at Jabotinsky House (party headquarters) in Tel Aviv. **imitated Jabotinsky's podium style:** YR. **differences ran deeper:** YS, HK, SM; also Kurzman and Schechtman. **Begin was none of this:** YR, YS, MS. **only history, politics, biogra-**

phy: YR, YS, YK. Begin's intellect was more derivative, less original than Jabotinsky's. Indeed, it was often derivative from Jabotinsky. Whenever MB is asked to name the men he most admires, he invariably includes Garibaldi. Outsiders are surprised at the non-Jewish candidate, and often cite the choice as evidence of MB's insight and originality. Garibaldi, in fact, is an inherited hero—Jabotinsky, who traveled and studied in Italy, came to admire the great liberator and passed on the admiration to Betar members. MB's main intellectual strengths were memory, recitation, oratory, languages. Over the years he came to judge others' intellectual qualities by these standards. Thus, when Moshe Dayan retired as foreign minister in 1979 and MB was searching for a successor, at one point he thought of the Liberal party's Yitzhak Modai. When aides argued that Modai lacked experience or qualifications for the post, ZC recalls Begin's having replied: "He speaks excellent English." **By instinct combative:** YR, YS, SM MSt.

one Begin admirer: Shimshon Yunitchman, who recounted the story in the Jewish New Year edition of the *JH* in 1955. He quotes Jabotinsky as having said of MB: "He is young, the youngest among you. He was nurtured and grew up in this land and he will continue to grow in stature for the future is his. He is worthy of the [Betar] command and the command is worthy of him." Yunitchman says he waited twenty years to divulge the conversation because he had agonized over violating its confidentiality. Whether Jabotinsky did so designate MB, even MB admirers interviewed for this book noted, is impossible to determine: No one else was present. No other of MB's associates, however, recall having heard Jabotinsky do so then or later. **Jabotinsky turned to an aide:** SM, the aide involved.

sent Begin to Czechoslovakia: Halevi's "History of Betar." **word of his exploits filtered:** Propes, quoted in Kanaan piece, says he had heard that Begin was "making do with one meal per day. I received reports he was sleeping in public parks." **heard delegates whisper:** Kanaan article. Propes's reference is to the Betar meeting that immediately preceded the Revisionist conference where MB confronted Jabotinsky. Interestingly, no other delegate to the Krakow meeting recalls such a whisper in the hall. YR, who grew up with Begin and later got to know Propes quite well, is convinced Propes "developed a fear" of MB during the Betar years in Poland. **Jabotinsky Zionists had responded:** Ben Ami, Katz, Schechtman, and

Tavin all provide excellent background on the IZL. The militants—who were not all Jabotinsky followers, though most were—formally broke from the mainstream Haganah in 1937 in protest over its policy of *havlaga,* or restraint. There had been a similar split in 1931, but during the Palestine violence of 1936, most of those who had left rejoined the Haganah. **Jabotinsky scolded:** Ben Ami; Schechtman. Further background of Jabotinsky-IZL tension from HK, MStr, and YS, who sees tension as evidence of a "split" inside Jabotinsky himself on the issue of violence. "How can your *Irgun* people," Jabotinsky asked an IZL officer, according to Schechtman, "throw bombs in Arab quarters at random, indiscriminately killing women and children? You must at least warn the Arabs in time to evacuate . . ." (p. 453).

He shared: YS. Not only did MB share that dislike, he brought it with him to Palestine, and the IZL there, in the 1940s. **Begin befriended the interloper:** HK. **"Within a year":** HK. **unsuccessful attempt to nudge:** Schechtman, p. 451. Reference is to MB during maiden congress of Jabotinsky's New Zionist Organization in Prague. MB "mentioned the Irgun and asked for directives" from Jabotinsky. Jabotinsky, says Schechtman, replied only: "One shouldn't ask one's father's permission." **Kook, who recalls him:** HK. **"staked out a militant":** DY. **"leave of absence":** DY; also Kanaan article. **Begin had no intention:** DY. "History of Betar" in Jabotinsky House archives says MB left for Galicia to "do his articles" in law in late 1937, was released from "administrative" duties he had been handling in Warsaw, but remained a member of Betar's central commission, or *netzivut.* **with Betar allies:** DY. **taking English lessons:** "Begin on Begin," *Yediot Aharanot.* MB says he found a tutor in Drohobych who provided "10 lessons in English grammar, and no more. From there I began to read and study English by myself." In *The Revolt,* p. 232, MB also credits BBC broadcasts during the 1940s. He says it was "mainly from the BBC" that he learned English. **fell in love:** DY, who knew Begin, Aliza, and MB's first romantic interest, Ela Neuberg, well at the time. **"very correct":** RBH. **Tsipora, remembers:** TI. **"prettier than Sara Braverman":** RS. **first girl Begin courted:** DY. **Aliza Arnold:** MB in *WN,* pp. 85–86; Kanaan article; DY. **mother did remark to Rachel:** RBH. **"the real reason":** DY.

Conference was a homecoming: RBH. **Hitler had convinced:** historical background from Ben Ami, Heller, Kurzman, Watt; YS, DY.

Begin spoke: Jabotinsky House archives account is main source for the congress confrontation; also Kanaan article; Dolav's "White Nights and Tempestuous Days"; DY, YS. **the delegates accepted:** DY; Jabotinsky House archives. **"world . . . Betar awaits":** Haber, p. 51. **"made Begin famous":** HK. **"Jabotinsky was a legend!":** YS. **Strelitz didn't even bother:**   MStr. **Jabotinsky tried to rescue:** Schechtman, p. 458, which is also source for Paris meeting. **agreement acknowledging the ascendancy:** Ben Ami, pp. 199–200. **Propes was sent:** Kanaan article; DY. **As successor:** HK.

Chapter Four: War

Books: Begin, Menachem, *White Nights (WN);* Bethell, Nicholas, *The Palestine Triangle;* Haber, Eitan, *Menachem Begin;* Heller, Celia, *On the Edge of Destruction: Jews of Poland Between the Two World Wars;* Keter, editors, *Encyclopaedia Judaica;* Medzini, Meron, editor, *Israel's Foreign Relations: Selected Documents;* Morse, Arthur D., *While Six Million Died;* Schechtman, Joseph B., *The Jabotinsky Story: Fighter and Prophet.*

Interviews: Michael Aviasher, Batya (Scheib) Eldad, Eliahu Ben Elissar, Rachel Begin Halperin, Yisrael Scheib, Bronka Stavsky (BSt), Moshe Stein (MS), Mordechai Strelitz (MStr), David Yutan, Tuvya and Tanya Zussman.

Articles, broadcasts, pamphlets, etc.: MB interview for Israel Television series, *Pillar of Fire;* Israeli, Amichai, "When I Was Sixteen"; Kanaan, Haviv, "Menachem Begin: First Station"; Schindler, Rabbi Alexander, "A Conversation with Menachem Begin."

Textual notes: **Begin moved:** MStr, who is main source, along with DY for first weeks of MB's tenure. **Begin dazzled Strelitz:** who lacked the IZL rank, wherewithal, or political savvy to mount the sort of challenge men like Kook had undertaken against Propes's authority. MStr says he hadn't even known about the Jabotinsky-Raziel agreement—under which he became head of the Military Department—until Kook passed on the news. **ordered . . . honor guard:** YS, who did not specify who the man was. However, other accounts of the period suggest it was probably Avraham Stern, the fiery philosopher-poet who broke with his friend David Raziel early in the Second World War over Raziel's and Jabotinsky's agreement to halt violence against the British until the end of British-Nazi fighting. Stern formed his own group, the Fighters for the Freedom of Israel—known by its Hebrew acronym LEHI or, simply, the "Stern group." MB, in the video interview with Rabbi Schindler, suggests that he befriended Stern when the latter visited Warsaw: "I knew [him] personally. I met him many times. He was a soldier, a fighter, a poet. I have deep sentiment for him, although I did not fight under his command or in his organization." The encounter or encounters can only have come about in Poland, since Stern was shot by the British in February 1942. MB was not yet in Palestine at the time. **invited Begin along:** MStr says he kept only one military detail from MB—as the IZL had kept it from Propes before MB. This was the location of IZL arms caches. Begin, notes MStr, seemed to have had only the most rudimentary grasp of such military detail anyway. Despite MB's delight in the martial side of Betar and the IZL, "he struck me more as a man of politics than of military matters." MB, for his part, seems to have kept considerably more from Jabotinsky. Schechtman (*Fighter and Prophet,* p. 457) tells of an encounter between Jabotinsky and a prominent Pole shortly after MB's elevation as Betar leader. The Pole complimented Jabotinsky on how well IZL training camps seemed to be doing. Jabotinsky, who seemed unaware of their existence, was left to inquire "angrily" of MB, "Are they ours?" **a new Betar High Command:** DY, who says, "Begin picked his closest friends to be in the command." DY was based in Katowice, southern Poland, at the time. MB summoned him to Warsaw. DY adds that MB pledged each of his new aides to remain in Poland for two years: After that, they would be free to leave for Palestine. **"There was coordination":** DY, MStr.

Begin enlisted: YS, MS, DY. **"The only other people":** YS. **dirty joke now and then:** DY. **increasingly rare visits:** RBH; background from Bethell, Heller, Morse. DY says MB did "not often" visit Brisk in the years immediately before the war. One earlier exception, says Begin in *Pillar of Fire* interview, came after an outburst of anti-Jewish rioting in Brisk. This "economic pogrom, against property" came in 1937 (details from MA, confirmed by Mr. and Mrs. TZ). A Jewish butcher had bribed a local policeman to keep mum about a batch of livestock he had slaughtered without paying the appropriate Polish taxes. The policeman took the money, reneged, showed up at the shop to confiscate the meat. The butcher stabbed him. "There was already tremendous anti-Jewish propaganda going on," recalls MA. "It was the background for a *pogrom.*" Several stores— including that of MA's family—were looted by mobs of Polish merchants, farmers, and youths. Most Jews huddled indoors. Eventually the Polish police called off the mobs. Both MB and MA say Begin visited Brisk after the violence. MB's account suggests the visit was not immediate, however: "There was a *pogrom*—in the fullest meaning of the word. Stores were destroyed, Jews were beaten. I was living in Warsaw then. I came after the *pogrom,* but I could still see signs. . . . They [Jews] defended themselves. But there were hundreds [of attackers], and the *pogrom* was evident in the whole city. This was in the late thirties. If I remember correctly, 1937 or 1938." MA says it was 1937: "I was seven at the time. It was May. I started to go to school that morning and I saw . . . this Jew running away, and a policeman lying hurt. . . . My parents hid me inside." Heller, pp. 285–286, also says it was in 1937. **handed Zionist envoys the draft text:** the White Paper was formally published some two months afterward, on May 17.

Barely was Begin home: RBH, who recalls the visit in great detail— and with credibility, since her chronology jibes perfectly with a calendar of Jewish holidays for 1939 (from *Encyclopaedia Judaica*). **with a warning:** MB, *White Nights,* p. 84. **Years later, Begin's memory:** "My first imprisonment," he says in Schindler video interview, "was in Poland, when I took part—I organized—a demonstration opposite the British embassy. . . . Some of us got arrested. I was among those apprehended, so I spent nearly two months in prison. . . . It was rather harsh, I must say. I was together with criminals. But somehow I managed." RBH's account puts MB's remarks about his cellmates in perspective. She also says MB was jailed for three weeks. She says she returned to Warsaw after Passover—having heard by letter from her husband that MB was in jail—and soon afterward visited the office of the prosecutor general to press for her brother's release. "Begin is being freed in one hour," she was told. Incredulous, she asked the official whether he was sure. "Miss," he replied, "you are speaking to the prosecutor general!" She says she went to wait outside the jail, where MB, head shaven, appeared as promised. RBH says MB's release had been arranged—over British objections—with the help of the U.S. ambassador. She states that Joseph Schechtman (the Jabotinsky aide who authored the biography and Revisionist history used as sources for this book) knew the ambassador and had intervened with him on MB's behalf. There is good circumstantial reason to believe RBH's chronology. Had MB been confined "nearly two months," this would have kept him in jail at least through early June. It seems likely he was out well before then, since DY says MB's wedding to Aliza took place on May 29. So do obituary tributes to Aliza Begin in the Israeli press in November 1982.

He contented himself: MB, in *Pillar of Fire* interview, says, "I remember Jabotinsky's speech in Warsaw after the publication of the White Paper—what a lion's roar! He spoke to an overflowing hall: 'The White Paper, it will be ripped to pieces!' " See also Schechtman, p. 478. **Scheib, unable to focus:** YS. **"I told her":** MB, *WN*, p. 86. **They were wed:** a photograph of the newlyweds, in uniform, is on file in the Jabotinsky House archives. Also see Haber's *Menachem Begin*, p. 51. **"I would wish for my own":** MB, *WN*, pp. 86–87. **stayed overnight:** MB, *WN*, p. 87. **"full of energy":** BS. **She understood the need:** DY, who saw much of MB and Aliza after she joined him in Warsaw, says that although the two were not physically demonstrative—"that was not their style, nor the era's"—one could "see that they were really in love; that they adored each other!"

Begin left for the Romanian port: EBE, who had a relative on the departing ship. **spent the . . . summer:** DY, MS. **suitcase of cash:** MA, Brisk native who ran into MB on train from Romanian border to Warsaw at the end of August. He says it was Stavsky who was sent with the suitcase. Stavsky's then wife, Bronka, confirms he had by now returned to Poland, indeed come back as MB's bodyguard. When MB spoke, says BSt, "Abrasha used to crack chairs . . ." **letter from Jabotinsky:** RBH. MS also mentions this, but says it was a telegram. To aides like MS, it appeared that MB "believed his [Jabotinsky's] statement, against a war's breaking out." Perhaps this was precisely what MB wanted them to believe: He was intent on keeping morale intact, as suggested in YS's account of MB's insistence that people must not let their pace of work flag. RBH, however, says it was clear MB thought Jabotinsky's assessment unrealistic. **British intervened:** DY. MB says the refugees were stopped by "intervention" of the British embassy in Bucharest (news conference, August 30, 1977, on return from a visit to Romania; Medzini, Vol. IV, p.

98.) MS says refugees were stopped on the initiative of two "British [police] officers [living] in Warsaw." He states they got in touch with Romanian border authorities, who said the refugees were "criminals" and had them stopped. **Begin summoned Stein:** MS. **Begin toyed:** MS. **he boarded a train:** MS says MB was reluctant to do so, and only arrived after urging by MS and other aides. **He arrived to find:** DY. **The Romanians had discreetly ... "into it!":** DY. **The next night ... he took the train:** MA. **As bombs rained:** account of first days of war from DY, YS, MS. Historical background of Nazi invasion from Watt. Further detail from MB in *Ma'ariv LaNoar;* WN, p. 87; and Yutan, quoted in Kanaan article. **"We are citizens":** YS. **set off to find the commander:** DY. **in strode Uri Zvi Greenburg:** YS. **It took two days:** MB says in *Ma'ariv LaNoar* that he left September 7. **decided to retreat:** DY, MS, YS. **"We figured":** DY. **"We were bombed":** YS. **bomb detonated a carload:** MS. **Well to the north:** DY. **parents and brother:** Rachel and her husband joined the exodus of Jews east into Russia.

Chapter Five: Flight

Books: Begin, Menachem, *White Nights (WN);* Watt, Richard M., *Bitter Glory: Poland and Its Fate—1918 to 1939.*

Interviews: Batya (Scheib) Eldad, Eliezer Fein, Yisrael Scheib, Moshe Steiner (MSt), Mordechai Strelitz (MStr), Yerachmiel Wirnik, David Yutan.

Articles, broadcasts, pamphlets, etc.: Farrell, William, "The New Face of Israel," interview-profile, in *New York Times Magazine,* July 17, 1977; Israeli, Amichai, "When I Was Sixteen"; Yutan, David, reminiscences of "Aliza Begin," in *At* magazine, November 1983, Hebrew.

Textual notes: **rail, cart, and foot:** YS, MS. In less detail, MB *White Nights,* p. 87. Also MB in "When I Was Sixteen." **Aliza's asthma:** MB, p. 87; MS. **She refused:** MB, p. 87. MStr confirms side trip to Aliza's hometown, during which he accompanied the Begins. **Soviet police:** MS. **Aliza agreed:** MB, p. 87. **Soviets closed:** DY, who had by this time rejoined Begin party from Brisk. Historical background in

Watt. **The best of bad options:** DY, MS. **"exhausting and perilous":** Yutan, *At* article.

moved in with Yutan's: Yutan, *At* article. **bagful of Polish zlotys:** MS. **trickle of hard currency:** YS. **He kept his men:** YS. DY, who are main sources for early period in Vilna. **Yutan told:** DY. **arrival of a letter:** YS. **news came that David Raziel:** YS. **Begin insisted he would not use one:** MS, YS. **Begin organized a rally:** YS. It was held at Vilna University, "a notoriously anti-Semitic university," says YS, who was there. **He closed:** YS. DY. **Begin saw to the forgeries:** DY. **"I felt . . . that the bearer":** MB, *WN*, p. 15. **summoned the High Command:** the meeting, recalls EF, was in Yutan's home. **comrades peeled off:** DY. **"words . . . were full of pain":** Yutan, *At* article. **"All of us were thinking":** DY. **came looking:** DY, who was not living there at the time. **village . . . outside town:** YS, DY. **reading politics:** YS. **the two men ventured . . . on vocabulary:** BSE. **"He and Aliza":** YS. **A *shtetl* ally:** YW. **got a letter:** DY, YS. **lunchtime on September 20:** MB, "When I Was Sixteen"; MB, *WN*, pp. 18–19; YS. **Begin retired to the bedroom:** YS. **"Tell Yisrael I concede":** MB, p. 19; YS. **He was . . . "ready":** MB to *NYT*'s Farrell. **"He wanted":** DY.

Chapter Six: Prison

Books: Begin, Menachem, *White Nights (WN)* and *The Revolt;* Brenner, Lenni, *The Iron Wall; The New Columbia Encyclopedia;* Niv, David, *History of the Irgun Zvai Leumi;* Silver, Eric, *Begin;* Solzhenitsyn, Aleksandr, *The Gulag Archipelago,* Volume 2.

Interviews: Ze'ev Chafets, Rachel Begin Halperin, Marek Kahan, Israel Lev, Yisrael Scheib, David Yutan.

Articles, broadcasts, pamphlets, etc.: Kanaan, Haviv, "First Station"; Yutan, David, reminiscences of "Aliza Begin," in *At* magazine.

Textual notes: **Begin was taken:** MB, *White Nights,* Ch. 2. This book, subtitled "The Story of a Prisoner in Russia," begins with MB's arrest and is by far the most detailed published account of his confinement. British writer Eric Silver, who interviewed MB's fellow prisoner Miron Sheskin in writing an earlier biography of Begin, says Sheskin "confirmed [MB's] description of conditions in the prison and the ... labor camp." Sheskin died in August 1983, about a year before I began work on this book. I did, however, check the credibility of MB's story through other sources: Polish-Zionist colleagues and contemporaries of MB imprisoned by the Russians in presumably similar camps; also Solzhenitsyn's two-volume history of the Gulag, which includes specific references to the Pechorlag complex, where MB was confined for part of his period in Russia. There seems little doubt that the major details of MB's account are accurate. It is equally clear, however, that Begin felt a need to exaggerate some aspects of the story—the length of confinement, the difficulties, his own responses. A later aide, ZC, is convinced that MB "never wrote a word in his career without some political motive." Since he published his first account of imprisonment—*The Revolt*—not long before Israel's second parliamentary election, the temptation to make the account heroic must have been strong. There may have been another motive for exaggeration. MB felt guilty, as we have seen in the previous chapter, at having fled Warsaw. The feeling must have remained strong in 1953, when he wrote *WN:* He knew that those he left behind—father, mother, brother—had been murdered by the Nazis. MB was not alone in his agony: Tens of thousands of other Polish Jews had fled east, been imprisoned by the Soviets, suffered, but survived. Fellow Brisk native Israel Lev, who also fled east and ended up in a Soviet labor camp near the one in which MB was confined, remarked to me: "I was taken to a camp near Archangelsk. I thought at one point of writing a book about the hell of that experience. Then, I realized that this 'hell' was paradise compared to what others suffered in the Holocaust!" MB's guilt—or at least the tendency to exaggerate in his prison accounts—seemed to grow over the years. In *WN*—and in the shorter version of his prison experience in the opening chapters of *The Revolt*—MB merely implies the experience was longer and more difficult than it was. Indeed, it is by combining scattered details offered in *WN* with historical evidence that I was able to calculate how long the imprisonment actually lasted. In later accounts—notably in his September 1981 video interview with Rabbi Schindler—MB explicitly says he was jailed for longer than he really was.

"I have read": *WN*, p. 27, which is source for other details in this section. **no beatings:** *WN, The Revolt*. **In the end:** *WN*. **Menachem missed:** *WN*. **Soon afterward:** *WN*, DY; also Yutan *At* article.

week's solitary confinement: *WN*, p. 125; *The Revolt*, p. 9. The joke was in Yiddish. **"intellectuals, with thin":** *WN*, p. 121. **"For a pillow":** *The Revolt*, p. 9. **On April 1:** *WN*, Ch. 12; *The Revolt*, pp. 1–11.

Begin told her: *WN*, p. 136. **left Vilna:** *WN*, p. 142; *The Revolt*, Ch. 2. **With seventy others:** *WN*, Ch. 15, which is source for details on trip and first days in labor camp.

good news came: *WN*. MB does not specify date, but says it was shortly after the Nazi attack on the USSR, which occurred on June 22 (*Columbia Encyclopedia*). **Polish prisoners . . . especially heartened:** *WN*, p. 147. **In mid-July:** or conceivably a week or so later. I have calculated the date by compiling details offered by MB in *WN* and *The Revolt*. He says he boarded the prison train from Vilna in the beginning of June. In *The Revolt,* he says the train had gone "half way" on its journey when news came of the Nazi attack on the USSR. By this ratio, the total journey should have lasted about six weeks. Counting from early June, that means MB should have arrived a bit after July 15. **"People don't get out":** *WN*. **Begin spent the first ten days:** "less than a fortnight" is MB's phrase, *WN*, p. 153. **a week later:** MB does not mention the date. The effect, if not intention, is to imply he was at Pechorlag longer than was the case. "Every ten days, we were given . . . ten night-shifts," he writes (*WN*, p. 182). But the chronological and historic references in his narrative make it clear MB can have had at most one of each shift. The Polish-Soviet pact was signed July 30 (Watt, p. 445). Given the history of mistrust, tension—and war—between Poland and Russia, there was, unsurprisingly, some delay before the Soviets freed the thousands of Poles hauled off to camps in 1939 and 1940. Observes Watt (p. 445): Four thousand Poles had been slaughtered and then buried in Katyn Forest, near Smolensk. For decades after the war, the Russians and Germans traded charges over who killed them. Yet the delay seems to have been brief. Brenner, in a detailed review of the fate of Polish Jews like Begin and Miron Sheskin (pp. 126–127), says most of the Polish-Jewish camp prisoners were freed "within a few weeks." In at least one area—Kolyma, in dreaded northeastern Siberia—releases seem to have begun almost "immediately . . . in August," after the accord (*Gulag*, Vol. 2., p. 131). **All Polish prisoners:** first word came from a camp guard, who told MB he had heard about it on Soviet Radio, *WN*, p. 189. **"We carried":** *WN*, Ch. 17. **The common criminals:** *WN*, Chs. 17–18. **helped him haul:** RBH, who, in an aside on MB's *modus vivendi* during his 1939 stay in Warsaw prison, says: "He gave lectures for the [Warsaw] prisoners. In prison! You know, when he was in concentration camp in Russia, the other prisoners wouldn't let him do hard labor—like unloading a truck full of bags. They didn't let him carry things like that. The prisoners were so friendly with him that they filled in for him. They did his work for him: the same thing here, in the Warsaw prison."

After barely a week's labor: again, MB does not provide exact dates, but again, details in the narrative and outside evidence make it possible to assemble a likely chronology. The illness came after at least seven days of labor, since he was on night shift when it struck. But it came before the guard passed on the radio bulletin about the Soviet-Polish rapprochement, which would have occurred sometime in early August. **temperature of almost 103:** *WN*, pp. 182–183. **helped those even frailer:** *WN*, Ch. 18. **touched even the *urki:*** *WN*, p. 199. **In late August:** MB, while again giving no exact dates, says in both *WN* and *The Revolt* that the transfer came "a little while before the winter set in." He says winter in northern Russia lasted nine months, the implication being that summer was June, July, and August, or, conceivably, July–September. Even if the latter—which I am assuming in order to avoid implying that MB's camp stay was *shorter* than it really was—the transfer would have come by the end of August. This seems true especially in light of the fact that MB says the riverboat move northward lasted about three weeks—still, MB suggests, before winter set in. **to a second camp:** *WN*, Ch. 19; *The Revolt*, pp. 19–21. **The boat left:** *WN*, Ch. 19. **nearly three weeks:** *WN*, p. 195. **crawled with lice:** *WN*, Ch. 27. **suddenly, the voyage:** *WN*, pp. 201–202; *The Revolt*, p. 23.

confinement had lasted a year: see above notes, citing references to *WN, The Revolt,* relevant historical background. Brenner says that Miron Sheskin, who was released with MB, had made his way to the Volga region—the "staging area" for General Wladyslaw Anders's Polish army-in-exile—by September 1941. ***summer* month, adds one disciple:** Marek Kahan. He was a Jabotinsky follower and Yiddish newspaper editor from Warsaw, and spent well over a year as a prisoner in the Pechora region. He was freed about the same time as MB, and, like Sheskin, made his way to the Anders army staging point. Later, MK was an underground aide to MB in Palestine. Says MK, "He [MB] spent the *winter* in Vilna." MB fudges this issue. The title of his prison memoir—*White Nights*—connotes the Arctic summer. But in *The Revolt,* he writes: "The [north Russian] winter goes on for eighteen to twenty hours and the temperature goes down to 60 and 70 degrees below zero," adding only several paragraphs later that "by good fortune, our transfer [from the labor camp] took place a little while before winter set in." Conditions, he adds, "were hard enough." **most murderous winter ever:** Solzhenitsyn (p. 221) says that in the six Arctic winter months after MB's release in autumn 1941, Pechorlag's population dropped from fifty thousand to ten thousand. "During this period," he writes, "not one prisoner transport was sent out of Pechorlag anywhere—so where did the *forty thousand* prisoners go?" **confinement . . . was agony:** YS, often critical of MB, says the camp experience and MB's survival of it do "reflect a genuinely enormous mental discipline, strength, in the man." **He moved south:** *WN,* Ch. 21. **located Rachel:** *WN,* p. 213, in the Uzbek town of Dzhizak. **Bader, was . . . some five hundred miles away:** MB, typically exaggerating detail in his recollections of the war years, says Bader "traveled thousands of kilometers" to see him. In fact, nine hundred kilometers lay between Mari—where MB says Bader was—and MB, by then in the town of Margelan. **when Begin tried to enlist:** for background on Jews in the Anders army, including the negotiations by Sheskin and Marek Kahan with the Poles, see Brenner, pp. 126–127. **He didn't have to:** Brenner (p. 127) explains the Anders army move to Iran, then the British rerouting of the Anders force to Palestine. About fourteen thousand Polish Jews left the USSR in early 1942, either as civilians or in the Anders army. On the move toward Iran, MB's troop train went through the town where RBH and her husband were staying. MB sent word from the station, telling people on the platform he would "give them anything if they would bring his sister," says RBH. But she recalls—"Although he could have taken us with him as the family of a soldier"—that he dared not tarry and try to rejoin the unit. "I missed the train. It had already left." She adds that "I was happy he didn't stay on. After he left, the NKVD [Stalin's political police] came looking for him." **in May 1942:** *The Revolt,* p. 25. **Once across:** DY. Also, Yutan *At* article. **learned something else:** Kanaan article says MB learned about Raziel in Transjordan. Niv, in his six-volume official history of the Irgun Zvai Leumi, says MB found out about both Raziel's and Stern's deaths at Mafraq (northern Transjordan) and that as soon as MB crossed to Jerusalem he "made contact with the [Jabotinsky Zionist] movement."

Chapter Seven: Home

Books: Begin, Menachem, *The Revolt;* Ben Ami, Yitshaq, *Years of Wrath, Days of Glory; Brisk-de-Lita Volume: Encyclopedia of the Diaspora;* Keter, editors, *Encyclopaedia Judaica;* Niv, David, *History of the Irgun Zvai Leumi.*

Interviews: Yaakov Amrami, Batya (Scheib) Eldad, Eliezer Fein, Yehiel Kadishai, Marek Kahan, Hillel Kook, Eliahu Lankin (EL), Yehuda Lapidot, Shlomo Lev-Ami, Eitan Livni (ELi), Yaakov Meridor, Shmuel Merlin, Yehoshua Ophir, Esther Raziel-Naor, Yisrael Scheib, Moshe Stein, Eli Tavin, David Yutan.

Articles, broadcasts, pamphlets, etc.: MB interview for Israel TV series, *Pillar of Fire;* Bashan, Raphael, "Begin on Begin"; Ben Eliezer, Arye, "Twenty Years Ago," in *Herut* newspaper, 1963, Hebrew; Bethell, Nicholas, interview with MB for *The Palestine Triangle,* March 1976, transcript in Israel Government Archives, Jerusalem; Dolav, Aharon, "White Nights and Tempestuous Days"; Yutan, David, reminiscences of Aliza Begin.

Textual notes: **Begin reunited:** Yutan's magazine article says he, Aliza, and various Betar comrades were living in southern Palestine when word came of MB's arrival. MB and Aliza moved into an apartment in Jerusalem. Benjamin, or Benny, Begin was born in March 1943. **attended their meetings:** YK, EL, ELi are among those who recall meeting MB in such encounters. **fidding with his wedding ring:** YS, who was one of the former Betar colleagues with whom MB reestablished contact on arrival. YS was teaching at a Tel Aviv high school when MB showed up and remarked, "We must complete our game of chess!" **celebrity in his own right:** EL, YM, ERN, YS. **cap tilted:** source is photographs of Private Begin from the period. **"I met him":** quoted in "White Nights and Tempestuous Days." BSE, in interview, adds, "I remember when Begin came with Anders's army. He was in uniform, and projected an image of self-pride. He was a 'gentleman' " **Begin briefly ran:** Niv, who says he remained in the post for about six months, aided by old Warsaw colleagues, including Epstein, Yutan, and Moshe Stein. **pseudonym "Ben Ze'ev":** Niv. **But when the British:** MB, quoted in Niv. **Visiting Arye Altman:** ERN, who is also source for her first meeting with MB.

Irgun had been at loose ends: EL, ELi, YL, ET, HK. It is from lengthy conversations with them and other Irgun veterans that the portrait of Meridor is taken. HK remarks, "The Irgun wasn't doing anything. The Revisionist party was running what little there was to be run," adding, "People weren't ready to *die* for the Revisionist party." Adds ELi, "We were looking for someone with authority" to assume the IZL leadership. ET concurs: "We were looking for someone to bring together this small group of people and make something of it—mainly because of our frustration." **One IZL novice:** YK. **"We were frustrated":** EL, who is source for other details of his group's overture to MB. **Whatever the newcomer's strengths:** MS, who is source for lobbying effort on MB's behalf. **Lankin group took its case:** EL, MS, YM. **Meridor had not met him, but:** YM. **summoned Moshe Stein:** YM, MS. **"amazed, embarrassed":** MS. **"serve . . . as a simple soldier":** YM, MS. **advice, and Meridor leaped:** YM.

It took only one meeting: ERN. **Meridor would say, years later:** YM. **rank and file's opposition lessened:** ERN, ET, ELi. **Rommel had only just:** ELi, ET. **From Europe came the first reports:** ELi, ET. MB, in Bethell interview, says, "We learnt as early as the end of 1942 that our people were being murdered in Europe." MB's father and brother were killed in July 1941—among five hundred Jews the Nazis marched out of Brisk and drowned in the Bug River, according to information from survivors in the *Brisk-de-Lita Volume* of *Encyclopedia of the Diaspora*. MB ("White Nights and Tempestuous Days") is quoted as saying he was told by survivors from Brisk-de-Lita that his ailing mother was taken from her hospital bed by the Nazis and killed. He says that learning of the fate of his family "was the most terrible moment in my life." **shouting a curse:** Brisk encyclopedia. **They were in America:** HK. **The name didn't even occur:** HK. **Ben Eliezer wrote back:** HK, SM; Ben Ami, p. 302. **Begin's name came up:** Ben Eliezer, in *Herut* article, says Meridor raised it. **had met him:** Ben Eliezer *Herut* article. **men met several times:** *The Revolt*, p. 63. **Begin unfolded:** Ben Ami, pp. 302–303. **refused to assume the IZL command as "deserter":** MK, YM; Ben Eliezer *Herut* article. **If the army:** Ben Eliezer *Herut* article; MK, HK; Ben Ami, pp. 302–303. MB, in various interviews, has mentioned the discharge from the army. In "Begin on Begin," he cites roles of Marek Kahan and Ben Eliezer, but does not mention the deal involved. "I refused to desert," he says. "I claimed any army fighting Nazi Germany must be assisted."

sped not to New York, but to Tel Aviv: Niv, who says MB was discharged December 1 and announced on arrival at Irgun headquarters: "I hereby present myself to you in IZL uniform: civilian clothing." **Altman's Revisionists:** ET, ELi, YO. **appealed for restraint:** YO, who was working for the aide, Benjamin Lubotsky, at the time. **asked for a vote of confidence:** ERN. **"Altman had wanted Lev-Ami":** YM. In separate interview, SLA counters: "Meridor would have stayed on . . . if we'd let him." Various IZL sources say Lev-Ami did seem to feel that he should have been made commander, including MS, HK. **"Ben David":** this is how MB is referred to in surviving records of IZL High Command meetings. **reference . . . was to Raziel:** SM, who says MB told him this. ELi confirms: "It was his *nom de guerre,* from Raziel's name." **roughly one hundred active members:** ET. **Few shared Begin's confidence:** EL, YA. **well over a month:** MB, in *Pillar of Fire* interview, says the draft declaration of revolt was ready before he assumed the IZL command. "But because of internal reasons and developments within the Irgun, publication of the declaration was delayed." **"Words. Just words!":** *The Revolt,* p. 44. MB says the printer's precise phrase—he was a Sephardic Jew—was *"palabra[s]."* **When Yutan brought:** Yutan's account, quoted in Dolav's "White Nights and Tempestuous Days."

Chapter Eight: Revolt

Books: Begin, Menachem; *In the Underground (ITU)* and *The Revolt;* Bell, J. Bowyer, *Terror out of Zion;* Ben Ami, Yitshaq; *Years of Wrath, Days of Glory;* Bethell, Nicholas, *The Palestine Triangle;* Cohen, Geula, *Woman of Violence;* Golan, Aviezer, and Shlomo Nachdimon, *Begin;* Hirschler, Gertrude, and Lester S. Eckman, *Menachem Begin;* Koestler, Arthur, *Promise and Fulfillment;* Kurzman, Dan, *Ben-Gurion: Prophet of Fire;* Lankin, Eliahu, *Tales of the*

Commander of the Altalena; Niv, David, *History of the Irgun Zvai Leumi;* Tavin, Eli, and Yona Alexander, editors, *Psychological Warfare and Propaganda: Irgun Documentation.*

Interviews: Yaakov Amrami, Marek Kahan, Eliahu Lankin (EL), Eitan Livni (ELi), Yaakov Meridor, Esther Raziel-Naor, Yisrael Scheib, Eli Tavin.

Articles, broadcasts, pamphlets, etc.: MB interview for Israel TV series, *Pillar of Fire;* Bethell, Nicholas, interview with MB for *The Palestine Triangle; Minutes of IZL High Command Meetings* (HC minutes), Jabotinsky House archives, Tel Aviv, 1944, Hebrew.

Textual notes: **"We are going":** MB in *Pillar of Fire* interview. **His poster:** on file at Jabotinsky House archives. Text in Begin's *In the Underground (ITU),* Vol. I, p. 21. Also, in English translation, in Tavin, pp. 259–262. **words fell flat:** ET. **into a Tel Aviv hotel:** It was really a simple, four-story pension called the Savoy Hotel. Near the Tel Aviv seashore, it was gutted in a Palestinian commando attack in 1975. **under an alias:** "Ben Ze'ev," "Son of Jabotinsky," the name MB had signed to his *Betar* newspaper articles after arriving in Palestine and by MB's own reckoning in *The Revolt* (pp. 109–110), one "not calculated to dispel suspicions." **After nightfall, February 12:** Bell's *Terror out of Zion* is by far the most meticulous history written so far about Jewish underground violence preceding Israeli independence and is a main source for background material in this chapter. See also communiqués on specific military actions in MB's *ITU.* **Begin claimed responsibility:** *ITU,* Vol. I, p. 25. **Ben Eliezer had Begin's grasp:** ELi, HK. **"How about hitting":** ELi. **On March 23:** Bell, pp. 115–117; *ITU,* Vol. I, pp. 36–37. **When Begin heard:** *The Revolt,* p. 63. **wall poster:** *ITU,* Vol. I, pp. 36–37. **Next morning, he traveled:** *The Revolt,* p. 49. **"Woe to the cause":** *The Revolt,* p. 48. **If the Arabs defied:** *The Revolt,* pp. 49–50. MB intermittently wrote such appeals to the Arabs from 1944 to 1948. One early example can be found in *ITU,* Vol. I, p. 116.

by a hair: MB, Bethell interview; Bethell, pp. 158–160. **caught a large number:** Bell, pp. 118–120. **Ben Eliezer and David Yutan:** DY. **"It seemed healthier":** *The Revolt,* p. 110. **Begin, Aliza, and their son:** *The Revolt,* pp. 110–113. **kitchen table, which Begin used:** underground meetings described by MK, ELi; also, Lankin, pp. 61–77. **drafted Yisrael Epstein:** Epstein, says MB in *The Revolt,* Ch. 8, was never a member of the IZL High Command (HC). But when Yutan was arrested in the spring of 1944, Epstein began handling publication of MB's wall-poster newspaper, *Herut.* Epstein, says MB, was also "one of the few who knew where I lived, and visited me frequently. . . . When our boys fell, it was to him I poured out my heart." **the returning Meridor:** Niv; minutes of IZL HC meetings. Meridor seems to have been absent for about a half year after MB's takeover. He is not mentioned as a participant in any HC meetings during the spring of 1944. His first entry on the roster comes in the HC minutes of August 23, 1944, with the note: "recently returned." Thereafter, he takes an active role and is listed second after MB. In a September 11 meeting dealing only with the technical details of a planned operation—against British police fortresses—MB is not in attendance. This is interesting for two reasons. It is a reflection of MB's function as *political* commander of the IZL, not field general. And in MB's absence, it is Meridor who chairs the session, which also includes Shlomo Lev-Ami, Lankin, and Livni. **was two months before:** Bell; Begin's *ITU.* **radio station:** *The Revolt,* p. 113. **amid taunts:** Bell, p. 121; Bethell, pp. 160–162; interviews with ET, YS. **including Yisrael Scheib:** on arrival in Israel, he had Hebraized his name to Yisrael Eldad. To spare readers unnecessary confusion, I have referred to him as "Scheib" throughout. **In July Begin chaired:** record of meeting, and MB's remarks at it, on file at Jabotinsky House. **"Western Wall Campaign":** Jabotinsky House archives. In *The Revolt,* pp. 88–91, MB adds that the idea for the campaign had germinated on Yom Kippur 1943—before he took over as IZL chief—when he saw "British police armed with rifles and batons" roughing up worshipers after a Jew had defied official restrictions and sounded the *shofar.* **"If the High Command is arrested":** Jabotinsky House archives. **many felt it was time:** minutes of HC sessions and other IZL meetings. I am grateful to Eli Tavin for telling me of the existence of these records. The minutes begin with the "promotion ceremony" on July 23, 1944, and stretch through the HC session of November 9, when the Haganah's campaign to turn over IZL members to the British forced an end to such written records. **fresh failure in the field:** Bell, p. 120. Also, *The Revolt,* pp. 84–86, in which MB says that the policy of announcing the precise results of such operations, however paltry, had the effect of gradually building up unshakable popular confidence in Irgun statements. **four British installations:** HC minutes, August 2, 1944. **Stern group hit one of them first:** HC minutes, August 5 and August 23, in which HC members contend that the Sternists preempted IZL plans in a vain effort to "add to their prestige" and thus increase their leverage in talks on a possible IZL-LEHI alliance. In minutes for an August 12 HC meeting, Livni complains that Haganah stakeouts of intended IZL targets are also complicating execution of IZL plans. **fourteen rifles:** *ITU,* Vol. I, p. 102.

Lankin . . . favored a truce: HC minutes, August 17 and August 23, 1944. **With any luck:** HC minutes, August 17. **did hedge his bets:** HC minutes, August 23. **grudging approval:** HC minutes, August 17, which note that "the rest of the command agree in principle with Ben David [Begin]" in his debate with Lankin, but that Shlomo Lev-Ami echoes Lankin's concern over the IZL's financial straits. HC minutes, August 23, note that Lankin "again raised the issue in principle of a pause" in military operations, sparking "a long and serious debate." Meridor, interestingly, raises another concern: the risk of harming Christian or Muslim Arabs in any confrontation with the British. MB incorporated in his wall-poster announcements an assurance that "no passerby, Muslim or Christian, will be disturbed." **staccato of escalating warnings:** *ITU,* Vol. I, pp. 126–129. **fall-back attacks:** Bell, pp. 122–123. **"intimidated into a humiliating withdrawal":** Bell, p. 123. **"I had always claimed":** EL. **"A change has occurred.":** *ITU,* Vol. I, p. 130.

He was no field general: ELi. **Drew excitement:** ELi. Also, observations on later meeting with MB from Koestler, p. 266. More trenchantly, Koestler is quoted in Bethell (pp. 191–192): "The meeting was 'a cops-and-robbers affair.' " MB's delight in the trappings of the underground permeates his prose in *The Revolt.* He devotes an entire chapter to the several different identities and aliases he assumed underground. The HC minutes read like a parody of a dimestore novel, full of code words that require something less than cryptographic genius to decipher. The IZL was "the company," and its six geographic subdivisions were "farms." Weapons and ammunitions sought in raids on British depots were dubbed "fruit." Military operations were "parties." Arrests were "illnesses." The Haganah was referred to as "the tourists," but the LEHI as "in-laws" in acknowledgment of their closer ideological affinity to Jabotinsky Zionism. **Begin as a "housewife":** MB evidently never noticed the quirk. In *The Revolt,* pp. 128–129, he mentions an ostensibly male alias, Dr. Yonah Koenigshoffer. He includes a similar reference in his interview with Bethell. The oddity came to light only in the late 1970s, with publication of an illustrated biography of Begin by two admiring journalists, Aviezer Golan and Shlomo Nachdimon. It includes a photograph of the ID document in question. Above a photo of a moustachioed MB is the name "Jona Konigshoffer. Also shown: "Height: 5 ft. 3 inches. Race: Jewish. Occupation: Housewife." **"an educator":** YA. **Rarely venturing outdoors:** YA, MK, ELi, ET. **broadcast brief bursts:** Bell, pp. 118–119. Esther Raziel-Naor was on the original radio team. She was among the first IZL activists detained during the revolt—in the spring of 1944. **He would enter the room:** Lankin, pp. 61–77; Hirschler-Eckman, pp. 79–80. **avoided detailed involvement:** HC minutes, August 2, 6, 17, and 31.

But when Tavin: ET, YM. MB, in *The Revolt,* pp. 102–103, also mentions the incident. But he refers to the suspect, a Revisionist party fund raiser named Yaakov Chylewicz, by the name he apparently was using at the time: Simon Tsorros. Begin is convinced Chylewicz-Tsorros was responsible for the arrest of Esther Raziel-Naor in March 1944. MB implies the man may also have been behind Begin's near arrest in Jerusalem after the March 23 IZL attacks. Not long afterward, ET managed to get his hands on a list of supposed IZL leaders that Chylewicz had given the British. He obtained the list by agreeing to arrange a meeting with Begin for Revisionist leader Altman—who was by now utterly overshadowed by Begin's IZL and also heartsick at the number of simple Revisionists erroneously arrested by the British as Irgun "terrorists." The meeting did nothing to slow the downward spin in relations between the Revisionists and MB's Irgun. The Chylewicz list turned out to be outdated. But, says MB in *The Revolt,* it did include "names, descriptions and addresses" of some major figures—notably, Meridor. MB, in the Bethell interview, refers to the man as Chylewicz and says he also gave the British Begin's name and Ben Eliezer's. Ben Ami (p. 308) says Chylewicz was responsible for the arrest of Ben Eliezer in April 1944. Sometime afterward, the IZL located Chylewicz's place of refuge: the United States. ET says the Irgun sent word to Hillel Kook's group of former IZL men in America to "prepare a reception for Aziv Chylewicz." The reference "Aziv" was to a vaunted double agent of the czarist police in Russia. But according to ET and to MB in the Bethell interview, the result was a laughable mix-up. Whoever received the cable did not understand the reference to "Aziv." A genuine reception was laid on, complete with an address of welcome to "Aziv Chylewicz." Chylewicz, who *did* understand the reference, went to ground again. ET says that about two years later there was some sentiment for sending a hit squad to assassinate him. But, says ET, "Begin didn't want to. . . . There were political considerations, since no matter who killed him, the FBI would have assumed we were responsible." **asked for permission to avenge:** HC minutes, August 2. **"He had erudition":** ET. HK, who was in the States but knew most of the principals and got to know the others on his return in 1948, is typically more trenchant: "Begin *knew* politics," he says. "None of the other guys did. Left to themselves, they couldn't organize a meeting of more than three people."

The British retaliated: Bell, p. 125; Bethell, pp. 174–175. **"We were revolutionaries":** YS. Scheib explains the difference in method, and mind-set, by comparing the Sternists to the fiery-eyed romantics who characterized Russian resistance cells under the czar. When asked, in a later interview, for help on confirming or scotching a longtime rumor of romantic involvement between MB and a female Sternist-veteran, Scheib replies, "Never! Never! . . . Begin can make jokes; he has a sense of humor; sometimes he can use Russian-style curses. But he has nothing *Bohemian* in his soul, no understanding of the arts, poetry. And I don't know, but I don't think he had a private love life." Then, chuckling, he adds, "Maybe that's another reason he could not be in LEHI!" One woman, Geula Cohen, who served in the IZL, was part of LEHI and later joined MB's Herut party, also touches on the difference between the Irgun and the Sternists. In *Woman of Violence*, Ch. 2, she says that at her LEHI initiation ceremony, a LEHI officer explained: "It is a question of style. Not just the style of living, but the style of dying as well. Two men, Raziel and Yair [Stern], set out on the same road. Raziel was killed in a military action in Iraq, on a secret mission for British intelligence. At about the same time, Yair was being riddled with bullets by British detectives in Tel Aviv." Cohen adds: "Raziel was a soldier who obeyed the law. Yair was a poet; he made the law." MB himself not only acknowledged but emphasized the distinction. He felt an affinity for LEHI, if only because it—like the Irgun—was fighting the British. This is abundantly clear in the HC minutes. It was the Sternists' "methods," MB said in the Bethell interview in 1976, that he rejected. MB—like the picture Geula Cohen paints of Raziel—was "a soldier who obeyed the law." He stressed this literally from the start of his tenure as IZL chief. In his wall-poster announcement of the March attacks on British police installations, for instance, MB notes that the victims—IZL and British—"fell in battle, in a planned attack. Soldiers of the Irgun Zvai Leumi do not shoot from ambush at accidental opponents." Almost invariably, this pattern held throughout the revolt. In September 1944, for instance, when IZL units hit police fortresses on Yom Kippur, he wrote that the attacks came "in direct battle," and added: "In all the attacks the principle of face-to-face fighting was preserved. We took every precaution not to harm civilians, Hebrew or foreign." The IZL, he said, was "an underground army" that observed "all regulations of war accepted throughout the world."

series of letters: cited in HC minutes. **did sign on . . . looser agreement:** letter from MB to LEHI, September 3, on file at Jabotinsky House; HC minutes, September 19 and November 9; *The Revolt,* p. 145. On October 16 the IZL and LEHI issued a "Common Manifesto." It listed eight shared principles of revolt, and encouraged "every loyal Israelite" at least tacitly to support them. The text appears in *ITU,* Vol. I, p. 161. **Revisionists . . . fumed:** ET, who as IZL intelligence chief maintained at least indirect contact with the party. **fury of David Ben Gurion:** Kurzman, pp. 253–254; Bell, pp. 126–127; Bethell, pp. 176–180.

Chapter Nine: The Finest Hour

Books: Frank, Gerold, *The Deed;* Kurzman, Dan, *Ben-Gurion: Prophet of Fire;* Niv, David, *History of the Irgun Zvai Leumi;* Slutsky, Yehuda, *History of the Haganah, Vol. III.*

Interviews: Yaakov Amrami, Yehuda Lapidot, Eitan Livni (ELi), Yaakov Meridor, M. Shengold, Eli Tavin.

Articles, broadcasts, pamphlets, etc.: MB interview for Israel TV series, *Pillar of Fire;* Bethell, Nicholas, MB interview for *The Palestine Triangle; Minutes of IZL High Command Meetings* (HC minutes).

Textual notes: **Begin thought Ben Gurion:** MB remarks to Haganah leaders, and in his wall-poster newspaper. See specific references below. **same was true of Dr. Altman:** MB to Altman's deputy, Lubotsky, nearly a year earlier (see my Chapter Seven). **he wasn't strong enough:** MB, at IZL promotion ceremony July 23 declares: "The [Revisionist] Movement is ours and not Dr. Altman's . . ." Account of ceremony, MB's remarks, on file at Jabotinsky House. **When the Revisionists refused:** HC minutes, August 17, and September 1 and 19, 1944. **vetoed a . . . putsch:** HC minutes, September 1. **"Either you head":** HC minutes, September 19.

resented and respected: this is evident from MB remarks and positions throughout 1944, as documented in HC minutes. Not only does he accept the idea of the IZL's incorporation in an eventually united Jewish underground under BG's overall command, but he seems to crave the chance to discuss the prospect man to man, equal to equal, with Ben Gurion. **man with whom Jabotinsky had reconciled:** MB, in *Pillar of Fire* interview, remarks: "For a certain period, Jabotinsky and Ben Gurion were friends. . . . I know this directly from Jabotinsky. There were affectionate letters exchanged between the two of them." Also, Kurzman, pp. 177–178 and 191–193. The two men were similar in at least one, fascinating sense: Both wanted to be seen as intellectuals. Neither was, in the full sense of the word (though MB had considerably more formal education and erudition). **There must be no illusion:** HC minutes, August 2, August 31, September 19. In August 31 HC minutes, MB says that ideological training inside the IZL must stress that an escalated Jewish uprising against the Mandate is inevitable. "We promise nothing," he said: "no power in the [Israeli] state, only war, a war of independence." In September 19 meeting, MB gets endorsement for proposal to BG of a "National Liberation Committee" under BG's chairmanship. MB says he will "emphasize [to BG] that we have no divisive ambitions." He says he will insist on IZL autonomy, adding, "It is enough that we agree to his leadership." **At first, he tried to avoid:** MB, at July 1944 promotion ceremony, says he refused "more than one" request by Haganah commander Eliahu Golomb for a meeting. "We have nothing to say to them at present. They are emotionally unprepared for war" against the Mandate. **They were staking out:** HC minutes, August 12 and 17. ET confirms. "We had trouble with them [the Haganah] long before the *saison*." The *saison*—open season—is Israelis' common term for the Haganah campaign, beginning in late 1944, to root out the IZL and turn over its members to the British. **For a while:** HC minutes, August 12 and 17. **confront the interlopers:** HC minutes, August 17. **directed Livni to draw up plans:** HC minutes, September 19.

Begin also, however, agreed: HC minutes, September 10, where idea of meeting with BG is accepted; HC minutes, September 19, where MB presents platform he intends to propose to Ben Gurion. **took his rivals' latest feelers:** MB makes this explicit in October 15 remarks to IZL instructors. In the speech, on file at Jabotinsky House archives, he notes that although he has assured the Labor Zionists he has no ambition to unseat them as the dominant political force among Palestine's Jews, the Labor Zionist leadership sensed that "mass sympathy" for the Irgun is growing and could "one day completely shatter the spiritual dominance of the left on the *yishuv.* . . . They [Labor] understand that"—regardless of MB's assurances to the contrary—"objective developments could bring this about." He added that "a great fear has overtaken" Palestine's Arabs as a result of the IZL military operations against the Mandate. **Dismissing warnings from Tavin:** ET. **known . . . in Warsaw:** MB, in Bethell interview, says, "We knew each other well at Warsaw University. He studied medicine and I studied law." MS recalls both MB and Sneh from debates at the Jewish students' dormitory near the Vistula. **assumed Ben Gurion himself would be there:** HC minutes, September 10 and 19. **would propose:** HC minutes, September 19.

Ben Gurion did not show: report on meeting in HC minutes, October 1944, and the official *History of the Haganah,* pp. 1887–1893. **"I don't know why":** MB, quoted by Sneh in *History of the Haganah.* **he would blame:** in Bethell interview. MB says, "The man who influenced Ben Gurion not to meet me was Moshe Sneh" (HC minutes). **Begin raised:** sources for details of meeting are reported in HC minutes, *History of the Haganah,* pp. 1887–1893; Niv, Vol. II, pp. 91–96. The IZL and Haganah accounts of the meeting are remarkably similar in substance, though they differ in tone. **For several hours:** MB version (HC minutes) is three hours. Haganah account says five. **Although not announcing:** minutes of a second MB meeting with Haganah, October 31, on file at Jabotinsky House. Niv (Vol. II, pp. 91–96) says a formal decision to cease fire was taken eight days after the meeting with Sneh—though "in order to build up arms stores and prepare cadres for action," and not in reply to the Haganah pressure. **It made no difference:** MB address to IZL instructors, October 15. **Three weeks later:** minutes of October 31 meeting, from Jabotinsky House archives. **sent . . . Golomb:** he was a founding leader of the Haganah. Sneh was also there. **patted Begin on the back:** minutes of October 31 meeting. **"We have no choice":** minutes which, says Golomb, added: "It is clear we are not talking about your physical annihilation. But developments could provoke even that: your outright destruction. And by that point it will no longer matter who started it: This will be merely an issue of propaganda, of explanation." Sneh, it seems, still hoped the worst could be averted. "I sense the day of our joining forces is not distant," he is quoted as saying. "Even if you still think we are mistaken, you must take stock of the fact that we are the *majority*. The majority of the Hebrew people abhors your activities." **Begin replied:** minutes of meeting.

pamphlet called "We Believe": *ITU,* Vol. I, p. 39. The date is given only as "1944," but pamphlet includes a lengthy riposte to Golomb's attempts to "threaten us [the IZL] with Hebrew force." **He told the High Command:** HC minutes, November 1. **two Stern group youths:** see Frank's *The Deed* for excellent rendering of the Moyne assassination and its background; *The Revolt,* pp. 145, 150–151. **Begin fumed:** HC minutes, November 9. In *The Revolt,* p. 145, MB says he and Meridor heard about the Moyne attack on the radio while waiting for Sternist leaders Nathan Yellin-Mor and Yitzhak Ysernitzky [Shamir] to arrive for a meeting aimed at furthering IZL–Stern group coordination. "We were very angry," adds MB (p. 150). **this was beside the point:** HC minutes, November 9. **Ben Gurion acted:** Kurzman, pp. 253–254; Bell, p. 127; Bethell, p. 184; *The Revolt,* pp. 145–148. Ben Gurion's first response came a day after Moyne's assassination, when he pushed a motion through the Jewish Agency Executive, saying: "The Jewish community is called upon to spew forth all the members of this harmful, destructive gang, to deny them any shelter or haven, not to give in to their threats, and to extend to the [British] authorities all the necessary assistance to wipe out [this] organization." The directive became more explicit, and more obviously directed as much at the IZL as at the Sternists, at a convention of the Labor Zionist trade union federation, the Histadrut, two weeks later. There, BG won endorsement for a four-point plan. It called on Jews to deny the IZL and Sternists work or shelter. Point three: "not to submit to their threats . . . that there should be no action against them lest we involve ourselves in civil war." Point four: that Jews should help the British in "crushing terrorism"—that is, the Sternists and the Irgun—in Palestine. **This left the Irgun:** Kurzman, pp. 253–254. He notes that BG's offensive "would strike not at the 'guilty' though compliant Stern Group, but at the 'innocent' though defiant Irgun." Also, Bell, pp. 127–138; YA, YL, YM, ET.

Begin ordered: MB passed the order through his field commanders, confirm YA, YL, ELi, ET. Days after BG's Histadrut announcement, MB used his wall-poster newspaper to proclaim: "There will be no civil war" (*ITU*, Vol. I, p. 169). Though lashing out against the Labor Zionist Establishment for having "done nothing, nor allowed anything to be done, while millions of Jews in the Diaspora are slaughtered," MB declared: "Be calm, loyal Jews. Jew will not fight Jew in this country. . . . We will not go to civil war, under no circumstances and in spite of all provocations. Whatever happens, our soldiers will not raise their guns against rival Jews." **"We** *ached"*: ET. **"orders were crazy":** YA. **"had come to accept":** YL. **held its fire:** ET, YA. MB, in Bethell interview, says, "It was one of the most wonderful things . . . that for nine months, in spite of the persecution, not one of them created a breach of my instructions. Not one of them took up arms against the men of the Haganah." **"I find it hard":** ET. **"we well remembered":** YL. **Begin recalls the period:** MB in *Pillar of Fire* interview. **reduced to warning:** MB in *Herut* wall newspaper, December 2, 1944; *ITU*, Vol. I, p. 169.

revolt went on hold: Bell, pp. 134–135. **Begin never left home:** ELi, who is source for other details in this section. Although Livni moved in with MB, he—like Scheib, the earlier roommate, and Yutan, the Warsaw protégé—says he always sensed a certain "distance" in the relationship. Even then, says ELi, "I never called him 'Menachem.' " **frustration finally boiled over:** IZL proclamation, February 1945, *ITU*, Vol. I, p. 221. **the assault began to slacken:** Bell, pp. 135–138. **even when Churchill:** Kurzman, pp. 260–262; Bell, pp. 137–138. The election was in late July. The reaction of BG and the Labor Zionists ranged from the cautious optimism of BG himself to elation among most others. MB said by wall-poster proclamation in August: "It is our duty, out of responsibility and free will, to give [the new British government] a chance to prove whether . . . it wishes to make good without delay on its public commitment." But such an implicit cease-fire pledge had little meaning at a time when the IZL was doing little fighting anyway. And the tone of MB's proclamation is—prophetically, it soon turned out—pessimistic. He said recent history demonstrated there was every possibility that Britain's Labour government would *not* live up to its platform, but would instead "follow the road of other British governments, the road of treachery and denial." He said that the IZL would not settle for mere verbal shifts either. The revolt "is not being run for 'friendly statements,' or for 'cancellation of decrees.' " Its aim: "Hebrew rule on Hebrew land." The uprising "will not cease until that goal is reached." **Begin tried to regain:** *The Revolt,* pp. 177–178; Niv, Vol. II, p. 161; YA interview. **no takers:** MB, in an IZL pamphlet in June, says, "Many days—weeks—have passed since our call, since we proposed the plan, the aim of which was to unite the forces of the Nation, to save and liberate the Nation. We were not answered." YA and *The Revolt* (p. 178) suggest that of the 250 people queried, only one or two replied with nibbles of curiosity. **autumn an exasperated Ben Gurion:** Kurzman, p. 262. In pp. 258–261, Kurzman provides excellent background to Ben Gurion's move from assault to uneasy alliance with MB.

a vindicated Begin: his central argument for restraint, besides the belief that Jews in Hitler's world must not kill Jews, had been that sooner or later BG would have no choice but to join the battle against the Mandate; Bell, pp. 134–136. **political terms, Begin had won:** Bell, p. 135. **"Begin had been proven prophetic":** YA. **most powerful endorsement:** ET. MB, in *Pillar of Fire* interview, says: "Not only had the crisis passed. But people [in the IZL] realized that this way [of restraint] had been correct, and the relationship between my soldiers and me became very deep."

Chapter Ten: To Unity and Back

Books: Begin, Menachem, *The Revolt* and *In the Underground (ITU);* Ben Ami, Yitshaq, *Years of Wrath, Days of Glory;* Bethell, Nicholas, *The Palestine Triangle;* Clarke, Thurston, *By Blood and Fire;* Frank, Gerold, *The Deed;* Katz, Shmuel, *Days of Fire;* Lankin, Doris, *The Lady Was a Rebel;* Niv, David, *History of the Irgun Zvai Leumi;* Tavin, Eli, and Yona Alexander, editors, *Psychological Warfare and Propaganda: Irgun Documentation.*

Interviews: Yaakov Amrami, Eliahu Ben Elissar, Hart Hasten, Marek Kahan, Hillel Kook, Yehuda Lapidot, Eitan Livni (ELi), Yaakov Meridor, Mordechai Raanan, Mordechai Strelitz (MStr), Shmuel Tamir, Eli Tavin.

Articles, broadcasts, pamphlets, etc.: Bethell, Nicholas, MB article for *The Palestine Triangle;* Schindler, Rabbi Alexander, "A Conversation with Menachem Begin."

Textual notes: **Begin joined:** *The Revolt,* pp. 183–185; Bell, pp. 145–146; Niv, Vol. II, pp. 180–182. The first coordinated strike came on the final day of October. The agreement on a "joint resistance" was formally signed only in November, however, due to the Jewish Agency's delayed okay of the accord (Bell, Niv). **no guarantee:** *The Revolt,* p. 184. "We are anxious about the future," MB recalls explaining to the Haganah negotiators—the commander, Sneh, and his deputy, Israel Galili. "Yesterday they [the Agency leadership] told you to fight us. Who can tell what orders they will give tomorrow?" Yet MB told Ben Ami at the time (p. 364) that, all in all, the advantages of the new arrangement outweighed the dangers. **did give the Haganah veto power:** the terms of the agreement can be found in *ITU,* Vol. II, p. 7. Clause "b" states: "The IZL and LEHI will not execute their military plans unless approved by the [joint] command of the United Resistance." Clause "f" excludes "confiscation campaigns" from this rule. Clause "h," reflecting MB's skepticism, declares: "If one day the Haganah finds it necessary to desert the military struggle against British rule, the IZL and LEHI will continue to fight." **bomb attacks throughout Palestine:** Bell, pp. 145–146. **Begin moved to test:** Bell, pp. 151–152. **Ben Gurion was called on the carpet:** Bell, p. 152. **"fine and refined reply":** MB commentary, included in *ITU,* Vol. II, and quoted in Niv, Vol. II.

found its war feet: Bell, pp. 153–160. Also, list of military actions October 31, 1945–July 1946—the period of united resistance—in *ITU,* Vol. I. **arrest of Eitan Livni:** Bell, pp. 159–160; MB, *The Revolt,* p. 67, where he says his initial reaction was to feel "all was lost. . . . But the place of each [person arrested] was filled. The work was done, because it had to be done." In Livni's place, "Gideon came, our Giddy . . ." **growing Haganah tendency to veto:** *The Revolt,* pp. 198–199. In a wall-newspaper article later in April (*ITU,* Vol. II, p. 109), MB complains that the Haganah is trying to take credit for formation of the Joint Resistance. He recalls that only months earlier, the Jewish Agency leadership had been trying by "threat and force" to bring the IZL to heel. "Yet, rising above our feelings, we stretched out our hands when the moment of awakening arrived to those who did these things to us," Begin writes. He accuses the Labor Zionist Establishment of arrogance, "retrospective wisdom," and, above all, reluctance to escalate the revolt. "We have been bitterly disappointed by the pace and scope of the war as run by the leadership of the Haganah. . . . The Haganah leadership is preoccupied . . . with limiting the war."

Begin had started wooing: Clarke (pp. 33–41), whose section on Paglin is based mostly on a lengthy interview with him—an impossibility for this book, since Paglin died in an automobile accident in 1978. "Begin has heard about you and admires what you're doing," an IZL messenger is quoted as having told Paglin when conveying the invitation to join the Irgun. Also, Frank, pp. 57, 72, 114–120, 138–139. Virtually all IZL veterans interviewed stressed the special fondness MB had for Paglin. It was—the word comes up in interviews with various IZL veterans who knew MB and Paglin—a "love." **earning a reputation:** it was Paglin who led the audacious airfield assault a few weeks before Livni's capture. **fuse ran out on his temper:** YM, YA; Ben Ami, pp. 507–508. YM says of Paglin: "Giddy thought everything could be done. Sometimes he didn't realize there were some things that *should* not be done." **encounter in an orange grove:** Clarke, p. 40. **burst of energy:** Bell, pp. 161–164. Bell notes that about a third of the loot seized in the robbery—at the Barclays Bank branch in Nablus—was due to be taken out of circulation, and carried stamp marks indicating it was nonnegotiable. **two Irgun captives to the gallows:** Bell, p. 164; *The Revolt,* pp. 242–250; Bethell, p. 244.

ordered Paglin to find British: MB in Bethell interview: "I . . . ordered our men to capture as many British officers as possible. We went for officers deliberately, because we thought if we had British officers we would save our men." **considered the Irgun an army:** see reference in notes to Chapter Eight on MB's insistence, in his announcements of military operations, on the formal military status of the IZL. **swore an oath:** Clarke, pp. 23–24; Frank, p. 57. **demanded filial devotion:** typical of the patriarchal approach—to which YL, ELi, ET, and others refer—is MB's response to pressure in 1944 to avenge the murder of a Jewish truck driver. Ruling out such a reprisal, MB declared: "I take upon myself the moral responsibility for this issue, and release you" (HC minutes, August 2, 1944). **arrest of officers who might have shared:** Landau and Kahan, who gradually became MB's closest aides, were quintessential supporting players. The characterization of Landau comes from Katz and Lankin; also interviews (see list at start of Chapter Ten notes) with IZL vets, who requested anonymity on this point. MK—who is referred to as "Begin's close adviser" by Ben Ami (pp. 470, 479)—told me the book I was writing was especially important to him, personally, "because all my life, from 1925 onward—in the life of the [Revisionist] party to the present, I have played a role in the background. I was never on stage. My role was to make sure that everything went off well for the people on stage." The point about Landau and Kahan is especially important since it seems part of a lifelong pattern in MB's approach to politics and power. Indeed, back in Warsaw (see Chapter Four) he had a not dissimilar relationship with Yutan and Epstein. With one brief exception—his first several years as prime minister—the pattern holds. Kahan's specific duties included spiriting Aliza Begin from Jerusalem to Tel Aviv when MB tunneled underground in 1944. When MB grew a beard for cover and then decided to go shorn for the same reason, it was Kahan who shaved him. Mrs. Kahan played a similarly familial role in cooking sometimes for Begin, who, she recalls, was apt to be so absorbed in the weighty business of determining IZL policy that he would barely look up from his newspaper or notepad when she served the meal. **Begin recalled several years afterward:** *The Revolt,* p. 76. In pp. 73–76, he explains the concept and operation of his underground as a "fighting family." In the Schindler video interview, MB is asked to remark on the fact that one of his underground aliases was as Rabbi Sassover. Interestingly, MB replies, "You know, I became not so much a rabbi as an old man. I had a beard . . ." **"I admit I liked it":** *The Revolt,* p. 76, where he says his subordinates' use of the nickname "reflected good, heart-warming spontaneous affection."

confessed his anguish: in the wrenching, rambling preface to his public proclamation of restraint in late 1944, when Ben Gurion ordered his campaign against the IZL (*ITU,* Vol. I, p. 169). **Begin called a brief halt:** *The Revolt,* p. 247. In a later "internal memo" (*ITU,* Vol. II, p. 163), MB says world news media all "understood these officers would be executed if Ashbel and Simchon were." **warning the British to stop:** *ITU,* Vol. II, p. 154. The proclamation also reflected the importance MB attached to the propaganda aspect of his revolt—something to which he devoted the overwhelming majority of his underground time and energy. In May 1946 he had used his *Herut* wall newspaper to issue a similar warning on British attempts to prevent IZL youths from plastering Palestine's walls with his words. Citing an incident in which the British had opened fire on two youngsters who were putting up an IZL poster, MB said, "We must inform the rulers that we are used to answering fire with fire. Our [poster] stickers will henceforth carry their poster in one hand, and a live grenade in the other" (*ITU*, Vol. II, p. 141). **"We won't have to":** MK. **ordered Paglin to free two:** *The Revolt*, p. 247. The move came amid pressure from the Haganah to let all the captives go (MB internal memo; *ITU*, Vol. II, p. 163). MB, however, insists both in the internal memo and in *The Revolt* that he freed the two only to make it easier to hold those that remained. And in an IZL radio proclamation on June 23, he denied the Haganah had had anything to do with the release. **Breaking his silence:** June 23, *ITU*, Vol. II, p. 151. Until 1948 all MB statements on the IZL's underground radio, "The Voice of Fighting Zion," were read out by an announcer—one step ahead of the British police.

The British ordered: Bell, p. 166. **swooped down:** Bell, p. 167; Bethell, pp. 249–250; Clarke, Ch. 6; Katz, pp. 92–93. **Begin got a note:** *The Revolt*, p. 248. **"internal memo":** *The Revolt*, p. 250. The full text can be found in *ITU*, Vol. II, p. 163. "The case . . . is significant," the memo began, "because it put [the nation of] Israel and the Irgun in the center of international interest and established, if not forever at least for the near future, the status of every imprisoned Hebrew fighter." **gave Begin the green light:** *The Revolt*, p. 216; Clarke, Ch. 8. Clarke's book provides a thoroughly researched, and grippingly readable, account of the King David attack. **dreamed of two years earlier:** HC minutes, September 19, 1944.

The King David was: Clarke, pp. 25–32. The King David stands today—repaired, rebuilt, with an additional two stories—on the same rise across from the walled Old City. **Private Begin . . . had visited:** HH, to whom MB told the story over coffee in the King David years later. **Never one to meddle:** YA, ELi; Clarke, pp. 88, 106–108. MB's tendency to leave military detail to experts predated his tenure as IZL commander. MStr had noted this quality in Begin back in Warsaw Betar days. Indeed, in his Warsaw congress showdown with Jabotinsky, MB at one point rebutted Jabotinsky's taunt that a military uprising was impractical by saying that the crucial need was for political decisiveness, the *experts* could work out the details. Ben Ami, who was a member of Hillel Kook's wartime group of IZL veterans in the United States, recalls (p. 355) receiving a letter from MB saying, "I don't command . . . though I'm called 'commander.' " Observes Ben Ami: "He preferred . . . leaving operational details to expert associates." **Livni had come:** ELi. Livni was a political neophyte, in the sense that Strelitz had been in Warsaw. He was a no-nonsense military man, distinguished by determination and personal courage. ELi, in describing his typical briefing of subordinates before a field operation, remarks: "Here, I learned a lot from Begin: at the outset of my briefing, when I disclosed the target, I would deliver a *political* analysis of the situation—the timing of the attack, what it would produce politically. This kind of analysis was how Begin started meetings of the High Command, and this I learned from him." **Paglin sensed Begin's urge:** YA. Further insights into Paglin's approach and character from YL, who was one of several IZL men to remark that "Begin loved Giddy . . ." For the effect of Paglin's approach on MB, see *The Revolt,* pp. 67–72, which is source for MB quotes in this section. If Paglin's style and personality diluted MB's control over the military side of the revolt, it was watered down even further by a Paglin decision to give wider rein to area commanders. The issue had first come up when Livni was chief of operations, in 1944, and had never been resolved. Now, remarks ELi, "the area commanders, who had wanted to clip my wings, used the advent of Paglin to accomplish this. Paglin himself told me this later." **was only to ask:** ELi, YA, ET. **Paglin would answer, as Livni had:** ELi, YA.

Paglin intended: Clarke, who notes that Chaim-Toit, a member of the attack unit, also contributed to the planning. Clarke adds that MB had no role in such details, figuring they involved questions only Paglin could answer. Also, Bell, pp. 169–171. **Begin's code of battle:** MB had consistently stressed that, as a regular army, the IZL was committed to sparing civilian casualties wherever possible. **Begin okayed:** Clarke, Ch. 10. **Haganah had second thoughts:** The official Haganah history says the delay came after Chaim Weizmann ordered Haganah leaders to cease fire until a Jewish Agency session scheduled for Paris in August (Bethell, p. 254). MB, in *The Revolt,* p. 218, implies that in addition to written pleas from Moshe Sneh, he received—and agreed to—at least two requests to postpone the attack. **July 19, Sneh wrote:** *The Revolt,* p. 218; Clarke, p. 149. The Sneh notes are on file at Jabotinsky House.

Begin sat with Chaim Landau: Clarke, pp. 278–279. **In all, twenty-eight Britons . . . :** Clarke, p. 294. **Begin stared:** Clarke, pp. 278–279. MB, in *Pillar of Fire* interview, says, "The pain was inestimable. There was mourning; losses which we didn't want." **Begin cut him short:** Clarke, p. 277, based on interview with Paglin. **note arrived**

from the Haganah: *The Revolt,* p. 223. **Ben Gurion denounced:** Bell, p. 173; *The Revolt,* p. 223; Clarke, p. 285.

Begin issued: *ITU,* Vol. II, p. 191. **bristled with inaccuracies:** Clarke, Chs. 15–25, a painstakingly researched and documented account. Also, Bethell, Ch. 8, which includes further detail, notably from interviews with British protagonists in the controversy. **spoke of a pitched battle:** a phrase MB repeats, thirty years later, in the interview with Bethell. **ordered no investigation:** YA, who says the only IZL inquiry ordered was into Haganah behavior during the affair. There was a brief joint attempt by the IZL and Haganah to resolve precisely what operational details had been agreed on beforehand. But the Haganah said one thing, the IZL another, and there the controversy rested. A year after the attack, MB disclosed by wall poster (*ITU,* Vol. III, p. 214) that he had suggested there be an inquest to be judged by prominent, nonpartisan Jews—but that the Haganah had turned down the idea. **"rules of Land Warfare":** further IZL communiqué, broadcast on underground radio, cited in Tavin, p. 130.

"We mourn the Jewish victims": original communiqué, *ITU,* Vol. II, p. 191. **Meeting with the High Command:** Katz, p. 95. The group, further altered by the 1944–1945 Ben Gurion assault, now included Katz, Amrami, Landau, Paglin. **said he would not pretend:** Clarke, pp. 288–289. **condolence note:** Clarke, p. 288. Richard Mowrer, who wrote for a pro-Zionist newspaper in the United States, had won MB's undying gratitude for remarking earlier in the revolt: "I know your boys fight with their eyes [ideologically] open." MB reproduces the quote—yet makes no mention of the condolence note—in *The Revolt,* p. 98.

turned out, years later, to be false: Israel Galili provided the intelligence report, MB says in transcript of Bethell interview. Galili, when interviewed by Bethell for *The Palestine Triangle,* said his own source was a man named Boris Guriel, who had in turn received the information from American journalist Carter Davidson of the Associated Press. Guriel, interviewed by Clarke, denied that he had been Galili's source. Davidson died in 1958. Bethell (pp. 264–265) says that Shaw and other Britons are unanimous in denying the charge. When an American writer published a book alleging that Shaw had fled the building minutes before the explosion, leaving the others behind to die, Shaw sued for libel. According to Clarke (p. 303) the publisher withdrew the book from circulation and tendered an apology. **Begin repeated, and embellished:** wall-poster proclamation, August 7, including "additional facts" on the King David (*ITU*, Vol. II, p. 208). "It is clear," writes MB, "the guilty party is Shaw, himself, who prevented the evacuation." IZL communiqué, cited by Tavin, p. 130, says: "Sir John V. Shaw ignored the warnings and said, 'I am here to give orders to the Jews and not receive orders from them.' Sir John then gave strict orders to his guards to permit no one to either enter or leave the building. But Sir John and a few senior officers left and saved themselves." In a wall proclamation on the first anniversary of the attack, MB says he is setting straight "the facts" of the controversy. One of these, he says, is that a "representative of the Joint Resistance" had told the IZL that Shaw had received the telephoned warning but dismissed it, saying, "I do not take orders from Jews. I give them orders." MB complained that Haganah radio took its time about broadcasting the report, first allowing the Jewish Establishment media full rein in condemning the IZL (*ITU*, Vol. III, p. 214). MB repeats the alleged anti-Semitic barb in *The Revolt,* p. 221, though he refers to Shaw only as "a high official."

"enemy of the Jewish people": Bell, p. 173; *The Revolt,* p. 223; Clarke, p. 285. BG, in Paris at the time, made the remark to the newspaper *France-Soir.* **retorting that even before the King David:** wall proclamation, *ITU,* Vol. II, p. 210. Responding to BG's Paris denunciation of the King David attack, MB says: "We forgive him. . . . We have forgiven him—but not forgotten—something far worse. We mean deeds, done on the initiative and incitement of Mr. Ben Gurion"—that is, the anti-Irgun campaign of 1944–1945. **Years later, Begin would recall:** *The Revolt,* pp. 210–211. Of the post-King David period, MB, in *Pillar of Fire* interview, says: "They were terrible days. Suffice it to say that." **whole world was against:** interestingly, the Revisionists' Dr. Altman joined in conveying condolences to the British high commissioner, Sir John Shaw. Shaw, evidently unaware of the estrangement between Altman and Begin's IZL, wrote back: "I have received your letter for July 24 . . . which purports to express grief and sympathy in respect to the dreadful event of Monday July 22 which massacred more than one hundred of my faithful colleagues and friends. According to their own published boast this revolting crime was perpetrated by a national military organization [Irgun Zvai Leumi] which is associated with your Organization. In these circumstances I find myself unable to accept the expressions of regret and sympathy . . ." (Clarke, p. 290).

Chapter Eleven: Two Fronts

Books: Begin, Menachem, *In the Underground (ITU)* and *The Revolt;* Ben Ami, Yitshaq, *Years of Wrath, Days of Glory;* Bethell, Nicholas, *The Palestine Triangle;* Eban, Abba, *An Autobiography;* Garcia-Granados, Jorge, *The Birth of Israel: The Drama As I Saw It;* Katz, Shmuel, *Days of Fire;* Kurzman, Dan, *Ben-Gurion: Prophet of Fire;* Niv, David, *History of the Irgun Zvai Leumi;* Tavin, Eli, and Yona Alexander, editors, *Psychological Warfare and Propaganda: Irgun Documentation;* Wyman, David, *The Abandoment of the Jews.*

Interviews: Hillel Kook, Shmuel Merlin, Eli Tavin.

Textual notes: **Wanted posters:** reproduction of the British police's file photo and description of MB can be seen in Bethell, p. 208. Guatemalan UN envoy García-Granados, p. 155, describing an underground encounter with MB, writes: "One hundred thousand troops had been unable to find him; there was a price on his head; he was wanted dead or alive; his photograph was on every bulletin board in every post office in Palestine . . ." **latest underground persona:** *The Revolt,* p. 127. His then hideout was on Yehoshua Bin-Nun Street, described by MB, p. 122, as "a small side-street in North Tel Aviv, muddy in winter, and dusty in summer"—near both the city dog pound and its slaughterhouse. **Twenty thousand men:** Bethell, p. 271; Bell, p. 173. **another ersatz rabbi:** Bethell, p. 271; Bell, p. 173. **British unit camped:** *The Revolt,* pp. 227–230. **"We should have caught":** Lieutenant General Evelyn Barker, in Bethell, p. 271. He adds: "This is one of the problems of search operations. You have to rely on very junior people and . . . the whole operation can be damaged." **Ben Gurion called a truce:** Kurzman, pp. 267–268; Katz, pp. 96–97. **"partition" of Palestine:** when the question came to a vote by the Zionist executive, BG abstained (Kurzman, p. 268). **Britons seemed to start wondering:** Bell, Pt. III, Ch. 3; Bethell, Ch. 9. **its worst weather:** Eban, pp. 64–65.

Begin churned out: *ITU,* Vol. I, pp. 230–250; Tavin, pp. 132–139. **Paglin resumed:** Bell, pp. 181–182. **Begin was left to warn him:** MB, in an IZL radio statement October 30 (*ITU,* Vol. II, p. 274), charged that Labor Zionist leaders were not only falling in behind the idea of partition, but were once again obliging the British by denouncing the IZL and LEHI. On partition, MB said, "No Jewish institution will be permitted to sign on to such an historic crime." **"We will react":** *ITU,* Vol. II, p. 274. "The self-restraint we practiced two years ago will not be repeated," said MB in the radio statement. **Begin suddenly lost his appetite:** *The Revolt,* p. 127.

sent Eli Tavin: ET. **Ben Gurion toured the camps:** Kurzman, pp. 262–264. **formulated a legal argument:** MB in *Herut* wall newspaper March 1946 (*ITU,* Vol. II, p. 89). **might offer other commodities:** ET. **he sent Yisrael Epstein:** Katz, pp. 114–115. **Begin exulted in the prospect:** by IZL radio (November 6, 1946) and wall newspaper (November 10), MB celebrated the embassy attack. In the radio message, he termed the operation "a sign that the Hebrew War of Independence has become a world war, just as the war of Britain against the People of Israel is a world war." By wall newspaper he said: "The fire of the Hebrew revolt is getting hotter; and is spreading. . . . Our forces have grown. Our banner flies high . . ." (*ITU,* Vol. II, pp. 278, 284). **Epstein, who had tarried:** ET. **Lankin, who had escaped:** Katz, pp. 116–117. He arrived in Europe at the start of 1947. **both sides reject:** HK says he never had any desire to compete with MB with the Palestinian IZL, much less displace MB as IZL commander. He says only that he was determined to preserve the existence of the Hebrew Committee and other organizations that he and his colleagues had established in the United States independently of the Irgun. ET, for his part, remarks that one must not "overstate the [political] importance" of Kook's organization within the IZL. **They had resigned:** HK. **effectiveness then unprecedented . . . Roosevelt administration's willful neglect:** Wyman provides an eloquent—and deeply depressing—account of Kook's uphill effort to impress the Holocaust on the political psyche of America and its government. In the United States, Kook operated under the pseudonym of "Peter Bergson"—in order to spare the name of his late uncle, Avraham Yitzhak Kook, who had been the chief rabbi of Palestine. Kook's U.S. organization was generally known as the "Bergson Group." Ben Ami, pp. 382–397, 424–438, and HK, SM, and ET provided further background.

idea of a "Hebrew government": ET, HK; Ben Ami, pp. 382–383. **occasional, generally polite:** SM recalls that Kook wrote MB shortly after his elevation as IZL chief, saying, "I have the honor to present myself to you as a junior officer to his superior," whereupon Begin, says SM, wrote back: "It is I who should salute *you*, since you were in the Irgun long before me . . ." **secular and pluralistic:** HK. **managed to negotiate:** ET, HK. **fired off a letter:** ET. **Kook . . . rejected the agreement:** HK, who says that "I didn't want the committee to be above the Irgun, but neither did I want us to be subordinate to it." Ben Ami (p. 383) provides further background. **Begin was insistent:** Katz, pp. 114–118. **With Epstein, he sent:** Katz, pp. 114–115. **owed his escape:** Ben Ami, p. 396; Katz, pp. 116–117; HK. **early proclamation:** Ben Ami, pp. 356–357, 373–374, 388–389. **Begin resented . . . :** ET. **suspicious that the HCNL:** ET. Ben Ami (pp. 435–437) suggests at least some of Kook's HCNL colleagues shared this suspicion. He says: "I backed Merlin's opposing Kook's concept that the men of the HCNL are 'the political leaders of our national revolution [while the IZL leaders are] its technical commanders.' " **By letter, Begin rejected:** Ben Ami, p. 383. **"a shooting agency":** HK; Ben Ami, p. 436. **Begin ordered Paglin:** Niv, Vol. III, p. 64. He says MB agreed to a request for a truce from Haganah leaders. **had Shmuel Katz:** Katz, pp. 107–108. **The congress, however:** Kurzman, pp. 268–269; Eban, pp. 67–71. **Begin denounced:** he called it a step toward "partition." He also said the IZL cease-fire had been voluntary, temporary, and was now over. Declaration reproduced in Tavin, p. 138. **hesitated to declare:** Ben Ami, pp. 388–390. **Begin heard the news:** *The Revolt,* p. 132. **hours after:** Katz, pp. 108–109; Bell, pp. 184–185; Bethell, pp. 290–291. **"one had to go on":** *The Revolt,* p. 132. **stilted, yet perfectly understandable, English:** under normal circumstances, MB explains in *The Revolt,* the English-speaking Katz would have helped. Katz was still in Europe. **"We warn the occupation":** *ITU,* Vol. II, p. 318; Bell, p. 184.

He told the British: *ITU,* p. 318, the second of back-to-back MB proclamations. **Paglin promptly kidnapped:** Bell, p. 185. **Britons would be shot:** *ITU,* Vol. II, p. 318: "We shall no longer react with the cane; we shall react with fire." **amnestied the second:** they amnestied sixteen Arabs along with him, but this fooled no one. Churchill, in Parliament, declared: "This is the road to abject defeat . . ." (Bethell, p. 291). **political triumph:** Britain's Lieutenant General Barker later lamented that British soldiers in Palestine had been kidnapped, killed—even flogged. MB, in a wall proclamation reproduced in Tavin, p. 141, said, "We are confident that the historian of the future will devote more space to the evaluation of the [retaliatory flogging] act than to its dry details." He compared the IZL flogging to the Boston Tea Party and said, "This is the first time in two thousand years of Jewish history that such a reprisal has taken place." **to organize the creation:** HK. Further background in Ben Ami. **Receiving one of Kook's colleagues:** this was Ben Ami—a member of Kook's "Bergson Group" in the United States—and he describes the January 1947 encounter with MB in Palestine on pp. 388–392. **sent Katz to Paris:** Katz, pp. 114–115.

"without at least the Irgun's": HK. **purchasing two ships:** HK. The first, called the *Ben Hecht* in honor of the writer and influential HCNL supporter, was intercepted by the British and routed to Cyprus. The second, the *Altalena,* did make it to Palestine and would figure prominently in a later part of the story of Menachem Begin (see Chapter Thirteen). **"I am enraged":** Ben Ami, pp. 424–425.

To sell the immigration ships: HK. Wyman provides excellent background on opponents of Kook's activities in the United States. **alarm among some of Kook's comrades:** Ben Ami (pp. 435–437) says other HCNL colleagues still shared Kook's views in ideological issues, but "most of us soon parted ways with him . . . on the issue of our [agreeing to MB's insistence on] our unconditional commitment to back the Irgun's military struggle with all our resources. . . . I backed Merlin's opposing Kook's concept that the men of the HCNL are 'the political leaders of our national revolution [while the IZL leaders are] its technical commanders.' I agreed with Merlin's criticisms of the elements of bitterness that had crept into the dialogue between Kook [and] Eri Jabotinsky and the Irgun command." **named Merlin head:** Ben Ami, pp. 435–436. **tension did gradually subside:** several months after the move, MB wrote a note to the HCNL men categorically rejecting the idea of a provisional government. Merlin, who had been hesitating to bow to MB on the issue (Katz, p. 208), now went along (Ben Ami, pp. 436–437).

Chapter Twelve: Dissident Commander

Books: Begin, Menachem, *In the Underground (ITU)* and *The Revolt;* Bell, J. Bowyer, *Terror out of Zion*; Bethell, Nicholas, *The Pal-*

estine Triangle; Collins, Larry, and Dominique Lapierre, *O Jerusalem!;* García-Granados, Jorge, *The Birth of Israel: The Drama As I Saw It;* Gitlin, Jan, *Attack on Acre Prison;* Graves, R. M., *Experiment in Anarchy;* Haber, Eitan, *Menachem Begin;* Katz, Shmuel, *Days of Fire;* Lankin, Doris, *The Lady Was a Rebel;* Tavin, Eli, and Yona Alexander, editors, *Psychological Warfare and Propaganda: Irgun Documentation.*

Interviews: Yaakov Amrami, Yehiel Kadishai, Eitan Livni, Yehoshua Ophir, Mordechai Raanan.

Articles, broadcasts, pamphlets, etc.: Bethell, Nicholas, MB interview for *The Palestine Triangle.*

Textual notes: **wall poster and radio message:** *ITU,* Vol. II, pp. 319–365, and Vol. III. **Paglin organized assaults:** Bell, pp. 181–202; Bethell, pp. 289–299. **Begin boasted:** communiqué, broadcast on IZL radio, January 5, 1947, reproduced in Tavin, pp. 142–143. **quadrupled that pace:** on the average, with spurts and lapses. Calculated with help of Bell's detailed account (pp. 181–202) of IZL military operations. **"We in Palestine":** YA. **sentenced another IZL prisoner to hang:** *The Revolt,* Ch. 18, pp. 188–189; Bethell, pp. 297–298. **"Of course I want":** *The Revolt,* pp. 263–264. **took his case to the world:** *ITU,* Vol. II, pp. 336, 338, 339; Tavin, p. 145: "If there is any meaning in the word 'hero,' *you* are the hero. . . ." **delayed the execution:** Bell, p. 189; Bethell, pp. 300–301. **death sentences on three more:** Bell, p. 189; Katz, p. 123. Immediately after the Gruner delay, several thousand British civilians and dependents were also evacuated (Bethell, p. 301). **clamped under martial law:** *The Revolt,* p. 256; Bell, p. 189; Bethell, pp. 303–304; Katz, p. 125.

He issued a vow: via IZL radio, February 9, 1947 (Tavin, pp. 150–151): " 'Martial law is probably an unavoidable stage in our struggle and we will pass through it as we did all trials in our long history of tears, blood and toil. But the enemy must know that if he is going to turn our country into a hell, we shall turn his life into a hell . . ." In a proclamation several weeks earlier (Tavin, p. 146), MB had appealed to Palestine's Jews not to "permit yourselves to be frightened by the bogey of 'martial law.' Martial law will bring hardships and suffering, but it is no longer a question of suffering. The question is [one of] to-be-or-not-to-be . . . life or death . . . to the whole nation." **moved to a new safe house:** that of a sympathetic Jew serving in the Palestine police force (Bell, pp. 189–190). Only several weeks earlier MB had left his longtime hideout at Yehoshua Bin-Nun Street for a new abode, fearing discovery (*The Revolt,* p. 128). **turned full control:** Bell, p. 189; YK. ELi, who says, "Under martial law—I was in prison at the time, but I know that the area commanders were given a free hand." MB, interviewed by Gitlin (p. 86) says that during the martial-law period he barely saw Paglin. Giddy instead sent "reports" via intermediaries. **mounted sixteen separate attacks:** Bell, p. 190; Katz, p. 125. GOVERN OR GET OUT!: Bell, p. 190. **imposed martial law:** Bell, pp. 190–191; Katz, pp. 125–127. **martial law was lifted:** giving, notes Bethell (p. 305), "the impression of [British] weakness." Bell, for his part, pronounces the crackdown "a catastrophic failure" (p. 191). **"You've won":** *The Revolt,* p. 323.

British moved Dov Gruner: Bell, p. 196; *The Revolt,* p. 266. **A sobbing announcer:** the 7:00 A.M. newscast, MB recalls in interview with Bethell. The announcer, a woman, was Leah Porat. "Suddenly," recalls MB, "her voice broke down and she cried. It was one of the most bitter days of our lives." In fact, the news cannot have been a complete surprise. YA, then head of IZL intelligence, had managed via an informant to get a copy of the new execution directive several days earlier, and had gone to MB with the information. YA has kept a copy of the document—marked "Top Secret"—which he showed me.

Begin ordered Giddy: MB, in Bethell interview, says, "I gave an order to capture British officers and execute them just as our men had been executed." **directed Irgun units:** *The Revolt,* p. 275. The text of the announcement, as broadcast on IZL radio, is reproduced in Gitlin, p. 124 (French-language edition; volume was published in English with different pagination, but was unavailable at time of writing this book). MB said the Irgun was not embarking on a "revenge war," but would "no longer be bound by the normal rules of warfare." He said any British captive would be brought before the court-martial henceforth accompanying every IZL field unit. **foiled Irgun attempts:** *The Revolt,* p. 275: "The [British] military were literally not to be found. . . ." **okay the smuggling of a grenade:** the idea, initially, was for Dov Gruner to get the package and, if hanging was inevitable, pull the pin to deal "one last blow" to the British (*The Revolt,* pp. 272–273). **pulled the pin:** *The Revolt,* pp. 273–274. The prisoners acted the evening before their scheduled execution, in order to avoid killing a rabbi who, unaware of the plan, had insisted on being present to comfort the prisoners as they walked to the gallows.

publicized their heroism: years later, discloses YK, Begin stipulated in his will that he and Aliza should be buried on the Mount of Olives, adjacent to the tombs of the two youngsters who had blown themselves up rather than face a British hangman. **taunted the British:** on IZL radio he lashed out at the British for carrying out the hangings "at dead of night, like miserable cowards" (Bethell, p. 306). Also, *The Revolt,* p. 258. **bundled Amrami into a car:** YA. **breached the Acre fortress:** *The Revolt,* Ch. 21; Bell, pp. 204–218; Bethell, pp. 308–309. **"greatest prison break":** via IZL radio, May 7, 1947 (Tavin, pp. 155-156). **sentenced them to die:** Bell, pp. 221–222. **dismissed Britain's decision:** IZL radio declaration (Tavin, pp. 151–152). MB clearly did not expect the committee to accomplish anything of lasting value (Lankin, p. 46). In a later meeting with members of the committee (García-Granados, p. 156), MB is said to have remarked, "Even if your committee recommends termination of the Mandate, I feel the power of Great Britain in the United Nations will prevent a favorable vote in the General Assembly." **political recognition:** MB internal memo after the meeting; June 23, 1947; *ITU,* Vol. III, p. 150. **The envoys:** *The Revolt,* pp. 294–302. The Swede was Judge Emil Sandstrom, his Chinese colleague, Dr. Victor Hoo. Sources for quotes are *The Revolt,* and the official minutes of the session—vetted by both Begin and Sandstrom—which are reproduced in Tavin, pp. 215–228. **memorandum for his troops:** headed "Internal—TOP SECRET," *ITU,* Vol. III, p. 150.

British announced they would hang: Bell, p. 227. **this time two unarmed sergeants:** Bell, pp. 227, 236–245; Bethell, pp. 323–324, 336–338. **Begin denounced:** IZL radio, July 16, *ITU,* Vol. III, p. 203. **Pressure on Begin mounted:** Bell, p. 228; Bethell, p. 324; Haber, p. 187. **meeting of his High Command:** YA. **received two more UN envoys:** García-Granados (who was one), pp. 152–161. Also, *The Revolt,* pp. 304–307; Katz, pp. 161–163. The other South American delegate was Enrico Fabregat of Uruguay. **When both appealed:** García-Granados, p. 159. **Paglin hurried:** Bell, p. 237. **seemed nagged by doubts:** Bell, p. 237. He says MB's hesitation concerned only the question of whether the hanging was technically feasible. However, years later Paglin hinted privately to at least one associate

(YO) that the doubts had run deeper. According to YO, Paglin said MB "never gave the order to hang the sergeants" and that he, Paglin, had had to force the issue. But a much closer associate of the late Paglin, Mordechai Raanan, told me Paglin never said such a thing to *him*. Adds MR: "Paglin would *never* have acted on such a matter without Begin's approval. Never." Katz (pp. 168–169) says there was "neither dissension nor discussion" inside the HC on the matter of the hangings. The principle of retaliation had been set out publicly long before. "No special meeting of the High Command took place after the execution . . . to consider what action to take. In the close contact maintained among its members there was no further discussion. We had made our position clear." **Paglin, asking to see Begin:** Bell, p. 237.

"It is mortifying": Moshe Sharett—Ben Gurion's political adviser and, later, foreign minister—made the statement in Geneva. See Bell, pp. 238—239. **entry by the British mayor:** Graves, p. 68. **"Two British spies":** wall proclamation, *ITU,* Vol. III, p. 228. The Britons were, said the poster, "sentenced to hang by the neck until dead." This, the poster announced, "was not an act of revenge for the murder of our Hebrew prisoners of war; but a regular legal action of the underground court that tried—and will continue to try—criminals of the Nazi-British occupation force." **memo for field units:** August 1, 1947, *ITU,* Vol. III, p. 234. **"So you are the man!":** *The Revolt,* p. 307. **remembers no such:** García-Granados, pp. 154–160. **balding, pale from his indoor revolt:** Lankin, p. 33. **says the envoy:** García-Granados, p. 156. **"kidnapped, killed, even flogged":** Lieutenant General Barker, cited in Bell, p. 185. **"straw that broke the Mandate's back":** Bell, p. 238. **Ben Gurion went along:** Kurzman, p. 274. **majority of Jews danced:** Kurzman, p. 275; Collins, pp. 31–33.

Chapter Thirteen: Friendly Fire

Books: Begin, Menachem, *In the Underground (ITU)* and *The Revolt;* Bell, J. Bowyer, *Terror out of Zion;* Ben Ami, Yitshaq, *Years of Wrath, Days of Glory;* Bethell, Nicholas, *The Palestine Triangle;* Eliot, G. F., *Hate, Hope and High Explosives;* Gilbert, Martin, *Atlas of the Arab-Israeli Conflict;* Graves, R. M., *Experiment in Anarchy;*

Katz, Shmuel, *Days of Fire;* Koestler, Arthur, *Promise and Fulfillment;* Kurzman, Dan, *Ben-Gurion: Prophet of Fire* and *Genesis 1948;* Lankin, Doris, *The Lady Was a Rebel;* Levin, Harry, *Jerusalem Embattled;* Niv, David, *History of the Irgun Zvai Leumi;* St. John, Robert, *Shalom Means Peace;* Tavin, Eli, *The Second Front (SF);* Tavin, Eli, and Yona Alexander, editors, *Psychological Warfare and Propaganda: Irgun Documentation.*

Interviews: Yehiel Kadishai, Mr. and Mrs. Marek Kahan, Shmuel Katz, Hillel Kook, Doris Lankin, Yehuda Lapidot, M. Levine, Yaakov Meridor, Shmuel Merlin, Mordechai Raanan, Alex Rafaeli.

Articles, broadcasts, pamphlets, etc.: Bethell, Nicholas, MB interview for *The Palestine Triangle;* Merlin, Shmuel, "Bonjour Tristesse," retrospective on relations with MB, in *Monitin* magazine, October 1983, Hebrew; Paglin, Amichai, "Interview," recorded by Shlomo Lev-Ami, on MB and the IZL, on file at Hebrew University Institute for Contemporary Jewry, Jerusalem, Hebrew; Segal, Yisrael, "The Deir Yassin File," reprise based on Jabotinsky House archives material, in *Koteret Rashit*, January 1983, Hebrew.

Textual notes: **saw no place:** Kurzman, *Ben-Gurion,* pp. 292–293. **called on the IZL:** in a Tel Aviv news conference, October 1947 (Niv, Vol. II, p. 175). **alongside "our persecutors":** wall proclamation, December 1947, *ITU,* Vol. IV, p. 85. **Israel filling not only:** the vision was summarized in the Irgun insignia, which pictures a rifle superimposed on a map of this Greater Israel with the words *Rak Kach,* "Only Thus." **"We," by contrast:** *Herut* wall newspaper, November 1947, *ITU,* Vol. IV, p. 84. **vowed to retaliate:** wall communiqué, October 27, reproduced in Tavin, pp. 232–233. **After a clash:** Bell, p. 246; Katz, pp. 182–183. **"Have you held":** *Herut* wall newspaper, November 30, 1947, *ITU,* Vol. IV, p. 84. **betray their "sacred" homeland:** the phrases became refrains in MB wall-poster and radio proclamations of late 1947 and early 1948. (see *ITU,* Vol. IV) **vowed to oppose:** in the meeting with García-Granados and Fabregat of the UN committee. MB made the remark public via an IZL radio declaration, October 22, 1947, *ITU,* Vol. IV, p. 34. **"No majority of this":** minutes of MB remarks to Judge Sandstrom and his fellow UN committeemen (Tavin, pp. 224–225).

he figured: letter to Eliahu Lankin and the IZL's "European command" in Paris several days before the UN partition vote in late November, reproduced in Tavin's *SF.* MB says: "We cannot deny the possibility that even if we manage to expand our borders during this conflict [with the Arabs], the nation will still be forced back into her ghetto-state by international pressure. And there will be no choice but to wait for a time in the future when we will be stronger." **use IZL gunfire:** letter to Paris command, in which he speaks of the need for an "expansionist offensive" on the ground. **staging hit-and-run:** Bell, pp. 254–263; Bethell, pp. 352–353; Gilbert, pp. 41–42; Katz, Ch. 22. For a compelling day-to-day account of the period, also see Graves, Chs. 4 and 5. **ceding operational control:** YK; Bell, pp. 254–269. **last three weeks of December:** Gilbert, p. 41. **issued an Arabic-language:** IZL radio, December 3, 1947, *ITU,* Vol. IV, p. 90. The tone of the declaration proceeds from sweet reason to harsh caveat. He opens with the argument that the British—who have never seen Palestinian Arabs as anything more than "natives . . . to wait upon [them] bowing and scraping"—are looking for an excuse to stay put. This, MB said, they hoped to accomplish "via a bloody Hebrew-Arab war." He assured the Arabs: "All of us, without exception, want peace with you." But, he said, "if you force us, by further acts of murder, to go on the counterattack, God help the murderers and their accomplices!" He then rehearsed some of the IZL's past exploits, notably the attacks on British police headquarters (whose effect among Arabs he had heard almost firsthand on a bus the next day) and the Acre jailbreak. **still held to his view:** he told Sandstrom's committee in June the Arabs would not fight unless there was prodding and interference from outside (Tavin, p. 222). Further evidence of MB's mind-set comes from Paglin, who, in a statement on file in the archives of Hebrew University's Institute for Contemporary Jewry, says that he tried to get MB to take the offensive against the Arabs the very day after the UN vote. "I came to Menachem and said to him that this was a turning point for us. It was clear that there would be war with the Arabs now, that there was a need to forget the war with the British and concentrate all efforts on preparing for larger-scale war with the Arabs." Paglin says that MB replied "in these exact words: 'Forget the idea that an Arab will raise a hand against a Jew in the Middle East. The barrel [bomb] that you threw in Haifa and the great actions we undertook [mean] that no son of Yepheth will now dare raise his hands against the Jews. Do not worry. Such a thing will not be.' " **peaceful Arab acceptance:** MB told Bethell in 1976: "My greatest worry in those months was that the Arabs might accept the United Nations plan. Then we would have had the ultimate tragedy, a Jewish state so small that it could not absorb all the Jews of the world" (p. 354).

"This silly agreement": wall proclamation, December 1947, *ITU,* Vol. IV, p. 85. **Jewish "offensive":** *The Revolt,* p. 337.

He and Aliza spent: Lankin, pp. 73–75. **Begin would leave at dawn:** MK. MK's wife adds that during the day, MB and Aliza "were never together. . . . She never came with him: They had *children.* Just as my husband and me never went out together, they never went together. If both of us were caught, what would happen to the children?" Mrs. Lankin—then married to Shmuel Katz—recalls of her first meetings with Aliza in 1947 that "Ala [was] small, thin, and stooped from long, endless days and nights of knitting and reading to tide over the interminable solitude of life in the underground." Still, Aliza seemed irrepressibly cheerful, given the circumstances. Recalls Mrs. Lankin (p. 40): "Ala gave birth to two children in the days of the underground. No loving husband brought her flowers and gifts, no friends helped to while away the days. She lay alone, unvisited, unknown—and she returned home each time to tackle the additional burden, smilingly and cheerfully. . . . When in addition to these burdens, one adds the painful suffering and terrible debilitating effect of chronic asthma, then truly Ala's gaiety and fortitude were such as to command both the amazement and admiration of her friends." **"usually so engrossed":** Mrs. MK. "He lived in the clouds," she said in an interview not long before her death in 1985. "Once he was reading the newspaper in my house and remarked, 'What delicious food!' So I asked him what *kind* of food he thought it was. "Potatoes," he said. Mrs. Kahan chuckled, "You should be so lucky!" It was barley, she recalls, adding, "You couldn't *get* potatoes at that time." **Late at night:** generally, MB would arrive at 7:00 A.M. and leave at 11:00 P.M., says Mrs. Kahan. **Mograbi Square:** *The Revolt,* p. 341.

he scrawled a warning: broadcast on IZL radio, February 29, *ITU,* Vol. IV, p. 220. **hundreds of volunteers:** MR; Katz, p. 188. **job to Paglin:** Katz, p. 188. **called a joint session:** late January 1948, *The Revolt,* p. 348. **he joined Jewish Agency leaders:** Katz, pp. 203–204. He and Landau were with MB at the negotiations (Bell, pp. 263–264). **But Ben Gurion:** Katz, p. 204. **Begin, meanwhile, resented:** in March, for instance, he rehearsed on IZL radio (*ITU,* Vol. IV, p. 237) the IZL's long record of military activity. He said BG's men had taken the battlefield only because "events" had forced it on them. Ben Gurion, charged MB, was still preoccupied with his own political ambitions, his desire to uproot the [IZL and LEHI] "separatists," and that this explained why the just-concluded operational accord with Agency representatives did not seem likely to be ratified. **Irgun units in Jerusalem:** MR, who was Jerusalem commander. **told, in intermittent radio:** YL, who was deputy Jerusalem commander, says MB was told "plans to strike in the general [Jerusalem] area." **"We didn't like to talk":** YL. **week after the Haganah's:** Bell, pp. 292–293. Levin, who was working for Haganah radio, provides a compelling day-by-day account of the period, pp. 42–71. **unlike Castel:** Graves, p. 179. There is no reason to disbelieve his account—an entry in a diary marked generally by its abhorrence of violence on all sides and its willingness to criticize all offenders, his own British colleagues included. **The only hint of trouble:** MB, in an April 11 wall-poster proclamation (*ITU,* Vol. IV, p. 276) quotes an April 4 report in the pro-Labor newspaper *Davar* on overnight sniping from a series of Arab villages, including Deir Yassin. There is no indication of further such reports. **Raanan argued:** MR. **Haganah commander agreed:** quoted in Bell, p. 292. **trickling into Palestine since December:** Graves, in March 8 diary entry (p. 152), says that at Ras el-Ain on the road from Jerusalem to the Palestine coast, "six hundred Iraqis have installed themselves in some buildings just outside the water-supply station" and that the British "seem to have no intention of evicting them."

attackers struck at dawn: MR; Bell, pp. 294–296; MR, YL. **never got close enough:** Kurzman, *Genesis.* MR and other IZL men spoke to Kurzman in the late 1960s for this account, which MR told me he felt was the most accurate one published. Other accounts—like Collins's, p. 304—say the loudspeaker truck toppled into a ditch. It is a near-impossible task to assemble an authoritative account of the battle of Deir Yassin, so colored have become the recollections of all who were involved by the ideological debate that has raged around the killings at Deir Yassin for decades. Especially on the Irgun side, some of the details vary sufficiently from one IZL vet's account to another's to suggest a defensive tendency to rewrite history. The presence or lack of outside Arab troops provides an example. All sides, however, agree on some major details, and these represent the body of the account given here. I have also relied on the recollections of MR, YL, and secondary sources for further details—in the specific notes that follow. Where there are conflicting accounts, these have also been included in the notes. But crucially relevant to the story of Menachem Begin is his own role—or lack thereof—in the tragedy, and his own response to it. In earlier biographies this has been obscured in the fog of what did or did not occur at Deir Yassin. **Raanan, on a nearby:** MR. **"the method":** MR. **When the Haganah's:** Kurzman, *Genesis,* p. 147. Some IZL accounts—including Begin's on the day of the attack—say the Palmach at least briefly provided help to the attackers. But in the account offered by Ben Ami, himself an IZL veteran who cites his "many conversations with Mordechai Raanan" and other IZL or LEHI sources, there is no mention of any Haganah presence until three days after the attack. Still, when Harry Levin reported for Haganah radio-station duty that evening, he found an order to broadcast no details. "The commander [Haganah Jerusalem chief David Shaltiel] had a cold, furious look in his eyes," recalls Levin. "It seems the Haganah is also involved. During the attack the IZL found itself in difficulties and called on the Haganah to help extricate their wounded. That was in the earlier stage, before the butchery." **including at least some:** so suggest Haganah postmortems, Arab survivors, and a Red Cross report that figure in Collins's account, and at least one IZL officer's testimony, gathering dust at Jabotinsky House, which was exhumed in *Koteret Rashit*'s 1983 reprise of the battle. The officer, Yehoshua Gorodenchik, says in his Jabotinsky House archives testimony: "After we had suffered many wounded we thought of retreat. We had prisoners, and before the retreat we decided to kill them. We killed the wounded as well, since anyway we could not offer them first aid. . . . In one place, eighty Arab prisoners were killed, after some of them opened fire and killed one of the men who came to extend first aid to them. They [IZL-LEHI troops] also found some Arabs who had dressed up as women, so they opened fire on women who did not rush to get down to the prisoners' gathering area." MR, while not explicitly confirming this, implies excesses may have been committed in the heat of battle—all the more so since most of the force was made up of recent volunteers, many of them still in their teens and newcomers to the battlefield. Levin, who spoke with two Haganah photographers sent in afterward, says (p. 59) one "told me he saw a large pile of burned and half-burned bodies in a pit; another pile of children's bodies, about sixteen of them. In a room of one house were the bodies of a woman and child; in a second room the bodies of two villagers and two uniformed Syrians."

issued an exultant: written Saturday, the day after Deir Yassin fell (although broadcast from IZL radio in Tel Aviv only on Sunday),

ITU, Vol. IV, p. 274. **To Raanan:** Segal's 1983 reprise in *Koteret Rashit.* **British thought him:** a British voice, recalls Levin (p. 60), broke into Haganah radio's nightly transmission April 10 and barked, "What about Deir Yassin, you murderers!" **Ben Gurion evinced:** Kurzman, *Ben-Gurion,* p. 280. The Jewish Agency issued a statement expressing "horror and disgust at the barbarous manner in which this action was carried out" Koestler (p. 160), notes the reply to BG's condolence message from Transjordan's royal court: "Not without logic, that as the Jewish Agency spoke in the name of all the Jews of Palestine, it would have to take the responsibility for their acts." **Begin's critics charged:** a British government spokesman, quoted in Levin (p. 71), declared after the hospital convoy ambush, "A very important change has been brought about in the situation in Jerusalem due to the evil barbarities committed at Deir Yassin." Levin notes, however, that Arab statements on the ambush make no such link. **voted with their feet:** the panic was also fueled by Arab radio reports that exaggerated the truth, frightening enough, of what had happened at Deir Yassin. Recalls Koestler (p. 160): "The effect . . . was the exact opposite of its aim: the Arab population was seized with panic, and fled from villages and towns with the pitiful cry: 'Deir Yassin.' " **in a phrase that remains:** indeed, it was a staple of Palestine Liberation Organization statements once Begin became prime minister in 1977.

mix of defensiveness: wall proclamation, and April 14 radio transmission, *ITU,* Vol. IV, pp. 276, 282. **in fact, says Lapidot:** YL. Ben Ami, p. 441, says that attackers found "a Moslem colonel from Yugoslavia, a British sergeant, two Iraqi soldiers and other Britons" among the village's defenders. **unclear whether Begin knew:** typically, he seems to have little interest in such military detail—a lapse whose effect was exacerbated, YA and MR suggest, by the tenuous radio communication between MB in Tel Aviv and the Jerusalem battlefront. What is clear is that, even years afterward, he continued to blur or ignore such detail and to repeat errors of fact. In no account, for instance, does he mention dynamiting houses—saying, instead, that the attackers had been forced to toss grenades. He has continued to suggest that far greater numbers of Syrian or Iraqi troops were present than was the case according to even IZL witnesses. This is not unlike MB's insistence to Bethell, in recapping the King David episode, that his men had fought a "pitched battle" with British troops in the basement. Similar, too, is his recollected sense that the *intention* to give prior warning—whatever its effect, or lack thereof—was sufficient indication that the IZL did all it could to avoid casualties. "Loudspeakers were brought there—this is a very interesting fact about the ethics of the Irgun—to warn civilians to leave . . ." MB tells Bethell of Deir Yassin (p. 355). **He broadcast it:** IZL radio, April 14, *ITU,* Vol. IV, p. 282. **"From an Arab source":** *ITU,* Vol. IV, p. 282. Interestingly, Ben Gurion was not averse to seizing the benefits of this. (Kurzman, *Ben-Gurion,* p. 281). He ordered Jews to settle promptly in Deir Yassin and other Arab towns and villages vacated in the post–Deir Yassin panic. In the nearly four decades since, virtually none of the refugees has been allowed to return. **loyalty and responsibility:** MB would make this point explicit to Lapidot, years later in the circumstances of another tragedy (see Chapter 27).

attack on Jaffa: Bell, pp. 299–303; *The Revolt,* Ch. 29. **raiding a British armory:** Bell, p. 299; *The Revolt,* pp. 349–351. Both the armory and train attacks were in the same general area, around Pardess Hannah, in the north of the country. The armory attack provokes one of the most strident entries to date in Mayor Graves's diary (p. 174). "The IZL," he writes, "did a very dirty piece of work . . . when they robbed the armory, murdered the guard in cold blood, killed the C.O. and wounded seven soldiers. They got away with a lot of arms . . ." He adds: "The terrorists have often been likened to mad dogs, and rightly so, though they do not suffer from the red-eyed frantic form of rabies, which drives mad dogs like bullets down the middle of the street. Their madness is marked by a calculating, perverse form of reasoning based partly on the memory of ill-usage and partly on a blank inability to see anyone else's point of view. . . . The curious thing is that some of their leaders and spokesmen, if morally defective, are far from being mentally so. Their staff work and planning are first class, and their propaganda must be very heartening to their own adepts, though it would convert very few intelligent neutrals . . ." MB's report on the armory attack (*The Revolt,* p. 349) is strikingly different: a head-on battle between the IZL unit and "a first-rate regiment of British artillery; a few score fought against hundreds, and won." This seems a further example—along with the King David and Deir Yassin controversies—of MB's selective memory. Paglin, in the Hebrew University archives statement, says that during the armory attack, "a soldier [of the IZL] shot three or four colonels after having taken them prisoner, after they had surrendered and were in custody for somewhere between fifteen minutes and an hour. There was an [IZL] investigation and the man was kept away from active duty for a long time." Paglin says the man in question was a close friend of three of the four IZL boys hanged at Acre. **addressed the troops:** *The Revolt,* p. 354. **set up headquarters:** *The Revolt,* pp. 354–371; Katz, pp. 219–221. **Begin returned:** *The Revolt,* pp. 364–365. **British tanks:** Bell, pp. 302–303. **first news conference:** *The Revolt,* p. 369.

wanted Begin's men to disband: Kurzman (*Ben-Gurion,* p. 292) refers to BG's evolving "obsession with one army." **long since stopped:** MB at least briefly, in late 1947, had considered the possibility of keeping the IZL alive as an "underground" force against partition, even if and when Ben Gurion declared a state. He had suggested as much in his meetings with the UN committee envoys in the summer of 1947 *(ITU).* In his November 1947 letter to Lankin and the IZL Paris command (reproduced in Tavin), MB listed this possibility among future Irgun options, including the one he eventually chose, conversion of the IZL into the Herut party. But in the intervening months, he had come to see the "underground" option as impractical. In another letter to the Paris command, February 21, MB argued: "Any real attempt to seize official power would mean not only bloodletting but a defeat for the Irgun and catastrophe for the [Jewish] people" (quoted in Niv and Tavin). **might hesitate . . . amid pressure:** MB's taunts of "surrender" notwithstanding, BG had long represented the militant camp in an Agency leadership that included those more disposed to caution and compromise. When on May 12 the leadership endorsed proclamation of the State of Israel, it did so by a one-vote majority. **a series of appeals, demands:** notably, March 28, April 1, May 9, *ITU,* Vol. IV. **On May 9:** *ITU,* Vol. IV, p. 325. MB said if BG didn't proclaim a government, "we shall arise and rebel. There will be surrender, but only by the Vichy leadership. The Hebrew Government will be founded. . . . Leaders, beware your actions."

Begin replied: text of address in Tavin, pp. 240–246. **Paglin's Tel Aviv apartment:** AR, who was there. "It was in a little room in Paglin's apartment . . . near the railroad station." Lankin (p. 113) says she drove MB to the apartment, "a comfortably furnished, bourgeois flat . . ." **his own inner circle:** Lankin, pp. 112–114; AR. **recalls**

Katz's wife: Lankin, p. 113. Mrs. Lankin was married to Shmuel Katz at the time; they were later divorced.

When Begin finished: HK. **shmuck . . . named Cohen:** The reference appears to have been to the Haganah's David Cohen. **It was Ben Gurion:** see earlier chapters. Also, in a rare spillover of resentment that MB tried to keep to himself, his remark in Bethell interview that Moshe Sneh, back in 1944, had "influenced Ben Gurion not to meet me." The resentment cannot have been helped in this 1948 encounter with Kook by the fact Kook and Ben Gurion had had quite a friendly discussion in New York several years earlier (HK). **drew a carefully folded:** HK. **Begin met senior:** at IZL headquarters, then at Freund Hospital in Tel Aviv, which had served as field hospital during the Jaffa fighting (Katz, pp. 228–229; Ben Ami, pp. 464–465).

needed desperately: arms: typical is the observation of American reporter George Fiedling Eliot, newly arrived in Palestine in the spring of 1948 (p. 29). "The constant talk was of the need for getting in more weapons and equipment by sea . . ." The saga of the IZL arms shipment—like the King David attack and Deir Yassin—has been the subject of decades-long controversy in Israel. It is slightly less difficult, however, to assemble the facts of the arms-boat talks, in that Begin's critics have disputed not so much the facts as questions of intention and interpretation. **Ben Gurion replied by note:** Katz, p. 231.

sent Katz and Marek Kahan: Katz, p. 231; Ben Ami, p. 479; SK. **At the start of June:** Ben Ami, pp. 473–474. **news reached him:** in the form of a personal message from Arye Ben Eliezer on his return to Palestine (Ben Ami, pp. 475–476). **via the BBC:** *The Revolt*, p. 155. **Begin fired off a cable:** *The Revolt*, pp. 155–156; Ben Ami, p. 481; HK, who was in Paris with Katz. **met Haganah commander:** Kurzman, *Ben-Gurion*, pp. 292–293; Katz, pp. 237–238. **No more deals:** Kurzman, *Ben-Gurion*, pp. 292–293, based in large part on interviews with the Haganah's Galili. **"keep clear" messages:** though the *Altalena* could not respond, the messages (Ben Ami; *The Revolt*) were received. **received Galili:** Ben Ami, pp. 487–488; Kurzman, Ben-Gurion, p. 293. **Begin . . . seemed not:** Merlin, quoted in Ben Ami, p. 488. **Galili left, saying:** Ben Ami, p. 489; Kurzman, *Ben-Gurion*, p. 293. **Kfar Vitkin:** Ben Ami, pp. 490–491. **Begin also suggested:** Kurzman, *Ben-Gurion*, p. 293. **plowed south of Crete:** Ben

Ami, p. 492. **20 percent:** Kurzman, *Ben-Gurion,* p. 293. **"argued and pleaded":** Ben Ami, p. 492.

as Begin spoke: HK; Ben Ami, pp. 494–495. **"You're crazy!":** HK. **Begin said nothing:** HK; Ben Ami, pp. 494–495. **Before dawn:** Ben Ami, pp. 498–508; Kurzman, *Ben-Gurion,* pp. 293–294; Merlin *Monitin* article; HK. **Ben Gurion summoned:** Kurzman, *Ben-Gurion,* p. 293. Ben Ami, pp. 499–500. **recently laid camouflage netting:** Merlin article. **Begin went on by launch:** Ben Ami, pp. 502, 504. **showed up with a message:** Ben Ami, p. 505; Kurzman, *Ben-Gurion,* p. 294. **told his men to keep unloading:** Ben Ami, who was on the beach at the time, pp. 506–508. **Begin told Meridor:** YM says it was clear that Paglin, left to his own devices, might have done just about anything—up to and including "killing Ben Gurion and the cabinet." Interviewed by Kurzman for the BG biography, Paglin "admitted to the author that he and another Irgun leader, Bezalel Stolnitzky, conspired to overthrow the government" during the *Altalena* crisis. "They were prepared," Paglin said, "to 'wipe out' Ben Gurion and his cabinet if necessary" (p. 293). **Pacing the beach:** HK. **"These Haganah guys":** Merlin article. **"negotiate with these** *bozes*": Merlin article. The epithet, he explains, was Labor Zionist slang for reactionaries. **"I was a sergeant!":** HK. **"Don't worry":** Ben Ami, p. 509.

mayors returned: Ben Ami, p. 510. **more sympathetic ... foreign press:** Ben Ami, p. 508. **Merlin suggested:** Merlin article. **suggested that Meridor:** *The Revolt,* p. 173. **situation report:** YK. MB quotes are from Ben Ami, p. 511. "This was all I heard. Suddenly, gun fire opened on us from all sides. . . ." **wounded Merlin:** SM; Merlin article. On arrival at the *Altalena,* Merlin was taken below deck. **On the beach:** Ben Ami, pp. 514, 516–519; *The Revolt,* pp. 173–174; Kurzman, *Ben-Gurion,* pp. 294–296; Katz, pp. 243–246 (account by the boat's skipper, Monroe Fein, written immediately after the crisis at Katz's request and placed on file in Jabotinsky House archives). **When someone on deck:** Ben Ami, pp. 516–518. **On the terrace:** Arthur Koestler (pp. 245–254) was in Israel at the time and compiled forty pages of notes in search of an authoritative account. He said that by the time the crisis erupted in its final explosion, the whole of Tel Aviv's UN staff and foreign-correspondent population was watching from the Dan and other nearby hotels or café terraces.

short, wiry character": American reporter Robert St. John (Ch. 8), based on interviews at the time with Fein. **group of fellow navy**: St. John, pp. 48–49. **Begin shouted**: Ben Ami, p. 518. **no one listened**: the firing "back and forth," says Fein to St. John, went on "for a full hour." **requested a cease-fire**: Fein to St. John; Katz, p. 245. **army field gun**: Fein to St. John, p. 49; Katz, p. 246. **Begin had the IZL men**: Merlin article; Ben Ami, p. 519. **telling Fein**: St. John, p. 49. MB's assurance came when Fein buttonholed him and said, "We are going to lose our ship and our cargo and a lot of lives unless someone makes some sense out of the situation." **shell hit the cargo**: St. John, pp. 49–50. Also, Fein to Katz, pp. 246–247. **decided not to risk**: HK notes that virtually everyone in Israel knew IZL headquarters was at Freund Hospital. He says that years later he asked BG why he hadn't arrested Begin at the time. BG, says Kook, got extremely flustered. But the implication of his jumbled reply was that he had feared doing so. St. John, in his on-scene account of the period, says that once the *Altalena* crisis had cooled a bit, people started wondering why MB had not been arrested. "His [MB's] followers said that the government was afraid to arrest him. Government people said that arrest was just what Begin wanted. Then he could pose as a martyr. Then his fanatical followers could be whipped into a frenzy of violence" (p. 170). By St. John's account, both sides seemed to be saying more or less the same thing—and about what HK now says. **weeping into the microphone**: Ben Ami, p. 520; Katz, pp. 249–250; Koestler, p. 251. Quotes are from text of speech, on file at Jabotinsky House archives.

returned to Kfar Vitkin: ML, a native of Brisk-de-Lita, and an IZL soldier who was there. **"I still remember"**: ML. **"His charismatic image"**: Ben Ami, pp. 521–522. **Katz, back from Europe**: Katz, p. 250. **"Blessed be the cannon"**: Kurzman, *Ben-Gurion*, p. 296. Koestler, p. 249. **Begin wanted**: DL (then Mrs. Katz). **"He was a completely"**: Lankin, p. 153.

Chapter Fourteen: Terms of Peace

Books: Begin, Menachem, *In the Underground (ITU);* Bell, J. Bowyer, *Terror out of Zion;* Green, Stephen, *Taking Sides;* Katz, Shmuel, *Days of Fire;* Kurzman, Dan, *Ben-Gurion;* Lankin, Doris,

The Lady Was a Rebel; Levin, Harry, *Jerusalem Embattled;* McDonald, James, *My Mission in Israel: 1948–1951;* St. John, Robert, *Shalom Means Peace;* Slutsky, Yehuda, *History of the Haganah, Vol. III;* Tavin, Eli, and Yona Alexander, editors, *Psychological Warfare and Propaganda: Irgun Documentation.*

Interviews: Eliahu Ben Elissar, Eitan Haber, Yehoshua Ophir, Eli Tavin.

Textual notes: **toyed with moving:** Lankin, p. 154. She, in fact, raised the question in a bid to cheer Begin up during the few days MB stayed with her and her then husband, Shmuel Katz, after the *Altalena* incident. But the idea "began germinating and maturing in his brain and eventually emerged as a full-fledged plan." **But Meridor, Katz, and the others:** Katz, p. 252; Lankin, p. 154. **two ministers resigned:** Bell, p. 327. **Ben Gurion's version:** symptomatic was a diary entry by Levin, June 25: "Ben-Gurion is in town, on his first visit since *Pesach* [Passover]. Saw him in the street today, greyer than before, graver, unsmiling, striding along as though his eyes were fixed just above ground. . . . A bodyguard of two armed men walk some distance behind him. Talk is that the IZL, embittered by the Government's shelling of their secret arms ship near Tel Aviv last week, may try to kidnap him . . ." (p. 253). **more sadness than:** Koestler, p. 266. He says MB spoke "as thoughtfully and unfanatically as his propaganda is bombastic and violent"—not at all par for Begin, who in other circumstances (like the meeting with UN envoy García-Granados) often blurred that distinction. Lankin (p. 153) says Koestler's visit came during the few days immediately post-*Altalena* when MB was living at the Katzes. **some of the old fire:** St. John, pp. 171–188. Returning also was MB's tendency to speak with public bombast in a private forum. St. John's interview lasted for two July afternoons, interrupted at nightfall the first day when MB announced he had an "important conference" to attend. It was more a speech than an interview. At the start of the second afternoon's session, Begin picked up his narrative as if a switch on a record player had been flicked off and then on: "almost in the middle of a sentence. In the middle of a paragraph anyway."

He sent Katz: Katz, pp. 252–280; Lankin, pp. 155–188. **ran their own show:** even when it came to deciding the fate of five Britons—accused of being Arab "spies" and captured by the IZL in Jerusalem in early July. MB, by radio phone from Tel Aviv, suggested trading the five for five of the IZL men still in detention over the *Altalena,* including Meridor, Lankin, and Kook. Katz (p. 256) "turned down the idea. It would be an unequal exchange." Instead, he turned them over to the Haganah in return for a public announcement that the Israeli government would bring them to trial. In the event, the attorney general dropped charges against three of them for lack of evidence. The other two were tried. One was acquitted. The second was sentenced to seven years' imprisonment, but this was overturned by an Israeli appeals court. **"one of the most deadly":** Tavin, pp. 247–248. **Begin said no:** Katz, pp. 263–272. **visit to Jerusalem:** Lankin, pp. 177–180. Green (p. 35) says the visit was August 3, and that a crowd of some four thousand supporters packed Zion Square for the speech. **"Arab," or Sephardic Jews:** The term "Sephardic," from the Hebrew word for "Spain," literally refers to Jews who trace their roots back to medieval Spain and Portugal. In the modern Israeli political lexicon, however, the term has come to refer to Jews who came from Middle Eastern or North African countries—the area to which most Sephardim fled when forced out of Iberia in the fourteenth and fifteenth centuries. **Begin personally oversaw:** YO, who was one of the men overseen. **at an open-air theater:** EBE, EH; both were there. MB's appearance in Tel Aviv, like his Jerusalem visit, came in August (Koestler diary entry, p. 274). **"quiet, like a temple":** EH. **five words:** EBE. **Koestler recalls:** p. 274.

portrayed him as: Tavin, pp. 247–257. **party platform:** reproduced in Tavin, pp. 249–257. **The Soviets:** a reference in Green's *Taking Sides* suggests the relationship might conceivably have been more direct. He cites (p. 21) a Jewish Agency document captured by the British and passed on to the Americans. It alleges that Begin "regularly accepted funds from Eugenie Podvigin, the Second Secretary of the Soviet legation in Beirut." Green wisely points out that there is ample reason to suspect this may have been part of Mandate–Jewish Agency attempts to discredit MB—and thus must be taken with a grain of salt. Yet it is certain MB valued the Soviets, politically—as a lone voice of outside sympathy during the years underground. This is reflected in a succession of wall-poster and IZL radio declarations. In May 1945 (*ITU,* Vol. I, p. 226), MB celebrated a Moscow Radio transmission "of great importance to Zionism." The Soviet announcer, MB relates, said the Soviets would "not oppose the migration of Jews to Israel." This meant Jews in Russia could leave. Only British policy, MB argued, now kept them from reaching Palestine. "Exit [from the USSR] is allowed; entry [into Palestine] forbidden." In June 1945 (*ITU,* Vol. I, p. 243), MB defended the Soviets from Jewish Agency criticism of the treatment of Jews in Red Army-held territories. MB said that while of course there were some difficulties for Jews in Soviet areas, and would always be, the war had convinced Moscow that it was wiser politically to support the return of Jews to Zion than to deal with them domestically, where they "cause perpetual fermentation." MB hastened to add, "We are not engaging in pro-Soviet propaganda, just as we are not engaging in anti-Soviet propaganda. The days in which we could allow ourselves the luxury of such distinctions have passed. Our [foreign] relations today can be of only one sort: reciprocity; help for help; friendship for friendship; hostility in repayment for hostility." The British and not the Soviets were, in this context, the enemy. In March 1947 (*ITU,* Vol. III, p. 15), MB highlights Moscow Radio coverage of IZL attacks. "This is the first time that the peoples of the USSR are hearing about an open Hebrew uprising against the British regime." On March 6, says Begin, the Soviet radio announcer declared: "In spite of all these [British] measures, the Hebrew Underground Organization, the Irgun Zvai Leumi, continues its attacks . . ." Interestingly, when Soviet delegate Andrei Gromyko stunned the world later in 1947 by endorsing the UN partition plan, MB (*ITU,* Vol. IV, p. 30) called this a welcome and "noble statement," but most of his IZL radio declaration lashed out *against* partition. Most interesting of all—in the context of the Green book's reference—is a passage in the IZL High Command minutes, August 31, 1944. In these, MB says there are signs that the revolt against Britain will widen, to embrace all the Jews of Palestine. He adds: "This does not depend only upon us. We think that we will receive the support of an external ally—genuine support." He does not offer further detail, or name the external power. In the context of his policy statements, and the political situation at the time, the USSR may have been the power he had in mind. The other possibility is the United States. In Moshe Sneh's version of his October 1944 meeting with MB *(History of the Haganah),* MB is quoted as telling him, "The Americans will want peace in the Middle East when the war with Hitler ends, because the war in the Far East will continue, and it is the Americans, even more than the British, who want calm here, since Israel is the road to [political control of] the Orient. The Americans can awaken public opinion and force the British to change their minds." Sneh says the "considerable enthusiasm" with which MB made the remarks made him "suspicious that Begin has some kind of connection with the Americans." In the event, neither the Soviet nor the American connection materialized. ET does note, however, that a good, if unofficial, working relationship developed with the French and Italians.

Begin promised: Tavin, pp. 249–257. **set out to create:** Kurzman, *Ben-Gurion,* Ch. 10. **Begin, in negotiations:** Katz, pp. 273–274. **Begin assigned part:** at news conference. MB also categorically disassociated the IZL from the assassination, a move which Koestler (p. 281) saw as completing "the transformation of the former underground body into a political party." **ordered the Irgun to disband:** McDonald, the U.S. ambassador, met with BG the morning after the assassination. BG told him (pp. 72–74) that he saw no sign of IZL involvement and that the Irgun had in fact "through several channels disavowed any association." Still, BG said he "intended to force the Irgunists to choose between 'unqualified loyalty to the State' and 'elimination.' " **disbanded the IZL:** Katz, pp. 278–280.

Chapter Fifteen: The People Speak

Books: Chafets, Ze'ev, *Heroes and Hustlers, Hard Hats and Holy Men;* Haber, Eitan, *Menachem Begin;* Hurwitz, Harry, *Menachem Begin;* Katz, Shmuel, *The Hollow Peace;* Koestler, Arthur, *Promise and Fulfillment;* Kurzman, Dan, *Ben-Gurion: Prophet of Fire;* McDonald, James G., *My Mission in Israel 1948–1951;* Niv, David, *History of the Irgun Zvai Leumi;* Stock, Ernest, *Israel on the Road to Sinai: 1949–1956;* Tavin, Eli, *The Second Front.*

Interviews: Yaakov Amrami, Eitan Haber, Harry Hurwitz, Yehiel Kadishai, Hillel Kook, Yaakov Meridor, Shmuel Merlin, Arye Naor, Yehoshua Ophir, Esther Raziel-Naor, Yisrael Scheib, Eli Tavin.

Articles, broadcasts, pamphlets, etc.: Israel Government Press Office, "Government Coalitions in Israel's History," June 14, 1984; Merlin, Shmuel, "Bonjour Tristesse." Schindler, Rabbi Alexander, "A Conversation with Menachem Begin"; Shenker, Dr. Barry, and Dr. Henri Stellman, "The Israeli General Elections, July 23rd 1984—A Guide to the System, Parties, Electorate and Issues," The Academic Study Group, London, 1984.

Periodicals: The Jerusalem Post (JP).

Textual notes: **Eli Tavin was keeping:** ET. **Paglin had slipped out:** ET, SM. **as their rabbi:** letter, reproduced in Tavin book, to the IZL European command in November 1947. MB stressed that he wanted the displaced IZL men to be full participants in plotting the group's future course, going so far as to ask his men to consult Hillel Kook (given the "fateful" nature of the question) and "ask him to hold a special advisory meeting" of his Hebrew Committee for National Liberation. Though MB nominally advocated open discussion and said he would "not express my own opinion," he tipped his hand later in the note. First, the rabbinical sign-off left no doubt as to who would be the most equal among equals in deciding the matter. Second, he stated that the IZL must take note of political realities— among them, that the outside world would probably ensure that Ben Gurion's partitioned state became an unassailable reality no matter what the IZL did. "There will be no choice but to wait for a time in the future when we will be stronger . . ." **Tavin and others:** ET. Niv says that Lankin, Merlin, and Marek Kahan—before returning aboard the *Altalena*—had joined Tavin in assembling plans for a surviving "Supreme Council of Popular Liberation." **told his Paris comrades:** ET. See also Niv, Tavin. **added drily:** Niv. **with most of Tavin's:** ET. **to Begin's side:** Ben Eliezer returned to Paris in mid-October 1947 (Niv) to press Begin's case with Tavin. **Paglin was a big boy:** ET. **"got cables, letters, messages":** ET.

persuaded the U.S. ambassador: McDonald, pp. 133–134. **where Shmuel Merlin feted:** SM. **Tavin had gathered:** ET. **Begin returned home to campaign:** McDonald, pp. 121–122. **Altman, begged:** HK. **"Begin," he recalls:** HK. **despite misgivings:** ET, who says these surfaced in earnest only at Herut's first party convention, which was held after the election—in late June 1949. **parades, torchlight rallies:** McDonald, pp. 121–122; Kurzman, p. 333. **beyond telling friends:** YA. **a betting pool:** HK. **To the U.S. ambassador:** McDonald (p. 124) said MB "told me before the election that he confidently expected Herut to be the second strongest party, and so hold the balance of power." **Voting day:** McDonald, p. 122. **Begin finished fourth:** with 11.3 percent of the vote, some 50,000 of 440,000 ballots cast, McDonald, p. 122; Koestler, pp. 293–310. See also 1984 Israel Government Press Office survey, "Government Coalitions in Israel's History," and the Shenker-Stellman article's historical survey of Israeli election results. **Ben Gurion galloped:** McDonald, p. 123; Israel Government Press Office survey; Shenker-Stellman article. **comfort in the pundits' consensus:** McDonald, the then American ambassador, recalls writing in his journal (p. 124) after the election: "In the give-and-take of an open debate the one-time [IZL and LEHI] terrorists lost much of their glamor. It was primarily Begin's unusual capacity for leadership that saved his party from a worse showing." **Neither, of course:** in what became BG's postelection trademark when forming successive cabinets in the years ahead, he ruled out any government coalition that contained either Herut— which he portrayed as a bunch of reconditioned IZL terrorists—or the pro-Moscow Communists (Haber, p. 239). **consulted or commanded:** EH, a longtime Herut supporter who wrote a generally admiring biography of MB after Begin's 1977 election as prime minister but, when interviewed by me four years later, offered a much more nuanced view. **received IZL comrades:** YA, EH, YK. **go to the movies:** YK, HH; Hurwitz, p. 104. **driver Yoske Giladi:** acquired when MB emerged from underground, Yoske was the man who drove MB to Kfar Vitkin for the arrival of the *Altalena* (Merlin article). **traveled to rallies:** EH. **"I am just":** see MB's videotaped interview with Rabbi Schindler.

Party meetings: ERN. **"I don't understand":** YS, to whom Greenburg made the comment. Interestingly, YM agrees with the assessment, except he adds: "Landau was also part of the inner circle." YS, HK, YO, and others remark that Meridor, Ben Eliezer, and Landau shared at least two important qualities—IZL credentials and an admiring acceptance of MB's leadership. **offered something positive:** YM, EH. **Begin parted ways with them:** HK; Katz, p. 16. **omitted Kook and Jabotinsky:** Katz, pp. 15–16. To this day, Israel has no constitution. **Katz, who had been:** Katz, pp. 13–16. **co-opted the eldest:** HK, AN. **hosted a reception:** HK. Though not an IZL activist, Bader was one of the few men besides MB who wrote in significant quantity for his underground wall newspaper. MB also called on Bader to help draft a formal IZL policy brief for Sandstrom's UN committee (though Bader did not attend MB's talks with the committeemen). **prompted Begin to reject:** HK, who proposed the idea. MB told the American ambassador (McDonald, p. 133), however, that he felt an ideological affinity for America and that Herut was Israel's "only really pro-US party." **"tell us how":** Stock, p. 27. **Ben Gurion did not bother:** YO, longtime Herut supporter and reporter for party newspaper; Katz, p. 13. **"You left me alone!":** YO. **went to Begin and urged:** Katz, p. 13. **"Ben Gurion smiled":** HK.

reporter for the party: YO. **published his first volume:** *The Revolt.* Published in 1950, the book is often defensive in tone, vague, and sometimes inaccurate with detail, reading more like an IZL wall-poster proclamation than a memoir. **new issue:** Kurzman, pp. 332–334. See also excellent interpretive section in Chafets, pp. 117–120. **Election day:** *JP* archives. **shaved his fourteen seats:** Israeli Government Press Office survey; Shenker-Stellman article. **broken man:** YM, ERN, YO; Hurwitz, p. 63.

Chapter Sixteen: Underground Revisited

Books: Bader, Yohanan, *The Knesset and I;* Haber, Eitan, *Menachem Begin;* Hurwitz, Harry, *Menachem Begin;* Kurzman, Dan, *Ben-Gurion: Prophet of Fire;* St. John, Robert, *Ben-Gurion;* Stock, Ernest, *Israel on the Road to Sinai.*

Interviews: Yaakov Amrami, Batya (Scheib) Eldad, Eitan Haber, Mr. and Mrs. Marek Kahan, Yaakov Meridor, Shmuel Merlin, Arye Naor, Yehoshua Ophir, Esther Raziel-Naor, Shmuel Tamir, Eli Tavin, Chaim Zadok.

Articles, broadcasts, pamphlets, etc.: Israel Government Press Office, "Government Coalitions in Israel's History"; Shenker, Dr. Barry, and Dr. Henri Stellman, "The Israeli General Elections, July 23rd 1984—A Guide to the System, Parties, Electorate and Issues."

Periodicals: Herut (party newspaper); *The Jerusalem Post (JP).*

Textual notes: **Begin summoned:** YO. **did not even show:** *JP,* January 11, 1952. **shut himself:** EH, YM, ERN. **"Ben Eliezer":** YO. **"He said it was his *duty*":** ERN. **"In the Irgun":** YA. **Meridor, who spent hours:** YM. **Begin felt rejected:** Hurwitz (p. 63) says: "I was in Israel at the time and know that the [election] results affected Begin deeply. He had not expected this ingratitude from the nation so soon after the glorious Irgun struggle and victory."

The most frequent ... Ben Eliezer: YM, YO, and ERN, who says Ben Eliezer's main brief was obvious: bring Begin back. "Arye," she says, "tried very hard to convince him to come back." On the urging of his colleagues (Bader, pp. 282–289), Ben Eliezer also disobeyed

MB's directive to present Begin's letter of resignation formally to the Knesset. **retired into private business:** YM; *JP,* January 11, 1952. **sat with Aliza:** BSE, Mrs. MK. ERN's son, AN, cites private remarks by Yohanan Bader that MB also used the time to try to pass the Israeli bar exam—but failed it. The reported remark, however, came after Bader and MB had drifted apart in the 1970s. Other sources (YM, ERN) suggest that MB had little time, energy, or inclination to study law during his postelection retirement. CZ—the Labor lawyer-politician who knows MB from Warsaw days and the Knesset, and who also served as Israeli attorney general—strongly doubts MB took or failed the bar. Given MB's intellect—indeed, merely MB's near-photographic memory—Zadok says had MB wanted to pass the bar, he would have had not the slightest difficulty. **They rested:** YO. **reunited with Eli Tavin:** ET. Several of their meetings took place in the Paris home of MB's sister, Rachel, who was living there at the time.

Ben Gurion had raised: Kurzman, p. 336. **not been against reparations:** SM. **amid signs . . . :** Kurzman, pp. 336–337. **Begin and Tavin walked:** ET. **when Ben Eliezer collapsed:** ERN, whose startled husband happened to be the first on the scene. The Ben Eliezer crisis, ERN is convinced, "hastened Begin's return." **cold, cloudy Monday:** St. John, pp. 228–229; *JP,* January 1952. **stone building with curved edges:** The building still stands, amid the commercial bustle of a greatly more crowded Jerusalem. The Knesset, however, is quartered in a low-slung structure of marble and glass on a hilltop at the city's western edge. **crowd of several thousand:** MB supporters have estimated that as many as fifteen thousand were there. **Begin drew:** St. John, p. 229; *JP.* **supporters followed:** *JP.* "There, the real battle started," says S. Eliahu (*JP,* January 11) in a recap of the confrontation. **Inside . . . Begin charged:** main source for this section is the official Knesset record, January 7, 1952 (Vol. X). Also, *JP,* January 8–11, 1952.

Ben Gurion went on radio: St. John, pp. 231–232; Kurzman, p. 339; *JP,* January 8–11. **So was Arye:** Hurwitz, p. 65; Kurzman, p. 339; *JP.* **vote was close:** *JP.* **under suspension:** *JP,* January 22, 1952. He was suspended for the remainder of the session—until the Passover holiday, roughly three months ahead. **called the punishment "cowardly":** Haber, p. 237. **rally in Tel Aviv:** *JP*'s daily coverage used for background, quotes, in this section. **Tavin, in Paris:** ET. An

IZL-Herut veteran, who requested anonymity, confirms Landau was involved in this renewed underground. ET says the man who phoned him was not Landau, but another senior IZL-Herut figure. The dictionary was mailed in late February 1952. **Landau, contacted a party:** the man requested anonymity. He says Landau told him he was speaking in "the name of the *mefaked*." (This word—Hebrew for "commander"—was Begin's title in the IZL.) Landau's envoy showed up and, the source says, declared that "we have decided to establish an underground in Haifa, against ships carrying goods from Germany. But since we want to keep the party legal here, we shall have to do what is necessary in the ports of Europe." The Haifa Herut party member says he was told to hire a sailor on a departing ship to carry a small explosive device to "our people in Marseilles." The Herut man says he duly hired a Bulgarian seaman. In the spring of 1952, the French ordered Eli Tavin out of the country; and also expelled the Herut party newspaper Paris correspondent on suspicion of having been involved in sending a threatening letter to West German Chancellor Konrad Adenauer. On return to Israel, the reporter said *(JP)* only that if someone told him Adenauer had been killed, "I, and many other Jews, would not weep." ET, for his part, says: "We tried to stop—let's put it that way—these negotiations. . . . Some of my friends tried, until the French decided to expel me."

Dov Shilanski was stopped: *JP.* **"Shilanski is my regular client . . .":** Tamir, quoted in *JP,* October 8, 1952. In interview with me, ST acknowledged he had never met Shilanski before the man's arrest. In December Shilanski was sentenced to twenty-one months' imprisonment. **concluded Shilanski was part:** see, for example *JP,* October 7, 1952. **Begin himself shunned contact:** ST notes that Shilanski seemed personally hurt by this "cold shoulder. He [Shilanski] admired Begin greatly." **Bader and a few others:** ST. Also, *JP,* October 10. **Tavin, who returned:** ET. **youngster who had organized:** see earlier note. Source requested anonymity. **Merlin, as secretary:** SM. **"Many of the excited":** *JP,* January 11, 1952. **Begin admired the army's counterstrikes:** Stock, pp. 68–69, 155; Hurwitz, p. 69. Background in Kurzman, pp. 341–342, 360. In Herut's newspaper (February 19, 1954), for instance, MB rejected the need to apologize for the controversial attack by Sharon's antiterror unit on the Arab village of Kibya. The raid left more than fifty civilians dead and caused a diplomatic crisis with the Eisenhower administration. **He**

resigned after: YA. exhausted Ben Gurion: Kurzman, pp. 361–370. "Tomorrow, they will be": official Knesset record, August 30, 1954 (Vol. 16). "There is already": Knesset record, March 24, 1954. Summoning Meridor back: YM. shouts of support: YO. The election trimmed: details from Shenker-Stellman article and Israel Government Press Office coalition survey. "The people are dancing": Hurwitz, who got the phone call (p. 63). "Correct me if ": Knesset record, November 2, 1955.

Chapter Seventeen: Family Quarrels

Books: Bader, Yohanan, *The Knesset and I;* Chafets, Ze'ev, *Heroes and Hustlers, Hard Hats and Holy Men;* Dayan, Moshe, *Story of My Life;* Eban, Abba, *An Autobiography;* Gilbert, Martin, *Atlas of the Arab-Israeli Conflict;* Haber, Eitan, *Menachem Begin;* Hirschler, Gertrude, and Lester Eckman, *Menachem Begin;* Hurwitz, Harry, *Menachem Begin;* Katz, Shmuel, *The Hollow Peace;* Kurzman, Dan, *Ben-Gurion: Prophet of Fire;* Medzini, Meron, editor, *Israel's Foreign Relations: Selected Documents, 1947–1974;* Meir, Golda, *My Life;* Ophir, Yehoshua, *The Book of the National Worker;* St. John, Robert, *Ben-Gurion;* Stock, Ernest, *Israel on the Road to Sinai.*

Interviews: Yaakov Amrami, Mike Arnon, Eitan Haber, Yehiel Kadishai, Leo Marcus, Yaakov Meridor, Arye Naor, Esther Raziel-Naor, Zelman Shoval, Shmuel Tamir.

Articles, broadcasts, pamphlets, etc.: Israel Government Press Office, "Government Coalitions in Israel's History"; Shenker, Dr. Barry, and Dr. Henri Stellman, "The Israeli General Elections, July 23rd 1984—A Guide to the System, Parties, Electorate and Issues."

Periodicals: The Jerusalem Post (JP); the *Jewish Herald (JH),* Johannesburg.

Textual notes: **raid and reprisal was building:** Stock, pp. 70–75; Gilbert, p. 60. Stock, using UN figures, says 148 Israelis were killed in Arab cross-border violence in 1955—118 of these on the Egyptian front. Gilbert gives a higher figure—278 dead, concurring that the great majority of Israeli casualties came on the Egyptian frontier. Earlier in the decade, the violence had been concentrated near Jordan. **Nasser suddenly announced:** Stock, p. 75; Kurzman, p. 382;

Dayan, p. 190. Dayan explains that although Nasser's shopping list—including tanks, armored personnel carriers, self-propelled guns, jet fighters, transport planes, minesweepers, and torpedo boats—"may not seem startling by today's standards, [it] represented a stunning acceleration of the pace of rearmament in the Middle East." The view in Israel, says Dayan, was that "the primary purpose . . . was to prepare Egypt for a decisive confrontation with Israel in the near future." **"There are no territories":** Stock, p. 168. **the idea of "security guarantees":** official Knesset record, November 2, 1955. **seminal statement of his views:** Knesset record, January 2, 1956.

spring of 1956: Stock, pp. 179–181. **"You," Ben Gurion shot back:** St. John, p. 273. **In mid-1956 he forced:** Kurzman, pp. 385–389. **truculent Egyptian demands, and tacit U.S.:** Nasser demanded that Israel pay for any peace by ceding to Egypt the part of the Negev Desert, which had lain outside the UN partition boundaries. The Egyptians also intermittently cut off shipping into Israel from the Red Sea. The Suez Canal—owned by Europeans but situated in Egypt—was barred to Israel. The Americans tacitly backed Egypt's demands on the Negev. **sealing an arms deal with the French:** both the Americans and British had spurned similar overtures. The French began secret deliveries to Israel in the summer. The British also swung behind Ben Gurion after Nasser announced in July he was nationalizing the Suez Canal. **grasped Ben Gurion's hand:** Kurzman (p. 391), based on interview with Bader. In a March 1957 speech, MB recalls digressing from an attack on Ben Gurion: "You remember the day before the Sinai Campaign when you invited me to your house, when you offered me your hand and told me of the Sinai Campaign, I did not refuse to accept the hand which you offered me. I did not hesitate to offer you my hand . . ." (Hurwitz, p. 80).

"if our teacher": Knesset record, November 7, 1956. **Israel came under pressure:** Kurzman, pp. 393–398; Eban, pp. 234–258; Meir, pp. 249–251; Stock, pp. 209–215. **Moscow warned Israel:** letter from Soviet leader Nikolai Bulganin, text in Medzini, pp. 557–558. **Ben Gurion told the Knesset:** text in Medzini, pp. 559–563. Eban (pp. 228–229), who was Israeli ambassador to both Washington and the UN at the time, says BG's declaration was "a political error. There was no chance whatsoever that Ben Gurion could maintain those positions. . . ." **United Nations call:** text in Medzini, p. 566. **Eisen-**

hower warned: text of president's letter in Medzini, pp. 563–564. **Ben Gurion told the Knesset:** text in Medzini, pp. 567–568. **State Department official:** Kurzman, p. 394. **had in mind:** Kurzman, p. 396. See also BG speech to Knesset, January 23, 1957 (text in Medzini, pp. 581–584). **Begin . . . tried and failed:** St. John, p. 294. **provincial capital, Begin again:** Knesset record, January 15, 1957. **Golda Meir, at the UN:** text in Medzini, pp. 604–607. **he pronounced an end:** MB speech reproduced in Hurwitz, pp. 74–82.

peace on Israel's borders: Kurzman, p. 398. **series of trips:** Hirschler-Eckman provide excellent detail on his journeys, pp. 220–221. **did not criticize:** LM, MA. **The Moroccans:** *Ha'aretz*, translation from Chafets, pp. 117–118. **"The primitive element":** Kurzman, p. 430. Eban (p. 265) says there was "concern at what seemed to be the rising support for the conservative . . . party under Menachem Begin, who was developing expansionist concepts together with a populist image. He was benefiting from the social protest in the [largely Sephardic] slum quarters of large towns, such as the Hatikvah Quarter in Tel Aviv . . ." **bolted Ben Gurion's:** Ophir, pp. 166, 175–185. **suggested a new alliance:** MB seems to have envisaged a distinctly one-sided alliance (not unlike that proposed to LEHI in his underground days), with MB and Herut dominant. "One party, one program, one leadership, one path, one fate" (Ophir, pp. 175–185). **In mid-1958:** Kurzman, p. 426. **"Israel . . . was born":** Knesset record. **"The General Staff":** Knesset record, which also notes that a week later, an embarrassed MB proposed a parliamentary inquiry into the radio bulletin. Ultimately responsible, MB insisted, must be the minister of defense, a post held at the time by Prime Minister Ben Gurion. **Begin misstepped again:** *JP*'s election coverage. **Begin picked up:** Shenker-Stellman article.

first public sign: *JP*. ST also recalls the stir caused at a political meeting he addressed shortly after the election. Tamir at the time was chairman of a public affairs lobby called the "New Regime," advocating the creation of a new centrist political movement. Among its members was Eri Jabotinsky, and Hillel Kook was a silent partner. In the post-election meeting, Tamir at one point was heckled by a group of Herut youngsters. He fired back: "If this is how you behave in opposition, God forbid that you should ever come to power!" **Katz . . . in a letter:** Katz, p. 17, calls it a "memorandum analyzing the connection between the atmosphere he had

generated around himself [within the party], and the party's failure
in the Knesset elections." YM says there was similar private criticism from other sources, notably from onetime party executive
Chairman Nahum Levine. **Shostak . . . had favored:** Ophir.

assist from Ben Gurion: Kurzman, pp. 433–437. **eroded by five seats:**
Shenker-Stellman article. **"microbes to our enemies":** Kurzman, p.
440. **refused to fire her:** AN. **insulted himself with the abiding adoration:** YA, ST, EH. **"It was a tradition":** EH, who was often there. He
had begun his involvement with Herut in the early 1950s when he
was thirteen, serving as a copy boy on the party newspaper. One of
his first jobs, he recalls, was to drop by Begin's Rosenbaum Street
apartment after school each Thursday and pick up the hand-
scrawled text of his weekly political article for the party organ.
Gradually Haber drifted into close friendship with Begin's son,
Benny. And gradually Haber came to Rosenbaum Street not only
on Thursdays but on Saturdays.

revived talk of an alliance: ZS, in background discussion on the
widening of Herut's electoral alliances several years later; Haber,
pp. 257–259. **parting charge that:** Kurzman, pp. 442–443; Knesset
record. **Begin liked Tamir:** ERN, YK.

family ties: his uncle, among other relatives, was a prominent Labor
Zionist. **first met him:** ST. **Tamir won:** although the verdict would
later be overturned on appeal. **Begin was delighted:** and offered him
a place on the Herut ticket, which ST says he declined. **Begin included Tamir:** ST. **image was tarnishing further:** Kurzman, pp.
444–449. **"It is a sad thing":** *JH.* **At the signing:** Haber, p. 258.
grooming him: ERN. **one of the veterans who objected:** Bader, p.
186. **got only twenty-six seats:** Shenker-Stellman article. **"Begin has
always said":** Ophir, ST. **margin of two to one:** of the roughly six
hundred convention delegates. **party's student leader:** Ehud Olmert,
who would later become a Herut member of the Knesset. Details of
convention from JP, June 28–July 3, 1966.

message, recalls Yaakov Meridor: YM. **"You could** *see***":** YM. **bared
a soul:** JP, July 3; ST. **announced he was leaving:** YM, ST. **Meridor,
with Begin's okay:** YM. **He withdrew:** ST, recalling abortive attempts to convey the message to MB that he had meant no personal
injury, remarks that MB seemed either unwilling or incapable to see

the proposed party changes were anything except "treachery." **dropping more than twenty pounds:** ST. **"He seemed so hurt!":** ERN. **Even Paglin:** source is close Herut-IZL friend of Paglin who requested anonymity. **Meridor convened:** YM.

Chapter Eighteen: A Taste of Power

Books: Brenner, Lenni, *The Iron Wall;* Dayan, Moshe, *Story of My Life;* Eban, Abba, *An Autobiography;* Golan, Matti, *Shimon Peres;* Hurwitz, Harry, *Menachem Begin;* Katz, Shmuel, *Days of Fire;* Kissinger, Henry, *White House Years;* Medzini, Meron, editor, *Israel's Foreign Relations: Selected Documents, 1947–1974;* Meir, Golda, *My Life;* Nixon, Richard, *The Memoirs of Richard Nixon;* Rabin, Yitzhak, *The Rabin Memoirs;* Weizman, Ezer, *On Eagles' Wings* and *The Battle for Peace (BFP).*

Interviews: Yaakov Amrami, Mike Arnon, Eliahu Ben Elissar, Yehiel Kadishai, Hillel Kook, Yehuda Litani, Meron Medzini, Yaakov Meridor, Arye Naor, Moshe Pearlman, Ephraim Poran, Zelman Shoval.

Articles, broadcasts, pamphlets, etc.: Bashan, Raphael, "Begin on Begin"; Goldstein, Dov, "Interview of the Year: Prime Minister Menachem Begin," in *Ma'ariv,* September 12, 1977, Hebrew; Segal, Mark, "Memories of Unity," interviews with Yohanan Bader, Moshe Baram, Arye Dulzin, Simcha Dinitz for retrospective on Israel's late 1960s national unity government, in *Jerusalem Post,* September 7, 1984; Schindler, Rabbi Alexander, "A Conversation with Menachem Begin"; Shenker, Dr. Barry, and Dr. Henri Stellman, "The Israeli General Elections, July 23rd 1984—A Guide to the System, Parties, Electorate and Issues."

Periodical: The Jerusalem Post (JP).

Textual notes: **Nasser moved:** background in Dayan, Meir, Rabin. The blockade of Sharm came, as MB had predicted, despite the U.S. guarantees offered in tandem with Israel's retreat in 1957. It is unclear whether Nasser's call, May 18, for the removal of the UN force was made in the expectation that the UN would comply. Nasser, like MB, was at least as much a rhetorician as a statesman. But comply the UN did—on May 22. **Begin wanted an ultimatum:** Knesset record. **The press called:** Dayan, pp. 333–335. **summoned Begin for consultations:** YK. **every bit as crucial:** see Knesset record, November 2, 1955, for just one of many such statements. **acquiesced in Herut's:** MA; Brenner, p. 153. *if* **Ben Gurion returned:** YK; Dayan, p. 335; Bader in Segal *JP* interview, September 7, 1984. This was in spite of MB's Knesset vow after BG's retreat from the Sinai in 1957 (Hurwitz, p. 80) that he and BG would remain opponents until Judgment Day.

call on Ben Gurion: YK; Eban, pp. 387–388; Haber, pp. 266–267. **enticed by the chance:** YA, HK. Bader also implies this in Segal *JP* interview. **Ben Gurion, now in his eighty-first:** MB would not *necessarily* have known that BG opposed the war, although he had made that abundantly clear to Chief of Staff Rabin (pp. 75–76) nearly a week earlier. But Ben Gurion's general decline was no secret. Recalls Eban (p. 388): "No one who had spoken to him or had watched his public appearances could believe that he had the power of objective analysis which had distinguished him in the past." HK remarks: "Begin didn't even check [out BG's position], so blind was his admiration for the old man!" YA recalls feeling embarrassed for MB: "The visit to Ben Gurion was foolish." **"It emerged":** YK, who says BG clearly did not fathom how far the Egyptian build-up had gone, and suggested that the army take Sharm el-Sheikh, as if that would finish the business once and for all. Bader, in Segal *JP* article, recalls Begin's abruptly abandoning mention of the Ben Gurion option. **went on radio:** Dayan, p. 333; Eban, p. 375. **Now he insisted:** YK: "He was adamant that any true national unity must embrace Rafi." **His political secretary:** YK. **appointed Dayan:** Dayan, p. 337; Eban, p. 392. **Begin summoned Meridor:** YM; Bader in *JP* interview; Haber, pp. 267–268. **delivered a biblical:** Dayan, p. 338. **"Sir, we have come":** Haber, p. 268.

Begin's initial role: only two ministers, from the left-wing Mapam faction, opposed the preemptive strike (Dayan, p. 347). Begin agreed: Simcha Dinitz in Segal *JP* retrospective, September 7, 1984. **embarked on a war of his own:** YK, who was summoned back from army reserve duty and spent the duration of the war at MB's side. **Allon, the former Palmach commander:** YK. Ironically, it was Allon who had carried out BG's order to shell the *Altalena* two decades earlier. **gave Begin what he wanted:** YK; Eban, p. 410. Dayan (pp. 367–368) recalls heading for the Knesset session only to find Jerusalem under shellfire and "everyone in the shelter." He suggests he did not attend the broom-closet session, but "hung around for a while, grew impatient, and returned to General Headquarters." **stayed overnight:** YK. **A Dayan aide recalls:** MP. EP, an army general who would later become military aide to Prime Minister Begin, notes: "For him to see the IDF [Israeli Army]—as a Jew from Poland, where you couldn't be more than maybe a corporal; and a general was always a figure far removed from you—here to see *Israeli* generals, respected by all the world, it was something he was very proud of, something he respected—something also that unsettled him."

At sunrise: YK. MB video interview with Rabbi Schindler. **Needing no convincing:** Dayan, in his version of events on June 7, does not even mention the early-morning cabinet session. He says only that later in the morning Israeli forces completed their encirclement of Jerusalem, and that "on the Mount of Olives, brigade commander Motta Gur issued the order to his battalion commanders to . . . enter the Old City." **"I cried":** MB video interview with Rabbi Schindler. **He feared Israel would find:** MM, who was present when Eshkol dampened the spirit of an office victory party by sharing his misgivings. **Israeli journalist recalls:** YL. **approved several settlements:** notably Kiryat Arba, on a hilltop outside Hebron, although he refused the settlers' bid to live in the city itself. Hebron, burial place of the Jewish patriarchs, had been the scene of the 1929 massacre that rid the city of a Jewish presence for the first time since that burial. It was now the second largest Arab town on the West Bank, after Nablus.

Begin loved his cabinet work: MA, who became cabinet secretary in 1968. **access to diplomatic cables:** MB interviews, September 1977, in *Ma'ariv* and *Yediot Aharonot*. There were some suggestions in the Israeli press (Eban, p. 428) that MB join Foreign Minister Eban for the postwar emergency session of the UN General Assembly. "This reflected a traumatic memory of the 1956 Sinai Campaign, when the General Assembly had been the arena of Israel's enforced retreat from its conquered territories." But Eban insisted on going without such baggage, or not at all. The prime minister got the point and resisted suggestions that MB or other ministers go along. **picture of a Polish gentleman:** MA. **"he would speak at great length":** MA. **Eban ignored:** except when issues of central importance to Israel's Mideast diplomatic policy were involved. In early July, for instance, Eban (p. 442) joined MB in drafting Israel's claim to sovereignty over all of Jerusalem, including a distinction between her "national rights" to the city and control of the holy sites. Under a peace accord, the statement said, Israel would be ready to give "appropriate expression" to the idea that other parties might have jurisdiction over non-Jewish holy places there. **"Begin and Galili":** MA. **made no effort to short-circuit:** Simcha Dinitz in Segal *JP* article, 1984; Eban in *JP* interview, 1982; Eban, pp. 446, 454.

spring, however, Israel came under pressure: Meir, pp. 319–323. Kissinger, pp. 558–593; Eban, pp. 465–468; Weizman, pp. 251–252, 257–265. **Egypt was getting:** Kissinger; and Weizman, who says (p. 261) that from March through June, "20,000 Soviet advisers poured into Egypt, penetrating into the lowest command echelons. . . . Soviet planes, with Russian pilots, were stationed in Egypt." Kissinger (p. 585) recalls a dogfight on July 30 of the following year (1970) in which the Israelis downed four "Russian-piloted aircraft"—an incident confirmed by a senior Egyptian diplomat in an interview with me "The Russians," he remarks, "were always blaming *our* pilots for the losses against Israel! Some of us nearly *celebrated* when they got shot down." **observed his self-imposed stricture:** MA. **victory of sorts:** Shenker-Stellman article.

For weeks he spurned: Segal *JP* article, based on interviews with unity government figures; YK, MA. **never before had Begin:** AN suggests one explanation: "Begin knew that he was choosing the Liberals' domestic issues as the reason for holding out. He was trying to be more Liberal than the Liberals—so that they would have to go along with him later on the issues he cared about, such as territorial compromise with the Arabs." **reflect deeper misgivings:** MA remarks that Begin "seemed to operate better in opposition." Also, Segal *JP* article; Weizman *(BFP)*, p. 45. **assured him he was needed:** Arye Ben Eliezer (according to Bader, in Segal *JP* article on the period), argued that MB would be minister for "safeguarding the integrity of Eretz [the Land of] Israel."

For Yaakov Meridor: YM; Weizman, pp. 266–268. Weizman says he was contacted by phone—by Yosef Kramerman, a Herut MK and Meridor's son-in-law. The offer came at Kramerman's home that same evening. **piecework for the Irgun:** Weizman was a student in London at the time and had a bit part in an abortive IZL plan to execute its "death sentence" against the now-repatriated Lieutenant General Evelyn Barker (Katz, pp. 119–121). **hawkish on:** For instance, Weizman says (p. 266) that "I repeatedly called for an end to the War of Attrition by sending in ground forces ..." **but knew he was too:** Weizman (page 266) says the Herut "in-laws" approach was blunt. They told him they had no idea what his chances were of being chief of staff, but "we are about to join a widely based National Unity Government. How would you like to join the Cabinet as a Herut representative?" **Chaim Weizmann's nephew:** although his branch of the family spelled the name with one less *n*. **he leaped:** the decision, Weizman recalls (p. 266), took at most "forty seconds." **Ben Eliezer was nearing death:** he died near the end of January 1970. **won two seats:** the Free Center party, see Shenker-Stellman article. **bringing ... younger blood:** YM. **Liberals were threatening:** Bader in Segal *JP* article.

Rogers announced: Nixon, pp. 592–593; Eban, pp. 466–467. **"Perhaps this," Sapir remarked:** Haber, p. 277. **Bader heard the news:** Bader in Segal *JP* article. He had opposed joining Mrs. Meir's government, arguing that MB could not hope to prevent territorial concessions but instead would be maneuvered into rubber-stamping them. **"I slept on the issue":** Bader in Segal *JP* article. **Begin initially chose:** YM. **pressed Meridor:** YM, whom he called a "lazy boy" for wanting to retreat to business. **"The mere name 'Weizman' ":** EBE. **"He should go through the motions":** YM. **"the man is still":** YK, to whom MB made the remark. **He suggested:** YM, YK. **Begin said he would play:** YK. **most open of secrets:** YK. **next day Weizman:** Weizman, p. 267. Weizman (*BFP*, p. 42) recalls MB's welcoming remarks at a meeting of the Herut central committee that evening: "My friend, my general, my companion."

"Begin enjoyed the cabinet": MA. Simcha Dinitz (Mrs. Meir's chief aide) in Segal *JP* article. **"our senior sister":** MA. **"You didn't say":** YK, MA. **Some 250:** Weizman, p. 261. **in June, Rogers proposed:** Eban, p. 467; Kissinger, pp. 578–585. **Nasser unexpectedly:** July 22, after an initial silence (Kissinger, p. 582). **Begin agreed:** Meir, pp. 322–323; Eban, p. 467; Haber, p. 282. **"we won't have":** Meir, pp. 322–323. "I couldn't get it through to him," writes Golda (p. 322), "that although the American commitment to Israel's survival was certainly great, we needed Mr. Nixon and Mr. Rogers much more than they needed us, and Israel's policies couldn't be based entirely on the assumption that American Jewry either would or could force Mr. Nixon to adopt a position against his will or better judgment." **Knesset accepted:** the vote was 67–28, with the rest abstaining. **Golda . . . let the matter:** Moshe Baram (chairman of Labor-coalition executive at the time) in Segal *JP* article; Meir, p. 323. **From the Liberals:** YK. Arye Dulzin (a Liberal party leader, who was a minister without portfolio in the Meir unity government) in Segal *JP* article. **not least from Meridor:** *JP*, August 7, 1970; Weizman, *BFP*, pp. 44–46; YK. **Reminding the Liberals:** *JP*, August 7, 1970. At one point, MB stared down the Liberal mayor of Ramat Gan and declared: "Where were you when the six million went to their deaths?" **by a whisker:** YK; *JP*, August 7, 1970. Weizman abstained. **"I swear to you":** Haber, p. 285. **foreign minister recalls thinking:** Eban, p. 468. **cabinet vote not long before:** MA; AN, who was aide to Minister of Development Chaim Landau at the time; Weizman, *BFP*, p. 44. **Dulzin, adds:** in Segal *JP* article. Weizman (*BFP*, p. 45) seconds the point: "The urge to resign, whatever the cost, was equally a product of his [MB's] long years in the opposition. All his life he'd been number one to his followers, and in Golda's cabinet he played second fiddle." **asked Begin why:** Moshe Baram in Segal *JP* article.

Chapter Nineteen: The Battle Within

Books: Dayan, Moshe, *Story of My Life;* Eban, Abba, *An Autobiography;* Green, Stephen, *Taking Sides;* Hurwitz, Harry, *Menachem Begin;* Kissinger, Henry, *White House Years;* Kurzman, Dan, *Ben-Gurion: Prophet of Fire;* Meir, Golda, *My Life;* Stock, Ernest, *Israel on the Road to Sinai;* Weizman, Ezer, *The Battle for Peace;* White, Theodore, *Breach of Faith.*

Interviews: Eliahu Ben Elissar, Ze'vev Chafets, Yaakov Meridor, Arye Naor, Zelman Shoval, Ezer Weizman.

Articles, broadcasts, pamphlets, etc.: Dolav, Aharon, "White Nights and Tempestuous Days"; Raanan, Nathan, "Refusing to Fade Away," profile on Ariel Sharon, in *Spectrum,* November 1983; Shenker, Dr. Barry, and Dr. Henri Stellman, "The Israeli General Elections, July 23rd 1984—A Guide to the System, Parties, Electorate and Issues"; Walker, Christopher, "A Fighter Back in the Front Line," profile on Sharon, London *Times*, August 6, 1981.

Periodicals: The Jerusalem Post (JP); the *Jewish Herald (JH);* Johannesburg; *Ma'ariv*, in which MB wrote twice-monthly political columns; *Yediot Aharonot*.

Textual notes: **initiative collapsed:** Eban, pp. 468–470; Kissinger, pp. 585–593. **warned President Nixon:** *JH,* quoting MB Knesset remarks. **resisted the Americans':** MB, *Ma'ariv* article, October 30, 1970. **"We remember Hitler":** *JH.* **promoted Weizman:** Weizman, p. 46; YM. **"chief executive officer":** YM, who had held the position himself. **"Begin felt only *one*":** AN. **saw no point:** Weizman, pp. 46–47. **"a party that wins":** EW. **Touring local branches:** Weizman, pp. 45–48. **Among the dozens:** EBE. Ben Elissar was reared by a cousin who arrived in Palestine on a Betar immigration boat that had been personally seen off by MB in 1939. **united in resentment:** *JP,* December 17, 1972. Kramerman was senior in this circle—as head of the Tel Aviv Herut branch and overall party treasurer. There were literally dozens of others, mostly officials in local party branches. The Ramat Gan branch was among the most energetic in backing what Weizman later called his attempt to "rearrange the furniture." Within the executive, Weizman promoted his protégés. As secretary of the body, he named Ben Amidror, who, alleges one senior party member close to MB, was "a zero, in party terms." As head of Herut's Organizational Department, he chose Petahya Shamir, another Weizman protégé, who ironically was also the brother of onetime Brisk schoolteacher Moshe Steiner, the man who brought MB into Betar.

held its convention: *JP.* **"No one in Begin's position":** EW. **Weizman also had:** *JP,* whose day-by-day accounts are used as background for this section, along with EW, EBE. **panic and protest from the old guard:** among Weizman's major adversaries were Chaim Landau, Eitan Livni, and Yohanan Bader, who had special reasons to oppose him. **developed the tradition:** EBE. **He went personally:** going so far, recalls EBE, as to scrawl a note formally "requesting to be received" by the group. **"I will find it":** *JP,* December 21, 1972; EBE. **went to Begin:** EBE. **buttonholed Weizman's candidate:** *JP,* December 22; EBE. The candidate was Petahya Shamir. **Weizman upbraided:** *JP,* December 22. **"Imagine, Eli!":** EBE. **Calling Weizman:** *JP,* December 21 and 22; EBE. **Ezer was in no position:** *JP,* December 22. **"We weren't used":** EBE. **Begin told the convention:** *JP.*

Interviewed on Israel Television: EBE; *JP.* Says one MB protégé, who asked to remain anonymous, "Compare the situation with Tamir's challenge. To wipe out Tamir took Begin seven months. Tamir had deep roots in the party. Even after seven months Begin didn't win an airtight victory. With Ezer, it took twenty-four hours. In Herut terms, Ezer was a lightweight . . ." **he chuckled:** EBE. **leaked reports that Landau:** *JP.* **Begin purged Weizman's protégés:** *JP,* January 8, 10, 11, 1973. **"We have never changed":** MB in *Ma'ariv,* January 1973. **one Labor official:** Aharon Yadlin, the Labor party's secretary general. **pro-government newspaper added:** *JP,* December 26, 1972. **barred the offending reporter:** Mark Segal, the *Jerusalem Post's* political reporter (*JP,* January 16, 1973). MB's sensitivity to media comment—exacerbated by his almost fanatical drive to read domestic and foreign-newspaper commentary—would remain keenly in evidence even after he became Israel's prime minister (ZC, who was head of the Israel Government Press Office for most of MB's tenure as prime minister). **Yigal Hurwitz drew up a chair:** EBE, who was there.

In the 1950s: background from Kurzman, also Raanan and Walker articles. **Begin had sided:** both in the Knesset (August 30, 1954, Knesset record), and in *Herut,* the party newspaper (February 19, 1954), for instance, he stressed the positive effects of Sharon's controversial attack on the Arab village of Kibya, on the West Bank of the Jordan River—in which more than fifty civilians were killed. In his Knesset speech, MB asked rhetorically why the Arabs hadn't retaliated for Kibya. "Because," he said, "they knew that we were strong." In the *Herut* article, he compared Sharon's antiterror strikes with the IZL's revolt. Kibya, in particular, had had "important psychological effects" on Israel's enemies—and might "jolt them away from their continuous acts of murder." **Sharon had attempted:** Raanan. EBE, who says Liberal leader Sapir "was furious, and went to Begin to complain." **Sharon struck on several fronts:** ZS, who was a Hurwitz protégé and a participant in the Sharon coalition talks. **"Sharon was not only":** EBE. **a *big* alliance:** ZS. **"I'm afraid of Begin!":** EW, who says he phoned Sharon, then in charge of Israel's Southern Command, in "1971 or '72" to suggest that Sharon hang up his uniform and join Herut. "I reached him in a command post in the Sinai." Sharon said no. Weizman says when he asked why not, Sharon replied: "I'm afraid of Begin!" **more curiosity than allure:** AN suggests that Sharon's parents' drift into the Labor Zionist orbit in Palestine was at least an equal allure. **"His approach to Begin":** EBE.

Begin called the bluff: *JP,* September 1973. "I have never taken part in such an ugly and disgraceful process in a body that should set an example of honesty and leadership," Weizman charged in a note that Begin's camp promptly leaked to the press. Acknowledging that he, too, must share the blame, Weizman wrote: "All of us created this negative spectacle. We all took part in bickering over *Knesset* seats in which slander was slung around and terrible untruths uttered." To which MB answered, in effect, that if Weizman's conscience dictated that he pull out of the exercise, a man must do what his conscience told him. So tense were the homestretch coalition talks that at one point Begin (*JP,* September 3) said he, too, was shelving the enterprise and advocating that each of the potential coalition partners run separately. Whether by design or intention, the prospect of the coalition's presumed standard-bearer's calling off bets promptly jolted the talks back on track. **an accidental encounter:** EW, who was there and has a photograph of the encounter on his office wall. **"I was very much":** text of letter, provided by Kadishai, appears in Dolav *Ma'ariv* article. **"Begin did, after all":** ZS. **Sharon's shotgun marriage:** AS, in an interview with me in my capacity as *Christian Science Monitor* correspondent in 1984, says of his creation of the Likud alliance: "I was working here, on my farm, and I got the idea." He said he feels that his status as an outsider, with "no experience in political life" helped the endeavor to succeed, adding: "Maybe that was my greatest single contribution to Israeli democracy. Labor had been in power, pre-independence, and for twenty-nine years." **Begin proposed:** ZS. **His younger daughter:** Haber, pp. 292–293; YK; Meir, p. 359; Hurwitz, pp. 95–97. **It took roughly:** background on war from Dayan, Kissinger, Nixon. **when Dayan sent a note:** ZS, who was an admirer and close associate of Dayan's from Rafi days and, later, during Dayan's tenure as foreign minister. **in a last gasp:** White, Ch. 10.

"well in advance": Knesset record, November 13 and 14, 1973; *JP,* November 4. Mrs. Meir said that opposition speeches, by MB and Shmuel Tamir, "tore me apart. They were so full of rhetoric and theatricality that I couldn't stand it. . . . If only [they] had stammered or hesitated occasionally. . . . Begin and Tamir were talking about a near catastrophe, about men who had been killed or crippled, about terrible things, but they spoke smoothly, without as much as a pause, and I was disgusted." **"best brains in Israel":** ZS. **did well in the election:** results in Shenker-Stellman article. **from the** *moshavim:* ZS. **"Even if Labor":** ZS, who was present.

Chapter Twenty: The Matter of Time

Books: Brenner, Lenni, *The Iron Wall;* Dayan, Moshe, *Story of My Life;* Golan, Matti, *Shimon Peres;* Haber, Eitan, *Menachem Begin;* Hurwitz, Harry, *Menachem Begin;* Meir, Golda, *My Life;* Nixon, Richard, *The Memoirs of Richard Nixon,* Volume 2; Rabin, Yitzhak, *The Rabin Memoirs.*

Interviews: Eliahu Ben Elissar, Ze'ev Chafets, Alexander Haig, Jr., Yehiel Kadishai, Yona Klimovitzki (YKl), Leo Marcus, Arye Naor, Ephraim Poran, Yisrael Scheib, Zelman Shoval, Bronka Stavsky (BSt), Ezer Weizman, David Yutan.

Periodicals: The Jerusalem Post (JP); Ma'ariv (in which MB wrote twice-monthly political articles).

Textual notes: **venom of the crowd:** Meir, p. 380; Golan, p. 141. **charged the government:** Knesset record; *Ma'ariv; JP.* MB, in his capacity as an increasingly respectable leader-of-the-opposition and veteran member of the Knesset's foreign affairs and defense committee, got to meet Kissinger during his postwar Mideast diplomatic period. On one occasion, according to an anecdote MB liked to tell, Kissinger joked: "You really gave me hell in the Knesset," to which Begin replied: "Not at all, sir. I want you to go to heaven. . . . I just want you to earn it!" (ZC) In the summer of 1974, MB was also invited to attend a state banquet for President Nixon, who was on what would prove to be his swan-song exercise in presidential glamour. MB's dinner partner was Nixon's White House chief of staff, Alexander Haig, a man with whom Begin would deal in matters of Mideast peace and war when MB had become prime minister and Haig, U.S. secretary of state. The two men talked at length, AH recalls, of Mideast politics and history. (See Chapter 26.) **They resigned:** Mrs. Meir left in April, after the Agranat Commission had issued a preliminary report. Dayan left with her, at the nadir of his popularity. The new government's minister of defense was his long-time Rafi colleague, Shimon Peres.

tried, and failed: Knesset record. **Golda's successor:** background from Golan, and from Rabin, whose memoir is so peppered with testy references to Shimon Peres that later it would form a rich source of anti-Labor copy for Likud election campaigns. **Begin quickly challenged:** *JP,* July 26, July 28, August 1, October 15, 1974. Among MB's follow-up moves were a [failed] attempt to get the Knesset to endorse the settlement, and a 150,000-name petition opposing "foreign rule of Judea and Samaria." **Rabin felt secure:** *JP,* December 1974. **"Mr. Rabin says":** *JP,* December 19, 1974. **first convention:** *JP,* which provides detailed day-to-day coverage, including the text of MB's January 12 keynote address. **Dayan, in the audience:** when Rafi-State's Yigal Hurwitz rose to speak, he dropped a wide hint that Dayan—the man whom, only months earlier, MB had savaged with Knesset rhetoric for the Yom Kippur War and its aftermath—might make a nice coalition member. Motioning toward Dayan, Hurwitz declared: "It is time for the pupils of Jabotinsky and the pupils of Ben Gurion to join forces to defend the country. All differences are irrelevant."

offered General Ariel Sharon: in July 1975. The move seemed a slap not only at Begin and the Likud, but at two colleagues with whom Rabin was locked in an increasingly acrimonious rivalry: Peres and Chief of Staff Motta Gur (Golan, pp. 166–169). In raising the subject with Peres, Rabin is quoted as saying: "Arik [Sharon] wants to be my adviser." Rabin said he had mixed feelings, but "could see the political advantage of bringing Sharon, a Likud man, into the establishment." Sharon's title was "general adviser," but the appointment included a written stipulation that he would "accompany the Prime Minister to any military or political forum in which he takes part." **Sharon, who had now taken to:** ZS. **"I will yet teach":** ZS. **"I think we are really":** BSt. **deferred to his partners:** ZS, who participated in coalition meetings. **soothing assurance:** ZS, who remarks that MB "treated Landau like a child." **A Liberal aide recalls:** ZC, who would later become director of the Israel Government Press Office.

passed over both Landau: after the January 1975 convention, Shamir was made chairman of the Herut executive, replacing the "interim chairman," Landau. Livni (*JP*) had also wanted the job. **new inner circle:** in addition to Kadishai and Ben Elissar, MB later took other "new guarders" under his wing. These included Esther Raziel-Naor's son, Arye, and a boyish-looking law graduate named Dan Meridor. Dan was no relation to Yaakov Meridor, but was the son of Eliyahu Meridor, a Herut deputy in the fourth, fifth, and sixth Knessets. **Begin had hired:** YK. **No one in the office:** YK and YK1, MB's office secretary. **used Kadishai to answer:** YK. **twice-a-month political commentaries:** EBE, who recalls that MB "used to make an appointment with himself. Every second Tuesday morning, from nine until about twelve, he would set aside for the *Ma'ariv* article, which he would dictate to Yehiel." **took issues of enormous starkness:** YK. **"Yehiel was the one person":** ZC. **Kadishai arranged:** YK.

last quality, always important: ZC, EBE, ST, YK1. Among others who personally experienced the effects of MB's preoccupation were David Yutan and Yisrael Scheib. DY, who sided with Tamir in the 1960s challenge, recalls being frozen out of MB's circle thereafter. "He cannot understand that one can have differing opinions and still be friends," says DY. YS, who had taken to writing on politics and was often acutely critical of Begin, recalls having toyed with the idea of joining Herut and running for the Knesset. MB received him and said that since Herut was a democratically run party, Scheib was free to join but that he would get no personal backing from MB. **"He would remark":** YK1. **"was like a kid":** a Likud official who worked with Ben Elissar and requested anonymity. **"a man who played":** EBE. **responded as a kind:** YK1 remarks that Begin always called Ben Elissar "Eli," and Kadishai "Yehiel." Ben Elissar called MB "Mr. Begin." Kadishai, says YK1, usually dodged the issue by "not using any title of address at all." **when Begin took:** EBE, who adds that Begin himself did not seem to attach much importance to such strictures. "I remember once when I was traveling in Europe and had dinner with him and with Aliza. The waiter brought Begin bacon and eggs. He didn't send it back. He simply pushed the bacon to one side of the plate, and ate the eggs." But there were limits, and during Ben Elissar's later tenure as Israel's first ambassador to Egypt, he had to do some quick thinking to avoid breaching them. "It was during a Begin visit to Egypt and we—the Israeli delegation—were having a private working lunch at one of the presidential palaces. Yehiel [Kadishai] and Freuke [MB's military adviser, Gen-

eral Ephraim Poran], Begin, and I were around the table," says
EBE. The Egyptian waiters served shrimp cocktails! Yehiel and
Freuke looked at each other in shock, but Begin dug in, saying,
"This is delicious! What is it?" As the other two aids went pale, Ben
Elissar replied, "Yes, the Egyptians make such good tuna cocktail!"
Whereupon everyone ate happily. **"I had** *ambitions***":** EBE. **authen-
tic, absolutely beyond doubt:** EBE; YKl, who remarks of Kadishai's
relationship with MB: "Yehiel has a mind of his own; he just doesn't
have a *will* of his own."

asked a reporter: *JP,* July 1976. **Entebbe hijack:** Palestinian gunmen
hijacked Air France's Tel Aviv–Paris flight. It landed briefly in
Libya, then went on to Entebbe in Idi Amin's Uganda. **Begin took
the high road:** EP, who was Rabin's chief military adviser. Rabin (p.
285) says: "To tell the truth, I was moved by Begin's support . . ." **"I
understand the problem":** EP. **was taking Begin:** MB's initial support (Rabin, p. 285) had come at a briefing of the Knesset's foreign
affairs and defense committee. When Rabin decided the following
day to order a rescue mission, he invited (p. 287) MB and a Liberal
party colleague, Elimelech Rimalt, for an updated briefing. **similar
crisis:** EP. **IZL veteran:** Yonatan Netanyahu, who led the assault on
the air terminal. **Recalls one Rabin aide:** EP, who was among several
Begin kept on his staff after becoming prime minister. **a series of
scandals:** background in *JP.* Also, Brenner, pp. 158–159; Haber, p.
297. **allegations that Abba Eban:** Haber (p. 297) who notes that no
supporting evidence, much less proof, for the accusations was ever
presented. **in the polls:** Golan, p. 188. **Orthodox partners:** the National Religious Party, which abstained in a Knesset vote of confidence on the Sabbath jets. **feelers to Peres:** Golan, p. 188. Begin and
the Liberals' Simcha Ehrlich approached Peres with the suggestion.
a crisis of his own: EBE, AN; *JP.* **Herut's coffers:** the party fund,
known as *Tel Chai.* **neck-deep in debt:** one estimate at the time (*JP*)
was that *Tel Chai* was eighty million Israeli pounds in the red. **"I
take and took":** *JP.* The statement, in December 1976, was read out
on MB's behalf by Yitzhak Shamir, following remarks evidently
leaked by Herut officials explicitly disassociating MB from the financial mess.

"He felt that finally": EBE. **invite Ezer Weizman back:** ZS, EW; *JP,*
April 30, 1976, and January 3, 1977. **had extended a measure:** EW.
Now he relented: ZS. Among Weizman's supporters was Yaakov

Meridor (EW, YK). YK makes it clear that MB acquiesced in, rather than actively sought, Weizman's return: "When they started to prepare the elections, the movement tried to consolidate forces, and among the activists brought back was Ezer. It was a fact of life, a *fait accompli.*" **keynote Likud's campaign:** *JP,* January 8, 1977. MB said that if elected, his top priority would be to prevent war. **softened position:** AN, who was with Landau in the drafting sessions. The platform (reproduced in Hurwitz, Ch. 24) issued an explicit Israeli claim only to the formerly Jordanian West Bank: "Judaea and Samaria [the area's biblical name] shall therefore not be relinquished to foreign rule; between the sea and the Jordan, there will be Jewish sovereignty alone." But it made no such stipulation for the Sinai, and moreover it advocated formal treaties of peace with Arab neighbors. In such pacts, "borders shall be determined." EBE remarks that, although many outsiders missed the implication at the time, it was an important reminder that "we had never defined the Sinai as part of the biblical Land of Israel." He notes that another area captured from Egypt in 1967, however, was considered biblically Jewish: the Gaza Strip.

pro-Labor newspaper: *JP.* **help from ... sympathizers:** including, says AN, the American Hart Hasten and the Canadian Nathan Silver, whom AN describes as "the man who saved Tel Chai." **"The trouble with most":** *JP,* January 28, 1977. **When Shamir phoned:** EW. **hired a friend:** ZC, who attended the campaign strategy sessions. The friend in question was Eliezer Zurabin. ZC notes that advertising experts had helped with Israeli campaigns before, but that Weizman and Zurabin ran the country's first U.S.-style public-relations blitz. ZC recalls an early strategy session, devoted to mapping out how best to market the candidate. Zurabin declared: "Your biggest problem will be Begin's image. People are scared stiff of him!" It was an image the Weizman-Zurabin duo promptly set out to remake.

when Weizman excluded: YK, who adds, "The financial mess had weakened him. . . . Begin accepted the campaign. He was put in a position where it was an accomplished fact. He accepted this. He had no choice. He was not in a position to say: don't do this, don't do that." **"What do you want?":** EBE. **"We're relying on him":** *JP,* February 25, 1977. Weizman remarked: "The Labor party has chosen its image—gray and unimaginative." **"I will soon":** LM. **rushed**

to the hospital: *JP* daily reports; EBE. **deliver on his earlier assurances:** EBE, AN. **Begin received his prodigal:** *JP*, April 12–13, 1977. **"He was," recalls:** EBE. **refused to let Yitzhak Shamir:** ZC, who is also the source for the Weizman quote; Chafets, p. 79. **Summoning Kadishai, he handed:** YK. **scold Weizman for airing:** *JP*, May 13, 1977, series of interviews with MB, Shimon Peres, and Yigael Yadin. **Weizman's advertising friend . . . :** ZC, *JP*, and Haber (pp. 3–9) are sources for election-night section.

Chapter Twenty-one: The 180 Days

Books: Begin, Menachem, *The Revolt;* Brzezinski, Zbigniew, *Power and Principle;* Carter, Jimmy, *Keeping Faith;* Churchill, Colonel Charles, *The Druzes and the Maronites;* Dayan, Moshe, *Breakthrough;* Egyptian Ministry of Foreign Affairs, *White Paper on the Peace Initiatives Undertaken by President Anwar al-Sadat (1971–1977);* Haber, Eitan, et al., *The Year of the Dove;* Katz, Shmuel, *The Hollow Peace;* Medzini, Meron, editor, *Israel's Foreign Relations: Selected Documents, 1977–1979;* Randal, Jonathan, *Going All the Way;* Vance, Cyrus, *Hard Choices;* Weizman, Ezer, *The Battle for Peace.*

Interviews: Ilana Beaninstock, Eliahu Ben Elissar, Jimmy Carter, Ze'ev Chafets, Batya (Scheib) Eldad, Abe Foxman, Hart Hasten, Harry Hurwitz (HHu), Yehiel Kadishai, Mr. and Mrs. Marek Kahan and daughter, Brurya (BK), Shalom Kital, Yona Klimovitzki (YKl), Samuel Lewis, Leo Marcus, Arye Naor, Ephraim Poran, Ezer Weizman.

Articles, broadcasts, pamphlets, etc.: Shenker, Dr. Barry, and Dr. Henri Stellman, "The Israeli General Elections, July 23rd 1984—A Guide to the System, Parties, Electorate and Issues."

Periodical: The Jerusalem Post (JP).

Textual notes: **squatter site of Elon Moreh:** Weizman, p. 217. **U.S. alarm:** *JP* quotes a U.S. official remarking, "Our worst fears [about Begin] are coming true." **Labor had lost:** results in Shenker-Stellman article. **Weizman advised Begin against:** Weizman, p. 217. **"In a few weeks":** *JP*. **rushed back to the hospital:** *JP*. **While Weizman and other:** joining him were Yitzhak Shamir, Simcha Ehrlich, and

Yigal Hurwitz. **Liberals' Simcha Ehrlich:** *JP.* **set out to assemble:** EBE, who quips that there "was no 'transition team.' First, the 'team' was Begin. But besides that, we'd never had a transition in Israel!" **two eager contenders:** ZC is source for Landau candidacy. Dulzin's was, courtesy of the Israeli media, no secret. **When the U.S. ambassador:** SL. **All three said:** EBE, YK. Indeed, much of the party's old guard was opposed. Katz (pp. 29–30) remembers walking in on a hospital room meeting between MB and "leading members of the Herut Movement, who were stunned and resentful at [the] sudden appointment of Dayan . . ." **Dayan had always:** MB, in *The Revolt,* recalls (p. 314) having met Dayan early in the IZL underground days. "He made some encouraging remarks." Dayan, a Haganah luminary, praised MB for his policy of not "hurting Jews" and also said the IZL was "proving to the whole Jewish youth that it was eminently possible to smite the ruling authorities." MB harked back to that meeting in explaining the Dayan choice to aides (YK). **so blemished:** EP, who knew Dayan well, remarks that Begin "brought Dayan back from the political desert, brought him back to life. . . . You have to *understand* what Dayan *was*—what he was before the Yom Kippur War, and what he was after, fallen, without position. I think this period between 1974 and 1977, those three years, shortened his life by a decade." **"Yes,"** **Begin told Kadishai:** YK. **"checking to make sure his pants":** EBE notes that the phrase was borrowed from Jabotinsky, who had used it in the 1930s to describe a European statesman. **Dayan accepted:** Dayan, Ch. 1. **"Who was Dulzin?":** EBE.

no word of gratitude: EBE. **Begin chuckled to an aide:** EBE. **At least three were lobbying:** YM says he, for one, was just as happy to get on with his life in private business. EBE says Begin did, briefly, think of giving the Ministry of Immigration and Absorption to an old guarder instead of to Levy. **spent much of his life:** he emigrated to Israel and started teaching at Haifa's Technion math and science institute. Chaim Landau's son was at the institute with Arens, and the elder Landau brought Arens into Herut (AN). **Telling almost no one:** SL. When Lewis asked for names of people he should keep in touch with on foreign affairs, MB listed Dulzin and Arens. **promises to put Ben Elissar and Arye Naor:** EBE, AN. Begin hired only two IZL veterans—both defectors, asked back as prodigal sons. The first was Shmuel Katz, whom Begin earmarked to head a new ministry of overseas information, but then froze out when Dayan objected.

The second, as adviser on Arab terrorism, was Paglin. Paglin died shortly afterward in an automobile accident. **Chafets, twenty-nine years old:** ZC. For several weeks of the transition period, Chafets also answered Begin's mail—and brought comic relief to the early Begin administration. Every letter had to be answered, said Begin, since to leave a letter unanswered was like ignoring someone who greeted you on the street. Chafets wrote the replies, although Begin signed every one, including a series of notes Chafets exchanged with a jailed Australian convict named Anthony. "It was great!" recalls ZC. "First the guy signed the letters 'Anthony.' But in a short time—I had the letters brought to me even when I became Press Office director—it was: 'Dear Menachem' . . . and 'Love, your pal, Tony!' " While passing over old guarders in favor of newer faces, Begin also retained several Labor-era aides, notably General Ephraim Poran as military adviser and Dan Patir as press spokesman.

ready to jettison: EBE. Begin had for years argued the need to keep the police under the tightest possible rein in a free society. He had even cried foul, for instance, when Labor favored spying on members of the Israeli Communist party. **Kadishai and Ben Elissar—and Dayan:** EBE. Ben Elissar, usually reticent to offer his opinion to Begin on such matters, recalls having protested that the Sharon appointment—no matter what its intention or effect—"will be seen as an arrangement more appropriate to Russia. Especially with Sharon in charge, everyone will assume this ministry is not only to control the police, or to deal with law and order . . ." **confided to Kadishai:** EBE. **took office:** he began work, recalls EBE, with a ceremony in late June in Rabin's office. Begin shook hands, thanked Rabin. Then he turned to Ben Elissar and gave his first order as prime minister: to send word to an Israeli freighter that had taken aboard a boatload of Vietnamese refugees, that the passengers should be brought to Israel for resettlement—he told EBE that Israel must display the kind of welcome the world had *denied* boatloads of *Jewish* refugees during the Holocaust. **"There will be no smoking":** EBE. Begin had stopped smoking some years earlier on a dare—from Kadishai, who was also stopping. Kadishai, recalls EBE, had gradually weakened and was now intermittently requesting cigarettes from smoking friends. MB, by contrast, never resumed. **meetings were brief:** AN. **"Begin ran the cabinet":** EP. **told reporters he would . . . retire:** among others, see MB interview with *Yediot Aharonot* (Jewish New Year edition), September 12, 1977. **crystal-clear vision:** EBE, HHu. **Item one was Middle East peace:** EBE, AN. **to visit Romania:** via the ambassador, whom he had buttonholed at a reception.

preparing his pitch: EBE; Dayan, pp. 19–21. **pored through transcripts:** EBE. The transcripts indicated, above all, a lack of chemistry between the two men—a suggestion confirmed by Carter (pp. 279–280). Carter found Rabin "very timid, very stubborn and somewhat ill-at-ease . . ." MB devoured other material as well. EBE recalls that he and other aides, knowing Begin's voracious reading appetite, passed him a mountain of routine embassy cables, intelligence reports, and other background documents. "He read them all." But it was a one-man show: "He didn't ask for any briefings. He is not a team worker, in that sense . . ." **drafted a preemptive strategy:** AN. **To invite suggestions:** AN. MB took the Carter-Rabin transcripts as proving the point. Rabin (p. 317) notes that Begin "instituted a departure" from past practice. "I had always believed—as Labor prime ministers before me—that prior to embarking on any political initiative, it was imperative for our two [Israeli and U.S.] governments to reach an understanding, even though in order to do so we might be called upon to make certain compromises."

arrived in Washington: background in Vance, pp. 180–184; Carter, pp. 288–292; Dayan, pp. 18–21; Brzezinski, pp. 98–101; Katz, pp. 119–127. Text of public remarks by Begin and Carter throughout visit in Medzini, pp. 27–50. **gray suit:** ZC. **"You had to know":** EBE. Moments after the Ribicoff visit, adds AF, Begin was handed a message from a startlingly different source: Ethiopia's Marxist strongman, Mengistu Haile Mariam. Mengistu, playing to Begin's presumed concern for Ethiopia's many thousands of Falasha Jews, suggested a trade-off. In the first of several messages in the years ahead, he asked Begin to press the United States to reconsider taking Somalia's side in the Horn of Africa conflict. (Begin said he would pass on the word. Doing so, he made what he himself later characterized to AF as an impassioned plea, contending that Mengistu was being pushed by U.S. policy into a Soviet embrace. Carter said he would think it over. The Israel-Ethiopia link—with assists from the Sudan and Ronald Reagan's White House—resulted nearly a decade later in the evacuation of large numbers of Falashas to Israel.) **"pleasant surprise"**: JC. **"strong leader, quite different"**: Carter diary entry, p. 290. **"The president assured"**: text in Medzini, pp. 31–32. **told aides:** AN.

high spirits, and top form: transcript in Medzini, pp. 39–47. **"I was informed"**: transcript in Medzini, pp. 51–54. In keeping with his mood—and his bent for superlatives—MB remarked to the waiting reporters: "I had the privilege of being in close proximity for eight years with Ze'ev Jabotinsky, and so I am not easily impressed by people. I wish to say, upon my return home, that I was profoundly impressed by the extraordinary personality of President Carter." **The next day:** text of government announcement on settlements in Medzini, pp. 54–55. **Carter was upset:** Carter (p. 291) remarks that his "feelings of optimism" over the Washington talks were abruptly halted by the settlement announcement. **Carter ... said only:** Carter, July 28, 1977, news conference (transcript in Medzini, pp. 67–70). Carter said Begin hadn't mentioned the plans at the summit, or offered "any commitments" on settlements. "I think it is not fair to overly criticize Prime Minister Begin. ... I think he is in a position now of great strength in Israel. I think his voice would be honored by the Israeli people. But he, like myself, has run on campaign commitments and I think he is trying to accommodate the interest of peace as best he can. That doesn't mean that the settlements are right, but I think it would not be proper to castigate him unnecessarily about it." **"As free men"**: Knesset speech (Medzini, pp. 55–67). **"made the settlement move"**: EBE. **enjoyed remarking:** EBE. **He would rise:** EBE. **morning newspapers:** including, says EBE, journals like the Histadrut's *Hamishmar* and *Hatzofeh* of Mapam—"papers we never used to read."

"I didn't like": IB, who adds that her loyalty to Begin became irreversible one morning a few weeks after he had taken office: "Some newspaperwoman came to interview me. ... The interview was nothing. But the *headline*—the article was okay, but the headline I didn't like. So I called Yona [Klimovitzki, Begin's longtime office secretary] and I said I wasn't coming to work anymore, because of that interview. ... And Yona said to Begin: 'Ilana is very upset.' And at that point he didn't know me personally. So when I arrived at the office all the girls said, the prime minister is on the phone for you. I got really scared! This is the end of my career! And he said to me: 'Ilana, I really want to thank you for the beautiful work you are doing. I heard you are upset by this article. It's okay.

The newspaperwoman didn't act correctly. . . .' And I thought: this is a great man."

change had come slowly: YK. **"What is this?":** EBE. **she was interviewed:** ZC. **emphysema—though family and friends:** HH, LM. **confiding to a friend:** Mrs. MK. **disliked the constant presence:** Mr. and Mrs. MK, who recall visiting Aliza shortly after the Begins had moved into the prime minister's residence. They were stopped by security guards outside. Aliza, when informed, promptly sped her old friends through, remarking: "Up until now I didn't believe it. Now that I see these guards outside, I believe it." **shared the dislike:** YK, to whom Begin would complain, "I feel like a prisoner." MB felt particularly uncomfortable with the idea of bodyguards trailing him in public, says YK. **barred them:** BK says Aliza was insistent on keeping the upper floor of the two-story official residence "private . . . for no one but family." **"Now that Menachem":** LM. **"I have an aptitude":** LM. **array of volunteer projects:** YK, IB, BSE.

Begin relied on Aliza: "I consult with her about everything," he told *Yediot Aharonot* (September 12, 1977). After the cabinet's regular Sunday morning session, he would often tell the reporters waiting outside: "My wife is waiting for lunch with me . . ." YK observes that Begin "would never consider participating in a particular event without having Aliza by his side." **"That was Mr. Begin":** IB. **role was to listen:** BSE, Mrs. MK, BK, YS, YK. In exploring the extent and limits of Aliza's role, YK notes that Begin's wife "almost never" came to see him at the office. "In all the years he was prime minister, she came to the office and left with him for lunch together once or twice." Nor does YK—who, with his own wife, spent many hours with the Begins—feel that MB's remark about "consulting" with Aliza should be taken literally. Perhaps, says YK, Aliza would "in passing express an opinion on some issue. . . . But they understood each other without talking. There *were* certain occasions—let's say, the appointment of Dayan—when she opposed what he was doing, or was not happy about it. He knew this." BSE, who was among Aliza's close friends, comments that "for Ala, Begin had no defect. I criticize my husband [Yisrael Scheib]. I tell him if I agree or disagree . . ." Not so Aliza. **"his *foundation*":** Mrs. MK.

"like a close aunt": IB. **voice suited the role . . . :** YS. **Targets of her wrath:** YS, DY. **Scheib says he sensed . . . :** YS. **Yutan, excluded:** DY. ZC recalls a later example, at the time of the 1978 Camp David summit talks. Zelman Shoval had set up camp at the Israeli embassy, with the idea that he would help handle a damage-containment campaign with the U.S. media should the talks fail. However, recalls, ZC, "Mrs. Begin was convinced that Shoval *wanted* the summit to fail, that he was undercutting her husband." No sooner had they succeeded, says ZC, than word of Mrs. Begin's ire fanned through the prime ministerial bureaucracy and, says ZC, "None of us even *talked* to Shoval!" **Begin, says one:** YKl. A friend of Mrs. Begin's, BSE, adds: "Ala would travel [abroad] with Menachem. . . . The children were left here with a nanny or a baby-sitter. She joined him. She would go with him to his lectures. She was the loyal friend. She was the one who always encouraged him. She protected him." **sudden, steep loss of weight:** Mrs. MK. **At Rosenbaum Street:** EBE. **"a man like Menachem Begin needs":** YS.

Ignored domestic issues: ZC, EBE. See Medzini for background: MB interviews, Knesset declarations, news conferences; also, *JP*. **foreign minister held:** Dayan, Ch. 3; Haber et al., pp. 9–14; EBE, AN. **"gloated," recalls an aide:** EBE; AN made a similar remark to me. **secret visit of his own:** EBE. **shrugged off:** see Medzini declarations, interview transcripts. **draft peace treaty:** EBE. Begin interview with Israel Army radio (Medzini, pp. 105–106): "We built the peace treaty on the basis of the well-known precedents after the two world wars, as well as on other precedents, as we read and studied the documents." Also, MB interview with Israel Radio (Medzini, p. 121). Among those assigned to the treaty committee were MB's cabinet generals (Dayan, Weizman, Sharon), Attorney General Aharon Barak, and Foreign Ministry legal adviser Meir Rosenne. **note for U.S. eyes only:** MB, Israel Army radio interview (Medzini, p. 106). **ordered "equalization":** *JP*, August 15, 1977. **An aide recalls:** EP, who remarks of Begin that he would sometimes make a public statement on a particular issue "and think, 'That's it. I don't have to do anything more. It's done.' "

under Rabin: Randal, pp. 195–204. **converted Rabin's commitment:** the first public step in the conversion process had come in a statement MB made in New York, July 1977, after meeting with UN Secretary General Kurt Waldheim en route home from the White House summit. Referring to south Lebanon's Christian villages as "an island surrounded by a sea, an ocean of Muslim" territory, he declared: "We will go on defending the Christian minority—we have been a minority for many ages . . ." On his return to Israel, he elaborated further before the Knesset (Medzini, pp. 55–57), and noted that he had raised the Lebanon issue at the White House talks, too. As the weeks and months passed, the vision would become even more clear. In September 1977, for instance, MB would say in an interview with *Yediot Aharonot:* "I regard Israel as the protector of the minorities in all the Middle East." **The Christians, Begin said:** MB address to an Israel Bonds delegation (Medzini, pp. 76–78). **maltreated and massacred each other:** Randal provides an excellent and splendidly written historical survey of the conflict. Colonel Churchill offers a fascinating contemporary account of Lebanon's confessional strife in the nineteenth century. (For passages on Lebanon I have also drawn upon my own experiences, reading, research, and conversations during the three years that I was based in Beirut as a UPI reporter and, later, as the *Christian Science Monitor* Middle East correspondent.) **"We help them":** MB Israel Bonds address (Medzini).

trip to Romania: *JP* daily coverage. MB news conference on return (transcript in Medzini, pp. 98–101). SK and a second Israeli reporter who accompanied MB but requested anonymity. **carload of Israeli reporters:** SK. **"a big, fat baby!":** source is Israeli reporter, who requested anonymity. **sent Dayan on:** Dayan, Ch. 4. **backed off, and sent an envoy:** Hassan Tohamy, a Sadat confidant and member of a prominent and deeply conservative family of intellectuals and diplomats. **read him the riot act:** Dayan, pp. 59–74; Brzezinski, pp. 107–108. **summoned Ambassador Lews:** Dayan, p. 65. **Begin okayed a request from Weizman:** Defense Ministry communiqúe (text in Medzini, p. 127). **now insisted he be allowed:** Dayan, p. 66. **"working paper":** in talks with Carter and Vance, Dayan agreed to the idea of a joint Arab negotiating team—including non-PLO Palestinians— for eventual peace talks. He went further, saying these Palestinians could participate in specific talks on the future of the West Bank and Gaza. **promised to stop phoning:** Begin disclosure in April 11, 1979, interview with *JP*. **assumed personal control:** Says AN: "He set out to become 'Mr. Settlements.' " **"No," Begin said, but:** MB interview with Israel Radio, September 12, 1977 (Medzini, p. 124).

briefly rehospitalized: in late September (Katz, p. 159). **"military" encampments:** Dayan, Ch. 5; Vance, p. 191. MB announced it to the Gush Emunim settlement movement (*JP,* September 29, 1977).

fooled no one: except, briefly, the Americans, who were on balance relieved when Dayan suggested the plan. Their relief, like the restraint on the Begin government's settlement expansion, lasted only a matter of weeks. **"It was not":** EBE. **adding DASH:** AN. **objections to making Shmuel Tamir:** AN observes that Begin got in a dig at Tamir, however, by inviting Israeli Attorney General Aharon Barak to continue attending cabinet sessions and speak up when legal issues arose. MB had initially included Barak—the first time the attorney general had been made part of cabinet discussions—as an interim measure until the Justice Ministry post had been filled. Beyond the implicit slap at Tamir in continuing this arrangement, it no doubt also reflected that MB had come to like Barak immensely. The relationship would have a major effect a year later during the Camp David summit with Presidents Carter and Sadat.

Begin went home: EBE. Background for this section comes from Dayan, Carter, Vance; *JP.* **plans for the further meeting . . . :** when Dayan and Sadat's envoy parted in mid-September, they had tentatively agreed to reconvene two weeks later (Dayan, pp. 54, 91). But other diplomatic developments—the U.S.-Soviet statement, the U.S.-Israel working paper, and inter-Arab efforts to arrive at a common position on Palestinian representation at an eventual Geneva conference—soon overshadowed this. **Israeli reporter phoned:** EBE. **Sadat . . . at one point:** excerpts from Sadat address in Egyptian *White Paper,* p. 151. **But, he told an aide:** Katz, p. 183. **government and TV networks:** EBE. Texts of relevant statements and transcripts of U.S. television interviews with Begin and Sadat in Medzini. **Begin was more certain:** EBE. **"After all the years":** Katz, p. 183.

Chapter Twenty-two: Waging Peace

Books: Carter, Jimmy, *Keeing Faith;* Dayan, Moshe, *Breakthrough;* Egyptian Ministry of Foreign Affairs, *White Paper on the Peace Initiatives Undertaken by President Anwar al-Sadat (1971–1977);* Medzini, Meron, editor, *Israel's Foreign Relations: Selected Documents, 1977–1979;* Silver, Eric, *Begin;* Vance, Cyrus, *Hard Choices;* Weizman, Ezer, *The Battle for Peace.*

Interviews: Eliahu Ben Elissar, Samuel Lewis, Leo Marcus, Arye Naor, William Quandt, Harold Saunders.

Periodicals: The Jerusalem Post (JP); Yediot Aharonot.

Textual notes: **felt to do otherwise:** EBE. **Knesset, where Begin likened:** MB address, November 15, 1977 (text in Medzini, pp. 166–169). **hoped "soon" to:** MB at impromptu news conference, November 17 (transcript in Medzini, pp. 180–182). In private, Begin did permit himself occasionally to enjoy the magnitude of the event. LM, who was scheduled to leave for a trip overseas, recalls having dropped in on Begin to say good-bye. The Sadat visit had not been confirmed publicly, but Begin said with a playful smile that he had a pretty good idea LM would decide to stay in Israel for a few more days. **"no more war":** the phrase, which MB would repeat often in the weeks ahead, was included in an English-language radio broadcast "to the Egyptian people" (Medzini, pp. 162–163). **refused Weizman's pressure:** Chief of Staff Mordechai Gur made the remarks to *Yediot Aharonot.* Sadat, said Gur, "should realize that if what he has in mind is another deception like that on the eve of the Yom Kippur War, his intentions are quite clear to us." MB reprimanded Gur sternly (EBE, who walked in on the exercise), but made no move to dismiss him. **"It was the first time":** EBE. **Begin greeted him:** texts or transcripts of MB's, Sadat's, and others' statements during the visit are found in Medzini, pp. 182–212. Text of Sadat's Knesset speech in Egyptian *White Paper,* pp. 167–182. Further background from Dayan, Weizman, Carter, and Vance. **"hot line" to Cairo, but:** Dayan, pp. 79–80. **Weizman scribbled:** Weizman, p. 33. **speech . . . startling for what *wasn't* there:** text in Medzini, pp. 191–196. **no advance copy:** Dayan, p. 81. **omitted explicit claims:** except to remark, generally, that Israel had taken "no foreign land."

protective of Sadat: transcript of the Begin-Sadat news conference, which was held in the auditorium of the Jerusalem Theater a few leafy blocks from the prime minister's residence, is reproduced in Medzini, pp. 204–210. **follow-up peace conference:** Midlevel talks, to build on the summit. All the major Arab parties to the Arab-Israeli dispute, including the PLO, were invited. All refused, in protest against Sadat's Jerusalem visit. Text of November 26, 1977, invitation in Egyptian *White Paper,* p. 217. **relayed through Washington:** an "urgent message," recalls Carter, pp. 298–299. Sadat passed on a similar message to Vance (p. 197) when the secretary of state visited Egypt and Israel December 10–14. **withdrawal from Sinai:** Dayan

(Ch. 7) says the offer stipulated there be an Israeli civilian presence at the port and airstrip in Sharm el-Sheikh and at the airfield near El Arish in northern Sinai, as well as a "police defense force" in Israeli border settlements inside Sinai. **on a yellow legal pad:** AN. **"Autonomy Plan":** drafted in intermittent consultation with Attorney General Barak (Katz, p. 193), it originally contained twenty-one paragraphs. It was made public, with some amendments, by MB before the Knesset, December 28, 1977 (Medzini, pp. 272–279). MB had refined the autonomy concept, piecemeal, over the years. At the 1975 Herut convention in Hebron, for instance, he had stipulated that Arabs could choose either Jordanian or Israeli citizenship and vote accordingly. He now gave the plan detail, listing sixteen local-policy areas—ranging from education to tourism and agriculture to "supervision of the local police"—in which "administrative autonomy" was admissible. He said the functions could be exercised through an elected council. The only things he didn't say—was determined not to say—were that Palestinians could aspire to sovereignty, or national rights, over any portion of the West Bank or Gaza; or that Israel would surrender or compromise her own claims in that regard. **convinced Carter:** Carter (p. 299) says MB responded to Sadat's pressure for concessions with "a request to come to Washington to present a new proposition, which, he said, could break the deadlock."

Weizman was furious: Weizman, pp. 116–117: "It never occurred to me that Dayan, with Begin's backing, would discuss giving up the whole of the Sinai without so much as consulting the defense minister." Of the autonomy plan, Weizman says it was "flung at the cabinet lock, stock and barrel." Weizman went so far—says Katz (p. 199), who passed him in the hallway of the government office complex—as to call on Begin, "trembling with rage, to inform the Prime Minister that he was resigning." He retreated, however, from the threat. **felt the Palestinian autonomy:** Katz, pp. 193–195: "I was amazed. . . . Here was Begin suddenly pulling out of his hat a program which did not predicate Jewish sovereignty, or Israeli sovereignty in territory in which the Arabs would enjoy self-government . . ." **Begin surprised Carter:** Carter, p. 299; Brzezinski, p. 115. **he agreed—over Katz's:** details of talks in Katz, pp. 201–215, and Brzezinski, pp. 115–120.

phoned Sadat and persuaded: see MB interview on CBS's *Face the Nation* (Medzini, pp. 254–257). **Carter . . . jotted:** Carter, p. 300. Interviewed by the author, JC says he does not feel this protectiveness survived. But he did get the feeling despite "moments of extreme bitterness" which had already soured the peace process, that Begin was "concerned" about the isolation and physical danger to which Sadat had thrown himself open. **resented the Egyptian's:** based on remarks on MB's ties with Sadat from EP, ZC, EW. Begin himself scattered only intermittent public hints at this resentment. See, for example, MB's November 28, 1977, statement to the Knesset on the Sadat initiative (Medzini, pp. 224–229). MB praises Sadat's visit, says it was a move without historic precedent, then adds: "But there is no precedent either to the way we welcomed the President of Egypt . . ." **When Ben Elissar phoned:** EBE. **having Katz stay on:** Katz, pp. 210–211. **joined Sadat Christmas Day:** Sadat was still not ready to have Begin visit Cairo. MB seemed sufficiently elated by becoming the first Israeli leader to visit Egypt to ignore Sadat's demonstratively low-key welcome for him even in Ismailiya (Dayan, Weizman).

got Sadat's instant agreement: addressing reporters on his return to Israel (transcript in Medzini, pp. 268–272), Begin said Sadat's okay had come "within a few minutes." **He emerged beaming:** accounts of summit come from Weizman, pp. 126, 128–135, and Dayan, pp. 103–106. **hundreds of reporters:** press conference transcript in Egyptian *White Paper,* pp. 228–239, and Medzini, pp. 261–268. **"Within the first five":** MB report and debate in Knesset, December 28 (Medzini, pp. 272–279).

it was painful: transcript of remarks in Medzini, pp. 275–276. **fellow backbencher:** Moshe Shamir. **Showing up at Begin's:** Katz, pp. 216–219. **Begin opened the central committee:** text in Medzini, pp. 290–291. **would reserve "the right to":** however, when dissenter Moshe Shamir rose in the Knesset a few days later to press Begin to make good on this threat, Begin made it clear he would not. **heard Begin whisper:** Katz, p. 222. **a quality he contrasted:** Katz, p. 225. **"It was . . . a very small":** EBE. **Sadat pulled out:** the Egyptians charged that Begin had insulted Egypt's chief delegate, Foreign Minister Mohammed Kamel, at a welcoming banquet. The Egyptians argued that MB had erred in using a toast to deliver what amounted to a political speech. They were also offended by MB's referring to Kamel as "a young man." Vance (p. 201) is convinced that any slight Begin made was "unwitting." A senior Egyptian negotiator, requesting anonymity, says the MB toast was merely a convenient public pretext for making a move based on more profound policy considerations. He suggests Sadat had concluded from MB's continued unwillingness to offer concessions on the Palestinian question or on settlements that it was time to stand back and reconsider the two-month-old peace initiative. **Begin was more relieved:** EBE, who had rushed to MB's office with news of the break-off, culled from Arabic-language radio monitors. Begin, recalls EBE, "didn't look unduly annoyed." See also MB remarks to visiting French-Jewish study group, January 19 (Medzini, pp. 301–306). **issued a statement:** January 19 (in Medzini, p. 301). **jaunty address:** Medzini, pp. 301–306. *kalt und fest:* MB was true to the slogan. A few days later when Sadat retreated from the diplomatic brink by allowing the other follow-up committee—for military matters—to start meeting in Cairo, Begin used the occasion to dress down Cairo's government-controlled media for a spate of anti-Semitic articles since the Ismailiya summit. In one, Begin himself had been likened to Shakespeare's Shylock. He said if the diatribes didn't stop within a week, no Israeli negotiators would travel to Egypt. In the end MB did send the military delegation to Cairo, where it opened talks (January 31) that almost immediately adjourned.

it seemed to Carter: Carter, pp. 304–306; Vance, pp. 202–203; Brzezinski, pp. 237, 245. **declared illegal:** Vance, in a February 10 news conference, said the Sinai settlements should be removed. **announcing a package deal:** announced by Vance February 14. **"so *wanted* Carter to":** HS. **"goodwill and understanding":** MB interview on U.S. TV (Medzini, pp. 254–257). **felt cheated:** AN. **considered ... lightweight:** EP, ZC, EW. Another senior Israeli participant in the peace process, who requested anonymity, remarks: "Begin did not appreciate Sadat's role. Privately, he would, for instance, call Sadat a 'liar.' And he felt he, Begin, was being called on to give up something concrete, while Sadat was giving only declarations ..." MB himself was asked (September 12, 1977, interview with *Yediot Aharonot*) to "define your attitude toward the Arabs." He replied: "As for my personal relations with Arabs, I will answer you frankly: Ze'ev Jabotinsky wrote: 'I relate to Arabs as to all other [non-Jewish] peoples, with a certain degree of respect and indifference.' He wanted [said Begin] to emphasize love: I love my people. As for the rest—I respect them but I cannot relate to them as to my own people ..." MB seemed additionally, however, to retain his IZL-era conviction that Arabs were backward, that they lacked the "Jewish brain." Weizman (pp. 143–144) recalls that at one point in mid-1978 MB wanted to invite "the Egyptians to tour the [Israeli Sinai] Rafah settlements, apparently convinced that their hearts would soften when they saw those green oases . . ." Says the senior Israeli official who requested anonymity: "Begin hated Arabs, in the sense that for him, they were not even a second-echelon people, but a fifth-echelon people. He never *knew* the Arabs." And Sadat? "He *never* liked Sadat. Never." **"Sadat says":** MB interview with PBS's Robert MacNeil, January 25, 1978 (Medzini, pp. 318–322). **Knesset, he complained:** MB Knesset speech, February 15, 1978 (Medzini, pp. 338–340).

Summoning his generals: AN. The reference is to the cabinet's defense committee, which included Dayan, Sharon, Yadin, military aide Ephraim Poran, Chief of Staff Gur, and a civilian, the Liberals' Simcha Ehrlich. Weizman, who was in the United States, conferred by phone, then hurried home (Weizman, pp. 269, 272–279). AN, who was at the defense committee session, says there was little discussion. No one challenged Begin's sense that a swift counterstrike was needed. The Defense Ministry's staff had already drawn up the appropriate contingency plans. "Freuke [Poran] phoned Ezer in the States and told him what had happened, using code words for the retaliation plans. Ezer asked whether 'the whole thing' was being ordered—that is, an incursion well into southern Lebanon. Freuke replied, 'No. Half.' " This referred to a planned drive six miles into Lebanon—with due care to avoid clashes with Syrian troops just above that zone. At one point during the incursion, Weizman recalls standing on a southern Lebanese hill and peering northward toward the coastal city of Tyre. Weizman wondered aloud whether he should order the army to take Tyre—as an "imposing final chord." Gur talked him out of it, warning, among other things, that the move might draw Syrian intervention. Weizman assented. **"gone forever":** MB to Knesset, March 13 (Medzini, pp. 359–362). **struck into Lebanon:** background from Weizman; also from my own experiences and recollections (I covered the incursion into south Lebanon, at one point getting caught between the advancing Israelis and retreating Palestinians along with two colleagues. We came under shell and mortar fire for hours, took refuge at nightfall in a southern Lebanese village, and "surrendered" the next morning to an Israeli column on the town's edge).

plea for concessions: Carter (p. 310) recalls that he had felt saddened by the PLO terror strike, but saw the Israeli invasion as "a terrible overreaction." **"wounded in the heart":** Carter diary entry, p. 311. Further detail on the Carter-Begin talks in Carter, pp. 311–312, and in Dayan, Vance, Brzezinski. **Begin looked dumbstruck:** Dayan and Brzezinski. **"drawn and ashen":** Dayan, p. 126.

honeymoon with the Israeli media: over a period of weeks, major Israeli newspapers had begun to run analyses, commentaries, and punditry with a remarkably similar "we-told-you-so" theme. MB did little to help the situation when, at the end of Israeli President Ephraim Katzir's term of office, he was called on to recommend a successor. Begin decided to break new ground by proposing a Sephardic candidate. But the Sephardim—like the Arabs—were a people MB knew more in the collective than as individuals. Having been told that a professor named Yitzhak Shaveh was a particularly gifted Sephardi, MB had Kadishai offer him the job. The man was on sabbatical in Paris and, though flattered at the offer, had no particular background or interest in politics. So embarrassing was the ensuing flap that Herut had no choice but to back Labor's candidate for the presidency (also Sephardic)—Yitzhak Navon. Typical of the media assault that built up during the first half of 1978 was the *JP*. On the eve of MB's departure for the White House talks, the *JP* ran a commentary by former Foreign Ministry Director General Shlomo Avineri, entitled WHO'S RUNNING THE SHOW? On March 9, the *JP*'s economics editor opined: "Disillusionment [with Begin] is setting in with a speed astonishing even in volatile Israeli politics." Not long after came a commentary on MB and the cabinet headlined: IN DEEP TROUBLE. **cabinet in disarray:** the signs were abundant. One of them confronted Begin literally upon landing. During his absence, Weizman had dramatized his criticism of some of his colleagues' allegedly ungenerous attitudes toward the Sadat initiative by calling for establishment of a "peace government" in Israel. MB, when asked for comment, replied that Israel "already has" such a government (MB news conference on return to Israel, Medzini, pp. 378–380). **Sharon drew up:** AN. **caught the government:** Shlomo Avineri in *JP*. **Once leakproof:** AN.

nor his body: the physical lapse came in May and early June (AN; *JP*). **confiding to a BBC:** Michael Elkins, quoted in Silver, p. 182. **When Sharon suggested:** Weizman, pp. 143–145. **Lebanon he**

flouted: background in Randal, and from my own period as *CSM* Mideast correspondent there. **His one concession:** WQ; Vance, p. 209. **a top U.S. official:** WQ, who feels the impact of the Carter message was intensified by the fact that Ambassador Lewis, with whom MB had established considerable personal rapport, was unavailable to deliver it. The substitute messenger, says WQ, was embassy Chargé d'Affaires Richard Viets, who conveyed the Carter message with neither smiles nor frills. **"consider and agree":** cabinet communiqué, June 18, 1978 (Medzini, pp. 434–435). **"Delphic sidestepping":** Vance, p. 214. **turned down a fresh:** cabinet statement, June 25 (Medzini, p. 441). **In July he rejected:** Weizman, pp. 329–330. **"Sam, no one gets":** SL. **from Dayan, not Begin:** Vance, pp. 215–216; Dayan, pp. 138–148. **rest of the cabinet berated:** AN.

prevented Peres: MB Knesset remarks, July 19, 1978 (Medzini, pp. 467–471). **"Peres can have":** YK, ZC. **tale of its origin:** YK. **quoting back ... a battery:** MB remarks and debate in Knesset, July 24 (Medzini, pp. 482–490). **that he was a better bargainer:** based on interview remarks by AN, EBE, and ZC. **Begin told the nation:** MB television address, September 2, 1978 (excerpts transcribed in Medzini, pp. 510–511).

Chapter Twenty-three: Camp David

Books: Brzezinski, Zbigniew, *Power and Principle;* Carter, Jimmy, *Keeping Faith;* Dayan, Moshe, *Breakthrough;* Medzini, Meron, editor, *Israel's Foreign Relations: Selected Documents, 1977–1979;* U.S. Government Policy Statement Series: *A Framework for Peace in the Middle East; Documents Related to the Camp David Accords;* Vance, Cyrus, *Hard Choices;* Weizman, Ezer, *The Battle for Peace.*

Interviews: Yaakov Amrami, Eliahu Ben Elissar, Jimmy Carter, Leo Marcus, Arye Naor, Ephraim Poran, Harold Saunders, Cyrus Vance.

Periodical: The Jerusalem Post.

Textual notes: **helicopter arrived last:** two hours after Sadat's, Carter, pp. 328–330. Background detail for this section comes from Carter, Vance, Brzezinski, Dayan, and Weizman; and from interviews with Camp David participants, including JC, CV, HS, SL. Also, an interview with an Egyptian participant, who requested anonymity. Accompanying Begin to Camp David were Dayan, Weizman, Attorney General Barak, Ephraim Poran, and several other officials and diplomats. **He asked Carter:** Carter, pp. 329–330. **interfaith prayer:** Weizman, p. 345. **Begin told the Israeli delegation:** Weizman, p. 344. **Begin insisted on addressing them by title:** JC. "Begin," he recalls, "was meticulous in reminding me and Sadat that we were heads of states and he was not. He was [just] a prime minister." **Carter joked to Begin:** Carter, p. 345. **"What** *chutzpah!***":** Weizman, p. 354. MB's specific reference was to Sadat's demand that Israel pay compensation, a provision Weizman and Dayan also found almost ridiculously presumptuous. **proposed drafting:** Dayan, pp. 161–162.

Begin refused: Carter, pp. 347–350; Weizman, pp. 356–357; Brzezinski, p. 257. **"We broke the ice":** Dayan, p. 163. **shelved the idea:** Carter, p. 356. **dropped by and suggested ... chess:** Brzezinski, p. 259. **Begin lied that it was the first time:** MB had often played chess in the intervening years: with YA on Saturday afternoons, to name but one example. In any case, Aliza emerged from the Begin cabin near the end of the game with Brzezinski and (p. 259) blew her husband's cover: "Menachem," she exclaimed, "just loves to play chess!" **as if the board:** Dayan, p. 157. **strategy was to prick:** CV, HS. **"I would draft":** Carter, p. 356. **"staking out a very":** HS. Another senior diplomat. He requested anonymity.

"I do not see": Carter, p. 365. **rebutted the draft:** Carter, pp. 373–379; Weizman, pp. 363–365; Brzezinski, pp. 260–262; Vance, pp. 220–221. The stormy session lasted, with a break, about seven hours and ended well after midnight. Weizman, a rare note of awe slipping into his narrative, remarks (p. 364) that Begin "faced Carter and the others, his voice raised to eliminate any doubts or misunderstandings. He rejected or amended considerable portions of the American proposal." **"no threats, please":** Weizman, p. 365. **"obstacle to progress":** Carter, p. 378. **Carter was more blunt:** Brzezinski (to whom Rosalynn repeated the remark), p. 262. **"You've** *got* **to see":** source is a senior U.S. official, who requested anonymity.

Americans began working: JC. **would have to consult:** Dayan, pp. 153–154. **prestige of the American presidency:** Dayan, p. 173. Weizman's account also includes references to U.S. pressures. **Weizman had long since:** CV and HS accounts both make it clear that Dayan and Barak were the key actors in the U.S. efforts to secure agreement with Begin. JC does remark: "You shouldn't overlook Ezer Weizman." However, he says that on matters of detail it was Aharon Barak who most often helped secure a compromise. **Begin respected Dayan:** An and EP. EP notes that Dayan had built up a special relationship with the prime minister—largely by forgoing Weizman-like confrontation tactics for a more quiet approach: "Dayan knew how to deal with Begin. He could get from Begin anything he wanted. But he would do it in private, face to face. He used to come to him before a [cabinet] meeting and tell him, 'Look, I think we should do so-and-so. And once he'd got Begin's approval, even if in the cabinet session there were many voices against, Begin would hold to what he had decided with Dayan in his office an hour before." Still, Dayan—like Sharon—seemed also cowed by MB at times. One senior U.S. official involved in the peace negotiations, who requested anonymity, remarks: "I don't know how many times Dayan and I would be talking and would agree that Begin has to be persuaded on such and such an issue, and Dayan would then say, 'But why don't *you* go in and raise it with him?' "

even more at ease with Barak: JC. Background on MB's relationship with Barak from AN, EBE. MB had relied on Barak to help draft the Palestinian autonomy plan in December 1977, had taken him along to the White House talks, then to Ismailiya and back to Washington for the additional U.S. summit in March 1978. Dayan, too, took Barak with him for the summer 1978 talks with Vance. **"You had Begin":** HS, who adds of Barak: "He was the kind of lawyer who *solved* problems rather than created them." **Begin would get "angry":** Dayan, p. 154. **"most serious talk":** Carter, pp. 385–387. **Americans embarked on:** JC, HS; Carter, pp. 387–389; Vance, pp. 222–223. **emerging draft proposed:** HS; Carter, pp. 387–388. Also, text of Camp David accords. **"I dealt primarily with":** JC, who remarks: "My impression was that on a personal basis, for some reason, Barak was more successful in getting Begin to accept proposals, and to modify his previous position than ... Dayan." **"My right eye":** Brzezinski, p. 263. **When Carter sought out:** Carter (p. 388) says: "Barak refused to discuss the Israeli settlements at all, saying that it was a subject only Begin could address." **Carter braved Begin:** Carter, p. 388. **Sadat ... began packing:** in reply (Carter, p.

392) to a meeting with Dayan in which discord over settlements (Dayan, p. 172) had predominated. **The Israelis met:** Weizman, pp. 369–370. **Sharon—back in Israel:** Weizman, p. 370.

Begin was alone: Carter (p. 394) recalls Dayan's remarking that "Begin was feeling somewhat excluded from the negotiating process, since I had not seen him lately." **the Americans knew it:** the Israelis (AN) were and are convinced that phone communications, including the Sharon call, were tapped. HS flatly denies this. In any case, the Americans did sense in the final days of the summit that MB was being urged by his own delegation to cede to U.S. pressure for a settlement compromise. JC remarks that Weizman, Dayan, and Barak—"all of his [Begin's] major advisers were inclined to accept the proposals that we were putting forward. . . . He [Begin] was the most recalcitrant member of the Israeli delegation." **relieved when he showed:** Carter, p. 395. **Begin, recalls the president:** also, Brzezinski, p. 270. **assured the other Israelis:** Weizman, p. 373. **set off for Sadat's:** Carter, pp. 400–401. **first meeting since:** except for a testy tourist excursion to Gettysburg. **"stretched almost to the breaking point":** HS: "stretched . . . by the pressures on him from his own people, particularly Barak and Dayan, and by the circumstances, of being in that kind of negotiation." **"We were all in a state":** JC, who recalls the helicopter flight as the single "closest moment" in his relationship with Begin. **Begin declared at the signing ceremony:** MB remarks at White House ceremony (text in Medzini, pp. 526–527). **old friend, who found:** LM.

Chapter Twenty-four: Full Stop

Books: Bethell, Nicholas, *The Palestine Triangle;* Brzezinski, Zbigniew, *Power and Principle;* Carter, Jimmy, *Keeping Faith;* Dayan, Moshe, *Breakthrough;* Medzini, Meron, editor, *Israel's Foreign Relations: Selected Documents, 1977–1979;* Vance, Cyrus, *Hard Choices.*

Interviews: Jimmy Carter, Ze'ev Chafets, Arye Naor, Ephraim Poran, Harold Saunders, Michael Sterner, Shmuel Tamir, Eli Tavin, Cyrus Vance.

Articles, broadcasts, pamphlets, etc.: Bethell, Nicholas, MB interview for *The Palestine Triangle;* Quandt, William B., "Menachem Begin: A Past Master at Negotiation," in *The Brookings Review,* Winter 1983.

Periodicals: The Jerusalem Post (JP); Ma'ariv; Time magazine.

Textual notes: **refused to sign:** HS, CV; Carter, p. 397; Vance, p. 229. After the late-night session in which the freeze was ostensibly agreed, Saunders was asked to draft the letter—by Carter, who clearly felt MB had signed onto the settlement moratorium. **endorsed by the U.S. diplomat:** HS. **"hear selectively":** HS, who remarks, "You could have a two-hour conversation between him and Carter, and then when you heard him describe it to the press or somebody else, you wondered whatever happened to the *other* two hours and fifty-nine minutes! Because he would go out and characterize it as the most marvelous conversation he'd ever had. He'd say, 'The president said this . . . ,' fixing on one nice element, and you'd wonder what happened to all the *rest* of the stuff the president had said." **Sadat addressing him as "friend":** Sadat used the term loosely—embracing all sorts of people, up to and including me and other foreign reporters who met and interviewed him. Begin took it literally. Sadat had called him "friend," MB said to a variety of audiences—the Knesset, Jimmy Carter, journalists—whenever it was suggested that Israel was being insufficiently forthcoming to Sadat in the negotiations.

Americans and Sadat saw: HS, CV; an Egyptian participant at Camp David, who requested anonymity. **"insignificant change":** JC. **once Begin had concluded:** based on discussions of Begin and the peace process with CV, HS. See also Vance, p. 229. **"Legitimate rights":** MB to *Ma'ariv,* September 20, a report naturally picked up by international wire services from Tel Aviv and fanned back worldwide. Similarly, Begin *(JP,* September 20) told a U.S. House of Representatives committee that Israeli troops would remain on the West Bank indefinitely. **When Carter warned:** Carter (p. 406) notes: "The next day in New York, Begin continued his disruptive comments. . . . I had a feeling that he really did not want any early talks involving the Palestinians and other Arabs." **Inviting Eli Tavin:** ET. **Begin struck back:** AN, ST. Landau tried again to say his piece later in the cabinet meeting, and this time MB acquiesced. **recalls one minister:** he requested anonymity. "If anyone had been loyal to Menachem Begin," the minister told me, "it was Landau. Almost embarrassingly loyal! Now he had no choice but to protest, if he was to be faithful to all the principles Begin had taught him over the years." **facing the cabinet:** Dayan, p. 191. **near-unanimous endorsement:** Of seventeen ministers, eleven voted in favor of the accords—and the Sinai settlement assurance. Two ministers voted against them: the Rafi-State's Yigal Hurwitz and a rehabilitated Eliezer Shostak. Four ministers—three Orthodox religious party members, and the Liberals' Yitzhak Modai—abstained. **He said the accords:** MB speech to Knesset, September 25, and remarks in debate, September 28 (text in Medzini, pp. 544–554). **in a single vote:** having toyed briefly with staying neutral on the Sinai settlement issue, Begin had now decided the best defense was a good offense, and waged an energetic battle for packaged passage of the accords, as in the cabinet. **maybe in two months:** in an interview with *Time,* MB said "98 percent" of the problems in signing a treaty had already been resolved, a figure he cut back to 90 percent in his Knesset remarks, yet which still left his two-month target seemingly in reach. **"What makes this night":** MB remarks in closing debate, September 28 (Medzini).

Yet if assailed: MB's swift riposte to Tavin and Landau; the new-guard cabinet he had assembled eighteen months earlier; and background remarks from ZC, AN, and EP; all suggest that MB's pain was tempered by a strong sense that he had progressed farther than his old comrades in political thinking and world vision. The bond he felt with his underground soldiers was no doubt heartfelt, as was the hurt at the strains it was now under. But so was the Knesset explanation of his treaty concessions. MB, moreover, told a *Time* magazine interviewer after the Camp David signing that it seemed inevitable that "some of my best friends, my most beloved friends" would reject the accord. But he added that "the Frenchmen have a philosophical expression: *c'est la vie . . .*" **acceptance he had . . . craved:** the perennially pro-Labor *JP* wrote (September 22) of the Camp David accords: "Menachem Begin has risen above himself. His critics, more than anyone else, owe him a tribute . . ." **In the airport crowd:** *JP,* September 24. **Opinion polls:** quoted in *JP,* September 21. **shuttles, telegrams, even videocassettes:** HS; Vance, p. 237. **sent Harold Saunders:** HS. Details of letter in Vance, pp. 230–231. **Begin was waiting:** HS. Similarly, when an MB announcement on future West Bank settlement shocked and angered the Americans later in the fall, MB wrote to Carter (p. 408) saying that "his actions on the West Bank settlements were designed to assuage the feelings of

some of his political allies, who had now turned against him."
Shrewdly, MB focused his public ire on the messenger (Saunders)
and not on the man who had made a point of personally signing the
document (Carter). HS recalls that on meeting Carter upon return
from his scathing reception in Israel, the president smiled and said,
"Well, I guess there has to be a villain in every piece!"

Begin sent Dayan: Dayan, pp. 199–221. The talks opened at Blair
House, the guest residence across Pennsylvania Avenue from the
White House, on October 12. Also in the delegation was Weizman.
Begin announced preemptive: Dayan, p. 225; Vance, p. 235. **unveil-
ing plans:** Carter, p. 408. Vance (p. 235) says: "We were very angry
. . . This step was contrary even to Begin's version of the Camp
David accords." **leaked his intention:** Carter, p. 408. **and Sadat:**
Sadat, who had no intention of sharing a podium with Begin, had an
envoy collect his share of the peace prize. **a personal vindication:**
Dayan (p. 228) says Begin called him in the United States shortly
afterward and "informed me with understandable emotion" of the
honor. **"What can a member":** MB to Israel TV (Medzini, pp.
574–576).

laureate met America's: Vance, pp. 236–237; Dayan, pp. 232–233.
needed U.S. money to relocate: typically, MB lacked mastery of the
detail involved. Weizman had already been hard at work securing a
grant for the transfer, but Begin shocked his fellow Israelis (and the
Israeli news media when the development became public) by beating an unwitting retreat: He pressed for a *loan*. **Vance reverted:**
Dayan, pp. 240–243. Carter, after hearing Vance's report on the
Begin talks, wrote in his diary (p. 409): "It is obvious that the Israelis
want a separate treaty with Egypt; they want to keep the West Bank
and Gaza permanently. . . . And they use the settlements and East
Jerusalem as issues to prevent the involvement of the Jordanians
and the Palestinians." **second encounter:** Dayan, pp. 244–246;
CV, who recalls having felt before the airport meeting that "Dayan
and I had basically reached agreement." However, during the encounter—which CV recalls was unique in the long negotiating
process—"Begin really blew up at Dayan, really chewed him out in
my presence, verging on publicly embarrassing him. . . . Begin
thought Dayan had gone too far."

phoned Carter, announcing: Carter (p. 411) recalls that MB had
"agreed to accept the month-old treaty draft, but had ruled out any

[linkage] timetable for discussions of agreement on the West Bank. Sadat too had hardened his position ...";. Vance, p. 239. **Sadat wrote Begin:** Vance, p. 240. The letter was relayed by the Americans. **Vance flew:** Vance, pp. 240–242; Carter, p. 411. **"very generous":** Carter to reporters, December 13 (transcript in Medzini, pp. 603–604). **Begin shouted:** AN; Vance, pp. 241–242. MS, who was with the Vance delegation, remarked to me (as *CSM* correspondent) after the talks that Begin had raised a battery of specific objections: "We expected there might be problems. But this was something right out of Saint Thomas Aquinas!" **Vance—despondent at:** this account is from a senior U.S. official, who requested anonymity. **Still, Begin would not give:** Vance, on the plane back, permitted himself a rare burst of frustration and anger in remarks to the traveling press. Speaking in the transparent guise of a "senior State Department official," he accused Israel of misleading the world by "claiming it was ready to sign" the draft treaty. "I think I was saddened," he added in a TV interview back in the United States, "at the fact—and disappointed—that the proposals were apparently turned down so flatly at the end of my trip." **"We now have an example":** MB Knesset statement (text in Medzini, pp. 613–618). **group of Israeli:** MB interview (transcript in Medzini, pp. 623–626). **sent Dayan back:** Dayan, pp. 259–267; Vance, p. 243. **Dayan protested:** the issue had come to a head during the Blair House talks (Dayan, pp. 209–210).

Summoning Dayan: Dayan, pp. 265–267; Carter, p. 413. Further details from MB Knesset speech and debate, March 20, recapping this period of the negotiations (Medzini, pp. 665–686). **give the foreign minister more leeway:** which, Dayan recalls (p. 266) replying with a smile, was unlikely in the extreme. **Begin told them:** MB Knesset recap of the negotiating process, March 20. He explained: "We already knew what the latest proposals were—submitted by Egypt, and supported by the United States." Begin said that he was determined not to accept them—and knew that the rejection could have caused an indefinite break in the peace talks, with the onus on Israel. **upset the conference's symmetry:** the argument was ironic, considering Begin's past insistence on pointing out that Presidents Carter and Sadat outranked him, a mere prime minister. **Begin grudgingly agreed:** to have done otherwise, notes Vance (p. 243), "would have openly ruptured his already tense relationship with Carter. For Begin, or any Israeli prime minister, to appear to be on such bad terms with the president of the United States would have been deeply disturbing to Israeli public opinion . . ." **added that he, too:** Carter diary entry, p. 413. MB, says Carter, refused to meet at Camp David and sent word "he was not even bringing his Foreign Minister or other cabinet ministers with him—and even said he would not discuss substantive issues."

gave him authority: Dayan, p. 267. **visit was merely "personal":** statement by the prime minister's office (Medzini, p. 644). **two legal aides:** Meir Rosenne and Yehuda Blum. **despite "hints":** MB news conference, March 1 (Medzini, pp. 644–645). **On arrival:** *JP;* Carter, p. 414. **Begin at first tried:** Carter, pp. 414–416; Vance, pp. 243–245; Brzezinski, pp. 280–281. **even one or two:** Carter diary entry, March 2, p. 415. **After a fitful sleep:** MB to Carter after the talks had ended, p. 416. **verbal formulas:** MB Knesset recap, March 20 (text of remarks in Medzini). **took Begin aside:** Carter, p. 416. **accept the "goal":** MB Knesset recap, March 20; Vance, p. 244. **had won, he said:** Dayan, p. 268. **right to buy Sinai oil:** Vance, pp. 244–245.

Carter phoned Sadat: Carter, p. 416. **beg Sadat's support:** Carter, p. 417; Brzezinski, p. 282: "The President . . . told me to tell Sadat very privately that the President's domestic political situation was becoming more difficult and that Begin might even wish to see the President defeated." Carter wrote in his diary (p. 418) when in Cairo: "Sadat understands that Begin may wish to back out if he gets a chance, or wait until after 1980 when there is a President in the White House who may not be so equally balanced between the Israeli and Arab interests . . ." **let "Begin have his way":** Carter, p. 417. **Egyptian . . . still wanted:** Vance, p. 246. **Sadat substituted:** MB Knesset recap, March 20 (Medzini, pp. 665–685).

unshakable preference for Sadat: two senior U.S. officials, who requested anonymity on this point. **drove directly:** JC. **said he thought:** JC; Carter, pp. 420–421. **"doing everything . . .":** Carter diary entry, March 10, p. 421. **"very dejected, and angry":** JC, who remarks: "I arrived at his home . . . having already derived from Sadat adequate concessions on previous Israeli demands, and found that Begin had no intention of reaching agreement at that time." JC says this was the single lowest point in his relations with Begin. **"go over Begin's head . . .":** JC, who explains: "I always looked upon Mr. Begin . . . as the most recalcitrant of the Israeli leaders. And when I went over in March and met privately with Begin at his home, I was convinced that he did not want to go further with the peace process at that time." **flanked by his:** AN; Vance, p. 247; Dayan, p. 270. **Carter opened:** Dayan, pp. 270–271. **rejected even this:** Quandt, who recalls that "the only thing we accomplished during the entire afternoon was to agree on 'contravene'!" calls the debate "one of his [Begin's] most remarkable performances. . . . The spectacle of the president, the secretary of state, the secretary of defense, the assistant to the president for national security affairs, and half a dozen of their top aides trying to find a word acceptable to Begin must have given him a sense of power and importance . . ." Quandt notes that the effect, if not the intention, was to reduce the amount of time, energy, and diplomatic pressure they could devote to the major substantive issues.

Begin did . . . seem fearful: Dayan, p. 273. **"The heavens will not fall":** Dayan, p. 272. **resumed arguing:** Dayan, p. 274; Vance, p. 248. **"You must agree":** AN. Also, Dayan (p. 274) recalls: "Carter demanded with brutal insistence that we should agree to Egyptian liaison officers . . . so that Egypt could influence her people to support the autonomy program." **"All right. Let us proceed":** AN. JC remarks: "Had I exploded in the cabinet meeting, had I gotten angry, and lost control of my equilibrium, it is likely I would have alienated other members of the cabinet"—that is, lost any hope at all of a treaty. **"the leaders have not yet":** text in Medzini, pp. 652–656. **Carter sat them out:** Vance, pp. 248–249; Dayan, p. 275. **nod from his colleagues, Dayan:** Vance, p. 249; Dayan, pp. 275–276. **Begin awoke:** Dayan, p. 276. **Carter gently suggested:** Carter, pp. 424–425. **When they arrived:** Vance, p. 251; Dayan, p. 277. **announced history's first:** he said—in a statement on the airport tarmac—that all the major elements for a treaty signing now seemed in place.

sailed the draft: Dayan, p. 278. **said he had weathered:** MB Knesset speech and debate, March 20 (Medzini, pp. 665–685). **Begin ended the session:** MB closing statement, March 22 (Medzini, pp. 685–689). **"Would *any* of you":** departure remarks (Medzini, p. 728). **startled Israeli radio correspondent:** SK, the correspondent. **On landing:** arrival remarks (Medzini, pp. 728–729). **Phoning Carter, he said:** Carter, p. 428. **addressed the Knesset:** text in Medzini, pp. 729–732.

Chapter Twenty-five: Fortress Peace

Books: Carter, Jimmy, *Keeping Faith;* Dayan, Moshe, *Breakthrough;* Feld, Ovadia, editor in chief, *The Israel Yearbook—1980;* Haig, Alexander, Jr., *Caveat;* Katz, Shmuel, *The Hollow Peace;* Medzini, Meron, editor, *Israel's Foreign Relations: Selected Documents, 1979–1980;* Randal, Jonathan, *Going All the Way;* Weissman, Steve, and Herbert Krosney, *The Islamic Bomb;* Weizman, Ezer, *The Battle for Peace.*

Interviews: Eliahu Ben Elissar, Ze'ev Chafets, David Garth, Alexander Haig, Jr., Yona Klimovitzki (YKl), Samuel Lewis, Sol Linowitz, Eitan Livni, Arye Naor, Ephraim Poran, Zelman Shoval.

Periodicals: Ha'aretz (Ha); The Jerusalem Post (JP); The New York Times; Yediot Aharonot (Yed). Also Israel Government Press Office transcripts of MB statements (provided by press office from its archives).

Textual notes: **drafted a policy statement:** Dayan, p. 305; Medzini, p. 27. **quoted back the hedges:** for instance, in a May 19 interview (Medzini, pp. 20–26), MB noted that the next round of peace talks would not be "negotiations on autonomy" but merely on "arrangements" to implement the "administrative autonomy" already defined by the letter of the Camp David accords. He added: "We will carry out each and every word of the accord as we signed it." But he said they had agreed to autonomy only for the *inhabitants* of the territories, noting that during the Camp David talks, either the U.S. or Egyptian negotiators had "twice" tried to remove that hedge. "Twice . . . we reentered it." **"Anwar Sadat," he crowed:** ZC. One former Begin aide, who requested anonymity on this point, adds that an emerging difference between MB and Dayan was that the foreign minister felt Sadat was genuinely concerned with achieving an overall Mideast peace settlement embracing the Palestinians. Weizman, notes ZC, felt similarly. Begin, for his part, felt that Sadat protested too much, that deep down inside all he wanted was a separate treaty that would give him back the Sinai. ZC adds that Begin seemed to delight in the fact that he often succeeded in wearing down Sadat and the Americans, while self-proclaimed *sabra* "Arab experts" like Dayan and Weizman kept insisting that "Sadat would never accept" the position, statement, or demand in question.

sure of himself: at the Washington treaty signing, MB proclaimed that Jimmy Carter, too, deserved a Nobel Peace Prize. Back in Israel, he wrote a letter nominating Carter for the accolade. **forbade Landau to raise:** *Ha,* April 27, 1979; *Yed,* April 27. **froze Dayan out:** ZS; Dayan, pp. 305, 312–314. Notably, Begin diluted Dayan's influence in framing Israeli strategy for the Palestinian autonomy talks with Egypt and the United States. The task was given to a six-member cabinet committee. Dayan, as early as one month after Camp David, had been seeking MB's assurance that the foreign minister would direct Israel's delegation. **Begin rejected that option:** Dayan, p. 305. MB made the point explicit, at a meeting with Israeli editors, December 21, 1979, (Medzini, pp. 160–166) that: "I am not in favor of unilateral action. I am in favor of abiding by the agreements ..." **In early June ... he announced:** June 3 (Medzini, p. 48). Dayan (p. 313) and Weizman (pp. 227–230) opposed the move. The Americans issued a statement saying, "We deeply regret the Israeli government's action. ... Establishing new settlements is harmful to the peace process and is particularly regrettable at this time with the negotiations just beginning ..." **"vital security need":** MB statement, June 11 (Medzini, pp. 55–56). MB sent a similar message to the chairman of the U.S. Senate Foreign Relations Committee, Charles Percy. **group of Palestinians:** Weizman, pp. 227–230. Additional background for Elon Moreh and settlement issue in general from my notes (I was covering the situation as *CSM* Mideast correspondent). Beyond MB's general support for settlement, Elon Moreh seemed to occupy a special place in the prime minister's heart. Perhaps this was due to his pre-1977 involvement with Jewish settlers' efforts to move there. Weizman quotes MB telling the cabinet at one stage, "Gentlemen, when my time comes to face the heavenly tribunal and I am asked: 'What is the good deed you have done which makes you worthy of entering paradise?' I shall reply: 'Elon Moreh.' "

inaugural voyage: key stages in "normalization" process included in Medzini's foreign-policy chronology (pp. xvii–xxii). **rebuffed U.S. proposals:** in late July. Background from *CSM* notes; Medzini chronology. **"tried to jolly him up":** The source is a senior U.S. diplomat, who requested anonymity. **Begin respected him:** Linowitz took over from Strauss at the start of November 1979. MB had called the canal treaty "an example for the settlement of disputes between nations, with good will overcoming differences of opinion . . ." (September 29, 1977, Medzini). Further background of MB-Linowitz relationship from SL. **one Linowitz aide:** who requested anonymity. **Dayan . . . felt powerless:** Dayan, p. 303. ZS, a close associate, recalls that Dayan would return from each successive meeting with Begin, increasingly frustrated and despondent. **On October 2:** Dayan, pp. 312–314. **Begin did so:** after the October 21 cabinet session and, formally, in the Knesset two days later. Dayan, interviewed October 21, explained: "The central topic of foreign policy [autonomy and the Palestinians] is not dealt with by the Foreign Ministry or the foreign minister. So the foreign minister is left to deal with marginal subjects—ceremonies, cocktails, things like that . . ." **ordered a survey:** ZC says this was a largely unnoticed but crucial turning point in Israel's West Bank policy.

implored him: source is the aide, who requested anonymity on this point. **did summon Gush:** MB interview, May 19, with Israel Army radio (transcript from Israel Government Press Office). **"The ladies should not":** MB remarks at Israel Foreign Press Association luncheon, February 7, 1980 (transcript in Medzini, pp. 177–180). **foreign minister's post to Yitzhak Shamir:** March 10, 1980. **hamstrung by the seizure:** see Iran section of Carter memoirs. The degree to which the hostage crisis overshadowed other foreign-policy issues was inescapably clear to all who watched it unfold, myself included, since I was covering the crisis from Tehran at the time. **Carter had been in a position:** background on this section from ZC, CV, Katz. Carter (pp. 494–496) noted in his diary before MB's arrival that he hoped to use "the same tactical approach as we had at Camp David . . . to devise proposals . . . acceptable to me, Sadat and to the Israeli people." The hope was to "force him [Begin] to join in with us." Yet Carter adds that Dayan, before resigning, had told him "there would be no more progress [on the Palestinian question] as long as Begin was heading the government." **Begin offered none:** MB interview after talks, *Yed;* Carter, pp. 495–496: "It did become clear that . . . the Camp David accords had now become almost like the Bible, with the words and phrases taking on special importance." **"No pressure":** MB toast at state dinner (text in Medzini, pp. 232–236). **an American interviewer:** Barbara Walters, April 20 (transcript in Medzini, pp. 236–241). **Begin barely blinked:** MB interview with small group of foreign journalists, myself included, June 5, 1980. In an upbeat, almost jaunty mood, MB quoted back passages from Camp David and remarked: "We are not in a ... *souk*. We don't start with a certain statement and [say] perhaps it will cost $1,000 and then we will be prepared to sell it for $600 ...." Also, to the visible surprise of press aide Dan Patir, MB went public with Dayan's 1977 meeting with King Hussein. Calling Hussein "the little king," MB said the talks had taken place "in a fine city ... and a fine hotel."

To friends, he referred: from two Israeli sources, who requested anonymity. **had gone on Israel Television:** AN; MB (interview in *Yed*, April 25). **In a letter:** text of Weizman letter, and MB reply, in *JP*. AN says Begin seemed especially incensed that Weizman had sent the resignation letter by messenger. **score that had rankled:** AN, EBE, SL. **he would take over:** at least in part, this was due to the difficulty of finding a successor all his coalition partners could agree on. The most palatable contender, Moshe Arens, turned down the job. **IZL veterans, it seemed:** EL. **inherited Labor aide:** EP, who was MB's military adviser. MB, in a June 20 interview with Israel Army radio, remarked: "I have a military secretary, a dear friend, Brigadier General Poran. And he conveys reports to me [on defense matters] ten times a day. Sometimes, even more ..." **trade his tie and jacket:** ZC. **"Certainly, I enjoy":** MB interview, June 20, 1980 (transcript from Israel Government Press Office). **he and Poran would ride:** EP. **"Look at me!":** Israel Army radio interview; June 20, 1980.

accused them of "anarchy": Israel Army radio interview, June 20, 1980. **"10,000 ... or even":** MB Israel TV interview, March 26, 1980 (transcript in Medzini, pp. 214–220). ZC says that Begin privately was similarly bothered by the raucous rightists of Gush Emunim, sometimes fuming: "What do these little Messianists think they can teach *me* about loyalty to the Land of Israel?" But publicly he never dismissed or upbraided Gush as he had Peace Now. **cautioned against assuming Jews:** until the matter was settled in court. When it was—several years later—Jews did turn out to have been responsible. **At least one aide:** source is the aide, who requested anonymity on this point. **collapsed on the Knesset:** *NYT*, July 1, 1980. **order a reduction:** MB told an Israeli interviewer at the time that he, Begin, had been "the first to suggest to Finance Minister Simcha Ehrlich that we abolish foreign-currency controls. I was the first man to hear from Ehrlich what his decontrol program was. I approved the program, and for a while we were the only two men in the cabinet to know about it." **first finance minister:** YKl recalls that Ehrlich "used to say to Begin, 'You take care of the big issues, and leave the details to me ...' " **told Herut officials:** in late April 1979, MB had (*Ha,* April 27) "absolved Ehrlich of responsibility for the inflation and the failure of economic policy over the past two years, and placed the blame squarely on the [Labor party] Alignment. ..." But on June 3, 1979, keynoting Herut's first national convention since the 1977 elections, MB remarked (transcript from Israel Government Press Office): "A government established two years ago cannot use as an excuse the ills of the past for not repairing those [economic] ills, if it does not demonstrate by tangible deeds that it has begun the task of repair." **ordered a price freeze:** *JP*'s daily coverage is source of background. The price freeze (*JP,* September 14, 1979) was imposed after the June Herut convention.

hard times awaited: said Hurwitz (*Israel Year Book,* 1980, pp. 109–110): "I have no good news for you." **Begin balked:** MB interview with Israel Army radio, June 20, 1980. **Hurwitz wanted 10 percent:** *JP,* December 15, 1980; January 4 and 12, 1981. **elections, for June:** shortening the government's term by five months. **rating in the polls:** *JP;* DG. **stalwart, Yoram Aridor:** who did have the distinction of being the first Israeli finance minister with a degree in economics. **"from three digits to two":** MB interview on Israel TV, April 16, 1981 (transcript from Israel Government Press Office). **election of Ronald Reagan:** who, argues SL, provided an opportunity, ultimately lost, to turn a new administration's mandate and energy to the Palestinian autonomy talks. **lost weight, gave fewer:** AN. **"He was in quite a deep":** the source requested anonymity. **An aide recalls Begin:** He requested anonymity.

Meridor, back in private business, who mounted: DG, whom Meridor sought out. **Garth, to map out:** DG. In the U.S. political arena, Garth had handled campaigns for John Lindsay, Ed Koch, and John Anderson. **flew to Israel:** DG says he initially had misgivings about taking the assignment. He feared possible Israeli voter backlash against American involvement in the campaign. But in the interim, Labor hired a U.S. campaign expert of its own, obviating Garth's worries. DG met and took a liking to Begin and, moreover, felt that only a reelected Begin would be strong enough to counter right-wing resistance to Israel's final withdrawal from the Sinai settlements. **shift started in April:** AN, SL. **"We can really win":** AN. **"Relax, David":** DG. **"If you sell":** Haig, p. 179. **town of Zahle:** Haig, p. 180. Background in Randal, pp. 224–232. **data would no doubt be:** MB Israel TV interview, April 16, 1981, just after the Haig visit (transcript from Israel Government Press Office). **Haig counseled caution:** Haig, p. 181. **played down that issue:** MB Israel TV interview, April 16. **he ordered the air force:** MB Israel Radio interview, May 7. He says he consulted with the cabinet defense committee on the decision (transcript from Israel Government Press Office). Displaying his customary freewheeling approach to military detail, MB said erroneously that the Syrian craft were helicopter gunships. **hinted that Israel would bomb:** MB, in May 7 Israel Radio interview, remarked: "If this conflict is not resolved through the diplomatic efforts of the United States . . . we will do what we have to do." **summoned diplomat Philip Habib:** Haig, p. 180. *Syrians* **could achieve "nothing":** MB Israel Radio interview, May 7. **told Knesset members, aides:** *JP* daily coverage; SL. **"I have never felt better":** MB Israel Radio interview, May 7. **cheering Likud audience:** *JP,* May 15. **On May 19:** *JP.* **"The prime minister":** *JP,* May 29.

To aides, recalls Naor: AN, who notes that the election had taken on such importance to Begin that he even toyed briefly with trying to bring Shmuel Tamir back into his coalition—an idea MB jettisoned when he sensed the furor of opposition among old-line Herut members. **Likud had narrowed:** DG. **"We found":** DG is source for this section. **"can't think of anybody":** DG. ZC says of Begin's style of leadership, "He had a 'cold warmth.' He had set up this concept of the Fighting Family," quite early on, "and then defined it in such a way so that the kids would always be vying for their father's approval." (The remark bears an uncanny resemblance to Brisk-de-Lita colleague Yehuda Rosenman's recollections of MB's Betar leadership in high school.) Adds SL of Begin's government period: "He had an extraordinary instinct of how to play other people. Instinctively. He managed to inspire tremendous loyalty. . . . He would give lots of little marks of encouragement. This was instinct but also [Ambassador Lewis is convinced] partly calculation. He *manipulated* people. Subconsciously, he knew how to play on fears and hopes—to tantalize with rewards—and also how to come up with an explanation when sometimes he couldn't deliver the rewards."

campaign more vitriolic: the vitriol sometimes even spilled over into the Knesset. Garth drafted a series of campaign ads citing Rabin's recently published memoirs as a source for anti-Peres invective. MB, amid howls of protest from Labor parliamentarians, at one point read excerpts into the Knesset record. As the shouts of protest got louder, Begin declared coolly from the podium: "This will not avail you. You will have to listen sooner or later." **Labor lost its cool ... "Khomeini-ism":** ZC; Chafets, pp. 136–137. **in May the prime minister ordered:** *JP*, June 2, 1981. **By month's end, Garth's:** DG. **Begin summoned the cabinet:** EP; Weissman-Krosney, pp. 3–10, 275–286. **A few, having never:** EP. **mission had taken root:** Weissman-Krosney, pp. 7–8; AN and EP say there was considerable opposition to the attack from both cabinet ministers and military officers. Among the questions raised (EP recalls): "Do we have the right to bomb or destroy a reactor that is civilian, at least for the time being? Does this mean that from now on we'll destroy every civilian nuclear reactor built in the Middle East?" Even some traditional hawks, adds AN, were at least initially opposed—among them, Yitzhak Shamir. **late autumn ... says one expert:** who requested anonymity. He added that there had been a number of earlier Israeli sabotage "operations like this," against less potentially perilous targets, that have never been made public. **Military aide Poran feels:** EP. LM recalls a meeting with Begin right after the successful attack; Begin's mood, says LM, was pensive, not celebratory. EP insists that Begin had originally planned to keep the operation secret. The official announcement came the day after the attack, on Begin's directive— and only, says EP, when an Arab radio station had accused Israel of siding with Iran in the Gulf War. The radio allegation, however, had made no explicit mention of the reactor bombing—plus there was some international speculation that Iran might have been responsible. Acknowledges EP: "It turned out it was a mistake; the report didn't refer to our operation. But by then it was too late ..." Be that as it may, Israel's ambassador in Washington made no bones about acknowledging Israeli responsibility for the reactor attack when addressing a naturally distraught Haig (p. 182) only hours afterward. **As the planes sped:** EP; Weissman-Krosney, p. 10. **telling Poran to phone:** EP. **So was President Reagan:** "and angry" (AH).

"There will not": *JP*. **Shouts of "Begin":** *JP*, June 19, 1981. The aftermath of the reactor attack provided yet another example of MB's imperfect grasp of military detail. While chatting with a Reuters reporter at a British embassy reception after the attack, MB said the Israeli strike had targeted a supersecret bunker "forty meters" underground. He phoned to apologize later: He had meant "four meters." MB's lack of understanding of military detail seemed often a result of a lack of *interest* in such things, which he felt were best left to the experts. EP, who was at the final military briefing before the reactor attack, recalls that Begin showed no visible interest in issues like the Israeli planes' approach route, when the attacking jets might show up on enemy radar, how they would get back. As in the IZL days, he was concerned with a more general question: Would there be casualties? The Israeli brass—like Livni and Paglin of old—said they had taken all possible precautions. **Lashing out at America:** although, as when he focused his anger at President Carter on Harold Saunders, MB blamed Reagan's defense secretary, Caspar Weinberger. **only a bleep:** DG, who says, "One of the great misconceptions of that campaign was that the Iraqi bombing had turned things around. It caused a bleep—I thought it was going to [do more], but it didn't . . ." **a fatal miscue:** DG, ZC, AN; Chafets, pp. 136–137. **next morning, when a reporter:** AN, who was in Begin's office at the time. **his own closing rally:** ZC. **"David, you're a very nice":** DG.

Chapter Twenty-six: Vision of Victory

Books: Haig, Alexander, *Caveat;* Randal, Jonathan, *Going All the Way;* Schiff, Ze'ev, and Ehud Yaari, *Israel's Lebanon War;* Weizman, Ezer, *The Battle for Peace.*

Interviews: Yitzhak Berman, Ze'ev Chafets, Bill Claiborne, Morris Draper, Batya (Scheib) Eldad, David Garth, Alexander Haig, Jr., Rafi Hurwitz, David Ignatius, Mrs. Marek Kahan and daughter, Brurya (BK), Yona Klimovitzki (YKl), Samuel Lewis, Leo Marcus, Dan Meridor, Arye Naor, Ephraim Poran, Zelman Shoval, Ehud Yaari, Mordechai Zippori.

Articles, broadcasts, pamphlets, etc.: Goldstein, Dov, "Interview of the Year: Prime Minister Menachem Begin," *Ma'ariv.*

Periodicals: Ha'aretz (Ha); The Jerusalem Post (JP); Yediot Aharonot (Yed).

Textual notes: **For months the hero:** indeed, so avid was Sharon's thirst for a renewed military role that, after Weizman's resignation, he declared (*JP,* June 6, 1980) his readiness to give up the Agriculture Ministry if made *deputy* defense minister—"so that his 'military expertise' would be at the disposal of whoever eventually receives the Defense portfolio.' " **questioning how an aging:** on Israel TV in the spring of 1981. **"I never argue":** MB Israel TV interview, April 15, 1981 (transcript from Israel Government Press Office). **Begin quipped: "He'll ring":** *Ha,* January 1, 1981. MB's office said later the comments had been taken out of context, but they were never explicitly retracted. MB made an almost identical remark, privately, to DG. **When Garth suggested:** DG. **did feel a debt:** AN. **a vision:** based on MB statements; background interviews with ZC, AN, SL. As the June 1982 war approached, MB's own articulation of the vision became gradually more explicit. In an NBC TV appearance in late April, he digressed from discussing Israel's stand toward the PLO in Lebanon, and remarked: "If they attack us again, we shall hit them; because we will not allow in our generation of the Holocaust and redemption to [be] shed again Jewish blood, while those responsible for its shedding enjoy impunity and even luxury. It happened in the Holocaust. It will never happen again . . ." (transcript from Israel Government Press Office). **memoir he said he would write:** In the September 1977 *Ma'ariv* interview, MB said, "I would like, and intend, to write a book called *The Generation of Holocaust and Redemption.*" He said it would begin with World War I, cover Jabotinsky's interwar activity, "the Holocaust, the underground movements in Israel, and all that has happened since the foundation of the State." **contemplated bombing Syria's . . . missiles:** Haig, p. 186. **ordered air attacks:** *JP;* Randal, pp. 236–237. **bombing of a PLO headquarters:** in the Fakhani neighborhood of Beirut, a warren of shops and five- to six-story stone buildings near the city's southwest edge. Details in *JP;* Randal, pp. 237–238; Haig, p. 186. **Americans fumed:** the *JP's* highly respected Washington correspondent, Wolf Blitzer, produced a stark survey of the "really terrible things being said about Begin"—some of the invective emanating from voices generally more friendly toward Israeli leaders. He quoted, for instance, the generally pro-Israeli *New Republic:* "Begin's actions are a threat both to the moral fibre of Israel and to the support Israel still enjoys in the West among those who have not wearied of its cause or sold out to Arab oil . . ." **"Ah, so you'd been":** DI. **"placed themselves":** MB added: "We do regret the civilian casualties" (transcript of interview, from Israel Government Press Office). **for the first time sending thousands:** RH, a career military man then working with Ze'ev Chafets in the Israel Government Press Office, remarked to me (I was on a visit to Israel at the time) that "you must not underestimate the domestic political significance of this bombardment in the north, and of the fact that for the first time thousands have either been driven into shelters or have left . . ." **When Philip Habib rushed:** Haig, p. 186; Randal, p. 239. **secure a cease-fire with the PLO:** with the stipulation that the Americans would have to negotiate with Arafat indirectly (which they did) via the very Saudis whom Begin had striven to paint as dangerous to the Reagan administration.

Ben Elissar, Naor . . . : AN, EBE, ZC, SL. **Yadin, who had retired:** AN. **Dayan, who won:** ZF recalls attending a Begin-Dayan meeting after the election that made clear how frayed were the ties between the two men. When Dayan professed willingness to rejoin the government if his views on the West Bank were accepted, Begin shot back: "If I didn't accept them when you were foreign minister, why should I do so when you represent a splinter party in the *Knesset*?" **Rounding out the new cabinet:** *JP.* In an irony of Israeli coalition politics, the minister of health—politically revived via the La'am splinter component of Likud—was Eliezer Shostak. **government program stated:** *JP.* **Begin opened the talks:** MB interview with *Yed,* September 28, 1981, on return from Washington. **military intelligence, who unfurled:** Major General Yehoshua Saguy; MB *Yed* interview; Haig, p. 187. **a man, he told Ambassador:** SL. **Begin played down:** MB *Yed* interview, September 28. **Haig, Begin had been warned:** Haig, p. 188. **"Permit me not":** MB *Yed* interview.

Begin had met Alexander Haig: AH. **outrage at American pressure:** "I rarely differed with President Eisenhower," AH explains. "But on that, I did. I thought Eisenhower was wrong . . . and that this had profound strategic implications, inside the NATO alliance. I felt that whatever one's own judgment of what had happened, that the price of reversal of what had happened" was exorbitant politically. AH recalls of that first dinner conversation with Begin that "we did not, I think, clash in any way, in terms of strategic views, of the [Mideast] regional dynamics in the wake of the Yom Kippur War." **grasped the Egyptian's hand:** MB Knesset speech, November 2,

1981; MB interview with French TV correspondent, November 25 (text of both from Israel Government Press Office). **When Haig, also in Cairo:** Haig, p. 326. **"Israel is but":** MB Knesset speech, November 2. MB said he was willing and ready to go ahead with the Palestinian talks on "establishment and the operation of the self-governing authority [administrative council] as agreed upon after the lengthy deliberations at Camp David." But there could be no place for the "peace plan . . . as she [Saudi Arabia], together with the misled or the other misleaders," called the Saudi proposal. **says Haig, Begin:** Haig, p. 174. **Said Reagan:** when, amid Israel's efforts to convince friendly congressmen of its position, he sent the AWACS sale to the Senate for approval in October.

a two-man government: SL notes that MB's mood after the 1981 vote seemed very different than in 1977, when he had felt the need or desire to have men like Dayan and Weizman around. "This time there wasn't any Weizman to take credit. It was his victory. It was an extraordinary comeback, and it was *his* oratory, and his savvy, that had enabled him to pull it off. . . . He was so self-confident that he really ceased to listen to anyone." **Sharon had allegedly leaked:** AN, cabinet secretary at the time, notes that Sharon's responsibility for leaks had been rumored, alleged, assumed, but never proven, and that MB vetoed an investigation to determine responsibility for the leaks. **denounced or threatened:** at one point vowing to strip the demure Yigael Yadin "naked on the cabinet table"—a remark MB had stricken from the cabinet minutes. **obscene hand gesture:** *JP,* September 14, 1979. **a reprimand, its tone:** AN; Weizman, pp. 223–224. **A Begin aide:** he requested anonymity on the point. But AH, then secretary of state, adds: "Sharon, who is not a humble man, nevertheless always gave clear deference to Mr. Begin. And Sharon can be very charming . . ." **if Begin still feared:** see MB keynote to 1975 Herut convention at Kiryat Arba, and earlier reference in text to MB's remark shortly thereafter that he would yet manage to teach even this fearsome general a lesson in tactics. One eloquent reflection of this complex relationship was Begin's response to Sharon's occasionally expressed view that a "Palestinian state" already existed—in Jordan—and that that was where the Palestinian nationalists' demands could best be redeemed (I was among reporters to whom Sharon made this remark). Asked by an Israeli interviewer if he agreed with Sharon's assessment, MB replied confidently: "Why should I? . . . Yes, I know that several of my colleagues believe [that Jordan is a 'Palestinian state'] as you have quoted them. That is their perfect right. [But] I want peace with Jordan . . ." Asked the same question shortly afterward by Israel Radio, MB declared more coyly that his colleagues "have the right to make that claim," but that he, Begin, preferred to envisage peace between "us and the ruler of east Transjordan [sic]."

Sharon froze out: principal source for background in this section is Schiff-Yaari. The authors are Israel's premier defense-affairs newsmen, and their account of the Lebanon War is by far the most thorough yet written. Sharon, whom I have interviewed twice when I was *CSM* Mideast reporter, declined two separate requests for an interview in connection with this book. He told me by phone in the summer of 1986 that he was reluctant to do so because, among other reasons, he did not like contributing in any way to a book over whose content he could not exercise control. He said he would prefer to write his own story. Sharon added that among the subjects he was particularly reluctant to address in an interview was "Mr. Begin." **When General Poran resigned:** ZC, SL. **Deputy Defense Minister Mordechai Zippori:** MB sweetened the pill for Zippori by making him minister of communications, but excluded Zippori from the cabinet's ministerial defense committee. **effect, recalls Ambassador Lewis:** SL. **"It seemed":** the official requested anonymity. **Begin returned home:** detailed account by MB, in the letter dictated to Kadishai and printed in *Ha,* December 4, 1981. **Then he summoned:** AN. **annexed Syria's Golan:** this possibility had been envisaged in the 1981 government program, but it was seen at the time as a mere exercise in verbal brashness. The *JP* (August 13) wrote: "Nowhere [in the clause] is it stated that it [the government] must so decide—ever." **Begin convened the cabinet:** AN, who says that most of the ministers seemed stunned and that only one broke ranks when it came time to vote: the Liberals' Yitzhak Berman, who abstained.

Begin summoned Ambassador Lewis: AN; Haig, pp. 328–329 (text of the lecture to Lewis was released by the Israel Government Press Office). **told the ministers:** AN. **motioned for Sharon:** Schiff-Yaari, pp. 47–48; AN. **Modai, asked for:** AN. **"I see . . . how feelings":** Schiff-Yaari, p. 48. **He mentioned the war plan:** Schiff-Yaari; AN. **"There are people around":** YB. **In January Sharon:** Schiff-Yaari, pp. 48–49. Sharon, the authors report, summed up the visit to aides, saying: "We'll make Bashir president!" **In February Begin sent word:** via Major General Saguy. (Haig, pp. 332–333). **Begin was determined they must leave:** in a succession of interviews and statements throughout 1981, he had vowed strictly to implement the treaty obligations with Egypt. At the Sadat funeral he had told Haig (p. 326) of the Sinai withdrawal: "I will meet my commitment or resign—and there may be such turmoil over the issue that I will have to resign." He did, however, turn down Haig's suggestion of a good-faith move to withdraw ahead of schedule. **equally intent:** DM, who succeeded Arye Naor as cabinet secretary in the spring of 1982. **"The question that is being asked":** *Yed,* January 25, 1982.

Begin received their parents: DM. **Begin drafted a cabinet:** DM. **Sharon did most:** U.S. official, who requested anonymity, to *CSM* colleague, who shared notes of the interview. **then asked the president:** DM. **On April 16, Mubarak:** MB recap in April 28 interview with Israel Army radio (transcript from Israel Government Press Office). **In effect if not by intention:** a U.S. official involved in drafting the Reagan reply, who requested anonymity, suggests the Americans believed the note was "just one more of these formal things Begin used to always insist upon . . ." Adds another U.S. diplomat: "They [officials in Washington] came to expect this kind of thing of him. But they didn't admire him for it . . ." **affirm Washington's commitment:** letter quoted by MB to Knesset, May 3, 1982 (text from Israel Government Press Office). **no promises on *quantity:*** it said only that Reagan was "mindful as well of your concerns with respect to quantitative factors." **tendered "important American commitments":** MB to Knesset, May 3.

Pain gnawed at him: SL. **More often than not, he chose pain:** Kadishai told LM that when clearing out Begin's desk after the prime minister had resigned, he had found a large quantity of the prescribed medicines—unopened, unused—in its drawers. In the immediate aftermath of his hip accident, however, MB did crave pain-killers. A hospital staff member involved in his treatment, requesting anonymity, told me: "He was on a pain-killer called Percodan; one every four hours. After such an accident everyone gets such pain-killers. Some want more, some less. Begin, in relative terms, wanted more . . ." **Aliza was ill:** BSE, MK, BK, who says Aliza was intermittently hooked up to medical machinery from 1981 onward. When up and about, she "had a little inhalator with oxygen in her purse. It was hard for her to breathe . . ." **she confided a dream:** YK1. **move back:** YK1. **write his epic:** MB, in a variety of interviews after the 1977 election, had made this pledge. In the September 1977 *Ma'ariv* interview, for instance, he notes that the decision was not "merely capricious. . . . True, a man of seventy can usually be active in state affairs. Gladstone, who put together his last government when he was eighty-six, must always be borne in mind. But if God gives me many years to live, I would like, and I intend, to write a book called *The Generation of Holocaust and Redemption.*" But during the hard-fought 1981 election campaign (*JP*, May 4, 1981), MB briefly retreated from the prospect of retiring precisely at seventy.

In May, he glared: MB Knesset address, May 4 (text from Israel Government Press Office). **"A vital danger":** this, said MB, was the return of the Land of Israel to Arab rule. "You stopped settling [Judaea and Samaria], and I will prove it," MB told parliament. "Five years ago, there was one settlement in Samaria. Today, there are thirty-nine settlements. . . . We established thirty-eight settlements . . ." MB could not resist adding that only a year earlier, Peres, leading in the polls, had appointed his cabinet: "He appointed Abba Eban [prospective] foreign minister—which he is not today . . ." **proclamation that Israel:** "In future negotiations on a peace treaty between Israel and its neighbors, any proposal to remove or dismantle any settlement in which Israeli citizens and Jews have settled and live will be rejected."

diplomatic foundations for war: Haig, pp. 330–331; Schiff-Yaari, pp. 65–68, Randal, pp. 245–248. Schiff and Yaari suggest that Sharon, rather than MB, played the leading role—or at least the more vocal one—in the ground-laying process. Senior U.S. officials—AH, SL, MD—say this is true, and that Sharon had privately felt out U.S. representatives on the idea of a deep push toward Beirut, months before the actual June 1982 invasion. But the U.S. sources say, equally, that Begin conveyed at least tacit backing for Sharon's belligerent mien all along. Remarks AH: "I didn't find any evident tension [between MB and Sharon] . . . I know some people say Sharon didn't tell Begin what was going on in Lebanon. I have a hard time buying that . . ." EY remarked to me that he and Schiff, conscious of potential obstacles from Israel's military censorship, had sensed they could not tell all they knew about all aspects of the war in their book. Says EY, a decision was made to focus on

Sharon's role—which they saw as primary—at the price of sometimes excluding detail on MB's. Not all details, however. Schiff-
Yaari (p. 39) do not skimp on MB's vision of victory, citing his remarks at a private meeting with "a high-ranking Israeli general" in
late 1981: "I want Arafat in his bunker!" **"Can anyone imagine"**: MB
Yed interview, April 13; Haig, p. 330. **"carefully selected"**: MB appearance on NBC's *Meet the Press,* April 25 (transcript from Israel
Government Press Office). **"hit them much harder"**: MB to Israel
Army radio, April 27 (transcript from Israel Government Press Office.) **the cabinet "has not"**: MB *Yed* interview, April 13.

Poran, heard whispers that Sharon: EP. **In May Israeli sappers**:
Schiff-Yaari, p. 55. **summoned the cabinet, and gave Sharon**: Schiff-
Yaari, pp. 58–60. Government ministers YB, MZ confirm Schiff-
Yaari's account of cabinet sessions before and during the war. **Labor
leadership to brief**: Schiff-Yaari, p. 60. **Americans summoned Begin**:
Haig, pp. 335–336. **ordered the chief of staff**: Rafael Eitan. Sharon
(Schiff-Yaari explain, p. 97) was out of Israel "on a secret visit to
Romania." **"We will not stand"**: Schiff-Yaari, p. 97. **He had Sharon
outline**: Schiff-Yaari, pp. 102–108; DM, MZ, YB. **"This time"**: DM.
"Who knows?": DM. **"May I have your"**: Schiff-Yaari, pp. 104–106.
In an Israel Army radio interview in late April, MB had remarked:
"I believe the Syrians will be very careful [in Lebanon]. They know
Israel is very strong . . ." **He won it, unanimously**: the Liberals' Simcha Ehrlich and Yitzhak Berman abstained. Zippori—because, AN
is convinced, of residual IZL loyalty—voted in favor. **most powerful
military machine**: EP is a background source for this section. **most
fearsome Fighting Jew**: AN. **Had only the Palestinians**: or had
Yasser Arafat been Hitler, and the PLO, the Nazis. See text, notes of
next chapter for MB's personalized vision of the Lebanon imbroglio
and the PLO.

Chapter Twenty-seven: Fighting Jew

Books: Begin, Menachem, *The Revolt;* Haig, Alexander, Jr., *Caveat;*
Kahan, Yitzhak et al., *The Commission of Inquiry into the Events at
the Refugee Camps in Beirut—Final Report;* Linowitz, Sol, *The*

Making of a Public Man; Randal, Jonathan, *Going All the Way;* Schiff, Ze'ev, and Ehud Yaari, *Israel's Lebanon War.*

Interviews: Ilana Beaninstock, Eliahu Ben Elissar, Yitzhak Berman, Avraham Burg, Morris Draper, Batya (Scheib) Eldad, Roberta Fahn, Alexander Haig, Jr., Harry Hurwitz, Yehiel Kadishai, Mrs. Marek Kahan and daughter, Brurya (BK), Yehuda Lapidot, Samuel Lewis, Dan Meridor, Arye Naor, Yisrael Scheib, Mordechai Zippori.

Articles, broadcasts, pamphlets, etc.: Naor, Arye, "The Israel Cabinet in the Lebanon War," in *The Jerusalem Quarterly,* No. 39, 1986; Abraham Rabinovich, "Fire in the Streets," in *The Jerusalem Post,* February 18, 1983; Shacham, Orit, "The Silence Connection," in *Ha'aretz,* November 2, 1984, Hebrew.

Periodicals: The Jerusalem Post (JP); Ha'aretz (Ha); Ma'ariv; Newsweek.

Textual notes: **Ambassador Lewis had:** Schiff-Yaari, pp. 115–116. **pledge from Arafat:** A UN official, who requested anonymity, says one of Secretary General Waldheim's top deputies had conveyed a unique personal message from Arafat to Begin shortly before the war. Arafat, sure an invasion was coming, called on Begin to reconsider, and declared that he, Begin, would not be able to crush the PLO by force of arms. But the UN source rejects a published account that the Arafat message included a note of admiration for MB's own record as an underground leader. **He wrote Reagan:** MB Knesset address, June 9 (text from Israel Government Press Office); Schiff-Yaari, p. 106. Haig (p. 337) says Begin indicated the operation would last "no more than three or four days." **about twenty-five miles:** the Israelis defined the target as "forty kilometers"—twenty-four miles. The formal communiqué following the cabinet meeting that approved the war plan did not, however, explicitly mention the forty-kilometer limit. **failing to notice:** or at least to mention, in the cabinet, to the Americans or to the Israeli public. **"tactic worthy of Hannibal!":** Schiff-Yaari, p. 112. Much of the detail, and exact quotes, for this chapter are taken from Schiff-Yaari, confirmed in interviews with YB, MZ, DM.

Begin helicoptered north: Schiff-Yaari, pp. 115–116. **with Sharon, to celebrate:** Schiff-Yaari, pp. 129–131. **Begin kept him waiting:** Schiff-Yaari, p. 152. Haig, and the Naor article, say that the meeting in fact took place only on the morning of June 8. Among other items

MB stipulated in the message to Assad was that the Syrians must withdraw all troops and equipment transferred to Lebanon since the Israeli attack. Naor argues that all three points were worded as requests, not explicit conditions. That in a June 8 Knesset address MB did not present the offer as conditional seems to bear out Naor's interpretation. But as we shall see, the argument almost immediately became academic. **limited his operational involvement:** Schiff-Yaari; MZ. **veto Sharon's urge:** MD, who was part of the Habib mission. **address the Knesset:** MB Knesset address (text from Israel Government Press Office); Schiff-Yaari, pp. 154–163. "We want our soldiers to come home," declared MB. Announcing that twenty-five Israeli troops had already died, he said the attack was not a full-scale war, but added: "It is a battle, and we knew that it would not be a [nature] hike." Of Syria, he said: "From this podium I call on President Assad to instruct the Syrian army not to harm Israeli soldiers. And then nothing will happen to them. We actually do not want to harm anyone. . . . We do not want any clash with the Syrian army. If we achieve the forty-kilometer line from our northern border, the job is done. All fighting will cease." **Sharon urged field units:** Schiff-Yaari, pp. 164, 182–184. **At least two ministers:** YB; Schiff-Yaari, pp. 164–166. **ridiculed Zippori:** from now on, scoffed Sharon, every cabinet minister would be showing up at meetings with rulers! YB says not only did Begin tolerate such assaults on Zippori, but he himself implied that Zippori's consistent opposition to the Israeli battle plan was rooted not in expertise (Zippori, besides Sharon, was the only cabinet member with military experience, in stark contrast to MB's first-term cabinet) but in jealousy at not having been named defense minister instead of Sharon. **Begin intervened:** Schiff-Yaari, p. 166. **screamed north, knocked out:** Schiff-Yaari, p. 167.

call for a cease-fire, Begin summoned: Ambassador Lewis relayed the Reagan message in the early hours of Thursday, June 10. The Begin-Haig conversation came around dawn June 10 (Haig, p. 340; Schiff-Yaari, pp. 169–170; MD). Haig says Begin phoned him. Schiff-Yaari says Haig initiated the call. **Reagan refused:** Haig (pp. 340–341) says he himself refused and ordered Lewis to call on the prime minister. AH, in an interview, says the Begin request came after a long and steady erosion of his own position within an administration dominated by people "less sympathetic" to Israel. These, he says, included Defense Secretary Weinberger, National Security Adviser William Clark, and Vice-President Bush, who "led the pack." AH says that at one point after the Israeli invasion, he was "told I was not allowed to *see* Begin." He adds that this was a result of intervention by Clark, "who was colluding with Weinberger." AH called Reagan, who sided with Haig. **Sharon—reporting intermittently:** Schiff-Yaari; Naor article; YB, MZ. **When the Americans:** MD.

Begin heard the news: Schiff-Yaari, pp. 193–194. **"In the old Austrian Empire":** *The Revolt,* p. 188. **ordered him to go no farther:** though they could provide "help" to the Phalangists, who, MB said, would now have to take the PLO-dominated western sector of the city (Schiff-Yaari, pp. 199–200). **"IDF forces will not":** quoted in Kahan Commission report, p. 11. **dispatched a message:** Schiff-Yaari, p. 200.

"occupied capital" was home: based on my experiences and observations while based in Beirut (1977–1980). For background on Lebanon and Beirut, also see Randal. **air and artillery attacks:** Schiff-Yaari, pp. 201–203; Haig, p. 344. **tried to portray the thrashing:** Schiff-Yaari, pp. 202–203; Haig, pp. 344–345. **reading from file cards:** Haig, pp. 344–345. **told ... Weinberger:** "Be quiet! You're wrong again!" (Haig, p. 344). AH notes that Begin (in a reflection of the old Carter-Saunders syndrome) was faultlessly careful to be polite to Reagan. "As for Weinberger, he did say to Cap's face—and to anyone who would listen—how he felt ..." **Begin declared that the summit:** MB Israel Radio interview, June 22 (transcript from Israel Government Press Office). In an airport statement (transcript from Israel Government Press Office), MB was similarly upbeat, referring to Sharon as "my friend, the minister of defense." **recalls Ambassador Lewis:** SL.

Sharon continued to bombard: Haig, pp. 346–347; Randal, p. 251. **Israelis were alerted:** Schiff-Yaari, p. 205. **informed Washington that Israel:** Haig, p. 347. He says he replied to Begin: "If Israel went into Beirut, the United States would abandon her." **A narrow majority:** Schiff-Yaari, pp. 212–213. **kept silent or defended Sharon:** YB. **"my friend":** MB airport statement on return from White House talks. **tightened his noose:** Randal includes a graphic account of the siege of West Beirut, a substantial portion of which he experienced firsthand. **hoped this would prod:** *JP,* June 24. **assured Habib of support:** MD. **sympathetic U.S. congressman:** Congressman Charles Wilson, from Texas. RF, who attended the meeting, recalls in a report written immediately afterward that when Wilson suggested Begin "go in and finish the job" against the PLO, MB said he preferred caution. MB "confided . . . the latest developments: Morris Draper arrived in Israel and indicated to Begin that the PLO will in fact surrender and that Habib is on the verge of concluding a settlement. He [Draper] pleaded for a little more time." "In light of this [writes RF of the meeting], Begin cancelled Friday's (tomorrow's) cabinet meeting and will hold it on Sunday morning instead, in order to give Habib these extra 48 hours. Begin also told [Wilson had told] Ambassador Lewis that if any developments occur even during Shabbat or Friday night, that he should call him. . . . Begin seemed very optimistic." **Lewis relayed news:** Haig, pp. 348–349; Schiff-Yaari, p. 209. Also relayed was Reagan's readiness to include U.S. marines in an international force to oversee the arrangements.

"He must back it": Schiff-Yaari, pp. 212–213. **president sent a letter:** *Newsweek* recap, September 13, 1982. **Begin was not among them:** Schiff-Yaari, p. 213. **Colonel Eli Geva:** Schiff-Yaari, pp. 215–216. **August 1—with the Americans:** Schiff-Yaari, p. 221; Randal, p. 256; *JP*. **greeting from Menachem Begin:** text in *JP*, August 4. **Begin's riposte:** EBE. **presented an analysis:** the text of a lecture he delivered at Israel's National Defense College, it was then published by the Israeli press. **August 4, Sharon resumed:** *JP*, August 5; Randal, p. 254. **Begin backed Sharon, declaring:** Schiff-Yaari, pp. 221–222; *JP*, August 6. **call-up of reserve units:** AB: *JP* retrospective on war, June 10, 1983. Further details for this chapter from other Israeli press retrospectives. See *Ma'ariv*, June 3, 1983. **"I know about all":** DM; *JP*, June 10, 1983; Schiff-Yaari, p. 223.

Sharon pushed the cabinet: Schiff-Yaari, pp. 225–227. **divested the defense minister of authority:** AN; Schiff-Yaari, p. 227. **awakened by a phone call:** Schiff-Yaari, pp. 225–226; *Newsweek*, September 13, 1982. **ended the bombardment except:** Randal, pp. 270–272; Schiff-Yaari, pp. 226–229. **dotted the "i":** Randal, pp. 143–145. **victory soured quickly:** DM; *Newsweek*, September 13; Schiff-Yaari, pp. 233–236. **Begin tried to put:** Linowitz, p. 232. **"Sam, I'm on vacation,"** MB reportedly told Lewis when he phoned. **advance text:** *Newsweek*, September 13, details the peace plan and its background. **"This . . . is the saddest":** *Newsweek*. MB repeated the phrase to Linowitz (p. 232). **turned to aides:** Schiff-Yaari, p. 233. **when Ge-**

mayel was ushered in: DM. **"Welcome, Mr. President":** background for section on Begin-Gemayel greeting is from Sharon news briefing during New York libel trial against *Time* magazine at the end of 1985. Notes provided to me by a colleague who attended. **perceived insult:** as related by Gemayel to MD afterward in Beirut. "Begin treated me like a bellboy!" Gemayel said. The president-elect also seemed offended by the fact that—in contrast to earlier visits to Israel when he had received VIP treatment—he was taken to the talks in a most undistinguished-looking car. **determined to end:** from background interviews I had with Phalangists, Lebanese politicians, newspaper editors, and others during visits to Beirut in 1984. Also, Randal, Ch. 1. **When Begin asked:** Schiff-Yaari, pp. 233–236. **shaken, telling one:** DM. **pleaded for a few days':** MB to Linowitz, p. 232. **seemed to feel:** SL. **pushed his address forward:** *Newsweek*, September 13. **communiqué of rejection:** *JP; Newsweek.* To drive home the point (*JP,* September 6), the cabinet announced plans to found eight additional West Bank and Gaza settlements. **wrote the president:** text in *JP,* September 6.

PLO left Beirut: Randal, p. 271. **afternoon of September 14:** DM. **Begin insisted:** DM; Kahan Commission report, pp. 13–14, 64–67. **gave Sharon expanded:** Kahan, p. 13; DM. **capture the teeming:** Kahan, pp. 13–15. **days before . . . by Gemayel's:** MD, who says Gemayel told him of the Sharon suggestion and response shortly before his assassination. **charged that "2,000 terrorists":** MD. **Begin kept in phone contact:** Kahan, pp. 15, 64. **Begin assured Lewis:** Kahan, p. 16. **Phalangists entered:** Kahan, p. 20. **no resistance to speak:** Kahan (pp. 20–21) says there were indeed "armed terrorist forces" in the camps and that these forces did open fire. But Western reporters in Beirut at the time say such resistance was slight. Neither from these sources nor in Kahan comes any evidence supporting the Sharon charge that "2,000 terrorists" were inside the camps. Kahan (p. 23) quotes a briefing by an Israeli military-intelligence officer some four hours after the Phalangists' entry: "It seems there are no terrorists there, in the camp. Sabra camp is empty. On the other hand, they [the Phalangists] have amassed women, children, and apparently also old people, with whom they don't exactly know what to do . . ." **late that night:** Kahan, pp. 24–25.

convened the cabinet: Kahan, pp. 25–27. **Begin did not hear:** Kahan, pp. 27, 65. **contacted Zippori:** Schiff-Yaari, pp. 268–269. **took no action:** he conferred with a Foreign Ministry aide, was told there was "nothing new" from Beirut, and dropped the matter (Kahan, p. 32). **"gone too far":** Kahan, p. 37. **No one phoned Begin:** Kahan, p. 39. Kahan (p. 40) does say that Chief of Staff Eitan testified that Begin had phoned him Saturday morning, saying that "the Americans had called him and complained that the Phalangists had entered" a hospital in one of the camps "and were killing" people. MB denied this to the commission. MD says that as far as he knows there was no American communication with Begin before sundown Saturday, although he, Draper, did protest in the bluntest possible terms to an Israeli representative in Beirut. **switched on the BBC:** Kahan, p. 43. **Begin phoned:** Kahan, pp. 43–44.

next morning—in a meeting: YL. **Writing an American:** California Senator Alan Cranston. Excerpts published in *JP,* October 3, 1982. **late September 400,000:** *JP,* September 26. **did grudgingly acquiesce:** *JP,* September 29. MB declared himself *(JP,* September 30) "fully responsible" for Israeli actions in Beirut, but denied that either he or other Israelis deserved any blame for the massacres. **Lewis, who continued:** SL.

a while he leaned on Aliza: SL, whose wife had become close to Mrs. Begin. **getting weaker:** BSE, BK. **"The two of them":** BSE. **confided a fear:** SL. **"I must devote":** SL. **looked weak, only slightly:** Account is from Judy Donner, an American artist employed to sketch the proceedings for a U.S. television network. **"My name is Begin . . .":** *JP,* November 9, 1982, carries a detailed report, including a verbatim transcript of key exchanges between Begin and commission members. **asking for a notepad:** IB, YK. **"He *went!*":** IB. **Begin flew first:** YK, HH, who were there, are main sources for this section. **Scheib, who grasped:** YS. **To Morris Draper:** MD. **Among a later batch:** IB. **"She always stood by me":** YK, HH, SL. **Begin tried to get them:** DM. **"How will I explain":** DM. **Meridor, who tried:** DM.

Kahan Commission warned: *JP,* December 10. The text of the Begin letter was made public December 9. **"We find no reason":** Kahan, pp. 66–67. **hinted broadly that Sharon:** the Kahan report (p. 105) said: "We have found, as has been detailed in this report, that the Minister of Defense bears personal responsibility. In our opinion, it is fitting that the Minister of Defense draw the appropriate personal conclusions arising out of the defects revealed with regard to the manner in which he discharged the duties of his office—and if necessary, that the Prime Minister consider whether he should exercise his authority under Section 21-A(a) of the Basic Law: the Government, according to which 'the Prime Minister may, after informing the Cabinet of his intention to do so, remove a minister from office.' " **Begin refused to sack:** telling visitors (*JP,* February 9) that he would rather quit himself than fire the defense minister. **removed him from the Defense Ministry:** and again took over the post himself for a few days—until he passed it to Moshe Arens. **"This man":** MB Knesset address, February 14, 1983 (text from Israel Government Press Office).

shouts of support: indeed, throughout Israel's 1984 election campaign, which I covered, having been reposted to the Mideast. For an excellent piece on the immediate street and social reactions to the publication of the Kahan report, see *JP,* February 18 (Rabinovich article). **recalls Dan Meridor, ruled with:** DM. **nationwide doctors' strike:** it began in early March. Not until late June did MB enter the fray. **"He was less":** DM. **"much less able to deal":** the diplomat requested anonymity. **"He tried hard":** SL. **suggested that the United States:** MB address to a meeting of the World Assembly of Jewish War Veterans (text from Israel Government Press Office). **Begin said the country:** MB address, April 17, 1983 (text from Israel Government Press Office). **infuriating Finance Minister:** MB summoned Aridor and Health Minister Shostak (*JP,* June 20) to his office. Aridor was "fuming" after the conference, recalls AN, who saw him shortly afterward. **he would say simply, "I cannot":** *Ma'ariv,* June 6, 1983. **cared deeply, too:** the roots of the preoccupation ran deep. HHu tells of accompanying MB on a tour of African countries during Herut's long stint in the opposition when, shortly after touchdown at one African airport, a large welcoming crowd appeared. MB, however, had disappeared. HHu found him in the airport bathroom, shaving. Explained MB: "I can't appear before these people unshaven!" The concern with appearance sometimes suggested his mixed feelings about that appearance. There are intermittent references in MB's written recollections of imprisonment to being conscious of having a "puny" physique and "white hands" that contrasted with other prisoners' muscles and calluses. But ZC says Begin sometimes seemed proud of those hands, which were delicate almost to the point of sculpted perfection. When photographed, he would occasionally half-jokingly insist on getting his hands in the picture. **"he said he could not"**: DM. **"Keep writing those"**: source is a Jerusalem-based aide to the lobbyist, who requested anonymity. **military officer recounts**: Shacham article, based on interviews with two dozen officials who met and worked with MB during his 1983 decline. **remained most people's choice**: and, by an enormous majority, top choice as leader of the Likud. *Ha,* in a survey published April 1, 1983, found MB's rating as party leader had actually increased since January, from 58.7 percent to 60 percent of respondents. On the question of who would make the best prime minister, Begin's rating had dropped off slightly—from 49.4 percent, in January, to 44.8 percent. *Ma'ariv* reported on April 27 that a separate survey on popular choices for prime minister had found MB's rating to be 46 percent—down from 62 percent in the early part of the Lebanon War, and from 50 percent in February 1983. *Ha,* in early May, quoted a poll saying MB's "popularity rating" had slipped from 55.3 percent of respondents in early 1983 to 54.5 percent. By the end of May, a *JP* poll found MB the top prime-ministerial choice of 41.1 percent of respondents—a drop of 4.5 percent from the previous month. Yet, in all of these surveys, Israeli President (and former Ben Gurion protégé) Yitzhak Navon ranked a distant second choice for prime minister—notching anywhere from 15 percent to about 25 percent of respondents' votes. (The *JP* survey published in late May gave Navon 20.3 percent.) As Likud leader, MB remained unassailably top choice. An August 21 *JP* poll found him the top choice of 42.1 percent of respondents. His closest rival—Ezer Weizman—rated 8.7 percent. **sometimes drifted off**: Shacham article. **from the newly created**: Shacham article; *JP,* August 29, 1983. The minister in question, Aharon Uzan, had been a minister in an earlier, Labor government. **Marcus visited Begin**: LM. **told his three closest**: *JP,* August 29. **A few followed him downstairs**: HHu.

Chapter Twenty-eight: Underground Farewell

Interviews: Eitan Haber, Rachel Begin Halperin, Hart Hasten, Harry Hurwitz (HHu), Yehiel Kadishai, Mr. and Mrs. Marek Kahan, Yona Klimovitzki, Dan Meridor, Yaakov Meridor, Arye Naor, Esther Raziel-Naor, Ehud Yaari, Mordechai Zippori.

Periodicals: Hadashot; the *International Herald Tribune (IHT); The Jerusalem Post (JP); Ma'ariv.*

Textual notes: **could hear the crowd:** *JP,* September 2 and September 4, 1983. **attended no:** *JP*'s daily coverage is source of background for this section. **democratic political party, not a monarchy:** a phrase he revived (*JP,* September 4) to aides and colleagues in the days after his departure. **By December, Kadishai:** source is MB colleague who requested anonymity. **skeletal-looking:** Israeli news photographers, staking out the residence, captured the scene. **lay in bed, in his pajamas:** HH. **Kadishai came practically:** YK, HH, HHu. **sister, Rachel, was largely:** AN, HH. **cottage industry:** see *JP, Ma'ariv,* other Israeli newspapers. Also, Op-Ed articles in American press. **an American academic:** Amos Perlmutter, in a *Newsday* opinion article reprinted in *IHT,* September 2, 1983. **Begin's admirers:** Israeli press background, plus a variety of interviews I conducted while covering the 1984 campaign as *CSM* correspondent.

Begin sent word: EY. **began conducting:** YK, HH. **offered occasional, terse comments:** *JP,* and my notes on actual broadcasts. **politely but firmly:** source, who would seem in a position to know, requested anonymity. **prodded by the wife:** HH. **Shamir's campaign:** my notes on campaign. **Shamir was reduced:** *JP.* **Mrs. Raziel-Naor:** ERN. **Kadishai, Meridor:** HHu, HH. *"Yesh zman":* HHu, HH. **Hasten pushed harder:** HH. **did not vote:** *JP.* **told an American news agency:** the Associated Press. MB said, "There are very serious problems in the country as such, and under the circumstances I think it would be a good idea ..." To Israel Radio, he added that the prime minister of such a coalition should be "my friend" Shamir. **he added, "very well":** to Israeli newspaper *Hadashot,* August 1984. **old guard fumed:** typical was the private remark one old guarder made to me the day after the 1984 election: "I would never have said this before. But I really think he has got mental problems. ... To have not even said anything during the campaign, to me that means Menachem Begin has gone over the wall. For two segments of the electorate—the Orthodox and the Sephardim—Begin is a real god. He could have made the difference between the present outcome and victory." **hoped to build:** based on conversations with aides and associates, including YK, HH, HHu.

rushed to Shaarei: *JP,* September 11, 1984. **though the ailment:** YK. **Begin paused at:** I was among the reporters present. **"The crisis**

was": YK. **two months later**: YK. **November 23 he emerged**: generally tipped off by YK that Begin would probably emerge, I attended. **Sharon, whom he**: *JP;* HH. After the libel-case decision was handed down in early 1985—finding that *Time* had printed an inaccuracy about Sharon, but stopping short of finding deliberate libel—Sharon phoned Begin in Israel. MB, in remarks to Israel Radio, celebrated what he termed an "absolute moral victory." **He told me**: MB phone conversation. **might start**: HHu. **lost weight again**: background from conversations with YK, HH. **When she later**: source is a family friend, who was at Benny's home during the conversation and requested anonymity. **March 1986 the party faithful**: *JP* and other Israeli news reports. **"I will say nothing"**: DM. **Mordechai Zippori wrote**: MZ.

a reporter's impish suggestion: Begin interview, *JP,* April 11, 1979. **still saw it**: based on conversations with HH, HHu. **"Begin will never"**: DM. **when one Begin admirer**: *JP,* July 17, 1984. *He, not Sharon*: AN adds that in earlier tussles with then Defense Minister Weizman, Begin had been wont to remind Weizman that under Israel's system, the entire government, not merely the defense minister, was responsible for the military. After the Sabra and Shatila massacres, MB coupled rejection of any blame with a declaration *(JP)* that he, as prime minister, assumed ultimate responsibility for all Israeli actions in Beirut. **misjudged his own nation's torment**: ZC. **"*goyim* killing *goyim*"**: one MB cabinet colleague, who requests anonymity, recalls remarking to a friend on hearing of the camp massacres that "Begin's response, I promise you, will be to say this was *goyim* and that the world is again blaming Jews." Further background for this section from conversations with EH, YM, AN. **not written his promised tome**: Or so, at least, said aides. HH remarked in July that Begin seemed to have sunk back into his combination of mental sharpness and physical surrender. "He still is up-to-date on every last detail of the political situation, here and overseas. He is mentally the same Begin ..." But, added HH, he did not bother changing from pajamas into clothes, and seemed unalterably opposed to reentering the outside world, much less resuming any public political role. RBH, who said she unfailingly spoke with her brother by phone each weekend, offered a similar picture, but also declared, "Why *should* he go out? I sympathize with him in this ..." **remarked to his wife**: Mrs. MK. **"A man"**: Mrs. MK.

Bibliography

Bader, Yohanan. *The Knesset and I* (Hebrew). Jerusalem: Edanim, 1979.

Begin, Menachem. *In the Underground* (Hebrew), 6 vols. Tel Aviv: Hadar, 1977.

———. *The Revolt.* Tel Aviv: Steimatzky's, 1983.

———. *White Nights: The Story of a Prisoner in Russia.* Tel Aviv: Steimatzky's, 1977.

Bell, J. Bowyer. *Terror out of Zion.* New York: St. Martin's Press, 1977.

Ben Ami, Yitshaq. *Years of Wrath, Days of Glory.* New York: Shengold, 1983.

Bethell, Nicholas. *The Palestine Triangle.* London: Steimatzky-André Deutsch, 1979.

Brenner, Lenni. *The Iron Wall: Zionist Revisionism from Jabotinsky to Shamir.* London: Zed Books, 1984.

Brzezinski, Zbigniew. *Power and Principle.* New York: Farrar, Straus & Giroux, 1985.

Carter, Jimmy. *Keeping Faith: Memoirs of a President.* New York: Bantam Books, 1982.

Chafets, Ze'ev. *Heroes and Hustlers; Hard Hats and Holy Men.* New York: William Morrow, 1986.

Churchill, Colonel Charles. *The Druzes and the Maronites.* London: Bernard Quaritch, 1862.

Clarke, Thurston. *By Blood and Fire.* London: Arrow, 1982.

Cohen, Geula. *Woman of Violence.* New York: Holt, Rinehart & Winston, 1966.

Collins, Larry, and Dominique Lapierre. *O Jerusalem!* New York: Pocket Books, 1973.

Columbia University Press. *The New Columbia Encyclopedia.* New York and London: 1975.

Dayan, Moshe. *Breakthrough.* London: Weidenfeld & Nicolson, 1981.

———. *Story of My Life.* London: Sphere Books, 1977.

Dobroszycki, Lucjan, and Barbara Kirshenblatt-Gimblett. *Image Before My Eyes—A Photographic History of Jewish Life in Poland, 1864–1939.* New York: Schocken Books, 1977.

Eban, Abba. *An Autobiography.* Tel Aviv: Steimatzky's, 1977.

Egyptian Ministry of Foreign Affairs. *White Paper on the Peace Initiatives Undertaken by President Anwar al-Sadat (1971–1977).* Cairo: 1978.

Eliot, G. F. *Hate, Hope and High Explosives.* Indianapolis: Bobbs-Merrill, 1948.

Frank, Gerold. *The Deed.* London: Jonathan Cape, 1964.

Garcia-Granados, Jorge. *The Birth of Israel: The Drama As I Saw It.* New York: Alfred Knopf, 1948.

Gervasi, Frank. *The Life and Times of Menachem Begin.* New York: G. P. Putnam's Sons, 1979.

Gilbert, Martin. *Atlas of the Arab-Israeli Conflict.* New York: Macmillan, 1974.
Gitlin, Jan. *Attack on Acre Prison* (French). Tel Aviv: Hadar, 1971.
Golan, Aviezer, and Shlomo Nachdimon. *Begin* (Hebrew). Jerusalem: Edanim, 1978.
Golan, Matti. *Shimon Peres.* London: Weidenfeld & Nicolson, 1982.
Graves, R. M. *Experiment in Anarchy.* London: Victor Gollancz Ltd., 1949.
Green, Stephen. *Taking Sides: America's Secret Relations with a Militant Israel.* New York: William Morrow, 1984.
Greenfield, Richard Pierce and Irving A. *The Life Story of Menachem Begin.* New York: Manor, 1977.
Haber, Eitan. *Menachem Begin.* New York: Delacorte, 1978.
Haber, Eitan, et al. *The Year of the Dove.* New York: Bantam Books, 1979.
Haig, Alexander, Jr. *Caveat.* New York: Macmillan, 1984.
Heller, Celia. *On the Edge of Destruction: Jews of Poland Between the Two World Wars.* New York: Schocken Books, 1980.
Herzl, Theodor. *The Jewish State.* Trans. Harry Zohn. New York: Herzl Press, 1970.
Hirschler, Gertrude, and Lester S. Eckman. *Menachem Begin.* New York: Shengold, 1979.
Hurwitz, Harry. *Menachem Begin.* Johannesburg: Jewish Herald Ltd., 1977.
Interpress (Polish Government Press Agency). *The Polish Jewry: History and Culture.* Warsaw: 1982.
Kahan, Yitzhak, et al. *The Commission of Inquiry into the Events at the Refugee Camps in Beirut—Final Report* (authorized translation). Jerusalem: 1983.
Katz, Shmuel. *Days of Fire.* Tel Aviv: Steimatzky's, 1968.
———. *The Hollow Peace.* Jerusalem: Dvir, 1981.
Keter, eds. *Encyclopaedia Judaica.* Jerusalem: Keter Publishing House, 1972.
Kissinger, Henry. *White House Years.* Boston: Little, Brown, 1979.
Koestler, Arthur. *Promise and Fulfillment: Palestine 1917–1949.* London: Macmillan, 1949.
Kurzman, Dan. *Ben-Gurion: Prophet of Fire.* New York: Simon & Schuster, 1983.
———. *Genesis 1948.* New York: World, 1970.
Lankin, Eliahu. *Tales of the Commander of the Altalena* (Hebrew). Tel Aviv: 1966.
Levin, Harry. *Jerusalem Embattled.* London: Victor Gollancz Ltd., 1950.
Linowitz, Sol. *The Making of a Public Man.* Boston: Little, Brown, 1985.
McDonald, James. *My Mission in Israel: 1948–1951.* London: Victor Gollancz Ltd., 1951.
Medzini, Meron, ed. *Israel's Foreign Relations: Selected Documents,* 6 vols. Jerusalem: Ministry for Foreign Affairs, 1976–1984.
Meir, Golda. *My Life.* London: Futura, 1976.
Mendelsohn, Ezra. *The Jews of East Central Europe Between the World Wars.* Bloomington: Indiana University Press, 1983.
Milosz, Czeslaw. *The History of Polish Literature.* Berkeley: University of California Press, 1983.
Morse, Arthur D. *While Six Million Died.* New York: Hart, 1968.
Naor, Arye. *Cabinet at War.* Tel Aviv: Lahav, 1986.
Neugroschel, Joachim, ed. and trans. *The Shtetl: A Creative Anthology of Jewish Life in Eastern Europe.* New York: G. P. Putnam's Sons, 1979.
Niv, David. *History of the Irgun Zvai Leumi* (Hebrew), 6 vols. Tel Aviv: Klausner Institute, 1980.

Nixon, Richard. *The Memoirs of Richard Nixon.* New York: Warner, 1979.

Oz, Amos. *The Hill of Evil Counsel.* London: Fontana Paperbacks, 1980.

Peretz, Isaac Loeb. *Selected Stories.* New York: Schocken Books, 1974.

Rabin, Yitzhak. *The Rabin Memoirs.* Boston: Little, Brown, 1979.

Randal, Jonathan. *Going All the Way.* New York: Viking, 1983.

Roskies, Diane K. and David G. *The Shtetl Book.* Ktav, 1975.

St. John, Robert. *Ben-Gurion.* London: Jarrolds, 1959.

———. *Shalom Means Peace.* New York: Doubleday, 1949.

Schechtman, Joseph B. *The Jabotinsky Story: Fighter and Prophet—The Last Years.* New York: A. S. Barnes, 1961.

Schechtman, Joseph B., and Yehuda Benari. *History of the Revisionist Movement.* Tel Aviv: Hadar, 1970.

Schiff, Ze'ev, and Ehud Yaari. *Israel's Lebanon War.* New York: Simon & Schuster, 1984.

Silver, Eric. *Begin.* London: Weidenfeld & Nicolson, 1984.

Slutsky, Yehuda. *History of the Haganah, Vol. III* (Hebrew). Tel Aviv: Am Oved, 1973.

Smith, Denis Mack. *Garibaldi.* Westport, Conn.: Greenwood Press, 1982 (reprint, Knopf, New York, 1956).

Solzhenitsyn, Aleksandr. *The Gulag Archipelago,* 2 vols. New York: Harper & Row, 1973–1975.

Steinman, Eliezer, ed. *Encyclopedia of the Diaspora: Brisk-de-Lita Volume* (Hebrew). Jerusalem: Encyclopedia of the Jewish Diaspora, 1954.

Stock, Ernest. *Israel on the Road to Sinai: 1949–1956.* Ithaca N.Y.: Cornell University Press, 1967.

Tavin, Eli. *The Second Front* (Hebrew). Tel Aviv: Ron, 1973.

Tavin, Eli, and Yona Alexander, eds. *Psychological Warfare and Propaganda: Irgun Documentation.* Wilmington, Del.: Scholarly Resources, Inc., 1982.

Trotsky, Leon. *My Life.* Middlesex, England: Penguin, 1975.

United States Government Policy Statement Series. *A Framework for Peace in the Middle East: Documents Related to the Camp David Accords.* Washington, D.C.: 1978.

Vance, Cyrus. *Hard Choices.* New York: Simon & Schuster, 1983.

Watt, Richard M. *Bitter Glory: Poland and Its Fate—1918 to 1939.* New York: Simon & Schuster, 1982.

Weissman, Steve, and Herbert Krosney. *The Islamic Bomb.* New York: Times Books, 1981.

Weizman, Ezer. *The Battle for Peace.* New York: Bantam Books, 1981.

———. *On Eagles' Wings.* Tel Aviv: Steimatzky's, 1979.

White, Theodore. *Breach of Faith.* New York: Dell, 1976.

Wyman, David. *The Abandonment of the Jews.* New York: Pantheon, 1984.

Index